Practical Lexicography

Practical Lexicography

A Reader

Edited by

THIERRY FONTENELLE

OXFORD
UNIVERSITY PRESS

OXFORD
UNIVERSITY PRESS

Great Clarendon Street, Oxford OX2 6DP

Oxford University Press is a department of the University of Oxford.
It furthers the University's objective of excellence in research, scholarship,
and education by publishing worldwide in

Oxford New York

Auckland Cape Town Dar es Salaam Hong Kong Karachi
Kuala Lumpur Madrid Melbourne Mexico City Nairobi
New Delhi Shanghai Taipei Toronto

With offices in

Argentina Austria Brazil Chile Czech Republic France Greece
Guatemala Hungary Italy Japan Poland Portugal Singapore
South Korea Switzerland Thailand Turkey Ukraine Vietnam

Oxford is a registered trademark of Oxford University Press
in the UK and in certain other countries

Published in the United States
by Oxford University Press Inc., New York

British Library Cataloguing in Publication Data

Data available

Library of Congress Cataloging in Publication Data

Data available

Typeset by SPI Publisher Services, Pondicherry, India
Printed in Great Britain
on acid-free paper by
Biddles Ltd., King's Lynn, Norfolk

ISBN 978–0–19–929233–2 (hb)
ISBN 978–0–19–929234–9 (pb)

1 3 5 7 9 10 8 6 4 2

Contents

Acknowledgements

I am indebted to a number of people without whom this *Reader* would not exist. Sue Atkins and Michael Rundell were instrumental in the genesis of this book, since it is a companion volume to their own *Oxford Guide to Practical Lexicography*, to be published in the same series. Their advice, recommendations, and suggestions have been much appreciated. Sue deserves a special mention: without her encouragements, her contagious enthusiasm, and her wonderful energy, the book would never have been brought to fruition. This is probably true of a large number of lexicography-related projects in which she was involved and this project is no exception. To a large extent, she is responsible for all the evenings and weekends I spent on this project and I am glad she encouraged me to take it on.

I am also grateful to John Davey and Karen Morgan for their guidance in Oxford and for seeing the *Reader* through to publication. Malcom Todd's expert eye has proved immensely useful for spotting inconsistencies or missing references and I thank him for his most helpful contribution. I also wish to express my gratitude to the Series Editors and to Tony Cowie who provided me with invaluable advice.

I also want to thank all the authors and the publishers who allowed me to reuse their papers. A similar vote of thanks goes to Jack Lynch, who allowed me to reuse the version he had edited of Johnson's *Plan of a Dictionary of the English Language,* and to Alain Duval, who agreed to translate his article into English. A special mention goes to the late Penny Stock's sister, Mrs. Wendy J. F. Nast, and to the late Dwight Bolinger's son, Mr. Bruce Bolinger, for their cooperation.

Finally, I want to thank my wife, Cécile. A little over twelve years ago, when completing my doctoral dissertation, I had indicated that she had 'suffered uncomplainingly and had tried to put up with my idiosyncratic behaviour during the genesis of [that] book'. I am not sure the situation has been different this time. I shirked lots of parental responsibilities to be able to complete the project and, as always, she has been there to help, encourage, and stimulate me. Our sons, Olivier, Marc-Antoine, and Pierre, also deserve a special mention. It is not always easy to live with a father who has a passion for dictionaries and linguistics. I know they have not always found that passion as 'cool' as their Xbox games, yet they displayed genuine interest in the progress I was making and Marc-Antoine even keyed in one or two papers for me. He now knows a lot more about frame semantics, phraseology, and polysemy. I thank him for giving me the opportunity to introduce him to these notions. In a nutshell, this *Reader* is dedicated to my family for their constant support.

Introduction

THIERRY FONTENELLE

Lexicography is neither a new science nor a new craft. Dictionaries have existed for hundreds of years and have been compiled to meet very practical needs (for example those of travelers who needed lists of words in multiple languages). At the same time, dictionaries can also be seen as cultural artifacts conveying a vision of a community's language. This explains why, in addition to being commercial objects, dictionaries have also been studied by linguists who find in them a treasure trove of information about language in general and vocabulary in particular. A revival in lexical studies over the past twenty-five years has revolutionized the art of dictionary-making and of dictionary analysis. The advent of computer technology, which makes it possible to manipulate large amounts of textual data and to store and retrieve lexical information in novel ways, has enabled linguists and lexicographers to question assumptions that had been taken for granted for decades. Do word senses really exist, for instance, or are they simply constructs and oversimplifications which come in handy because we tend to work best with clear-cut distinctions and categories that we like to classify into distinct, well-defined boxes? How should we account for polysemy in dictionaries? What kinds of examples are most effective when trying to show how a word is typically used? Should lexicographers invent their own examples or should they rather use real sentences excerpted from large bodies of running texts? How should definitions be structured and written in learners' dictionaries and in dictionaries for native speakers? Should the *definiendum* (the word being defined) be included in a full-sentence definition, or should such definitions be reserved for a limited number of cases? What are collocations and how can they be identified in corpora? How should collocations be represented in monolingual and in bilingual dictionaries? How can we speed up the compilation of dictionaries and provide lexicographers with tools enabling them to sort the wheat from the chaff and to identify what is common and typical, instead of being blinded by exceptional, anomalous cases? Now that concordances and KWIC lines (Key Word In Context) are routinely made available to dictionary makers, how can we make sure that the lexicographer is not as powerless as a person standing underneath Niagara Falls, holding a rainwater gauge while the evidence sweeps by in immeasurable torrents, to quote Church *et al.* (1994: 153)? Now that the World Wide Web enables us to nearly instantaneously access billions of words in dozens of languages, do we still need dictionaries to make sense of words? Do we even still need lexicographers to tap the evidence, extract lexicographically relevant facts, and distill them into dictionaries? And, if we do, how do we make sure that the dictionaries they compile really meet users' needs? Do we even know how people use dictionaries and what we can do to help them find their way about these resources?

These are some of the questions we hope will be answered in this *Reader*, which should be seen as a companion volume to Sue Atkins and Michael Rundell's *Oxford Guide to Practical Lexicography* (forthcoming, 2008). Lexicography has now become a well-established field of research, as is testified by the number of publications (journals, conference proceedings, books...) that deal with this topic. Lexicographers, lexicologists, and linguists interested in lexical matters regularly participate in meetings organized by international associations such as the *European Association for Lexicography* (Euralex), the *Dictionary Society of North America* (DSNA), the *African Association for Lexicography* (Afrilex), the *Asian Association for Lexicography* (Asialex), the *Australasian Association for Lexicography* (Australex), or regional and national associations such as *SeaLex* (Southeast Asian Lexicography) or the *Spanish Association for Lexicography*. Other scientific organizations such as the *European Association for Phraseology* (Europhras) or the *Special Interest Group on the Lexicon* (SIGLEX) of the *Association for Computational Linguistics* also testify to the widespread interest in specialized aspects of lexicographical issues. Scores of universities now offer courses on lexicography and lexicology, lexical semantics, and corpus linguistics, realizing that building dictionaries is a time-consuming and costly activity that requires very special linguistic skills. Publishing houses also need to train their lexicographers. Identifying lexicographically relevant facts in big corpora is far from a trivial task and compiling dictionaries assumes an in-depth understanding of linguistic concepts like subcategorization, collocations, phraseology, polysemy, homonymy, or lexical semantic relations, to give only a few examples. It also presupposes a good knowledge of how people actually use dictionaries. While there is no dearth of excellent articles discussing all these issues, it must be acknowledged that many of these papers are often published in hard-to-access conference proceedings. The present collection of articles attempts to meet the need for a coherent and easily accessible compilation of papers, many of which have become classics in the field of lexicography. Aspiring lexicographers as well as students in linguistics and lexicography should find in this anthology a wealth of material and a lot of food for thought which should help them make the appropriate decisions in their present and future projects, be they academic research projects or dictionary-writing activities. More seasoned lexicographers as well as researchers and teachers will find in these articles basic as well as advanced descriptions of some of the most crucial issues and hot topics discussed in lexicography circles.

I METALEXICOGRAPHY, MACROSTRUCTURE, MICROSTRUCTURE, AND THE CONTRIBUTION OF LINGUISTIC THEORY

The structure of this *Reader* reflects the structure of Atkins and Rundell's *Oxford Guide to Practical Lexicography* (forthcoming, 2008). The anthology includes many articles they grant recommended reading status. The first chapters deal with metalexicography and the contribution of linguistic theory to the dictionary-making process. Chapter 2, Samuel Johnson's "Plan of a Dictionary of the English Language", is obviously the oldest article, since it was addressed to Lord Chesterfield in 1747. Yet, more than 250 years later, it is still so modern, so true, so relevant that it should be considered a must-read article for every lexicographer. Johnson discusses all the issues which lexicographers are faced with when embarking on a dictionary project, ranging from inflectional and derivational morphology, to pronunciation and etymology. The representation of syntactic information (which corresponds to what modern linguistics would call subcategorization) attracts Johnson's attention when he points out that one dies *of* one's wounds while one may perish *with* hunger, stressing that "every man acquainted with our language would be offended with a change of these particles". While Johnson's *Dictionary of the English Language*, published in 1755, was to be primarily for native speakers of English, many of his preoccupations are still very much at the heart of the creation of current learners' dictionaries. Johnson was aware of the need to establish clear criteria for selecting words to be included in a dictionary, or distinguishing between general language and specialized terminology. As McDermott and Moon (2005: 153) point out, "Johnson was innovative in many of his dictionary's features since he was the first to deal systematically with such fundamental features of the English language as phrasal verbs, common polysemous verbs such as *take*, compound nouns, participial adjectives, verbal nouns, etc". Moreover, he was the first to base his dictionary on actual examples of usage, which probably made him the first "corpus lexicographer", even though the term did not exist at the time. After reading Johnson's "Plan", edited by Jack Lynch, included in this volume, as well as Johnson's "Preface", interested readers will read the various papers included in the June 2005 special issue of the *International Journal of Lexicography* edited by Anne McDermott and Rosamund Moon to know more about Johnson's *Dictionary of the English Language* and his contribution to modern lexicography. Hanks' contribution (2005), in particular, will make it abundantly clear that Johnson was a radical thinker who was well ahead of his time and managed to shed light on the nature of language and of meaning, long before philosophers like Wittgenstein started addressing the crucial issue of word meaning.

In Chapter 3, Sue Atkins addresses the issue of theoretical lexicography and its relation to dictionary making. The paper, originally published in a special issue of *Dictionaries*, the journal of the Dictionary Society of North America, was one of two position papers written for a forum on the theory and practice of lexicography (the other position paper was Wierzbicka 1992). Considering dictionaries from the point of view of form and of content, Atkins argues that linguists who criticize many aspects of dictionaries are wrong when they imply that the errors they notice can be corrected out of context. The notion of context is very large indeed and "theoretical lexicographers" should be aware that changes in editorial policy they are sometimes quick to recommend may have a domino effect on many aspects of the dictionary-making process. She then discusses the various design decisions in the planning of trade dictionaries, ranging from the pre-lexicographical decisions (user groups, physical features, sources of evidence, etc.), to macrostructure decisions (list of headwords, subentry criteria...), to microstructure decisions. It is at this last level, she claims, that linguistics has most to contribute to theoretical lexicography. Editors need to decide how to present lexical entries and what lexical information should be recorded. This is where lexicographers need criteria for identifying "dictionary senses", an area which can benefit from linguists' analyses of systematic linguistic variation. Scholars such as Fillmore, Levin, or Cruse, who routinely discuss lexical semantics issues and the intersection between syntax and semantics, have a lot to offer to practical lexicographers. Other groups of linguists, who specifically deal with lexicographical matters, such as Apresjan (1973), Mel'čuk (1998), Zgusta (1971), or Wierzbicka (1992), may also help practitioners with their studies of word sense relationships and their insights into word meaning.

Atkins' reference to the contribution of scholars like Apresjan provides an appropriate transition to Chapter 4, in which Juri Apresjan discusses the principles of systematic lexicography. In an attempt to bridge the gap between lexicography and linguistic theory, he outlines five principles which are relevant to systematic lexicography: the reconstruction of what he calls the naïve picture of the world, the integrated theory of linguistic description (unifying grammar and lexis), the discovery of lexical classes whose members behave systematically, the characterization of all the relevant properties of lexemes (individuation), and the formulation of rules accounting for the meaning interaction of language units in texts. Apresjan (2000) goes into deeper discussions, and readers will also benefit from other articles such as Apresjan (1973) on regular polysemy, which is of direct relevance to lexicographers who need to capture systematic alternations and need criteria to address the question of sense differentiation. Ostler and Atkins (1992), as well as Nunberg and Zaenen (1992), will also usefully complement this article by providing insights into lexical implication rules and systematic polysemy, which are necessary to account for phenomena such as the Count/Mass or the Container/Contents alternations ("He dropped the bottle" vs. "He drank the whole bottle").

II   ON CORPUS DESIGN

The next two chapters deal with corpus design. Gone are the days when lexicographers were relying upon their intuition to compile dictionaries. Corpora are now routinely used to extract linguistic evidence to be distilled into dictionary entries. They are now considered an essential component of the dictionary-making process. While the use of corpus material was still considered a novelty in the 1980s and, in the field of bilingual lexicography, even in the early 1990s, no dictionary could be published today without mentioning that it is based upon a (preferably very large) electronic text corpus. Several papers in this *Reader* address the issue of how corpora should be used and why they are needed to identify relevant, central, and typical facts (examples, collocations, etc). However, before talking about concordances, KWIC lines, or "Word Sketches", it is important to discuss what it means for a corpus to represent a language. Since it is impossible to have access to everything that has ever been written in a given language, it is crucial to consider the kinds of texts which will be included in the corpus that is constructed. Douglas Biber addresses these issues in Chapter 5. For generalizations concerning a language to be possible, a corpus must be representative, which means that a sample should include the full range of variability in a population. Differences in the distribution of linguistic features have implications for corpus design which cannot be ignored at the planning stage. Interested readers will also want to read Atkins *et al.* (1992) on corpus design criteria, which was written at the beginning of the 1990s, like Biber's article, that is, in a pre-Web era. In "The Web as Corpus" (Chapter 6), Kilgarriff and Grefenstette introduce a special issue of *Computational Linguistics* devoted to the "fabulous linguist's playground" that the Web has now become with its hundreds of billions of words of texts which can be used for language research as well as for the development of practical natural language processing (NLP) systems. While arguing that the web is not representative of anything other than itself and acknowledging that no corpus is representative either, Kilgarriff and Grefenstette also address the issue of sublanguages in corpora and conclude with a number of proposals to remedy the shortcomings of current search engines which are ill-suited to linguistic research.

III   ON LEXICOGRAPHICAL EVIDENCE

Electronic corpora have revolutionized the field of dictionary-making exactly in the same way as they have revolutionized the world of linguistics. Does this mean all lexicographers or all linguists should be turned into "corpus lexicographers" or "corpus linguists"? Does this mean that intuition and introspection no longer play any role in linguistic analysis? Charles Fillmore tries to answer these types of questions in Chapter 7 and argues very convincingly that the armchair linguist and the corpus linguist should actually coexist in the same body. While there is no way of avoiding reliance upon intuitive knowledge about language, it cannot be denied that what can be found in a corpus is normally authentic data. It is this authenticity which makes corpora so valuable, since they teach us facts that we cannot discover in any other way. Fillmore taps corpora because he is interested in finding out about lexical and structural features of a language which he would most certainly miss, were he exclusively relying upon his own intuition and speculations. To make his point, he discusses the lexical description of the English words *risk* and *home*. His analysis of *risk*, discussed in the present paper as well as in Fillmore and Atkins (1982, 1994), provides an excellent introduction to frame semantics, a linguistic theory which has been popularized over the last few years thanks to the FrameNet project (Atkins *et al.* 2003a and 2003b; Fillmore *et al.* 2003a and 2003b; Fontenelle 2003), although the concepts were already formulated earlier (e.g. in Fillmore 1977b, 1977c, and 1982b). The work of Fillmore and Atkins reveals discrepancies between the ten monolingual dictionaries they used in their study of *risk*. He identifies a linguistic category making up a "frame", as well as "frame elements" which are present in some or all situations involving a risk. "Deeds", "Harms", and "Valued Possessions" are the frame elements which gravitate around the concept of *risk* and the task of the linguist (or the lexicographer writing a dictionary entry) is to capture the possible groups of frame elements and describe how they may be realized along the syntactic axis. The analysis he proposes, based upon authentic evidence from the 100-million-word British National Corpus, makes it possible to account for differences between *taking risks* and *running risks*, a difference about which none of the dictionaries he examined with Sue Atkins had anything to say. Readers interested in the relationship between intuition and corpus-based evidence will find additional and useful information in Atkins *et al.* (1996, 2003a), Hanks (1990), or Sinclair (1987c).

IV ON WORD SENSES AND POLYSEMY

The next section deals with the crucial issue of word senses and polysemy. While Patrick Hanks asks the Wittgensteinian question "Do word meanings exist?" in Chapter 8, Adam Kilgarriff answers, in a very no-nonsense way, that he "does not believe in word senses", in Chapter 9. As Hanks points out, the question may seem odd since, as a lexicographer, he has spent over thirty years writing and editing monolingual definitions. Yet, both Hanks and Kilgarriff arrive at the same conclusion that word meanings do not exist as a checklist, if they do exist at all. Dictionaries are based on a huge oversimplification which posits that words have enumerable, listable meanings which are divisible into discrete units. If there is anything that corpus linguistics and the systematic analysis of authentic evidence have taught us, it is certainly that the concepts of polysemy and word meaning are a lot more mysterious than we may think. The polysemous nature of the noun *bank* (financial institution vs. the steep side of a river) has been analyzed to death and Hanks prefers to see this as two different words (with different etymologies and uses) that happen to be spelled the same, rather than two senses of the same word. Meanings do not seem to exist outside the context in which they are used, which is why he prefers to talk about "meaning potentials" ("potential contributions to the meanings of texts and conversations in which the word is used and activated by the speaker who uses them"). Dictionaries only contain lists of meaning potentials, while corpora contain traces of meaning events. Word sense disambiguation eventually boils down to trying to map the one onto the other. It is therefore essential for computational lexicographers to devise systems to discover the contextual triggers that activate the components making up a word's meaning potential. Hanks' more recent work on Corpus Pattern Analysis (CPA) to build up an inventory of syntagmatic behavior that may be useful for automatic word sense disambiguation is an attempt to contribute to the development of such a system (Hanks and Pustejovsky 2005).

    Kilgarriff shares a similar view and argues that the concept of "word sense" is not a workable one. He rather demonstrates that occurrences of a word in context, in the form of citations or key-word-in-context (KWIC) concordances, provide a much more operational definition and he sees word senses as abstractions over clusters of word usages. The lexicographer's data-driven task is therefore to examine large numbers of concordances and divide them into clusters, working out the elements that explain why the members of a cluster belong together. It is also crucial to note that this impacts the way in which many linguists view the concept of idiom. Idioms are still often defined as multi-word entries whose meaning is not equal to the sum of the meanings of the words they are made up of. This notion of non-compositionality is a moot point because compositionality itself is very hard to define operationally. The multi-word entry is simply one of the various contexts in which a given word can be used and therefore contributes to the set of clusters that need to be identified and described. Readers who are interested in more traditional, less extreme approaches to polysemy will turn to Cruse (1986) for a good overview of the homonymy/polysemy distinction and for useful tests for distinguishing word senses.

The late Penelope Stock shows in Chapter 10 how working lexicographers cope with the polysemy issue and divide lexical items into different meanings. Her view is clearly influenced by the large body of data to which she had access when she was working as a lexicographer for the Cobuild project at the University of Birmingham (Sinclair *et al.* 1987). She is also aware of the oversimplification criticized by Kilgarriff and Hanks in the preceding chapters. Since she is working on a concrete project where she is expected to come up with (preferably numbered) word meanings and definitions, however, she proposes a number of procedures for distinguishing clear-cut cases of different senses for a dictionary headword. The material she uses is obviously the same as what all corpus lexicographers resort to (concordanced citations extracted from large corpora). The procedures she advocates include syntactic analysis (e.g. the distinction between count and uncount uses), which often make it possible to disambiguate meanings. Collocational patterns also provide the lexicographer with clues to distinct meanings. To identify co-occurrence preferences, it is essential to consider the immediate environment of a given item, which frequently provides contextual evidence that can be used as a tool to disambiguate meanings. She tries to offer practical suggestions for describing words that have blurring between senses, which should be useful to lexicographers who are frequently confronted with clines between two or more meanings.

V   ON COLLOCATIONS, IDIOMS, AND DICTIONARIES

Collocations and phraseology are at the heart of the contextual triggers that need to be identified and exploited to disambiguate word meanings. Cowie (1998a: 2) notes that "recognition of phraseology as an academic discipline within linguistics is evident not only from vigorous and widespread research activity, but also from the publication of several specialized dictionaries reflecting one theoretical perspective or another and from the attention increasingly given to the subject in textbooks on lexical semantics, lexicology, and vocabulary in language teaching." In Chapter 11, Cowie discusses the status of a whole range of word combinations, from collocations, seen as associations of two or more lexemes occurring in a range of grammatical constructions, to idioms, which tend to resist a number of syntactic manipulations and are usually a lot more "opaque" (although we have seen above this reference to the opacity of idiomatic expressions may be a moot point when one tries to identify meaning potentials by clustering concordances). There are many definitions of collocations and many linguists would argue that the distinction between collocations and idioms is actually a cline, a continuum rather than a clear-cut dichotomy. An expression like *foot the bill* is generally regarded as a collocation and not as an idiom; yet, it cannot be passivized, while *spill the beans*, which many would recognize as a true idiom, can. Cowie discusses some of the syntactic tests and manipulations linguists have used to classify idioms and measure their resistance to variation (cleft sentence, insertion of material, passivization . . .). He notes that some transformations are more indicative of idiomaticity than others, which is a useful element to help lexicographers identify those combinations which should be granted entry status in a dictionary. Cowie also mentions routine formulae, speech-act formulae (*good morning* . . .), and gambits (*if you must know* . . .), which are structurally a lot more complex than the traditional collocations like *pay attention* or *confirmed bachelor*. The diversity of phraseological combinations and the notion that proficiency in a language depends upon prefabricated material are also described at length in the various chapters of Cowie (1998a), several of which directly deal with dictionaries and lexicography (Mel'čuk 1998; Fontenelle 1998; Cowie 1998b).

Collocations are a hot topic in linguistics and in lexicography. There is no dearth of descriptions and definitions (see Sinclair 1991 – and more particularly its Chapter 8 – for a purely statistical view of co-occurrence knowledge). Computational linguists even regularly organize conferences and workshops on the topic (Daille and Williams 2001) and excellent introductions to the field exist, covering the pedagogical or the computational perspectives (Cowie 1986 or Cowie in this volume; Cowie *et al.* 1983; Čermak 2001; Heid 1994; Fernando 1996; Benson 1985, 1989, to name but a few). Collocations are at the heart of Mel'čuk's Meaning-Text Theory, whose lexical component, the Explanatory Combinatory Dictionary (ECD), describes "restricted lexical co-occurrence" via lexical functions. These functions account for a whole range of collocational and paradigmatic relations. Mel'čuk (1998) offers an in-depth description of lexical functions. In Chapter 12, Fontenelle shows how a bilingual dictionary can be exploited to build a lexical-semantic database using this mechanism of lexical functions. He extracts the collocational material from the machine-readable version of the dictionary, tapping its microstructure and making use of the metalinguistic indicators used by the lexicographers to indicate that a particular collocate enters into a Subject–Verb, a Verb–Object, an Adjective–Noun, or a Noun–Noun relation. After enriching the data extracted from the dictionary, the resulting database can be searched via sophisticated semantic specifications, which makes it possible for instance to group all collocates that have the same specification (list the adjectives that express the Magn (intensifying) function or list verbs that express the 'deletion/nullification' (Liqu) function applied to the noun *law*, like *abolish*, *repeal*, *rescind*, or *do away with*). Fontenelle shows how such a database adds a thesauric, onomasiological dimension to an electronic dictionary, making it possible to extract semantic networks in which items that share a common meaning component are grouped and the relationship between the members of a collocation are labeled in terms of lexical functions (Mult(arrow) = *cloud/rain/sheaf/shower/storm* or Son(arrow) = *zing*). While this dictionary typically aims for breadth of description, a corpus is more useful to analyze frequent phenomena in depth, and Fontenelle (1992) points out that one of the major problems with intuition-based dictionaries such as the first edition (1978) of the Collins–Robert dictionary is that the collocations they include are often arbitrary and we have no evidence that they reflect the actual behavior of words. In the second part of Chapter 12, he therefore shows how the database can be linked to corpus data in order to allow the lexicographer to validate the existence of the collocational material tagged with the lexical function apparatus. This work was carried out in the framework of a series of projects focusing on lexical acquisition from electronic corpora and from machine-readable dictionaries to try to automatically extract co-occurrence knowledge and integrate it into lexicons usable by natural language processing applications. The semantic networks displayed in this article illustrate the Firthian principle that "words shall be known by the company they keep" (Firth 1957).

VI   ON DEFINITIONS

Lexicographers are often judged by their ability to write definitions for dictionaries. Definitions are an essential component of monolingual dictionaries, since users tend to turn to dictionaries mainly to look up words in order to find out about their meanings. Zgusta (1971), Ayto (1983), Stock (1988), or Landau (1984 – especially Chapter 4) all provide highly relevant information about definitions, Zgusta pointing out that the specification of meaning is the central task for the lexicographer (1971: 23). In most cases, dictionaries adopt the classical Aristotelian model of definitions based upon the distinction between *genus* and *differentiae*, the difficulty being to choose a genus term that is neither too general nor too specific. In many cases, dictionaries tend to define by synonym and antonym, as noted by Bolinger, who, in Chapter 13, tries to tackle the difficult task of defining what appears to be indefinable. He takes the example of the suffix *-less*, which, on the surface, seems to be easily defined as "the equivalent of the negative prefix *un-* attached to an adjective in *-ful*". Such a definition does not say anything about additional characteristics of adjectives in *-less*, however. While many adjectives in *-ful* are gradable (*very grateful, very insightful*...), most adjectives in *-less* are not (**very countless*, **very ceaseless*...). The study of minimal pairs also shows that a word in *-less* is not necessarily the exact antonym of the same word in *-ful* (*sinful* and *sinless* being cases in point). How should lexicographers render the hyperbolic sense of extremity found in *fathomless, countless* or even in *supperless*, which is probably worse than "without supper"? How do they indicate that *-less* is closer to "free from something undesirable" in *fearless* or *blameless,* while *doubtless* is not free from doubt at all? Dictionaries should serve as "a reminder of forgotten knowledge and an organizer of diffuse knowledge", Bolinger concludes.

The first edition of the Cobuild dictionary (Sinclair *et al.* 1987) introduced an innovation in the way definitions were written. Criticizing the over-use of parentheses to indicate likely objects and subjects, Hanks (1987) argues that the traditional conventions used in most modern dictionaries make definitions difficult reading for ordinary readers. The full-sentence definitions (FSDs) introduced by the Cobuild lexicographers were considered a real revolution at the time, with a first part placing the word being explained in a typical structure (A **brick** is...; **Calligraphy** is... – Hanks 1987: 117), and the second part identifying the meaning. In his discussion of the pros and cons of the traditional definitions, which are supposed to be substitutable in any context for the *definiendum,* Hanks stresses the importance of collocational and syntactic information and argues that full-sentence definitions make it possible to suggest much more easily whether collocates are obligatory, common but variable, or simply open. Selection preferences are easier to integrate into such definitions, he claims, giving the example of an "ergative" verb like *fuse,* that is, a verb that undergoes the so-called causative–inchoative alternation, as in the following definition taken from Cobuild1 (Sinclair *et al.* 1987):

2 When a light or some other piece of electrical apparatus **fuses** or when you **fuse** it, it stops working because of a fault, especially because too much electricity is being used.

The revolution created by the introduction of full-sentence definitions attracted a lot of attention and certainly influenced other learners' dictionaries. However, the relatively dogmatic approach proposed by the Cobuild team also attracted some criticism. In Chapter 14, Michael Rundell tries to explain why such defining conventions have not been adopted universally. This paper, which can be seen as an answer to Sinclair (2004) and Hanks (1987), acknowledges that the FSD model works better than alternative models in a number of cases (for instance if a verb is nearly always used in the passive form, like *lay up*, a full sentence definition is clearly better – "If someone is **laid up** with an illness, the illness makes it necessary for them to stay in bed"). The disadvantages of the FSD model cannot be ignored, however, and Rundell shows that, for instance, the coverage of an FSD-based dictionary is reduced because these definitions are on average much longer than traditional definitions. The complexity of these longer definitions can also be the source of a number of problems and can be challenging for learners. To some extent, the additional complexity entailed by full-sentence definitions is similar to the one that is sometimes created by the use of a controlled defining vocabulary in learners' dictionaries, which encourages the lexicographer to resort to syntactically more complex, convoluted (or less natural) constructions in order to avoid non-"core" vocabulary (Fontenelle, forthcoming). Rundell shows that pronoun references in *if*-definitions can also be unclear or that the redundancy found in some long-winded structures is sometimes not very informative ("You use X to describe something that . . . "). The solution he advocates is to use hybrid approaches, recognizing that FSDs work in some cases, but that, in a large number of other cases, simplicity and economy are more adequate.

VII   ON EXAMPLES

Definitions are not the only component of dictionary entries that generate a lot of heated discussions among lexicographers. Examples can also be controversial. Should they be based on authentic material or should they be written (invented) by the lexicographer? If they are excerpted from a corpus, should they be left unchanged or is the lexicographer allowed to edit them? What is an effective example? Batia Laufer discusses these issues in Chapter 15, showing that examples made up by lexicographers may be pedagogically more beneficial for language learners than authentic ones. There is clearly a difference between interesting examples and authentic examples, as is shown by Fox (1987: 142–143). One of the major difficulties for the lexicographer is to select ordinary, typical examples illustrating common usage and to resist the temptation to focus on abnormal, idiosyncratic, rare usages. Learners should not be distracted with unintelligible examples. Capitalizing on earlier studies focusing on the perceived value of invented and authentic examples, Laufer examines the real pedagogic values of examples by testing the comprehension of new words. She concludes that definitions and examples contribute to a better comprehension than examples alone and that examples made up by lexicographers enable learners to understand better than unedited examples that have really occurred. Readers who are interested in the Cobuild approach to examples or in a general comparison between Cobuild1 and LDOCE2 will consult Hausmann and Gorbahn (1989). Herbst (1996) also points out that, in this corpus era, even made-up examples tend to be based upon corpus research, which means that they are closer to authentic usage than twenty years ago, when the controversy about the relative merits of authentic and invented examples was raging.

VIII   ON GRAMMAR AND USAGE IN DICTIONARIES

The primary function of monolingual dictionaries is to provide information about meaning. Users also expect to find guidance about usage, however, which is why dictionaries, especially monolingual learners' dictionaries (MLDs), have tried to come up with systems to represent information about the grammatical properties of lexical items. Cowie (forthcoming) shows that systems for encoding grammatical patterns go back to Palmer and Hornby's pioneering work, which led first to the publication of the *Grammar of English Words* (Palmer 1938), and subsequently to that of the *Idiomatic and Syntactic English Dictionary* (Hornby 1942), later to become the *Oxford Advanced Learners' Dictionary* (see also Cowie 1999a for a good survey of the various generations of learners' dictionaries; Fontenelle (forthcoming) analyzes the specific contribution of the first edition of the *Longman Dictionary of Contemporary English* (Procter 1978) to linguistic research and natural language processing). The systematic description of complementation patterns and the "vocabulary control movement" promoting the use of a controlled defining vocabulary have been major milestones in the field of pedagogical lexicography, which, to a large extent, has been confined to English (and more specifically British) lexicography. In Chapter 16, Michael Rundell analyzes recent trends in English pedagogical lexicography. Advances in the area of computer technology (notably in the field of corpus storage and exploitation) as well as dictionary publishers' efforts to better meet the needs of users have resulted in deep changes. Rundell wonders whether all these revolutions have actually improved the products and to what extent the latest versions of MLDs are different from the first generation created by the above-mentioned pioneers. He argues that advances have been real and can be measured, both with respect to the quality of information (the linguistic description of how words are used) and the way this information is presented to the users. One of the most visible changes is certainly the systematic use of corpus-based examples, although, as we see in Chapter 15, there is some tension between the choice of lexicographer-invented examples or of exclusively corpus-based, unedited data. While most modern MLDs make use of authentic data, they differ in the extent to which sentences are processed and modified by the lexicographer to meet the users' needs. The use of electronic corpora has also enabled dictionary publishers to include reliable information on the frequency of occurrence of the entries, of their senses and their synonyms. This also makes it possible to organize polysemous entries on the basis of the frequency of their meanings, an approach which was pioneered by the Cobuild project and which most other MLDs have now adopted. Modern learners' dictionaries also pay more attention to phraseology, collocations, and the systematic inclusion of lexical relations such as synonymy, antonymy, and hyponymy, reflecting current research in psycholinguistics. Rundell also points out that the syntactic description of the environment in which a given lexical item can be inserted has been simplified after dictionary publishers realized that the obscure grammar codes used in the earlier editions of dictionaries such as OALD or LDOCE assumed too much grammatical knowledge on the part of the users and required them to consult separate tables of grammar codes to make sense of often cryptic complementation patterns such as V3, D2, T5a or VP11 and Dn.pr, to give only a few examples. While dictionary users and pedagogues agree that, as Fontenelle (forthcoming) puts it, a sound linguistic description of the complementation properties of lexical items does not always lead to an intelligible and usable scheme, those who suffer most from this evolution may be the computational linguists who are interested in exploiting these grammar codes when building parsers and for whom such delicate distinctions are crucial to build the lexical components of their NLP systems. Rundell argues, however, that the delicacy of the linguistic description is sacrificed to the need for maximum clarity, but that the losses are outweighed by the gains, users benefiting from the publishers' better understanding of the learners' needs and capabilities (see also the various papers in Herbst and Popp 1999).

IX   ON BILINGUAL LEXICOGRAPHY

The corpus revolution has not only affected the field of pedagogical lexicography. Bilingual dictionaries have also benefited from very large monolingual and multilingual corpora and from sophisticated corpus query tools. In Chapter 17, Sue Atkins shows how the lexicographer's work has changed over the last thirty years and how entries are (or could be) written at the beginning of the twenty-first century. She describes the use of KWIC concordances to discover the grammatical and combinatorial properties of lexical items. She shows how "word sketches" (described in more details in Chapter 20) enable the lexicographer to find out about grammatical relations and statistically significant co-occurrence patterns, something which the time-consuming manual scanning of thousands of concordances does not easily allow. Starting from the word *cook* and its French equivalents (*cuire, cuisiner, cuisine, cuisson*...), she then embarks on a clear demonstration of the benefits of a "frame semantic" analysis of the cooking frame. This application of the insights of theoretical linguistics to a concrete example of a bilingual entry makes it clear that the French translation part of the entry (and hence lexicography in general) can benefit from a detailed analysis by resorting to concepts such as beneficiary, duration, or causativity/inchoativity. For instance, it is essential to understand the notion of beneficiary if one wants to understand why *cook* is best translated as *préparer* when the person for whom the food is cooked is mentioned. For *She cooked me a wonderful breakfast* (= *elle m'a préparé un merveilleux petit déjeuner*), the verbs *cuire* and *cuisiner* are not possible, *faire* is possible and *préparer* is much more common. Yet, the translation *préparer* does not appear anywhere in the Collins–Robert English–French entry Atkins is analyzing. She also shows how the FrameNet database makes it possible to distinguish several senses of *cook* associated with the two main frames which it instantiates (the Apply_heat frame as opposed to the Cooking_creation frame). Nothing in the existing entry indicates that the causative–inchoative alternation, which is typical of change-of-state verbs, applies only to cases where *cook* refers to the Apply_heat frame with raw food (*cook the onions* vs. *the onions are cooking*), which again demonstrates that lexical semantics can contribute to lexicography and help lexicographers extract salient and relevant facts from the mass of linguistic data that is made available to them.

Atkins was the main editor of the English–French part of the first edition of the Collins–Robert dictionary (1978). Alain Duval was her opposite number for the French–English part of the same dictionary. In Chapter 18, he discusses the difficult problem of equivalence in bilingual dictionaries. Difficulties arise as soon as the reality referred to by the source language entry does not belong to the cultural universe of the target language user. The relationship between the structure of a bilingual entry and an encyclopedic article is also explored and the concepts of connotation and denotation are introduced. The examples he uses illustrate various degrees of equivalence, making it abundantly clear that perfect equivalence (which entails equal levels of denotation and of connotation) is far less frequent than one imagines. In other cases, translation equivalents are examined from the point of view of extension (the set of objects to which a concept applies) and comprehension (the set of features peculiar to a concept). Duval also introduces the concepts of language events (which record normalized, unbiased, and neutral translations) and of speech events (which correspond to creative coinages). He concludes by arguing for systematic and meticulous use of metalinguistic labels in bilingual dictionaries to guide users and warn them against dangerous generalizations. Such metalinguistic labels are found systematically in the best bilingual dictionaries. Readers interested in bilingual dictionaries will usefully consult Zgusta (1979, 1984), Snell-Hornby (1984, 1986, 1990), or Béjoint and Thoiron (1996).

X   ON TOOLS FOR LEXICOGRAPHERS

Gathering data is one thing; making sense of it is another. As Atkins stresses in Chapter 17, dictionaries packed with "cognitively salient" items do not necessarily provide a good description of naturally occurring language. Lexicographers need to be able to identify typical, natural patterns. While the primary material they work from is made up of KWIC lines, they need to go beyond these concordances to be able to identify frequent multi-word entries, typical collocations, or selection preferences. One of the major problems which the lexicographer faces is no longer the scarcity of the data. Rather, the analyst is confronted with a wealth of data which, beyond a given threshold, can no longer be analyzed manually. Twenty or even a hundred KWIC lines are manageable. 5000 lines cannot be read and "digested" by any human being working under the time constraints imposed by publication deadlines. Yet, with corpora of more than 100 million words (the HarperCollins Bank of English comprises over 400 million words), most queries are likely to generate several thousand lines. The lexicographer needs to process these "immeasurable torrents of evidence", to paraphrase Church *et al.* (1994: 153). In addition to sorting facilities, computational linguists have therefore worked with lexicographers to propose a number of statistical methods whose aim is precisely to help lexicographers separate the wheat from the chaff and identify central and typical usages. One such method, proposed by Ken Church and Patrick Hanks in Chapter 19, is centered on the concept of *mutual information*, which is used to identify relations between words which co-occur more often than chance. This paper, originally published in 1990, has been cited extensively and revolutionized the field of phraseology and collocation studies. It should be read by anybody who wonders how collocations can be extracted from corpora and what kind of (simple but ingenious) computation underlies this extraction process. In a later study, Church *et al.* (1994) show that mutual information (MI) values may be used in deciding whether a sequence of two words such as *requested and* is more or less interesting than the sequence *requested anonymity*. Lexicographers intuitively feel that the former sequence is linguistically (and lexicographically) uninteresting, while the latter combination probably deserves more attention and is a suitable candidate for inclusion in a dictionary (whether as an example of what one can typically *request* or as an example of which verb typically combines with *anonymity*). The problem is that this intuition is not reliable and cannot be readily tapped to discover that one typically requests *anonymity, permission* (to do something), *asylum* (and more specifically *political asylum*), *copies* (of a document) or *documents* themselves. The very first applications of such identification techniques in printed dictionaries can be found in the Cobuild dictionary (Sinclair *et al.* 1987; see also Sinclair 1991 for a very clear introduction to the concept of statistical collocations studies). Variations of MI scores were then adapted and refined, for instance by taking into account the relative frequencies of the words, because the original MI statistics unfortunately gave too much weight to low-frequency collocates. For instance, Baugh *et al.* (1996) describe in detail the statistical indices they used to measure the strength of collocations and to choose which collocations were included in the Cambridge CIDE dictionary (Procter 1995).

Statistical tools to extract collocations have become such a hot topic that several workshops and conferences have been organized over the last few years to address the role of collocations in lexicography, in applied and computational linguistics, and to compare the various approaches that have been proposed (see, for instance, Daille and Williams 2001; Krenn and Evert 2001, Evert and Krenn 2001 ...). A major objection is that MI scores reveal heterogeneous material and that no distinction is made between paradigmatic (vertical) and syntagmatic (horizontal) relations. They can be used to show that the words *doctor* and *nurse* often occur in similar contexts. This is probably interesting to show that the two words are semantically related, but whether this is a linguistically interesting piece of information is probably a moot point. On the other hand, collocations of a noun such as *rose* will include items like *red, orange, lovely, bunch, thorns*, or *petals*. The lexicographer who analyzes the output of these statistical techniques will have to abstract away from these raw results to try to come up with generalizations and regroupings into meaningful classes (*rose* is often accompanied by a <color> adjective; *bunch* will occur in an *N1 of N2* combination and *petals* and *thorns* are prototypical parts of a rose). To help lexicographers summarize concordances, Adam Kilgarriff and his colleagues present, in Chapter 20, the concept of a *Sketch Engine*, based upon *Word Sketches*, which can be seen as distinct collocate lists for subjects, direct objects, adjectives, *N of N* constructions, et cetera. A prerequisite here is the availability of a lemmatized and parsed corpus. Kilgarriff uses a lemmatized and part-of-speech tagged version of the British National Corpus (BNC), which is made up of 100 million words of contemporary British English. The Sketch Engine combines grammatical relations identified via shallow-parsing techniques and statistically significant frequencies of occurrence. Using such a tool, the lexicographer gets an instant snapshot of the environment of a given lexical item, which facilitates the decision-making process and helps her identify relevant and typical linguistic information to be included in the dictionary entry she is preparing. The successful use of this type of tool in large-size lexicographical projects such as the Macmillan English Dictionary (Rundell 2002; Kilgarriff and Rundell 2002); shows that researchers are on the right track. One of the next steps will be to create tools that help lexicographers identify relevant lexical items whose collocates are worth including in a dictionary. This area of research is still in its infancy, but the results of preliminary investigations seem to be promising (Kilgarriff 2006).

The provocative title of Chapter 21 ("The Future of Linguistics and Lexicographers: Will there be Lexicographers in the Year 3000?") will not leave lexicographers indifferent. In this article, originally presented as a keynote speech at the Euralex'98 Conference in Liège, Gregory Grefenstette discusses what computational linguistics can offer lexicographers to help them in their everyday tasks. He argues that a lot can be achieved with approximate linguistic tools. But Grefenstette is mainly concerned with abstracting away from surface differences in text and his approach probably works best when it is limited to the structural processing of texts (morphological analyses, POS tagging, shallow parsing...). The highest level of abstraction, that of semantic tagging, is still in its infancy because, as he puts it, "the problem is no longer one of simple structure, but also of meaning". His multi-dimensional view of the lexicon may mean that future lexicographers might no longer deal with some of their current tasks. Computers are very good at counting and, as we can see in Chapters 19 and 20, are becoming increasingly better at filtering KWIC lines, extracting patterns of usage, and clustering them in coherent ways. This might sound depressing for lexicographers, but Grefenstette concludes, very optimistically, that explaining what makes a cluster coherent is beyond the scope of a computer. Drawing distinctions and contrasts, condensing the facts in an intelligible way and making sense of the masses of data at our disposal is still something for which lexicographers will always be needed.

XI   ON SEMANTIC NETWORKS AND WORDNETS

NLP researchers have been trying to construct very large lexicons for over twenty-five years, first by trying to reuse existing machine-readable dictionaries, then by exploiting large corpora and developing machine-learning techniques to overcome the so-called lexical acquisition bottleneck. Two lexical databases have proved to be extremely popular among researchers as sources of lexical information. The *Longman Dictionary of Contemporary English* (Procter 1978) has probably been the most widely used database derived from a printed dictionary (see Boguraev and Briscoe 1989, Wilks *et al.* 1996, and Fontenelle (forthcoming) for details about why this dictionary has revolutionized the field of computational lexicography). Another lexical database, created from scratch and used in a large number of NLP projects, is the WordNet database developed by George Miller and his colleagues at the University of Princeton. Chapter 22 is an introduction to this on-line lexical database, originally published in a special issue of the *International Journal of Lexicography* (Miller *et al.* 1990). WordNet has undergone many changes in between, but anyone who is not yet familiar with this database should certainly start with this paper. Inspired by psycholinguistic theories of human memory, WordNet is a database organized in several categories corresponding to the main parts of speech: nouns, verbs, adjectives, adverbs, and function words. Very much like a thesaurus à la Roget, WordNet organizes lexical information in terms of word meanings, instead of word forms, which provide the main access key in a traditional printed dictionary. In this schema, words are assigned to "synsets", that is, sets of synonyms like {*revoke, annul, lift, countermand, reverse, repeal, overturn, rescind, vacate*}. Synonymy is therefore the core relation and it is argued that meanings can be represented by synsets. The whole database is organized by semantic relations (synonymy being the most important one) and these semantic relations can be seen as pointers between synsets. Antonymy (*light–dark*), hyponymy (a *sardine* is a *fish*), meronymy (part–whole relation – *finger* is a meronym of *hand*), and entailment (*succeed* entails *try*) are coded systematically, which explains why the database has been found so interesting by NLP researchers who cannot afford to spend a lot of time (or, more frequently, lack the lexicographical skills) to build a large-scale dictionary for information retrieval, word sense disambiguation, and other NLP tasks. Hanks and Pustejovsky (2005) note that one of the great merits of WordNet is that it is a full inventory of English words. Yet, they point out "that members of the NLP community seem to have accepted with little or no discussion WordNet's equation of synsets with senses. Closer inspection, however, shows that many of WordNet's senses are indistinguishable from one another by any criterion." The criticism leveled by Hanks and Pustejovsky at the database probably explains why the database has not been used by dictionary publishers and traditional lexicographers, mainly because it can be shown that the hierarchies are sometimes the product of the compilers' imagination and do not always correspond to anything that is empirically observable. For want of other resources, however, researchers (especially computational linguists) tend to turn to this free resource which definitely deserves more than a passing remark in a book about lexicography. Readers who are interested in this database will also turn to the other papers on WordNet in the Winter 1990 IJL Special Issue (Miller 1990a, 1990b; Gross and Miller 1990; Fellbaum 1990; Beckwith and Miller 1990). Fellbaum (1998) also gives an overview of more recent developments and has become the standard reference book on this database. It is also worth pointing out that the WordNet community of computational linguists, brought together in the Global WordNet Association, has also developed a number of similar (and parallel) databases in thirty languages (see Vossen 1998 on the EuroWordNet project), which testifies to the dynamic nature of these initiatives.

XII   ON DICTIONARY USE

The last section of this *Reader* deals with the way dictionaries are used. We know that, unfortunately, users hardly ever read the prefatory material lexicographers carefully prepare for their audience. Research has also shown that many users only read the first part of a dictionary entry and are unwilling to go over the other parts of the entry (Tono 2001: 161). In Chapter 23, Sue Atkins and Krista Varantola report on a study of the way people use dictionaries and consult them for help with translation tasks. Lexicographers and language teachers need to understand how people use dictionaries, when (and why) they decide to opt for an L2 dictionary instead of a bilingual one, what information they usually look for, which entries they look up, etc. Knowing which entries get looked up is especially important when lexicographers need to decide under which piece of a multi-word entry a definition or a translation should appear (see Bogaards 1990, 1998). Atkins and Varantola's purpose is to monitor the dictionary look-up process as naturally as possible when users try to translate a text, whether from their mother tongue into a foreign language or the other way round. The findings are interesting, since the analysis of the database they compiled shows that the types of expressions which caused most of the problems were very general words, and not what people usually consider "hard words". Combinations of extremely basic terms forming multi-word units are also a constant source of frustration. Is it also surprising to find out that students are interested in getting more information about collocations in English and about the combinatory properties of basic lexical items? The increased attention paid by the latest learners' dictionaries to collocations is a direct response to such requests and to those findings.

Atkins and Varantola also point out the amount of weight accorded by users to bilingual dictionaries compared with monolingual dictionaries. While teachers tend to encourage their students to use monolingual dictionaries (whether for native speakers or for learners), it is impossible to ignore this overwhelming preference for bilingual dictionaries (although they observed that a large number of people moved from bilingual dictionaries to monolingual dictionaries in the middle of a search).

The authors conclude by pleading for careful and thorough teaching of dictionary skills to help dictionary users make sense of entries and extract the information they need. Teachers also need to be aware of how their students use these reference works and lexicographers need to understand what users' pain points are, typically in the field of collocation and complementation. Similar studies on dictionary use can be found in Atkins (1998), Atkins and Hulstijn (1998), Thumb (2004), or Tono (2001).

PART I

Metalexicography, Macrostructure, Microstructure,
and the Contribution of Linguistic Theory

2

The Plan of a Dictionary of the English Language

SAMUEL JOHNSON*

THE PLAN OF A DICTIONARY OF THE ENGLISH LANGUAGE; Addressed to the Right Honourable PHILIP DORMER, Earl of CHESTERFIELD, One of His Majesty's Principal Secretaries of State

My LORD,

WHEN first I undertook to write an English Dictionary, I had no expectation of any higher patronage than that of the proprietors of the copy, nor prospect of any other advantage than the price of my labour; I knew that the work in which I engaged is generally considered as drudgery for the blind, as the proper toil of artless industry, a task that requires neither the light of learning, nor the activity of genius, but may be successfully performed without any higher quality than that of bearing burthens with dull patience, and beating the track of the alphabet with sluggish resolution.

WHETHER this opinion, so long transmitted and so widely propagated, had its beginning from truth and nature, or from accident and prejudice, whether it be decreed by the authority of reason, or the tyranny of ignorance, that of all the candidates for literary praise, the unhappy lexicographer holds the lowest place, neither vanity nor interest incited me to inquire. It appeared that the province allotted me was of all the regions of learning generally confessed to be the least delightful, that it was believed to produce neither fruits nor flowers; and that after a long and laborious cultivation, not even the barren laurel had been found upon it.

YET on this province, my Lord, I enter'd with the pleasing hope, that, as it was low, it likewise would be safe. I was drawn forward with the prospect of employment, which, tho' not splendid, would be useful, and which tho' it could not make my life envied, would keep it innocent, which would awaken no passion, engage me in no contention, nor throw in my way any temptation to disturb the quiet of others by censure, or my own by flattery.

I HAD read indeed of times, in which princes and statesmen thought it part of their honour to promote the improvement of their native tongues, and in which dictionaries were written under the protection of greatness. To the patrons of such undertakings, I willingly paid the homage of believing that they, who were thus solicitous for the perpetuity of their language, had reason to expect that their actions would be celebrated by posterity, and that the eloquence which they promoted would be employed in their praise. But I considered such acts of beneficence as prodigies, recorded rather to raise wonder than expectation; and content with the terms that I had stipulated, had not suffer'd my imagination to flatter me with any other encouragement, when I found that my design had been thought by your Lordship of importance sufficient to attract your favour.

* London: J. and P. Knapton, 1747. Edited by Jack Lynch and reprinted with his permission. http://andromeda.rutgers.edu/~jlynch/Texts/plan.html

How far this unexpected distinction can be rated among the happy incidents of life, I am not yet able to determine. Its first effect has been to make me anxious lest it should fix the attention of the public too much upon me, and as it once happened to an epic poet of France, by raising the reputation of the attempt, obstruct the reception of the work. I imagine what the world will expect from a scheme, prosecuted under your Lordship's influence, and I know that expectation, when her wings are once expanded, easily reaches heights which performance never will attain, and when she has mounted the summit of perfection, derides her follower, who dies in the pursuit.

Not therefore to raise expectation, but to repress it, I here lay before your Lordship the plan of my undertaking, that more may not be demanded than I intend, and that before it is too far advanced to be thrown into a new method, I may be advertised of its defects or superfluities. Such informations I may justly hope, from the emulation with which those who desire the praise of elegance or discernment must contend in the promotion of a design that you, my Lord, have not thought unworthy to share your attention with treaties and with wars.

In the first attempt to methodise my ideas, I found a difficulty which extended itself to the whole work. It was not easy to determine by what rule of distinction the words of this dictionary were to be chosen. The chief intent of it is to preserve the purity and ascertain the meaning of our English idiom; and this seems to require nothing more than that our language be considered so far as it is our own; that the words and phrases used in the general intercourse of life, or found in the works of those whom we commonly stile polite writers, be selected, without including the terms of particular professions, since, with the arts to which they relate, they are generally derived from other nations, and are very often the same in all the languages of this part of the world. This is perhaps the exact and pure idea of a grammatical dictionary; but in lexicography, as in other arts, naked science is too delicate for the purposes of life. The value of a work must be estimated by its use: it is not enough that a dictionary delights the critic, unless at the same time it instructs the learner; as it is to little purpose, that an engine amuses the philosopher by the subtilty of its mechanism, if it requires so much knowledge in its application, as to be of no advantage to the common workman.

The title which I prefix to my work has long conveyed a very miscellaneous idea, and they that take a dictionary into their hands have been accustomed to expect from it a solution of almost every difficulty. If foreign words therefore were rejected, it could be little regarded, except by critics, or those who aspire to criticism; and however it might enlighten those that write, would be all darkness to them that only read. The unlearned much oftener consult their dictionaries, for the meaning of words, than for their structures or formations; and the words that most want explanation, are generally terms of art, which therefore experience has taught my predecessors to spread with a kind of pompous luxuriance over their productions.

The academicians of France, indeed, rejected terms of science in their first essay, but found afterwards a necessity of relaxing the rigour of their determination; and, though they would not naturalize them at once by a single act, permitted them by degrees to settle themselves among the natives, with little opposition, and it would surely be no proof of judgment to imitate them in an error which they have now retracted, and deprive the book of its chief use by scrupulous distinctions.

Of such words, however, all are not equally to be considered as parts of our language, for some of them are naturalized and incorporated, but others still continue aliens, and are rather auxiliaries than subjects. This naturalization is produced either by an admission into common speech in some metaphorical signification, which is the acquisition of a kind of property among us, as we say the *zenith* of advancement, the *meridian* of life, the *cynosure*[1] of neighbouring eyes; or it is the consequence of long intermixture and frequent use, by which the ear is accustomed to the sound of words till their original is forgotten, as in *equator, satellites*; or of the change of a foreign to an English termination, and a conformity to the laws of the speech into which they are adopted, as in *category, cachexy, peripneumony*.

OF those which yet continue in the state of aliens, and have made no approaches towards assimilation, some seem necessary to be retained, because the purchasers of the dictionary will expect to find them. Such are many words in the common law, as *capias, habeas corpus, præmunire, nisi prius*; such are some terms of controversial divinity, as *hypostasis*; and of physick, as the names of diseases; and in general all terms which can be found in books not written professedly upon particular arts, or can be supposed necessary to those who do not regularly study them. Thus when a reader not skilled in physick happens in Milton upon this line,

> ——————pining atrophy,
> *Marasmus*, and wide-wasting pestilence.

he will with equal expectation look into his dictionary for the word *marasmus*, as for *atrophy*, or *pestilence*, and will have reason to complain if he does not find it.

IT seems necessary to the completion of a dictionary designed not merely for critics but for popular use, that it should comprise, in some degree, the peculiar words of every profession; that the terms of war and navigation should be inserted so far as they can be required by readers of travels, and of history; and those of law, merchandise and mechanical trades, so far as they can be supposed useful in the occurrences of common life.

BUT there ought, however, to be some distinction made between the different classes of words, and therefore it will be proper to print those which are incorporated into the language in the usual character, and those which are still to be considered as foreign in the Italick letter.

ANOTHER question may arise, with regard to appellatives, or the names of species. It seems of no great use to set down the words *horse, dog, cat, willow, alder, daisy, rose*, and a thousand others, of which it will be hard to give an explanation not more obscure than the word itself. Yet it is to be considered, that, if the names of animals be inserted, we must admit those which are more known, as well as those with which we are, by accident, less acquainted; and if they are all rejected, how will the reader be relieved from difficulties produced by allusions to the crocodile, the camæleon, the ichneumon, and the hyæna? If no plants are to be mentioned, the most pleasing part of nature will be excluded, and many beautiful epithets be unexplained. If only those which are less known are to be mentioned, who shall fix the limits of the reader's learning? The importance of such explications appears from the mistakes which the want of them has occasioned. Had Shakespeare had a dictionary of this kind, he had not made the *woodbine* entwine the *honeysuckle*; nor would Milton, with such assistance, have disposed so improperly of his *ellops* and his *scorpion*.

BESIDES, as such words, like others, require that their accents should be settled, their sounds ascertained, and their etymologies deduced, they cannot be properly omitted in the dictionary. And though the explanations of some may be censured as trivial, because they are almost universally understood, and those of others as unnecessary, because they will seldom occur, yet it seems not proper to omit them, since it is rather to be wished that many readers should find more than they expect, than that one should miss what he might hope to find.

---

[1] Milton.

WHEN all the words are selected and arranged, the first part of the work to be considered is the ORTHOGRAPHY, which was long vague and uncertain, which at last, when its fluctuation ceased, was in many cases settled but by accident, and in which, according to your Lordship's observation, there is still great uncertainty among the best critics; nor is it easy to state a rule by which we may decide between custom and reason, or between the equiponderant authorities of writers alike eminent for judgment and accuracy.

THE great orthographical contest has long subsisted between etymology and pronunciation. It has been demanded, on one hand, that men should write as they speak; but as it has been shewn, that this conformity never was attained in any language, and that it is not more easy to persuade men to agree exactly in speaking than in writing, it may be asked with equal propriety, why men do not rather speak as they write. In France, where this controversy was at its greatest height, neither party, however ardent, durst adhere steadily to their own rule; the etymologist was often forced to spell with the people; and the advocate for the authority of pronunciation, found it sometimes deviating capriciously from the received use of writing, that he was constrained to comply with the rule of his adversaries, lest he should lose the end by the means, and be left alone by following the crowd.

WHEN a question of orthography is dubious, that practice has, in my opinion, a claim to preference, which preserves the greatest number of radical letters, or seems most to comply with the general custom of our language. But the chief rule which I propose to follow, is to make no innovation, without a reason sufficient to balance the inconvenience of change; and such reasons I do not expect often to find. All change is of itself an evil, which ought not to be hazarded but for evident advantage; and as inconstancy is in every case a mark of weakness, it will add nothing to the reputation of our tongue. There are, indeed, some who despise the inconveniencies of confusion, who seem to take pleasure in departing from custom, and to think alteration desirable for its own sake; and the reformation of our orthography, which these writers have attempted, should not pass without its due honours, but that I suppose they hold singularity its own reward, or may dread the fascination of lavish praise.

THE present usage of spelling, where the present usage can be distinguished, will therefore in this work be generally followed, yet there will be often occasion to observe, that it is in itself inaccurate, and tolerated rather than chosen; particularly, when by the change of one letter, or more, the meaning of a word is obscured, as in *farrier*, for *ferrier*, as it was formerly written, from *ferrum* or *fer*; in *gibberish* for *gebrish*, the jargon of Geber and his chymical followers, understood by none but their own tribe. It will be likewise sometimes proper to trace back the orthography of different ages, and shew by what gradations the word departed from its original.

CLOSELY connected with orthography is PRONUNCIATION, the stability of which is of great importance to the duration of a language, because the first change will naturally begin by corruptions in the living speech. The want of certain rules for the pronunciation of former ages, has made us wholly ignorant of the metrical art of our ancient poets; and since those who study their sentiments regret the loss of their numbers, it is surely time to provide that the harmony of the moderns may be more permanent.

A NEW pronunciation will make almost a new speech, and therefore since one great end of this undertaking is to fix the English language, care will be taken to determine the accentuation of all polysyllables by proper authorities, as it is one of those capricious phænomena which cannot be easily reduced to rules. Thus there is no antecedent reason for difference of accent in the two words *dolorous* and *sonorous*, yet of the one Milton gives the sound in this line,

> He pass'd o'er many a region *dolorous*,

and that of the other in this,

> *Sonorous* metal blowing martial sounds.

IT may be likewise proper to remark metrical licenses, such as contractions, *generous*, *gen'rous*, *reverend*, *rev'rend*, and coalitions, as *region*, *question*.

BUT it is still more necessary to fix the pronunciation of monosyllables, by placing with them words of correspondent sound, that one may guard the other against the danger of that variation, which to some of the most common has already happened, so that the words *wound*, and *wind*, as they are now frequently pronounced, will not rhyme to *sound*, and *mind*. It is to be remarked that many words written alike are differently pronounc'd, as *flow*, and *brow*, which may be thus registered *flow*, *woe*, *brow*, *now*, or of which the exemplification may be generally given by a distich. Thus the words *tear* or lacerate, and *tear* the water of the eye, have the same letters, but may be distinguished thus, *tear*, *dare*; *tear*, *peer*.

SOME words have two sounds, which may be equally admitted, as being equally defensible by authority. Thus *great* is differently used.

> For Swift and him despis'd the farce of state,
> The sober follies of the wise and *great*. POPE.

> As if misfortune made the throne her seat,
> And none could be unhappy but the *great*. ROWE.

The care of such minute particulars may be censured as trifling, but these particulars have not been thought unworthy of attention in more polished languages.

THE accuracy of the French, in stating the sounds of their letters, is well known; and, among the Italians, Crescembeni has not thought it unnecessary to inform his countrymen of the words, which, in compliance with different rhymes, are allowed to be differently spelt, and of which the number is now so fixed, that no modern poet is suffered to encrease it.

WHEN the orthography and pronunciation are adjusted, the ETYMOLOGY or DERIVATION is next to be considered, and the words are to be distinguished according to the different classes, whether simple, as *day*, *light*, or compound as *day-light*; whether primitive, as, to *act*, or derivative, as *action*, *actionable*, *active*, *activity*. This will much facilitate the attainment of our language, which now stands in our dictionaries a confused heap of words without dependence, and without relation.

WHEN this part of the work is performed, it will be necessary to inquire how our primitives are to be deduced from foreign languages, which may be often very successfully performed by the assistance of our own etymologists. This search will give occasion to many curious disquisitions, and sometimes perhaps to conjectures, which, to readers unacquainted with this kind of study, cannot but appear improbable and capricious. But it may be reasonably imagined, that what is so much in the power of men as language, will very often be capriciously conducted. Nor are these disquisitions and conjectures to be considered altogether as wanton sports of wit, or vain shews of learning; our language is well known not to be primitive or self-originated, but to have adopted words of every generation, and either for the supply of its necessities, or the encrease of its copiousness, to have received additions from very distant regions; so that in search of the progenitors of our speech, we may wander from the tropic to the frozen zone, and find some in the valleys of Palestine and some upon the rocks of Norway.

BESIDE the derivation of particular words, there is likewise an etymology of phrases. Expressions are often taken from other languages, some apparently, as to *run a risque*, *courir un risque*; and some even when we do not seem to borrow their words; thus, to *bring about* or accomplish, appears an English phrase, but in reality our native word *about* has no such import, and it is only a French expression, of which we have an example in the common phrase, *venir à bout d'une affaire*.

IN exhibiting the descent of our language, our etymologists seem to have been too lavish of their learning, having traced almost every word through various tongues, only to shew what was shewn sufficiently by the first derivation. This practice is of great use in synoptical lexicons, where mutilated and doubtful languages are explained by their affinity to others more certain and extensive, but is generally superfluous in English etymologies. When the word is easily deduced from a Saxon original, I shall not often inquire further, since we know not the parent of the Saxon dialect, but when it is borrowed from the French, I shall shew whence the French is apparently derived. Where a Saxon root cannot be found, the defect may be supplied from kindred languages, which will be generally furnished with much liberality by the writers of our glossaries; writers who deserve often the highest praise, both of judgment and industry, and may expect at least to be mentioned with honour by me, whom they have freed from the greatest part of a very laborious work, and on whom they have imposed, at worst, only the easy task of rejecting superfluities.

BY tracing in this manner every word to its original, and not admitting, but with great caution, any of which no original can be found, we shall secure our language from being overrun with *cant*, from being crouded with low terms, the spawn of folly or affectation, which arise from no just principles of speech, and of which therefore no legitimate derivation can be shewn.

WHEN the etymology is thus adjusted, the ANALOGY of our language is next to be considered; when we have discovered whence our words are derived, we are to examine by what rules they are governed, and how they are inflected through their various terminations. The terminations of the English are few, but those few have hitherto remained unregarded by the writers of our dictionaries. Our substantives are declined only by the plural termination, our adjectives admit no variation but in the degrees of comparison, and our verbs are conjugated by auxiliary words, and are only changed in the preter tense.

To our language may be with great justness applied the observation of *Quintilian*, that speech was not formed by an analogy sent from heaven. It did not descend to us in a state of uniformity and perfection, but was produced by necessity and enlarged by accident, and is therefore composed of dissimilar parts, thrown together by negligence, by affectation, by learning, or by ignorance.

OUR inflections therefore are by no means constant, but admit of numberless irregularities, which in this dictionary will be diligently noted. Thus *fox* makes in the plural *foxes*, but *ox* makes *oxen*. *Sheep* is the same in both numbers. Adjectives are sometimes compared by changing the last syllable, as *proud*, *prouder*, *proudest*; and sometimes by particles prefixed, as *ambitious*, *more* ambitious, *most* ambitious. The forms of our verbs are subject to great variety; some end their preter tense in *ed*, as I *love*, I *loved*, I have *loved*, which may be called the regular form, and is followed by most of our verbs of southern original. But many depart from this rule, without agreeing in any other, as I *shake*, I *shook*, I have *shaken*, or *shook* as it is sometimes written in poetry; I *make*, I *made*, I have *made*; I *bring*, I *brought*; I *wring*, I *wrung*; and many others, which, as they cannot be reduced to rules, must be learned from the dictionary rather than the grammar.

THE verbs are likewise to be distinguished according to their qualities, as actives from neuters; the neglect of which has already introduced some barbarities in our conversation, which, if not obviated by just animadversions, may in time creep into our writings.

THUS, my Lord, will our language be laid down, distinct in its minutest subdivisions, and resolved into its elemental principles. And who upon this survey can forbear to wish, that these fundamental atoms of our speech might obtain the firmness and immutability of the primogenial and constituent particles of matter, that they might retain their substance while they alter their appearance, and be varied and compounded, yet not destroyed?

BUT this is a privilege which words are scarcely to expect: for, like their author, when they are not gaining strength, they are generally losing it. Though art may sometimes prolong their duration, it will rarely give them perpetuity, and their changes will be almost always informing us, that language is the work of man, of a being from whom permanence and stability cannot be derived.

WORDS having been hitherto considered as separate and unconnected, are now to be likewise examined as they are ranged in their various relations to others by the rules of SYNTAX or construction, to which I do not know that any regard has been yet shewn in English dictionaries, and in which the grammarians can give little assistance. The syntax of this language is too inconstant to be reduced to rules, and can be only learned by the distinct consideration of particular words as they are used by the best authors. Thus, we say according to the present modes of speech, the soldier died *of* his wounds, and the sailor perished *with* hunger; and every man acquainted with our language would be offended with a change of these particles, which yet seem originally assigned by chance, there being no reason to be drawn from grammar why a man may not, with equal propriety, be said to die *with* a wound or perish *of* hunger.

OUR syntax therefore is not to be taught by general rules, but by special precedents; and in examining whether Addison has been with justice accused of a solecism in this passage,

> The poor inhabitant——
> Starves in the midst of nature's bounty curst,
> And in the loaden vineyard *dies for thirst*,

it is not in our power to have recourse to any established laws of speech, but we must remark how the writers of former ages have used the same word, and consider whether he can be acquitted of impropriety, upon the testimony of Davies, given in his favour by a similar passage.

> She loaths the wat'ry glass wherein she gaz'd,
> And shuns it still, although *for thirst she dye*.

WHEN the construction of a word is explained, it is necessary to pursue it through its train of PHRASEOLOGY, through those forms where it is used in a manner peculiar to our language, or in senses not to be comprised in the general explanations; as from the verb *make*, arise these phrases, to *make love*, to *make an end*, to *make way*, as he *made way* for his followers, the ship *made way* before the wind; to *make a bed*, to *make merry*, to *make a mock*, to *make presents*, to *make a doubt*, to *make out an assertion*, to *make good* a breach, to *make good* a cause, to *make nothing* of an attempt, to *make lamentation*, to *make a merit*, and many others which will occur in reading with that view, and which only their frequency hinders from being generally remarked.

THE great labour is yet to come, the labour of interpreting these words and phrases with brevity, fulness and perspicuity; a task of which the extent and intricacy is sufficiently shewn by the miscarriage of those who have generally attempted it. This difficulty is increased by the necessity of explaining the words in the same language, for there is often only one word for one idea; and though it be easy to translate the words *bright*, *sweet*, *salt*, *bitter*, into another language, it is not easy to explain them.

WITH regard to the INTERPRETATION many other questions have required consideration. It was some time doubted whether it be necessary to explain the things implied by particular words. As under the term *baronet*, whether instead of this explanation, *a title of honour next in degree to that of baron*, it would be better to mention more particularly the creation, privileges and rank of baronets; and whether under the word *barometer*, instead of being satisfied with observing that it is *an instrument to discover the weight of the air*, it would be fit to spend a few lines upon its invention, construction and principles. It is not to be expected that with the explanation of the one the herald should be satisfied, or the philosopher with that of the other; but since it will be required by common readers, that the explications should be sufficient for common use, and since without some attention to such demands the dictionary cannot become generally valuable, I have determined to consult the best writers for explanations real as well as verbal, and perhaps I may at last have reason to say, after one of the augmenters of Furetier, that my book is more learned than its author.

IN explaining the general and popular language, it seems necessary to sort the several senses of each word, and to exhibit first its natural and primitive signification, as

To *arrive*, to reach the shore in a voyage. He *arrived* at a safe harbour.

THEN to give its consequential meaning, *to arrive*, to reach any place whether by land or sea; as, he *arrived* at his country seat.

THEN its metaphorical sense, to obtain any thing desired; as, he *arrived* at a peerage.

THEN to mention any observation that arises from the comparison of one meaning with another; as, it may be remarked of the word *arrive*, that in consequence of its original and etymological sense, it cannot be properly applied but to words signifying something desirable; thus we say, a man *arrived* at happiness, but cannot say, without a mixture of irony, he *arrived* at misery.

Ground, the earth, generally as opposed to the air or water. He swam till he reached *ground*. The bird fell to the *ground*.

THEN follows the accidental or consequential signification, in which *ground* implies any thing that lies under another; as, he laid colours upon a rough *ground*. The silk had blue flowers on a red *ground*.

THEN the remoter or metaphorical signification; as, the *ground* of his opinion was a false computation. The *ground* of his work was his father's manuscript.

AFTER having gone through the natural and figurative senses, it will be proper to subjoin the poetical sense of each word, where it differs from that which is in common use; as, *wanton* applied to any thing of which the motion is irregular without terrour, as

> In *wanton* ringlets curl'd her hair.

To the poetical sense may succeed the familiar; as of *toast*, used to imply the person whose health is drunk; as,

> The wise man's passion, and the vain man's *toast*. POPE.

THE familiar may be followed by the burlesque; as of *mellow*, applied to good fellowship.

> In all thy humours whether grave, or *mellow*. ADDISON.

OR of *bite,* used for *cheat*.

>——More a dupe than wit,
>Sappho can tell you, how this man was *bit*. POPE.

AND lastly, may be produced the peculiar sense, in which a word is found in any great author. As *faculties* in Shakespeare signifies the powers of authority.

>——This Duncan
>Has born his *faculties* so meek, has been
>So clear in his great office, that, *&c.*

THE signification of adjectives may be often ascertained by uniting them to substantives, as *simple swain*, *simple sheep*; sometimes the sense of a substantive may be elucidated by the epithets annexed to it in good authors, as the *boundless ocean*, the *open lawns*, and where such advantage can be gained by a short quotation it is not to be omitted.

THE difference of signification in words generally accounted synonymous, ought to be carefully observed; as in *pride, haughtiness, arrogance*: and the strict and critical meaning ought to be distinguished from that which is loose and popular; as in the word *perfection*, which though in its philosophical and exact sense, it can be of little use among human beings, is often so much degraded from its original signification, that the academicians have inserted in their work, *the perfection of a language*, and with a little more licentiousness might have prevailed on themselves to have added *the perfection of a dictionary*.

THERE are many other characters of words which it will be of use to mention. Some have both an active and passive signification, as *fearful*, that which gives or which feels terror, a *fearful prodigy*, a *fearful hare*. Some have a personal, some a real meaning, as in apposition to *old* we use the adjective *young* of animated beings, and *new* of other things. Some are restrained to the sense of praise, and others to that of disapprobation, so commonly, though not always, we *exhort* to good actions, we *instigate* to ill; we *animate*, *incite* and *encourage* indifferently to good or bad. So we usually *ascribe* good, but *impute* evil; yet neither the use of these words, nor perhaps of any other in our licentious language, is so established as not to be often reversed by the correctest writers. I shall therefore, since the rules of style, like those of law, arise from precedents often repeated, collect the testimonies on both sides, and endeavour to discover and promulgate the decrees of custom, who has so long possessed, whether by right or by usurpation, the sovereignty of words.

IT is necessary likewise to explain many words by their opposition to others; for contraries are best seen when they stand together. Thus the verb *stand* has one sense as opposed to *fall*, and another as opposed to *fly*; for want of attending to which distinction, obvious as it is, the learned Dr. Bentley has squandered his criticism to no purpose, on these lines of Paradise Lost.

>——In heaps
>Chariot and charioteer lay over-turn'd,
>And fiery foaming steeds. What *stood, recoil'd*,
>O'erwearied, through the faint satanic host,
>Defensive scarce, or with pale fear surpris'd,
>*Fled* ignominious——

"Here," says the critic, "as the sentence is now read, we find that what *stood, fled*," and therefore he proposes an alteration, which he might have spared if he had consulted a dictionary, and found that nothing more was affirmed than that those *fled* who did *not fall*.

IN explaining such meanings as seem accidental and adventitious, I shall endeavour to give an account of the means by which they were introduced. Thus, to *eke out* any thing, signifies to lengthen it beyond its just dimensions by some low artifice, because the word *eke* was the usual refuge of our old writers when they wanted a syllable. And *buxom*, which means only *obedient*, is now made, in familiar phrases, to stand for *wanton*, because in an ancient form of marriage, before the reformation, the bride promised complaisance and obedience in these terms, "I will be bonair and *buxom* in bed and at board."

I KNOW well, my Lord, how trifling many of these remarks will appear separately considered, and how easily they may give occasion to the contemptuous merriment of sportive idleness, and the gloomy censures of arrogant stupidity; but dulness it is easy to despise, and laughter it is easy to repay. I shall not be solicitous what is thought of my work by such as know not the difficulty or importance of philological studies, nor shall think those that have done nothing qualified to condemn me for doing little. It may not, however, be improper to remind them, that no terrestrial greatness is more than an aggregate of little things, and to inculcate after the Arabian proverb, that drops added to drops constitute the ocean.

THERE remains yet to be considered the DISTRIBUTION of words into their proper classes, or that part of lexicography which is strictly critical.

THE popular part of the language, which includes all words not appropriated to particular sciences, admits of many distinctions and subdivisions; as, into words of general use; words employed chiefly in poetry; words obsolete; words which are admitted only by particular writers, yet not in themselves improper; words used only in burlesque writing; and words impure and barbarous.

WORDS of general use will be known by having no sign of particularity, and their various senses will be supported by authorities of all ages.

THE words appropriated to poetry will be distinguished by some mark prefixed, or will be known by having no authorities but those of poets.

OF antiquated or obsolete words, none will be inserted but such as are to be found in authors who wrote since the accession of Elizabeth, from which we date the golden age of our language; and of these many might be omitted, but that the reader may require, with an appearance of reason, that no difficulty should be left unresolved in books which he finds himself invited to read, as confessed and established models of style. These will be likewise pointed out by some note of exclusion, but not of disgrace.

THE words which are found only in particular books, will be known by the single name of him that has used them; but such will be omitted, unless either their propriety, elegance, or force, or the reputation of their authors affords some extraordinary reason for their reception.

WORDS used in burlesque and familiar compositions, will be likewise mentioned with their proper authorities, such as *dudgeon* from Butler, and *leasing* from Prior, and will be diligently characterized by marks of distinction.

BARBAROUS or impure words and expressions, may be branded with some note of infamy, as they are carefully to be eradicated wherever they are found; and they occur too frequently even in the best writers. As in Pope,

> ——in endless error *hurl'd*.
> *'Tis these* that early taint the female soul.

In Addison,

> Attend to what a *lesser* muse indites.

And in Dryden,

> A dreadful quiet felt, and *worser* far
> Than arms.———

If this part of the work can be well performed, it will be equivalent to the proposal made by Boileau to the academicians, that they should review all their polite writers, and correct such impurities as might be found in them, that their authority might not contribute, at any distant time, to the depravation of the language.

WITH regard to questions of purity, or propriety, I was once in doubt whether I should not attribute too much to myself in attempting to decide them, and whether my province was to extend beyond the proposition of the question, and the display of the suffrages on each side; but I have been since determined by your Lordship's opinion, to interpose my own judgment, and shall therefore endeavour to support what appears to me most consonant to grammar and reason. Ausonius thought that modesty forbad him to plead inability for a task to which Caesar had judged him equal.

Cur me posse negem posse quod ille putat?[2]

And I may hope, my Lord, that since you, whose authority in our language is so generally acknowledged, have commissioned me to declare my own opinion, I shall be considered as exercising a kind of vicarious jurisdiction, and that the power which might have been denied to my own claim, will be readily allowed me as the delegate of your Lordship.

IN citing authorities, on which the credit of every part of this work must depend, it will be proper to observe some obvious rules, such as of preferring writers of the first reputation to those of an inferior rank, of noting the quotations with accuracy, and of selecting, when it can be conveniently done, such sentences, as, besides their immediate use, may give pleasure or instruction by conveying some elegance of language, or some precept of prudence, or piety.

IT has been asked, on some occasions, who shall judge the judges? And since with regard to this design, a question may arise by what authority the authorities are selected, it is necessary to obviate it, by declaring that many of the writers whose testimonies will be alleged, were selected by Mr. Pope, of whom I may be justified in affirming, that were he still alive, solicitous as he was for the success of this work, he would not be displeased that I have undertaken it.

IT will be proper that the quotations be ranged according to the ages of their authors, and it will afford an agreeable amusement, if to the words and phrases which are not of our own growth, the name of the writer who first introduced them can be affixed, and if, to words which are now antiquated, the authority be subjoined of him who last admitted them. Thus for *scathe* and *buxom*, now obsolete, Milton may be cited:

> ——The mountain oak
> Stands *scath'd* to heaven——
> ——He with broad sails
> Winnow'd the *buxom* air——

By this method every word will have its history, and the reader will be informed of the gradual changes of the language, and have before his eyes the rise of some words, and the fall of others. But observations so minute and accurate are to be desired rather than expected, and if use be carefully supplied, curiosity must sometimes bear its disappointments.

THIS, my Lord, is my idea of an English dictionary, a dictionary by which the pronunciation of our language may be fixed, and its attainment facilitated; by which its purity may be preserved, its use ascertained, and its duration lengthened. And though, perhaps, to correct the language of nations by books of grammar, and amend their manners by discourses of morality, may be tasks equally difficult; yet, as it is unavoidable to wish, it is natural likewise

---

2 Why should I say that I cannot do what he thinks I can? (Ausonius, *Preface to the Emperor Theodosius*, line 12).

to hope, that your Lordship's patronage may not be wholly lost; that it may contribute to the preservation of ancient, and the improvement of modern writers; that it may promote the reformation of those translators, who for want of understanding the characteristical difference of tongues, have formed a chaotic dialect of heterogeneous phrases; and awaken to the care of purer diction, some men of genius, whose attention to argument makes them negligent of style, or whose rapid imagination, like the Peruvian torrents, when it brings down gold, mingles it with sand.

WHEN I survey the Plan which I have laid before you, I cannot, my Lord, but confess, that I am frighted at its extent, and, like the soldiers of Cæsar, look on Britain as a new world, which it is almost madness to invade. But I hope, that though I should not complete the conquest, I shall at least discover the coast, civilize part of the inhabitants, and make it easy for some other adventurer to proceed farther, to reduce them wholly to subjection, and settle them under laws.

WE are taught by the great Roman orator, that every man should propose to himself the highest degree of excellence, but that he may stop with honour at the second or third: though therefore my performance should fall below the excellence of other dictionaries, I may obtain, at least, the praise of having endeavoured well, nor shall I think it any reproach to my diligence, that I have retired without a triumph from a contest with united academies and long successions of learned compilers. I cannot hope in the warmest moments, to preserve so much caution through so long a work, as not often to sink into negligence, or to obtain so much knowledge of all its parts, as not frequently to fail by ignorance. I expect that sometimes the desire of accuracy will urge me to superfluities, and sometimes the fear of prolixity betray me to omissions; that in the extent of such variety I shall be often bewildered, and in the mazes of such intricacy be frequently entangled; that in one part refinement will be subtilised beyond exactness, and evidence dilated in another beyond perspicuity. Yet I do not despair of approbation from those who knowing the uncertainty of conjecture, the scantiness of knowledge, the fallibility of memory, and the unsteadiness of attention, can compare the causes of error with the means of avoiding it, and the extent of art with the capacity of man; and whatever be the event of my endeavours, I shall not easily regret an attempt which has procured me the honour of appearing thus publickly,

My Lord,

    Your Lordship's

        Most Obedient

            and

        Most Humble Servant,

                        SAM. JOHNSON.

3

Theoretical Lexicography and its Relation to Dictionary-making [1]

B. T. S. ATKINS*

I   INTRODUCTION

Does *theoretical lexicography* exist? If this forum is to discuss its nature, we must at least grant it the benefit of the doubt, although its counterpart, *practical lexicography,* has a tautological ring to it. I propose here to interpret the term *theoretical lexicography* in the very general sense of "a body of theory related to lexicography," and, drawing inspiration from the title of Landau (1984), to define *lexicography* as "the art and craft of dictionary-making."

A more traditional definition of this latter term is to be found in the 1990 *Concise Oxford Dictionary* (COD): "the compiling of dictionaries." That plural form is very important. Abstract terms like *lexicography* and generic concepts like *the dictionary* form a smoke screen between theoretical discussions and the real, hard world of dictionary-making. What I have to say here concerns making dictionaries, not making "the dictionary."

Dictionaries may be considered from the point of view of form or of content, and both are relevant to this discussion. First, FORM: a dictionary (to quote the COD again) is "a book that lists...and explains the words of a language..." Much is written nowadays in artificial intelligence circles about electronic dictionaries, but almost the whole of dictionary production still consists of books—and I know no publisher who sees an imminent profitable market for custom-built electronic dictionaries. The electronic dictionaries that exist today all started life as books, with the tiny exception of lexicons built expressly *for* a computer. To my knowledge, apart from the Japanese EDR Electronic Dictionaries, none of these is even as big as a small pocket dictionary. Books are the focus of professional lexicography, and the dictionaries discussed, reviewed, praised, or criticized are books. Theoretical lexicography must be relevant to books.

Second, CONTENT: along this axis, there are two main types. The first is the scholarly and historical dictionary, a work often with few length constraints, and sometimes little pressure to complete within a specific time period—but also with a tendency to run out of money around letter C, or take 50 years to get there. The second type is the trade dictionary, a product created to be sold in the marketplace. I am principally concerned here with this type of dictionary,

* Atkins, B.T.S. (1992/3). 'Theoretical lexicography and its relation to dictionary-making', in Frawley, W. (ed.), *Dictionaries: the Journal of the Dictionary Society of North America*, 14: 4–43. Reproduced with permission of the Dictionary Society of North America.

[1] My thanks go to Beth Levin and Nicholas Ostler for their comments on a preliminary version of this paper, and especially to Patrick Hanks, for many helpful discussions. However, this is a practical lexicographer's personal view of a field where there is a lot of theoretical activity, and errors and unfortunate glimpses into an abyss of theoretical ignorance are entirely my own.

partly because all my experience lies in this area,[2] and partly because once again these are the dictionaries on which scholars traditionally focus their attention. A trade dictionary, as the name implies, is a commercial object. If it is to be of any real value today (and not simply in some future when the computerized dictionary is commonplace), then theoretical lexicography must be relevant to books created by a publishing house to sell the product in a competitive market.

The theory of dictionary-making is, however, too vast a canvas for this forum. Although theoretical lexicography is certainly not synonymous with lexicology (the study of the lexicon), nor with its daughter science lexical semantics (the study of word meaning), a large proportion of the decisions made by the lexicographer are linguistic decisions, and so we should consider particularly, but not exclusively, the contribution of theoretical linguistics to theoretical lexicography, and hence the role of the theoretical linguist in dictionary-making.

Many people in contemporary lexicography deal with theoretical linguists by keeping their heads down below the barricades and getting on with writing dictionary entries. Sometimes an academic title whistles past, like "What linguists might contribute to dictionary-making if they could get their act together" (McCawley 1986); or a plaintive sentence crashes onto one's desk, such as "Lexicography has no theoretical foundations, and even the best lexicographers, when pressed, can never explain what they are doing, or why" (Wierzbicka 1985: 5).

I am happy to put the case for the practical lexicographers, although Dr. Johnson has already done so far better than I could ever do. Discerning linguists in search of a *raison d'être* will find in his "Plan of a Dictionary," addressed to Lord Chesterfield in 1747, many suggestions about what they might contribute to dictionary-making if only they "could get their act together" [see Johnson's "Plan" in this volume—*Ed.*]. In this work Johnson rehearses the major problems of a lexicographer writing "a dictionary design'd not merely for critics but for popular use." In the intervening years, some of these problems have been addressed by scholars, to the considerable benefit of lexicographers, who no longer puzzle much over orthography ("in which ... there is still great uncertainty among the best critics"), although hyphenation still gives us pause for thought; pronunciation ("the stability of which is of great importance to the duration of a language"); etymology ("in search of the progenitors of our speech, we may wander from the tropics to the frozen zone, and find some in the vallies of Palestine and some upon the rocks of Norway"); derivational morphology ("our language ... now stands in our dictionaries a confused heap of words without dependence, and without relation"); or inflectional morphology ("how [our words] are inflected through their various terminations").

Other problems discussed by Johnson persist to this day. These include establishing criteria, though he did not use the word, for the selection of a word list ("to determine by what rule of distinction the words of this dictionary were to be chosen"), and the inclusion in it of specialist vocabulary ("the peculiar words of every profession") or of basic vocabulary ("the words *horse, dog* ... and a thousand others, of which it will be hard to give an explanation not more obscure than the word itself"). Johnson foresaw difficulties with syntax, and valency in particular:

Words having been hitherto considered as separate and unconnected, are now to be likewise examined as they are ranged in their various relations to others by the rules of syntax or construction, to which I do not know that any regard has been yet shewn in English dictionaries, and in which the grammarians can give little assistance.

---

[2] For the same reason, I will draw my examples mainly from dictionaries of English, and some of my more specific comments may be valid only for English or closely related languages.

He was aware of the quagmire of collocation and idiom that awaited him and his amanuenses ("phraseology ... where it is used ... in senses not to be comprised in the general explanations; as, from the verb *make,* arise these phrases, *to make love, to make an end, to make way. . .* "). He raised the subject of explaining word meaning, or defining ("interpretation"). He had a detailed plan of action for the division into senses and ordering of these senses in the dictionary ("it seems necessary to sort the several senses of each word, and to exhibit first its natural and primitive signification ... "), and noted the need for a systematic differentiation of near synonyms ("the difference of signification in words generally accounted synonymous ... as in *pride, haughtiness, arrogance*"). He was aware of the connotation of words ("some are restrained to the sense of praise, and others to that of disapprobation, so commonly, though not always, we *exhort* to good actions, we *instigate* to ill"), and touched on many other aspects of language, such as style, register, currency, and regional variations of language, which the lexicographer has to deal with.

Every editor of every new dictionary must make decisions on how to manage every one of these aspects of lexicography, and more. Theoretical lexicography must provide a theoretically sound, yet practical, basis for such decision-making. To do so requires awareness of those points in the dictionary design process where there is editorial choice and those where there is none.

2 THE PROCESS OF LEXICOGRAPHY

Consideration of the steps in the design of a new dictionary must be set in the context of the process of lexicography. In the first stage—the ANALYSIS process—the lexicographer analyzes the word, trying to discover as many relevant linguistic facts as possible, record them, understand them, and order them. This calls for skills of observation and perception, for a high degree of linguistic knowledge and awareness, and for the ability to impose order on chaos.

The sources of lexicographical evidence—the input to this process—may vary from a large electronic corpus with sophisticated software tools of manipulation, through citations gathered during a reading program, and the contents of one's own and other people's published dictionaries, down to back-of-an-envelope jottings. The output of the analysis process may vary from rough notes to a structured, computerized text. In large projects, analyzing the data and creating such a text may constitute a phase of the project quite distinct from the compilation of the actual dictionary text; it may even be carried out by a different group of compilers from those who write the dictionary entries proper.

Whatever the size and ambition of the analysis process, it should furnish the lexicographer with all the facts needed for the second stage of the process, which I will call SYNTHESIS. The same analysis will serve for many different syntheses—and indeed, with the advent of electronic databases, such an approach is becoming more common in large publishing houses. Each new synthesis produces a different dictionary, a different book aimed at a different market and designed with a different group of users in mind. Within the framework of the publisher's specifications, the dictionary user drives the lexicography, and if the lexicographer has no clear idea of the person the entry is being written for, that entry is not likely to be of much use to anyone.

During the synthesis stage, the compiler extracts from the collection of ordered facts those that are relevant to the particular dictionary being written.[3] In large projects, these are

---

[3] In bilingual dictionary-making, the transfer process can straddle both the analysis and the synthesis stages. Often the same lexicographer will be responsible for the material in both languages, usually with a network of informants

described in a STYLE GUIDE drawn up by senior editors. The style guide not only identifies the types of data to be recorded and gives guidance on how to recognize them but also sets out in detail the way in which the dictionary entry must be constructed and presented. The synthesis process, the actual writing of the dictionary entries, calls for skills of interpretation, evaluation, selection, compression, and communication, and a certain amount of linguistic knowledge.

One clear, albeit indirect, contribution that the theoretical linguist may make to the synthesis process is to give the would-be lexicographer language skills and language awareness. The basic subject matter of theoretical and applied linguistics—in particular, lexical semantics and syntax—is highly relevant to all lexicography, and if nothing else, heightens the linguistic awareness of those who practice it (see Atkins 1992).

3   A HOLISTIC APPROACH TO DICTIONARY ASSESSMENT

At bottom, however, it is the senior editors at the design stage of a dictionary project who can benefit most from the work of the theoretical linguist. These are the people who carry responsibility for the ultimate content and presentation of the dictionary, and for the policy that is implemented by the compiling team. Let us briefly consider three examples (among very many, from very many linguists) of comments that, however constructive, simply do not take account of the fact that the text results from a coherent design policy and that suggested changes must be set in that context.

If, as McCawley (1986: 4) claims, the respective entries for *bean* and *rice* in the *American Heritage Dictionary of the English Language* (AHD) "provide no clue to the reader that *bean* is a count noun and *rice* is a mass noun," then that is because such a distinction is precluded at the dictionary design stage by the defining style chosen by the editor for such words as these. Of course, this begs the question of whether the AHD, designed principally for native speakers of American English, needs to hold such information. Is that the best use of the space available? Would it make the entries more intelligible and useful? Such a comment on dictionary policy is, I would argue, valid only if set in the context of the design policy as a whole, which of course is intended to give a specific user group what it is looking for.

If, as Wierzbicka (1985) claims, the four-line entry for the main sense of *cup* in W2 is inadequate because, among other defects, it includes the phrase "with or without a handle"[4] (which could apply to any concrete object), and if it must be replaced by the 80-odd line entry that she proposes, then that fault again lies with the definition policy and can be corrected only if the whole definition policy is altered. But I doubt if Wierzbicka would wish to be thought of as writing about the synthesis stage of a trade dictionary. Her work, however, is of relevance to the education of lexicographers and to the analysis stage of lexicography, of which more later.

If, as Hausmann and Gorbahn (1989) claim, difficult examples in the *Collins Cobuild Dictionary* make less intelligible the entries for quite common words (they quote "I had always

in the second language. In a few large publishing houses, for works in two major languages, the preparatory analysis and the dictionary compilation may be carried out by teams of lexicographers from both linguistic communities working in partnership. It takes special skills to compile an entry that must serve both types of user, the "encoding" source-language speaker and the "decoding" target-language speaker. This type of dictionary makes economic sense from the publisher's point of view; the same text, often the same book with only a cover change, sells in two markets. From each type of user's point of view, of course, such a book contains a lot of redundant material, and the space it occupies could be put to better use.

[4]   This comment of Labov's (1973), which Wierzbicka quotes, is not an appropriate criticism of dictionary defining techniques, nor did Labov present it as such.

considered Anthony priggishly above the rest of us" for *above)*, this results from a deliberate editorial policy not to adapt the corpus citations selected for dictionary use, and criticism of it should include some mention of alternative approaches to the use of corpus material in learners' dictionaries.

My point is that linguists may criticize many aspects of published dictionaries, and in many cases they are right to do so. However, they are wrong if they imply that the particular error noticed may be corrected out of context. The context is a very large, very complex, very labor-intensive, very expensive publication. A one-volume collegiate dictionary compiled from scratch will take over 100 person-years of work, and cost up to four million dollars. A change in editorial policy that affects one aspect of the lexicography will have a domino effect on almost every other. Theoretical lexicographers must be aware of this and place their commentaries in the context of the dictionary as a whole.

Consider, for instance, Frawley (1989) who, in a thought-provoking evaluation of the information structure of definitions, suggests (239) that two lines be added to every entry to hold facts relating to the historical development and relative frequency of the word senses described in it. In view of the overall effect that such a design decision would have, it would be useful if he were also to suggest a method of incorporating it into the specifications of the dictionary itself. How would the editor make space for 100,000 lines of text (assuming a dictionary with a 100,000-word word list in which one in two entries had more than one sense)?[5] Adding approximately 500 pages to a dictionary aimed at a specific market slot is not feasible.

The dictionary as a whole, an artifact designed with care to fit precise specifications, is the context in which theoretical work on lexicography must be set. The commercial specifications place iron constraints upon the compiler. A holistic approach to dictionary design decisions is essential.

What are these design decisions? When is each taken, what are the options at each point, and how great an effect does each have on the subsequent compiling? These decisions must be firmly rooted in theory, and theoretical lexicography, if it is to be effective, must have something to contribute to them.

4 DECISION POINTS IN THE LEXICOGRAPHICAL PROCESS

A typology (very much abridged in this description) of the design decisions in the planning of a trade dictionary is shown in Fig. 1. The left-to-right linearity of the diagram reflects the chronology of the decision-making process. The first set of decisions to be made falls into the category of PRE-LEXICOGRAPHY; later come the decisions to be made about the dictionary MACROSTRUCTURE; lastly those regarding the MICROSTRUCTURE. Decisions on the macrostructure relate principally to how "words"[6] are handled in the dictionary, while those under the microstructure heading concern "senses."[7] Once all these principled decisions have been

---

[5] Frawley (1989: 239) claims that "no precious space is lost" if entries are adapted in that way, but since his proposal is to add two lines of new information to every multi-sense entry, I cannot follow his reasoning here.

[6] Terminology here is a minefield. By "word" in this context lexicographers mean a single orthographical form, which may have several meanings, lexemes, and/or lexical units, as the terms are used in Cruse (1986). This high-level item is sometimes called a "lemma," although in corpus linguistics this term is mostly restricted to the context of inflectional morphology. A "word" may represent several lexical items, if the latter term is taken to mean an orthographical form combined with a specific set of meanings; the notion of citation form (as in Lyons 1977, here and there) relates to the morphological aspect of the word.

[7] This term is used here rather more loosely than in Cruse (1986), where it designates the semantic component of a lexical unit.

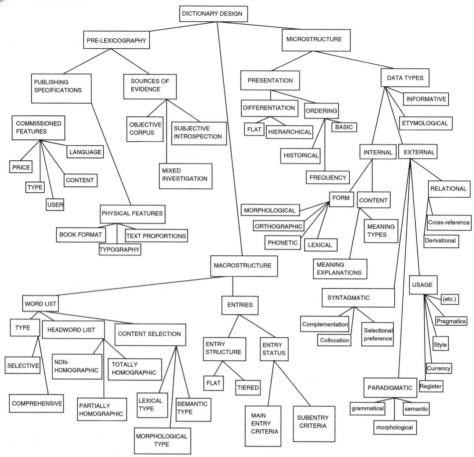

FIG. 1   Typology of dictionary design decisions

made and many sample entries have been written to test them, the work is ready to move into the synthesis stage. The style guide, already drafted, is completed as far as possible (although this is rather an organic entity and will change marginally throughout the whole compilation process), and compiling begins in earnest. I propose to look systematically at the decision points in this progression (nodes in the diagram in Fig. 1), for it is at these points that the dictionary editor may look to theoretical lexicography to guide the decisions.

4.1   Pre-lexicographical decisions

The principal decisions made during the pre-lexicography stage are those relating to PUB-LISHING SPECIFICATIONS and those relating to SOURCES OF EVIDENCE. They are made, not by dictionary editors, but by publishers, and result largely from the publisher's judgment of the market. The commissioning publisher identifies a "market slot" and commissions a dictionary to fill it. This slot is described in terms of the COMMISSIONED FEATURES. Of these, the PRICE—what the dictionary would sell for if it entered the market today—is by far the most important: it constrains all decisions on the physical features of the book and, in particular, delimits the space available to the editors. A great number of the purely lexicographical decisions are affected by this. The price of the finished book and the estimated sales figures set the project budget, which in turn sets the time to be spent on production, the size of the team involved (the editors and the management, and computing, keyboarding, secretarial, and clerical staff who support and complement them), the compiling process (on-line or not), and the formatting of text files to drive the typesetter (word-processed, tagged, or relational database format). And so on.

As well as the price, the commissioning publisher's specification of the dictionary to be produced will include details of the TYPE (whether the book will deal with general language or some field-specialized word-stock), and the LANGUAGE (monolingual, bilingual, or multi-lingual).

One of the most influential factors at this stage is the definition of the USER GROUP (e.g., adult or child, mother-tongue speaker or learner) for whom the book is intended, because lexicographers have clearly defined obligations toward the users of the dictionary they are writing. The user opens a dictionary with a set of reasonable expectations: that the book will not fall apart while it is being used; that the print will be visible; that the facts sought will be there; that the entry will be intelligible; that the information needed will be discernible in all the other information in the entry; that it will be accurate; that it will be usable.

The lexicographer and the dictionary user play a game with strict rules, not all to the user's advantage: italic type indicates one kind of information, roman type another; headwords are selected according to a known set of criteria, faithfully followed; there is a predictable structure to the entries; there is a finite, listed set of abbreviations; everyone is assumed to know the meaning of "noun" and "verb" and other parts of speech, and to understand concepts like transitivity. And so on. It is a game in which the dictionary compilers hold all the trump cards. But they must not break their own rules, even for a single word (and if they do, the computational lexicologists scanning their on-line version of the dictionary will find them out); and the users must not complain if they cannot find what they are looking up, as long as it is in there somewhere, however deeply buried. The lexicographer gets to define the specific rules of the game for any particular dictionary and sets these out in the introduction. Unfortunately, in some dictionaries, it can appear that the lexicographer thinks, "Now I've told them what the rules are. If they can't manage them, well, my conscience is clear." That is not good lexicography (but only latterly have people come to think so). There is no virtue in blindly following the style guide to the point where an entry, however systematic it may be, is so concise and so tightly packed with information as to be entirely hermetic.

We must ask, in planning a dictionary, how much we expect the dictionary user to put in to get anything out. There are decisions that make the successful use of the dictionary contingent upon skills that by definition the user will not have (such as a knowledge of the meaning of the word being looked up), or is not likely to have (such as the ability to decode abstruse abbreviations, or to interpret the information values of typeface changes in a 6-point type entry containing eight typefaces). Such decisions may result in a rigorously systematic and theoretically sound text, but will leave the user bewildered and frustrated: the dictionary has failed in its primary purpose. Above all else, it must function as a successful act of communication between the compiler who wrote it and the person consulting it. It is a tool for the reader to use. If the tool does not work when used intelligently, then it is the toolmaker's fault, not the user's.

The last item in this section, CONTENT SPECIFICATION, is not usually explicit at this early stage of design, but the type of content is nonetheless implicitly defined at this point. The editors of a new dictionary will carefully assess the market slot matching the product to the intended users to ensure a good fit. They study its competitors and know it has to sell against dictionaries with a certain number of "entries" (or "references," or whatever term its publisher uses for statistical claims); the market slot constrains the editors' freedom to decide whether or not the dictionary will have illustrations, how its pronunciations will be treated, what appendices it may have, and other questions of that ilk. The new dictionary may be one of a series already under way, in which case much of its content and many aspects of the lexicography will be defined by that fact.

The PHYSICAL FEATURES of the dictionary are already at least partially defined in the pre-planning stages of the project, often, like the content, implicitly rather than explicitly. These include the BOOK FORMAT (size, type of cover, etc.), TYPOGRAPHY (typefaces, fonts, type sizes, etc.), and TEXT PROPORTIONS (how many pages available for dictionary text, as opposed to the front matter and back matter).

When the publishing board approves the project, therefore, the editors have a very specific task before them: to produce a clearly defined dictionary of a specified size and type, in a specified period, with specified staff and facilities. Most of the lexicographical decisions stem directly or indirectly from these facts. A body of theory relating to dictionary-making must take account of the context in which the craft is practiced. Perhaps its principal role is to give editors criteria on which to base the linguistic decisions that have to be made in this context.

The remaining pre-lexicographical decisions that have an effect on dictionary content are those regarding the SOURCES OF EVIDENCE that will inform the lexicography. Objectivity here should be interpreted as a gradient rather than a definable point. It is of course possible to be entirely subjective in one's assessment of language, and many dictionaries (the cheapest kind) are written entirely by INTROSPECTION, without the benefit of any kind of citations file or, at the least, discussion with others. Probably the majority of dictionaries, however, combine the subjective and objective approaches, called here INVESTIGATION, and rely on citation files (ranging from notes taken by a solitary editor to the extensive files resulting from a systematic and comprehensive reading program) and informants (face-to-face questioning, questionnaires, tests, and so on). Some of the larger, richer, and more progressive publishing houses are now actively engaged in providing a third type of source of evidence, the ELECTRONIC CORPUS: a collection of electronic texts (in a standardized format with certain conventions relating to the content), which is selected in a principled way in order to furnish a store of linguistic data for lexicographical work. Of course, as long as the text selection is performed by human beings, this evidence cannot be totally objective. The pre-lexicographical decisions relating to evidence (Fig. 1) differ from the others in one important respect: the critical contribution that theoretical lexicography can make. The basis on which text (or transcribed speech) is selected to serve as lexicographical evidence must be a sound theoretical one. A citations file holding humanly selected extracts from works already humanly pre-selected for searching is doubly biased towards subjectivity. I know of little theoretical work relevant to the selection of materials to be incorporated into a publisher's reading program, although the work on corpus text typology and selection must be of interest here.

Theoretical work on corpus design is of considerable relevance to lexicographical corpus builders, e.g., Biber (1989), Biber and Finegan (1986), Leitner (1990), Engwall (1994), and Atkins *et al.* (1992). The larger the corpus, the less likely it is to be biased by the subjective element of text selection (see Clear 1988; 1992), but the more difficult it becomes for lexicographers to analyze manually. Two thousand citations for one word are about as much as any compiler can cope with, but not enough to yield all the useful facts about a common word. Moreover, the 20 million-word general language corpus, that offers 2,000 instances of the lemmas *list, extra,* or *save,* will swamp compilers with 10,000 for *pay, same,* or *again,* yet offer only 10 or so citations for *malady* or *proclivity.*

The problem, of course, is how to handle a corpus large enough to provide enough evidence for the infrequent words. There is a real need for a body of theory that will underpin corpus-handling tools smart enough to pre-select lexicographical evidence without distorting it or losing hard facts. The work of sociolinguists and psycholinguists is highly relevant here, as well as that of lexical semanticists, syntacticians, morphologists, dialectologists (almost everyone, in fact). I know of no one who has addressed this problem specifically, although there is much of interest to lexicographers in the computational analysis of word frequency by Francis and Kučera (1982), and Hofland and Johansson (1982), and the statistically based research into words-in-use by Church and his colleagues (Church and Hanks 1990—see also in this volume, *Ed.*—Church *et al.* 1990, 1994), Jelinek (1985), and the research described in Biber (1988) into linguistic variation across spoken and written texts.

However, the foundations have to be in place before large-scale corpora can be tamed. Existing automatic part-of-speech taggers, though not perfect, are already of great benefit to corpus lexicographers; a foolproof parser is the corpus-handling tool we need most urgently. Francis (1980), Johansson (1980, 1982), Church (1988), Hindle (1994), Marcus (1980), Magerman and Marcus (1990), and Garside, Leech, and Sampson (1987) are among those whose research truly belongs to theoretical lexicography, since they are working towards the corpus-handling tools we are all waiting for.

In short, the pre-lexicographical phase involves the principal constraints of space (number and length of entries) and time (time available for analyzing and compiling the text). Severe space restrictions impose a prioritizing of information; theoretical lexicography, if it is to have any value at all, must help us to do this. If it is to be done well, this in turn demands thorough, theoretically informed, initial research, for which there is no time. This is the lexicographer's dilemma. While theoretical lexicography has an important contribution to make to the pre-lexicography in connection with the gathering and pre-processing of lexicographical evidence, neither linguists nor lexicographers have any real say in the decisions that affect the lexicography most radically, namely, the business decisions made by publishers. Realistically, there is little that any of us can do to change these, and our task is to see how a dictionary written under such conditions may be true to the language and helpful to the user.

4.2   Macrostructure decisions[8]

The macrostructure is the basis of the dictionary—the walls, roof, rooms, windows, plumbing, and drains, indeed all that holds and shapes the linguistic information. It has traditionally lacked the glamour of the living inhabitants. The living, changing, challenging, bewildering meanings and uses of the microstructure capture the linguistic limelight. Yet everything that shapes and molds the information in the dictionary will surely repay theoretical study and must have a powerful claim on our attention. A theory of lexicography must include research into the basis of the editorial decisions on the macrostructure outlined in Fig. 1.

These decisions fall into two groups: those relating to the WORD LIST (list of headwords in the dictionary) and those relating to the LEXICAL ENTRIES. The editors must first decide if the TYPE of word list is to be COMPREHENSIVE or SELECTIVE. In the latter case, the only possible one in trade dictionaries, principled decisions must be made about what should constitute the main text of the book (normally lexical information indexed by the word list); what, if anything, is to be treated as "intra-textual" material, e.g., inset usage and grammar notes; and what as "extra-textual," i.e., the front and back matter, including any appendices of tables and lists to which dictionary entries may be cross-referred.

The editors must then decide how to structure the vocabulary to be treated in the text of the dictionary. They must choose the type of HEADWORD LIST. It may be NON-HOMOGRAPHIC,

---

[8] I am glad to acknowledge here the contribution that the work of Robert Ilson (personal communication) and Alain Rey (1977) has made to my thinking on macrostructure and microstructure decisions.

with each headword a unique orthographical form and all lexical units with the same form considered as constituents of a unique polysemous headword. It may be TOTALLY HOMO-GRAPHIC, where each headword is a unique unity of form and content and a single ortho-graphical form may be shared by many headwords, none of which is polysemous. Between these two extremes lies the type of headword list used in trade dictionaries, the PARTIALLY HOMOGRAPHIC, where a single form may be shared by several headwords, each of which may itself be polysemous. Of the three, the last puts most demands on a theory, in terms of criteria for the decisions that have to be made.

Criteria for headword status are also needed for the actual CONTENT SELECTION of the headword list. The first set of criteria relates to LEXICAL TYPE, with some dictionaries restrict-ing the headword list to single whole words (no multiword items, alphabetisms, hyphenated forms, etc.). The second set of criteria relates to MORPHOLOGICAL TYPE, specifically including or excluding derivatives or inflected forms, affixes, etc. The third set of criteria relates to SEMANTIC TYPE, selecting for inclusion or exclusion items such as proper names, taboo words, and so on.

The second group of decisions affecting the macrostructure of the dictionary relates to the actual dictionary ENTRIES. The ENTRY STRUCTURE may be FLAT, where every item has its own main entry, or TIERED, where the subentries may be "nested" within a main entry, or even within other subentries. Subentries may be defined or be left undefined, and other types of information may be systematically included or excluded for these lexicographical second-class citizens. Of course the ideal format is one in which there are no subentries, but the space penalty that this imposes is always severe in trade dictionaries.

If the entry structure is tiered, the editor must give the lexicographers a way of deciding the ENTRY STATUS: whether an item is to be a main entry or a subentry. (This is not to be confused with the criteria for content selection discussed above.) MAIN ENTRY CRITERIA may be on morphological (base or derived form), grammatical (part of speech), or orthographical (solid word, hyphenated form, or multiword item) grounds. SUBENTRY CRITERIA within a group of related lexical items may be morphological (e.g., adverbs in -ly and nouns in -ness), or lexical (locating compounds, phrasal verbs, or other multiword items within the appropriate headword entries).

The macrostructure decisions in dictionary-making are already constrained by the publish-ing decisions in the pre-lexicographical phase of a project, which limit the size and scope of the dictionary. If a systematic approach to the macrostructure is to be implemented, the style guide must set out clear criteria by which the word list may be selected and headword status and main entry status may be allocated to each lexical item. The works of Apresjan (1974, 1995a), Mel'čuk and his colleagues (Mel'čuk 1988; Mel'čuk and Zholkovsky 1988; Mel'čuk et al., 1984/1988/1992), Cruse (1986), Lyons (1969), and many other scholars are all relevant in a rather general way to macrostructure decisions, but there is certainly room here for theorists to tackle this lexicographical problem more directly.

4.3   Microstructure decisions

At the detailed level of decisions on the dictionary microstructure, linguistics has most to contribute to theoretical lexicography.[9] It is certainly also here, the province of the "sense" as opposed to the "word," that dictionaries attract most attention from theoretical linguists. The more systematic the approach to the lexicography, the more systematic the finished dictionary.

---

[9] One of the most useful and comprehensive works of reference encompassing the whole field is Lyons (1969).

Here we can benefit from theoretical work, for instance that of Apresjan (1973, 1992a and b, 1995a), Clark and Clark (1979), Fillmore and his colleagues (Fillmore 1975b, 1977a, 1978; Fillmore *et al.* 1988), Householder *et al.* (1964, 1965), Lakoff (1987), Levi (1982), Levin (1993), Mel'čuk (here and there), Pustejovsky (1991), and others, whose analysis of syntax and semantics allows us to predict, and plan for, systematic linguistic variation. Systematicity is useful both at the analysis and the synthesis stages. During analysis, it brings order to chaos. During synthesis (by a large team, over several years), it leads to a more consistent text.

The editors at the planning stage of a new dictionary have two distinct but related problems: what to record and how to identify it. They must decide what in the context of word meaning constitutes a relevant lexical entity: what is a "dictionary sense," what criteria can be used to check whether a construction should or should not be recorded as relevant to a particular headword (designated as "syntagmatic: complementation" in Fig. 1), and so on. They must also give their compiling team criteria for identifying these.

The editors' first two decisions are how to handle lexical units in the dictionary (PRESEN-TATION), and what lexically relevant information (DATA TYPES) to record for each of these. The type of presentation of lexical units depends on two factors: (1) the way in which the headword is divided into senses (sense DIFFERENTIATION), and (2) the order in which these senses are set out in the dictionary entry.

4.3.1   Dictionary senses

One of the primary tasks of the lexicographer is to identify the lexical units (or dictionary "senses") that together constitute the lexical item (or headword) for which an entry is being compiled—the *differentiation of senses*. (It is rare for a dictionary style guide to give the lexicographers criteria for identifying a valid dictionary sense, but, through team discussions and detailed editing of the compilers' output, the editors attempt to achieve a consensual approach to this difficult task.) The sense structure selected by the editor at the design stage may be FLAT, in which case all senses will have equal status and the sense numbers run 1, 2, 3, 4, etc., and only proximity or lack of it will show closeness or distance in meaning; or it may be HIERARCHICAL, allowing for a grouping of senses in a more intuitively satisfying way: for instance, 1, 1a, 1b, 2, 2a, etc., or some more complex variant such as 1, 1a1, 1a2, 1b1, 1b2, 1b3, etc. The four entries for *taste* in Appendix 1 illustrate these choices: the COD and CED have a flat structure, the others a hierarchical one.

Having decided what these senses are, the compiler must decide how to order them within the entry.[10] A principled decision on the ORDERING of senses must be made by the editor at the design stage. Is the ordering to follow the HISTORICAL development of the senses or their perceived relative FREQUENCY, or is it to run from the sense intuitively believed to be BASIC (or "core", "literal," etc.) to the more metaphorical usages?[11] There is great opportunity here for theorists to offer guidance on how senses may be differentiated, how "closeness" of meaning may be evaluated and indicated, how predictable meaning shifts may be analyzed and used in lexicography, and how all this may be shown in a two-dimensional dictionary entry. The broad canvas of Lyons (1977) offers a background in which to set more lexicographically oriented work, such as that of Mel'čuk (1988) and Apresjan (1974, 1992a and b, 1995a),[12] who address specifically the question of sense differentiation and sense relationships, and whose

---

[10]   After years of corpus lexicography, I am inclined to believe, with Moon (1987a, 1988) and others, that many words are basically monosemous, and it does the user a disservice to suggest otherwise by dividing them into "senses."

[11]   There are other ways of differentiating and ordering senses. In a bilingual dictionary, for instance, these often reflect the amount of semantic overlap between the source-language word and its principal target-language equivalent.

[12]   I give the 1974 work as the basic Apresjan reference, although my knowledge of Apresjan's work comes principally from personal communications and references in the work of others, notably that of Mel'čuk.

"heuristic criteria for definitions" are extremely useful. Among other works on meaning that I have personally found helpful are Cruse (1986) and Leech (1974), although more for their consciousness-raising discussion than for immediate applicability, as most of the words one has to deal with when working through the alphabet turn out to be more recalcitrant than those chosen as examples in works on semantic theory.

Faced now with the overwhelming richness and subtlety of the language in a computerized corpus, I no longer believe that it is possible to give a faithful, far less a true, account of the "meaning" of a word within the constraints of the traditional entry structure (see Atkins 1991b, and Fillmore and Atkins 1994). Perhaps such a "true" account is an overambitious aim for a lexicographer, whose job is to give an account of word meaning that is intelligible and helpful to a user schooled in traditional dictionary use, although I would not wish to posit it as a constraint on the theoretical lexicographer. The lexical analysis of Wierzbicka (1985, 1987, 1988), and of Apresjan, Mel'čuk, and those who work with them on immensely detailed lexicographical entries, of Jackendoff (1990), and Fillmore (here and there) and Kay (1984, 1989, 1990) and their colleagues shows us what lexicography could be like if we had the time (and the talent). The work of Lakoff and Johnson (1980) and Lakoff (1987) is also relevant to practical lexicography, in particular on radial categories, prototypes (inspired by the work of Rosch), and the pervasion of metaphor throughout the vocabulary.

All this is inspiring. How can we pack such insights into a standard dictionary entry? How can we adapt the dictionary entry to take account of them? The problem that faces us daily is illustrated by the material in Appendix 2, which shows a set of corpus citations for the word *taste,* drawn from the Oxford Pilot Corpus, built by the Oxford University Press as part of a pilot study for the British National Corpus.[13] As Appendix 1 demonstrates, four current dictionaries of about the same size and scope take four different positions on the presentation and ordering of the meanings of this word.

It is reasonable to expect a body of lexicographical theory to provide some guidance on how to tackle the following questions in the light of the corpus evidence and within the context of a dictionary of similar size and scope to those listed above:

(1) On what basis should the senses of *taste* be differentiated? How many, and which senses, should be distinguished? Are some senses more closely related than others?
(2) On what basis may we decide which sense structure is more appropriate (flat or hierarchical)? If hierarchical, how can we decide what depth of "nesting" is appropriate?
(3) On what basis should the senses identified for this word be ordered? How should they be numbered in the entry?
(4) Should this entry have anything in common with the entries for other words of perception, such as *see, look, hear, listen, smell, feel,* etc.? If so, what should the lexicographer be aware of while writing the *taste* entry?

Theoretically based answers to the above questions should allow a lexicographer analyzing the corpus data in Appendix 2 to identify senses appropriate to a dictionary entry, and to make decisions like the following:

---

[13] The British National Corpus is at present being constructed [now available at http://www.natcorp.ox.ac.uk/ – *Ed.*] with the help of government funding by a consortium led by Oxford University Press, and including Longman Publishers, Chambers Publishers, the Universities of Lancaster and Oxford, and the British Library. Begun in January, 1991, the project aims at providing a research resource in electronic form of 100 million words of general British English, together with some basic text-handling tools.

(1) If line 3 is one sense ("sample flavor of") and line 14 another ("perceive flavor of"), should the following lines be assigned to the "sample" group, the "perceive" group, or to another sense entirely: 5, 16, 19, 20, 21, 22, and 23?

(2) Should lines 4, 9, 15, 17, and 18 all be instances of the same sense or different senses, and if the latter, which senses?

(3) Should lines 2 and 24 be instances of the same sense or different senses?

(4) Should lines 2, 6, 7, and 8 be instances of the same sense or of several different senses; and, if the latter, which senses?

(5) Should lines 31 to 43 inclusive be instances of the same sense or of different senses; and, if the latter, which senses?

4.3.2   Lexically relevant data internal to the headword[14]

Many decisions on lexically relevant data types must be made by the designers of a new dictionary. These relate to four different kinds of information: INTERNAL, about the word or the word sense itself; EXTERNAL, about its relationships with other words or word senses; ETYMOLOGICAL, in a sense a diachronic subset of external, but such a clear-cut area in lexicography that it is useful to treat it quite distinctly; and INFORMATIVE, a motley collection of useful comments that the compiler may make in order to clarify a particular entry. Internal and external information is the province par excellence of linguistics today and I will look at these in more detail. Space precludes any further reference to etymology (whether this is the historical development of a word's orthographical form or its meaning, or the meaning of an idiom, phrasal verb, or compound), or to the various types of informative usage notes and comments in entries.

The "internal" facts about a word or word sense may relate either to its form or to its sense. A certain amount of information on the FORM of the headword is routinely provided in every dictionary: the MORPHOLOGICAL base form is always given, and sometimes inflected forms as well; standard and variant spellings, and possibly syllabification, constitute the usual ORTHOGRAPHIC information; there are different ways (IPA, orthoepic rewriting systems, etc.) of displaying PHONETIC information; and of course the dictionary shows whether the LEXICAL form is a sublexical item, a single word, a hyphenated word, or a multiword item.

As for the semantic CONTENT of the word, the lexicographer must analyze and describe for the user the meaning component of each lexical unit (or dictionary "sense"). There is a large body of philosophical and linguistic writing on meaning analysis, in addition to the work already mentioned. This is important to lexicographers, because anything related to word meaning is interesting, but to my mind does not fall into the category of theoretical lexicography. Lexicographers need no convincing that word meaning is variable and probabilistic and highly context-dependent, and cannot be convinced that it is capable of binary analysis.

There is, however, one particular question on the semantic content of words that theoretical lexicography could usefully address: what is the most appropriate information to be included in the explanation of meaning? At the stage in the planning of a new dictionary when thought is being given to the actual compiling process, an invaluable resource would be a body of theoretical literature that would help in sorting the contents of the word list into various types of vocabulary, and identifying for each type (e.g., "natural kind terms," "diseases," "verbs of perception," and so on) the essential semantic (and other linguistic) facts that should be recorded for them, and from which the contents of the eventual dictionary entry could

---

[14] I say "lexically" rather than "lexicographically" because the problem arises in the analysis stage of lexicography rather than in the synthesis stage when the content of a specific dictionary entry is selected from the known information.

be selected. This would allow "template" (or model) entries to be compiled for each type, bringing systematicity to the lexicography, hence to the dictionary, as they are used to inform the compiling of other members of the set, although not to impose content or structure on any individual entry. To a certain extent this approach is being implemented in some dictionary projects (it accelerates the compilation process) but, alas, often in a theoretical vacuum.

This is one of the areas where lexical semantics has greatest potential for lexicography. Apresjan, Mel'čuk, and Wierzbicka address the question of lexically appropriate information. Apresjan (1992a and b) comes closest of all, in my view, to offering the kind of structured information that lexicographers need from linguists. Mel'čuk is too abstract and complex for instant commercial application;[15] Wierzbicka's approach is extremely useful in providing a summary of the lexically appropriate information for certain classes of vocabulary item (e.g., Wierzbicka 1985, for *vehicle,* its function, mode of operation, construction, and size), but her work is a drop in the ocean of the average dictionary's 100,000-word word list. Cups and mugs, bikes and cars, cats and dogs, and names of fruits and vegetables are not the words that cause us intractable problems as do most of the polysemous verbs (e.g., *taste),* or nouns whose usage swings between countability and uncountability (e.g., *taste* again), or "relational" words like *sister* or *bride* or *enemy*—the list is endless. I do not even know where to begin the task of classifying the vocabulary into "sets" of words (apart from obvious sets like days of the week, or measures, or those mentioned above).

As regards meaning CONTENT, there are two major kinds of decision to be made. The first, shown in Fig. 1 as MEANING TYPES, covers the various types of meaning to be included in different types of entry—denotation and connotation, reference, literal and figurative meaning, cognitive and affective meaning, and so on. Discussion of the relation of abstract meaning types to dictionary entries tends to take place among theorists, rather than among editors planning a new dictionary. However, this is clearly a subject to which all editors should give some thought, and it would be helpful to have an extensive body of theoretical writing (as, for instance, Wierzbicka 1988) to which they could turn for guidance.

This topic is closely linked to the second, MEANING EXPLANATIONS. The term is intended to designate all the information in a dictionary entry that the lexicographer employs in order to transmit the meaning of an item to the dictionary user: not only the definition, and near-synonyms (if distinct from the definition), but glosses and commentaries, examples of usage, formulae (in the entries for chemical terms, for instance), references to extra-textual listings of lexical sets (e.g., military ranks, weights and measures, prefixes, chemical elements, nationality adjectives and nouns, etc.), notes and cross-references drawing the user's attention to related but contrasting entries, other types of usage notes, and even pictorial illustrations.

I am principally concerned in this paper with monolingual dictionary-making, but cannot, while discussing meaning, entirely ignore in this regard the special responsibilities of the bilingual dictionary editor. Bilingual lexicography shares with monolingual lexicography the processes of analysis, but poses quite different problems when it comes to transmitting word meaning and usage. While writers such as Zgusta (1979, 1984), Steiner (1971, 1984), Iannucci (1975), and Snell-Hornby (1984, 1986, 1990) have offered helpful comments on this complex matter, there is one major topic that is still largely unexplored. Many scholars criticize equivalents in bilingual dictionaries from the point of view of text translation. There is considerable difference between the context-sensitive equivalence sought by the translator and the context-free equivalence that must be offered in a bilingual dictionary entry. A

---

[15] Mel'čuk's work is of exemplary systematicity and as such provides a model for lexicographers at the analysis stage. However, its very rigor makes it difficult to apply in a finite dictionary not only because space precludes this but because the rich diversity of usages to be found in corpus material tends not to lend itself to an analysis based on a rigorous differentiation of senses.

dictionary must above all not lead its users into error. When space cannot be spared for detailed metalinguistic indications, the lexicographers must choose a safe, general translation in preference to one that may be perfect in some contexts but perhaps erroneous in others. This is a fruitful furrow for theoretical lexicography to plow.

In a monolingual dictionary, the basic responsibility for explaining the meaning of an expression falls of course on the definition, although psycholinguists doubt the efficacy of this, particularly for children (see Miller 1986; Miller and Gildea 1987); however, it is not clear how to make use of their findings in a print dictionary. Specific decisions on the form and content of definitions of general language items are rarely part of the planning of a dictionary project (although they ought to be); scientific and other specialized terms are often defined under more formal constraints.

The content and structure of definitions are often discussed in the theoretical literature. Most of this discussion is of interest, but often unfortunately only of theoretical interest to the working lexicographer. Our principal (and I fear insoluble) problem is to pack enough information into a definition to suit the needs of a wide range of users, and to do so succinctly enough to fit it into the dictionary format, yet express it intelligibly enough for the user to be able to grasp the meaning of the word and (optimistically) to know how to use it. In that arena, the professional lexicographer often perceives as self-indulgent a discussion of whether or not the inclusion of encyclopedic information is against the rules, or whether anaphora is to be frowned on, or whether the "best" definitions have the Aristotelian structure of genus term and differentiae (as if all definitions had that form),[16] or any other similarly abstract question.

There is little to be gained if practitioners respond to theoretical discussions with variations on the theme of the impossibility of doing better—or even sometimes doing at all—what they do for a living. This is certainly not what I want to say. Without untrammeled theoretical work, there is surely no way forward. But just as lexicography will improve if more lexicographers read theoretical papers, so the value of theoretical papers will increase if the theorists try some real-world lexicography. Papers that discuss definition structure or content at a high level of abstraction can in the end contribute only to the advancement of linguistics. Theoretical linguists can become theoretical lexicographers only by thinking and writing about linguistic theory in the context of the harsh world of practical dictionary-making ("If you want to put that in, what are you going to leave out?"). As it is, the most helpful and common-sense papers on defining that I know are those written by practicing and practical lexicographers, e.g., Ayto (1983, 1984, 1988), Hanks (1979, 1988, 1990), Landau (1984), and Zgusta (1971, 1979, 1984), who are able to bring to their discussions a knowledge of the pressures of time and space that lexicographers must contend with daily. Not for nothing did James Murray's granddaughter call one of the chapters in her book "The Triple Nightmare: Space, Time and Money" (Murray 1977).

Frawley (1988) takes Ayto to task for "a dubious inclination towards vagueness" and "prefer[ring] to abandon rigor so as to avoid definitions that are 'merely dumb monuments to arcane speculations'" (Ayto's phrase). Here Frawley speaks for theorists to whom the abandonment of rigor means the abandonment of intellectual standards and hence the debasing of the work. Ayto, on the other hand, speaks for the practitioners to whom a dictionary is something people open in an attempt to find out what a word means and how to use it, and for whom "rigor" often collocates with "mortis." We do not see the dictionary as a rigorous, exhaustive, theoretically consistent account of a subset of the words of the language. (We would have to be mad to believe that such an account can be accomplished in the confines of

---

[16] Perhaps some on-line dictionary-cruncher can tell me how many senses of how many nouns and verbs in our general vocabulary are in fact treated this way in dictionaries—not all, by any means, and certainly very few adjectives and adverbs, and probably no conjunctions, prepositions, or interjections.

one book.) If to be rigorous means to be opaque, then rigor must be sacrificed to intelligibility. As Hanks (1979) puts it: "Precision in lexicography is a matter of style and judgment, not construction by theory." Zgusta (1971) is more explicit:

> The lexicographic definition overlaps to some extent with the logical definition, but there are some striking differences . . . whereas the logical definition must unequivocally identify the defined object . . . in such a way that it is both put in a definite contrast against everything else that is definable, and positively and unequivocally characterized as a member of the closest class, the lexicographic definition enumerates only the most important semantic features of the defined lexical unit, which suffice to differentiate it from other units. (252)

Landau (1984) goes further, and in *Dictionaries: the Art and Craft of Lexicography* points out that:

> if a definition fails in its basic purpose of giving the reader enough immediate information to enable him to surmise, at least approximately, its meaning in context, it is of no value whatsoever. (131)

Commenting on Gove's advice to rigorously avoid the "broadening" of definitions,[17] Landau (1984: 126) speaks for the lexicographical community when he says, "I did not think it was the function of a dictionary to rigorously avoid anything that might help the reader grasp meaning better."

There is one aspect of meaning explanation that linguists could usefully address much more specifically: the many different defining techniques that are needed to cope with the whole word-stock of the language. One of the biggest challenges to the theoretical lexicographer is to devise a typology of vocabulary items and a parallel typology of defining strategies suited to each. A list of such vocabulary items should include referring expressions, non-referring expressions, action words, qualifying adjectives, classifying adjectives, deictics, quantifiers, transitive and intransitive prepositions, modal verbs, and so on.

4.3.3   *Lexically relevant data external to the headword*

The lexically relevant data that I have called EXTERNAL to the headword cover all the facts that a dictionary may contain that have to do with the headword's relationship with other words in the language. These fall into four classes, which I will consider in reverse order of difficulty for lexicographers, and I believe for theoretical linguists as well.

RELATIONAL information consists of a fairly straightforward set of facts about morphological DERIVATION, and under this heading I also include all the various types of CROSS-REFERENCES to other entries in the dictionary. PARADIGMATIC information may be GRAMMATICAL (e.g., part of speech, etc.), SEMANTIC (e.g., hyponymy), or MORPHOLOGICAL (e.g., conjugation). Neither relational nor paradigmatic information presents great difficulty to the editor planning a new dictionary, and there is much linguistic writing to which we can go for more facts if we need them.

Much more complex is USAGE information, and sociolinguists, stylistics specialists, and other linguists have produced a large and useful body of literature to which editors may turn when they have to decide, at the planning stage of a dictionary, exactly what types of facts will be labeled in that dictionary. The choice includes information on REGISTER ([formal], [familiar]), CURRENCY ([obsolete], [old-fashioned]), STYLE ([poetic], [technical]), PRAGMATICS ([expressing pleasure], [used to express surprise]), STATUS ([dialect], [slang], [jargon]), and FIELD ([architecture], [music]).

Register is the most difficult. Theoretical lexicography must be able to offer a set of criteria that may be applied in the assignment of register labels to lexical items and usages, for the

---

[17] For example, by defining *tubbable* as 'suitable for washing' rather than 'suitable for tubbing'.

dictionary style guide must not only enumerate the labels to be used but also describe their use in such a way as to induce consistency across a whole team of individual compilers. Native-speaker's intuition is not enough. Intuition may suggest that expressions of annoyance in British English, such as *bother!, blast!, damn!,* and *shit!* belong to different registers, and that they are listed here in ascending order of "strength." However, if a dictionary has a three-way register labeling system (say, "informal," "familiar," and "taboo") one lexicographer would ignore the register difference between *bother!* and *blast!,* but others would wish to class *blast!* and *damn!* together. Intuition does not extend to a consensus on register labeling among a team of a dozen people of different ages, backgrounds, and speech patterns. The word-stock of the language is so large and so diverse that even in a dictionary written over a number of years by a single lexicographer it is impossible to ensure consistency in the marking of register. Computerized compiling allows all the register labels to be compared at the end of the project, although in real life there is never time for this. If there were, we could make our labeling superficially more consistent, but we would still have no theoretical basis for our decisions.

At the design stage of a dictionary project, however, the editor's greatest problems with external facts lie in SYNTAGMATIC relationships. What Hanks (1990) calls "selectional preference" (or "selectional restrictions," though that seems too rigorous a term to most corpus lexicographers) is not one that often concerns conventional lexicography. The same cannot be said for COMPLEMENTATION, a term that I use in its broadest sense, to designate the range of syntagmatic environments in which a word's full semantic potential may be expressed. These are the constructions and vocabulary that the native speaker selects unconsciously and unerringly in any context. These facts lie at the heart of lexical analysis and are an important part of the synthesis process of certain dictionaries, such as those for the language learner, including the ultimate learner, the computer.

This is a problem that has become sharply focused with the use of electronic corpora as lexicographical evidence. The wealth of citations available for each headword poses more questions than it answers. Discussions of valency and subcategorization abound in the theoretical literature, but I have searched in vain for something that can be used to give lexicographers criteria for selecting from corpus evidence the constructions to be recorded as part of the "active scope" of the headword: the core of this problem is reflected in the linguists' eternal debate over arguments versus adjuncts. Among theorists, Mel'čuk's work is the most relevant. A concrete example of the decisions that have to be made in this area may be found in the discussion of the complementation of the verb *risk* in Fillmore and Atkins (1994).

Of equal complexity for the lexicographer, and again, much more so since the advent of corpus evidence, is the question of COLLOCATION, which I use in the broadest sense to designate the significant co-occurrence of two or more words (either because such a grouping happens more frequently than the statistical norm, or because it represents a semantically opaque lexical item, like *red herring*—or both). It is the editor's task, at the design stage of a dictionary, to classify the collocations to be noted in the corpus, and to identify these clearly enough to enable a team of lexicographers systematically to exclude some classes and include others. But our language is so fine and flexible and subtle and complex that such a task seems doomed to failure. Theoretical linguistics abounds in writings on phraseology; there is no dearth of interesting and perspicacious commentaries on this aspect of language. But the challenge to the theoretician is still open: how may an editor classify the collocations of the language, and, having done so, devise criteria for assigning each multiword item encountered to its appropriate class? One example of the problem will suffice: a team of lexicographers working through a corpus must consistently decide which verbal usages with prepositions are to be treated as "phrasal verbs" (and therefore given special treatment as lexical units) and which are to be considered as instances of the use of the base verb form with a prepositional complement. This is a problem to which theoretical writings have so far offered no solution.

At the design stage, unless an editor is able to predict all the various classes of collocations that will be found and that must be identified and dealt with in a specific way according to that identification, there will be no real consistency in the dictionary's treatment of the language. It is reasonable to doubt if it will ever be possible to classify these multiword items as we now try to do, but until another option presents itself, we are forced to continue in this task.

This makes me wary of the responsibilities being laid in this paper on theoretical lexicography. We are doing our best in adverse circumstances, but it is naive to hope for instant solutions from theoretical lexicographers. At best, they can only help us devise an acceptable compromise. Those who have done some practical lexicography, with all the space constraints involved, will in my view be better placed to do this.

5   CONCLUSION

For me, there are three kinds of theoretical linguists, who may or may not consider themselves theoretical lexicographers. The work of the first group is too theoretical, too abstract, or too difficult, or shows too little conception of what practical lexicography is all about, for it to be of any immediate use in dictionary-making. I believe most working lexicographers share this opinion, although of course individuals will draw the boundaries in different places.

The second group discusses aspects of lexical semantics (particularly the intersection of syntax and semantics) that have a great bearing on practical lexicography. It is not the role of these linguists to tell lexicographers what to do, or how to solve problems, nor do they try to do this; they show us different ways of looking at language and word meaning, which we can take and adapt to our needs. I am thinking of scholars like Fillmore, Lakoff, Levin, Cruse, and others mentioned already in this paper, whose work I personally have found inspiring and useful. These linguists have a crucial contribution to make to theoretical lexicography, particularly as the day of the electronic dictionary approaches, when we must gather resources for a wholly new description of the language, unrestricted by space constraints, with relationships among word meanings at the heart of the database.

The third group of linguists deals with specifically lexicographical matters, in a way that is not always directly applicable to practical lexicography but from which we can learn much; psycholinguists, sociolinguists, and specialists in stylistics and text analysis fall into this category, and central to it are scholars like Apresjan, Mel'čuk, Wierzbicka, and Zgusta. Here again, we must not ask them for instant solutions to our problems, but rather see how much we can use of their structured approach to the lexical entry and its contents, their theory-based insights into word meaning, and their rigorous factoring out of word sense relationships.

Theorists and practitioners certainly need to work together if dictionaries are to be improved, or if electronic dictionaries are to rise to the challenge of the new medium. But I am not sure that I speak for many, let alone all, of my colleagues. One senior and respected dictionary editor, on hearing Cruse's definition of a lexical unit, responded, "That sounds like good sound common sense dressed up in pompous verbiage." Is that all that linguistic theory is? Of course not. Inherent lexicographical aptitude is essential (and quite distinct from other linguistic skills, and quite independent of theoretical knowledge), but it is not enough.

This paper is an attempt to explain why we need more than the traditional "intuitive, atheoretical, approach to lexicography." The forum itself is a way of establishing better communication between working lexicographers and their theoretical counterparts. The language is bigger than both of us.

APPENDIX I   TASTE

taste /teɪst/ *n. & v.* — n. **1 a** the sensation characteristic of a soluble substance caused in the mouth and throat by contact with that substance (*disliked the taste of garlic*). **b** the faculty of perceiving this sensation (*was bitter to the taste*). **2** a small portion of food or drink taken as a sample. **3** a slight experience (*a taste of success*). **4** (often foll. by *for*) a liking or predilection (*has expensive tastes: is not to my taste*). **5** aesthetic discernment in art, literature, conduct, etc. esp. of a specified kind (*a person of taste, dresses in poor taste*). — *v.* **1** *tr.* sample or test the flavour of (food etc.) by taking it into the mouth. **2** *tr.* (also *absol.*) perceive the flavour of (*could taste the lemon; cannot taste with a cold*). **3** *tr.* (esp. with *neg.*) eat or drink a small portion of (*had not tasted food for days*) **4** *tr.* have experience of (*had never tasted failure*). **5** *intr.* (often foll. by *of*) have a specified flavour (*tastes bitter, tastes of onions*). □ a bad (or bitter etc.) taste *colloq.* A strong feeling of regret or unease. **taste blood** see BLOOD. **taste bud** any of the cells or nerve-endings on the surface of the tongue by which things are tasted. **to taste** in the amount needed for a pleasing result (*add salt and pepper to taste*), □□**tasteable** adj. (ME. - touch, taste, f. OF *tast. taster* (touch. try. taste. ult. perh. f. L *tangere* touch + *gustare* taste) **tasteful** /teɪstfʊl/ *adj.* having, or done in good taste. □□ **tastefully** adv. **tastefulness** *n*
tasteless /teɪstlɪs/ *adj.* **1** lacking flavour. **2** having, or done in, bad taste. □□ **tastelessly** adv. **tastelessness** n.
taster /teɪstə(r)/ *n.* **1** a person employed to test food or drink by tasting it. esp. for quality or *hist.* to detect poisoning. **2** a small cup used by a wine-taster. **3** an instrument for extracting a small sample from within a cheese, (ME f AF *tastour*. OF *tasteur* f *taster*. see TASTE)|
tasting /teɪstɪŋ/ a gathering at which food or drink (esp. wine) is tasted and evaluated.
tasty/teɪstɪ/ *adj.* (**tastier**; **tastiest**) (of food) pleasing in flavour; appetizing. □□ **tastily** adv. **tastiness** n.

Concise Oxford Dictionary (1990)

taste (teɪst) *n.* 1. the sense by which the qualities and flavour of a substance are distinguished by the taste buds. 2. the sensation experienced by means of the taste buds. 3. the act of tasting. 4. a small amount eaten, drunk, or tried on the tongue. 5. a brief experience of something:*a taste of the whip.* 6. a preference or liking for something; inclination: *to have a taste for danger.* 7. the ability to make discerning judgments about aesthetic, artistic and intellectual matters; discrimination: *to have taste.* 8. judgment of aesthetic or social matters according to a generally accepted standard: *bad taste.* 9. discretion; delicacy: *that remark lacks taste.* 10. *Obsolete,* the act of testing. — *vb.* 11. to distinguish the taste of (a substance) by means of the taste buds. 12. (*usually tr.*) to take a small amount of (a food, liquid, etc.) into the mouth, esp, in order to test the quality: *to taste the wine.* 13. (often foll. by *of*) to have a specific flavour or taste: *the tea tastes of soap; this apple tastes sour.*14. (when *intr.* usually foll. by *of*) to have an experience of (something):*to taste success.* 15. (*tr.*) an archaic word for enjoy. 16. (*tr.*) *Obsolete,* to test by touching. [C13; from Old French *taster.* ultimately from Latin *taxare* to appraise) —'**tastable** *adj.*
taste bud *n.* any of the elevated oval-shaped sensory end organs on the surface of the tongue, by means of which the sensation of taste is experienced.
tasteful ('teɪstfʊl) *adj.* 1. indicating good taste: *a tasteful design.* 2. a rare word for **tasty**. —'**tastefully** adv. —'**tastefulness** n.
tasteless ('teɪstlɪs) *adj.* 1. lacking in flavour; insipid. 2. lacking social or aesthetic taste. 3. *Rare,* unable to taste. —'**tastelessly** adv – '**tastelessness** n.
taster ('teɪstə) *n.* 1. a person who samples food or drink for quality. 2. any device used in tasting or sampling 3. a person employed. esp. formerly, to taste food and drink prepared for a king, etc., to test for poison
tasty ('teɪstɪ) *adj.* **tastier, tastiest.** 1. having a pleasant flavour. 2 *Brit. informal* attractive: used chiefly by men when talking of women. —'**tastily** adv. —'**tastiness** n.

Collins English Dictionary (1991)

---

¹**taste**\ˈtāst\ *vb* **tast·ed**; **tast·ing** [ME *tasten* to touch, test, taste, fr. MF *taster,* fr. (assumed) VL *taxitare.* freq. of L *laxare* to touch — more at TAX]*vt* (14c) **1** : to become acquainted with by experience (has *tasted* the frustration of defeat) **2** : to ascertain the flavor of by taking a little into the mouth **3** : to eat or drink esp. in small quantities <the first food I've *tasted* in days> **4** : to perceive or recognize as if by the sense of taste **5** *archaic :* APPRECIATE.ENJOY—*vi* **1** : to eat or drink a little **2** : to test the flavor of something by taking a small part into the mouth **3** : to have perception, experience, or enjoyment : PARTAKE — often used with *of* **4** : to have a specific flavor (the milk ~s sour)
²**taste** *n* (14c) **1** *obs* : TEST **2 a** *obs* : the act of tasting **b** : a small amount tasted **c** : a smalt amount : BIT.esp : a sample of experience (her first ~ of success) **3** : the one of the special senses that perceives and distinguishes the sweet, sour, salty, or salty quality of a dissolved substance and is mediated by taste buds on the tongue **4** : the objective sweet, sour, bitter, or salty quality of a dissolved substance as perceived by the sense of taste **5 a** : a sensation obtained from a substance in the mouth that is typically produced by the stimulation of the sense of taste combined with those of touch and smell : FLAVOR **b** : the distinctive quality of an experience (the attempt to cheat left a bad ~ in my mouth) **6** : individual preference : INCLINATION **7 a** : critical judgment, discernment, or appreciation **b** : manner or aesthetic quality indicative of such discernment or appreciation
taste bud *n* (ca. 1890) : an end organ mediating the sensation of taste and lying chiefly in the epithelium of the tongue
taste·ful\ˈtāst-fəl\ *adj* (1611) **1** : TASTY la **2** : having, exhibiting, or conforming to good taste—**taste·ful·ly**\-fa-le*adv* —**taste·ful·ness** *n*
taste·less\ˈtāst-ləs\ *adj* (1603) **1** : having no taste : INSIPID <~ - vegetables) **b** : arousing no interest : DULL **2** : not having or exhibiting good taste—**taste·less·ly** *adv*—**taste·less·ness** *n*
taste·mak·er\-,mā-kər\ *n* (1954): one who sets the standards of what is currently popular or fashionable
tast·er\ˈtā-stər\ *n* (15c) **1** : one that tastes; *esp* : one that tests (as tea) for quality by tasting **2** : a device for tasting or sampling
tasty\ˈtā-stē\ *adj* **tast·i·er, -est** (1617) **1 a** : having a marked and appetizing flavor **b** : strikingly attractive or interesting < a ~bit of gossip) **2** : TASTEFUL *syn* see PALATABLE —**tast·i·ly**\-stə-lē *adv* —**tast·i·ness**\-stē-nəs\ *n*

Webster's Ninth New Collegiate Dictionary
(1983)

taste (tāst) *v.* **tast·ed, tast·ing, tastes**—*tr.* 1. To distinguish the flavor of by taking into the mouth. 2. To eat or drink a small quantity of. 3. To experience or partake of, esp. for the first time: *finally tasted real success.* 4. *Archaic.* To appreciate; enjoy.—*intr.* 1.To distinguish flavors in the mouth. 2. To have a distinct flavor: *The stew tastes salty.* 3. To eat or drink a small amount. 4. To have an experience; partake.—*n.* 1. a. The sense that distinguishes the sweet, sour, salty, and bitter qualities of dissolved substances in contact with the taste buds on the tongue. b. This sense in combination with the senses of smell and touch, which together receive a sensation of a substance in the mouth. 2. a. The sensation of sweet, sour, salty, or bitter qualities produced by or as if by a substance placed in the mouth. b. The unified sensation produced by any of these qualities plus a distinct smell and texture; flavor. 3. The act of tasting. 4. A small quantity eaten or tasted. 5. A limited or first experience; sample: *"Thousands entered the war. got just a taste of it. and then stepped out"* (Mark Twain). 6. A personal preference or liking for something: *a taste for adventure.* 7. a. The faculty of discerning what is aesthetically excellent or appropriate, b. A manner indicative of the quality of such discernment: *furnished with superb taste.* 8. a. The sense of what is proper, seemly, or least likely to give offense in a given social situation, b. A manner indicative of the quality of this sense. 9. *Obs.* The act of testing; trial. [ME *tasten* < OFr. *taster. 'taxitare,* freq. of Lat. *taxare,* to touch.] —**tast'a·ble** *adj.*
taste bud *n.* Any of numerous spherical or ovoid nests of cells that are distributed over the tongue and embedded in the epithelium, consisting of gustatory cells and supporting cells and constituting the end organs of the sense of taste.
taste·ful (tāst'fəl) *adj.* 1. Exhibiting good taste 2. Tasty.—**taste'ful·ly** *adv.*—**taste'ful·ness** n.
taste·less (tāst'lis) *adj.* 1. Lacking flavor; insipid. 2. Exhibiting poor taste. —**taste'less·ly** *adv.* —**taste'less·ness** n
tast·er (tā'stər) *n.* 1. One who tastes, esp. a person who samples a food or beverage for quality. 2. Any of several devices or implements used in tasting.
tast·y (tā'ste) *adj.* **–i·er. -i·est.** 1. Having a pleasing flavor; savory. 2. Having good taste; tasteful. —**tast'i·ly** *adv* —**tast'i·ness** n.

American Heritage Dictionary
(1985)

APPENDIX 2   SOME CITATIONS FOR TASTE

<1>	Classicism of detail and proportion, the needs and	tastes of her clients, and the fit of the bui	<1>
<2>	sight. Sheer paradise! If fishing is not to your	taste, Craigendarroch offers the irresistible	<2>
<3>	summon our courage to enter the cluster. Touch it,	taste it, feel it. Such intimacy requires car	<3>
<4>	om nowhere all had their hands up." He now began to	taste the horror of the war. The corpses ever	<4>
<5>	" said the doctor. "Thanks. The only grapes I ever	taste are the ones I nick from my patients."	<5>
<6>	Really the same thing but in different sizes. To my	taste, none of these have a particularly dist	<6>
<7>	Which, unfortunately, is not to her mother-in-law's	taste! Tabitha wanted to cook some British di	<7>
<8>	l vinegar to the meat during cooking and sweeten to	taste with a little blackcurrant jam. Add a f	<8>
<9>	nal plan to build a new Bay City Rollers. Those who	taste instant success usually falter quickly	<9>
<10>	a bottle). Blanquette de Limoux has a lovely creamy	taste, with a full, rounded flavour. A new i	<10>
<11>	d to the demand. Most converts have their favourite	taste in mineral water & dash unless, like a	<11>
<12>	e affection as he discovers that they share certain	tastes: a liking for Graeco-Roman art and the	<12>
<13>	ation, confuses discrimination in the sense of good	taste with discrimination as social intoleran	<13>
<14>	acquired taste; the more you acquire, the less you	taste it. Too much, and the taverna starts d	<14>
<15>	harnel house of a butcher's van &dash, the price of	tasting the fruit of knowledge. As a precis t	<15>
<16>	hills the better the flavour. Then, and only then,	taste it and adjust your seasoning. <hdl> SH	<16>
<17>	Bill, simply wiped the two locals out. But having	tasted blood, the government was not satisfie	<17>
<18>	community, Eleanor Thorne decided, I should like to	taste the fruits of life in a small home, a	<18>
<19>	crow." The girl laughed. "Is that all?" "No." He	tasted his brandy. "You smell." "What do I f	<19>
<20>	ts, including vodka, which could not immediately be	tasted. Mr Lumb said: "Originally my clients	<20>
<21>	oducts of olive pressing as a weedkiller. "If you	taste the oils on their own, they can be very	<21>
<22>	ip. blub!" She made the kind of face she made when	tasting sour milk. "For God's sake, Henry," s	<22>
<23>	se, when I'm eating a box of candy, I can't wait to	taste the last piece." "I want to start a ch	<23>
<24>	developing awareness of the other senses—touch,	taste and smell. Such a room can be used as a	<24>
<25>	steaming. Ideally, it will be long-grained, rich in	taste and slightly sticky. The grains will be	<25>
<26>	up the dishes at home after putting her food to the	taste test. She'll be dishing out ideas, info	<26>
<27>	d who had behaved so badly that he was forbidden to	taste what turned out to be deadly toadstools	<27>
<28>	dness. When the roast beef appeared, even before he	tasted it, he decided that the reason for all	<28>
<29>	e at Boots, was the first Acesulfame sweetener.It	tastes just as good as sugar but has no calor	<29>
<30>	e. He was thinking bleach. His toast in the morning	tasted of bleach, his pint at the Rose tasted	<30>
<31>	domestic architecture is well suited to a feminine	taste, for if we even allow the objections &e	<31>
<32>	enges in their DIY projects. This refinement in the	taste of homeowners and prospective owner-occ	<32>
<33>	es. I love Frank Sinatra. I love Def Leppard. My	taste is pretty catholic!" From the start, J	<33>
<34>	eau. "Altogether "a really rather lovely" book. His	taste is altogether for suffering rather than	<34>
<35>	lanting scheme was gaudy and banal. It followed the	taste of Queen Victoria and Prince Albert, fo	<35>
<36>	mired by John Fowler (of Colefax &and.). A woman of	taste and energy, Mrs Baer goes right to the	<36>
<37>	se what he would wear, then positively preened. His	taste was individual: he had a pink suit and	<37>
<38>	als and banner ideas. Though for more sophisticated	tastes there was always the popular theme of	<38>
<39>	cess behind them, they used their eccentricities of	taste (and newly acquired cash) to move a lit	<39>
<40>	s of bands on smaller independent labels. As public	taste develops an acceptance of such modern n	<40>
<41>	holds good for the development in personal literary	taste of many another reader. "Parrot crit	<41>
<42>	ion had Albert Lewis not been a man of some musical	taste, who took the boys to the opera and the	<42>
<43>	use in an isolated setting, reflecting the romantic	taste of her time and her own desire to segre	<43>

4

Principles of Systematic Lexicography[1]

JURI D. APRESJAN*

For Sue Atkins from an admirer

Up till quite recently there has been a gap between lexicography and linguistic theory. Moreover, in some quarters lexicography was looked down upon as a purely practical enterprise unworthy of scholarly interest. I am convinced, however, that sound lexicography can only be based on sound linguistic theory and that recent theoretical developments are of paramount importance for practical dictionary making.

There are five principles inherent in modern linguistic theory that are of immediate relevance to systematic lexicography and may help to bridge the gap between the two:

1. The reconstruction of the 'naive' (language) picture of the world, or the pattern of conceptualizations underlying lexical and grammatical meanings of the given language.
2. The unification of grammatical and lexicological studies within what may be called an integrated linguistic description, or a fully coordinated description of dictionary and grammar. Such a description requires that grammatical rules should be geared to the entries of an 'integrated dictionary' and that the entries of such a dictionary should be sensitive to grammatical rules.[2]
3. The search for systematicity in lexicon as manifested in various classes of lexemes – lexicographic types, lexico-semantic paradigms, regular polysemy, and the like (a breakthrough into lexical macrocosm).
4. The emphasis on meticulous studies of separate word senses in all of their linguistically relevant properties (a breakthrough into lexical microcosm, or 'lexicographic portrayal'; a good example is Fillmore and Atkins 1992).
5. The formulation of rules governing the interaction of lexical and grammatical meanings in the texts (the so-called projection rules, semantic amalgamation rules, and the like).

Below I shall briefly outline each of the five principles.

* Apresjan, J. (2002). 'Principles of systematic lexicography', in Corréard, M.-H. (ed.), *Lexicography and Natural Language Processing – in Honour of B. T. S. Atkins*. Euralex, 91–104.

[1] This paper has been supported with grants from the Russian Research Foundation for the Humanities (No. 02-04-00306a) and the Russian Foundation for Fundamental Research (Nos. 02-06-80106 and 00-15-98866).

[2] For details see Apresjan (1995a: 21–27); for a more extensive treatment see Apresjan (1995b: 8–241) and Apresjan (2000).

I   RECONSTRUCTION OF THE 'NAIVE', OR LANGUAGE PICTURE OF THE WORLD

One of the most fascinating manifestations of a specific 'world-view' are the so-called obligatory meanings, i.e. meanings which a certain language *forces* its speakers to express no matter whether they are important for the essence of their messages or not. After F. Boas and R. Jakobson it has become customary to oppose grammatical and lexical meanings as obligatory and non-obligatory. Grammatical meanings, e.g. number in English substantives, are claimed to be obligatory in the sense that they must be expressed every time when the speaker uses the respective part of speech. For example, in the phrase *Telephone is a useful invention* the noun *telephone* is used in the singular, although quantity is absolutely immaterial for the essence of the speaker's thought. What is actually spoken of is not the number of concrete objects but a certain technical way of conveying messages. By contrast, lexical meanings were presumed to be optional in the sense that they are expressed only when there is actual communicative need for them.

Research of the last decades has shown that the opposition of grammatical and lexical meanings is not so sharp. Some elements of lexical meanings have also been demonstrated to be obligatorily and quite systematically expressed.

For instance, Russian forces its speakers, whenever they talk of locomotion, to specify the manner of locomotion (walking, flying, crawling and so on), although it may be irrelevant for their thought. In particular, the idea of 'a certain living being having left at the point of observation a certain place' is expressed in good Russian by the phrases *Sobaka vyshla iz konury* 'The dog walked out of its kennel', *Ptitsa vyletela iz gnezda* 'The bird flew out of its nest', *Zmeia vypolzla iz nory* 'The snake crawled out of its hole', *Ryba vyplyla iz grota* 'The fish swam out of the grotto'. On purely logical grounds the verb *pokinut'* 'to leave' seems to come closer to the required meaning, yet the phrases ?*Sobaka pokinula konuru* 'The dog left its kennel', ?*Ptitsa pokinula gnezdo* 'The bird left its nest', ?*Zmeia pokinula noru* 'The snake left its hole', ?*Ryba pokinula grot* 'The fish left the grotto' are at least doubtful. They sound unmotivatedly elevated with regard to the required meaning or else express an entirely different idea of 'leaving a certain place *for good*'.

In this respect Russian is opposed to French where the idea at issue is uniformly expressed by the same verb *sortir*: *Le chien est sorti de sa niche, le serpent est sorti de son trou*, etc. Only when it is necessary to emphasize the way of leaving a certain place does French allow to specify it by adding an adverbial phrase like *en marchant, à la nage* etc. English seems to be intermediate between Russian and French. The required idea can be quite idiomatically rendered by the verbs *to walk, to fly, to crawl, to swim*, specifying the ways of locomotion in precisely the same way as Russian does (see the English glosses above). On the other hand, one can freely resort to the indiscriminate verb *to leave*, which comes closer to the French way of thinking: *The dog left its kennel, the bird left its nest, the snake left its hole, the fish left the grotto.*

The same predilection of Russian for specifying the *way* things are done can be further substantiated by the vocabulary of spatial position. Russian forces its speakers, when talking about space orientation of certain physical bodies with regard to some other bodies, to specify the way they are positioned (e.g. whether they stand, lie or hang). Cf. *U okna stoial Ivan* 'John stood at the window', *Na stene viseli kartiny* 'Some pictures hung on the wall', *Knigi lezhali v uglu* 'The books lay in the corner'. What the speaker actually *means* to communicate may be limited to the idea of 'to be placed, to be located somewhere'. This idea is prototypically rendered in Russian by the verb *nakhodit'sia*. Yet the phrases *U okna nakhodilsia*

Ivan, Na stene nakhodilis' kartiny, V uglu nakhodilis' knigi would be odd or at least non-idiomatic.

French is again opposed to Russian because in similar circumstances it does not make any difference between the ways objects are positioned in space. It uses the neutral verb *se trouver* or the equally neutral construction *il y a*, unless it is necessary, for some reason or other, to specify their spatial positions. English is again intermediate between Russian and French, allowing for both forms of expression.

The *language picture of the world,* including language specific meanings, is thus the first keynote of systematic lexicography.

2   THE UNIFIED, OR INTEGRATED THEORY OF LINGUISTIC DESCRIPTION

Every complete linguistic description is ultimately made up of a grammar and a dictionary. It is reasonable to expect that these two documents should be mutually adjusted to each other, i.e. coordinated with regard to the types of information included and the formal devices used to record them.

Unfortunately, up till quite recently these natural principles have not been clearly formulated, much less adhered to. Originally dictionaries and grammars were produced by different people. The result was basically discordant grammars and dictionaries that did not give a coherent picture of the language at large. Below I shall quote one of the most intriguing examples of such a discrepancy.

English grammar has always recognized (cardinal) numerals as a part of speech in its own right, distinct from nouns and adjectives. Indeed, their morphological, derivational, syntactic and semantic properties are very different from those of true nouns and adjectives. (a) In such prototypical uses as *five books, twenty-five, room five, to divide <to multiply> five by five* and some others they can have no number marking – the basic morphological category of genuine nouns. (b) Derivationally they are set off from nouns and adjectives by such patterns as '*X + teen*', '*X + ty*', '*X + th*', '*X + fold*', as in *fifteen, fifty, fifth, fivefold*. (c) Syntactically they require that the nouns they combine with have the plural form, as in *five books*. They can also form the multiplicative construction *five by five* featuring a unique meaning of the preposition *by*. Prototypical nouns and adjectives have neither of these properties. (d) In co-occurring with one another they form a specific concatenated construction with an additive meaning: *twenty-five* = '20 + 5'. Semantically this construction is entirely different from the typically substantive or adjectival constructions conjoining two nouns or adjectives, like *cannon-ball, computer system, dark blue, English-Russian* and so on.

Within a scientific description of English, classing numerals as nouns or adjectives in the dictionary is bound to play havoc with the grammatical rules geared to genuine nouns and adjectives if we apply the rules literally. However, there is virtually no comprehensive dictionary of British, American, Australian or any other variety of English that has the grammatical label 'num'. In a host of most influential dictionaries numerals are labelled either as nouns or as adjectives. Most inconsistently many of them include an entry for *numeral,* with the definition 'a word <a name> denoting <expressing> a number', and some of them even quote *cardinal numerals* as an example.

As can be seen from this account, traditional grammar and dictionary at this point are glaringly incompatible. Insistence on the necessity of *integrated* linguistic descriptions, with perfectly coordinated dictionary and grammar, becomes thus the next major principle of systematic lexicography.

3 LEXICAL CLASSES

The vocabulary of any language has several principles of lexeme grouping at its disposal, of which I shall briefly discuss lexicographic types and lexico-semantic paradigms.

3.1 Lexicographic types

I use this term to refer to a group of lexemes with a shared property or properties, not necessarily semantic, which are sensitive to the same linguistic rules and which should therefore be uniformly described in the dictionary. I shall exemplify this concept with the classes of factive and putative predicates. Both of them will be narrowed down to the subclasses of verbs denoting mental *states* (not processes or actions).

Following Vendler (1972), the label of 'factive' is assigned to verbs *to know <to understand, to guess, to remember, ...> (that P)* and similar predicates which govern propositions denoting facts.[3] All of them are decomposable into semantic structures with the sense 'to know' at the bottom and presuppose the truth of the subordinate clause. That means that irrespective of whether the knowledge of P is asserted or denied, P always remains true. Such sentences as *He knew that he was under police surveillance* and *He didn't know that he was under police surveillance* are alike in asserting that he was under police surveillance.[4]

The label of 'putative' is assigned to verbs *to think <to believe, to consider, to find, to hold, to doubt, ...> that P* and similar predicates which denote opinions. Opinions, unlike knowledge, are not necessarily true. In other words, it cannot be deduced either from the sentence *He thought that he was under police surveillance*, or from the sentence *He didn't think that he was under police surveillance* whether he was in fact under surveillance or not.

Both groups of verbs share the common feature of all statives noted in Vendler (1967: 99–103), namely, a specific relation to the idea of duration. It manifests itself above all in the inability of *to know <to understand, to guess, to remember, ...> (that P)* and *to think <to believe, to consider, to find, to hold, to doubt, ...> that P* to occur in the progressive tenses (in the senses under consideration). Indeed, the phrases **When I entered he was knowing <understanding, guessing> that the meeting had been cancelled* or **When I entered he was believing <considering, doubting> that the meeting had been cancelled* are highly ungrammatical.

On other points factive and putative statives differ from one another. All of their formal differences are quite systematic, i.e. semantically motivated, so that two well-defined and consistently organized lexico-semantic classes emerge. To make them accessible to certain rules of grammar and other sufficiently general linguistic rules we have to posit two distinct lexicographic types which should be uniformly described throughout the dictionary. I shall exemplify these types mostly with the material of the verbs *to know* and *to think*.

There are a number of well-known and much discussed syntactic properties which distinguish factives from putatives. The most important of them is the ability of factives to govern

---

[3] In accordance with the treatment of knowledge in theoretical studies and the lexicographic description of the verb *to know* in major dictionaries I distinguish propositional knowledge (*I know that he has come*) from knowledge-acquaintance (*Do you know Sam?*), knowledge-familiarity (*He knows French literature very well*) and some other types of knowledge. All these uses of *to know* are considered to represent different lexical meanings (different senses, different lexemes) of the verb. In this article only propositional knowledge is at issue.

[4] In P. Kiparsky and C. Kiparsky (1971: 345) where the notion of factivity was first introduced prototypical factive predicates are exemplified with a different series of words – adjectives like (*It's*) *significant <odd, tragic, exciting> (that P)*, and verbs like (*It*) *suffices <amuses (me), bothers (me)> (that P)*. I side with Z. Vendler in ranking *to know* as a prototypical factive predicate.

an oblique question introduced by the *wh*-words like *what, who, which, where, when, how* and so on: *He knew what was in store for him <why his father kept silent, where to look for the mistake, how to do the job>*. Putatives do not govern oblique questions; in particular, they cannot replace factives in the above sentences.

The next syntactic peculiarity of *to know* and other prototypical factives is rooted in the fact that knowledge has a source, but not a reason. Therefore factives can govern nominal groups denoting sources of information and cannot subordinate adverbial modifiers of cause. Compare the well-formedness of *How do you know it?, I know it from the newspapers* and the ungrammaticality of **Why do you know it?*

By contrast, opinions have a reason, but never a source. Therefore putative verbs can subordinate adverbial modifiers of cause but not those denoting a source of information. Compare the well-formedness of *Why do you think so?* and the ungrammaticality of **I think so from the newspapers*.

Putatives allow of neg-transportation, with only a slight change of emphasis: *I didn't think he would cope with the task ≈ I thought he would not cope with the task*. With factives neg-transportation is impossible for semantic reasons: there is a fundamental difference between *I didn't know he had coped with the task ≠ I knew he had not coped with the task*.

Prototypical putative verbs denote all sorts of opinions, that is, evaluative judgements. Therefore most of them can in some way or other govern assessment constructions with the second complement denoting the essence of evaluation: *to think <to consider, to find> somebody young, to regard <to look upon> this marriage as a mistake* etc. For putatives the second complement is obligatory. Phrases like **I think him, *I consider him* (in the sense at issue) are ungrammatical.

At first sight factives like *to know* and *to remember* are also able to form this construction: *I knew <remember> her young*. However, the similarity is purely superficial. Phrases like *I knew her young* feature a different syntactic construction and a different lexical meaning of the verb. The second complement in this case does not fill in any semantic valency of the verb but fulfils the function of a co-predicative dependent. Syntactically it is optional, and its semantic relation to the verb is entirely different from that of the putative verbs. *I knew her young* means 'I knew her at a *time* when she was young'. This reference to time is totally alien to putatives. On the other hand, the construction at issue changes the lexical meaning of the verb *to know* from propositional knowledge (*I knew that she was young*) to that of acquaintance (*I knew her at the time when she was young*; see note 3). This is as much as to say that factives cannot be used in assessment constructions typical of putatives.

Let us now look at the combinatorial potential of the two lexicographic types at issue. Factive verbs freely co-occur with positive evaluation adverbs like *well, perfectly well*, and so on. To qualify knowledge in this way is just to emphasize its truth. Cf. *I know that you are against rigid measures ≈ I know perfectly well that you are against rigid measures*. Putatives in such contexts are absolutely ruled out: phrases like **I think perfectly well that you are against rigid measures* are totally ungrammatical.

In their turn, putative verbs co-occur freely with truth-adverbs like *correctly, rightly* and the like: *He rightly thought that it would be pointless to continue the conversation*. The respective phrases with factives are pleonastic and therefore ungrammatical: propositional knowledge cannot be wrong by definition.

There is at least one more formal feature which distinguishes factives and putatives – their prosodic and communicative properties. Curiously enough these have been almost totally neglected in theoretical studies, not to speak of dictionaries.

Factive words convey information about the real state of things. Therefore they can bear a strong phrasal accent (the so-called main phrasal stress) and serve as the rheme of the utterance, as in the phrase *I ↓knew she would marry him, I ↓remember how it all ended.* There is a rational motivation for it – it is pragmatically and psychologically reasonable to call the addressee's attention to the undoubtedly true information by phonically accentuating it.

Putative words express somebody's opinion about something which may be either true or false. Therefore they are never marked off by the main phrasal stress and are usually located in the thematic part of the utterance. The only type of phrasal stress they can bear is the so-called logical, or contrastive stress marking the contrastive rheme of the utterance, as in the sentence *Do you ↑↑believe you are under police surveillance, or do you ↓↓know it?*

These distinctions are so strong that they occur even within a single word if it happens to have a factive and a putative sense. Note the difference in the interpretation of the verb *to understand* in such sentences as *I ↓understand he is in trouble* (He *is* in trouble) and *I understand he is in ↓trouble* (I am doubtful about whether he is in trouble or not and am asking for information rather than asserting anything).

These differences carry over to all sorts of factives and putatives, in particular, to factive and putative adjectives and adverbs. For instance, a written sentence like *His son is a real gangster* is homographic and conceals two different propositions. The first is *His son is a ↓real gangster* (robs people and engages in all sorts of criminal activities, i.e. 'belongs to the class Y and has all its essential properties', factive). The second is *His son is a real ↓gangster* (naughty, disorderly, misbehaving, i.e. 'resembles an object of class Y but lacks its crucial property', putative).

3.2   Lexico-semantic paradigms

The division of vocabulary into multiple intersecting lexicographic types is the most important but not the only manifestation of the systematic character of vocabulary. Another noteworthy principle of lexeme organization is their grouping in lexico-semantic paradigms – compact word classes with the common core meaning and predictable semantic distinctions.

An interesting type of lexico-semantic paradigms are groups of converse terms. As is well known, such terms denote the same situation but assign different syntactic ranks to its actants and may therefore enforce different theme–rheme articulations of the utterance. For instance, the verbs *to buy, to sell, to pay* and *to cost* denote a four-actant situation with two human participants, X (recipient) and Y (source), and two objects, A (thing or service) and B (money), which they exchange. *To buy* assigns the highest syntactic rank to X, the second – to A, the third – to Y and the fourth – to B. The verb *to sell* assigns the highest rank to Y, and shifts X to the third place, while keeping intact the status of A and B. The verb *to pay*, on the contrary, preserves the ranks of X and Y but swaps those of A and B, making B the second ranking complement of the verb and shifting A to the fourth place. The verb *to cost* raises A to the highest rank and places B second, while X is ranked third. Y becomes syntactically inexpressible though it is fully preserved semantically: if something *cost* me a thousand pounds, that means there was someone whom I paid the sum.

A remarkable principle of vocabulary organization is that for every fragment of reality which is socially important language tends to develop as many converse verbs as are necessary to raise a step or more the rank of every actant. The same holds true of the lexico-semantic paradigms of substantives naming the actants of a many-actant situation; consider the nouns *buyer, article (goods), seller* and *cost* as (semantic) derivatives of the verb *to buy*, or the nouns *physician, patient*, and *illness* as (semantic) derivatives of the verb *to treat* (in the medical sense).

Lexico-semantic paradigms, like grammatical paradigms, allow us to predict all of their potential members on the basis of more general schemes underlying the given paradigm. For paradigms of de-verbal actant substantive derivatives this general scheme (which may be called a semantic paradigm) consists of the set of semantic roles for the given verb. For instance, as is clear from the foregoing discussion, the semantic roles for *to buy* are recipient (agent), object, source (counteragent) and second object. The degree of completeness of a lexico-semantic paradigm is an objective measure of systematicity of the respective fragment of lexicon.

To sum up, the third principle of systematic lexicography is the requirement that all salient *lexical classes* should be fully taken into account and uniformly described in a dictionary in all of their linguistically relevant properties.

4   LEXICOGRAPHIC PORTRAITS

To follow up the example considered in the preceding section, it should be noted that not all of the factives and not all of the putatives can be expected to display the prototypical properties of those two lexicographic types.

For instance, the factive verb *to understand* which, as noted above, is reducible in the long run to the idea of 'to know', has no valency of an outward source of information. Understanding is a process too deep-seated in the mind of the subject himself and involving too much of his own activity. That accounts for the ungrammaticality or the dubiousness of sentences like **Where do you understand it from?, ?I understand it from the newspapers.*

Various putative stative verbs display varying degrees of incompatibility with the idea of duration mentioned above. For instance, the verb *to think (that P),* which is a close synonym of *to believe* and *to consider,* can be used in the progressive tenses, especially when it is conjoined with a genuinely actional verb: *As I lay down thinking that my book was quite close to completion, I heard the phone ring.* Neither *to believe,* nor *to consider* can replace *to think* in such contexts.

The explanation is to be sought in the semantic structure of *to think* as a whole. The second basic sense of *to think* is purely actional: *I was thinking about tomorrow's session when the phone rang.* Now, closely related senses of a single word are apt to 'grow' into one another and impart to the neighbouring senses at least some of their properties. In such cases deviation from the prototype becomes highly probable.

This adds a new dimension to the facts discussed so far. It appears that in lexical description one should give equal attention to the shared properties of lexemes (the problem of lexico-graphic types, or *unification*) and to what distinguishes them (the problem of lexicographic portraits, or *individuation*).

A lexicographic portrait is an exhaustive characterization of all the linguistically relevant properties of a lexeme, with particular emphasis on the semantic motivation of its formal properties. A certain property is considered to be linguistically relevant if there is a rule of grammar or some other sufficiently general rule (semantic rules included) that accesses this property. Once the given lexeme is viewed against the whole set of linguistic rules, an entirely novel point of observation is created. It highlights new facets of lexemes and helps to uncover a number of their lexicographically relevant and semantically motivated properties that have never been recorded in dictionaries.

Consider the word *alone* in the following two uses: 1) *The house stands on the hillside all alone, He likes living alone*; 2) *Smith alone knows what happened, You alone can help me.* *Alone 1* is assigned the following definition in current dictionaries: 'by oneself, without the company or help of others'. *Alone 2* is defined as follows: 'and no other, no one else, the only one'.

It should be noted that *alone 1* and *alone 2* have different scopes. This is borne out by (a) the semantic contrast between *He lives there alone 1* and *He alone 2 lives there*; (b) the fact that *He lives alone 1* is grammatical while *?He alone 2 lives* is odd; (c) the fact that *He alone 2 knows the truth* is grammatical, while **He knows alone 1 the truth* is not. Yet the dictionary definitions cited above fail to bring out this difference in the scopes. I propose the following more explicit definitions: *X does P alone 1* = 'X does P; one could expect that someone else would do P simultaneously or together with X; no one else does P simultaneously or together with X'; *X alone 2 does P* = 'X does P; there is no one else that does P'.

These definitions account for the following more formal properties of *alone 1* and *alone 2* which should be recorded in a dictionary of lexicographic portraits.

Syntactically *alone 1* is an adverbial modifier, that is, a verbal dependent (*Don't go there alone*), whereas *alone 2* is a noun attribute (cf. *Smith alone, you alone*).

Communicatively *alone 1* has no permanent value. It may mark off the verbal group as the theme (topic) of the utterance, as in *Living alone 1* [theme] *is a nuisance <a pleasure>*. On the other hand, it may serve as the rheme (comment), as in *The house stands on the hillside all alone 1* [rheme]. Unlike it, *alone 2* always marks off the nominal group to which it refers as the rheme of the utterance; cf. *Smith* [rheme] *alone 2 knows what happened*.

The above distinctions are mirrored in the prosodic properties of the two lexemes. *Alone 1* can bear the main phrasal stress, as in *The house stands on the hillside all ↓alone 1*, or it may be left phrasally unstressed, as in *He ↓likes living alone 1*. Contrary to that *alone 2* always bears the main phrasal stress, cf. *Smith ↓alone 2 knows what happened, You ↓alone 2 can help me*.

Insistence on exhaustive *lexicographic portrayal* is the fourth major principle of systematic lexicography.

5   INTERACTION OF MEANINGS IN THE TEXTS

The word 'system', so much used in section 3, has two basic senses in technical language – taxonomic and operational. Systems in the taxonomic sense are all sorts of static classifications of objects, like the periodic table of chemical elements. The crucial feature of such systems is the reducibility of a large set of complex objects to a much smaller set of repetitive simpler components. Systems in the operational sense are sets of objects interacting with each other according to natural laws, like the system of blood circulation, or according to rules designed by humans to solve a certain task, like advanced information systems.

If one looks at the lexicon from this point of view it turns out to be a sufficiently well organized system in both these senses. The vocabulary of a language is, above all, a very large set of lexemes. Their meanings are decomposable into a much smaller set of simpler semantic components which give rise to a number of intersecting lexeme classes. Some of them have been illustrated above.

But lexemes are not only members of a taxonomic system. They have an operational dimension too, and start to live a full life in the texts where they interact with one another and with various grammatical items according to certain sufficiently general rules. In the remainder of this article I shall try to exemplify the nature of these rules and show their relevance for lexicography.

5.1   Interaction of lexical meanings

Consider the following Russian phrase: *Petr khorosho okharakterizoval svoikh odnoklass-nikov*, lit. 'Peter characterized well his class-mates'. It is two-ways ambiguous. On the first reading it means that the speaker estimated highly the mastery of Peter's description of his class-mates. On the second reading it means that Peter spoke with praise about his class-mates.

The ambiguity is rooted in the semantic structure of the verb *kharakterizovat'* 'to character-ize' and the scopes of the adverb *khorosho* 'well' within it. The Russian verb *kharacterizovat' A as X* can be defined as follows: 'to describe the essential properties of A and to assess them as X'. 'To describe' denotes an action, 'to assess' – evaluation. Both these components may fall within the scope of the adverb *khorosho*. The latter may serve as an adverbial modifier of *kharakterizovat'* and is then linked with the top sense 'to describe', yielding the interpretation of a good description. On the other hand, *khorosho* may fill in the third valency of the verb *kharakterizovat'* (i.e., valency X) and is then linked to the internal sense 'to assess', yielding the interpretation of a positive evaluation, on the part of Peter, of his class-mates.

Not every verb and not every evaluative adverb can produce this kind of ambiguity.

Consider the verbs *opisyvat'* 'to describe' and *otzyvat'sia* 'to estimate, to assess'. The phrase *Petr khorosho opisal svoikh odnoklassnikov* 'Peter described his class-mates well' can have only the first reading (that of the speaker praising the mastery of Peter's description), while the phrase *Petr khorosho otozvalsia o svoikh odnoklassnikakh* 'Peter estimated highly his class-mates' can have only the second reading (that of Peter praising his class-mates). These unambiguous interpretations can be accounted for by the fact that *opisyvat'* 'to describe' is just a designation of action, with no evaluative component within it, while *otzyvat'sia* is a purely evaluative verb, with no idea of action behind it.

Let us now turn to other types of adverbs, for example, the adverbs (a) *prekrasno* 'perfectly', *velikolepno* 'splendidly', on the one hand, and (b) *polozhitel'no* 'positively', *otritsatel'no* 'negatively', on the other. Even if combined with the verb *kharakterizovat'*, adverbs of group (a) produce only the first interpretation, while adverbs of group (b) produce only the second interpretation; cf. *Petr velikolepno okharakterizoval svoikh odnoklassnikov* 'Peter character-ized splendidly his class-mates' vs. *Petr polozhitel'no okharakterizoval svoikh odnoklassnikov* 'Peter gave a positive evaluation of his class-mates'.

Note that the same kind of ambiguity is inherent in such English phrases as *a good review* and the like: a *review* is a description accompanied by an evaluation, and the adjective *good* can have for its scope either the actional or the evaluative component in the semantic structure of this noun, yielding the two interpretations under consideration.

5.2   Semantic interaction of lexical and grammatical items

I shall quote one more example to illustrate a different type of semantic amalgamation rules and a different type of interaction, namely, the interaction of lexemes with grammatical items.

The Russian verbs *brosat'* 'to throw', *kidat'* 'to throw' and *shvyriat'* 'to hurl' govern two sequences of forms – (a) the accusative plus the indication of direction (*brosat' kamni v prud <na dorogu, cherez zabor>* 'to throw (the) stones into the pond <onto the road, over the fence>') and (b) the instrumental plus the indication of object (*brosat' snezhkami v prokhozhikh* 'to throw snowballs at the passers-by'). The first government pattern features the prototypical meaning of the verb embodied in its dictionary definition: 'to let fly or to drop object A onto surface or into space B'. In the second government pattern the verb regularly acquires a richer meaning: it points to a desire to hit a target and therefore implies a greater swing of the arm.

Both groups of facts considered in section 5 should be entered in dictionaries in some form or other and commented upon where necessary, probably with succinct explanations of how they arise. A dictionary which fails to record such facts (and this is the practice of most explanatory dictionaries of Russian in the case of *brosat'*) does the user a bad turn.

Attention to meaning interaction of various language units in the texts is thus the last important principle of systematic lexicography.

PART II
On Corpus Design

5

Representativeness in Corpus Design

DOUGLAS BIBER*

I   GENERAL CONSIDERATIONS

Some of the first considerations in constructing a corpus concern the overall design: for example, the kinds of texts included, the number of texts, the selection of particular texts, the selection of text samples from within texts, and the length of text samples. Each of these involves a sampling decision, either conscious or not.

The use of computer-based corpora provides a solid empirical foundation for general purpose language tools and descriptions, and enables analyses of a scope not otherwise possible. However, a corpus must be 'representative' in order to be appropriately used as the basis for generalizations concerning a language as a whole; for example, corpus-based dictionaries, grammars, and general part-of-speech taggers are applications requiring a representative basis (cf. Biber, 1993b).

Typically researchers focus on sample size as the most important consideration in achieving representativeness: how many texts must be included in the corpus, and how many words per text sample. Books on sampling theory, however, emphasize that sample size is not the most important consideration in selecting a representative sample; rather, a thorough definition of the target population and decisions concerning the method of sampling are prior considerations. Representativeness refers to the extent to which a sample includes the full range of variability in a population. In corpus design, variability can be considered from situational and from linguistic perspectives, and both of these are important in determining representativeness. Thus a corpus design can be evaluated for the extent to which it includes: (1) the range of text types in a language, and (2) the range of linguistic distributions in a language.

Any selection of texts is a sample. Whether or not a sample is 'representative', however, depends first of all on the extent to which it is selected from the range of text types in the target population; an assessment of this representativeness thus depends on a prior full definition of the 'population' that the sample is intended to represent, and the techniques used to select the sample from that population. Definition of the target population has at least two aspects: (1) the boundaries of the population—what texts are included and excluded from the population; (2) hierarchical organization within the population—what text categories are included in the population, and what are their definitions. In designing text corpora, these concerns are often not given sufficient attention, and samples are collected without a prior definition of the target population. As a result, there is no possible way to evaluate the adequacy or representativeness of such a corpus (because there is no well-defined conception of what the sample is intended to represent).

* Biber, D. (1993c). 'Representativeness in corpus design', *Linguistic and Literary Computing*, 8(4): 243–257. Reproduced with permission of Oxford University Press.

In addition, the representativeness of a corpus depends on the extent to which it includes the range of linguistic distributions in the population; i.e. different linguistic features are differently distributed (within texts, across texts, across text types), and a representative corpus must enable analysis of these various distributions. This condition of linguistic representativeness depends on the first condition; i.e. if a corpus does not represent the range of text types in a population, it will not represent the range of linguistic distributions. In addition, linguistic representativeness depends on issues such as the number of words per text sample, the number of samples per 'text', and the number of texts per text type. These issues will be addressed in Sections 3 and 4.

However, the issue of population definition is the first concern in corpus design. To illustrate, consider the population definitions underlying the Brown corpus (Francis and Kučera, 1964/79) and the LOB corpus (Johansson *et al.*, 1978). These target populations were defined both with respect to their boundaries (all published English texts printed in 1961, in the United States and United Kingdom respectively), and their hierarchical organizations (fifteen major text categories and numerous subgenre distinctions within these categories). In constructing these corpora, the compilers also had good 'sampling frames', enabling probabilistic, random sampling of the population. A sampling frame is an operational definition of the population, an itemized listing of population members from which a representative sample can be chosen. The LOB corpus manual (Johansson *et al.*, 1978) is fairly explicit about the sampling frame used: for books, the target population was operationalized as all 1961 publications listed in *The British National Bibliography Cumulated Subject Index, 1960–1964* (which is based on the subject divisions of the Dewey Decimal Classification system), and for periodicals and newspapers, the target population was operationalized as all 1961 publications listed in *Willing's Press Guide* (1961). In the case of the Brown corpus, the sampling frame was the collection of books and periodicals in the Brown University Library and the Providence Athenaeum; this sampling frame is less representative of the total texts in print in 1961 than the frames used for construction of the Lancaster–Oslo/Bergen (LOB) corpus, but it provided well-defined boundaries and an itemized listing of members. In choosing and evaluating a sampling frame, considerations of efficiency and cost effectiveness must be balanced against higher degrees of representativeness.

Given an adequate sampling frame, it is possible to select a probabilistic sample. There are several kinds of probabilistic samples, but they all rely on random selection. In a simple random sampling, all texts in the population have an equal chance of being selected. For example, if all entries in the *British National Bibliography* were numbered sequentially, then a table of random numbers could be used to select a random sample of books. Another method of probabilistic sampling, which was apparently used in the construction of the Brown and LOB corpora, is 'stratified sampling'. In this method, subgroups are identified within the target population (in this case, the genres), and then each of those 'strata' are sampled using random techniques. This approach has the advantage of guaranteeing that all strata are adequately represented while at the same time selecting a non-biased sample within each stratum (e.g. in the case of the Brown and LOB corpora, there was 100% representation at the level of genre categories and an unbiased selection of texts within each genre).

Note that, for two reasons, a careful definition and analysis of the non-linguistic characteristics of the target population is a crucial prerequisite to sampling decisions. First, it is not possible to identify an adequate sampling frame or to evaluate the extent to which a particular sample represents a population until the population itself has been carefully defined. A good illustration is a corpus intended to represent the spoken texts in a language. As there are no catalogues or bibliographies of spoken texts, and since we are all constantly expanding the universe of spoken texts in our everyday conversations, identifying an adequate sampling frame in this case is difficult; but without a prior definition of the boundaries and parameters of speech within a language, evaluation of a given sample is not possible.

The second motivation for a prior definition of the population is that stratified samples are almost always more representative than non-stratified samples (and they are never less representative). This is because identified strata can be fully represented (100% sampling) in the proportions desired, rather than depending on random selection techniques. In statistical terms, the between-group variance is typically larger than within-group variance, and thus a sample that forces representation across identifiable groups will be more representative overall.[1] Returning to the Brown and LOB corpora, a prior identification of the genre categories (e.g. press reportage, academic prose, and mystery fiction) and subgenre categories (e.g. medicine, mathematics, and humanities within the genre of academic prose) guaranteed 100% representation at those two levels; i.e. the corpus builders attempted to compile an exhaustive listing of the major text categories of published English prose, and all of these categories were included in the corpus design. Therefore, random sampling techniques were required only to obtain a representative selection of texts from within each subgenre. The alternative, a random selection from the universe of all published texts, would depend on a large sample and the probabilities associated with random selection to assure representation of the range of variation at all levels (across genres, subgenres, and texts within subgenres), a more difficult task.

In the present paper, I will first consider issues relating to population definitions for language corpora and attempt to develop a framework for stratified analysis of the corpus population (Section 2). In Section 3, then, I will return to particular sampling issues, including proportional versus non-proportional sampling, sampling within texts (how many words per text and stratified sampling within texts), and issues relating to sample size. In Section 4, I will describe differences in the distributions of linguistic features, presenting the distributions of several particular features, and I will discuss the implications of these distributions for corpus design. Finally, in Section 5, I offer a brief overview of corpus design in practice.

2   STRATA IN A TEXT CORPUS: AN OPERATIONAL PROPOSAL CONCERNING THE SALIENT PARAMETERS OF REGISTER AND DIALECT VARIATION

As noted in the last section, definition of the corpus population requires specification of the boundaries and specification of the strata. If we adopt the ambitious goal of representing a complete language, the population boundaries can be specified as all of the texts in the language. Specifying the relevant strata and identifying sampling frames are obviously more difficult tasks, requiring a theoretically motivated and complete specification of the kinds of texts. In the present section I offer a preliminary proposal for identifying the strata for such a corpus and operationalizing them as sampling frames. The proposal is restricted to western societies (with examples from the United States), and is intended primarily as an illustration rather than a final solution, showing how a corpus of this kind could be designed.

I use the terms genre or register to refer to situationally defined text categories (such as fiction, sports broadcasts, psychology articles), and text type to refer to linguistically defined text categories. Both of these text classification systems are valid, but they have different bases. Although registers/genres are not defined on linguistic grounds, there are statistically important linguistic differences among these categories (Biber, 1986, 1988), and linguistic

---

[1] Further, in the case of language corpora, proportional representation of texts is usually not desirable (see Section 3); rather, representation of the range of text types is required as a basis for linguistic analyses, making a stratified sample even more essential.

feature counts are relatively stable across texts within a register (Biber, 1990). In contrast, text types are identifed on the basis of shared linguistic co-occurrence patterns, so that the texts within each type are maximally similar in their linguistic characteristics, while the different types are maximally distinct from one another (Biber, 1989).

In defining the population for a corpus, register/genre distinctions take precedence over text type distinctions. This is because registers are based on criteria external to the corpus, while text types are based on internal criteria; i.e. registers are based on the different situations, purposes, and functions of text in a speech community, and these can be identifed prior to the construction of a corpus. In contrast, identification of the salient text type distinctions in a language requires a representative corpus of texts for analysis; there is no a priori way to identify linguistically defined types. As I show in Section 4, though, the results of previous studies, as well as on-going research during the construction of a corpus, can be used to assure that the selection of texts is linguistically as well as situationally representative.

For the most part, corpus linguistics has concentrated on register differences.[2] In planning the design of a corpus, however, decisions must be made whether to include a representative range of dialects or to restrict the corpus to a single dialect (e.g. a 'standard' variety). Dialect parameters specify the demographic characteristics of the speakers and writers, including geographic region, age, sex, social class, ethnic group, education, and occupation.[3]

Different overall corpus designs represent different populations and meet different research purposes. Three of the possible overall designs are organized around text production, text reception, and texts as products. The first two of these are demographically organized at the top level; i.e. individuals are selected from a larger demographic population, and then these individuals are tracked to record their language use. A production design would include the texts (spoken and written) actually produced by the individuals in the sample; a reception design would include the texts listened to or read. These two approaches would address the question of what people actually do with language on a regular basis. The demographic selection could be stratified along the lines of occupation, sex, age, etc.

A demographically oriented corpus would not represent the range of text types in a language, since many kinds of language are rarely used, even though they are important on other grounds. For example, few individuals will ever write a law or treaty, an insurance contract, or a book of any kind, and some of these kinds of texts are also rarely read. It would thus be difficult to stratify a demographic corpus in such a way that it would ensure representativeness of the range of text categories. Many of these categories are very important, however, in defining a culture. A corpus organized around texts as products would be designed to represent the range of registers and text types rather than the typical patterns of use of various demographic groups.

Work on the parameters of register variation has been carried out by anthropological linguists such as Hymes and Duranti, and by functional linguists such as Halliday (see Hymes, 1974; Brown and Fraser, 1979; Duranti, 1985; Halliday and Hasan, 1989). In Biber (1993a), I attempt to develop a relatively complete framework, arguing that 'register' should be specified as a continuous (rather than discrete) notion, and distinguishing among the range of situational differences that have been considered in register studies. This framework is overspecified for

[2] Actually, very little work has been carried out on dialect variation from a text-based perspective. Rather, dialect studies have tended to concentrate on phonological variation, downplaying the importance of grammatical and discourse features.

[3] Other demographic factors characterize individual speakers and writers rather than groups of users; these include relatively stable characteristics, such as personality, interests, and beliefs, and temporary characteristics, such as mood and emotional state. These factors are probably not important for corpus design, unless an intended use of the corpus is investigation of personal differences.

TABLE I   Situational parameters listed as hierarchical sampling strata

1. *Primary channel.* Written/spoken/scripted speech

2. *Format.* Published/not published (+ various formats within 'published')

3. *Setting.* Institutional/other public/private-personal

4. *Addressee.*
   (*a*) *Plurality.* Unenumerated/plural/individual/self
   (*b*) *Presence* (*place and time*). Present/absent
   (*c*) *Interactiveness.* None/little/extensive
   (*d*) *Shared knowledge.* General/specialized/personal

5. *Addressor.*
   (*a*) *Demographic variation.* Sex, age, occupation, etc.
   (*b*) *Acknowledgement.* Acknowledged individual/institution

6. *Factuality.* Factual-informational/intermediate or indeterminate/imaginative

7. *Purposes.* Persuade, entertain, edify, inform, instruct, explain, narrate, describe, keep records, reveal self, express attitudes, opinions, or emotions, enhance interpersonal relationship, . . .

8. *Topics.* . . .

corpus design work—values on some parameters are entailed by values on other parameters, and some parameters are specific to restricted kinds of texts. Attempting to sample at this level of specificity would thus be extremely difficult. For this reason I propose in Table I a reduced set of sampling strata, balancing operational feasibility with the desire to define the target population as completely as possible.

The first of these parameters divides the corpus into three major components: writing, speech, and scripted speech. Each of these three requires different sampling considerations, and thus not all subsequent situational parameters are relevant for each component.

Within writing, the first important distinction is publication.[4] This is because the population of published texts can be operationally bounded, and various catalogues and indexes provide itemized listings of members. For example, the following criteria might be used for the operational definition of 'published' texts: (1) they are printed in multiple copies for distribution; (2) they are copyright registered or recorded by a major indexing service. In the United States, a record of all copyright registered books and periodicals is available at the Library of Congress. Other 'published' texts that are not copyright registered include government reports and documents, legal reports and documents, certain magazines and newspapers, and some dissertations; in the United States, these are indexed in sources such as the *Monthly Catalog of US Government Publications, Index to US Government Periodicals*, a whole system of legal reports (e.g. the *Pacific Reporter*, the *Supreme Court Reports*), periodical indexes (e.g. *Readers' Guide to Periodical Literature, Newsbank*), and dissertation abstracts (indexed by University Microfilms International).

A third stratum for written published texts could thus be these 'formats' represented by the various cataloguing and indexing systems. Together these indexes provide an itemized listing of published writing, and they could therefore be used as an adequate sampling frame. With a large enough sample (see following section), such a sampling frame would help

---

[4] This parameter would not be important for many non-western societies, or for certain kinds of corpora representing different historical periods; quite different sampling strategies would be required in these cases.

achieve 'representativeness' of the various kinds of published writing. However, we know on theoretical grounds that there are several important substrata within published writing (e.g. purposes and different subject areas), and it is thus better to additionally specify these in the corpus design. This approach is more conservative, in that it ensures representativeness in the desired proportions for each of these text categories, and at the same time it enables smaller sample sizes (since random techniques require larger samples than stratified techniques).

Setting and format are parallel second-level strata: format is important for the sampling of published writing; setting can be used in a similar way to provide sampling frames for unpublished writing, speech, and scripted speech. Three types of setting are distinguished here: institutional, other public, and private-personal. These settings are less adequate as sampling frames than publication catalogues—they do not provide well-defined boundaries for unpublished writing or speech, and they do not provide an exhaustive listing of texts within these categories. The problem is that no direct sampling frame exists for unpublished writing or speech. Setting, however, can be used indirectly to sample these target populations, by using three separate subcategories: institutions (offices, factories, businesses, schools, churches, hospitals, etc.), private settings (homes), and other public settings (shopping areas, recreation centres, etc.). (For scripted speech, the category of other public settings would include speech on various public media, such as news broadcasts, scripted speeches, and scripted dialogue on television sitcoms and dramas.) Operational sampling frames for each of these settings might be defined from various government and official records (e.g. census records, tax returns, or other registrations). The goal of such sampling frames would be to provide an itemized listing of the members within each setting type, so that a random sample of institutions, homes, and other public places could be selected. (These three settings could be further stratified with respect to the various types of institution, types of home, etc.)

To this point, then, I have proposed the sampling frames shown in Table 2.

Before proceeding, it is necessary to distinguish between two types of sampling strata. The first, as above, actually defines a sampling frame, specifying the boundaries of the operationalized population and providing an itemized listing of members. The second, as in the remaining parameters of Table 1, identifies categories that must be represented in a corpus but do not provide well-defined sampling frames. For example, Addressee plurality (no. 4a: unenumerated/plural/individual/self) provides no listing of the texts with these four types of addressee; rather, it simply specifies that texts should be collected until these four categories are adequately represented.

Further, the remaining parameters in Table 1 are not equally relevant for all the major sampling frames listed in Table 2. Consider, for example, the parameters listed under 'Addressee'. Published writing always has unenumerated addressees,[5] is always written for non-present

TABLE 2   Outline of sampling frames

Writing (published). Books/periodicals/etc.
   (based on available indexes)
Writing (unpublished). Institutional/public/private
Speech. Institutional/public/private
Scripted speech. Institutional/public media/other

---

[5] Published collections of letters and published diaries are special cases—these originally have individual addressees, but they are usually written with the hope of eventual publication and thus with an unenumerated audience in mind.

addressees, and is almost always non-interactive (except for published exchanges of opinion). It can require either general or specialized background knowledge (e.g. popular magazines versus academic journals) but rarely requires personal background knowledge (although this is needed for a full understanding of memoirs, published letters, diaries, and even some novels and short stories). Unpublished writing, on the other hand, can fall into all of these addressee categories. The addressees can be unenumerated (e.g. advertisements, merchandising catalogues, government forms or announcements), plural (office circular or memo, business or technical report), individual (memo to an individual, professional or personal letter, e-mail message), or self (diary, notes, shopping list). The addressee of unpublished texts is usually absent, except in writing to oneself. Unpublished writing can be interactive (e.g. letters) or not. Finally, unpublished writing can require only general background knowledge (e.g. some advertisements), specialized knowledge (e.g. technical reports), or personal knowledge (e.g. letters and diaries).

Speech is typically directed to a plural or individual addressee, who is present. Speech addressed to self is often considered strange. Speech can be directed to unenumerated, absent addressees through mass media (e.g. a televised interview). Individual and small-group addressees can also be absent, as in the case of telephone conversations and 'conference calls'. (Individual addressees can even be non-interactive in the case of talking to an answering machine.) Private settings favour interactive addressees (either individual or small group conversations) while both interactive and non-interactive addressees can be found in institutional settings (e.g. consider the various kinds of lectures, sermons, and business presentations). General knowledge can be required in all kinds of conversation; specialized background knowledge is mostly required of addressees in institutional settings; personal knowledge is most needed in private settings.

Scripted speech is typically directed towards plural addressees (small groups in institutional settings and unenumerated audiences for mass media). Dialogue in plays and televised dramatic shows are examples of scripted speech that is directed to an individual but heard by an unenumerated audience. Addressees are typically present for scripted speech in institutional settings but are not present (physically or temporally) for scripted speech projected over mass media. Except for the lecturer who allows questions during a written speech, scripted speech is generally not interactive. Finally, scripted speech can require either general or specialized background knowledge on the part of the addressee, but it rarely requires personal background knowledge.

Addressors can vary along a number of demographic parameters (the dialect characteristics mentioned above), and decisions must be made concerning the representation of these parameters in the corpus. (Collection of texts from some addressor categories will be difficult for some sampling frames; e.g. there are relatively few published written texts by working class writers.) The second parameter here, whether the addressor is acknowledged or not, is relevant only for written texts: some written texts do not have an acknowledged personal author (e.g. advertisements, catalogues, laws and treaties, government forms, business contracts), while the more typical kinds of writing have a specific author(s).

Factuality is similar to assessments of background knowledge in that it is sometimes difficult to measure reliably, but this is an important parameter distinguishing among texts within both writing and speech. At one pole are scientific reports and lectures, which purport to be factual, and at the other are the various kinds of imaginative stories. In between these poles are a continuum of texts with different bases in fact, ranging over speculation, opinion, historical fiction, gossip, etc.

The parameter of purpose requires further research, both theoretical (as the basis for corpus design) and empirical (using the resources of large corpora). I include in Table 1 several of the purposes that should be represented in a corpus, but this is not intended as an exhaustive listing.

Similarly the parameter of topic requires further theoretical and empirical research. Library classification systems are well developed and provide adequate topic strata for published written texts. These same classifications might also serve as strata for unpublished writing, but they would need to be tested empirically. For spoken texts, especially in private settings, further research on the range of typical topics is required.

The spirit of the proposal outlined in this section is to show how basic situational parameters can be used as sampling strata to provide an important first step towards achieving representativeness. The particular parameter values used, however, must be refined, and the framework proposed here is clearly not the final word on corpus sampling strata.

3   OTHER SAMPLING ISSUES

3.1   Proportional sampling

In most stratified sample designs, the selection of observations across strata must be proportional in order to be considered representative (Williams, 1978; Henry, 1990); i.e. the number of observations in each stratum should be proportional to their numbers in the larger population. For example, a survey of citizens in North Carolina (reported in Henry, 1990, pp. 61–66) used two strata, each based on a government listing of adults: households that filed 1975 income tax returns, and households that were eligible for Medicaid assistance. These two lists together accounted for an estimated 96% of the population. In the selection of observations, though, these lists were sampled proportionately—89% from the tax list and 11% from the Medicaid list—to maintain the relative proportions of these two strata in the larger population. The resulting sample can thus be claimed to represent the adult population of North Carolina. Representativeness in this case means providing the basis for accurate descriptive statistics of the entire population (e.g. average income, education, etc.).

Demographic samples are representative to the extent that they reflect the relative proportions of strata in a population. This notion of representativeness has been developed within sociological research, where researchers aim to determine descriptive statistics that characterize the overall population (such as the population mean and population standard deviation). Any single statistic that characterizes an entire population crucially depends on a proportional sampling of strata within the population—if a stratum which makes up a small proportion of the population is sampled heavily, then it will contribute an unrepresentative weight to summary descriptive statistics.

Language corpora require a different notion of representativeness, making proportional sampling inappropriate in this case. A proportional language corpus would have to be demographically organized (as discussed at the beginning of Section 2), because we have no a priori way to determine the relative proportions of different registers in a language. In fact, a simple demographically based sample of language use would be proportional by definition—the resulting corpus would contain the registers that people typically use in the actual proportions in which they are used. A corpus with this design might contain roughly 90% conversation and 3% letters and notes, with the remaining 7% divided among registers such as press reportage, popular magazines, academic prose, fiction, lectures, news broadcasts, and unpublished writing. (Very few people *ever* produce published written texts, or unpublished written and spoken texts for a large audience.) Such a corpus would permit summary descriptive statistics for the entire language represented by the corpus. These kinds of generalizations, however, are typically not of interest for linguistic research. Rather, researchers require language samples that are representative in the sense that they include the full range of linguistic variation existing in a language.

In summary, there are two main problems with proportional language corpora. First, proportional samples are representative only in that they accurately reflect the relative numerical frequencies of registers in a language—they provide no representation of relative importance that is not numerical. Registers such as books, newspapers, and news broadcasts are much more influential than their relative frequencies indicate. Secondly, proportional corpora do not provide an adequate basis for linguistic analyses, in which the range of linguistic features found in different text types is of primary interest. For example, it is not necessary to have a corpus to find out that 90% of the texts in a language are linguistically similar (because they are all conversations); rather, we want to analyse the linguistic characteristics of the other 10% of the texts, since they represent the large majority of the kinds of registers and linguistic distributions in a language.[6]

3.2 Sample size

There are many equations for determining sample size, based on the properties of the normal distribution and the sampling distribution of the mean (or the sampling distribution of the standard deviation). One of the most important equations states that the standard error of the mean for some variable ($s_{\bar{x}}$) is equal to the standard deviation of that variable (s) divided by the square root of the sample size ($n^{1/2}$), i.e.

$$s_{\bar{x}} = s/n^{1/2}$$

The standard error of the mean indicates how far a sample mean can be from the true population mean. If the sample size is greater than 30, then the distribution of sample means has a roughly normal distribution, so that 95% of the samples taken from a population will have means that fall in the interval of plus or minus 1.96 times the standard error. The smaller this interval is, the more confidence a researcher can have that she is accurately representing the population mean. As shown by the equation for the standard error, this confidence interval depends on the natural variation of the population (estimated by the sample standard deviation) and the sample size (n). The influence of sample size in this equation is constant, regardless of the size of the standard deviation (i.e. the standard error is a function of one divided by the square-root of n). To reduce the standard error (and thus narrow the confidence interval) by half, it is necessary to increase the sample size by four times.

For example, if the sample standard deviation for the number of nouns in a text was 30, the sample mean score was 100, and the sample size was nine texts, then the standard error would be equal to 10:

$$\text{Standard error} = 30/\sqrt{(9)} = 30/3 = 10$$

This value indicates that there is a 95% probability that the true population mean for the number of nouns per text falls within the range of 80.4 to 119.6 (i.e. the sample mean of 100 ± 1.96 times the standard error of 10). To reduce this confidence interval by cutting the standard error in half, the sample size must be increased four times to 36 texts; i.e.

$$\text{Standard error} = 30/\sqrt{(36)} = 30/6 = 5$$

---

[6] A proportional corpus would be useful for assessments that a word or syntactic construction is 'common' or 'rare' (as in lexicographic applications). Unfortunately, most rare words would not appear at all in a proportional (i.e. primarily conversational) corpus, making the database ill-suited for lexicographic research.

Similarly, if the original sample was 25 texts, then we would need to increase the sample to 100 texts in order to cut the standard error in half, i.e.

$$\text{Standard error} = 30/\sqrt{(25)} = 30/5 = 6$$

$$\text{Standard error} = 30/\sqrt{(100)} = 30/10 = 3$$

Unfortunately there are certain difficulties in using the equation for the standard error to determine the required sample size of a corpus. In particular, it is necessary to address three problems:

(1) The sample size (n) depends on a prior determination of the tolerable confidence interval required for the corpus; i.e. there needs to be an a priori estimate of the amount of uncertainty that can be tolerated in typical analyses based on the corpus.

(2) The equation depends on the sample standard deviation, but this is the standard deviation for some particular variable. Different variables can have different standard deviations, resulting in different estimates of the required sample size.

(3) The equation must be used in a circular fashion; i.e. it is necessary to have selected a sample and computed the sample standard deviation before the equation can be used (and this is based on the assumption that the pilot sample is at least somewhat representative)—but the purpose of the equation is to determine the required sample size.

In Section 4, I consider the distribution of several linguistic features and address these three problems, making preliminary proposals regarding sample size.

3.3   A note on sampling within 'texts'

To this point I have not yet addressed the issue of how long text samples need to be. I will consider this question in more detail in Section 4, discussing the distribution of various linguistic features within texts. Here, though, I want to point out that the preference for stratified sampling applies to sampling within texts as well as across texts. Corpus compilers have typically tried to achieve better representation of texts by simply taking more words from the texts. However, these words are certainly not selected randomly (i.e. they are sequential), and the adequacy of representation thus depends on the sample length relative to the total text length. Instead it is possible to use a stratified approach for the selection of text samples from texts; i.e. especially in the case of written texts and planned spoken texts, the selection of text samples can use the typical subcomponents of texts in that register as sampling strata (e.g. chapters, sections, possibly main points in a lecture or sermon). This approach will result in better representation of the overall text, regardless of the total number of words selected from each text.

4   DISTRIBUTIONS OF LINGUISTIC FEATURES: PRELIMINARY RECOMMENDATIONS CONCERNING SAMPLE SIZE

4.1   Distributions within texts: length of text samples

In this section I consider first the distribution of linguistic features within texts, as a basis for addressing the issue of optimal text length. Traditional sampling theory is less useful here than for the other aspects of corpus design, because individual words cannot be treated as separate observations in linguistic analyses; i.e. since linguistic features commonly extend over more than one word, any random selection of words from a text would fail to represent many features and would destroy the overall structure of the text. The main issue here is thus the number of contiguous words required in text samples. The present section illustrates how this issue can be addressed through empirical investigations of the distribution of linguistic features within texts.

In Biber (1990) I approach this problem by comparing pairs of 1,000-word samples taken from single texts in the LOB and London–Lund corpora. (Text samples are 2,000 words in the LOB corpus and 5,000 words in the London–Lund corpus.) If large differences are found between the two 1,000-word samples, then we can conclude that this sample length does not adequately represent the overall linguistic characteristics of a text, and that perhaps much larger samples are required. If, on the other hand, the two 1,000-word text samples are similar linguistically, then we can conclude that relatively small samples from texts adequately represent their linguistic characteristics.

In the case of written texts (from the LOB corpus), I divided each original text in half and compared the two parts. In the case of spoken texts (from the London–Lund corpus), four 1,000-word samples were extracted from each original text, and these were then compared pairwise.

To provide a relatively broad database, ten linguistic features commonly used in variation studies were analysed. These features were chosen from different functional and grammatical classes, since each class potentially represents a different statistical distribution across text categories (see Biber, 1988). The features are: nouns, first person pronouns, third person pronouns, contractions, past tense verbs, present tense verbs, prepositions, passive constructions (combining by-passives and agentless passives), WH relative clauses, and conditional subordinate clauses. Pronouns and contractions are relatively interactive and colloquial in communicative function; nouns and prepositions are used for integrating information into texts; relative clauses and conditional subordination represent types of structural elaboration; and passives are characteristic of scientific or technical styles. These features were also chosen to represent a wide range of frequency distributions in texts, as shown in Table 3, which presents their frequencies (per 1,000 words) in a corpus of 481 spoken and written texts (taken from Biber, 1988, pp. 77–78). The ten features differ considerably in both their overall average

TABLE 3   Descriptive statistics for frequency scores (per 1,000 words) of ten linguistic features in a corpus of 481 texts taken from 23 spoken and written text genres

Linguistic feature	Mean	Min.	Max.	Range
Nouns	181	84	298	214
Prepositions	111	50	209	159
Present tense	78	12	182	170
Past tense	40	0	119	119
Third person pronouns	30	0	124	124
First person pronouns	27	0	122	122
Contractions	14	0	89	89
Passives	10	0	44	44
WH relative clauses	3.5	0	26	26
Conditional subordination	2.5	0	13	13

frequency of occurrence and in their range of variation. Nouns and prepositions are extremely common; present tense markers are quite common; past tense, first person pronouns, and third person pronouns are all relatively common; contractions and passives are relatively rare; and WH relative clauses and conditional subordinators are quite rare. (In addition, these features are differentially distributed across different kinds of texts; see Biber, 1988, pp. 246–269.) Comparison of these ten features across the 1,000-word text pairs thus represents several of the kinds of distributional patterns found in English.

The distributions of these linguistic features were analysed in 110 1,000-word text samples (i.e. fifty-five pairs of samples), taken from seven text categories: conversations, broadcasts, speeches, official documents, academic prose, general fiction, and romance fiction. These categories represent a range of communicative situations in English, differing in purpose, topic, informational focus, mode, interactiveness, formality, and production circumstances; again, the goal was to represent a broad range of frequency distributions.

Reliability coefficients were computed to assess the stability of frequency counts across the 1,000-word samples. In the case of the London–Lund corpus (the spoken texts), four 1,000-word samples were analysed from each text, and for the LOB corpus (the written texts), two 1,000-word subsamples were analysed from each text.

The reliability coefficient for each feature represents the average correlation among the frequency counts of that feature (i.e. a count for each of the subsamples). For the spoken samples, all coefficients were high. The lowest reliabilities were for passives (0.74) and conditional subordination (0.79), while all other features had reliability coefficients over 0.88. The coefficients were somewhat smaller for the written samples, in part because they are based on two instead of four subsamples. Conditional subordination in the written texts had a low reliability coefficient (0.31), while relative clauses and present tense in the written texts had moderately low reliability coefficients (0.58 and 0.61 respectively); all other features had reliability coefficients over 0.80. Overall, this analysis indicates that frequency counts for common linguistic features are relatively stable across 1,000 word samples, while frequency counts for rare features (such as conditional subordination and WH relative clauses—see Table 3) are less stable and require longer text samples to be reliably represented.[7]

These earlier analyses can be complemented by tracking the distribution of various linguistic features across 200-word segments of texts. For example, Fig. 1 shows the distribution of prepositional phrases throughout the length of five texts from Humanities Academic Prose— the figure plots the cumulative number of prepositional phrases as measured at each 200-word interval in these texts. As can be seen from this figure, prepositional phrases are distributed linearly in these texts. That is, there are approximately the same number of prepositional phrases occurring in each 200-word segment (roughly thirty per segment in three of the texts, and twenty-five per segment in the other two texts). (The linear nature of these distributions can be confirmed by lining up a ruler next to the plot of each text.) This figure indicates that a common feature such as prepositional phrases is extremely stable in its distribution within texts (at least Humanities Academic Prose texts)—that even across 200-word segments, all segments will contain roughly the same number of prepositional phrases.

Figure 2 illustrates a curvilinear distribution, in this case the cumulative word types (i.e. the number of different words) in five Humanities texts. In general, frequency counts of a linguistic feature will be distributed linearly (although that distribution will be more or less stable within a text—see below), while frequencies of different *types* of linguistic features (lexical or grammatical) will be distributed curvilinearly; i.e. because many types are repeated

---

[7] In Biber (1990) I also assess the representativeness of 1,000-word text samples by computing difference scores for pairs of samples from each text. This analysis confirms the general picture given by the reliability coefficients while providing further details of the distribution of particular features in particular registers.

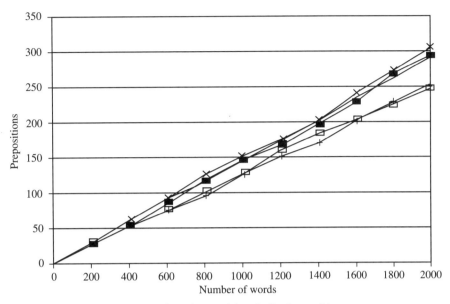

FIG. I Distribution of prepositions in five humanities texts.

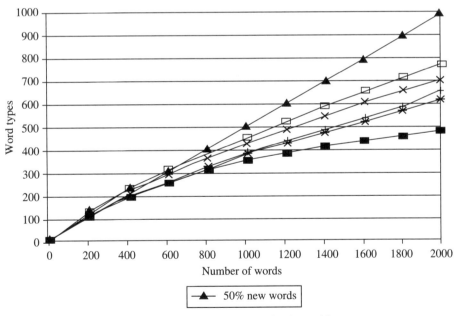

FIG. 2 Distribution of word types in five humanities texts.

across text segments, each subsequent segment contributes fewer new types than the preceding segment. In Fig. 2, the straight line marked by triangles shows the 50% boundary of word types (the score when 50% of the words in a text are different word types). In all five of these texts, at least 50% of the words are different types in the first 200-word segment (i.e. at least half of the words are not repeated), and two of the texts have more than 50% different types in the first three segments (up to 600 words). All of the texts show a gradual decay in the

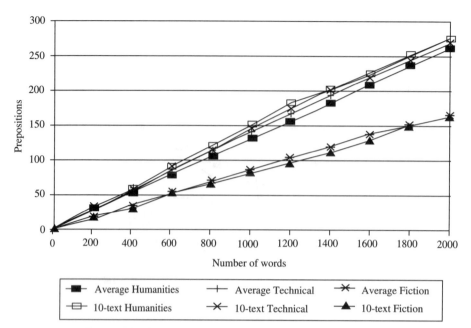

FIG. 3   Distribution of prepositions in texts from three registers.

number of word types, however. The most diverse text drops to roughly 780 word types per 2,000 words (39%), while the least diverse text drops to roughly 480 word types per 2,000 words (only 24%). These trends would continue in longer texts, with each subsequent segment contributing fewer new types.

These two types of distributions must be treated differently. In Figs. 3–9, I plot the distributions of seven linguistic features within texts representing three registers. Three of the features are cumulative frequency counts: Fig. 3 plots the frequencies of prepositional phrases, a common grammatical feature; Fig. 4 plots the frequencies of relative clauses, a relatively rare grammatical feature; and Fig. 5 plots the frequencies of noun–preposition sequences, a relatively common grammatical sequence. The other four figures plot the distributions of types in texts. Figures 6 and 7 plot the distribution of lexical types: word types (the number of different words) in Fig. 6 and hapax legomena (once-occurring words) in Fig. 7. Figures 8 and 9 plot the distribution of grammatical types: different grammatical categories or 'tags' in Fig. 8, and different grammatical tag sequences in Fig. 9. The figures thus illustrate lexical and grammatical features, with rare and common overall frequencies, having linear and curvilinear distributions.

The figures can be used to address several questions. First they present the overall distributions of these features. The stable linear distribution of prepositional phrases is further confirmed by Fig. 3. In contrast, the relatively unstable distribution of relative clauses, indicated above by a relatively low reliability coefficient, is further supported by the frequent departures from linearity in Fig. 4. That is, since relative clauses are relatively rare overall, even two or three extra relatives in a 200-word segment results in an aberration. Figure 5 shows that the distribution of noun–preposition sequences is similar to that of prepositional phrases in being linear and quite stable (although less frequent overall).[8]

---

[8] These are primarily prepositional phrases functioning as noun modifiers, as opposed to prepositional phrases with adverbial functions.

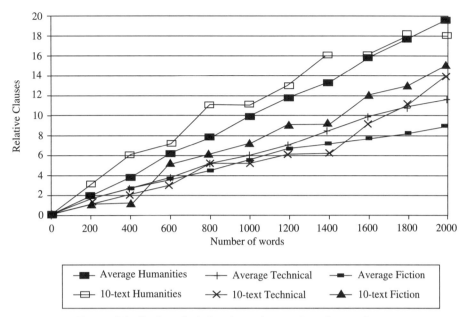

FIG. 4   Distribution of relative clauses in texts from three registers.

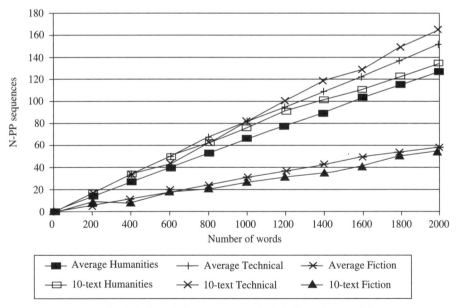

FIG. 5   Distribution of N-PP sequences in texts from three registers.

Figures 6–9 show different degrees of curvilinearity, with the grammatical and syntactic types showing sharper drop-offs than the lexical types. Grammatical tag types show the sharpest decay: most different grammatical categories occur in the first 200 words, with relatively few additional grammatical categories being added after 600 words.

Figures 3–9 also illustrate distributional differences across registers, although only three registers are considered here. For example, Figures 3 and 5 show fairly large differences

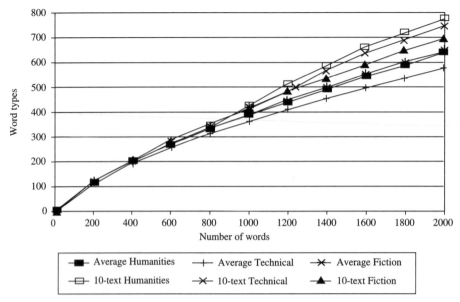

FIG. 6   Distribution of word types in texts from three registers.

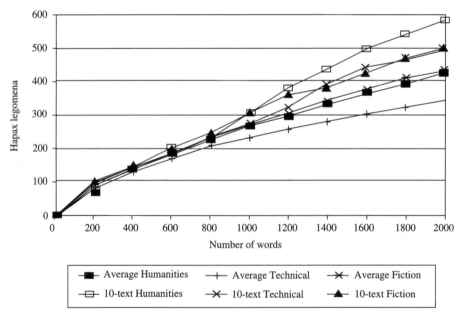

FIG. 7   Distribution of *hapax legomena* in texts from three registers.

between academic prose and fiction, with the former having much higher frequencies of prepositional phrases and noun–prepositional phrase sequences. The differences among registers are less clear-cut in Fig. 4, but humanities academic prose texts consistently have more frequent relative clauses than either technical academic prose or fiction.

Each register is plotted twice in these figures: the 'average' scores and the '10-text' scores. Average scores present the average value for ten texts from that register for the segment in

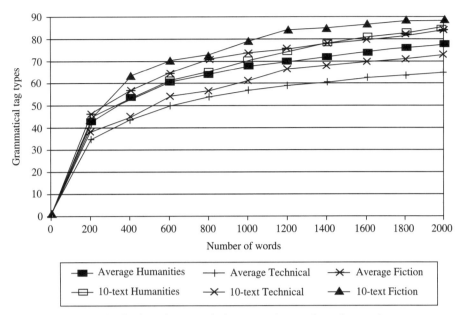

FIG. 8   Distribution of grammatical tag types in texts from three registers.

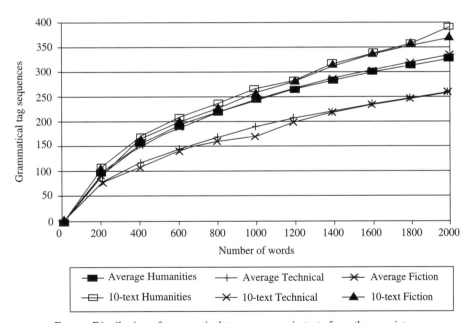

FIG. 9   Distribution of grammatical tag sequences in texts from three registers.

question. (For example, Fig. 3 shows that humanities texts have on average 130 prepositions in the first 1,000 words of text.) In contrast, the '10-text' scores are composite scores, with each 200-word segment coming from a different text. Thus, the score for 400 words represents the cumulative totals for the first 200 words from two texts, the score for 600 words sums the first 200-word totals from three texts, etc.

In the case of stable, linear distributions, there is very little difference between the average and 10-text scores. In fact, Figs 3 and 5 show a remarkable coincidence of average and 10-text values; a single distribution is found, within a register, regardless of whether subsequent 200-word segments are taken from the same text or from different texts. Figure 4 shows greater differences for relative clauses (a relatively rare and less stable feature). Here averaging over ten texts smooths out most aberrations from linearity, while the 10-text values show considerable departures from linearity.

In contrast, there are striking differences between the average and 10-text distributions for the curvilinear features (Figs 6–9). In these cases, the 10-text scores are consistently higher than the corresponding average score from the same register. In the case of word types, the 10-text scores for all three registers are higher than the average scores of the registers. The difference is particularly striking with respect to technical academic prose—after 2,000 words of text, 10-text technical prose has the second highest word type score (approximately 740, or 37%), while on average technical prose texts have the lowest word type score (approximately 570, or 28%). This shows that there is a high degree of lexical repetition within technical prose texts, but there is a high degree of lexical diversity across technical texts. The distribution of *hapax legomena*, shown in Fig. 7, parallels that of word types—again, all three 10-text scores are higher than the average scores; 10-text humanities prose shows the highest score; and the average technical prose score is by far the lowest. These distributions reflect the considerable lexical diversity found across humanities texts, and the relatively little lexical diversity within individual technical texts.

There is more similarity between the 10-text and average scores with respect to the distribution of grammatical types (Figs 8 and 9), although for each register the 10-text score is higher than the corresponding average score. Interestingly, these figures show that technical prose has the least grammatical diversity as well as the least lexical diversity.

In summary, the analyses presented in this section indicate the following:

(1) Common linear linguistic features are distributed in a quite stable fashion within texts and can thus be reliably represented by relatively short text segments.
(2) Rare linguistic features show much more distributional variation within texts and thus require longer text samples for reliable representation.
(3) Features distributed in a curvilinear fashion, i.e. different feature types, are relatively stable across subsequent text segments, but occurrences of new types decrease throughout the course of a text. The frequency of new types is consistently higher in cross-text samples than in single-text samples. These patterns were shown to hold for relatively short text segments (2,000 words total) and for cross-text samples taken from a single register; the patterns should be even stronger for longer text segments and for cross-register samples. These findings support the preference for stratified sampling—more diversity among the texts included in a corpus will translate into a broader representation of linguistic feature types.

With regard to the issue of text length, the thrust of the present section is simply that text samples should be long enough to reliably represent the distributions of linguistic features. For linearly distributed features, the required length depends on the overall stability of the feature. For curvilinear features, an arbitrary cut-off must be specified marking an 'adequate' representation, e.g. when subsequent text segments contribute less than 10% additional new types. Given a finite effort invested in developing a corpus, broader linguistic representation can be achieved by focusing on diversity across texts and text types rather than by focusing on longer samples from within texts.

Specific proposals on text length require further investigations of the kind presented here, focusing especially on the distributions of less stable features, to determine the text length required for stability, and on the distributions of other kinds of features (e.g. discourse and information-packaging features).

4.2 Distributions across texts: number of texts

A second major statistical issue in building a text corpus concerns the sampling of texts: how linguistic features are distributed across texts and across registers, and how many texts must be collected for the total corpus and for each register to represent those distributions?

4.2.1 *Previous research on linguistic variation within and across registers*

Although registers are defined by reference to situational characteristics, they can be analysed linguistically, and there are important linguistic differences among them; at the same time, some registers also have relatively large ranges of linguistic variation internally (see Biber, 1988, Chapters 7 and 8). For this reason, the linguistic characterization of a register should include both its central tendency and its range of variation. In fact, some registers are similar in their central tendencies but differ markedly in their ranges of variation (e.g. science fiction versus general fiction, and official documents versus academic prose, where the first register of each pair has a more restricted range of variation). In Biber (1988, pp. 170–98), I describe the linguistic variation within registers, including the linguistic relations among various subregisters.

The number of texts required in a corpus to represent particular registers relates directly to the extent of internal variation. In Biber (1990), I analyse the stability of feature counts across texts from a register by comparing the mean frequency counts for 10-text subsamples taken from particular registers. Five registers were analysed: conversations, public speeches, press reportage, academic prose, and general fiction. Three 10-text samples were extracted from each of these registers, and the mean frequency counts of six linguistic features were compared across the samples (first person pronouns, third person pronouns, past tense, nouns, prepositions, passives). The reliability analysis of these mean frequencies across the three 10-text samples showed an extremely high degree of stability for all six linguistic features (all coefficients greater than 0.95). These coefficients show that the mean scores of the 10-text samples are very highly correlated; that is, the central linguistic tendencies of these registers with respect to these linguistic features are quite stable, even as measured by 10-text samples. However, there are two important issues not considered by this analysis. First, the six linguistic features considered were all relatively common; rare features such as WH relative clauses or conditional subordination might show much lower reliabilities. Secondly, this analysis addressed how many texts were needed to reliably represent mean scores, but did not address the representation of linguistic diversity in registers.[9]

4.2.2 *Total linguistic variation in a corpus: total sample size for a corpus*

In Section 3, I discussed how the required sample size is related to the standard error ($s_{\bar{x}}$) by the equation:

$$s_{\bar{x}} = s/n^{1/2} \tag{4.1}$$

---

[9] Actually this latter question was addressed by computing difference scores, for the mean, standard deviation, and range, across the 10-text samples.

The actual computation of sample size depends on a specification of the tolerable error (*te*):

$$te = t * s_{\bar{x}} \qquad\qquad (4.2)$$

Equation 4.2 states that the tolerable error is equal to the standard error times the *t*-value. Given a sample size greater than thirty (which permits the assumption of a normal distribution), a researcher can know with 95% confidence that the mean score of a sample will fall in the interval of the true population mean plus-or-minus the tolerable error.

Equation 4.2 can be manipulated to provide a second equation for computing the standard error, i.e. $s_{\bar{x}} = te/t$. If the ratio *te/t* is substituted for $s_{\bar{x}}$ in Equation 4.1, and the equation is then solved for *n*, we get a direct computation of the required sample size for a corpus:

$$n = s^2/(te/t)^2 \qquad\qquad (4.3)$$

where *n* is the computed sample size, *s* is the estimated standard deviation for the population, *te* is the tolerable error (equal to 1/2 of the desired confidence interval), and *t* is the *t*-value for the desired probability level.

I note in Section 3 that there are problems in the application of Equation 4.3. In one sense, the equation simply shifts the burden of responsibility, from estimating the unknown quantity for required sample size to estimating the unknown quantities for the tolerable error and population standard deviation; i.e. in order to use the equation, there needs to be a prior estimate of the tolerable error or confidence interval permitted in the corpus and a prior estimate of the standard deviation of variables in the population as a whole.

The tolerable error depends on the precision required of population estimates based on the corpus sample. For example, say that we want to know how many nouns on average occur in conversation texts. The confidence interval is the window within which we can be 95% certain that the true population mean falls. For example, if the sample mean for nouns in conversations was 120, and we needed to estimate the true population mean of nouns with a precision of ± 2, then the confidence interval would be 4, extending from 118 to 122. The tolerable error is simply one side (or one-half) of the confidence interval. The problem here is that it is difficult to provide an a priori estimate of the required precision of the analyses that will be based on a corpus.

Similar problems arise with the estimation of standard deviations. In this case, it is not possible to estimate the standard deviation of a variable in a corpus without already having a representative sample of texts. Here, as in many aspects of corpus design, work must proceed in a circular fashion, with empirical investigations based on pilot corpora informing the design process. The problem for initial corpus design, however, is to provide an initial estimate of standard deviation.

A final problem is that standard deviations must be estimated for particular variables, but in the case of corpus linguistics, there are numerous linguistic variables of interest. Choosing different variables, with different standard deviations, will result in different estimates of required sample size.

In the present section, I use the analyses in Biber (1988, pp. 77–78, 246–269) to address the first two of these problems. That study is based on a relatively large and wide-ranging corpus of English texts: 481 texts taken from twenty-three spoken and written registers. Statistical analyses of this corpus can thus be used to provide initial estimates for both the tolerable error and the population standard deviation.

In the design of a text corpus, tolerable error cannot be stated in absolute terms because the magnitude of frequency counts varies considerably across features (as was shown in Section 3). For example, a tolerable error of ± 5 might work well for common features such as nouns, which have an overall mean of 180.5 per 1,000 words in the pilot corpus, but it

TABLE 4   Estimates of required sample sizes (number of texts) for the total corpus

	Mean score in pilot corpus	Standard deviation in pilot corpus	Tolerable error	Required *N*
Nouns	180.5	35.6	9.03	59.8
Prepositions	110.5	25.4	5.53	81.2
Present tense	77.7	34.3	3.89	299.4
Past tense	40.1	30.4	2.01	883.1
Passives	9.6	6.6	0.48	726.3
WH relative clauses	3.5	1.9	0.18	452.8
Conditional clauses	2.5	2.2	0.13	1,190.0

would be unacceptable for rare features such as conditional subordinate clauses, which have an overall mean of only 2.5 in the corpus (so that a tolerable error of 5 would translate into a confidence interval of −2.5 to 7.5, and a text could have three times the average number of conditional clauses and still be within the confidence interval). Instead I propose here computing a separate estimate of the tolerable error for each linguistic feature, based on the magnitude of the mean score for the feature; for illustration, I will specify the tolerable error as ± 5% of the mean score (for a total confidence interval of 10% of the mean score). Table 4 presents the mean score and standard deviation of seven linguistic features in the pilot corpus, together with the computed tolerable error for each feature. It can be seen that the tolerable error ranges from 9.03 for nouns (which have a mean of 180.5) to 0.13 for conditional clauses (which have a mean of only 2.5).

Given the tolerable errors and estimated standard deviations listed in Table 4, required sample size (i.e. the total number of texts to be included in the corpus) can be computed directly using Equation 4.3. Table 4 shows very large differences in required sample size across these linguistic features. These differences are a function of the size of the standard deviation relative to the mean for a particular feature. If the standard deviation is many times smaller than the mean, as in the case of common features such as nouns and prepositions, the required sample size is quite small. If, on the other hand, the standard deviation approaches the mean in magnitude, as in the case of rare features such as WH relative clauses and conditional clauses, the required sample size becomes quite large. Past tense markers are interesting in that they are relatively common (mean of 40.1) yet have a relatively large standard deviation (30.4) and thus require a relatively large sample of texts for representation (883). Overall the most conservative approach in designing a corpus would be to use the most widely varying feature (proportional to its mean—in this case conditional clauses) to set the total sample size.

4.2.3   *Linguistic variation within registers: number of texts needed to represent registers*
The remaining issue concerns the required sample size for each register. Although most books on sample design simply recommend proportional sampling for stratified designs (see Section 3), a few books discuss the need for non-proportional stratified sampling in certain instances; these books differ, however, on the method for determining the recommended sample sizes for subgroups. For example, Sudman (1976, pp. 110–111) states that non-proportional stratified sampling should be used when the subgroups themselves are of primary interest (as in the case of a text corpus), and that the sample sizes of the subgroups should be equal in that case (to minimize the standard error of the difference). This procedure is

appropriate when the variances of the subgroups are roughly the same. In contrast, Kalton (1983, pp. 24–25) recommends using the subgroup standard deviations to determine their relative sample sizes. This procedure is more appropriate for corpus design, since the standard deviations of linguistic features vary considerably from one register to the next.

Although I do not make specific recommendations for register sample size here, I illustrate this approach in Table 5, considering the relative variances of seven linguistic features (the same as in Table 4) across three registers: conversations, general fiction, and academic prose. As above, the data are taken from Biber (1988, pp. 246–269).

TABLE 5   Relative variation within selected registers

Conversations. Average normalized deviation = 0.37

	Mean score in pilot corpus	Standard deviation in pilot corpus	Ratio of standard deviation/mean (normalized deviation)
Nouns	137.4	15.6	0.11
Prepositions	85.0	12.4	0.15
Present tense	128.4	22.2	0.17
Past tense	37.4	17.3	0.46
Passives	4.2	2.1	0.50
WH relative clauses	1.4	0.9	0.64
Conditional clauses	3.9	2.1	0.54

General fiction. Average normalized deviation = 0.39

	Mean score in pilot corpus	Standard deviation in pilot corpus	Ratio of standard deviation/mean (normalized deviation)
Nouns	160.7	25.7	0.16
Prepositions	92.8	15.8	0.17
Present tense	53.4	18.8	0.35
Past tense	85.6	15.7	0.18
Passives	5.7	3.2	0.56
WH relative clauses	1.9	1.1	0.58
Conditional clauses	2.6	1.9	0.73

Academic prose. Average normalized deviation = 0.49

	Mean score in pilot corpus	Standard deviation in pilot corpus	Ratio of standard deviation/mean (normalized deviation)
Nouns	188.1	24.0	0.13
Prepositions	139.5	16.7	0.12
Present tense	63.7	23.1	0.36
Past tense	21.9	21.1	0.96
Passives	17.0	7.4	0.44
WH relative clauses	4.6	1.9	0.41
Conditional clauses	2.1	2.1	1.00

Table 5 presents the mean score, standard deviation, and the ratio of standard deviation to mean score, for these seven linguistic features in the three registers. The ratio represents the normalized variance of each of these features within each register—the extent of internal variation relative to the magnitude of the mean score. The raw standard deviation is not appropriate here (similar to Table 4) because the mean scores of these features vary to such a large extent.

Table 5 shows that the normalized standard deviation varies considerably across features within a register. For example, within conversations the counts for nouns, prepositions, and present tense all show relatively small normalized variances, while passives, WH relative clauses, and conditional clauses all show normalized variances at or above 50%. As shown earlier, features with lower overall frequencies tend to have considerably higher normalized variances.

There are also large differences across the registers. For example, past tense has a normalized variance of 46% in conversations and only 18% in general fiction, but it shows a normalized variance of 96% in academic prose. Conditional subordination also shows large differences across these three registers: it has a normalized variance of 54% in conversations, 73% in general fiction, and 100% in academic prose.

In order to determine the sample size for each register, it is necessary to compute a single measure of the variance within each register. This measure is then used to allot a proportionally larger sample to registers with greater variances. (This should not be confused with a proportional representation of the registers.) A certain minimum number of texts should be allotted for each register (e.g. at least twenty texts per register), and then the remaining texts in the corpus can be divided proportionally depending on the relative variance within registers.

To illustrate, consider Table 5 again. This table lists an average normalized deviation for each register, which represents an overall deviation score computed by averaging the normalized standard deviations of the seven linguistic features. Conversations and general fiction both have relatively similar overall deviations (37% and 39% correspondingly) while academic prose has a somewhat higher overall deviation (49%). To follow through with this example, assume that there were to be a total of 200 texts in a corpus, taken from these three registers. Each register would be allotted a minimum of twenty texts, leaving 140 texts to be divided proportionally among the three registers. To determine the relative sample size of the registers, one would solve the following equation based upon their relative overall deviations:

$$0.37x + 0.39x + 0.49x = 140$$
$$1.25x = 140$$
$$x = 112$$

and thus the sample sizes would be:

Conversation 0.37 * 112 = 41
General fiction 0.39 * 112 = 44
Academic prose 0.49 * 112 = 55
Total allocated texts = (41 + 20 for conversation) + (44 + 20 for general fiction) + (55 + 20 for academic prose) = 200 texts

To compute the actual values for register sample sizes, it is necessary to analyse the full range of linguistic features in all registers, computing a single average deviation score for each register. This could be done by averaging across the normalized variances of all linguistic features, as illustrated here. An alternative approach would be to use the normalized variances of the linguistic dimensions identified in Biber (1988). This latter approach would have a more solid theoretical foundation, in that the dimensions represent basic parameters of variation among registers, each based on an important co-occurrence pattern among linguistic features. In contrast, the approach illustrated in this section depends on the pooled influence of linguistic features in isolation, and thus relatively aberrant distributions can have a relatively strong influence on the final outcome. In addition, use of the dimensions enables consideration of the distributions with respect to particular functional parameters, so that some dimensions can be given more weight than others. In contrast, there is no motivated way for distinguishing among the range of individual features on functional grounds.

It is beyond the scope of this paper to illustrate the use of dimension scores for the linguistic characterization of registers (since I would first need to explain the theoretical and methodological bases of the dimensions). The same basic approach as illustrated in this section would be used, however. The major difference involves the analysis of deviation along basic dimensions of linguistic variation rather than with respect to numerous linguistic features in isolation.

5   CONCLUSION: BEGINNING

I have tried to develop here a set of principles for achieving 'representativeness' in corpus design. I have offered specific recommendations regarding some aspects of corpus design, and illustrations elsewhere (regarding issues for which final recommendations could not be developed in a paper of this scope). The bottom-line in corpus design, however, is that the parameters of a fully representative corpus cannot be determined at the outset. Rather, corpus work proceeds in a cyclical fashion that can be schematically represented as follows:

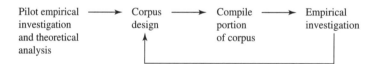

Theoretical research should always precede the initial corpus design and actual compilation of texts. Certain kinds of research can be well advanced prior to any empirical investigations: identifying the situational parameters that distinguish among texts in a speech community, and identifying the range of important linguistic features that will be analysed in the corpus. Other design issues, though, depend on a pilot corpus of texts for preliminary investigations. Present-day researchers on English language corpora are extremely fortunate in that they have corpora such as the Brown, LOB, and London–Lund corpus for pilot investigations, providing a solid empirical foundation for initial corpus design. The compilers of those corpora had no such pilot corpus to guide their designs. Similar situations exist for current projects designing corpora to represent non-western languages. For example, a recently completed corpus of Somali required extensive fieldwork to guide the initial design (see Biber and Hared 1992). Thus the initial design of a corpus will be more or less advanced depending on the availability of previous research and corpora.

Regardless of the initial design, the compilation of a representative corpus should proceed in a cyclical fashion: a pilot corpus should be compiled first, representing a relatively broad range of variation but also representing depth in some registers and texts. Grammatical tagging should be carried out on these texts, as a basis for empirical investigations. Then empirical research should be carried out on this pilot corpus to confirm or modify the various design parameters. Parts of this cycle could be carried out in an almost continuous fashion, with new texts being analysed as they become available, but there should also be discrete stages of extensive empirical investigation and revision of the corpus design.

Finally, it should be noted that various multivariate techniques could be profitably used for these empirical investigations. In this paper, I have restricted myself to univariate techniques, and to simple descriptive statistics. Other research, though, suggests the usefulness of two multivariate techniques for the analysis of linguistic variation in computerized corpora: factor analysis and cluster analysis. Factor analysis can be used in either an exploratory fashion (e.g. Biber, 1988) or for theory-based 'confirmatory' analyses (e.g. Biber, 1992). Both of these would be appropriate for corpus design work, especially for the analysis of the range and types of variation within a corpus and within registers. Such analyses would indicate whether the different parameters of variation were equally well represented and would provide a basis for decisions on sample size. Cluster analysis has been used to identify 'text types' in English— text categories defined in strictly linguistic terms (Biber, 1989). Text types cannot be identified on a priori grounds; rather they represent the groupings of texts in a corpus that are similar in their linguistic characterizations, regardless of their register categories. Ideally a corpus would represent both the range of registers and the range of text types in a language, and thus research on variation within and across both kinds of text categories is needed.[10]

In sum, the design of a representative corpus is not truly finalized until the corpus is completed, and analyses of the parameters of variation are required throughout the process of corpus development in order to fine-tune the representativeness of the resulting collection of texts.

6 ACKNOWLEDGEMENTS

I would like to thank Edward Finegan for his many helpful comments on an earlier draft of this paper. A modified version of this paper was distributed for the Pisa Workshop on Textual Corpora, held at the University of Pisa (January 1992), and discussions with several of the workshop participants were also helpful in revising the paper.

---

[10] For example, one of the most marked text types identified in Biber (1989) consists of texts in which the addressor is producing an on-line reportage of events in progress. Linguistically, this text type is marked in being extremely situated in reference (many time and place adverbials and a present time orientation). Unfortunately, there are only seven such texts in the combined London–Lund and LOB corpora, indicating that this text type is under-represented and needs to be targeted in future corpus development.

6

Introduction to the Special Issue on the Web as Corpus

ADAM KILGARRIFF AND
GREGORY GREFENSTETTE*

I   INTRODUCTION

The web is immense, free and available by mouse-click. It contains hundreds of billions of words of text and can be used for all manner of language research.

The simplest language use is spell checking. Is it *speculater* or *speculator*? Google gives 67 for the former (usefully suggesting the latter might have been intended) and 82,000 for the latter. Question answered.

Language scientists and technologists are increasingly turning to it as a source of language data, because it is so big, because it is the only available source for the type of language they are interested in, or simply because it is free and instantly available. The mode of work has increased dramatically from a standing start seven years ago with the web being used as a data source in a wide range of research activities: the papers in the Special Issue form a sample of the best of it. This introduction aims to survey the activities and explore recurring themes.

We first consider whether the web is indeed a corpus, then present a history of the theme in which we view it as a development of the empiricist turn which has brought corpora center-stage in the course of the 1990s. We briefly survey the range of web-based NLP research, then present estimates of the size of the web, for English and for other languages, and a simple method for translating phrases. Next we open the Pandora's Box of representativeness (concluding that the web is not representative of anything other than itself, but then nor are other corpora, and that more work needs doing on text types). We then introduce the papers in the Special Issue, and conclude with some thoughts on how the web could be put at the linguist's disposal rather more usefully than current search engines allow.

I.I   Is the web a corpus?

To establish whether the web is a corpus we need to find out, discover or decide what a corpus is. McEnery and Wilson (1996: 21) say:

In principle, any collection of more than one text can be called a corpus ... But the term "corpus" when used in the context of modern linguistics tends most frequently to have more specific connotations than this simple definition provides for. These may be considered under four main headings: sampling and representativeness, finite size, machine-readable form, a standard reference.

* Kilgarriff, A., and Grefenstette, G. (2003). 'Introduction to the special issue on the web as corpus', *Computational Linguistics,* 29(3): 333–348. Reproduced with permission of the Association for Computational Linguistics.

We would like to reclaim the term from the connotations. Many of the collections of texts which people use and refer to as their corpus, in a given linguistic, literary, or language-technology study, do not fit. A corpus comprising the complete published works of Jane Austen is not a sample, nor representative of anything else. Closer to home, Manning and Schütze (1999: 120) observe:

In Statistical NLP, one commonly receives as a corpus a certain amount of data from a certain domain of interest, without having any say in how it is constructed. In such cases, having more training data is normally more useful than any concerns of balance, and one should simply use all the text that is available.

We wish to avoid a smuggling-in of values into the criterion for corpus-hood. McEnery and Wilson (following others before them) mix the question "what is a corpus?" with "what is a good corpus (for certain kinds of linguistic study)?", muddying the simple question "is corpus *x* good for task *y*?" with the semantic question "is *x* a corpus at all?" The semantic question then becomes a distraction, all too likely to absorb energies which would otherwise be addressed to the practical one. In order that the semantic question may be set aside, the definition of corpus should be broad. We define a corpus simply as "a collection of texts". If that seems too broad, the one qualification we allow relates to the domains and contexts in which the word is used rather than its denotation: *a corpus is a collection of texts when considered as an object of language or literary study.*

The answer to the question "is the web a corpus?" is yes.

2   HISTORY

For chemistry or biology, the computer is merely a place to store and process information gleaned about the object of study. For linguistics the object of study itself (in one of its two primary forms, the other being acoustic) is found on computers. Text is an information object, and a computer's hard disk is as valid a place to go for its realization as the printed page or anywhere else.

The one-million-word Brown corpus opened the chapter on computer-based language study in the early 1960s. Noting the singular needs of lexicography for big data, in the 1970s Sinclair and Atkins inaugurated the COBUILD project, which raised the threshold of viable corpus size from one million to, by the early 1980s, eight million words (Sinclair 1987b). Ten years on, Atkins again took the lead with the development (from 1988) of the British National Corpus (hereafter BNC) (Burnard 1995), which raised horizons tenfold once again, with its 100m words, and was in addition widely available at low cost and covered a wide spectrum of varieties of contemporary British English.[1] As in all matters Zipfian, logarithmic graph paper is required. Where corpus size is concerned, the steps of interest are 1, 10, 100..., not 1, 2, 3.

Corpora crashed into computational linguistics at the 1989 ACL meeting in Vancouver: but they were large, messy, ugly objects clearly lacking in theoretical integrity in all sorts of ways, and many people were skeptical regarding their role in the discipline. Arguments raged, and it was not clear whether corpus work was an acceptable part of the field. It was only with the highly successful 1993 Special Issue of this journal [*Computational Linguistics – Ed.*]

---

[1] Across the Atlantic, a resurgence in empiricism was led by the success of the noisy channel model in speech recognition (see Church and Mercer 1993 for references).

on Using Large Corpora (Church and Mercer 1993) that the relation between computational linguistics and corpora was consummated.

There are parallels with web corpus work. The web is anarchic and its use is not in the familiar territory of computational linguistics. However, as students with no budget or contacts realize, it is the obvious place to obtain a corpus meeting their specifications, as companies want the research they sanction to be directly related to the language types they need to handle (almost always available on the web), as copyright continues to constrain "traditional" corpus development,[2] as people want to explore using more data and different text types, so web-based work will grow.

The web walked in on ACL meetings starting in 1999. Rada Mihalcea and Dan Moldovan used hit counts for carefully constructed search engine queries to identify rank orders for word sense frequencies, as an input to a word sense disambiguation engine (Mihalcea and Moldovan 1999). Philip Resnik showed that parallel corpora – until then a promising research avenue but largely constrained to the English-French Canadian Hansard – could be found on the web (Resnik 1999): we can grow our own parallel corpus using the many web pages that exist in parallel in local and in major languages. We are glad to have the further development of this work (co-authored by Noah Smith) presented in this Special Issue [see Resnik and Smith 2003 – *Ed*].

In the student session of ACL 2000, Rosie Jones and Rayid Ghani showed how you can build a language-specific corpus using the web from a single document in that language (Jones and Ghani 2000). In the main session Atsushi Fujii and Tetsuya Ishikawa demonstrated that descriptive, definition-like collections can be acquired from the web (Fujii and Ishikawa 2000).

2.1   Some current themes

Since then there have been many papers, at ACL and elsewhere, and we can mention only a few. The EU MEANING project (Rigau *et al.* 2002) takes forward the exploration of the web as a data source for word sense disambiguation, working from the premise that within a domain, words often have just one meaning, and that domains can be identified on the web. Mihalcea and Tchklovski complement this use of web as corpus with web technology to gather manual word sense annotations on the Word Expert website.[3] Santamaría *et al.* [2003 – *Ed*.] discuss how to link word senses to web directory nodes, and thence to web pages.

The web is being used to address data sparseness for language modeling. In addition to Keller and Lapata [2003 – *Ed*.] and references therein, Volk (2001) gathers lexical statistics for resolving prepositional phrase attachments, and Villasenor-Pineda *et al.* (2003) "balance" their corpus using web documents.

The Information Retrieval community now has a web track as a component of their TREC evaluation initiative. The corpus for this exercise is a substantial (around 100GB) sample of the web, largely using documents in the .gov top level domain, as frozen at a given date (Hawking *et al.* 1999).

---

[2] Lawyers may argue that the legal issues for web corpora are no different to those around non-web corpora. However, firstly, language researchers can develop web corpora just by saving web pages on their own computer without any copying on, thereby avoiding copyright issues, and secondly, a web corpus is a very minor sub-species of the caches and indexes held by search engines and assorted other components of the infrastructure of the web: if a web corpus is infringing copyright, then it is merely doing on a small scale what search engines such as Google are doing on a colossal scale.

[3] http://teach-computers.org/word-expert.html

The web has recently been used by groups at Sheffield and Microsoft among others as a source of answers for question-answering applications, in a merge of search engine and language-processing technologies (Greenwood *et al.* 2002; Dumais *et al.* 2002). AnswerBus (Zheng 2002) will answer questions posed in English, German, French, Spanish, Italian and Portuguese.

Naturally, the web is also coming into play in other areas of linguistics. Agirre *et al.* (2000) are exploring the automatic population of existing ontologies using the web as a source for new instances. Varantola (2000) shows how translators can use "just-in-time" sublanguage corpora to choose correct target language terms for areas where they are not expert. Fletcher (2004) demonstrates methods for gathering and using web corpora in a language-teaching context.

2.2   The 100m words of the BNC

One hundred million words is large enough for many empirical strategies for learning about language, either for linguists and lexicographers (Baker, Fillmore and Lowe 1998; Kilgarriff and Rundell 2002) or for technologies that need quantitative information about the behavior of words as input (most notably parsers – Briscoe and Carroll 1997; Korhonen 2000). However, for some purposes it is not large enough. This is an outcome of the Zipfian nature of word frequencies. While 100m is a vast number, and the BNC contains ample information on the dominant meanings and usage patterns for the 10,000 words that make up the core of English, the bulk of the lexical stock occurs less than 50 times in it, which is not enough to draw statistically stable conclusions about the word. For rarer words, rare meanings of common words, and combinations of words, we frequently find no evidence at all. Researchers are obliged to look to larger data sources (Keller and Lapata 2003; also Section 3.1 below). They find that probabilistic models of language based on very large quantities of data, even if that data is noisy, are better than ones based on estimates (using sophisticated smoothing techniques) from smaller, cleaner datasets.

Another argument is made vividly by Banko and Brill (2001). They explore the performance of a number of machine learning algorithms (on a representative disambiguation task) as the size of the training corpus grows from a million to a billion words. All the algorithms steadily improve in performance, though the question "which is best?" gets different answers for different data sizes. The moral: performance improves with data size, and getting more data will make more difference than fine-tuning algorithms.

2.3   Giving and taking

Dragomir Radev made the useful distinction between NLP "giving" and "taking".[4] NLP can give to the web technologies such as summarization (for web pages or web search results); machine translation; multilingual document retrieval; question-answering and other strategies for finding not only the right document but the right part of a document; and tagging, parsing and other core technologies (to improve indexing for search engines, the viability of this being a central Information Retrieval research question for the last twenty years). "Taking" is, simply, using the web as a source of data for any CL or NLP goal, and is the theme of this Special Issue. If we focus too closely on the giving side of the equation, we look only at short to medium-term goals. For the longer term, for "giving" as well as for other purposes,

---

[4] Remarks made in a panel discussion at the Empirical NLP Conference, Hong Kong, October 2002.

a deeper understanding of the linguistic nature of the web and its potential for CL/NLP is required. For that, we must take the web itself, in whatever limited way, as an object of study.

Much web search engine technology has been developed with reference to language technology. The prototype for AltaVista was developed in a joint project between Oxford University Press (exploring methods for corpus lexicography (Atkins 1993)) and DEC (interested in fast access to very large databases). Language identification algorithms (Beesley 1988; Grefenstette 1995), now widely used in web search engines, were developed as NLP technology. The Special Issue explores a "homecoming" of web technologies, with the web now feeding one of the hands that fostered it.

3   WEB SIZE AND THE MULTILINGUAL WEB

There were 56 million registered network addresses in July 1999, 125 million in January 2001, and 172 million in January 2003. A plot of this growth of the web in terms of computer hosts can easily be generated. Linguistic aspects take a little more work, and can only be estimated by sampling and extrapolation. Lawrence and Giles (1999) compared the overlap between page lists returned by different web browsers over the same set of queries and estimated that, in 1999, there were 800 million indexable web pages available. By sampling pages, and estimating an average page length of 7 to 8 kilobytes of non-markup text, they concluded that there might be 6 terabytes of text available then. In 2003, Google claims to search four times this number of web pages, which raises the number of bytes of text available just through this one web server to over 20 terabytes from directly accessible web pages. At an average of ten bytes per word, a generous estimate for Latin-alphabet languages, that suggests two thousand billion words.

The web is clearly a multilingual corpus. How much of it is English? Xu (2000) estimated that 71% of the pages (453 million out of 634 million web pages indexed by the Excite engine at that time) were written in English, followed by Japanese (6.8%), German (5.1%), French (1.8%), Chinese (1.5%), Spanish (1.1%), Italian (0.9%), and Swedish (0.7%).

We have measured the counts of some English phrases according to various search engines over time and compared them with counts in the BNC, which we know has 100 million words. Table 1 shows these counts in the BNC, on AltaVista in 1998 and in 2001, and then on Alltheweb in 2003. For example, the phrase *deep breath* appears 732 times in the BNC. It was indexed 54,550 times by AltaVista in 1998. This rose to 170,921 in 2001. And in 2003, we could find 868,631 web pages containing the contiguous words *deep breath* according to Alltheweb. The numbers found through the search engines are more than three orders of magnitude higher than the BNC counts, giving a first indication of the size of the English corpus available.

We can derive a more precise estimate of the number of words available through a search engine by using the counts of function words as predictors of corpus size. Function words, such as *the*, *with*, *in*, etc., occur with a frequency that is relatively stable over many different types of texts. From a corpus of known size, we can calculate the frequency of the function words and extrapolate. In the 90-million-word written-English component of the BNC *the* appears 5,776,487 times, around 7 times for every 100 words. In the American Declaration of Independence, *the* occurs 84 times. We predict that the Declaration is about $84 \times 100/7 = 1,200$ words long. In fact, the text contains about 1500 words. Using the frequency of one word gives a first approximation. A better result can be obtained by using more data points.

TABLE 1   Frequencies of English phrases in the BNC and on AltaVista in
1998 and 2001, and on AlltheWeb in 2003.

Sample phrase	BNC (100m)	WWW fall 1998	WWW fall 2001	WWW spring 2003
medical treatment	414	46,064	627,522	1,539,367
prostate cancer	39	40,772	518,393	1,478,366
deep breath	732	54,550	170,921	868,631
acrylic paint	30	7,208	43,181	151,525
perfect balance	38	9,735	35,494	355,538
electromagnetic radiation	39	17,297	69,286	258,186
powerful force	71	17,391	52,710	249,940
concrete pipe	10	3,360	21,477	43,267
upholstery fabric	6	3,157	8,019	82,633
vital organ	46	7,371	28,829	35,819

The counts for the BNC and AltaVista are for individual occurrences of the phrase.
The counts for AlltheWeb are page counts (the phrase may appear more than once
on any page.)

From the first megabyte of the German text found in the European Corpus Initiative
Multilingual Corpus,[5] we extracted frequencies for function words and other short, common
words. We removed from the list words that were also common words in other languages.[6]
AltaVista provided on its results pages, along with a page count for a query, the number
of times that each query word was found on the web.[7] Table 2 shows relative frequency
of the words from our known corpus, the index frequencies that AltaVista gave (February
2000) and the consequent estimates of the size of the German-language web indexed by
AltaVista.

We set aside words which give discrepant predictions – too high or too low – as (1)
AltaVista does not record in its index the language a word comes from, so the count for
the string *die* includes both the German and English occurrences, and (2) a word might
be under- or over-represented in the training corpus or the web (consider *here* which
occurs very often in "click here".) Averaging the remaining predictions gives an estimate of
3 billion words of German that could be accessed through AltaVista on that day in February
2000.

This technique has been tested on controlled data (Grefenstette and Nioche 2000) in which
corpora of different languages were mixed in various proportions, and gives reliable results.
Table 3 gives estimates for the number of words that were available in thirty different Latin
script languages through AltaVista in March 2001. English led the pack with 76 billion words,
and seven further languages already had over a billion.

From the table, we see that even "smaller" languages such as Slovenian, Croatian, Malay
and Turkish have more than one hundred million words on the web. Much of the research that
has been undertaken on the BNC simply exploits its scale and could be transferred directly to
these languages.

---

[5] http://www.elsnet.org/resources/eciCorpus.html

[6] These lists of short words and frequencies were initially used to create a language identifier.

[7] AltaVista has recently stopped providing information about how often individual words in a query have been
indexed, and now only returns a page count for the entire query.

TABLE 2 German short words in the ECI corpus and via AltaVista giving German web estimates

Word	Known-size-corpus relative frequency	AltaVista frequency	Prediction for German-language web
oder	0.00561180	13,566,463	2,417,488,684
sind	0.00477555	11,944,284	2,501,132,644
auch	0.00581108	15,504,327	2,668,062,907
wird	0.00400690	11,286,438	2,816,750,605
nicht	0.00646585	18,294,174	2,829,353,294
eine	0.00691066	19,739,540	2,856,389,983
sich	0.00604594	17,547,518	2,902,363,900
ist	0.00886430	26,429,327	2,981,546,991
auf	0.00744444	24,852,802	3,338,438,082
und	0.02892370	101,250,806	3,500,617,348
Average			3,068,760,356

The numbers in Table 3 are lower bounds for a number of reasons:

- AltaVista only covers a fraction of the indexable web pages available. The fraction was estimated at just 15% by Lawrence and Giles (1999).
- AltaVista may be biased to North American (mainly English language) pages by the strategy it uses to crawl the web.
- AltaVista only indexes pages that can be directly called by a URL, and does not index text found in databases that are accessible through dialog windows on web pages, the

TABLE 3 Estimates of web size in words as indexed by AltaVista for various languages

Language	Web size	Language	Web size
Albanian	10,332,000	Catalan	203,592,000
Breton	12,705,000	Slovak	216,595,000
Welsh	14,993,000	Polish	322,283,000
Lithuanian	35,426,000	Finnish	326,379,000
Latvian	39,679,000	Danish	346,945,000
Icelandic	53,941,000	Hungarian	457,522,000
Basque	55,340,000	Czech	520,181,000
Latin	55,943,000	Norwegian	609,934,000
Esperanto	57,154,000	Swedish	1,003,075,000
Romanian	86,392,000	Dutch	1,063,012,000
Irish	88,283,000	Portuguese	1,333,664,000
Estonian	98,066,000	Italian	1,845,026,000
Slovenian	119,153,000	Spanish	2,658,631,000
Croatian	136,073,000	French	3,836,874,000
Malay	157,241,000	German	7,035,850,000
Turkish	187,356,000	English	76,598,718,000

"hidden web". This hidden web is vast (consider MedLine,[8] just one such database, with more than 5 billion words; see also Ipeirotis, Gravano, and Sahami 2001), and it is not considered at all in the AltaVista estimates.

Repeating the above procedure over time, the second author and Nioche showed that the proportion of non-English text to English is growing. In October 1996 there were 38 German words for every 1000 words of English indexed by AltaVista. In August 1999, there were 71 and in March 2001, 92.

3.1   Finding the right translation

How can these great numbers be used for other language-processing tasks? Consider the compositional French noun phrase *groupe de travail*. In the MEMODATA bilingual Dictionary[9] the French word *groupe* is translated by the English words *cluster*, *group*, *grouping*, *concern* and *collective*. The French word *travail* translates as *work*, *labor* or *labour*. Many web search engines allow the user to search for adjacent phrases. Combining the possible translations of *groupe de travail* and submitting them to AltaVista in early 2003 gave the counts shown in Table 4.

The phrase *work group* is 15 times more frequent than any other, and is also the best translation among the tested possibilities. A set of controlled experiments of this form are described in Grefenstette (1999). A good translation was found in 87% of ambiguous cases from German to English and 86% of ambiguous cases from Spanish to English.

TABLE 4   AltaVista frequencies for candidate translations of *groupe de travail*

labor cluster	21	labour collective	428
labor grouping	28	work collective	759
labour concern	45	work concern	772
labor concern	77	labor group	3,977
work grouping	124	labour group	10,389
work cluster	279	work group	148,331
labor collective	423		

4   REPRESENTATIVENESS

We know the web is big, but a common response to a plan to use the web as a corpus is "but it's not representative".

There are a great many things to be said about this. It opens up a pressing yet almost untouched practical and theoretical issue for computational linguistics and language technology.

---

[8]   http://www4.ncbi.nlm.nih.gov/PubMed/

[9]   See http://www.elda.fr/cata/text/M0001.html. The basic multilingual lexicon produced by MEMODATA contains 30,000 entries for five languages: French, English, Italian, German, Spanish.

4.1   Theory

First, "representativeness" begs the question "representative of what?" Outside very narrow, specialized domains, we do not know with any precision what existing corpora might be representative of. If we wish to develop a corpus of general English, we may think it should be representative of general English, so we then need to define the population of "general English language events" of which the corpus will be a sample. Consider the following issues.

- Production and reception: is a language event an event of speaking or writing, or one of reading or hearing? Standard conversations have, for each utterance, one speaker and one hearer. A *Times* newspaper article has (roughly) one writer and several hundred thousand readers.
- Speech and text: do speech events and written events have the same status? It seems likely that there are orders of magnitude more speech events than writing events, yet most corpus research to date has tended to focus on the more tractable task of gathering and working with text.
- Background language: does muttering under one's breath or talking in one's sleep constitute a speech event, and does doodling with words constitute a writing event? Or, on the reception side, does passing (and possibly subliminally reading) a roadside advertisement constitute a reading event? And what of having the radio on but not attending to it, or the conversational murmur in a restaurant?
- Copying: if *I'd like to teach the world to sing*, and, like Michael Jackson or the Spice Girls, am fairly successful in this goal and they all sing my song, then does each individual singing constitute a distinct language production event?

    In the text domain, organizations such as Reuters produce news feeds which are typically adapted to the style of a particular newspaper and then re-published: is each re-publication a new writing event? (These issues, and related themes of cut-and-paste authorship, ownership and plagiarism, are explored in Wilks 2004.)

4.2   Technology

Application developers urgently need to know about what to do about sublanguages. It has often been argued that, within a sublanguage, few words are ambiguous and a limited repertoire of grammatical structures is used (Kittredge and Lehrberger 1982). This points to sublanguage-specific application development being substantially simpler than general-language application development. However, many of the resources that developers may wish to use are general-language resources, such as, for English, WordNet, ANLT, XTag, COMLEX and the BNC. Are they relevant? Can they be used? Is it better to use a language model based on a large general-language corpus, or a relatively tiny corpus of the right kind of text? Nobody knows. There is currently no theory, no mathematical models and almost no discussion.

A related issue is that of porting an application from the sublanguage for which it was developed to another. It should be possible to use corpora for the two sublanguages to estimate how large a task this will be, but again, our understanding is in its infancy.

TABLE 5   Possible language errors

pienso de que	388
pienso que	356,874
piensas de que	173
piensas que	84,896
piense de que	92
piense que	67,243
pensar de que	1,640
pensar que	661,883

Hits for Spanish *pensar que* with and without possible "dequeismos errors" (spurious *de* between the verb and the relative), from Alltheweb.com, March 2003. Not all items are errors, e.g. "…pienso de que manera…" *…think how….* The correct form is always at least 500 times more common than any potentially incorrect form.

4.3   Language modeling

Much work in recent years has gone into developing language models. Clearly, the statistics for different types of text will be different (Biber 1993b). This imposes a limitation on the applicability of any language model: we can only be confident that it predicts the behavior of language samples of the same text type as the training-data text type (and we can only be entirely confident if training and test samples are random samples from the same source).

When a language technology application is put to use, it will be applied to new text for which we cannot guarantee the text type characteristics. There is little work on assessing how well one language model fares when applied to a text type which is not that of the training corpus. Two studies are Sekine (1997) and Gildea (2001), both of which show substantial variation in performance when the training corpus changes. The lack of theory of text types leaves us without a way of assessing the usefulness of language modeling work.

4.4   Language errors

Web texts are produced by a wide variety of authors. Contrary to paper-based, copy-edited published texts, web-based texts may be produced cheaply and rapidly with little concern for correctness. On Google a search for "I beleave" has 3,910 hits, and "I beleive", 70,900 pages. The correct "I believe" appears on over 4 million pages. Table 5 presents what is regarded as a common grammatical error in Spanish, comparing the frequency of such forms to the accepted forms on the web. All the "erroneous" forms exist, but much less often than the "correct" forms. The web is a dirty corpus, but expected usage is much more frequent than what might be considered as noise.

4.5   Sublanguages and general-language-corpus composition

A language can be seen as a modest core of lexis, grammar and constructions, plus a wide array of different sublanguages, as used in each of a myriad of human activities. This presents a challenge to general-language resource developers: should sublanguages be included? The three possible positions are:

- no, none should
- some, but not all, should
- yes, all should.

The problem with the first position is that, with all sublanguages removed, the residual core gives an impoverished view of language (quite apart from demarcation issues, and the problem of determining what is left). The problem with the second is that it is arbitrary. The BNC happens to include cake recipes and research papers on gastro-uterine diseases, but not car manuals or astronomy texts. The third has not, until recently, been a viable option.

4.6   Literature

To date, corpus developers have been obliged to take pragmatic decisions about the sorts of text to go into a corpus. Atkins, Clear and Ostler (1992) describe the desiderata and criteria used for the BNC, and this stands as a good model for a general-purpose, general-language corpus. The word "representative" has tended to fall out of discussions to be replaced by the meeker "balanced".

The recent history of mathematically sophisticated modeling of language variation begins with Biber (1988), who identifies and quantifies the linguistic features associated with different spoken and written text types. Habert and colleagues (Folch *et al.* 2000; Beaudouin *et al.* 2001) have been developing a workstation for specifying subcorpora according to text type, using Biber-style analyses amongst others. In Kilgarriff (2001) we present a first pass at quantifying similarity between corpora, and Cavaglia (2002) continues this line of work. As mentioned above, Sekine (1997) and Gildea (2001) are two papers which directly address the relation between NLP systems and text type; one further such item is Roland *et al.* (2000). Buitelaar and Sacaleanu (2001) explores the relation between domain and sense disambiguation.

A practical discussion of a central technical concern is Vossen (2001), who tailors a general-language resource for a domain.

Baayen (2001) presents sophisticated mathematical models for word frequency distributions and it is likely that his mixture models have potential for modeling sublanguage mixtures. His models have been developed with a specific, descriptive goal in mind and using a small number of short texts: it is unclear whether they can be usefully applied in NLP.

While the extensive literature on text classification (Manning and Schütze, 1999: 575–608) is certainly relevant, it most often starts from a given set of categories and cannot readily be applied to the situation where the categories are not known in advance. Also, the focus is usually on content words and topics or domains, with other differences of genre or sublanguage not being examined. Exceptions focusing on genre include Kessler, Nunberg and Schütze (1997) and Karlgren and Cutting (1994).

4.7   Representativeness: conclusion

The web is not representative of anything else. But nor are other corpora, in any well-understood sense. Picking away at the question merely exposes how primitive our understanding of the topic is, and leads inexorably to larger and altogether more interesting questions about the nature of language, and how it might be modeled.

"Text type" is an area where our understanding is, as yet, very limited. While further work is required irrespective of the web, the use of the web forces the issue. Where researchers use established corpora, such as Brown, the BNC or the Penn Treebank, researchers and readers are willing to accept the corpus name as a label for the type of text occurring in it without asking critical questions. Once we move to the web as a source of data, and our corpora have names like "Aprilo3-sample77", the issue of how the text type(s) can be characterized demands attention.

5   INTRODUCTION TO PAPERS IN THIS SPECIAL ISSUE

One use of a corpus is to extract a language model: a list of weighted words, or combinations of words that describe (i) how words are related, (ii) how they are used with each other, and (iii) how common they are in a given domain. In speech processing, language models are used to predict which word combinations are likely interpretations of a sound stream; in Information Retrieval to decide which words are useful indicators of a topic; and in Machine Translation, to identify good translation candidates.

In this volume, Celina Santamaría, Julio Gonzalo and Felisa Verdejo (Santamaría *et al.* 2003) describe how to build sense-tagged corpora from the web by associating word meanings with web page directory nodes. The Open Directory Project (at dmoz.org) is a collaborative, volunteer project for classifying web pages into a taxonomic hierarchy. Santamaría *et al.* present an algorithm for attaching WordNet word senses to nodes in this same taxonomy, thus providing automatically created links between word senses and web pages. They also show how this method can be used for automatic acquisition of sense-tagged corpora, from which one could, among other things, produce language models tied to certain senses of words, or for a certain domain.

Unseen words, or word sequences – that is, words or sequences not occurring in training data – are a problem for language models. If the corpus from which the model is extracted is too small, there are many such sequences.

Taking the second author's work, as described above, as a starting point, Frank Keller and Maria Lapata (Keller and Lapata 2003) examine how useful the web is as a source of frequency information for rare items: specifically, for dependency relations involving two English words such as <*fulfil* OBJECT *obligation*>. They generate pairs of common words, constructing combinations that are and are not attested in the BNC. They then compare the frequency of these combinations in a larger 325-million-word corpus and on the web. They find that web frequency counts are consistent with other large corpora. They also report on a series of human-subject experiments, in which they establish that web statistics are good at predicting the intuitive plausibility of predicate–argument pairs. Other experiments show that web counts correlate reliably with counts recreated using class-based smoothing and overcome some problems of data sparseness in the BNC.

Other very large corpora are available for English. English is an exception, and the other three papers all exploit the multilinguality of the web. Andy Way and Nano Gough (Way and Gough 2003) show how it can provide data for an Example-Based Machine Translation (Nagao 1984) system. First, they extract 200,000 phrases from a parsed corpus. These phrases are sent to three online translation systems. Both original phrases and translations are chunked. From these pairings a set of chunk translations is extracted to be applied in a piecewise fashion to new input text. The authors use the web again at a final stage to re-rank possible translations by verifying which sub-sequences among the possible translations are most attested.

The two remaining papers present methods for building aligned bilingual corpora from the web. It seems plausible that this automatic construction of translation dictionaries can palliate the lack of translation resources for many language pairs. Philip Resnik was the first to recognize that it is possible to build large parallel bilingual corpora from the web. He found that one can exploit the appearance of language flags and other clues which often lead to a version of the same page in a different language.[10] Here, in this volume, Resnik and Noah Smith (Resnik and Smith 2003) present their STRAND system for building bilingual corpora from the web.

An alternative method is presented by Wessel Kraaij, Jian-Yun Nie and Michel Simard (Kraaij *et al.* 2003). They use the resulting parallel corpora to induce a probabilistic translation dictionary which is then embedded into a Cross Language Information Retrieval system. Various alternative embeddings are evaluated using the CLEF (Peters 2001) multilingual information retrieval testbeds.

6   PROSPECTS

The default means of access to the web is through a search engine such as Google. While the web search engines are dazzlingly efficient pieces of technology and excellent at the task they set themselves, for the linguist they are frustrating:

- The search engine results do not present enough instances (1000 or 5000 maximum).
- They do not present enough context for each instance (Google provides a fragment of around ten words).
- They are selected according to criteria which are, from a linguistic perspective, distorting (with uses of the search term in titles and headings going to the top of the list, and often occupying all the top slots).
- They do not allow searches to be specified according to linguistic criteria such as the citation form for a word, or word class.
- The statistics are unreliable, with frequencies given for "pages containing x" varying according to search engine load and many other factors.

If only these constraints were removed, a search engine would be a wonderful tool for language researchers. Each of them could straightforwardly be resolved by search engine designers, but linguists are not a powerful lobby and search engine company priorities will never perfectly match our community's. This suggests a better solution: do it ourselves. Then the kinds of processing and querying would be designed explicitly to meet linguists' desiderata, without any conflict of interest or "poor relation" role. A large number of possibilities open out. All those processes of linguistic enrichment which have been applied with impressive effect to smaller corpora could be applied to the web. We could parse the web. Web searches could be specified in terms of lemmas, constituents (e.g. noun phrase) and grammatical relations rather than strings. The way would be open for further anatomizing of web text types and domains. Thesauruses and lexicons could be developed directly from the web. And all for a multiplicity of languages.[11]

The web contains enormous quantities of text, in lots of languages and language types, on a vast array of topics. Our take on the web is that it is a fabulous linguists' playground. We hope the Special Issue will encourage you to come on out and play!

---

[10] For example, one can find Azerbaijan news feeds online at http://www.525ci.com in Azeri (written with a Turkish codeset), and on the same page are pointers to versions of the same stories in English and in Russian.

[11] The idea is developed further in Grefenstette (2001) and in Kilgarriff (2003a).

PART III

On Lexicographical Evidence

7

"Corpus Linguistics" or "Computer-aided Armchair Linguistics"

CHARLES J. FILLMORE*

Armchair linguistics does not have a good name in some linguistics circles. A caricature of the armchair linguist is something like this. He sits in a deep soft comfortable armchair, with his eyes closed and his hands clasped behind his head. Once in a while, he opens his eyes, sits up abruptly shouting, "Wow, what a neat fact!", grabs his pencil, and writes something down. Then he paces around for a few hours in the excitement of having come still closer to knowing what language is really like. (There isn't anybody exactly like this, but there are some approximations.)

Corpus linguistics does not have a good name in some linguistics circles. A caricature of the corpus linguist is something like this. He has all the primary facts that he needs, in the form of a corpus of approximately one zillion running words, and he sees his job as that of deriving secondary facts from his primary facts. At the moment he is busy determining the relative frequencies of the eleven parts of speech as the first word of a sentence versus as the second word of a sentence. (There isn't anybody exactly like this, but there are some approximations.)

These two don't speak to each other very often, but when they do, the corpus linguist says to the armchair linguist, "Why should I think that what you tell me is true?", and the armchair linguist says to the corpus linguist, "Why should I think that what you tell me is interesting?"

This paper is a report of an armchair linguist who refuses to give up his old ways but who finds profit in being a consumer of some of the resources that corpus linguists have created.

I have two main observations to make. The first is that I don't think there can be any corpora, however large, that contain information about all the areas of English lexicon and grammar that I want to explore; all that I have seen are inadequate. The second observation is that every corpus that I have had a chance to examine, however small, has taught me facts that I couldn't imagine finding out about in any other way. My conclusion is that the two kinds of linguists need each other. Or better, that the two kinds of linguists, wherever possible, should exist in the same body.

During the early decades of my career as a linguist, I thought of myself as fortunate for having escaped corpus linguistics. Of course, I wouldn't have used the term corpus linguistics in describing my good fortune: maybe I would have called it statistical linguistics.

The situation was this. When I showed up as a beginning graduate student at the University of Michigan's linguistics program, a long time ago, the first person I considered as a possible dissertation director was the kind of professor I myself would like to be able to be, namely,

* Fillmore, C. (1992). '"Corpus linguistics" or "Computer-aided armchair linguistics"', in Svartvik, J. (ed.), *Directions in Corpus Linguistics, Proceedings of Nobel Symposium 82*, Stockholm, August 1991. Berlin: Mouton de Gruyter, 35–66. Reproduced with permission of Walter de Gruyter GMBH.

someone with a well-articulated research agenda who asked each of the students who came under his wing to take on a predetermined assignment within that agenda.

If I wanted him to be my mentor, I was to carry out the following assignment.

First, I was to make extensive tape recordings – actually, at the time, it may have been wire recordings – of natural conversations in English and Japanese. After doing that, I was to choose and justify a set of empirical criteria for phonemic analysis that could be applied to each of these languages.

(Those were the days when, realizing that a single language could be given more than one phonemic analysis, people worried – correctly – that phonemic descriptions of different languages couldn't be considered comparable unless one applied, equally to each of the languages being compared, precisely the same set of decision-making criteria.)

Armed with a carefully justified phonemic analysis, for each language, I was then to prepare phonemic transcriptions of all the conversations that I had recorded.

That was the first part – maybe a year, maybe a year and a half. The next and more important part of the job was to take from each transcript cumulatively larger samples – say, the first 200 phoneme tokens, the first 400 phoneme tokens, the first 600 phoneme tokens, etc., and with each of these growing samples, to plot out the relative frequencies of the phonemes. I was to continue doing this until I had determined, for each of these languages, the mean length of discourse samples, in terms of stretches of phoneme tokens, at which the relative frequencies of the phonemes stabilized.

If the results, using this measure, turned out to be significantly different for English and Japanese, and if I could argue that such a difference could be related to, say, phonotactic characteristics of the two languages, then the results of the research could be seen as contributing, to phonological scholarship, some practical guidelines on how large a corpus of spoken language needs to be for it to be considered an adequate reservoir of the phonological phenomena of the language.

I rejected the assignment. But now, having recalled it for the sake of the opening paragraphs of this talk, I find that it doesn't sound quite as bad to me today as it did thirty-some years ago. There have been times when I've regretted the missed opportunity, since I now know that in the process of moving carefully through a text, of any sort, I would undoubtedly have learned a great deal about both of these languages. I must admit, of course, that I can imagine languages for which the relative frequencies of their phonemes would stabilize long before all their interesting phonological properties had checked in. The fact is, I couldn't really imagine myself becoming interested in such a project; nor could I imagine what I would be able to say in the section of the dissertation that was supposed to bear the title, "The Significance of the Present Research".

The year was 1957. I soon came to be subjected to other intellectual currents within linguistics; and, in fact, before long I was, without the encouragement of my Michigan teachers, converted to a way of doing linguistics which not only did not depend on the careful examination of corpora but whose practitioners often actively ridiculed such efforts.

There were two sorts of activities in those days that would have fit the category corpus linguistics: the first was the study of corpora that field linguists had gathered for poorly documented languages, with both descriptive-linguistic and ethnographic interests in mind; and the second was the study of the statistical properties of languages for which there was no scarcity of data. I was a good disciple, and I learned the correct things to say to linguists who pushed either of these kinds of studies on me. To the first I learned to say that the knowledge linguists need, in order to come up with an account of a language that met the requirements of a generative grammar, could not be derived from a corpus, however large. For that we need to appeal to the kind of intuitive knowledge of their language possessed only by native speakers, the people who know not only what one can say in the language, but also what one cannot say. And as long as we've got that, we don't need anything else.

To the second group of linguists I learned to quote the philosopher Michael Polanyi, author of *Personal Knowledge* (1958), who had said that if natural scientists felt it necessary to portion out their time and attention to phenomena on the basis of their abundance and distribution in the universe, almost all of the scientific community would have to devote itself exclusively to the study of interstellar dust. And I admired, and later shamelessly imitated, Morris Halle's performance in a debate with policy makers in foreign language education who sought funding for corpus building so that it could become possible to design programs in which one could teach a language's words and structures in the order of their frequency of occurrence in natural texts. Halle said that if driver education were handled according to such principles, nobody would be taught how to put an automobile into reverse gear, since the distance an automobile covers while moving backwards is a hardly noticeable fraction of the distance it covers when moving forward.

Later on I sometimes found myself arguing with people who were defending the superiority of corpus studies against those who kept pointing out that there were many important features of English that simply were not to be found in the corpora that were then available. I would hear my opponents say that this is a pointless objection: all it means is that we need a larger corpus. But the answer to that was easy: that the ability to judge that some corpus is not large enough to be representative of the phenomena of the language, is an ability based on the recognition that certain things which the linguist, as a native speaker, intuitively knows about the language are not exhibited in the corpus. In the end, there is simply no way to avoid reliance on intuitive knowledge.

The most convincing part of the case for using a corpus was that it makes it possible for linguists to get the facts right. Authenticity was the key word. There was a lot of evidence that linguistic intuition, so-called, isn't always reliable, but what one finds in a corpus more or less has to be taken as authentic.

On the question of the authenticity of one's data, I have in recent years been given reason to believe that my own position in linguistics is a confused one. A few years ago, my (I think) friend William Labov went around the world giving a lecture in which something that I had written was offered as a paradigm example of what he called "woolly minded introspectionism". In attempting to demonstrate certain kinds of fit between linguistic form and aspects of language use, I had suggested that a particular utterance form could not be used over the telephone. My example involved the colloquial gesture-requiring demonstrative *yea*, as in *It was about yea big*. For this sentence, the addressee has to be watching the speaker (Fillmore 1972). Labov, master observer of the language as he is, soon after reading my claim, heard somebody use just that expression over the telephone. I am convinced that the person Labov heard would have corrected himself instantly if he had realized what he had just said, but nevertheless I stand accused and convicted as a woolly minded introspectionist. In a recent meeting with some Soviet linguists I was informed that my work was admired in their group because I always concerned myself with real language as opposed to made-up language; but shortly before that, at a conference of non-generative linguists, after I had presented the results of some corpus-based research I'd been doing with Japanese, two different members of the audience spoke to me saying almost the same thing, something about how eye-opening it must have been for somebody like me to look at real data!

My own interest in corpora has so far been exclusively in respect to their ability to supply information about lexical or structural features of a language which the usual kinds of accidental sampling and armchair introspection could easily allow us to miss. The kind of work I have in mind proceeds like this. We extract, from a large corpus, passages exhibiting particular phenomena. We do manual processing of these examples: we record observations about them in some sort of structural database; we sort the examples by various criteria, we stare at the groups of examples we have collected, we speculate on relations among the phenomena that we observe, we consult the database in respect to our speculations, and so on. The basic rule is that we make ourselves responsible for saying something about each example that we find.

This is similar in a number of ways to traditional lexicographic methods, working off of a collection of citation slips accumulated by the lexicographer or by members of the dictionary's reading program team. The difference is that – before COBUILD[1] at least – the citation slips the lexicographers examined were largely limited to examples that somebody happened to notice; the corpus work I am talking about here requires a principle of total accountability.

I have worked with on-line corpora on several projects, all of them fairly recently. One involves English conditional sentences, in which I am using mainly brochures from the U.S. Department of Agriculture;[2] another involves Japanese clause connectives, for which the corpus is a series of textbooks on science used in Japanese middle schools.[3]

But today I want to discuss two research efforts aimed at the lexical description of two English words, *risk* and *home.*

The *risk* work,[4] which was carried out in collaboration with Beryl T. Atkins, lexicographical adviser at the Oxford University Press, began with a comparison of the *risk* entries – for both the noun and the verb – in ten monolingual English dictionaries, both British and American, and noticing certain discrepancies among them. We decided to find out what a large corpus could show us about the behavior of this word.

In the case of the verb, we can notice that there are three different kinds of direct objects. To see the differences, consider a setting in which we are talking about the advisability of your climbing up a particular cliff. I might tell you that as far as I'm concerned, *I wouldn't risk the climb.* To give a little content to my worries, I warn you that since the cliff is steep and slippery, *You would risk a fall.* To convince you that the matter is serious, I might warn you that *You would be risking your life.* The *climb* names what you might do that could put you in danger. The *fall* is what might happen to you. And *your life* is what you might lose.

The *Collins Cobuild English Language Dictionary* listed all three uses, as did *Longman Dictionary of Contemporary English,* but all the others had only two of them, not always the same two.

Mrs. Atkins had the *risk* KWIC concordances from the Birmingham corpus, but it soon became obvious that to be able to sort the examples according to the senses they exhibited, we needed sentence-long contexts. From IBM Hawthorne we received all of the sentences containing the word *risk* from a corpus they had acquired from the American Publishing House for the Blind, representing a 25,000,000 word collection of edited written American English. The number of *risk* sentences was 1,743.

---

[1] COBUILD: Collins Birmingham University International Language Database; also a metonymic name for the *Collins Cobuild English Language Dictionary,* 1987 (Editor-in-chief: John Sinclair).

[2] This is part of the DCI (Data Collection Initiative) corpus of the Association for Computational Linguistics; segments of the corpus were provided to the University of California at Berkeley through the courtesy of Mark Liberman of the University of Pennsylvania. (I am grateful to the Institute of Cognitive Studies for providing an electronic home for our campus's growing collection of linguistic corpora as well as facilities for accessing and processing them.)

[3] The corpus was provided by the Japanese Telecommunications firm NTT, in connection with an NTT-sponsored research project which I am directing.

[4] Two studies based on this work are Fillmore and Atkins (1992, 1994). The summary presented here repeats material found in those articles.

Since I have been working on a method of semantic description which emphasizes the background conceptual structures for describing word meanings,[5] the first thing I wanted to do was to characterize situations involving risk.

All situations for which the word *risk* is appropriate are situations in which there is a probability, greater than zero and less than one, that something bad will happen to someone or something. In talking about such a situation we need to be able to identify the individual who is likely to suffer if things go wrong – call that person the Protagonist in a risk scenario – and we need to be able to speak of the bad things that might happen to this individual – let's call that Harm. All risk situations involve the probability that from the point of view of some Protagonist something bad will happen.

The Harm could take the form of damage to or loss of something that the Protagonist cares about. We can refer to that as a Valued Possession of the Protagonist, meaning something that the Protagonist cares about which is endangered in the risk scenario.

The probability that something bad will befall a Valued Possession of a Protagonist might, or might not, be the result of some act performed by the Protagonist. We refer to such an act as the Deed. The Protagonist's Deed might be performed in order to achieve some goal. We refer to the goal the Protagonist had in performing the Deed as, simply, the Goal.

We speak of the structure of notions lying behind a linguistic category as making up a "frame", and of its elements as "frame elements". Since some of the frame elements were seen as present in all situations involving risk, and others only in some, we found it necessary to define three slightly different variants, or sub-frames, of the risk frame. The differences among them can be suggested by the following diagrams, adapted from a notation used in mathematical decision theory, in which branches in a directed graph represent alternative futures, and the nodes are either circles, representing chance, or squares, representing choices.[6]

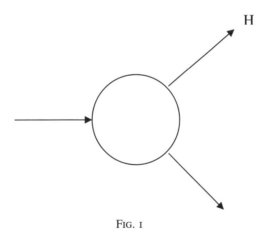

H

FIG. I

In Figure I we see a situation in which there is the possibility that some Harm will occur, but not necessarily as the result of someone's action:

If you stay here you risk getting shot.

---

[5] A discussion of this approach can be found in Fillmore (1985).
[6] For a representative work on decision theory, which uses the notation, see Raiffa (1970).

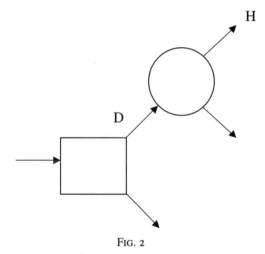

FIG. 2

In Figure 2 we see a situation in which the Protagonist's Deed puts the Protagonist on a path for which there is the possibility of Harm:

I had no idea when I stepped into that bar that I was risking my life.

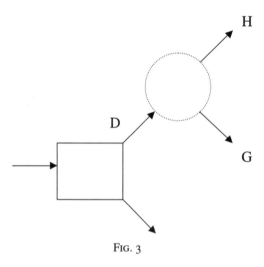

FIG. 3

In Figure 3, the dotted circle – not a standard part of decision theoretic notation – is intended to represent the deliberateness of the Protagonist's decision to perform the Deed. The idea is that the Protagonist chose the path because it is a way of reaching the Goal, while knowing that same path might lead to Harm:

I know I might lose everything, but what the hell, I'm going to risk this week's wages on my favorite horse.

Armed with this set of distinctions we went through all the verb examples in the corpus and each frame element that got expressed in it. The following is an example of the kind of description this work yields (Figure 4):

When		
you talk like that	Deed	Subclause
you	Protagonist	Subject
risk		
losing your job	Harm	Gerund

FIG. 4   "When you talk like that you risk losing your job."

All of the examples of *risk* were transitive. We found NP objects of the verb representing Deed, Harm, or Valued Possession.

Most of us decided to risk *the venture*. <D>
You would risk *death* doing what she did. <H>
Now he was prepared to risk *his good name*. <VP>

In the case of the Harm and Deed frame elements, we also found gerundial objects. In the Deed case the gerund was always a verbal gerund; in the Harm case there were also instances of clausal gerunds.

He risked *committing grave mistakes*. <H>
He had to risk *Pop getting mad at him*. <H>
She risked *going to the pool alone*. <D>

Almost all of the sentences in the corpus could be accounted for, in the sense that we could fit all of their complements and adjuncts into our view of the risk scenario, but there were a few hold-outs, sentences containing syntactic units whose interpretations didn't directly or simply fit into the risk frame. It was the corpus that forced us to deal with these examples, because I am very sure we would not have thought of them on our own. I am referring to adjunct prepositional phrases with *in*, *on*, and *to*. Examples:

Roosevelt risked fifty thousand dollars *in* Dakota ranch lands.
You risked a month's earnings *on* that stupid horse!
The captain risked his ship *to* torpedo attack.

Risking money *in* something is interpreted as investing, and we note that the preposition *in* is appropriate for investing. Risking money *on* something is seen as gambling, and we note that the preposition *on* is appropriate for gambling. The example here involving risking something *to* something is interpreted as exposing, and we note that the preposition *to* is appropriate for exposing.

What we see operating here is a kind of metonymy. Investing, gambling, and exposing all contain the notion of risk, so that *risk*, given the appropriate syntactic support, can be used to stand for each of them. Perhaps the ability of *risk* to participate in this metonymy is to be accounted for by the fact that this verb does not characterize any type of action on its own. It is the type of verb described by Yuri Apresjan as "evaluative" (personal communication): it reveals the evaluated consequences of an action, but it has no other content.

Most of the dictionaries we examined did not identify the three object types, and none of them contained any information, except in the examples they included, dealing with the gerundial complements. And of course none of the dictionaries had any way of relating the various individual senses to a single underlying semantic frame.

Turning briefly to *risk* as a noun, we note that the most frequent uses were as direct object of either the verb *run* or the verb *take*. *Running risks* and *taking risks* have meanings very similar to that of the simple verb *risk*, but they provide the possibility of expressing the evaluation only: since these phrases have no obligatory complement, it is not necessary to include mention of anything specific about the situation, whereas with the verb it is necessary to say something about either the Deed, the Valued Possession, or the Harm. These phrasal expressions welcome *of* + gerund complements expressing either Deed:

I took the risk of asking my boss for a raise.

or Harm:

I took the risk of losing my job.

and they also accept a *that*-clause complement expressing Harm:

Aren't you running the risk that your daughter will never speak to you again?

None of the dictionaries we surveyed told us anything useful about the difference between running and taking risks. Our conclusion was this: that when you speak of *running a risk* you have in mind the situation represented by Figure 1, but when you speak of *taking a risk* you have in mind a situation represented by one of the other two diagrams. Since Figure 1 is included in Figure 2 and 3, there are numerous situations in which either *run a risk* or *take a risk* could be used. In order to test the difference, you need to find a critical sentence which fits one of the diagrams but not the others. Such sentences can be imagined:

The newborn babies in that hospital run the risk of hypothermia.

or

A car parked here runs the risk of getting dented.

In neither of these cases can the version with *take* be used.

We are convinced that our analysis is correct, and that the existence of sentences with *run-risk* which do not allow substitution with *take-risk* supports our understanding of the contrast. However, we found no examples of that type in the actual corpus. And of course, even if we had found such sentences, we would still have to recognize that we cannot find corpus evidence that paraphrasability with *take* is impossible.

The work with *risk* convinced me of the value of the corpus, because, as I said, the simple requirement that we check all of the examples forced us to recognize things that we very probably wouldn't have noticed otherwise. But we could not depend on the corpus alone, since an important judgment that we wanted to be able to make did not receive support from the corpus.

The analysis of the data that we already have has not yet been completed, but it does in fact seem clear that we need more examples. There are mysteries with the count vs. noncount distinction with this word (*a risk* or *many risks*, vs. *much risk*). We are working with the hypothesis that the noncount form is compatible with *run* but not *take*:

You won't be running much risk if you follow my instructions.

versus

You won't be taking a big risk if you do that.

but not

You won't be taking much risk.

There are also some mysteries having to do with the contexts in which verbs with the different types of complements can occur. It seems that *risk* when accompanied by the Deed complement occurs very often in negative modal form (*I would never risk swimming here* etc.), but we need more examples to see whether this tendency is a real part of the data. In short, I find myself in the end simultaneously convinced (i) that many decisions we have to make about the description of this word cannot be supported by direct corpus evidence, and (ii) that there are decisions that we will be able to make only if we get additional data, from a much larger corpus.

In connection with the next study, I should explain that I have been interested for a long time in words whose grammatical and semantic properties struck me as being completely unique; and *home* is one such word. So when, quite recently, I got my hands on the WSJ section of the DCI corpus (the text of the 1989 *Wall Street Journal*, approximately 8 or 9 million running words), the first thing I did with it was to extract from it all of the sentences containing the word *home*.

Colleagues with access to other corpora who heard about my interest, and who probably worried about the representativeness of my corpus, sent me great quantities of further examples, these taken from the *Grolier's American Academic Encyclopedia* and from on-line newspapers in and around Oxford.

Each of these sources, from written English, produced many hundreds of examples. I work in a third-world university, so except for the London–Lund Corpus, which we bought in better days, we have only corpora that we could get for free. I have access to only relatively small corpora of spoken language data. I don't think that I will find big surprises when I take a careful look at the conversational data that I have, though there will undoubtedly be big differences in respect to relative frequencies of the usage I've found.

The word *home* has a number of distinguishable uses. Its central use is as a relational noun, seen in phrases like *my home*, *our home*, etc. where it can refer to any place where a person lives, with the resident or residents of the home indicated in a possessive modifier. It is in this central use that the phrase *my home* is to be interpreted as the place where I live, rather than, say, a home which I own.

For interpreting many of the uses of the word we need to appeal to a kind of prototype understanding of this particular cultural unit. A semantic prototype for *home* would probably run something like this:

- A home is a place where people live
- The people who live in the home are members of an intact family
- The home is comfortable and familiar
- Each member of the family has unquestioned use of at least some of the objects and facilities in the home
- One lives in the home throughout one's childhood and early youth
- There are many reasons to go away from the home temporarily (shopping, play, travel, education, work, military service, etc.) but after these temporary absences, the natural and expected thing is to return home
- When one reaches the age appropriate for seeking one's fortune, one leaves home and, sooner or later, founds or becomes part of a new home

A number of lexical and phrasal expressions containing the word *home* appeal to various aspects of such a prototype. A homeless person is someone who has no fixed place to go to after the day's wanderings. *Being homesick* is feeling bad when separated from the familiar and comfortable setting of home and from the people in it. If we remark about somebody that *she left home at age fifteen*, we recognize that this was out of the ordinary. We speak of children of divorced parents as coming from *broken homes*. If I say that I want you as a guest in my house, *to feel at home*, I am inviting you to treat the objects in my house as objects you can use and enjoy, to relax in the way you would relax in your own home, etc. (We never actually mean just that, but the phrase is intended to give that impression.)

The meaning of *home* that fits the prototype is very closely tied to the notion of family, and in this way *home* differs from *house*. The following contrast shows this distinction quite clearly. If I say that during the first ten years of my life I lived in five different houses, you will assume that my family moved a lot; but if I say that I lived in five different homes, you will assume that I was an orphan and I lived with five different families, or that I lived in various institutional settings.

In addition to what I spoke of as the central sense of *home*, there are other relational noun usages with meanings that depart in a number of ways from the prototype. With slightly different meanings, two of the other usages can be reflected by their occurrence with the prepositions *to* and *of*; and a third, carrying a considerably different meaning, takes the preposition *for*.

> The Barbican Centre provides a permanent home to both the London Symphony Orchestra and the Royal Shakespeare Company.

> The African continent was the home of one of the world's oldest civilizations, that of ancient Egypt.

> He spent his final years in a home for the aged.

In addition to the necessarily relational uses, *home* also occurs as a plain noun. In this function, not requiring any mention of actual or intended residents, the word is used as a kind of up-market name for *house*. For the noun in this sense, a modifying possessive construction has to identify a relationship other than residence, for example, that of the home's creator. This usage is said to be an American development, and it is noticeable mainly in the speech of real estate professionals. We see it in sentences like

> Our construction company specializes in luxury homes.
> Our homes were built with the busy executive in mind.

The focus of my interest in this word has concerned its use without an article, especially when functioning as a locative or directional adverb. Examples of adverbial *home* and its typical context are the following:

> Let's go home
> When did you leave home
> I just want to stay home
> The school principal sent the kids home early today
> Let's get out there and welcome the troops home
> Would anybody like to take the leftovers home
> I usually work at home
> I keep expecting letters from home
> I wonder what the folks back home are doing

The adverbial use descends from early dative and accusative case forms, which froze into particular colligations before determiners became popular. The word has both locative and directional adverbial functions, at least in American English. It occurs with the prepositions *at* and *from*, but not *to* when it is a complement of a verb. (That is, we can say *go home* but not *go to home*. However, in structures in which *to* is independently required, the combination of *to + home* is possible: *from work to home*, *close to home*, etc.)

The adverb behaves – most clearly in the case of its occurrence with transitive verbs – like a verbal particle. That is, as with other particles like *off*, *away*, etc., we find alternations between Object + Particle and Particle + Object orders.

> Would anybody like to take home the leftovers?
> Would anybody like to take the leftovers home?

There are numerous reasons for my interest in adverbial uses of *home*. One is that they present a problem in cohesion semantics: in the case of the noun *home*, the "resident" is identified by a possessive determiner, but in the adverbial use we have to figure out who lives in the house from the context. This fact is indirectly revealed in definitions of the word *home* through the use of the word *one* – and one of my interests in lexicographic traditions is the conventions for using the word *one* in defining phrases.

In the *Concise Oxford Dictionary* (1990) we find *home* defined as "the place where one lives"; in the *Chambers Twentieth Century Dictionary* (1983), it is "the residence of one's family"; in the *Collins English Dictionary* (1986), "the place or a place where one lives"; in *Webster's Third New International Dictionary* (1986), "one's principal place of residence"; in the *Random House Dictionary* (1987), "the place in which one's domestic affections are centered"; and so on. This definitional pattern distinguishes *home* from *house*, where the definers never use the word *one*, but are more likely to speak of something like "a structure in which people live" or "a building used as a home".

Because of the connection between the adverbial uses and the central sense of the noun, we can think of the prepositionless noun as meaning "the place where one lives", the locative adverb as "at the place where one lives", and the directional adverb as "to the place where one lives".

The felt appropriateness of the word *one* in these definitions reveals an anaphoric element in the meaning of the word. One part of the process of giving a semantic interpretation to expressions containing the adverb *home,* then, is that of establishing the cohesive link between this hidden anaphoric element and some other part of the text which can provide its antecedent. When I go home it's to my home; when the factory boss sends the workers home, it's to their homes, etc. One of my interests was in figuring out whether there are any strict principles determining what controls or binds the hidden anaphor in *home* and whether what we know about the anaphoric properties of *one* allows us to use it in formulating the definitions of adverbial *home* in a way which predicts which cohesive links are possible and which are not.

A second interesting fact about adverbial *home* is its participation in multiple contrast sets. One of the discussions of *home* in Quirk *et al.* (1985) points out the quasi-antonymy relation the word has with *abroad* and *out*:

> We were abroad during the last few summers, but this year we're staying *at home*.
> I've gone out the last few nights, but tonight I'm staying *at home*.

One question I'd like to ask is whether we are dealing with clearly distinguishable contrast sets here. The adjective *short* has very similar meanings in the contrast set in which it is opposed to *long* and in the one in which it is opposed to *tall*, but it is quite clear that it has separate if related senses precisely because of its participation in these two antonymy relations. What can we say about *home* in this respect?

A third point of interest relates to certain differences between American English and British English. The usage notes in some dictionaries tell us that in British English *be home* is used only to refer to a situation in which someone has freshly arrived from elsewhere. I wanted to see if there are any traces of this distinction in the American English examples.

A fourth reason for being interested in *home* relates to my interest in deixis. Twenty years ago, as a part of a series of lectures on deixis, I read a paper in which I presented what I then believed to be a true account of the English verbs *come* and *go* (see Fillmore 1975a). The connection with deixis is that in describing *come*, one has to say something about the presupposed location of one or both of the speech-act participants at the destination of the journey. Independently of that deictic feature, I claimed in my paper that a temporal adverb associated with a *come* expression identified the arrival time, whereas a temporal adverb adjoined to a *go* expression identified the departure time. To see what I mean, imagine Max at a late night party and people talking about his return home after the party. The sentence

Max went home at midnight

would be interpreted as telling us what time Max left the party, but

Max came home at three in the morning

said by somebody in his home, would inform us of the time at which he arrived at the house. The generalization I proposed is that a time-phrase with *go* indicates the departure time, a time-phrase with *come* indicates the arrival time.

I believed, then, that the interpretation differences I reported had to be described as a difference in the semantic structures of *go* and *come*. If anybody had asked me about it, I surely would have said that the fact that I used the word *home* in my examples to indicate the destination of the journey was purely accidental. Anything else would have done just as well, I would have said.

Once in a while, in the intervening years, I worried about the fact that a sentence like

He went to the dentist's at two o'clock

doesn't really mean the same thing as

He left for the dentist's at two o'clock

as my generalization would have predicted, but I tended to think that there must be some special problem with such sentences. I now believe, as you have guessed, that the difference has a lot to do with the word *home*.

There was still another reason for my interest in *home*. I have a general cross-linguistic interest in the concept of the "home base" as a feature in lexical semantic systems.

A home base feature is present in the semantic systems of many languages, and sometimes the home base category interacts with or contrasts with the other deictic categories in the verbs of motion. I know of several such systems in the native languages of the Americas, but the phenomenon might well be much more widespread than that.

In Japanese the idea of going home, coming home, returning home, getting home, etc., is expressed using the verb *kaeru*, which is usually translated as "return". And the idea of sending somebody home, bringing or taking somebody home, is expressed with the causative form of *kaeru*, namely *kaeraseru*. These verbs usually occur in construction with some secondary verb indicating the difference between coming and going, or that between sending and accompanying.

I have always thought that the Japanese verb *kaeru* really means what the English verb *return* means, but that it is simply conventionally used in the context of talking about going home. This seems reasonable, since every journey to one's home is an instance of returning.

I now think, however, that it really means "to go home" and that its use in some contexts with more temporary starting places is a separate development. The difference can be seen in talking to Japanese or foreigners about going back to Japan. If I want to ask a Japanese person when he's going back to Japan, I can use the word *kaeru*, because he is going home. But if I am talking to a foreigner who may have visited Japan many times to ask him if he is ever planning to return to Japan, I cannot use the verb *kaeru*. I have to say something that means "go again". Japan is not that person's home, and so *kaeru* is not appropriate.

The idea that *kaeru* and *return* mean the same is not only a mistake made by English-speaking people who are learning Japanese. It works in the other direction too. I recently learned about an anti-American demonstration in Japan in which the protestors carried plac-ards in English urging Americans to return. The addressees of this message might have found it quite friendly and welcoming, were it not for the accompanying shouting and clenching of fists.

The WSJ corpus yielded about 450 sentences with determiner-less instances of *home*, and I'll briefly survey the collection now. The examples sort themselves into literal and figurative, and I begin with the literal. Of these, the examples can be divided into those expressing location, those expressing going away from the home, and those expressing returning to the home. The location examples can express location at the home or location away from the home. The examples of returning to the home are further divided into those that express arrival at the home, those that express setting out on the homeward journey, and those that express transit. Superimposed on these path differences is the distinction between intransitive and transitive, i.e. between plain and caused movement.

One group of the location examples simply described things that were at the resident's home, expressed as objects of the verb *have* or objects of the preposition *with*.

He believes every family should have a Bible at home.

According to the poll, 19% of respondents already have computers at home.

It would be nice if each of us had a wife at home to anticipate and meet our needs . . .

I remembered being fired at age 44, with five children at home.

Sentences about the resident not leaving home used the verb-phrase *stay at home* and *stay home*. The latter possibility apparently does not exist in British English.

Mothers who work should be subsidized more than those who stay at home.

I don't have the personality to stay at home.

If I stayed at home, I'd be looking at the walls.

Friends criticized her for not staying at home.

Then maybe I could stay home and have seven children and watch Oprah Winfrey.

I think a lot of people got scared and stayed home.

ABC wanted comedies that would appeal to the kind of people who stay home Saturdays.

Kate Myers challenges the view . . . that men should work and married women should stay home with the children.

Stay specifically communicates the idea of not going out or away, but we also have expressions with *be*, simply indicating the fact of being at home. Both languages accept *at home*.

The company's chairman ... and another top official were at home yesterday.

Subscribers won't need to be at home during the day for in-home service calls.

There is a difference between the two languages when *be* is followed by *home* without a preposition. The usage notes tell us that there is no distinction in American English between *be home* and *be at home*, but that in British English *be home* is used only to express the idea of having freshly returned from somewhere. Another way to think about this is to say that in British English, *home* without a preposition is only a dynamic or directional adverb, never a static or purely locational adverb. Thus perhaps *he is home* has a structure that is a bit like *the ball is over the fence*, where we are indicating the location of something by saying that it just got there.

The following examples would presumably not be accepted by British speakers.

Japanese tradition says she should be home taking care of her two preschool children.

Because of her inability to be home to care for a kitten, she was counseled instead to adopt a cat.

"At least she can die knowing she is home."

For the fresh-return sense, American English also prefers the prepositionless form.

"Mona, I'm home!"

"Will he be home in time for dinner?"

He barely had time to tell the news media "I am happy to be back home" before one of his bodyguards tugged his elbow and said "Comrade, let's move".

If a speaker of American English comes home, sees nobody in the house, wants the people in the house to know that he is back, he will shout *I'm home*, and surely not *I'm at home*.

I am not sure, but I think we can summarize the difference by saying that in British English the prepositionless form requires the "fresh arrival" meaning, and in American English the "fresh arrival" meaning requires the prepositionless form.

There is another difference between *be home* and *be at home* in American English. The form without the preposition can only express the resident's location, the form with *at home* can express the location of some possession of the resident. Thus, it is possible for me to say that *my computer is at home*, but I can't say that *my computer is home*.

There are expressions talking about people not being at home. The most common phrase is *away from home*.

The children were away from home for 16 days altogether.

The ASPCA doesn't give young kittens, which are more in demand than cats, to people who are away from home during the day.

School administrators walk a tightrope between the demands of the community and the realities of how children really act when they are away from home.

The word *away* is interesting in this respect. Being *away from home* can signal a short absence or a long absence, but simply being *away* suggests an absence of at least one night. In this it contrasts with being *out*. Thus if somebody calls for my wife asking if she is at home – or, in America, if she is home – I could answer that she is away, the assumption being that she won't be back until at least tomorrow, or I could answer that she is out, the assumption being that she will return in the same day. The examples I mentioned from Quirk *et al.* (1985)

earlier contrasted *at home* vs. *abroad* and *at home* vs. *out*, but I think that *away* is a third alternative.

When you are away from home you can still communicate with your family. The "directionality" with the adverb *home* can also be that of a communicating act, as shown in two of the WSJ examples:

You can always call home if you're lonely.

In the spring of '40 they stopped writing home.

Another attested sentence, absent from the WSJ corpus, is *E.T., phone home*, illustrating the same point.

Leaving home can be for a short period or a long period. One can go shopping, one can go on a trip, or one can leave home for good. Examples of each type were found in the corpus:

Many residents leave home without locking doors.

Most travelers are leaving home for fun rather than business.

If you'd rather have a Buick, don't leave home without the American Express card.

Miss Johns ran away from home to California at age 14, got a job as a bank teller, earned a high school equivalency degree and became a trading assistant at Drexel Burnham Lambert.

At an early age, Wonda left home and married.

Verbs indicating arrival at home include *arrive, get, return*, and *come.*

Warner arrived home to tidy the house and prepare a nourishing meal for the brats.

Four months after he got home, he and his wife separated.

"I phoned my wife from there. 'Put on the coffee', I said, 'I'm coming home for good'."

"You can come home from work at 6 o'clock, and they call it 'abandonment'."

Verbs indicating "going home" included simple *go*, the general directional verb *head* (*heading home* is going in the direction of home), and manner and means verbs like *hurry, run, drive, ride a bike*, etc. We find that *home* is also a possible complement for nouns designating journeys:

On the flight home she kept worrying about the children.

The journey home was to take three days.

The transitive verbs we find in the corpus include *bring, take*, and a number of verbs suggesting the idea of carrying, and *send, order, summon*, etc., suggesting the idea of giving orders.

The remaining examples were metaphorical, with *at home* used in the meaning of being competent (*The pianist was at home with Chopin*); *pounding, driving, hammering, nailing*, or *pressing a point home*, meaning something like "try energetically to convince"; *hit home, strike home*, etc., meaning "to affect one deeply".

I turn now to the various semantic problems we left hanging. One was the question of interpreting the anaphoric element in *home*, and the appropriateness of the word *one* in the definition of *home*. Dictionary entries for idioms with variable possessive pronouns distinguish two types, along the lines of *to blow one's nose* and *to pull someone's leg*. The possessor, in the case of the idioms listed with *one's* is always the subject of the verb (*I blow my nose, you blow yours*), but in the case of the idioms listed with *someone's* it is distinct from the subject (*I'm pulling your leg, *I'm pulling my leg*).

I will allow myself to use the word "control" to express the relation between the antecedent and the anaphoric element in *home*. In all of the examples of intransitive verbs in the corpus the controller was the subject. With the transitive verbs the controller was the subject with some verbs – for example *send, bring, carry, tote,* and *take* – but the object with others – for example *send, summon, order,* etc. In the case of *be home* or *be at home* it was always the subject. However, this is a case where the corpus has let us down. It failed to show that the subject with *at home* wouldn't have to be the resident of the home (since I can say that I left my computer at home), and it failed to show that with *bring* and *take* the object could be the controller. (Actually there was one example with *take*, concerning a limousine that was waiting to take some judges home.) It is certainly possible to say things like

A policeman brought my husband home last night.

It is also possible for *send* to be used with the subject, not the object, controlling the anaphoric element of *home*, as in

If, when I travel, I buy books, I always send them home rather than carry them home.

But there's still more to say. In the case of both the intransitive verbs and the transitive verbs, there are contexts in which the resident of the home can be introduced with a *with* phrase: *My dog is so friendly he'll go home with anyone.* And we can imagine a sentence with three possible controllers of the anaphoric element of *home*. Consider the sentence *The teacher sent Jimmy home with Mary.* It could mean that she sent the kids to her own home; it could mean that she sent Jimmy to his own home, in Mary's company; or it could mean that she sent Jimmy to Mary's home (in Mary's company). The context for this last case might be that Jimmy's parents had had a family emergency and had to leave town, and that Mary's parents had agreed to take care of Jimmy during their absence. *The teacher sent Jimmy home with Mary*, then, would mean that it was to Mary's home.

It seems clear that the relationship between the anaphoric element of *home* and its antecedent is not controlled syntactically but semantically. The controller can always be the subject, but otherwise you simply have to know who the travelers are. Furthermore, paraphrasing *home* with "at one's home" or "to one's home" will not make it possible to identify the antecedent of the anaphoric element of *home*, because the referential anaphor *one* is always bound to the clause's subject.

You have undoubtedly noticed that I resorted to made-up examples and imagined contexts. But that, of course, is because I'm pretty sure that what I am claiming about the fact of the matter is right, but the corpus didn't give any evidence on it one way or the other.

I turn now to the paradigmatic semantics of *home*. A part of knowing what function a word performs in a given context is knowing what it is being used "in contrast with" in that context. Recall what we have already noticed about the ability of *at home* to be in contrast with *out, away,* or *abroad*.

In the WSJ corpus a great many of the sentences contained explicit indications of the alternative to *at home*, either in a way in which the contrast was presented directly (*at home and abroad, at home or at work, in school but not at home*), or in some less direct way. In fact, in just this respect it is clear that in the case of *home* we need more than a single sentence to learn the facts, since we had some sentences like *At home, however, things were different*. To understand the scale of the intended contrast for this sentence we have to know what the preceding sentence was.

These contrasts show us that the English category of home involves considerable variation of scale.

Advertisers claim virtues for their products overseas that they are forbidden by law to claim at home.

Senators and Representatives don't always say the same thing in Washington that they say at home.

The yen is powerful overseas but has little purchasing power at home.

Parents wonder if their children behave better at school than they behave at home.

These children speak one language at school and another language at home.

In many cases the contrast was covert, discoverable only by figuring out why it seemed relevant to use the adverb *at home*. It is relevant to say that some parents teach their children at home, since the usual thing is to have children educated at school. It makes sense to talk about people who shop at home with a computer, or that in bad times people tend to eat at home, because these activities are understood as things that one could carry out in shops or restaurants.

A Bulgarian linguist, Svillen Stanchev, who has been visiting the Berkeley campus this year, went through my WSJ examples, and concluded that the English word *home* was a translator's nightmare. Most of the sentences could not be translated using a Bulgarian equivalent of *home*. There seem to be three reasons for this. One is that Bulgarian does not have the scale variations that English has, which allows us to use *at home* to refer to being in one's house, neighborhood, town, state, country, or planet. A second is that Bulgarian doesn't seem to allow the distributive interpretation of adverbial *home* with multiple travelers. In a sentence about the director of a factory sending the workers home after an accident, a translation with *home* would suggest that they all went to the same home, but a translation that made explicit that each worker went to his own home sounded silly, since the point was that the workers had to leave the factory and in the context there was no reason to make sure that each one ended up in his own proper home. The third reason – and this was the biggest surprise I got from the corpus – is that many English expressions with *home* appear to be simply negations of the other member of the contrast set. That is, to say that *Joe is at home* **sometimes** means simply that Joe is not at the other place where he might instead relevantly be.

It appears that with the word *home* a potential three-way alternation has come to be seen as a two-way contrast. If on a given day I could be expected to be either at home or at work, that sounds like a two-way contrast, but we know, of course, that in reality there is a third possibility: I might go someplace else altogether – for example, to the beach, to a coffeehouse, or what have you. But we find in the corpus lots of expressions about *being at home* or *going home* or *being sent home* that give the impression of only a two-way contrast. We read that *in a bad business climate customers stay home in droves*. (There aren't many homes large enough for people to assemble in droves.) Because of an accident the factory workers stayed home. One of the most striking examples of this that I have noticed – not from the WSJ corpus but from a recent news report – was a sentence which described non-voters as people who stay home on election day. Since elections in the United States are traditionally held on Tuesdays, when most people work, it is not at all likely that the people who didn't vote stayed home.

It is this use that I now associate with the "departure time" interpretation of *go home*, since *go home* has to be interpreted as going away from the place where one is. Mr. Stanchev tells me that the slogan YANKEE GO HOME would not work in direct Bulgarian translation, since it focuses on the wrong end of the journey.

A careful study of sentences with *risk* and with *home* has revealed facts about the uses and meanings of these words that have not been well described in existing grammars or dictionaries, and has given me reasons to be absolutely committed to the use of corpus evidence. But it is also true that in thinking through the consequences of the various hypotheses that observed corpus data evoked, other judgments needed to be brought in. Atkins and I think that we understand the difference between *run a risk* and *take a risk*, but we didn't find the critical examples in the corpus. But even if we had found sentences which worked with *run* but which wouldn't have tolerated replacement of *run* with *take*, we still have to face the reality that there are no corpora of starred examples: a corpus cannot tell us what is not possible. The cohesion problem with *home* is not syntactically resolvable, but almost all of the examples in the actual corpus did suggest that antecedents could be found in the subjects or the objects. The possibility that they could also be found in the objects of the preposition *with* was not shown in the corpus, and this seems to be an accidental gap.

As I said at the beginning, my concern with corpora is with the possibility of amassing enough examples to cover a particular domain more thoroughly than an armchair linguist could possibly manage without this sort of help. So one kind of corpus linguist should find this encouraging: there are really good reasons for building corpora, and as far as I'm concerned, the bigger the better. But what I have been saying is probably not encouraging to people who want to do most of their analysis without expecting anyone to have to sit down and stare at the examples one at a time to try to work out just what is the intended cognitive experience of the interpreter, what are the interactional intentions of the writer, and so on. Should it ever come about that linguistics can be carried out without the intervention and suffering of a native-speaker analyst, I will probably lose interest in the enterprise.

PART IV
On Word Senses and Polysemy

8

Do Word Meanings Exist?

PATRICK HANKS*

1 INTRODUCTION

My contribution to this discussion is to attempt to spread a little radical doubt. Since I have spent over 30 years of my life writing and editing monolingual dictionary definitions, it may seem rather odd that I should be asking, do word meanings exist? The question is genuine, though: prompted by some puzzling facts about the data that is now available in the form of machine-readable corpora. I am not the only lexicographer to be asking this question after studying corpus evidence. Sue Atkins, for example, has said "I don't believe in word meanings" (cited as the title of a paper by Kilgarriff, 1997e–also in this volume, *Ed.*), and Eugene Nida (1997) is one of many who have insisted that words only have meaning in context.

It is a question of fundamental importance to the enterprise of sense disambiguation. If senses don't exist, then there is not much point in trying to "disambiguate" them – or indeed do anything else with them. The very term *disambiguate* presupposes what Fillmore (1975b) characterized as "checklist theories of meaning". Here I shall reaffirm the argument, on the basis of recent work in corpus analysis, that checklist theories in their current form are at best superficial and at worst misleading. If word meanings do exist, they do not exist as a checklist. The numbered lists of definitions found in dictionaries have helped to create a false picture of what really happens when language is used.

Vagueness and redundancy – features which are not readily compatible with a checklist theory – are important design features of natural language, which must be taken into account when doing serious natural language processing. Words are so familiar to us, such an everyday feature of our existence, such an integral and prominent component of our psychological makeup, that it's hard to see what mysterious, complex, vague-yet-precise entities meanings are.

2 COMMON SENSE

The claim that word meaning is mysterious may seem counterintuitive. To take a time-worn example, it seems obvious that the noun *bank* has at least two senses: "slope of land alongside a river" and "financial institution". But this line of argument is a honeytrap. In the first place, these are not, in fact, two senses of a single word; they are two different words that happen to be spelled the same. They have different etymologies, different uses, and the only thing that they have in common is their spelling. Obviously, computational procedures for distinguishing

* Hanks, P. (2000). 'Do word meanings exist?', *Computers and the Humanities*, 34: 205–215, originally given as a talk at the first SENSEVAL workshop, held at Herstmonceux Castle, Sussex, England on 2–4 September 1998. Reproduced with kind permission of Springer Science and Business Media.

homographs are both desirable and possible. But in practice they don't get us very far along the road to text understanding.

Linguists used to engage in the practice of inventing sentences such as "I went to the bank" and then claiming that it is ambiguous because it invokes both meanings of ***bank*** equally plausibly. It is now well known that in actual usage ambiguities of this sort hardly ever arise. Contextual clues disambiguate, and can be computed to make choice possible, using procedures such as that described in Church and Hanks (1990 – see also in this volume, *Ed.*). On the one hand we find expressions such as:

> people without bank accounts; his bank balance; bank charges; gives written notice to the bank; in the event of a bank ceasing to conduct business; high levels of bank deposits; the bank's solvency; a bank's internal audit department; a bank loan; a bank manager; commercial banks; High-Street banks; European and Japanese banks; a granny who tried to rob a bank

and on the other hand:

> the grassy river bank; the northern bank of the Glen water; olive groves and sponge gardens on either bank; generations of farmers built flood banks to create arable land; many people were stranded as the river burst its banks; she slipped down the bank to the water's edge; the high banks towered on either side of us, covered in wild flowers.

The two words *bank* are not confusable in ordinary usage.

So far, so good. In a random sample of 1000 occurrences of the noun *bank* in the British National Corpus (BNC), I found none where the "riverside" sense and the "financial institution" sense were both equally plausible. However, this merely masks the real problem, which is that in many uses NEITHER of the meanings of *bank* just mentioned is fully activated.

The obvious solution to this problem, you might think, would be to add more senses to the dictionary. And this indeed is often done. But it is not satisfactory, for a variety of reasons. For one, these doubtful cases (some examples are given below) do invoke one or other of the main senses to some extent, but only partially. Listing them as separate senses fails to capture the overlap and delicate interplay among them. It fails to capture the imprecision which is characteristic of words in use. And it fails to capture the dynamism of language in use. The problem is vagueness, not ambiguity.

For the vast majority of words in use, including the two words spelled *bank*, one meaning shades into another, and indeed the word may be used in a perfectly natural but vague or even contradictory way. In any random corpus-based selection of citations, a number of delicate questions will arise that are quite difficult to resolve or indeed are unresolvable. For example:

How are we to regard expressions such as "data bank", "blood bank", "seed bank", and "sperm bank"? Are they to be treated as part of the "financial institution" sense? Even though no finance is involved, the notion of storing something for safekeeping is central. Or are we to list these all as separate senses (or as separate lexical entries), depending on what is stored? Or are we to add a "catch-all" definition of the kind so beloved of lexicographers: "any of various other institutions for storing and safeguarding any of various other things"? (But is that insufficiently constrained? What precisely is the scope of "any of various"? Is it just a lexicographer's copout? Is a speaker entitled to invent any old expression – say, "a sausage bank", or "a restaurant bank", or "an ephemera bank" – and expect to be understood? The answer may well be "Yes", but either way, we need to know why.)

Another question: is a bank (financial institution) always an abstract entity? Then what about (1)?

(1)   [He] assaulted them in a bank doorway.

Evidently the reference in (1) is to a building which houses a financial institution, not to the institution itself. Do we want to say that the institution and the building which houses it are separate senses? Or do we go along with Pustejovsky (1995: 91), who would say that they are all part of the same "lexical conceptual paradigm (lcp)", even though the superordinates (INSTITUTION and BUILDING) are different?

The lcp provides a means of characterizing a lexical item as a meta-entry. This turns out to be very useful for capturing the systematic ambiguities which are so pervasive in language....Nouns such as *newspaper* appear in many semantically distinct contexts, able to function sometimes as an organization, a physical object, or the information contained in the articles within the newspaper.

a. The newspapers attacked the President for raising taxes.
b. Mary spilled coffee on the newspaper.
c. John got angry at the newspaper.

So it is with $bank_1$. Sometimes it is an institution; sometimes it is the building which houses the institution; sometimes it is the people within the institution who make the decisions and transact its business.

Our other *bank* word illustrates similar properties. Does the "riverside" sense always entail sloping land? Then what about (2)?

(2)   A canoe nudged a bank of reeds.

3   OCKHAM'S RAZOR

Is a bank always beside water? Does it have one slope or two? Is it always dry land? How shall we account for (3) and (4)?

(3)   Philip ran down the bracken bank to the gate.
(4)   The eastern part of the spit is a long simple shingle bank.

Should (3) and (4) be treated as separate senses? Or should we apply Ockham's razor, seeking to avoid a needless multiplicity of entities? How delicate do we want our sense distinctions to be? Are "river bank", "sand bank", and "grassy bank" three different senses? Can a sand bank be equated with a shingle bank?

Then what about "a bank of lights and speakers"? Is it yet another separate sense, or just a further extension of the lcp? If we regard it as an extension of the lcp, we run into the problem that it has a different superordinate – FURNITURE, rather than LAND. Does this matter?

There is no single correct answer to such questions. The answer is determined rather by the user's intended application, or is a matter of taste. Theoretical semanticists may be more troubled than language users by a desire for clear semantic hierarchies. For such reasons, lexicographers are sometimes classified into "lumpers" and "splitters": those who prefer – or rather, who are constrained by marketing considerations – to lump uses together in a single sense, and those who isolate fine distinctions.

We can of course multiply entities ad nauseam, and this is indeed the natural instinct of many lexicographers. As new citations are amassed, new definitions are added to the dictionary to account for those citations which do not fit the existing definitions. This creates a combinational explosion of problems for computational analysis, while still leaving many actual uses unaccounted for. Less commonly asked is the question, "Should we perhaps adjust the wording of an existing definition, to give a more generalized meaning?" But even if we ask this question, it is often not obvious how it is to be answered within the normal structure of a set of dictionary definitions.

Is there then no hope? Is natural language terminally intractable? Probably not. Human beings seem to manage all right. Language is certainly vague and variable, but it is vague and variable in principled ways, which are at present imperfectly understood. Let us take comfort, procedurally, from Anna Wierzbicka (1985):

An adequate definition of a vague concept must aim not at precision but at vagueness: it must aim at precisely that level of vagueness which characterizes the concept itself.

This takes us back to Wittgenstein's account of the meaning of *game*. This has been influential, and versions of it are applied quite widely, with semantic components identified as possible rather than necessary contributors to the meaning of texts. Wittgenstein, it will be remembered, wrote (*Philosophical Investigations*, 1953: no. 66):

Consider for example the proceedings that we call "games". I mean board games, card games, ball games, Olympic games, and so on. What is common to them all? Don't say, "There must be something common, or they would not be called 'games' " – but *look and see* whether there is anything common to all. For if you look at them you will not see something common to all, but similarities, relationships, and a whole series of them at that. To repeat: don't think, but look! Look for example at board games, with their multifarious relationships. Now pass to card games; here you find many correspondences with the first group, but many common features drop out, and others appear. When we pass next to ball games, much that is common is retained, but much is lost. Are they all "amusing"? Compare chess with noughts and crosses. Or is there always winning and losing, or competition between players? Think of patience. In ball games there is winning and losing; but when a child throws his ball at the wall and catches it again, this feature has disappeared. Look at the parts played by skill and luck; and at the difference between skill in chess and skill in tennis. Think now of games like ring-a-ring-a-roses; here is the element of amusement, but how many other characteristic features have disappeared! And we can go through the many, many other groups of games in the same way; can see how similarities crop up and disappear. And the result of this examination is: we see a complicated network of similarities overlapping and criss-crossing: sometimes overall similarities, sometimes similarities of detail.

It seems, then, that there are no necessary conditions for being a bank, any more than there are for being a game. Taking this Wittgensteinian approach, a lexicon for machine use would start by identifying the semantic components of *bank* as separate, combinable, exploitable entities. This turns out to reduce the number of separate dictionary senses dramatically. The meaning of $bank_1$ might then be expressed as:

- IS AN INSTITUTION
- IS A LARGE BUILDING
- FOR STORAGE
- FOR SAFEKEEPING
- OF FINANCE/MONEY
- CARRIES OUT TRANSACTIONS
- CONSISTS OF A STAFF OF PEOPLE

And $bank_2$ as:

- IS LAND
- IS SLOPING
- IS LONG
- IS ELEVATED
- SITUATED BESIDE WATER

On any occasion when the word "bank" is used by a speaker or writer, he or she invokes at least one of these components, usually a combination of them, but no one of them is a necessary condition for something being a "bank" in either or any of its senses. Are any of the components of *bank₂* necessary?

"IS LAND"? But think of a bank of snow.
"IS SLOPING"? But think of a reed bed forming a river bank.
"IS LONG"? But think of the bank around a pond or small lake.
"IS ELEVATED"? But think of the banks of rivers in East Anglia, where the difference between the water level and the land may be almost imperceptible.
"SITUATED BESIDE WATER"? But think of a grassy bank beside a road or above a hill farm.

4   PEACEFUL COEXISTENCE

These components, then, are probabilistic and prototypical. The word "typically" should be understood before each of them. They do not have to be mutually compatible. The notion of something being at one and the same time an "(ABSTRACT) INSTITUTION and (PHYSICAL) LARGE BUILDING", for example, may be incoherent, but that only means that these two components are not activated simultaneously. They can still coexist peacefully as part of the word's meaning potential. By taking different combinations of components and showing how they combine, we can account economically and satisfactorily for the meaning in a remarkably large number of natural, ordinary uses.

This probabilistic componential approach also allows for vagueness.

(5)   Adam sat on the bank among the bulrushes.

Is the component "IS SLOPING" present or absent in (5)? The question is irrelevant: the component is potentially present, but not active. But it is possible to imagine continuations in which it suddenly becomes very active and highly relevant, for example if Adam slips *down* the bank and into the water.

If our analytic pump is primed with a set of probabilistic components of this kind, other procedures can be invoked. For example, semantic inheritances can be drawn from superordinates ("IS A BUILDING" implies "HAS A DOORWAY" – cf. (1); "IS AN INSTITUTION" implies "IS COGNITIVE" – cf. (6)).

(6)   The bank defended the terms of the agreement.

What's the downside? Well, it's not always clear which components are activated by which contexts. Against this: if it's not clear to a human being, then it can't be clear to a computer. Whereas if it's clear to a human being, then it is probably worth trying to state the criteria explicitly and compute over them. A new kind of phraseological dictionary is called for, showing how different aspects of word meaning are activated in different contexts, and what those contexts are, taking account of vagueness and variability in a precise way. See Hanks (1994) for suggestions about the form that such a phraseological dictionary might take.

A corpus-analytic procedure for counting how many times each feature is activated in a collection of texts has considerable predictive power. After examining even quite a modest number of corpus lines, we naturally begin to form hypotheses about the relative importance of the various semantic components to the normal uses of the word, and how they normally combine. In this way, a default interpretation can be calculated for each word, along with a range of possible variations.

5   EVENTS AND TRACES

What, then, is a word meaning?

In the everyday use of language, meanings are events, not entities. Do meanings also exist outside the transactional contexts in which they are used? It is a convenient shorthand to talk about "the meanings of words in a dictionary", but strictly speaking these are not meanings at all. Rather, they are "meaning potentials" – potential contributions to the meanings of texts and conversations in which the words are used, and activated by the speaker who uses them.

We cannot study word meanings directly through a corpus any more satisfactorily than we can study them through a dictionary. Both are tools, which may have a lot to contribute, but they get us only so far. Corpora consist of texts, which consist of traces of linguistic behaviour. What a corpus gives us is the opportunity to study traces and patterns of linguistic behaviour. There is no direct route from the corpus to the meaning. Corpus linguists sometimes speak as if interpretations spring fully fledged, untouched by human hand, from the corpus. They don't. The corpus contains traces of meaning events; the dictionary contains lists of meaning potentials. Mapping the one onto the other is a complex task, for which adequate tools and procedures remain to be devised.

The fact that the analytic task is complex, however, does not necessarily imply that the results need to be complex. We may well find that the components of meaning themselves are very simple, and that the complexity lies in establishing just how the different components combine.

6   MORE COMPLEX POTENTIALS: VERBS

Let us now turn to verbs. Verbs and nouns perform quite different clause roles. There is no reason to assume that the same kind of template is appropriate to both. The difference can be likened to that between male and female components of structures in mechanical engineering. On the one hand, the verbs assign semantic roles to the noun phrases in their environment. On the other hand, nouns (those eager suitors of verbs) have meaning potentials, activated when they fit (more or less well) into the verb frames. Together, they make human interaction possible. One of their functions, though not the only one, is to form propositions.

Propositions, not words, have entailments. But words can be used as convenient storage locations for conventional phraseology and for the entailments or implications that are associated with those bits of phraseology. (Implications are like entailments, but weaker, and they can be probabilistic. An implicature is an act in which a speaker makes or relies on an implication.)

Consider the different implications of these three fragments:

(7)   the two men who first climbed Mt Everest
(8)   He climbed a sycamore tree to get a better view.
(9)   He climbed a gate into a field.

(7) implies that the two men got to the top of Everest. (8) implies, less strongly, that the climber stopped part-way up the sycamore tree. (9) implies that he not only got to the top of the gate, but climbed down the other side. We would be hard put to it to answer the question, "Which particular word contributes this particular implicature?" Text meanings arise from combinations, not from any one word individually. Moreover, these are default interpretations, not necessary conditions. So although (7′) may sound slightly strange, it is not an out-and-out contradiction.

(7′) *They climbed Mount Everest but did not get to the top.

Meaning potentials are not only fuzzy, they are also hierarchically arranged, in a series of defaults. Each default interpretation is associated with a hierarchy of phraseological norms. Thus, the default interpretation of *climb* is composed of two components: CLAMBER and UP (see Fillmore 1982a) – but in (10), (11) and (12) the syntax favours one component over the other. Use of *climb* with an adverbial of direction activates the CLAMBER component, but not the UP component.

(10) I climbed into the back seat.
(11) Officers climbed in through an open window.
(12) A teacher came after me but I climbed through a hedge and sat tight for an hour or so.

This leads to a rather interesting twist: (13) takes a semantic component, UP, out of the meaning potential of *climb* and activates it explicitly. This is not mere redundancy: the word "up" is overtly stated precisely because the UP component of *climb* is not normally activated in this syntactic context.

(13) After breakfast we climbed up through a steep canyon.

7   SEMANTIC INDETERMINACY AND REMOTE CLUES

Let us now look at some examples where the meaning cannot be determined from the phraseology of the immediate context. These must be distinguished from errors and other unclassifiables. The examples are taken from a corpus-based study of *check*.

Check is a word of considerable syntactic complexity. Disregarding (for current purposes) an adjectival homograph denoting a kind of pattern (*a check shirt*), and turning off many other noises, we can zero in on the transitive verb *check*. This has two main sense components: INSPECT and CAUSE TO PAUSE/SLOW DOWN.

Surely, as a transitive verb, *check* cannot mean both "inspect" and "cause to pause or slow down" at the same time? (14) and (15) are obviously quite different meanings.

(14) It is not possible to check the accuracy of the figures.
(15) The DPK said that Kurdish guerrillas had checked the advance of government troops north of Sulaimaniya.

But then we come to sentences such as (16)–(18).

(16) Then the boat began to slow down. She saw that the man who owned it was hanging on to the side and checking it each time it swung.

Was the man inspecting it or was he stopping it? What is "it"? The boat or something else? The difficulty is only resolved by looking back through the story leading up to this sentence – looking back in fact, to the first mention of "boat" (16′).

(16′) "Work it out for yourself," she said, and then turned and ran. She heard him call after her and got into one of the swing boats with a pale, freckled little boy ...

Now it is clear that the boat in this story has nothing to do with vessels on water; it is a swinging ride at a fairground. The man, it turns out, is trying to cause it to slow down ("checking" it) because of a frightened child. This is a case where the relevant contextual clues are not in the immediate context. If we pay proper attention to textual cohesion, we are less likely to perceive ambiguity where there is none.

(17)   The Parliamentary Assembly and the Economic and Social Committee were primarily or wholly advisory in nature, with very little checking power.

In (17), the meaning is perfectly clear: the bodies mentioned had very little power to INSPECT and CAUSE TO PAUSE. Perhaps an expert on European bureaucracy might be able to say whether one component or the other of *check* was more activated, but the ordinary reader cannot be expected to make this choice, and the wider context is no help. The two senses of *check*, apparently in competition, here coexist in a single use, as indeed they do in the cliché *checks and balances*. By relying too heavily on examples such as (14) and (15), dictionaries have set up a false dichotomy.

(18)   Corporals checked kitbags and wooden crates and boxes ...

What were the corporals doing? It sounds as if they were inspecting something. But as we read on, the picture changes.

(18')   Sergeants rapped out indecipherable commands, corporals checked kitbags and wooden crates and boxes into the luggage vans.

The word *into* activates a preference for a different component of the meaning potential of *check*, identifiable loosely as CONSIGN, and associated with the cognitive prototype outlined in (19).

(19)   PERSON check BAGGAGE into TRANSPORT

No doubt INSPECT is present too, but the full sentence activates an image of corporals with checklists. Which is more or less where we came in.

8   WHERE COMPUTATIONAL ANALYSIS RUNS OUT

Finally, consider the following citation:

(20)   He soon returned to the Western Desert, where, between May and September, he was involved in desperate rearguard actions – the battle of Gazala, followed by Alamein in July, when Auchinleck checked Rommel, who was then within striking distance of Alexandria.

Without encyclopedic world knowledge, the fragment ... *Alamein in July, when Auchinleck checked Rommel* is profoundly ambiguous. I tried it on some English teenagers, and they were baffled. How do we know that Auchinleck was not checking Rommel for fleas or for contraband goods? Common sense may tell us that this is unlikely, but what textual clues are there to support common sense?

Where does the assignment of meaning come from?

- From internal text evidence, in particular the collocates? Relevant are the rather distant collocates *battle*, *rearguard actions*, and perhaps *striking distance*. These hardly seem close enough to be conclusive, and it is easy enough to construct a counterexample in the context of the same collocates (e.g. **before the battle, Auchinleck checked the deployment of his infantry*).

- From the domain? If this citation were from a military history textbook, that might be a helpful clue. Unfortunately, the extract actually comes from an obituary in the *Daily Telegraph*, which the BNC very sensibly does not attempt to subclassify. But anyway, domain is only a weak clue. Lesk (1986) observed that the sort of texts which talk about pine cones rarely also talk about ice-cream cones, but in this case domain classification is unlikely to produce the desired result, since military texts do talk about both *checking equipment* and *checking the enemy's advance*.
- From real-world knowledge? Auchinleck and Rommel were generals on opposing sides; the name of a general may be used metonymically for the army that he commands, and real-world knowledge tells us that armies *check* each other in the sense of halting an advance. This is probably close to psychological reality, but if it is all we have to go on, the difficulties of computing real-world knowledge satisfactorily start to seem insuperable.
- By assigning *Auchinleck* and *Rommel* to the lexical set [GENERAL]? This is similarly promising, but it relies on the existence of a metonymic exploitation rule of the following form:

$$\text{[GENERAL}_i\text{] checked [GENERAL}_j\text{]} = \text{[GENERAL}_i\text{]'s army checked}$$
$$(= \text{halted the advance of) [GENERAL}_j\text{]'s army.}$$

We are left with the uncomfortable conclusion that what seems perfectly obvious to a human being is deeply ambiguous to the more literal-minded computer, and that there is no easy way of resolving the ambiguity.

9 CONCLUSION

Do word meanings exist? The answer proposed in this discussion is "Yes, but..."

Yes, word meanings do exist, but traditional descriptions are misleading. Outside the context of a meaning event, in which there is participation of utterer and audience, words have meaning potentials, rather than just meaning. The meaning potential of each word is made up of a number of components, which may be activated cognitively by other words in the context in which it is used. These cognitive components are linked in a network which provides the whole semantic base of the language, with enormous dynamic potential for saying new things and relating the unknown to the known.

The target of "disambiguation" presupposes competition among different components or sets of components. And sometimes this is true. But we also find that the different components coexist in a single use, and that different uses activate a kaleidoscope of different combinations of components. So rather than asking questions about disambiguation and sense discrimination ("Which sense does this word have in this text?"), a better sort of question would be "What is the unique contribution of this word to the meaning of this text?"

A word's unique contribution is some combination of the components that make up its meaning potential, activated by contextual triggers. Components that are not triggered do not even enter the lists in the hypothetical disambiguation tournament. They do not even get started, because the context has already set a semantic frame into which only certain components will fit.

A major future task for computational lexicography will be to identify meaning components, the ways in which they combine, relations with the meaning components of semantically related words, and the phraseological circumstances in which they are activated.

The difficulty of identifying meaning components, plotting their hierarchies and relationships, and identifying the conditions under which they are activated should not blind us to the possibility that they may at heart be quite simple structures: much simpler, in fact, than anything found in a standard dictionary. But different.

9

"I Don't Believe in Word Senses"[1]

ADAM KILGARRIFF*

I INTRODUCTION

There is now a substantial literature on the problem of word sense disambiguation (WSD). The goal of WSD research is generally taken to be disambiguation between the senses given in a dictionary, thesaurus or similar. The idea is simple enough and could be stated as follows:

> Many words have more than one meaning. When a person understands a sentence with an ambiguous word in it, that understanding is built on the basis of just one of the meanings. So, as some part of the human language understanding process, the appropriate meaning has been chosen from the range of possibilities.

Stated in this way, it would seem that WSD might be a well-defined task, undertaken by a particular module within the human language processor. This module could then be modelled computationally in a WSD program, and this program, performing, as it did, one of the essential functions of the human language processor, would stand alongside a parser as a crucial component of a broad range of NLP applications. This point of view is clearly represented in Cottrell (1989):

> [Lexical ambiguity] is perhaps the most important problem facing an NLU system. Given that the goal of NLU is understanding, correctly determining the meanings of the words used is fundamental.... The tack taken here is that it is important to understand how people resolve the ambiguity problem, since whatever their approach, it appears to work rather well. (p. 1)

Word meaning is of course a venerable philosophical topic, and questions of the relation between the signifier and the signified will never be far from the theme of the paper. However, philosophical discussions have not addressed the fact of lexicography and the theoretical issues raised by sense distinctions as marked in dictionaries. We often have strong intuitions about words having multiple meanings, and lexicography aims to capture them, systematically and consistently. The philosophy literature does not provide a taxonomy of the processes underpinning the intuition, nor does it analyse the relations between the word sense distinctions a dictionary makes and the primary data of naturally-occurring language. This is a gap that this paper aims to fill.

* Kilgarriff, A. (1997e). 'I don't believe in word senses', *Computers and the Humanities*, Kluwer Academic Publishers, 31(2): 91–113.

[1] Sue Atkins – Past President, European Association for Lexicography; General Editor, Collins-Robert English/French Dictionary; Lexicographical Adviser, Oxford University Press – responding to a discussion which assumed discrete and disjoint word senses, at "The Future of the Dictionary" workshop, Uriage-les-Bains, October 1994.

I show, first, that Cottrell's construal of word senses is at odds with theoretical work on the lexicon (section 2); then, that the various attempts to provide the concept "word sense" with secure foundations over the last thirty years have all been unsuccessful (section 3). I then consider the lexicographers' understanding of what they are doing when they make decisions about a word's senses, and develop an alternative conception of the word sense, in which it corresponds to a cluster of citations for a word (section 4). Citations are clustered together where they exhibit similar patterning and meaning. The various possible relations between a word's meaning potential and its dictionary senses are catalogued and illustrated with corpus evidence.

The implication for WSD is that there is no reason to expect a single set of word senses to be appropriate for different NLP applications. Different corpora, and different purposes, will lead to different senses. In particular, the sets of word senses presented in different dictionaries and thesauri have been prepared, for various purposes, for various human users: there is no reason to believe those sets are appropriate for any NLP application.

2   THESIS AND ANTITHESIS: PRACTICAL WSD AND THEORETICAL LEXICOLOGY

2.1   Thesis

NLP has stumbled into word sense ambiguity.

Within the overall shape of a natural language understanding system – morphological analysis, parsing, semantic and pragmatic interpretation – word sense ambiguity first features as an irritation. It does not appear as a matter of particular linguistic interest, and can be avoided altogether simply by treating all words as having just one meaning. Rather, it is a snag: if you have both river *bank* and money *bank* in your lexicon, when you see the word *bank* in an input text you are at risk of selecting the wrong one. There is a practical problem to be solved, and since Margaret Masterman's group started examining it in the 1950s (see, e.g., Sparck Jones, 1986), people have been writing programs to solve it.

NLP has not found it easy to give a very principled answer to the question, "what goes in the lexicon". Before the mid-1980s, many systems made no claims to wide coverage and contained only as many words in the lexicon as were needed for the "toy" texts that were going to be analysed. A word was only made ambiguous – that is, given multiple lexical entries – if it was one that the researchers had chosen as a subject for the disambiguation study. This was clearly not an approach that was sustainable for wide coverage systems, and interest developed in dictionaries, as relatively principled, wide-coverage sources of lexical information.

As machine-readable versions of dictionaries started to become available, so it became possible to write experimental WSD programs on the basis of the dictionary's verdict as to what a word's senses were (Lesk, 1986; Jensen and Binot, 1987; Slator, 1988; Véronis and Ide, 1990; Guthrie *et al.*, 1990; Guthrie *et al.*, 1991; Dolan, 1994). Looked at the other way round, WSD was one of the interesting things you might be able to do with these exciting new resources.

Since then, with the advent of language corpora and the rapid growth of statistical work in NLP, the number of possibilities for how you might go about WSD has mushroomed, as has the quantity of work on the subject (Brown *et al.*, 1991; Hearst, 1991; McRoy, 1992; Gale, Church, and Yarowsky, 1992; Yarowsky, 1992). Clear (1994), Schütze and Pederson (1995) and Yarowsky (1995) are of particular interest because of their approach to the issue of the set of word senses to be disambiguated between. Schütze and Pederson devised high-dimensionality vectors to describe the context of each occurrence of their target word, and then clustered these vectors. They claim that the better-defined of these clusters correspond to word senses, so a new occurrence of the word can be disambiguated by representing its context as a vector and identifying which cluster centroid the vector is closest to. This system has the characteristic that a context may be close to more than one cluster centroid, so at times it may be appropriate to classify it as more than one sense.

Both Clear (1994) and Yarowsky (1995) provide a mechanism for the user to input the senses between which they would like the system to disambiguate. They ask the user to classify a small number of statistically-selected "seed" collocates, so the user determines the senses to be disambiguated between when deciding on the senses he or she will assign seed collocates to.[2] Clear then finds all the words which tend to co-occur with the node word in a large corpus, and quantifies, for a very large number of words, the evidence that it occurs with each of the seeds, and thus indirectly, with each sense of the node word. Disambiguation then proceeds by summing the evidence for each sense provided by each context word.

Yarowsky's method is iterative: first, those corpus lines for the node word which contain one of the seed collocates are classified. Then the set of corpus lines so classified is examined for further indicators of one or other of the senses of the word. These indicators are sorted, according to the strength of evidence they provide for a sense. It will now be possible to classify a larger set of corpus lines, so producing more indicators for each sense, and the process can be continued until all, or an above-threshold proportion, of the corpus lines for the word are classified. The ordered list of sense-indicators will then serve as a disambiguator for new corpus lines.

In the Semantic Concordance project at Princeton a lexicographic team has been assigning a WordNet (Miller, 1990a – see also Miller *et al.* 1990 reprinted in this volume, *Ed.*) sense to each noun, verb, adjective and adverb in a number of texts, thus providing a "gold standard" disambiguated corpus which can be used for training and evaluating WSD programs (Landes, Leacock and Tengi, 1998).

In 1994–95, there was an extended discussion of whether WSD should be one of the tasks in the MUC program.[3] This would have provided for competitive evaluation of different NLP groups' success at the WSD task, as measured against a "benchmark" corpus, in which each word had been manually tagged with the appropriate WordNet sense number (as in the Semantic Concordance). Some trials took place, but the decision was not to proceed with the WSD task as part of the 1996 MUC-6 evaluation, as there was insufficient time to debate and define detailed policies. The theme has recently been taken up by the Lexicons Special Interest Group of the Association for Computational Linguistics, and a pilot evaluation exercise is taking place in 1998: a milestone on the road from research to technology (Resnik and Yarowsky, 1997; Kilgarriff, 1997a).

2.2   Antithesis

Since the publication of *Metaphors We Live By* (Lakoff and Johnson, 1980) and *Women, Fire, and Dangerous Things* (Lakoff, 1987), there has been one approach to linguistics – cognitive linguistics – for which metaphor has been a central phenomenon. Metaphor is, amongst other things, a process whereby words spawn additional meanings, and cognitive linguists are correspondingly interested in polysemy. Lakoff's analysis of the polysemy of

---

[2] In Yarowsky's work, this is just one of the options for providing seeds for the process.

[3] The MUC (Message Understanding Conference) is a series of US Government-funded, competitive, quantitatively-evaluated exercises in information extraction (MUC-5, 1994).

mother is hugely cited. Word sense ambiguity can often be seen as a trace of the fundamental processes underlying language understanding (Sweetser, 1990). The structures underlying the distinct meanings of words are at the heart of the cognitive linguistics enterprise (Geeraerts, 1990; Taylor, 1989).

Working in this framework, Cruse (1995) gives a detailed typology of polysemy. He distinguishes polysemy, defined according to distinctness of meaning, from polylexy, which is where, in addition to distinctness of meaning, distinct lexical entries are required. A word is polysemous but not polylexic where its non-base meanings are predictable, so they can be generated as required and need not be stored. He also addresses where readings are antagonistic and where they are not, and the characteristics of the different semantic properties, or "facets", of a sense. He uses ambiguity tests to tease out a number of issues, and a full Cruse lexical entry would contain: a specification of polysemous senses; their lexical relations including their relations to each other; whether they were antagonistic or not; the facets, shared or otherwise, of each, and the extent to which distinct facets of meaning could operate autonomously, so approach the status of senses on their own. He considers several varieties of "semi-distinct" readings.

Lexical ambiguity has also moved centre-stage within theoretical and computational linguistics. Both AAAI and ACL have recently devoted workshops to the topic.[4] When Pustejovsky and others discuss the generative lexicon (Pustejovsky, 1991; Briscoe, Copestake, and Boguraev, 1990), the generative processes they have in mind are, again, ones whereby words spawn additional meanings (or, at least, additional uses). Regular polysemy (Apresjan, 1974) has recently been discussed, and computational mechanisms for addressing it proposed, by Ostler and Atkins (1992), Kilgarriff and Gazdar (1995) and Copestake and Briscoe (1995), *inter alia*. Levin and colleagues have also been finding systematicity in lexical ambiguity, in relation to verb classes, their patterns of subcategorisation, and their patterns of alternation (Levin and Rappoport Hovav, 1991; Levin, 1993; Levin, Song, and Atkins, 1997).

This combination of circumstances leads to an odd situation. Much WSD work proceeds on the basis of there being a computationally relevant, or useful, or interesting, set of word senses in the language, approximating to those stated in a dictionary. To the WSD community, word senses are, more or less, as the dictionary says.[5] (This is not, of course, to say that WSD authors have not noted the theoretical problems associated with dictionary's word senses.) WSD research has gone a long way on this basis: it is now common for papers to present quantitative comparisons between the performance of different systems. Meanwhile, the theoreticians provide various kinds of reason to believe there is no such set of senses. To get beyond this impasse, we need to look more closely at the question, "what is a word sense?".

3   WHAT IS A WORD SENSE?

No entity without identity (Quine, 1969)

Or, to know what something is, is to know when something is it. To know what a word sense s_1 is, is to know which uses of the word are part of s_1 and which are not, probably because they are part of s_i where $i \neq 1$. If we are to know what word senses are, we need operational criteria for distinguishing them.

---

[4] The AAAI Spring Symposium on Representation and Acquisition of Lexical Information, Stanford, April 1995 and the ACL SIGLEX Workshop on The Breadth and Depth of Semantic Lexicons, Santa Cruz, June 1996.

[5] Sometimes not all the sense distinctions recognised in the dictionary are viewed as salient to the program. WSD researchers tend to be lumpers, not splitters (Dolan, 1994).

3.1   Selection and modulation

A good starting point is Cruse's textbook on Lexical Semantics (Cruse, 1986). "Lexical units" are the object of his enquiry, and he devotes two substantial chapters to specifying what they are. He states the heart of the problem thus:

> One of the basic problems of lexical semantics is the apparent multiplicity of semantic uses of a single word form (without grammatical difference).

He addresses in some detail the difference between those cases where the context **selects** a distinct unit of sense, from those where it **modulates** the meaning. In the pair

> Have you put the money in the bank?
> The rabbit climbed up the bank.

the two sentences select different meanings of *bank*, whereas in

> Raphael doesn't often oil his bike.
> Madeleine dried off her bike.
> Boris's bike goes like the wind.

different aspects of the bicycle – its mechanical parts; its frame, saddle and other large surfaces; its (and its rider's) motion – are highlighted in each case. The meaning of *bike* is modulated differently by each context.[6]

3.2   Ambiguity tests

The selection/modulation distinction is closely related to the distinction between ambiguity and generality, also referred to as "vagueness", "indeterminacy" and "lack of specification".[7] Where a word is ambiguous, a sense is selected. Where a word-meaning is general between two readings, any particular context may or may not modulate the word-meaning to specify one or other of the readings. Thus, *hand* is unspecified between right hands and left hands; some sentences modulate the meaning to specify a right or left hand, as in "When saluting, the hand should just touch the forehead", while others do not.[8]

Clearly, *bank* is ambiguous between the readings demonstrated above; *bike* is not. But for many reading-pairs, the answer is not clear:[9]

- I planted out three rows of beans yesterday.
  Cook the beans in salted water.
- The cottage was charming.
  Our hosts were charming.
- Bother! I was about to talk to John, but now he's disappeared! (NOT-HERE)
  I can't find it anywhere, it seems to have disappeared. (CAN'T-FIND)

---

[6] Cruse identifies two major varieties of modulation, of which highlighting is one.

[7] See Zwicky and Sadock (1975) for a fuller discussion of the terms and their sources.

[8] Also related to this distinction is the polysemy/homonymy distinction: when do we have two distinct words, and when, one word with two meanings? Most commentators agree that there is a gradation between the two, with the distinction being of limited theoretical interest. For some purposes, the distinction may be more useful than the vagueness/ambiguity one (Krovetz, 1996). In practice, similar difficulties arise in distinguishing homonymy from polysemy, as in distinguishing vagueness from ambiguity.

[9] The examples are taken by comparing four state-of-the-art English learners' dictionaries (LDOCE, 1995; OALD5, 1995; COBUILD, 1995; CIDE, 1995) and finding words where the lexicographers in one team made one decision regarding what the distinct word senses were, whereas those in another made another. This immediately has the effect of introducing various factors which have not been considered in earlier theoretical discussions.

A number of tests have been proposed for determining whether a word is ambiguous or general between two meanings. They are catalogued in Zwicky and Sadock (1975), Cruse (1986), ten Hacken (1990), Kilgarriff (1992) and Geeraerts (1993). Here, I shall describe only one of the more successful tests, the "crossed readings" one.

Mary arrived with a pike and so did Agnes.

could mean that each arrived with a carnivorous fish, or that each arrived bearing a long-handled medieval weapon, but not that the one arrived with the fish and the other with the weapon. On the other hand, in

Tom raised his hand and so did Dick.

each might have raised a right hand, each might have raised a left, or one might have raised his right, and the other, his left. The question now is, in

Ellen bought some beans, and so did Harry.

is it possible that Ellen bought plants and Harry, food? If so, then the conclusion to be drawn from the test is that *bean* is ambiguous between the readings, and if not, then it is not.[10]

3.2.1   Criticisms of the tests

The tests are generally presented with the aid of an unproblematical example of ambiguity and an unproblematical example of vagueness. This is done in order to demonstrate what the test is and what the two contrasting outcomes are. However, this is not to use the tests in anger. What we want of a test is that it is consistent with our intuitions, where our intuitions are clear, and that it resolves the question, where our intuitions are unclear. The cross-reading test fares tolerably well in meeting the consistency condition (though see Geeraerts 1993 for a contrary view). But do the tests help where intuitions are unclear? There is little if any evidence that they do. Here I discuss three classes of problems.

Firstly, it must be possible to construct a plausible test sentence. The word in its two uses must be able to occur with the same syntax and the same lexico-grammatical environment. Consider the transitive and intransitive uses of *eat*, as in "John ate the apple" and "John ate". Is this a case of ambiguity or vagueness?

*Mary ate, and John, the apple.

is unacceptable, but the reason is that elided constituents must have the same syntax and subcategorisation in both their expressed and elided occurrences. It might be desirable to treat all words with alternative subcategorisation possibilities as ambiguous. But whether or not that is done, the test still fails to elucidate on the topic of a word's meaning, where the word has different syntax in different uses. The test can only be posed where the two uses are syntactically similar.

---

[10] For many putatively ambiguous reading-pairs, there are intermediate cases. A sprouting bean, or one bought for planting, is intermediate between FOOD and PLANT. But the possibility of intermediate cases does not preclude ambiguity: whether two readings of a word are completely disjoint, permitting no intermediate cases, is a different question to whether a word is ambiguous. This imposes a further constraint on ambiguity tests. A speaker might say, "Ellen and Harry must have bought the same kind of *bean*, unless, say, Ellen bought plants and Harry bought beans sold at the supermarket but which he was intending to plant". We should not infer that *bean* is vague. Rather, we must insist that both of the crossed readings are prototypical. (There are of course further difficulties in making this constraint precise.)

The *disappear* example displays a different variant of this problem. The CAN'T-FIND and NOT-HERE readings have different aspectual characteristics: CAN'T-FIND is stative while NOT-HERE is a punctual "achievement" verb.

Martha disappeared and so did Maud.

does not permit a crossed reading, but that is because we cannot construct a viable aspectual interpretation for the conjoined sentence, compare

? I evicted and knew her.[11]

It is not evident whether there is a conclusion to be drawn regarding polysemy.

In general, one can apply more or less effort into trying to find a test sentence (and associated context) in which the crossed reading is plausible. A test is clearly flawed if, the more ingenuity the investigator displays, the more of one particular outcome he or she will get. (The crossed reading test is the test which suffers least from this flaw, but it is nonetheless in evidence.)

The second point is more general and theoretical. A certain amount of interpretation of an utterance must have been undertaken before an acceptability judgement can be made. Three parts of the interpretation process are lexical access, parsing, and "pragmatic interpretation", the final stage of incorporating the new information into the discourse model. The premise behind acceptability judgements is that a subject can report on the outcome of the first two stages, irrespective of what goes on in the third. For a wide range of syntactic questions, the methodology is widely used and has proved its worth.

Nunberg (1978)'s arguments illustrate the hazards of the premise for questions in lexical semantics. Consider

The newspaper costs 25p and sacked all its staff.

It is anomalous. We cannot place the origin of the anomaly in the lexicon unless we grant the word two lexical entries, one for a copy of the newspaper and one for the owner or corporate entity. Then the size of our lexicon will start to expand, as we list more and more of the possible kinds of referent for the word, and still it will never be complete. So the origin of the anomaly must be the interpretation process. But the anomaly seems similar to the anomaly that occurs with *bank*. In a case lying between *newspaper* and *bank*, how would we know whether the source of the anomaly was the lexicon or the interpretation process? In the general case the point at which the lexical process becomes a general-purpose interpretative one cannot be identified. There is no accessible intermediate representation in which lexical ambiguities are resolved (for acceptable sentences) but in which the contents of the sentence have not been incorporated into the hearer's interpretation of the discourse. Geeraerts (1993) presents an extensive critique of the tests along these lines, presenting evidence that the different tests give contradictory results, and that even if we constrain ourselves to looking at just one of the tests, they can all be made to give contradictory results by manipulating the context in which the item under scrutiny is set.

The third problem is simply the lack of evidence that the tests give stable results. It will sometimes happen that, for the same reading-pair, an informant will deem crossed readings possible for some test sentences and not for others. Or different informants will have conflicting opinions. There are, remarkably, no careful discussions of these issues in the literature. The merit of the method of acceptability judgements for syntax rests on the relative stability

---

[11] Eight out of ten informants found the related sentence, "I loved and married her", odd. The two who found it acceptable were reading *and* as an indicator of temporal sequence.

of their outcomes: they work (to the extent they do) because linguists agree where the stars belong. Preliminary investigations into the stability of outcomes in lexical semantics suggest that it is severely lacking.

3.3   Psycholinguistics and "semantic priming"

There is a set of findings in psycholinguistics which might allow us to base an account of "word sense" directly on the mental lexicon. The experimental paradigm is called "semantic priming". It is well-established that, if I have just heard the word *doctor* (the "prime"), and then a sequence of letters (the "target") is flashed up on a screen and I am asked to identify whether it is a word or not, I respond faster if it is a word and it is *nurse* than if it is a word but unrelated to *doctor*.[12]

If an ambiguous prime such as *bank* is given, it turns out that both *river* and *money* are primed for. If *bank* is presented in isolation, priming for both *river* and *money* is found for another second or two. In a context which serves to make only one of these appropriate, after something between 50 and 200 ms a choice is made and after that only the appropriate target is primed for.

So, for ambiguous words, priming behaviour has a distinct "signature". Perhaps it is possible to identify whether a word is vague or ambiguous by seeing whether it exhibits this signature.

The hypothesis is explored by Williams (1992). He looked at adjectives, for example *firm*, for which the two readings were represented by *solid* and *strict*. After confirming that the prime, *firm*, in isolation, primed equally for *solid* and *strict*, he tested to see if *solid* was primed for when *firm* occurred in a STRICT context, and *vice versa*, after delays of 250, 500 and 850 ms.

His results were asymmetrical. He identified central meanings (SOLID) and non-central ones (STRICT). Where the context favoured the central reading, the non-central-sense targets were not primed for. But when the context favoured the non-central reading, central targets were. The experiments provide evidence that the various meanings of polysemous words are not functionally independent in language comprehension, and that not all senses are equal, in their representation in the mental lexicon. Williams discusses the asymmetrical results in terms of hierarchical meaning structures.

Priming experiments do show potential for providing a theoretical grounding for distinguishing ambiguity and generality, but more work needs to be done, and the outcome would not be a simple, two-way, ambiguous/general distinction. Also, the method would never be practical for determining the numbers of senses for a substantial number of words. The results of the experiments are just not sufficiently stable: as Williams says, the priming task "suffers from a large degree of item and subject variability" (p. 202).

4   LEXICOGRAPHERS, DICTIONARIES, AND AUTHORITY

What set of procedures do lexicographers have available to them to pin down those protean entities, "meanings"? Faced with the almost unimaginable diversity of the language they are trying to describe, with the knowledge that what for the sake of convenience we are pleased to call a language is in many ways a synthesis of shifting patterns that change from year to year, from locality to locality, from idiolect

---

[12] This is the "lexical decision" task in a mixed, visual and auditory procedure. It is one of a variety of versions of semantic priming experiments. The basic effect is robust across a number of experimental strategies.

to idiolect, how do they arrive at those masterpieces of consensus, dictionaries? How do they decide what, for the purposes of a dictionary, constitutes the meaning of a word, and where, in the case of polysemous words, one meaning ends and the next begins? (Ayto, 1983: 89).

In the middle of this debate stand the lexicographers. The word senses that most WSD researchers aim to discriminate are the product of their intellectual labours. But this is far from the purpose for which the dictionary was written.

Firstly, any working lexicographer is well aware that, every day, they are making decisions on whether to "lump" or "split" senses that are inevitably subjective:[13] frequently, the alternative decision would have been equally valid. In fact, most dictionaries encode a variety of relations in the grey area between "same sense" and "different sense": see Kilgarriff (1993) for a description of the seven methods used in LDOCE2 (1987).

Secondly, any particular dictionary is written with a particular target audience in mind, and with a particular editorial philosophy in relation to debates such as "lumping *vs.* splitting", so the notion of specifying a set of word senses for a language in isolation from any particular user group will be alien to them.

Thirdly, many are aware of the issues raised by Lakoff, Levin, Pustejovsky and others, with several lexicographers bringing valuable experience of the difficulties of sense-division to that literature (see below).

Fourthly, the weight of history: publishers expect to publish, bookshops expect to sell, and buyers expect to buy and use dictionaries which, for each word, provide a (possibly nested) list of possible meanings or uses. Large sums of money are invested in lexicographic projects, on the basis that a dictionary has the potential to sell hundreds of thousands of copies. Investors will not lightly adopt policies which make their product radically different to the one known to sell. However inappropriate the nested list might be as a representation of the facts about a word, for all but the most adventurous lexicographic projects, nothing else is possible.[14]

The division of a word's meaning into senses is forced onto lexicographers by the economic and cultural setting within which they work. Lexicographers are obliged to describe words as if all words had a discrete, non-overlapping set of senses. It does not follow that they do, nor that lexicographers believe that they do.

---

[13] **Lumping** is considering two slightly different patterns of usage as a single meaning. **Splitting** is the converse: dividing or separating them into different meanings.

[14] The format of the dictionary has remained fairly stable since Dr. Johnson's day. The reasons for the format, and the reasons it has proved so resistant to change and innovation, are explored at length in Nunberg (1994). In short, the development of printed discourse, particularly the new periodicals, in England in the early part of the eighteenth century brought about a re-evaluation of the nature of meaning. No longer could it be assumed that a disagreement or confusion about a word's meaning could be settled face-to-face, and it seemed at the time that the new discourse would only be secure if there was some mutually acceptable authority on what words meant. The resolution to the crisis came in the form of Johnson's Dictionary. Thus, from its inception, the modern dictionary has had a crucial symbolic role: it represents a methodology for resolving questions of meaning. Hence "the dictionary", with its implications of unique reference and authority (cf. "the Bible") (Leech, 1974). Further evidence for this position is to be found in McArthur (1987), for whom the "religious or quasi-religious tinge" (p. 38) to reference materials is an enduring theme in their history; Summers (1988), whose research into dictionary use found that "settl[ing] family arguments" was one of its major uses (p. 114, cited in Béjoint (1994: 151); and Moon (1989) who catalogues the use of the UAD (Unidentified Authorising Dictionary) from newspapers' letters pages to restaurant advertising materials (pp. 60–64).

The implications for ambiguity are this: to solve disputes about meaning, a dictionary must be, above all, clear. It must draw a line around a meaning, so that a use can be classified as on one side of the line or the other. A dictionary which dwells on marginal or vague uses of a word, or which presents its meaning as context-dependent or variable or flexible, will be of little use for purposes of settling arguments. The pressure from this quarter is for the dictionary to present a set of discrete, non-overlapping meanings for a word, each defined by the necessary and sufficient conditions for its application – whatever the facts of the word's usage.

4.1   Lexicographical literature

Lexicographers write dictionaries rather than writing about writing dictionaries. Little has been written that answers the challenge posed by Ayto in the quotation above. Zgusta's influential *Manual* (1971), while stating that the specification of word meaning is the central task for the lexicographer (p. 23) and the division of a word's meanings into senses is a central part of that, gives little guidance beyond admonishments to avoid making too many, or too few, distinctions (pp. 66–67).

Ayto's own offering in the 1983 paper is the "classical" or "analytic" definition, comprising genus and differentiae. In choosing the genus term, the lexicographer must take care to select one that is neither too general – *entity* would not do as a genus term for *tiger* – nor too specific, if the specific genus term is likely to be unknown by the dictionary users. Where two meanings of a word have different genus terms, they need treating as different senses. The next task is to identify the differentiae required to separate out senses falling under the same genus term. He discusses *cup*, and argues that there are three senses, one for the "trophy" sense, one for the varieties standardly made of china or earthenware, and one for the prototypically plastic or paper varieties. But his consideration of the arguments for treating the second and third of these as distinct ends in a welter of open questions.

Stock (1984 – see also in this volume, *Ed.*) is a response to Ayto's piece, and finds it wanting, firstly, in the circularity involved in using different genus terms to identify distinct senses – the lexicographer will only look for distinct genus terms after determining there are distinct senses – and secondly, in that the model cannot be applied to many words. She looks closely at *culture*, noting how different dictionaries have divided the territory that the word covers in quite different ways, and observes,

It is precisely the lack of clarity in our use of the word *culture* which makes it such a handy word to have at one's disposal. It offers, as it were, semantic extras just because in most uses its possible meanings are not clearly disambiguated.... What can the dictionary maker do to reflect this state of affairs?... They do not, cannot by their very structure, show that there is slippage between some of the senses that they give but not between others. (p. 139)

Hanks (1994), looking at *climb*, and Fillmore and Atkins (1992), studying the semantic field centred on *risk*, make similar comments about the inadequacies of dictionary conventions, and appeal to prototype theory and frame semantics for richer frameworks to describe the relationships between the different ways a word (or word-family) is used.

Stock, Hanks and Atkins were all involved in the early stages of the COBUILD project, which, in the early 1980s, broke new ground in lexicography through its use of very large computerised language corpora (Sinclair *et al.*, 1987). Good lexicographic practice had long used huge citation indexes, but being able to see hundreds of instances of a word in context, ordinary and extraordinary examples thrown together, was a radical development. It has changed how lexicographers think about meaning. Where Ayto's paper offers semantic analysis, Stock presents corpus evidence. The lexicographer's primary source of evidence for how a word behaves switches from subjective to objective; from introspection to looking at contexts.

4.2   A corpus-based model of word senses

This suggests a quite different answer to the question, "what is a word sense?" Corpus lexicography proceeds approximately as follows. For each word, the lexicographer

1. calls up a concordance[15] for the word;
2. divides the concordance lines into clusters, so that, as far as possible, all members of each cluster have much in common with each other, and little in common with members of other clusters;
3. for each cluster, works out what it is that makes its members belong together, reorganising clusters as necessary;
4. takes these conclusions and codes them in the highly constrained language of a dictionary definition.

Putting the concordance lines into clusters is data-driven rather than theory-driven. The lexicographer may or may not be explicitly aware of the criteria according to which he or she is clustering.[16] (It is a requirement for corpus lexicography software that it supports manual clustering (Atkins, 1993; CorpusBench, 1993; Schulze and Christ, 1994).) Stage 3 is just a fallible *post hoc* attempt to make the criteria explicit. The senses that eventually appear in the dictionary are the result, at several removes, of the basic clustering process.

Ambiguity tests failed to provide us with an account of what it meant for two uses of a word to belong to the same word sense. Once we operationalise "word sense" as "dictionary word sense", we now have a test that meets the challenge. The identity test for a word sense in a particular dictionary is that two usages of the word belong to it if and only if the lexicographer would have put them in the same cluster.[17]

We can now present a different perspective on the ambiguity/generality debate. Where a word's uses fall into two entirely distinct clusters, it is ambiguous, but where the clusters are less well-defined and distinct, "vague" or "unspecified" may be a more appropriate description. There is no reason to expect to find any clear distinction between the two types of cases.

5   USE, FREQUENCY, PREDICTABILITY AND THE WORD SENSE

"Clustering" is a metaphor. It regards corpus lines as points in space with measurable distances between them. To give the account substance, more must be said about the ways in which corpus lines may be "close". In this section, I classify the types of relationships that hold between a word's patterns of usage, and consider how these considerations relate to lexicography.[18]

There are five knowledge sources which come into play for understanding how a word contributes to the meaning or communicative intent of the utterance or discourse it occurs in. If a word in context is interpretable by a language user, it will be by virtue of these knowledge sources.

Whether a dictionary provides a word sense that matches an instance of use of the word, is dictated by considerations of frequency and predictability: if the instance exemplifies a pattern of use which is sufficiently frequent, and is insufficiently predictable from other meanings

---

[15] By "concordance" I mean a display which presents a line of context for each occurrence of the word under scrutiny in the corpus, with all occurrences of the key word aligned. Fuller details are, of course, system specific, but it has rapidly become evident that this kind of display is the basic requirement for any corpus lexicography system.

[16] The interactions between the lexicographers' clusters and the automatic clusters produced for Information Retrieval purposes (Schütze and Pederson, 1995), and the potential for automating some of the clustering that the lexicographer performs, are subjects of current research.

[17] A psycholinguistic investigation along these lines is presented in Jorgensen (1990).

[18] I do not dwell on cases of simple similarity, where there is a straightforward match between corpus lines, or between a corpus line and a word's core meaning. While it is a major language-engineering problem to operationalise even "simple similarity", it is not a problematic matter, either theoretically or for lexicographers or other human language users.

or uses of the word, then the pattern qualifies for treatment as a dictionary sense. A use is predictable, to the extent that a person reading or hearing it for the first time can understand it (in all its connotations). Clearly, different dictionaries have different thresholds of frequency and predictability.

To illustrate the various processes whereby new types of usage may be added to the repertoire for a word, let us consider the simple single-sense word, *handbag*:

a small bag, used by women to carry money and personal things (British; American English translation: purse)   (LDOCE3)

As the 715 examples in the British National Corpus (BNC)[19] make plain, typical uses involve things being put into, or taken out of, or looked for in handbags, or handbags being lost, found, stolen, manufactured, admired, bought or sold. But a couple of dozen examples stretch the limits of the definition or fall outside it altogether.

First, a proper name, and a reference to a unique object:

the Drowning Handbag, an up-market eatery in the best part of town
an inimitable rendering of the handbag speech in The Importance of Being Earnest

Next, metonymy, visual metaphor, simile:

She moved from handbags through gifts to the flower shop
"How about you? Did the bouncing handbag find you?"[20]
a weird, menacing building with bats hanging in the trees like handbags
Skin generally starting to age like old handbag or bodywork of car

Next, Mrs Thatcher:

from Edward Heath's hip-pocket to Margaret Thatcher's handbag and on to Mr Major's glass of warm beer
"Thousands . . . will be disgusted at the way she [Thatcher] is lining her handbag"
send out Mrs Thatcher with a fully-loaded handbag
"If you want to define the Thatcher-and-after era in a single phrase", he muses, " 'accountants with plenary powers' says it." Well now – I would have gone for something a little snappier: 'A mad cow with a handbag,' comes to mind as a first attempt.
She [Thatcher] cannot see an institution without hitting it with her handbag.

The last of these is cited in another citation as the launching-point of verbal *handbag*. Of the three verbal citations, all were species of hitting and in two of them, Mrs Thatcher was the perpetrator.

Next, and closely related to Mrs Thatcher, "handbag as weapon":

Meg swung her handbag.
determined women armed with heavy handbags
it was time to race the old ladies back to the village for the tea and scones of Beck Hall. I beat them, but only just – those handbags are lethal.
old ladies continue to brandish their handbags and umbrellas at the likes of Giant Haystacks

---

[19] For the BNC see http://info.ox.ac.uk/bnc. Counts were: *handbag* 609, *handbags* 103, *handbagging* 1, *handbagged* 2.

[20] This turns out to be a (sexist and homophobic) in-group joke, as well as a case of both metonymy and of a distinct idiomatic use of the word. Interestingly, in the text, "the bouncing handbag" succeeds in referring, even though the idiom is not known to the addressee, as is made explicit in the text.

the blue rinse brigade . . . will be able to turn out in force without having to travel and give poor Louis Gerstner the handbagging of his life.

Peterborough manager Chris Turner added: "Evidently one of their players caught one of our players and it was handbags at 10 paces and then someone threw a punch."

The final, quite distinct group relates to discos, and the lexical unit *dance round your handbag*, a pejorative phrase for the behaviour of certain exclusively female groups at discotheques and dances where – prototypically – they dance in a circle with their handbags on the floor in the middle. The conversational speech subcorpus of the BNC provides two instances of the full form while in the written corpus, the two related corpus lines, both from music journalism, make only fleeting references to the collocation, and strikingly indicate a process of lexicalisation:

The shoot was supposed to be a secret, but word got out and Hitman regulars travelled down to Manchester. Two thousand couldn't get into the club, and tension mounted between trendy regulars (locked out of their own club) and the Hitman's handbag brigade (shut out of their programme).

   New Yawk drawling rap over Kraftwerk's 'The Model' just does not work, no way, no how. Handbag DJs will love it.

All these uses can be traced back to the standard sense: the potential for using the word in the nonstandard way is (in varying degrees) **predictable** from

- its standard meaning and use
- general linguistic knowledge (e.g. of processes of metonymy, regular polysemy, and ellipsis, etc., and, in this case, the relation between words for goods and words for shops or departments of shops where those goods are sold)
- general world knowledge (e.g. regarding Mrs Thatcher, or juvenile female behaviour at discotheques)
- knowledge of related collocations (e.g. "lining their pockets", "WEAPON at NUMBER paces")
- taxonomic knowledge

These five knowledge sources define the conceptual space within which lexical creativity and productivity, and the idea of a "word sense", are located.[21]

Needless to say, they frequently interact in complex ways. In "handbags at ten paces", the speaker[22] assumes the addressee's awareness of handbag-as-weapon. Note that "*briefcases at ten paces" and "*shoulder-bags at ten paces" do not carry the same meaning. Although briefcases and shoulder-bags are just as viable weapons as handbags, the words *briefcase* and *shoulder-bag* do not carry the "weapon" connotations which make the citation immediately understandable. Handbag-as-weapon is a feature of the word, over and above the extent to which it is a feature of the denotation.

In the citation's context, there is no overt reason for a reference to *handbag*; the people involved are men, not women, so not prototypical handbag-users, and there is no other reference to femininity. It would appear that the speaker is aiming to both distance himself from and minimise the significance of the incident by treating it as a joke. The "duel" metaphor is itself a joke, and the oddity of *handbag* in the context of either football or duel, along

---

[21] In Kilgarriff (1992), in the context of an analysis of polysemy, I call the first four knowledge types HOMONYMY, ALTERNATION, ANALOGY and COLLOCATION. (Taxonomy is addressed separately.)

[22] This is presented as a quotation of a football manager's spoken comment; quite whether it is verbatim, or the *Daily Telegraph* journalist's paraphrase, we shall never know.

with its associations with femininity and Mrs Thatcher, contributes to the effect. Moreover, there is a sexist implication that the men were behaving like women and thereby the matter is laughable.

Interpreting "handbags at ten paces" requires lexical knowledge of "handbag-as-weapon", collocational knowledge of both form and meaning of "WEAPON at NUMBER paces", and (arguably) knowledge of the association between handbags and models of masculinity and femininity.

The "music journalism" use displays some further features. *Handbag* was lexicalised in the clubbing world in ca. 1990 as a music genre: the genre that, in the 1970s and 1980s, certain classes of young women would have danced round their handbags to.[23] The coinage emanates from the gay and transvestite club scene and is redolent with implications, from the appropriation of the handbag as a symbol of gay pride, to changes in the social situation of women over the last twenty years (and its expression in fashion accessories), to transvestite fantasies of being naive seventeen-year-old girls in a more innocent age.

To restrain ourselves to more narrowly linguistic matters: the licence for the coinage is via the "dance round your handbag" collocation, not directly from handbags. As shown by the spoken corpus evidence, the regular, non-ironic use of the collocation co-exists with the music-genre use. It is of much wider currency: all but two of a range of informants knew the collocation, whereas only two had any recollection of the music-genre use. Also, "handbag" music (or at least the use of that label) was a 1990–91 fashion, and the term is no longer current: 1996 uses of it will probably refer back to 1990–91 (as well as back to the 1970s and 1980s).

Syntactically, the most information-rich word of the collocation has been used as a nominal premodifier for other nouns: in the music-genre sense, it is used as other music-genre words, as an uncountable singular noun, usually premodifying but potentially occurring on its own: "Do you like jazz/house/handbag?"

5.1   Frequency

These arguments make clear that there is a *prima facie* case for including handbag-as-weapon and handbag-as-music-genre as dictionary senses, and "dance round your handbag" as an only partially compositional collocation. Each exhibits lexical meaning which is not predictable from the base sense. So why do the dictionaries not list them? The short answer is frequency. Around 97% of *handbag* citations in the BNC are straightforward base sense uses. The music-genre sense is certainly rare, possibly already obsolete, and confined to a subculture. The collocation is partially compositional and occurs just twice in the corpus: for any single-volume dictionary, there will not be space for vast numbers of partially compositional collocations. Not only is a lexicographer "a lexicologist with a deadline" (Fillmore, 1988) but also a lexicologist with a page limit.[24]

---

[23] Thanks to Simon Shurville for sharing his expertise.

[24] It is an interesting question, touched on in Kilgarriff (1993) but worthy of a much fuller investigation, what the percentage of "anomalous" uses might be for various classes of words. One would expect the figures to be highly corpus-dependent. A large proportion of the BNC is material written by novelists and journalists – who earn their living, in some measure, through their skills in the original and engaging use of language. (The music-genre use of *handbag* probably first occurred in advertising material, probably the most fecund discourse of all.) Also one might expect spoken material to have a higher proportion of set phrases, owing to the time constraints on the production of spoken language.

5.2   Analytic definitions and entailments

The handbag-as-weapon sense is rather more common, and a further consideration comes into play. The denotations of base-sense *handbag* and handbag-as-(potential)-weapon are the same. Correspondingly, the lexical fact that there is a use of *handbag* in which it is conceptualised as a weapon does not render the LDOCE definition untrue. A lexicographer operating according to the classical approach whose goal was simply to provide necessary and sufficient conditions for identifying each word's denotation would say that the "weapon" aspect of meaning was irrelevant to his or her task. A more pragmatic lexicographer might also follow this line, particularly since space is always at a premium.

The situation is a variant on autohyponymy (Cruse, 1986: 63–65), the phenomenon of one sense being the genus of another sense of the same word. The prototypical example is *dog* (canine *vs.* male canine). *Dog* is a case where there clearly are distinct senses. For *knife* (weapon *vs.* cutlery *vs.* bladed object), Cruse (1995: 39–40) argues for "an intermediate status" between monosemy and polysemy, since, on the one hand, "bladed object" is a coherent category which covers the denotation, but on the other, in a scenario where there was a penknife but no cutlery knife at a table setting, one might reasonably say "I haven't got a knife". COBUILD2 distinguishes "weapon" and "cutlery" senses, while LDOCE3 provides a single, analytically adequate, "bladed object" sense.

In a discussion of the polysemy of *sanction*, Kjellmer (1993) makes a related observation. His goal is to examine how language breakdown is avoided when a word has antagonistic readings. Nominal *sanction* is such a word: in "sanctions imposed on Iraq" the meaning is akin to punishment ("PUN") whereas in "the proposal was given official sanction" it is related to endorsement ("END"). A first response is that the context disambiguates – punishment, not support, is the sort of thing you "impose", whereas "give" implies, by default, a positively-evaluated thing given. Syntax is also a clue: the plural use is always PUN, whereas determinerless singular uses suggest END. Kjellmer then finds the following instances:

The process of social control is operative insofar as sanction plays a part in the individual's behaviour, as well as in the group's behaviour. By means of this social control, deviance is either eliminated or somehow made compatible with the function of the social group.

Historically, religion has also functioned as a tremendous engine of vindication, enforcement, sanction, and perpetuation of various other institutions.

Here the context does not particularly favour either reading against the other. In the second case, the co-ordination with both an END word (*vindication*) and a PUN one (*enforcement*) supports both readings simultaneously. How is this possible, given their antagonism? How come these uses do not result in ambiguity and the potential for misinterpretation? The answer seems to be that,

we may operate, as readers or listeners, at a general, abstract level and take the word to mean "control, authority" until the context specifies for us which type of control is intended, if indeed specification is intended. In other words, faced with the dual semantic potentiality of the word, we normally stay at a higher level of abstraction, where the danger of ambiguity does not exist, until clearly invited to step down into specificity. (p. 120)[25]

---

[25] Kjellmer implies that the further specification is a temporal process, there being a time in the interpretation process when the lexical meaning of the word is accessed but specified for "control" but not for either PUN or END. I see no grounds for inferring the temporal process from the logical structure.

Citations where *sanction* is unspecified for either PUN or END are rare, and there is no case for including the unspecified "control" sense in a dictionary.

The example demonstrates a relationship between a lexicographer's analytic defining strategy and the interpretation process. There are occasions where a "lowest common denominator" of the usually distinct standard uses of a word will be the appropriate reading, in a process analogous to the way an analytically-inclined lexicographer might write a definition for a word like *charming* or *knife*, which would cover the word's uses in two or more distinct corpus clusters. Some dictionaries use nested entries as a means of representing meanings related in this way.

6   IMPLICATIONS FOR WSD

The argument so far exposes a lack of foundations to the concept of "word sense". But, a WSD researcher might say, "so what?" What are the implications for practical work in disambiguation?

The primary implication is that a task-independent set of word senses for a language is not a coherent concept. Word senses are simply undefined unless there is some underlying rationale for clustering, some context which classifies some distinctions as worth making and others as not worth making. For people, homonyms like *pike* are a limiting case: in almost any situation where a person considers it worth their while attending to a sentence containing *pike*, it is also worth their while making the fish/weapon distinction.

Lexicographers are aware of this: the senses they list are selected according to the editorial policy and anticipated users and uses of the particular dictionary they are writing. Until recently, WSD researchers have generally proceeded as if this was not the case: as if a single program – disambiguating, perhaps, in its English-language version, between the senses given in some hybrid descendant of Merriam-Webster, LDOCE, COMLEX, Roget, OALD and WordNet – would be relevant to a wide range of NLP applications.

The argument so far shows that there is no reason to expect the same set of word senses to be relevant for different tasks.

The handbag data shows how various the non-standard uses of *handbag* are. These uses are sufficiently predictable or insufficiently frequent to be dictionary senses (in a dictionary such as LDOCE). They are licensed by a combination of linguistic principles, knowledge of collocations and lexico-syntactic contexts, and world knowledge. Only in a single case, the department store metonym, is there a plausible linguistic principle for extending the base meaning to render the non-standard use interpretable. The data suggest that little coverage will be gained by an NLP system exploiting generative principles which dictate meaning potential. The non-standard uses of words tend to have their own particular history, with one non-standard use often built on another, the connections being highly specific to a word or lexical field.

The handbag data also indicates how the corpus dictates the word senses. The BNC is designed to cover a wide range of standard English, so is consonant with a general purpose dictionary. The common uses in the one should be the senses in the other. But, were we to move to a music journalism corpus, the music-genre sense would be prominent. A 1990s music-journalism dictionary would include it.

The practical method to extend the coverage of NLP systems to non-standard uses is not to compute new meanings, but to list them. Verbal *handbag* can, if sufficiently frequent, be added to the lexicon as a synonym for *beat*; "WEAPON at NUMBER paces" as one for "have an argument". Given the constraints of the sublanguage of a given NLP application, and the usually much narrower confines of the knowledge representation (which defines the meaning distinctions the system can provide an interpretation for) the proliferation of senses is not a problem. For the medium term future, the appropriate language-engineering response to a use of a word or phrase, for which there is a valid interpretation in the knowledge representation but where the system is currently getting the wrong interpretation because the word or phrase's use does not match that in the lexicon, is to add another lexical entry.[26]

The implications of this account of word senses for different varieties of NLP application are addressed in fuller detail in Kilgarriff (1997b, 1997c).

7 CONCLUSION

Following a description of the conflict between WSD and lexicological research, I examined the concept, "word sense". It was not found to be sufficiently well-defined to be a workable basic unit of meaning.

I then presented an account of word meaning in which "word sense" or "lexical unit" is not a basic unit. Rather, the basic units are occurrences of the word in context (operationalised as corpus citations). In the simplest case, corpus citations fall into one or more distinct clusters and each of these clusters, if large enough and distinct enough from other clusters, forms a distinct word sense. But many or most cases are not simple, and even for an apparently straightforward common noun with physical objects as denotation, *handbag*, there are a significant number of aberrant citations. The interactions between a word's uses and its senses were explored in some detail. The analysis also charted the potential for lexical creativity.

The implication for WSD is that word senses are only ever defined relative to a set of interests. The set of senses defined by a dictionary may or may not match the set that is relevant for an NLP application.

The scientific study of language should not include word senses as objects in its ontology. Where "word senses" have a role to play in a scientific vocabulary, they are to be construed as abstractions over clusters of word usages. The non-technical term for ontological commitment is "belief in", as in "I (don't) believe in ghosts/God/antimatter". One leading lexicographer doesn't believe in word senses. I don't believe in word senses, either.

ACKNOWLEDGEMENTS

This research was supported by the EPSRC Grant K18931, *SEAL*. I would also like to thank Sue Atkins, Roger Evans, Christiane Fellbaum, Gerald Gazdar, Bob Krovetz, Michael Rundell, Yorick Wilks and the anonymous reviewers for their valuable comments.

---

[26] A well-organised, hierarchical lexicon will mean that this need not introduce redundancy into the lexicon.

10

Polysemy

PENELOPE F. STOCK*

I INTRODUCTION

The aspect of polysemy which I wish to address in this paper concerns the issue of how work-ing lexicographers divide lexical items or words into different, usually numbered, meanings. It is not infrequently stated that lexicographers are somewhat shy of explaining their own techniques – or are perhaps too busy to do so – or even that they are unaware of what they are doing, working from some intuition that cannot be stated. The most recent discussion that I am aware of on the subject of sense division is that by John Ayto (1983). In his paper Ayto gives an account of one accepted working method.[1]

His argument is as follows: firstly the lexicographer should consider the superordinates of each of the meanings of the lexical item (that is, the appropriate genus word which will be selected on which to base an analytic definition). This is, so to speak, the first sifting process: where meanings require quite distinct genus words they are ipso facto different senses. If one meaning of *fly* has the general superordinate term 'move through the air' and one has the superordinate 'an insect', then they are clearly different senses of *fly*. Distinct superordinates or genus words suggest distinct senses. The second move is to disambiguate those meanings which have the same superordinate. Ayto uses *cup* as an example, in which several meanings may have definitions which begin with the same genus word: 'vessel'. These are two or three differently described vessels for drinking liquids from, and the sports trophy. The second sifting process takes place when the lexicographer considers the various differentiae that will be required in a definition to distinguish these meanings from each other such that, for example, the sports trophy has a different function from other cups, is differently shaped, and so on. Considerations of shape, size, the material used in construction, etc., are used to disambiguate two further meanings, which are roughly speaking (1) a bowl-shaped vessel with a handle typically presented to the drinker with a saucer, and (2) a straight-sided vessel usually made from plastic and typically presented to the drinker from a vending machine.

Clearly the problem that arises here is that of knowing when to stop eliciting differentiae which individuate different instances of the object in question. Is a separate sense needed for green cups, one for blue, etc? At this stage the lexicographer should consider the near-synonyms of the word in question. The extent to which he or she must consider the individual features of particular instances of things called *cups* is precisely the extent to which they cease to be called *cups* and become instead *mugs* or *glasses*. The lexicographer is required

---

* Stock, P. (1984). 'Polysemy', in Hartmann, R.R.K. (ed.), *LEXeter '83 Proceedings*. Tübingen: Niemeyer, 131–140. Reprinted with permission of Mrs W.J. Nast.

[1] On 'sense division' in the English dictionary and 'meaning discrimination' in the bilingual dictionary, see Dolezal (1984) and Kromann *et al.* (1984).

only to posit sufficient differentiae to distinguish cup from mug and glass and then to review those features which still present distinctly separate types of cup and divide them into senses accordingly.

After a theoretical model of sense division has been achieved, a practical decision can be made about how many senses there are actually room for in a dictionary, and if space constraints are powerful the lexicographer can, as it were, climb back up the ladder toward ambiguity again until a satisfactory number of definitions can be established which cover the main meanings of the word.

Ayto puts this model forward not as the sole answer to a lexicographer's needs but as one basic tool of sense division: a strict semantic analysis, which provides an initial theoretical basis on which lexicographers can work, using their judgment as to how best to present the information at their disposal to meet the dictionary's user's needs. This analysis of how meaning can be disambiguated is clear, neat, and not a hundred miles removed from the working practices of large numbers of lexicographers.

Yet it seems to me that as a theoretical model it is insufficiently detached. For in order to obtain the appropriate superordinates for related senses of a word the lexicographer must, first, have already distinguished the senses in his or her mind, and, second, have decided at what level of superordination the genus word will be chosen. Further, although the model seems to work very satisfactorily with respect to concrete nouns referring to fairly common objects in the real world, it is not at all clear that it would be so satisfactory with words which are more abstract, for example *degree* or *culture*, or with words which are highly polysemous such as *do* or *say*, or with words of other word classes than noun or verb. So there are two problems which arise with this technique. First, it does not free lexicographers from the charge of working purely from some mysterious intuition, in a state of circular subjectivity. Second, it does not have sufficiently wide applicability.

I should like to put forward the basis, at least, of an alternative model. This model has been derived from the experiences of lexicographers at the University of Birmingham, who are working with a large body of recorded instances of uses of words in the language. For the purposes of lexicological research the material has been concordanced so that we are examining a number of instances of the use of a word with what can fairly be described as 'minimal context' (see Figure 1).

What is immediately striking about working with citation material in this form is that a surprising number of concordanced instances of words are quite unambiguous. Lexicographers are able to read through a large number of usages and determine distinct senses in a significant proportion of cases. This was, to me, quite unexpected. I became interested in considering what it was in the minimal contexts available that enabled lexicographers to decide without apparent trouble which meaning of a polysemous word was being used, or, alternatively, what techniques we were using to make such a decision. At the same time I became interested in the difference between such cases and cases which were baffling, or at least perplexing. I shall look at the former case first.

2   CLEARLY DISTINGUISHABLE MEANINGS

It would be my contention that language users do not generally speak or write ambiguously, where ambiguity depends upon confusion of meanings in a polysemous word. People misunderstand each other, but rarely because they cannot distinguish between different meanings of individual words. The fact that we can make and recognize puns successfully depends on such a state of affairs. The use, by linguists, of the word *bank* as an example to demonstrate

2	delineation	
s and values. the elaboration of negritude, the	delineation	and celebration of a distinctively
ied, too, to catholic social philosophy); the	delineation	of a distinct African personality
2	delinquency	
ir fathers and the love they could have given,	delinquency	is often blamed on the fact that mor
are taken into care, sometimes because of their	delinquency	, or often because their parents becom
8	delinquent	
m locked up until he's twenty-one as a juvenile	delinquent	. and he can. that's four years. And d
re regularly unemployed in later life, are more	delinquent	, and might become poor parents them
one parent show greater signs of disturbed or	delinquent	behaviour, are less likely to do well
ing to de-pendent, neglected, incorrigible and	delinquent	children. while i stand gripping the
lishment, in which he is treated as if he were a	delinquent	child. the whip may be cruel compare
nder monique, as she was for a minute or two: a	delinquent	nymphet shining through the matter of
dren tend to be more rebellious, aggressive and	delinquent	than the moral, conforming pupils in
e time, boys may run a greater risk of becoming	delinquent	. the case for more equal relationship
1	delions	
where i happily belched and laboured. the dan	delions	perished. a reek of sap mingled with the
1	deliquescent	
sh-moo, what with little dictionaries; candle;	deliquescent	rock salt figure from salt mine whi
5	delirious	
treasures to mary…. no doubt, i was a little	delirious	- and on the following day I was still
that with all blocks removed and a prospect of	delirious	and unlimited delights before me, i wo
her hair, and we gently kissed. Her kiss, to my	delirious	embarrassment, had some rather comical
at her tennis game produced in me - the teasing	delirious	feeling of teetering on the very brink
ir geoffrey harmsworth attributed northcliffe's	delirious	mental state in the last months solely
1	delirium	
ermere feared became a reality. long before his	delirium	northcliffe was pursued by the daemons
15	deliver	
lasses and had attempted to get me over once to	deliver	a lecture. i had no intention of doing
g, knowing she was coming, watching her come to	deliver	herself in curiosity and lust, knowing w
ial place. Then i heard the old-timer cough and	deliver	himself of some sepulchral mucus. i left
hen put the dress down. how come he got you to	deliver	it? she asked rudolph. I happened to m
icated the little overnight bag. 'i was asked to	deliver	it to you.' 'what is it?' gretchen asked
power of luck the sense of magical forces which	deliver	omens in commonplace encounters: this be
i see, boylan said. 'i suppose somebody has to	deliver	rolls.' he laughed. 'you just don't seem
nyone do up at five o'clock in the morning?' 'i	deliver	rolls on a bicycle for my father.' Rudol
five o'clock in the morning, rain or shine, to	deliver	rolls to the depot hotel and the ace din
had to get up at five o'clock every morning to	deliver	the bread in the cart attached to a bicy
big commercial bakery stopped every morning to	deliver	the cakes and pastries and axel confined
oblems had totally failed, where democracy does	deliver	the goods, in africa, or elsewhere, the
e of hypocrisy as well. finally, its failure to	deliver	the goods made it appear increasingly ir
that, said my mother, and turned toward me to	deliver	the message with full force (i said she
he end of my name. and i did not like having to	deliver	x amount of achievement every single ter
5	deliverance	
ng planks on their heads in relief at britain's	deliverance	, all displays being funded by the ar
ky that it seemed to promise hope, and possibly	deliverance	, for the most unhappy of the world's
e lion's den again, with no guarantee of divine	deliverance	. his tormentor's next and final cove
catch in a door that would ensure his physical	deliverance	.rothermere's daemons were more tang
virtue, loses the power of flight which is its	deliverance	; there is no longer anything to rais
28	delivered	
's best under- graduate speech, and excellently	delivered	.'' after a year at university benn join

FIG. I

ambiguity in word meaning would strike many non-linguists as curious. People do not, outside linguistic texts, confuse the senses of 'a place to deposit money' and 'one side of a river'. It must be rare indeed that the situation arises in which 'I'm just going to the bank' means 'I'm just going to the river bank'.

Given that it is the case that sufficient distinction between the meanings of polysemous words is made, somehow, for communication between language users to be successful, the obvious point to consider is that the case of normal discourse disambiguation is effected by the context of the discourse and the specific situation of the speakers and hearers involved. However, the experience of lexicographers working at Birmingham shows that it is, in fact, possible to disambiguate meanings from written material with minimal, and purely linguistic, context. Furthermore, with reference to the *bank* example mentioned above, I should go so far as to suggest that 'I'm just going to the bank' means unambiguously 'I'm just going to Lloyds/the NatWest/Coutts' or what you will. There would normally be some onus on a speaker or writer to clarify that, in a given situation, 'I'm just going to the bank' refers to a river bank. The language user has to make it clear which sense of a polysemous word is being used at any one time.

What techniques are available for language users to do this? It is clear that, in a large number of cases when working from concordanced citational material, an examination, sometimes even a fairly cursory examination, of the syntactic and collocational patterns in the environment of the node word (the word under analysis), clarifies which meaning is being used (cf. Jones and Sinclair 1974).

I would therefore like to suggest the following procedures for distinguishing clear-cut cases of different senses for a dictionary headword. (These procedures have been numbered but are not taken as necessarily proceeding in the order given.)

Procedure 1 constitutes an analysis of the syntactic behaviour of each instance of the word in use. The broadest and most obvious move is to distinguish word classes. But of great interest also are the syntactic structures or patterns in which the word functions. In the following two examples of *operate*:

(1) Human beings will simply be unable to operate them.
(2) They operated but it was too late.

the example using the transitive verb in (1) must mean 'to control and run' something, say machinery, and the example using the intransitive verb in (2) must mean 'to wield a knife in order to effect internal repairs on animate bodies'.

The following extracts featuring the noun *bite* are taken from the Birmingham corpus:

1. We teach the youngsters to develop competitive bite.
2. ...gives each of them a quick bite to immobilize them.
3. The crude Italian Rosso could not compare for bite with the Algerian Pinard that sloshes...
4. ...their bites leave itching red spots on the skin.
5. It seems indifferent to insect bites.
6. ...knees wide apart, in a clump of water mint. 'A bite! A bite! You've got a bite!
7. Madeleine took a bite. 'It is delicious' she agreed.
8. And dinner was the last bite you had tonight?
9. I'm allergic to dog bites.
10. Brody was in the midst of swallowing a bite of egg salad sandwich.
11. Meadows took a bite of meat, chewed it, savoured it...
12. ...he barely tasted the four bites he managed to wrest away for himself.
13. Young Lionel lacked bite and grasp.
14. ...had been walking fast too for the bite of the cold air...

Immediately one notices the clear distinction between the 'count' and the 'uncount' senses. The lexicographer will want to distinguish 'competitive bite', 'the bite of Italian

Rosso', and young Lionel's inadequacies from the insect bites, dog bites, and the egg salad sandwich. Thus even the broadest syntactic analysis can be useful in disambiguating meanings.

Procedure 2 consists of reviewing the data in the light of collocational patterns and the general co-occurrence of lexical items in different semantic areas. Returning to the examples of *bite* above, one would want to say that the examples of the countable noun cover more than one meaning of *bite*. Consideration of the lexical items in the immediate environment of the node word, however, immediately shows broad groups. Examples 2 and 4 discuss the effects of biting: immobilizing the victim or leaving itching spots; we can infer snakes and insects. Examples 5 and 9 are premodified by the giver of the bites, *insect* and *dog*, and in these cases *bite* means 'wound' of some kind. Examples 7, 10, 11, and 12 have the lexical items *delicious, swallow, sandwich, meat, chew, taste* – all to do with food, the savouring of food. These cases have the synonym 'mouthful'.

The above two procedures can be used as primary tools for disambiguating senses with minimal contextual evidence. They are useful in working from concordanced material in which the level of syntactic and collocational patterning thus far discussed is largely accessible within a few words each side of the node word.

However, the account of these procedures given is somewhat crude and is intended to be only a general outline of methods which need considerable further refinement. In particular the combination of a syntactic and collocational approach is one which suggests promising avenues for further research. Example 7 of *bite* above illustrates this point. The four words *Madeleine took a bite* followed by a full-stop, when taken alone, are sufficient to give the meaning 'mouthful'. The word *take* regularly co-occurs in collocation with *bite*, although the collocation is not restricted to the sense of *bite* which has the synonym 'mouthful'. *Madeleine* does not regularly so co-occur. In this case a combination of the syntactic structure (subject, predicate, nominal group, without a following adjunct), the collocational pattern which lexically realizes the predicate and nominal group (*took a bite*) and the fact that the subject is human (*Madeleine*) are sufficient context to provide the necessary clues to meaning. Further analysis along these lines, which are based on Firth's notion of colligation (cf. Palmer 1968), should take account of the habitual patterns in grammatical categories in relation to a word, in addition to the actual lexical realizations of the categories in these patterns.

Procedure 3 consists of dealing with citations which can be given more than one reading. These present no lexicographic problems. The lexicographer merely has to perform the linguistic counterpart of the visual trick where a vase can be seen as two profiles or vice versa. That is, the lexicographer has to define the meaning of the word in each of its readings. This last procedure is thus a kind of mopping-up operation for those senses which can be clearly distinguished.

I should now like to turn to some more baffling cases.

3   MEANINGS WHICH ARE NOT CLEARLY DISTINGUISHABLE

I have proceeded thus far without questioning various premises which tend to be accepted by working lexicographers. One of these is that there are such things as distinct and distinguishable senses of polysemous words which can be clearly defined and which are, as it were, separable from each other in terms of dictionary presentation. This premise is questioned by Professor Roy Harris in an article (1982) in which he reviewed the latest published *Supplement to the Oxford English Dictionary* (OED). He describes OED lexicography as 'black and white' lexicography for a number of reasons. One of them is the following:

It (that is OED lexicography) takes for granted the validity of the assumption that the many varying shades of semantic grey which in practice language presents us with can without distortion be reduced to a clearly determinate number of verbal meanings. This assumption was accepted without question by the philologists of Murray's generation. It no longer is today. But it is an assumption very necessary to the whole enterprise of presenting the vocabulary of a language as a list of separate items, each with a fixed set of possible interpretations. Is that in practice how language works? Anyone who reflects carefully upon his own speech for a while without prejudging the issue will quickly come to doubt whether it is, unless he has become so brainwashed by a dictionary-based education that he literally cannot conceive that words could be anything else than what they are represented as being in dictionaries.

I have already argued, of course, that there are, in fact, cases where different senses can be disinterred from a mass of citational material, complete with moderately clear boundaries, and which are susceptible to definition of the analytic kind. However, not all citational evidence can be clearly disambiguated in terms of lexicographic senses. In some cases the meanings blur into each other or are otherwise indistinct from each other. Yet the lexicographer must, given the existing methods of presenting dictionary information, make some sort of job of sorting them out into different meanings, normally numbered meanings. There are two different types of blurring between senses. One is the case of figurative or metaphorical extensions of literal senses. My proposed procedures are simply no use for handling distinctions of meaning in this area, since it would seem that figurative extensions typically take the same syntactic and collocational environments as the literal senses from which they are derived.

The second type of blurring is where a word seems either to operate on a cline between two or more meanings, or to bring in its train various extra nuances so that any individual utterance might suggest one strong aspect of a meaning but is, as it were, strengthened or supported by various other possible close meanings.

Given below are a number of examples of the word *culture*.

1. ...as one person of culture to another...
2. There does seem evidence that Eastern cultures have more right brain emphasis.
3. ...a multicultural society where cultures can live side by side.
4. Blood cultures were done because of the possibility of...
5. You're a person of international culture.
6. ...desire to live as a nation that has its own culture and individuality.
7. ...by removing all traces of black ethics and culture.
8. ...the Ministry of Culture.
9. Man dresses the part his culture tells him he is called upon to play.
10. Newspaper reading, word-and-trade-conscious urban culture.
11. ...nevertheless absorbed enough of Spanish political culture to build authoritarian principles...
12. ...to give value and literate dress to an oral culture we have forgotten how to appreciate.
13. ...the great cultures of Japan and China.
14. I have shown how Caro's work belongs to the culture of the early 1960's.
15. ...the big colloquium on African culture and African civilization that's to be held...
16. ...has led to the development of a specific 'pop' culture.
17. ...the culture of machismo.
18. ...culture shock.
19. Infanticide was practised by many early cultures.
20. One of his assistants was careless about a culture of chicken cholera germs...

21. ... the extension of the throw-away culture.
22. ... traceable local accents and a person of genuine culture wouldn't find all that much difference.

Two of these, Examples 4 and 20, can be separated from the others using my proposed procedures. They have no semantic link with the rest of the examples. The lexicographer can whip these out straight away and deal with this meaning in the style appropriate to the dictionary he or she is working on.

The remaining twenty examples suggest three or four general semantic areas. Some are in the general area of the arts, and perhaps include a dash of the notion that the arts appeal to the sophisticated. Some relate to something like a society or a civilization – something which is either broader or narrower than these terms, or perhaps both, e.g. Example 2. A few suggest the notion of a shared heritage or tradition in a group. Finally there are a group in which the term is used to pick out a section of society which is being identified, perhaps temporarily, by some feature of the lifestyle of its members, e.g. Example 21.

This, I think, accounts for the broad range of semantic areas which should be covered by a dictionary. Yet I have elicited four semantic areas which do not correlate with the semantic areas offered in either the *Collins English Dictionary* (CED) or in the *Longman Dictionary of Contemporary English* (LDOCE, Procter 1978). Neither do the definitions in these dictionaries suggest that the meanings have been analysed in exactly the same way in each (see entries E_1 and E_2 below).

E_1:

cul.ture [...] n. **1.** the total of the inherited ideas, beliefs, values, and knowledge, which constitute the shared bases of social action. **2.** the total range of activities and ideas of a group of people with shared traditions, which are transmitted and reinforced by members of the group: *the Mayan culture*. **3.** a particular civilization at a particular period. **4.** the artistic and social pursuits, expression, and tastes valued by a society or class, as in the arts, manners, dress, etc. **5.** the enlightenment or refinement resulting from these pursuits. **6.** the cultivation of plants, esp. by scientific methods designed to improve stock or to produce new ones. **7.** *Stockbreeding*. The rearing and breeding of animals, esp. with a view to improving the strain. **8.** the act or practice of tilling or cultivating the soil. **9.** *Biology*. **a.** the experimental growth of microorganisms, such as bacteria and fungi, in a nutrient substance (see **culture medium**), usually under controlled conditions. **b.** a group of microorganisms grown in this way. ~*vb*. (*tr.*) **10.** to cultivate (plants or animals). **11.** to grow (microorganisms) in a culture medium. [C15: from Old French, from Latin *Cultura* a cultivating, from *colere* to till; see CULT]-' **cul.tur.ist** *n.*-'**cul.ture.less** *adj*.

E_2:

cul.ture/.../ *n* **1** [U] artistic and other activity of the mind and the works produced by this: *The aim of our library service is to bring culture to the people* **2** [U] a state of high development in art and thought existing in a society and represented at various levels in its members: *the development of culture|a man of little culture* **3** [C;U] the particular system of art, thought, and customs of a society; the arts, customs, beliefs, and all the other products of human thought made by a people at a particular time: *ancient Greek culture|a tribal culture, never studied before* **4** [U] development and improvement of the mind or body by education or training **5** [U] the practice of raising animals and growing plants or crops: *bee culture|The culture of this uncommon flower is increasing in Britain* **6** [C;U] (a group of bacteria produced by) the practice of growing bacteria for scientific use or use in medicine

It is precisely the lack of clarity in our use of the word *culture* which makes it such a handy word to have at one's disposal. It offers, as it were, semantic extras just because in most uses its possible meanings are not clearly disambiguated. We use it in a rather 'vague' way. What can the dictionary maker do to reflect this state of affairs? CED's and LDOCE's entries

E_1 and E_2 demonstrate one thing very clearly. They do not, cannot by their very structure, show that there is slippage between some of the senses that they give but not between others.

The convention of giving analytic definitions which detail the boundaries of word meaning for any one sense is perhaps a hindrance rather than an aid in showing where senses merge. It may be worthwhile to consider alternatives to the conventional structure of dictionary entries for some words and expressions. For example, an entry which looked more like a thesaurus extract with strings of related near-synonyms but well supported by citational exemplification, or a short statement about the variety of usages of one word, might be preferable in indicating a range of meaning. However, such styles may present too many problems to the dictionary maker who has, still, to conform to the constraints of the page and present meanings linearly. Yet with words such as *culture*, even if definitions resembling analytic ones are used, it would be more realistic were the genus word and some differentiae directed toward the centre of a semantic area, rather than attempting to cover its blurred boundaries. In this case the question then arises: how to show the dictionary user that there is a functional difference between two types of definition which apparently operate identically?

There is nothing in the LDOCE entry E_2 for *culture* to show that there is a complete break in meanings between definition Numbers 4 and 5, but no such break between 1 and 2. The CED entry E_1 has interposed a label after their definition Number 9 which has the effect of orientating the reader to a new semantic area, but this kind of technique is by lexicographic convention only used for senses which fall within technical subjects or fields.

The convention of sub-sense numbering (1, 1a, 1a(i), etc.) has been used before in dictionaries, notably the OED, the Webster dictionaries, and the *Longman New Universal Dictionary*. All these dictionaries follow a broadly etymological or historical sense ordering pattern.[2] With the advent of synchronically orientated dictionaries, however, the notion of the subsense might profitably be released from its diachronic bonds and be used to convey range in meaning and the idea of the semantic cline. For example, definitions numbered 1; 1a; 1b; 1c; 2 could be used to convey the information that there are three senses being presented which shade into each other, all under the heading (1), with (2) a separate sense, not blurring in syntactic, collocational, or colligational patterning with any of the meanings covered under (1).

4   CONCLUSION

In conclusion I should like to suggest that it is now necessary for lexicographers to reconsider the ways in which they analyse meanings and the ways in which they present their analyses. It seems to me, firstly, that Ayto's account of distinguishing the senses of polysemous words is too partial since it cannot handle satisfactorily a very large number of these words. Secondly, Professor Harris is right, in general terms, to criticize lexicographers for fudging the issue of meaning clines, but he does not, apparently, accept the case that some meanings of polysemous words can be clearly isolated and defined, and he fails to offer any positive suggestions for alternative methods of defining or describing words which have blurring between senses. I hope that I have been able to offer a method which can be used to determine isolable meanings of polysemous words and, further, some suggestions for presenting meanings in such a way as to show the 'many varying shades of semantic grey which in practice language presents us with...without distortion', or at least with less distortion.

---

[2] On convention and ordering, see Ilson (1984) and Kipfer (1984).

PART V
On Collocations, Idioms, and Dictionaries

Phraseology

ANTHONY P. COWIE*

Throughout the 1980s and into the 1990s, there has been a quickening of interest among theoretical linguists, and among specialists in lexicography, discourse analysis, language acquisition, and foreign language teaching, in what were traditionally known as 'idioms', and are variously called 'word-combinations' (Zgusta 1971), 'fixed expressions' (Alexander 1987), and 'phrasal lexemes' (Pawley 1985; Lipka 1990). The interest reflects a keener awareness than before of the pervasiveness of ready-made memorized combinations in written and spoken language and a wider recognition of the central part they play in first and second language acquisition and in speech production (Bolinger 1976, 1985; Peters 1983; Pawley and Syder 1983). The notion that native-like proficiency in a language depends crucially on knowledge of a stock of prefabricated units, varying in complexity and internal cohesion, can also be seen as a necessary corrective to the atomistic view that the workings of language can be explained by a system of rules of general applicability, a lexicon largely made up of minimal units, and a set of basic principles of semantic interpretation (Fillmore *et al.* 1988).

This shift of perception is partly the outcome of a steady accumulation of descriptive studies throughout the 1970s and 1980s, and questions of analysis and classification will be the chief focus of this survey. Phraseology, as the study of the structure, meaning, and use of word-combinations, is not a commonly recognized field of activity among British and American linguists (for an East European view, see Arnold 1986; Gläser 1988); but that it has become a significant focus of research, especially perhaps in Europe, is apparent from the attention given to word-combinations in textbooks on lexical semantics (Cruse 1986), lexicology (Carter 1987; Lipka 1990), and vocabulary in language teaching (Carter and McCarthy 1988), and from the publication of a number of phraseological dictionaries (e.g., Cowie *et al.* 1983; Benson *et al.* 1986). It is noticeable, too, that despite the continuing influence in collocational analysis of neo-Firthian lexical theory (Sinclair 1987b), with its emphasis on observed frequency of co-occurrence within stated distances (or 'spans') in large computerized corpora, the dominant influences in work are a more directly Firthian strain (Mitchell 1971) and East European (specifically Soviet) phraseological theory, first mediated to non-Russian-speaking students through the work of Klappenbach (1968); Weinreich (1969); Arnold (1973); and Lipka (1974).

The main features of this general approach are:

(a) Recognition of a broad spectrum of phraseological categories, including those with a speech-act or discourse-structuring function (Mitchell 1971; Alexander 1978, 1987; Pawley 1985; Gläser 1986, 1988; Cowie 1988).

* Cowie, A.P. (1994). 'Phraseology', in Asher, R.E., and Simpson, J.M.Y. (eds.), *The Encyclopedia of Language & Linguistics*, Vol 6. Oxford: Pergamon Press, 3168–3171. Reprinted with permission from Elsevier.

(b) An acknowledgment that categories with a referential (or 'nominative') function are ranged along a continuum or scale, from transparent, freely recombinable collocations at one end to formally invariable, unmotivated idioms at the other (Klappenbach 1968; Aisenstadt 1979; Cowie 1981; Fernando and Flavell 1981). Idioms are also seen to form the end-point of a *historical* process, by which word-combinations first establish themselves through constant re-use, then undergo figurative extension and finally petrify (Cowie *et al.* 1983: xii).

(c) Recognition that complex lexical units of various types should be studied in relation to their grammatical and pragmatic functions, and not simply in terms of the textual proximity and frequency of co-occurrence of their components (Mitchell 1971; Cowie 1981). Analysis within specified constructions (e.g., of transitive verb + object pronoun, or attributive adjective + head noun), often to some degree of delicacy, is in fact crucial. As Greenbaum has demonstrated, statements of collocational restriction call for syntactic information in at least some cases. Referring to verb + intensifier collocations, he shows that the acceptability of certain of these (e.g., *prefer* + *much*) depends on the positioning of their components relative to other clause elements (1974: 82). Compare:

> I much prefer a dry wine
> * I prefer a white wine much

A grammatical perspective is also essential for purposes of tracing idiom development. Provided collocations and idioms of the same construction type are compared, it is possible to identify many idioms which have developed from specific stable collocations, some of which subsequently remain in use. (Consider, for example, the 'figurative' idiom *let off steam*, which has evolved from a formally identical, and extant, technical collocation.)

Any approach to the analysis of word-combinations is beset by terminological difficulties. In the brief survey that follows, 'word-combination' is used as the most inclusive term (thus, *jog someone's memory, kick the bucket, how do you do?* and *that reminds me...* are all word-combinations), 'composite' being reserved to refer collectively to those with a denotative or naming function. 'Formula' will be used generically to denote any expression with a speech-act or discourse-structuring function.

I   COLLOCATIONS

Collocations are associations of two or more lexemes (or roots) recognized in and defined by their occurrence in a specific range of grammatical constructions. HEAV- + RAIN is one such abstract composite, realized in the patterns *heavy rain* and *raining heavily* (Mitchell 1971). Though transparent and (usually) lexically variable (cf. *light rain, a heavy shower*), they are characterized by arbitrary limitation of choice at one or more points, as in *light exercise/heavy exercise* (Cowie 1981). Collocations are to be distinguished from 'free' or 'open' combinations such as *drink one's tea* or *dismiss an employee*, in which selection restrictions on the choice of object nouns can be stated in terms of features denoting general properties (Hausmann 1989). In *dismiss an employee*, for example, the verb can be recombined with nouns having the features 'human', 'employed' and 'subordinate', a specification which will account for the acceptability of *dismiss a secretary* or *dismiss a cleaner*, and for the oddness of *dismiss one's boss* and *dismiss a guard-dog* (Cruse 1986).

Occasionally, combinations whose elements have neutral meanings can display arbitrary limitations on choice (cf. *cut one's throat, slash one's wrists* with **slash one's throat, ?cut one's wrists*), but such restrictions are more usual when one of the constituents is used in a figurative sense (cf. *break a stick, branch, twig*, etc., *with break one's journey, *trip, *voyage* – Aisenstadt 1979; Cowie 1981, 1986; Benson 1989). The two related properties highlighted in that instance are, first, the well-worn figurative meaning of one element (the verb in *break one's journey*) and, second, the arbitrary restriction by that sense of the range of choice (the 'collocational range') at the place of the other element. Collocations in which one element is now a dead metaphor are widespread in English and other languages (for parallel instances in French and German, see Hausmann 1979, 1989; Benson 1989). Another example is *wholesome fare*, where the specialized element is *fare* (in the sense of 'food') and there are few options at the place of the adjective: *wholesome / plain / simple fare*.

The strong tendency in language use – often dominant over analogical reshaping – to reuse existing collocations goes some way towards explaining the anomaly of **break a voyage* or **nourishing fare*. This tendency is nowhere more clearly demonstrated than when the collocabilities of two or more synonymous words are compared. Consider *perform, carry out*, and *conduct*. While all three (in given sense) collocate with *test* and *experiment*, only the first two collocate with *task* and only the last two with *survey*: **conduct a task* and **perform a survey* seem equally unacceptable (Cowie 1986).

Figurative meaning is not the only factor constraining open choice; and the verb in a verb + noun collocation need not be the determinant of limited collocability. An important sub-class of verb + noun + preposition collocations contains a so-called 'delexical' verb, e.g., *bring, have, make, send, take* (Moon 1987a). Consider *have an influence on someone/something*. Here the specific action or process is conveyed by the noun. Moreover, it is the noun which constrains the choice of verb, rather than the other way about. The collocability of *influence* (*on someone/something*) is limited to *have / exercise / exert*, but *have* in the appropriate sense has a much wider privilege of occurrence: *have control / power over someone, have an effect on someone / something, have a hold on someone*, etc.

2   IDIOMS

Some collocations of the delexical verb + noun + preposition type come close to idiomaticity, since not only is part-for-part substitution impossible but a special passive transformation shows the verb and the two following elements to form a close idiomatic unit (Quirk *et al.* 1985: 1159):

> They took (good) care of the children → The children were *taken* (good) *care of*

Despite the efficacy of such tests, the most familiar approach to the definition of idioms, and one that linguists as well as lexicographers have helped to popularize, focuses on the difficulty of understanding idioms in terms of the meanings of their constituents. The following definition (from the *Collins English Dictionary*, second edition, 1986) represents this tendency:

> ... a group of words whose meaning cannot be predicted from the meanings of the constituent words, as for example (*It was raining*) *cats and dogs*.

But this formulation (and similar definitions could be culled from a range of dictionaries now in print) is open to serious challenge. As Cruse clearly demonstrates, such definitions are circular. Since 'meanings of the constituent words' must be understood to imply 'meanings the constituent words have in other, non-idiomatic contexts', one finds that to apply the definition one must already be able to distinguish between idiomatic and non-idiomatic expressions (Cruse 1986: 37). Fortunately, idioms can be defined without circularity by applying procedures such as those demonstrated earlier. Since idioms in the strict sense are semantic units, they should resist replacement of their components by words which are themselves semantic units. Compare in this respect *blow the gaff / *puff the gaff* and *kick the bucket / *kick the pail*, where the effect of substitution is to produce nonsense or a non-idiom (Cowie *et al.* 1983: xii).

A second weakness of the traditional definition, with its stress on the semantic opaqueness of combinations, is its exclusiveness. It leaves out of account a large class of expressions which have figurative meaning (i.e., in terms of the whole combination) but which also keep a current literal interpretation. Examples of such 'figurative idioms' are *close ranks, do a U-turn*, and *die a natural death*. (There are also marginal cases, such as *run off the rails* and *reach the end of the line*, where interpretation may or may not benefit from knowledge of an original technical sense.) The semantic evidence suggests a gradation, and this is underlined by the possibility of lexical or pronominal substitution in individual cases. Consider, for instance, a *closed / sealed book, a dry / dummy run*, and *I had a close shave but Bill had an even closer one*. Idioms in the narrow sense (i.e., invariable opaque combinations) are clearly related to figurative idioms and the looser, more transparent collocations along a cline or continuum (Cowie 1981; Alexander 1987).

True idioms were taken up in the 1960s and 1970s by generative grammarians, who were concerned with the theoretical difficulties of accounting for their interpretation and syntactic properties in terms of a transformational-generative grammar (Weinreich 1969; Newmeyer 1972). Fraser (1970) used a battery of transformations as a means of establishing degrees of idiomaticity (or a 'frozenness hierarchy'), judging as most frozen those items which were resistant to most transformations. The difficulty with such an approach is that specific restrictions do not apply evenly to idioms of a given structural type (idiomaticity having been established on independent semantic grounds) and may affect some collocations as well (Cowie 1981: 230). Thus, while *spill the beans* (true idiom) can be passivized, *mark time* (figurative idiom) cannot, and neither can *foot the bill* (restricted collocation). Perhaps the most useful approach is to accept that while no transformation will prove diagnostically reliable in every case, some types of transformation are more indicative of idiomaticity than others. For instance, grammatical processes whose function is to highlight a specific clause element will often not be applicable if that element also forms part of the idiom (Cruse 1986: 38). Thus the following pseudo-cleft construction has no idiomatic reading:

*What John did to the beans was spill them

3   FORMULAE

Routine formulae, of which *Good morning* and *You can say that again* are examples, differ from both collocations and idioms ('composites') in regard to the kinds of meaning they convey and the structural levels at which they operate. Whereas composites tend to develop more or less unitary referential meanings through recurrent use below the rank of sentence, formulae evolve meanings which largely reflect the way they are used in discourse (Coulmas 1981; Cowie 1988). Consider the familiar social formula *How do you do*. Like *spill the beans*, say, this has with time become less susceptible to interruption, substitution, or the rearrangement of parts. Both are now units of meaning. In the case of *How do you do*, however, a meaning has developed which is largely indicative of the way the combination is *used* (as a formal response to being introduced for the first time).

Word-combinations with a discourse function have come into prominence through the work of linguists concerned with analyzing the highly patterned expressions used in routine social encounters (Ferguson 1976; Keller 1979; Coulmas 1981). Two major types will be mentioned here: expressions used to perform such functions as greetings, apologies, and invitations, and those involved in organizing turn-taking, indicating a speaker's attitude to his interlocutor, and generally ensuring smooth interaction between speakers (Cowie 1988). The first will be referred to as 'speech-act formulae' (Pawley 1985) and the second as 'gambits' (Keller 1979). While speech-act formulae are often set expressions (*Good morning, nice day, see you soon, pleased to meet you*), gambits commonly lack the stereotyping which tends to go hand in hand with specialization in a discourse function. In this respect, the 'checking' gambit *Are you with me?* (cf. *Are you following me?, Do you follow?*) can be compared with *If you must know*, which is a fixed gambit used to introduce a piece of information given to someone who has been asking for it inquisitively or tiresomely, as in this exchange:

'Come on, where did you meet him?'
'If you must know, I met him at a conference in Moscow.'

Gambits are found in a great variety of grammatical constructions. The structuring devices *Do you follow?* or *You can say that again!*, span complete sentences. But in other cases the gambit may be a dependent clause introducing or rounding off some larger unit whose illocutionary force it helps to establish. One such gambit is *if you must know* (above). Another is *if you please*, usually in final position (and with an intonational fall from *if*), and signaling that the preceding clause is judged by the speaker to be an absurd or unreasonable claim:

The parents want some say in the fate of their children, and these days even the children demand to be heard, if you please.

4   THEORETICAL DEVELOPMENTS

Though detailed analyses of multiword units of particular types continue to appear, often linked to the compilation of dictionaries (Cowie 1986; Sinclair 1987b; Benson 1989), a number of attempts have been made to tackle certain of the theoretical problems posed by their diversity and prevalence. Following Bolinger's seminal paper of 1976, several authors have challenged commonly held assumptions about the scale of the phrasal lexicon (Pawley 1985) and the incidence of the ready-made in speech and writing (Cowie 1988). Writing of 'lexicalized sentence stems', which correspond closely to the collocations, idioms, and formulae described here, Pawley and Syder (1983) suggest that such familiar expressions as *I think a lot of X* and *Come to think of it ...* probably amount to several hundred thousand, and point to their role as the main building-blocks of connected speech. They take the view that lexicalized stems have a more or less individual grammar, each being subject to a somewhat different range of phrase structure and transformational restrictions. One could argue that the spectrum of complex units whose properties have to be acquired independently is wider still. In a 1988 study, Fillmore *et al.* focus on 'formal' idioms such as *Him mind the baby!* The peculiarity of such idioms is that while indefinitely many sentences can be modeled on the appropriate construction (e.g., *Them borrow the flat! Her write a novel!*), so that they cannot simply be listed in the phrasal lexicon, their syntactic form and meaning cannot be derived from knowledge of the wider grammar of English. Formal idioms call for individual mini-grammars embedded within the general grammar to account for their syntactic, semantic, and, where relevant, pragmatic properties.

Using a Bilingual Dictionary to Create Semantic Networks

THIERRY FONTENELLE*

I   INTRODUCTION

In this paper, I plan to tackle the complex problem of the use and exploitation of bilingual lexical resources available in machine-readable form. The reusability of lexical resources has indeed attracted a lot of attention in the past few years but NLP researchers have tended to concentrate mainly on monolingual English learners' dictionaries, somewhat neglecting bilingual dictionaries. The less structured format of the magnetic tapes of the latter is probably partly responsible for this lack of interest. The reluctance of publishers to distribute the machine-readable versions of their bilingual dictionaries has also contributed to the concentration of efforts on the exploitation of monolingual (and predominantly English) machine-readable dictionaries (MRDs). However, it has to be admitted, as Atkins and Levin (1991: 255) point out, that "the explicit treatment accorded to restrictions on subjects/objects of verbs in dictionaries for the foreign learner (i.e. bilingual dictionaries) renders such works a valuable source of material for the semi-automatic construction of a lexical database". In this paper, I wish to describe the construction of a lexical-semantic database from the computerized version of the Collins–Robert English–French dictionary (Atkins and Duval 1978). I will pay special attention to the retrieval programs which make it possible to readily extract the collocational and thesauric information it contains. The emphasis will also be laid on the manual lexicographical work which was required in order to enrich the database with lexical-semantic information based on Mel'čuk's descriptive apparatus of lexical functions (Mel'čuk et al. 1984/1988/1992). Attention will also be paid to potential exploitations of this bilingual database, ranging from applications in a word sense disambiguation or translation selection perspective to the integration of the lexical database (LDB) into a series of corpus-based tools for collocation extraction, using the dictionary and its lexical-semantic information as an external resource linked to corpus query tools.

2   LEXICAL ACQUISITION AND MACHINE-READABLE DICTIONARIES

In a paper that was originally written for the Grosseto workshop on "Automating the Lexicon" in 1986, Boguraev (1994) carried out a survey of MRD-based research and showed that the exploitation of machine-readable commercial dictionaries can be traced back to two doctoral dissertations which exerted a profound influence on the field of computational lexicography. Amsler's seminal work on the structure of the Merriam-Webster Pocket Dictionary

* Fontenelle, T. (1997). 'Using a bilingual dictionary to build semantic networks', *International Journal of Lexicography*, 10(4): 275–303. Reprinted with permission of Oxford University Press.

(Amsler 1980) described various procedures for connecting definition texts and for revealing implicit semantic information buried in the microstructure of the dictionary entries. His basic assumption was that most definitions comply with the traditional Aristotelian distinction between genus and differentiae and that the very structure of these definitions could be used as a starting point to semi-automatically create taxonomies usable in Natural Language Processing (NLP). Shortly after Amsler's thesis, Michiels's dissertation (1982) explored the elaborate grammatical coding system of LDOCE (Procter 1978), which he then described as the first truly computerized dictionary of English. In his dissertation, Michiels proposed a database organization of the lexical data which would make it possible to reuse the syntactic and semantic information of LDOCE entries to feed the lexical component of a parser of English. Such proposals have been recently put into practice in HORATIO, an experimental definite-clause grammar parser for a subset of English whose lexical material is directly imported from LDOCE (Michiels 1995 a,b,c).

Amsler's and Michiels's work led to the worldwide recognition that MRDs house a lot of NLP-relevant information the extraction of which could be partly automated. Several research groups managed to obtain the tapes of these and other dictionaries, attempting to construct computational lexicons which provide syntactic and semantic information to NLP systems (Boguraev and Briscoe 1989; Chodorow *et al.* 1985; Byrd 1989; Byrd *et al.* 1987; Klavans *et al.* 1993; Ide *et al.* 1994; Briscoe *et al.* 1993, to quote only a few).

Disambiguation is undoubtedly a key concept in computational linguistics and most efforts to extract lexical information from MRDs stem from the recognition that disambiguation should be done at word-sense level. In this context, a key lexical relation is definitely hyperonymy, which corresponds to the lexicographical notion of genus or superordinate term in a definition. This explains why researchers have long been trying to collect all hyperonym links in a dictionary to produce complete taxonomies of concepts (see Michiels and Noël 1984 who search for items belonging to the thesauric "instrument" set in LDOCE; see also more recent work by Vossen *et al.* 1989, Vossen 1992, 1996, Wilks *et al.* 1989, 1996 or Calzolari 1984, 1988. Some pitfalls related to these approaches are described by Ide *et al.* 1991, 1994). One of the main stumbling blocks which hampers the automatic generation of taxonomies is that the language used in definition texts is usually not disambiguated and basic genus filiation techniques such as those described by Amsler (1980) or Michiels (1982), or implemented by Guthrie *et al.* (1990), need to rely on a previously disambiguated defining vocabulary (Kilgarriff 1992: 17). One of the ultimate goals of lexical knowledge acquisition is to make it possible for a user to navigate within a lexical knowledge base through concepts and lexical relations (this term covering more than the three basic relations of synonymy, antonymy and hyperonymy).

At this juncture, it should be stressed that most projects focus on monolingual dictionaries (LDOCE – Procter 1978, Cobuild – Sinclair 1987, or OALD 4 – 1989). Relatively little work has been done on the exploitation of bilingual dictionaries, which is probably due to two factors:

(1) Few research teams have been granted access to the tapes of bilingual MRDs. The English department at the University of Liège and the IBM Yorktown Heights Lexical Systems Group (see Byrd 1989; Byrd *et al.* 1987; Klavans and Tzouk-ermann 1995) managed to acquire a copy of the large Collins–Robert English–French dictionary (henceforth CR). Interestingly, the IBM group has also used the Collins English–German dictionary as one of the lexical components of the LMT machine translation system (Neff and McCord 1990). Other teams have had access to some bilingual dictionaries in the Collins series. Farwell *et al.* (1993)

describe a practical MT project using a bilingual lexicon derived from LDOCE and a Collins Spanish–English dictionary. The Pisa group has also used the Collins English–Italian pocket dictionaries as lexical resources to establish links between parallel texts and hence align sentences in bilingual corpora (Picchi *et al.* 1992). The ISSCO group in Switzerland has used the pocket machine-readable versions of the English–French Collins–Robert dictionary to implement a network-based dictionary consultation tool on the campus of the University of Geneva (Petitpierre *et al.* 1994). However, it should be borne in mind that some of these projects make use of the pocket versions of these bilingual MRDs, which means that the collocational knowledge they contain cannot compete with what can be extracted using traditional corpus-based statistical tools.

(2) A second, perhaps more fundamental, reason for which bilingual dictionaries tend to have been somewhat neglected by the research community is the less structured format of the typesetting tapes. In this respect, it is important to bear in mind the traditional distinction between "computerized" dictionaries, which display a logical organization making them suitable for transformation into a lexical database (LDB), and "machine-readable dictionaries" (MRDs), which are usually hardly more than flat text files with codes aimed at driving the typesetting process. The former dictionaries are of course easier to process since their logical format makes it possible to identify each piece of information more readily (definitions, parts of speech, grammar codes, etc. are already partly formalized and identifiable). The Collins–Robert dictionary used in this paper (see also Fontenelle 1997) clearly belongs to the latter class insofar as what was made available to us was the typesetting tape, which means that the transformation of this file into a relational database was far from trivial. The new generation of dictionaries, which now usually rely on an SGML or SGML-like system of tags and codes, is easier to exploit (see Segond and Zaenen 1994 and Bauer *et al.* 1994 who, in the Compass project, exploit the tapes of the recent Oxford–Hachette dictionary – Corréard and Grundy 1994 – in order to build the context-sensitive look-up component of an interactive text comprehension aid for advanced language learners).

3   CONSTRUCTING A LEXICAL-SEMANTIC DATABASE FROM THE COLLINS–ROBERT DICTIONARY

The idea which underlies the work described here was to reuse the machine-readable version of the English–French part of the CR dictionary in order to exploit the collocational knowledge contained in it. This research started after I had realized that the CR metalinguistic apparatus is a treasure trove of information on the combinatory properties of lexical items. It is important to note, as Michiels (1996) points out, that bilingual and monolingual dictionaries share a number of oversimplifications, the most important being the following:

- words have enumerable, listable meanings, so that
- meaning is divisible into discrete units.

A further simplification is that a bilingual dictionary such as CR divides the semantic space of source items as a function of the target language. Thus, a word which is considered as monosemic in a monolingual dictionary may be regarded as polysemic in a bilingual dictionary because the target language makes distinctions which are non-existent in the source language. Consider the entry for **croak** in CIDE (Procter 1995) below, which offers one definition to cover the general SOUND meaning (grammar codes appear between square brackets; e.g. [I]= intransitive use):

> **croak** [SOUND] *v* (of animals) to make deep rough sounds such as a FROG or CROW makes, or (of people) to speak with a rough voice because of a sore or dry throat. *I could hear frogs croaking by the lake.* [I] *"Water, water", he croaked.* [+ clause]

In comparison, CR makes distinctions which are based solely on the existence of different potential translations:

> **croak 1** *vi* **(a)** *[frog]* coasser; *[raven]* croasser; *[person]* parler d'une voix rauque; *(*grumble)* maugréer, ronchonner.

These examples point to the all-important nature of the metalinguistic indicators (*frog, raven, person, grumble*) in a good bilingual dictionary (see also Duval 1986, 1990). The CR dictionary partly owes its reputation to the extensive use it makes of this italicized metalinguistic information about the semantic, syntactic and combinatory properties of words. A systematic approach has been adopted by the CR lexicographers to account for a whole range of collocational constraints and selection restrictions:

– typical noun subjects of a verb headword appear in square brackets [ ];
– nouns which usually complement a noun headword appear in square brackets or parentheses;
– typical objects of a verb headword or nouns typically modified by an adjective headword appear unbracketed;
– adjectives, verbs and adverbs modified by an adverb are unbracketed.

The following examples illustrate this approach:

- Typical subjects (N+V combinations)

glance off *vi [bullet etc]* ricocher, dévier; *[arrow, sword]* dévier
zing 2 *vi [bullet, arrow]* siffler **the bullet ~ed past his ear** la balle lui a sifflé à l'oreille; **the cars ~ed past** les voitures sont passées dans un bruit strident.

- Typical objects (V+N combinations)

discharge 1 *vt* **(a)** *ship, cargo* décharger; *[bus etc] passengers* débarquer; *liquid* déverser; *(Elec)* décharger.
(b) *employee* renvoyer, congédier; *(Mil) soldier* rendre à la vie civile; *(for health reasons)* réformer; *(Jur) prisoner* libérer, mettre en liberté, élargir...
(c) *gun* décharger, faire partir; *arrow* décocher
shoot 3 *vt (fire) gun* tirer *or* lâcher un coup de (*at* sur); *arrow* décocher, lancer, tirer (*at* sur); *bullet* tirer (*at* sur); *rocket, missile* lancer (*at* sur)
barb 2 *vt arrow* garnir de barbelures, barbeler; *fish hook* garnir de barbillons.

- N+N combinations

cloud 1 *n* **a** *(Met)* nuage, nuée *(liter)*; *[smoke, dust etc]* nuage; *[insects, arrows]* nuée; *[gas]* nappe...
quiver *n (for arrows)* carquois

shaft *n* **(a)** *(stem etc)* *[arrow, spear]* hampe; *[tool, golf club]* manche; *[feather]* tuyau; *[column]* fût; *[bone]* diaphyse ...
sheaf *n, pl* **sheaves** *[corn]* gerbe; *[papers]* liasse; *[arrows]* faisceau.

* Adj+N combinations

barbed I *adj arrow* barbelé; *(fig) words, wit* acéré
gnawing *adj sound* comme une bête qui ronge; *(fig) remorse, anxiety etc* torturant, tenaillant; *hunger* dévorant, tenaillant; *pain* harcelant

A few remarks ought to be made at this juncture. First, most of the examples above illustrate collocational constraints of the restricted type (Aisenstadt 1979). Applying Hausmann's terminology (1979), it is easy to notice that the base of the collocations, i.e. the main element which is responsible for the selection of the other member of the combination, appears in italics while the collocator itself is the headword (the element whose meaning is modified or "tailored" to fit the meaning of the base). It should be borne in mind that, in an encoding perspective, this way of presenting these polar collocations may not prove very useful if one wants to start from the base in order to discover a collocator which expresses a given meaning. Imagine, for example, that a translator or a student wishes to know which verbs can take the noun *arrow* as subject and express the typical noise made by arrows. The entry for *arrow* in the dictionary is not going to provide any useful answer but a quick glance at the first category of combinations above reveals that the verb *zing* might be appropriate because it includes some reference to a possible collocation with *arrow* which appears in italics and between square brackets to indicate its subject status. Working with the printed version of the dictionary and trying to locate all occurrences of the italicized bracketed item *arrow* would undoubtedly provide a partial answer to the question above but it would boil down to looking for a needle in an 800-page haystack. The availability of the machine-readable version of the dictionary, however, makes it possible for the user to access information via any element of the dictionary, including – though not exclusively – the element in italics. Focusing on the occurrences of a given italicized base makes it possible to answer such lexicographically interesting questions as:

* What can one do to arrows? (= which verbs can take *arrow* as direct object?)
* What can arrows do? (= which verbs can take *arrow* as subject?)
* What can arrows be like? (= which adjectives can modify *arrow*?)

These issues have been at the crux of AI/NLP semantic studies for some time and are increasingly attracting the attention of lexicographers who realize that, next to the traditional question of what things glance off or zing, inverse questions (such as "what can arrows do?" or "what does one normally do with books?") are equally crucial and worth answering. Many computational linguists are therefore trying to develop sophisticated statistical techniques to acquire collocational knowledge from large textual corpora (Choueka 1988; Smadja 1991, 1993; Grefenstette 1994 a,b; Church and Hanks 1990 [also in this volume – *ed.*]; Church *et al.* 1994 ...). Potential areas of application range from the development of novel types of lexical resources to the construction of computational lexicons for natural language generation (Smadja 1993).

Starting from the hypothesis that co-occurrence knowledge is spread across the entire MRD, it is therefore possible to retrieve a given base and its collocators by concentrating on the occurrences of a given italicized item, say *arrow*, in the whole English–French part of the dictionary. Doing so yields a list of 21 items (with *shaft* appearing twice – see Figure 1). If we use Boolean operators to refine the queries against the dictionary and search for the occurrences of the part-of-speech (POS) label *vt* and the italicized item *arrow*, we come up with the following list of verbs which can take *arrow* as direct object:

- *barb, discharge, feather, loose, poison, send, shoot, speed*

Similarly, *arrow* appears as possible subject of the following verbs:

- *glance off, zing*

Along the same lines, arrows can be *barbed* and the item *arrow* appears under the following noun entries:

- *barb, cloud, head, quiver, rain, shaft, sheaf, shower, storm*

The above lists of items which contain some reference to the noun *arrow* in the microstructure of the entries are indisputably most useful since they contain the type of decision-making material any translator or writer would like to have at his or her fingertips. As noted by Cop (1988), someone writing a text about a given concept, in this case arrows, frequently needs a list of contextual partners to jog his or her memory or to spark his or her imagination. It should be realized, however, that this list of verbs is rather heterogeneous and resembles what can be found in a traditional collocational dictionary such as the BBI dictionary (Benson *et al.* 1986 – note that the entry for *arrow* in this dictionary is very poor: the only collocating verb is *shoot* and there are no N+N collocations). The compilations extracted from the CR dictionary do not provide any semantic interpretation and the user is left in the lurch when it comes to working out the exact nature of the link which unites the various components of the collocation. The verbs *discharge, shoot, poison* or *barb* all appear in the same category of V+N collocations but it hardly needs to be pointed out that they do not express the same meaning and are far from being interchangeable. Most collocational dictionaries also fail to differentiate between collocations, and corpus-based studies drawing on sophisticated statistical techniques often yield the same type of heterogeneous data, even if tagged and parsed data are used. Smadja (1991) admits that the type of semantic interpretation he has in mind to distinguish sub-classes cannot be performed automatically. In the example under scrutiny here, this semantic interpretation would be based on the recognition that the relationship between the base of the collocation (*arrow*) and the collocator is variable. *Discharge* and *shoot* (together with *loose, send* or *speed*) could be considered as near synonyms, while *barb* and *feather* would both belong to a class of verbs referring to what must be done to arrows before they can be used properly. In order to allow more flexible queries and semantically-motivated questions, I therefore decided to embark on the construction of a lexical database in which the relationship between the base (the metalinguistic indicator) and the collocator would be made explicit in terms of lexical-semantic labels. Mel'čuk's apparatus of lexical functions was chosen to assign these semantic tags because it provides the linguist with a powerful descriptive tool, not only based on sound theoretical research but also capable of coping with a wide range of lexical-semantic relations, whether paradigmatic (on the vertical axis) or syntagmatic (on the horizontal axis).

4   ENRICHING THE DATABASE

It should be realized that enriching an MRD with lexical-semantic relations involves *adding* information and hence changing the dictionary files. Since the structural properties of the dictionary entries had to be identified, which would make it possible to display only selected types of information (headwords, translations, collocates, parts of speech...), a flexible representation model was required to enable us to update the dictionary, change the contents and have powerful searching and retrieving facilities at our disposal to formulate fine-grained queries against the database. The relational model was opted for because it would enable us to make full use of the retrieval and indexing facilities of standard relational database management systems.

As pointed out by Michiels (1995b), some criticism has been leveled against the use of the relational database model for the implementation of lexical databases (see Boguraev *et al.* 1992 and Ide *et al.* 1994). Arguments countering this criticism are put forward by Michiels (1995b: 94) as follows: "It is pointed out that the restrictions of the relational model (fixed number of fields, fixed field length, etc.) make it extremely difficult to implement a lexical database in such a model. For instance, lexical items have different numbers of homographs; homographs have different numbers of associated definitions; definitions have different numbers of associated examples; definitions and examples are of varying length, from a single word to a full sentence. However, it is in the very essence of the relational model to work with a series of tables rather than a single one. Consequently, the fact that one definition has one example, whereas the following has six, is not really a problem if the definition table and the example table are distinct tables related by one or several common fields."

The Collins–Robert dictionary is now in relational database format. The database design and the transformation of the CR typesetting tapes into dBaseIII+ relational tables was carried out by Jacques Jansen. The retrieval software consists of a series of application programs, written in C for DOS and Unix (Sun) platforms (by Luc Alexandre) and in Clipper (by myself). I also wrote a Clipper program for enriching the database with lexical-semantic labels à la Mel'čuk. The structure of the database is fully described in Fontenelle (1997).

Basically, the enrichment of the database consisted in creating two new fields, one for the lexical-semantic relation holding between the italicized metalinguistic item and the headword under which it appears, and another one for the French translation of the italicized item. The latter field was meant to provide partial disambiguation of these indicators, which are sometimes used in their various senses across the dictionary. Since this has strong implications for the study of the collocational environment of a given lexical item, it was decided to systematically translate the italicized items (e.g. arrow = flèche in the examples above), which offered the additional advantage that the database now contains information about the collocators and the bases for both languages while, in the original version, only English bases, English collocations and French collocations could be accessed.

At this juncture, it is useful to briefly introduce the underlying framework chosen to represent the lexical-semantic relation coded in a separate field of the database. Mel'čuk's Meaning-Text Theory (MTT) is probably famous enough and there is no need to introduce it at great length here (see Mel'čuk *et al.* 1984/1988/1992, Mel'čuk and Zholkovsky 1988. Mel'čuk *et al.* 1995 and Wanner 1996 present most useful introductions to MTT and lexical functions). Suffice it to say here that the Meaning-Text Theory and more specifically the lexical component of MTT, viz. the Explanatory Combinatory Dictionary (ECD), offer a systematic description of the syntactic, semantic and combinatory potential of lexical items. Syntactic information and constraints are found in the so-called Government Pattern section of an ECD entry. To describe "restricted lexical co-occurrence", i.e. the lexical combinability of a keyword, in other words the company it keeps, Mel'čuk uses the concept of lexical function (LF), which accounts for a whole range of collocational (but also purely paradigmatic) relations. The notation f(X)=Y is used to indicate that a lexical-semantic relation f holds between a keyword X (which corresponds to Hausmann's bases) and a value Y (the "collocator"). Mel'čuk's contention is that most of the systematic and recurrent lexical-semantic relationships in a general-language lexicon can be formalized in terms of a set of around 60 lexical functions. The Magn function, for instance, links a keyword to items that express the highest degree of the concept denoted by this keyword (intensifier), as in:

Magn (thirst) = unquenchable
Magn (liar) = arrant, confirmed, hopeless
Magn (pain) = excruciating

Another function, $Oper_n$, provides for the keyword X a semantically impoverished verb Y that takes X as its direct object (the subscript refers to the nth semantic actant, or participant/role, which is taken as subject). Consider the following expressions:

$Oper_1$ (complaint) = lodge $Oper_1$ (attention) = pay
$Oper_1$ (support) = lend $Oper_2$ (attention) = draw, attract
$Oper_1$ (question) = ask

The relevance of the concept of LFs in a multilingual perspective, more specifically in a generation perspective, is obvious as it provides a systematic and consistent way of representing restricted collocations (see Heylen 1995 or Wanner 1996). Other examples of such LFs are given below:

Liqu (to refer to verbs expressing destruction or nullification): Liqu (file) = erase, delete; Liqu (marriage) = annul; Liqu (law) = abolish, do away with, abrogate . . .
Son (refers to the typical sound or noise): Son (duck) = quack; Son (elephant) = trumpet . . .
$Fact_0$ (for verbs expressing the "realization" of something – be realized): $Fact_0$ (dream) = come true
Mult (refers to a regular group, set or multitude): Mult (key) = bunch; Mult (fish) = school, shoal; Mult (cattle) = herd . . .
Sing (refers to a regular portion or unit): Sing (grass) = blade; Sing (dust) = grain, speck . . .
S_{loc} (refers to the typical place or location of the keyword): S_{loc} (bee) = hive; S_{loc} (pig) = sty; S_{loc} (lion) = den . . .

Lexical functions can combine to form complex LFs. Causativity can be denoted in terms of the Caus LF, for instance, while aspect can be conveyed through the use of the functions Incep (start), Cont (continuation) or Fin (end) which express the phases of a process:

CausPredMinus (anger) = assuage, soften, soothe (Pred = "be" the keyword)
$IncepOper_1$ (habit) = get into
$FinOper_1$ (influence) = lose

Similarly, S_0Son will yield the substantive (S_0) expressing the typical sound (Son) of the keyword: S_0Son (elephant) = trumpeting.

The list of standard lexical functions was then used to populate the CR database. An application program taking the linguist/lexicographer through a series of pull-down menus was written to facilitate the encoding procedure. The menus provided the coder with a list of potential lexical functions and the appropriate LF for a given pair of items (metalinguistic indicator considered as the argument of the LF; headword considered as the value) was selected by moving the arrow keys and placing the cursor on the desired function. By providing a predetermined list of LFs, the coder did not have to type in the lexical-semantic label, which considerably reduced the risk of typos and inconsistencies. Moreover, the lists the coder was provided with were context-sensitive: lexical functions linking two nouns are indeed not the same as those linking a noun and its collocating intransitive verbs. The menus were therefore designed so as to present the coder with lists of potential LFs selected as a function of the part of speech of the headword and the typographical information contained in a special field of the database (indicating whether the metalinguistic item appeared between parentheses, in square brackets or unbracketed).

It is clear that the application program which was written in order to assign the LF labels and the translation equivalents of the metalinguistic items could only ensure a reduction in the number of typographical inconsistencies by offering automatic checking facilities. The linguistic decisions concerning the choice of LFs have been impossible to automate, however, except for a number of cases where a definition pattern could be used as a clue to assign a specific relation (e.g. *sound of* in "**zip** *n (sound of bullet)* sifflement" signals the S_0Son lexical function for substantives expressing noises and sounds: S_0Son (bullet) =zip). In most cases, the semantic interpretation was then carried out manually for the entire English–French part of the dictionary, which represents over 70,000 pairs of items. For each italicized item appearing in the metalinguistic part of the dictionary, a semantic network was then created in which the base is connected to the various entries under which it appears by means of the Mel'čukian LFs. To come back to the example of *arrow* analyzed above, the semantic network for this noun and its 21 partners can be represented as follows:

part (arrow / flèche) = barb (barbelure <f>) [C]
$preparfact_0$ (arrow / flèche) = barb (garnir de barbelures) [S]
$qual_0$ (arrow / flèche) = barbed (barbelé) [S]
mult (arrow / flèche) = cloud (nuée) [C]
$causfact_0$ (arrow / flèche) = discharge (décocher) [S]
$preparfact_0$ (arrow / flèche) = feather (empenner) [S]
$antifact_0$ (arrow / flèche) = glance off (dévier) [C]
part (arrow / flèche) = head (pointe <f>) [C]
$causfact_0$ (arrow / flèche) = loose (tirer (<on><or><at><sb>sur qn)) [S]
causnocer (arrow / flèche) = poison (empoisonner) [S]
sloc (arrow / flèche) = quiver (carquois <m>) [P]
mult (arrow / flèche) = rain (pluie <f>) [C]
$causfact_0$ (arrow / flèche) = send (lancer) [S]
part (arrow / flèche) = shaft (hampe <f>) [C]
syn (arrow / flèche) = shaft (flèche <f>) [P]
mult (arrow / flèche) = sheaf (faisceau <m>) [C]
$causfact_0$ (arrow / flèche) = shoot (décocher) [S]
mult (arrow / flèche) = shower (pluie <f>) [C]
$causfact_0$ (arrow / flèche) = speed (lancer) [S]
mult (arrow / flèche) = storm (pluie <f>) [C]
son (arrow / flèche) = zing (siffler) [C]

As can be noticed, the network preserves the standard notation of lexical functions $f(X)=Y$. A slash separates the metalinguistic item (arrow) and the French equivalent which was added when enriching the database. The last item of information refers to the content of a field indicating that *arrow* originally appeared between square brackets (C for "crochets" in French) under *barb, glance off, rain*, etc. [S] indicates that *arrow* appeared unbracketed (at "surface" level) under *barbed, discharge, feather*, etc. [P] indicates that *arrow* originally appeared in a parenthesized string as in the following example:

quiver *n (for arrows)* carquois *m*

The structure "for + Noun" in the "micro-definition" above was used to semi-automate the coding of "place" (S_{loc}) or "instrument" (S_{instr}) relations, in keeping with Ahlswede and Evens's contention that recurring defining formulae – or definition patterns – are valid clues to identify lexical-semantic relations (1988).

The semantic network for *arrow* can be represented diagrammatically in Fig. 1:

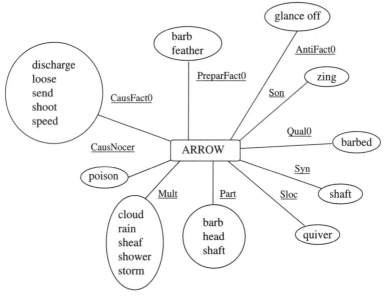

FIG. 1   Semantic network for *arrow*

Several remarks are in order here. First, such representation makes it possible to group items which share a common meaning component, like the exponents of the CausFact$_0$ LF which means that one "causes the keyword to realize the inherent objective associated with it", while AntiFact$_0$ means that this objective is not realized. The GROUP relationship is represented by the Mult LF while PreparFact$_0$ yields verbs indicating the type of preparation which is necessary before an arrow can be used properly. Second, it should be stressed that the semantic networks generated by the Collins–Robert dictionary are by no means comprehensive. One might argue that the work described here, and any attempt at analyzing dictionary data, represents only the beginning of a description of the semantic networks based on lexical functions (see also Fontenelle 1992). For instance, the database can inform the user that arrows can zing or that *cloud/rain/sheaf/shower/storm of arrows* are valid collocations illustrating a group (Mult) relationship because these forms are attested in the CR dictionary (s.v. *zing, cloud, rain*, etc.). The database will not inform users that arrows can hiss, however, because there is no information whatsoever in the English–French part of the dictionary (the only typical subjects listed for *hiss* are *person, smoke, gas, steam*). One way of improving on the CR lists of collocations, which is currently being investigated by the DEFI team (Michiels 1996; Michiels and Dufour 1996; Dufour 1997), is to combine the CR database with the Oxford–Hachette dictionary (Corréard and Grundy 1994) to create a single machine-tractable dictionary usable for word sense disambiguation. Corpus analysis would obviously also complement the data and would for instance make it possible to add the following relations to the diagram above:

PerfFact$_0$ (arrow) = hit, strike, wound, pierce [a target]
Func$_0$ (arrow) = fly, speed
S$_{instr}$ (arrow) = bow
S$_0$Func$_0$ (arrow) = flight
Gener (arrow) = weapon

It should also be noted that the range of relations used in my database is slightly different from the list advocated by Mel'čuk. The part–whole relationship, for instance, is not accounted for in Mel'čuk's model of LFs because it is not a function in its strict sense (it is a semantic, one-to-many relation). The availability of this type of material in the CR dictionary and its potential use in information retrieval or in (machine) translation was so obvious that I have decided to treat it in the database like other types of relations. Coding it systematically across the entire dictionary then makes it possible to answer such questions as:

Q: What are the main parts of an arrow?
A: Part (arrow) = barb (Fr. barbelure), head (Fr. pointe), shaft (Fr. hampe)

The use of the term "function" may be considered inappropriate since one argument can clearly yield two or more values (CausFact$_0$ (arrow)=discharge, loose, send. . . .) The term "lexical-semantic relation" would probably be more appropriate since the material contained in the database includes $1 \rightarrow 1$ and $1 \rightarrow n$ relations. Moreover, it should also be stressed that, unlike the standard network representations used by AI specialists, the relational networks depicted above do not offer transitivity (e.g. *arrow* implies *weapon* but *cloud of arrows* does not imply *cloud of weapons). The usefulness of these relations in an NLP perspective should be obvious, however. Part–whole relations, instrumental relations or hyperonymy links, for instance, are essential in solving PP attachment problems (i.e. deciding on where to attach a given prepositional phrase). To illustrate the complexity of this task, consider the following two sentences:

(1) John painted the jeep with the new brush.
(2) John painted the jeep with the new wheels.

It is clear that (1) and (2) should be assigned different constituent structures. *With the new brush* in (1) is an immediate constituent of the larger constituent *painted the jeep with the new brush*. Conversely, *the jeep with the new wheels* in (2) forms a constituent. The two analyses may be arrived at on the basis of the distinct types of lexical-semantic relationship playing a role in (1) and in (2). While *brush* is undoubtedly the typical instrument associated with the process of painting, *wheel* participates in a strong semantic relationship with *jeep* (and with most vehicles in general), viz. a part-of relationship. Solving such potential ambiguities presupposes the description of such relations in the lexicon, possibly in the form of lexical functions which specify the following information:

S$_{instr}$ (paint) = brush
Part (vehicle) = wheel . . .
Spec (vehicle) = jeep . . .

To avoid specifying that wheels are parts of jeeps, ambulances, lorries, cars, etc., it is much more economical to mention this information only once for the general hyperonym (vehicle) and to make sure that the taxonomy of vehicles is captured through the function Spec (specific term), which was introduced in the CR database whenever a hyperonym was used in the microstructure of an entry (see section 5 below).

5   RETRIEVING DATA FROM THE BILINGUAL DATABASE

Several application programs were written to enable the user to update the database, search it or export data. A retrieval program was written in order to provide users with multiple access keys and to give them maximal freedom by means of a command line interface. The user simply has to type the name of the program, viz. robcol, and the conditions on the fields he or she wishes to formulate (the symbol "*" can also be used for wildcards). The fields which can be queried have to be preceded by a hyphen:

-i: italicized metalinguistic item
-h: headword
-pos: part of speech (of the headword)
-lex: lexical function
-tdt: French translation of the italicized item
-fre: French translation of the headword
-frm: register (formal, informal . . .)

If we are interested in retrieving headwords which contain the item *pig* in italics, we may type the following command:

robcol -i pig

which yields the following results:

boar (n) : pig => verrat <m> (porc,male)
dig (vi) : pig => fouiller (porc,)
food (n) : pig => pâtée <f> (porc,)
geld (vt) : pig => châtrer (porc,)
grunt (vi) : pig => grogner (porc,son)
keep (vt) : pig => élever (porc,)
mash (n) : pig => pâtée <f> (porc,)
nuzzle (vi) : pig => fouiller du groin (porc,)
root (vi) : pig => fouiller (avec le groin) (porc,)
root up (vt sep) : pig => déterrer (porc,)
rout (vi) : pig => fouiller (porc,)
slop (n) : pig => pâtée <f> (porc,)
snout (n) : pig => museau (porc,part)
sow (n) : pig => truie <f> (porc,female)
sty (n) : pig => porcherie <f> (porc,sloc)
swill (n) : pig => pâtée <f> (porc,)

The format is here the following:

headword + part of speech + italicized item => French translation of the headword + French translation of the italicized item (here, *porc*) + standard lexical function or lexical-semantic relation, if any.

The program makes it possible to retrieve collocational information by combining different types of criteria. In the following query, for instance, the user is interested in extracting the verbs which can take *law* as direct object and whose meaning in the vicinity of *law* can be expressed in terms of the lexical function Liqu (liquidate, eradicate):

robcol -i law -lex liqu
Output:

abolish (vt) : law => abroger (loi,liqu)
annul (vt) : law => abroger (loi,liqu)
do away with (vt fus) : law => supprimer (loi,liqu)
repeal (vt) : law => abroger (loi,liqu)
rescind (vt) : law => abroger (loi,liqu)
revoke (vt) : law => rapporter (loi,liqu)

Focusing on the transitive verbs which can take *law* as direct object would yield a heterogeneous and much larger list of verbs including the six verbs above, but also other verbs such as *carry out, elude, enact, enforce, obey, override, promulgate, vote in . . .*

The flexibility of the retrieval interface enables the user to select, say, transitive phrasal verbs with a separable particle (part of speech = vt sep) which can be described as semantically impoverished "support" verbs (LF = $Oper_1$) for bases beginning with "a":

robcol -i "a*" -pos "vt sep" -lex oper1
Output:

bring forward (vt sep) : argument => avancer (argument,oper1)
pull out (vt sep) : argument => sortir [informal] (argument,oper1)
put forward (vt sep) : argument => avancer (argument,oper1)
put in (vt sep) : application => faire (candidature,oper1)

The following command retrieves verbs which can take the noun *sail* as direct object and which mean that the inherent purpose associated with sails is realized (LF = $Real_1$):

robcol -i sail -lex real1

get up (vt sep) : sail => hisser (voile,real1)
haul up (vt sep) : sail => hisser (voile,real1)
hoist (vt) : sail => hisser (voile,real1)
put up (vt sep) : sail => hisser (voile,real1)
shake out (vt sep) : sail => déployer (voile,real1)
spread (vt) : sail => déployer (voile,real1)

Roughly speaking, the verbs above correspond to Pustejovsky's "telic" role in the Generative Lexicon model (Pustejovsky 1991). It should be noted that the mechanism of compound functions makes it possible to formalize the relationship between *sail* and verbs which express the opposite meaning in terms of the $AntiReal_1$ LF (the typical purpose associated with sails is no longer realized):

robcol -i sail -lex antireal1

haul down (vt sep) : sail => affaler (voile,antireal1)
lower (vt) : sail => abaisser (voile,antireal1)
strike (vt) : sail => amener (voile,antireal1)

The data extracted above include a sizeable number of phrasal verbs used in a semi-technical sense. Extracting such collocations from corpora requires a previously analyzed (tagged and, preferably, parsed) corpus. Since no tagger can be considered as infallible (most surveys report success rates of around 90%) and parsers are even more error-prone, standard collocation extraction programs may fail to identify combinations which, to a human eye, would inevitably be considered as interesting collocations. Consider the sentence *This law was done away with in 1992*. It combines several difficulties which may hinder the automatic recognition of the collocation: passivization, use of a complex phrasal verb (most collocation extraction programs work best with bi-grams, i.e. pairs of words co-occurring within a given span of items). The phrasal verb *do away with* is actually made up of three "words" and the combination with *law* involves four highly frequent items, which makes the identification of this V-N collocation very difficult (consider *put up, shake out* or *haul down sails*, which feature the same type of complexity, to a lesser extent).

The retrieval program can of course also be used to extract information as if one were simply looking up a headword in the printed dictionary. The primary access key is then the headword field and the information which is displayed is similar to what can be found in the dictionary, although the output is reformatted (and can obviously be customized). The interest of such information in a generation perspective is evident.

robcol -h confirmed -pos adj

> confirmed (adj) : drunkard => invétéré (ivrogne,magn)
> confirmed (adj) : liar => invétéré (menteur,magn)
> confirmed (adj) : smoker => invétéré (fumeur,magn)
> confirmed (adj) : bachelor => endurci (célibataire,magn)
> confirmed (adj) : sinner => endurci (pécheur,magn)
> confirmed (adj) : habit => incorrigible (habitude,magn)

The lexical function linking *confirmed* and *liar* above is Magn because the adjective can be seen as an intensifier ("magnification"), as in *heavy smoker*. Focusing on this function and on the noun *liar* enables us to extract other adjectives which, when combined with *liar*, have a similar meaning:

robcol -i liar -lex magn

> arrant (adj) : liar => fieffé (menteur,magn)
> bare (cpd) [barefaced] : liar => éhonté (menteur,magn)
> chronic (adj) : liar => invétéré (menteur,magn)
> confirmed (adj) : liar => invétéré (menteur,magn)
> habitual (adj) : liar => invétéré (menteur,magn)
> hopeless (adj) : liar => invétéré (menteur,magn)
> out (cpd) [out-and-out] : liar => fieffé (menteur,magn)
> rank (adj) : liar => fieffé (menteur,magn)
> straight (cpd) [straight-out] : liar => fieffé (<before> <n>) (menteur,magn)
> unqualified (adj) : liar => fieffé (<before><n>) (menteur,magn)

6   AN INHERITANCE MECHANISM

It may be useful to stress that the database is not a collocational database proper, but should be described more aptly as a lexical-semantic network. The thesauric and alphabetical organizations of the dictionary are no longer incompatible in a computerized dictionary, which is very much in keeping with prevailing ideas about the psycholinguistic organization of the lexicon. As a matter of fact, the Liège database features some characteristics which are typical of WordNet, the on-line lexical network developed at the University of Princeton (Miller *et al.* 1990 – also in this volume, *Ed.*). It should not be forgotten, however, that the metalinguistic indicators in the bilingual dictionary often function as heads of thesauric classes. Consider the following query, which extracts nouns designating a regular group (Mult < multitude) of fish:

robcol -i fish -lex mult
Output:

> school (n) : fish => banc <m> (poisson,mult)
> shoal (n) : fish => banc <m> (<de><poissons>) (poisson,mult)

The database contains the appropriate answer to our question because the printed dictionary includes the following entries:

school *n [fish]* banc *m*
shoal *n [fish]* banc *m* (de poissons)

Consider the following example sentences in two major monolingual learner's dictionaries (s.v. *school, shoal*):

- A school of tiny, glittering *fish* (Cobuild)
- *Piranhas* often feed in shoals (CIDE)
- Shoals of *whiting* (CIDE)

It is clear that, in the Collins–Robert dictionary, *fish* between square brackets can refer to the English word *fish*, but is also the head of a thesauric class comprising several types of fish. *A school of fish* is of course a well-formed phrase and need not necessarily refer to big fish, as the Cobuild example shows (a school of *tiny*, glittering fish). The problem here is that *a school of sardines, of herring* or *a shoal of whiting* are clearly equally well-formed. Lexicographers usually only use a superordinate term because exhaustive listing of all the hyponyms would be too space-consuming in most cases. One solution, described and implemented by Michiels (1996), is to link the bilingual dictionary to the WordNet database in order to be able to compute the tightness of the link between *school/shoal* and *sardine, whiting*, etc. Keeping track of this information is of cardinal importance if one wants to avoid translating the above phrases as *une école de sardines/merlans* . . .

  In addition to linking the CR database to an external resource, we have also tried using CR-internal information. The dictionary indeed contains a large number of synonyms and hyperonyms which we have captured using the mechanism of lexical functions (see section 3 above). Information about hyperonymy is represented as follows in the printed dictionary:

sole *n (fish)* sole *f*
perch *n (fish)* perche *f*
whiting *n (fish)* merlan *m*

The function Spec (specific term) has been introduced in order to formalize the link between the parenthesized item *fish* and the headwords *sole, perch*, etc. Hyponyms of *fish* can therefore be extracted from the dictionary itself, using the following command:

robcol -i fish -lex spec

(sample list)

    angel (cpd) [angelfish] : fish => chétodon <m> (poisson,spec)
    barbel (n) : fish => barbeau <m> (poisson,spec)
    bass (n) : fish => bar <m> (poisson,spec)
    bass (n) : fish => perche <f> (poisson,spec)
    carp (n) : fish => carpe <f> (poisson,spec)
    char (n) : fish => omble <m> (chevalier) (poisson,spec)
    dab (n) : fish => limande <f> (poisson,spec)
    dory (n) : fish => dorée <f> (poisson,spec)
    flounder (n) : fish => flet <m> (poisson,spec)
    gudgeon (n) : fish => goujon <m> (poisson,spec)
    ling (n) : fish => lingue <f> (poisson,spec)
    ling (n) : fish => lotte <f> de rivière (poisson,spec)
    marlin (n) : fish => makaire <m> (poisson,spec)
    perch (n) : fish => perche <f> (poisson,spec)
    pike (n) : fish => brochet <m> (poisson,spec)
    ray (n) : fish => raie <f> (poisson,spec)
    sea (cpd) [sea dog] : fish => roussette <f> (poisson,spec)

An inheritance mechanism has been implemented to allow more fine-grained queries. The following command (in which "inherit" is the name of the inheritance program):

    inherit sole mult

might be paraphrased as:

    "list nouns referring to a group/set (multitude) of soles – if *sole* does not appear explicitly as a metalinguistic indicator, move up the hierarchy and search for a group relationship (LF=Mult) for hyperonyms of *sole* (using the Spec function: Spec(X)=sole → X= fish; Mult(fish)=school, shoal)"
    Output: Mult (sole) = school/shoal

The experiment has revealed that the CR database cannot compete with hierarchies of hyper- and hyponyms à la WordNet, however, because the explicit indication of synonyms and hyperonyms in a bilingual dictionary depends on a target-oriented division of the semantic space covered by a source language entry (see section 3). Therefore, hyperonyms tend to be mentioned only when they are translationally relevant (Eng. *piranha* is translated as Fr. *piranha* without any metalinguistic indicator because a French-speaking user of the dictionary does not need to be told that this monosemic item refers to a kind of fish). Moreover, the WordNet database offers the additional advantage that hyponymy and other relations hold between word senses and not words, since the various types of relations used by the WordNet lexicographers link synsets, i.e. sets of synonyms for a given word meaning (see also Vossen (1996), who describes the EuroWordNet project, an EU-funded project which aims at creating wordnets from existing machine-readable dictionaries for Spanish, Dutch and Italian and linking them to the English WordNet database).

7 COMBINING THE LEXICAL DATABASE AND CORPUS-QUERY TOOLS

In this section, I would like to describe experiments carried out in the framework of the DECIDE project. The basic idea underlying this project was to link the Liège lexical-semantic database with other existing tools developed at the *Rank Xerox Research Centre* in Grenoble (Grefenstette 1994 a,b) and at the *Institut für maschinelle Sprachverarbeitung* at the University of Stuttgart, in particular the IMS Corpus Workbench and the Xkwic tools, which produce KWIC (keyword in context) concordances and feature very powerful sorting and collocate search facilities (Atkins and Christ 1995; Schulze and Christ 1994). The idea of combining corpus tools and external resources (see Christ (1994) who links the Xkwic tools to WordNet) makes it possible to formulate more specific queries, ultimately aiming to reduce the amount of data which has to be browsed manually by a lexicographer in his or her everyday work.

It is a well-known fact that dictionary compilers usually receive workpacks consisting of a list of entries to be compiled within a given period of time. If the lexicographers do not work interactively with a corpus, the entries they have to deal with are sometimes accompanied by corpus extracts which are to serve as lexicographical evidence. Appropriate corpus sentences can then be used to extract or tailor a dictionary example and, of course, to bring to the fore relevant linguistic facts to be included in the entry. Usually, however, the entries given to the compilers are arranged in alphabetical order. For the sake of consistency, however, one might imagine that the compilers would be provided with a list of entries belonging to given semantic sets (verbs of sound emission, verbs of cooking, body parts, adjectives of colour, etc), in keeping with some prevailing ideas on the organization of the lexicon (see Levin 1993). As is argued by Atkins (1996), selecting lexicographers' workpacks on the basis of semantics leads to faster compiling and better and more contrastive entries for near synonyms. Such an approach also provides a checklist for revising, updating or enlarging the initial list. We tried to examine this approach by using data extracted from the Collins–Robert database and searching for relevant evidence in a corpus annotated with part-of-speech and morphosyntactic information (i.e. each word form in a sentence has been "tagged" with the most probable category – see Heid (1996) who discusses the collocation *issue a warning* in which both *issue* and *warning* can, in isolation, be morphologically analyzed as nouns or verbs and for which a tagger would produce a pattern such as issue/VB a/DET warning/NSing).

In our experiment, we were interested in examining to what extent the lexical function mechanism of our CR database could be exploited to extract semantically coherent sets of concordances from a tagged corpus. Because verbs of sound display interesting phonaesthetic, collocational and lexical-semantic properties, it was decided to extract from the CR database verbs which had been labeled with the Son LF (Son refers to the verb expressing the typical sound or noise of a keyword; CausSon is the LF linking the keyword and the transitive-causative verb of sound taking this keyword as direct object). In the original printed version of the dictionary, sound verbs looked as follows:

bray 2 *vi [ass]* braire; *[trumpet]* résonner, éclater
crow^2 (…) **2** *vi* **a** *[cock]* chanter. **b** *[baby]* gazouiller; *[victor]* chanter victoire
drone *vi [bee]* bourdonner; *[engine, aircraft]* ronronner, *(louder)* vrombir…
hum *vi* **a** *[insect]* bourdonner; *[person]* fredonner, chantonner; *[aeroplane, engine, machine]* vrombir…

Such information was used to generate the following triples in the database:

Son (bee / abeille) = drone (bourdonner)
Son (aircraft / avion) = drone (ronronner, vrombir)
Son (baby / bébé) = crow (gazouiller)
Son (ass / âne) = bray (braire)

<ita>	<headword>	<ita>	<headword>
aeroplane	hum	baby	fret
aircraft	drone	bagpipes	wail
alarm clock	ring	band	snap
animal	bellow	bee	drone
animal	cry	bell	chime
animal	growl	bell	go
animal	howl	bell	jangle
animal	squeal	bell	peal
ape	gibber	bell	ring
arrow	zing	bell	ring out
article	rattle	bell	sound
ass	bray	bell	toll
baby	babble	clock	tick
baby	coo	telephone	ring
baby	crow	train	hoot

FIG. 2   Lexical function = Son (verb for typical sound of)

Using the customizing facilities offered by the retrieval program, we extracted pairs of items for which the LF Son had been assigned. Formatting the output in columns, a small sample of collocates contained in the CR database and meeting this criterion looks as above (Figure 2; <ita> refers to the originally italicized item, i.e. the subject of the verb of sound).

Such a word list would undoubtedly be of use to a lexicographer working on a specialized type of dictionary, a thesaurus, for instance, or to make sure that near synonyms or semantically similar items are treated consistently. The list above, containing several hundred pairs of collocates, was then submitted to the Corpus Query Processor developed at the University of Stuttgart and, more specifically, to the MacroProcessor (MP), a flexible query generator which uses macros and template files for complex search patterns (Schulze 1996). The corpus used in the experiment was a 255,000-word subset of the BROWN corpus and the following template file was used:

```
$1_$TNAME =
[word = "$1" & uppos = "N.*"]
[]*
[lemma="$2" & uppos = "V.*"]
within s;
```

This template searches the corpus for a noun and a verb separated by an unspecified number of words, indicated by []*, within sentence boundaries (within s). The noun and the verb are taken from an input file consisting of CR data as in Figure 2 above. Each line containing a Noun+Verb collocation is then evaluated against the corpus, using the template as a filter mechanism ($1, i.e. the first item of the list must be a noun; $2, i.e. the item appearing in the second column must be tagged as a verb in the corpus; elements are separated by tabs in the input file). The following output file was obtained:

166514: not touching anything. The <clock on the mantel_piece was scandalized and ticked> so loudly that he glanced at it over his shoulder

165923: _from the hall. Between the <telephone and the wall_plug there was sixty feet of cord, and when the conversation came_to_an_end, Eugene carried the instrument with him the whole length of the apartment, to his bathroom, where it rang> three more times while he was shaving and

179779: active imagination. When the <telephone rang> on the day after Hino went down to the village

148882: as shouting triumphantly. A <train hooted>. Instantly , he chilled. They were pursuing him

The concordances above clearly show that this approach can be used with a variety of applications in mind:

(1) Since the whole extraction chain has been automated, it is easy to retrieve potential collocates from the Collins–Robert dictionary and check whether these combinations are attested in a corpus and with which frequency (evaluating dictionary material against corpus data).
(2) A dictionary compiler could be provided with a compact collection of instances of a keyword or of word combinations. This can greatly facilitate and speed up the compiling process since the extraction of collocations has been carried out according to semantic criteria in order to reduce the noise. All occurrences of the item *ring* (and its inflected forms) above necessarily illustrate the sound meaning of the verb because the lexical function Son has been used as a primary access key in the lexical database.

To give a last example of the vistas opened up by this combination of dictionary-based extraction and corpus analysis in the field of information retrieval or lexicon building, one may imagine that a lexicographer wishes to extract sentences referring to a "group" of trees, without knowing which collocates can express this relationship. The lexical function at stake here is Mult and the CR database contains the following information:

clump (n) : tree => bouquet <m> (arbre,mult)
cluster (n) : tree => bouquet <m> (arbre,mult)
line (n) : tree => rangée <f> (arbre,mult)
row (n) : tree => rangée (arbre,mult)
stand (n) : tree => bouquet <m> (arbre,mult)

Modifying the template above accordingly (we are searching the corpus for Noun+Noun combinations, hence $2 must be tagged as "N.*"), we obtain the following concordances in the small (and non representative) subset of the BROWN corpus:

157953: ked with sweat . There was a <clump of trees> that appeared to provide cover right up
215343: st out_of_sight in the first <stand of trees> , fed by a half dozen springs that popped_out of

8   CONCLUSIONS

In a paper presented at a workshop in Grenoble on "The Future of the Dictionary" in 1994, Véronis and Ide (1994) wonder whether the 15 years of research on machine-readable dictionaries constitute wasted effort, considering the fact that the "extraction of semantic information has proved to be a far greater problem than originally envisaged, and, as a result, not a single large-scale knowledge base has been created from MRDs to date". Véronis and Ide suggest that the answer to their question depends on the point of view one wishes to adopt. It is true that original goals – i.e. automatically turning the MR version of a dictionary into a lexical database directly usable by NLP systems – have not been met. However, even though lexical information has proved harder to extract from MRDs than was thought 15 years ago, some taxonomies based on genus terms extracted from definitions have been created and are used successfully in some NLP systems (Guthrie *et al.* 1990; Wilks *et al.* 1996). Moreover, MRD research has made an outstanding contribution to the study of word meaning. What I have discussed in this paper (and in Fontenelle 1997) should be seen as a contribution to the study of lexical-semantic relations and, more specifically, of collocational knowledge. The vast resource of linguistic data which is now available in the form of a flexible bilingual database will provide linguists and lexicographers with another testbed for their linguistic hypotheses. The exploitation of this database of 70,000 contextual pairs of English and French items has only begun and is only limited by the researcher's imagination. The flexibility of the retrieval programs and the multiple access paths they provide open up new and exciting vistas of research into the structure of the lexicon, offering almost endless possibilities for exploring the dictionary data and the manifold semantic links between words. Although some of the ideas about lexical acquisition are not necessarily new, it may be useful to stress that this work on the Collins–Robert dictionary departs from earlier research on MRDs in several respects, which can be summarized as follows:

(1) Most research projects in computational lexicography have concentrated on mono-lingual learner's dictionaries. Bilingual dictionaries have often been neglected, with only a few recent exceptions (see Neff and McCord 1990; Farwell *et al.* 1993; Meyer 1990; Segond and Zaenen 1994; Bauer *et al.* 1994; Segond and Breidt 1996).

(2) In most cases, research on MRDs has focused on the extraction of syntactic information (subcategorization). The collocational potential of an MRD, whether bilingual or monolingual, had, to my knowledge, never been made so explicit and accessible.

(3) Most attempts to generate relational lexicons from MRDs are based on the use of defining formulae as clues to lexical-semantic relations (Amsler 1980; Michiels 1982; Ahlswede and Evens 1988; Calzolari 1988). Interpreting and making explicit the semantic links between metalinguistic indicators and the headwords under which they appear required a different methodology and a wider range of labels than the standard relations of synonymy and hyperonymy used in exploiting defin-ing formulae.

(4) On-line lexical databases such as WordNet and monolingual dictionaries are undoubtedly much more useful than bilingual dictionaries for generating taxo-nomical hierarchies. The situation is reversed, however, in the case of colloca-tional knowledge. The few MRD-based systems which offer some possibility of retrieving collocations are limited to very basic questions, even though they may be important from a lexicographical point of view. Boguraev (1991: 251) cites the following query against the IBM version of the Collins–Robert dictionary: What does one normally do with books? (= List the transitive verbs which can take *book* as direct object). More sophisticated, semantically-motivated queries are usually not possible with existing systems because the relationship between the metalinguistic items and the headwords has not been figured out, as is the case in the database described here.

(5) Mel'čuk's theory of lexical functions is usually applied to limited semantic domains or to very small fragments of the lexicon (note, however, that extensive lexical structures using the Meaning-Text model have been produced for Niren-burg's generation system (1989)). Testing this theory against a huge corpus of

general-language, "pre-digested" bilingual data extracted from an MRD had never been attempted. Furthermore, existing explanatory combinatory dictionaries offer only limited access paths. Bases are listed in alphabetical order, which means that collocators or lexical functions cannot be taken as primary access keys, as is the case in the CR database. Starting from existing pairs of lexical items and trying to discover which function relates the members of these pairs has brought to light a number of shortcomings in the mechanism of lexical functions (some of the problems related to the formalizable nature of LFs are discussed at greater length in Fontenelle 1997 and in Alonso Ramos and Tutin 1992). Despite these limitations, the descriptive power of Mel'čuk's lexical functions has proved most useful to structure the Collins–Robert combinatory and paradigmatic knowledge into lexical-semantic networks. This descriptive capacity has enabled me to add a thesauric dimension to the dictionary, even if the resulting database is incomplete and lacks the systematic descriptions of the specific government patterns associated with collocations. The significance of this thesauric, onomasiological dimension should be obvious to translators, who are constantly (and often desperately) seeking the appropriate term in context, to lexicographers, who are faced with the gnawing problem of extracting lexicographically relevant facts, or to computational linguists working in the field of information retrieval or machine translation for which access to large repositories of co-occurrence knowledge is an absolute must.

9   ACKNOWLEDGEMENTS

This work was carried out at the University of Liège (English Department) partly within the framework of the DECIDE project (*Designing and Evaluating Extraction Tools for Collocations in Dictionaries and Corpora* – MLAP 93/19), which was in part financed by the European Commission. I wish to thank Jacques Jansen, who analyzed the typesetting tapes of the Collins–Robert dictionary and constructed the relational database. Luc Alexandre, who wrote some of the retrieval programs, has also been most helpful. His energy is especially appreciated. A similar vote of thanks goes to Sue Atkins, Ulrich Heid, Gregory Grefenstette, James Steele, Yorick Wilks, Robert Ilson and Archie Michiels for stimulating discussions, feedback and critical comments, though the usual disclaimer applies since I am solely responsible for errors and inconsistencies and the views expressed here are not necessarily shared by them. Finally, thanks are also due to the publishers for granting the University of Liège access to the tapes of the Collins–Robert dictionary for research purposes.

PART VI
On Definitions

13

Defining the Indefinable

DWIGHT BOLINGER*

Picture an overzealous gardener who broadcasts onion seed at the rate of a dozen per square inch, lets the plants grow to a tangled mass, and extracts one to describe. Its central stalk is more or less intact but its roots are torn and the resulting description, while grossly true, will forever stand in need of repair because of those missing tendrils.

Lexicography is an unnatural occupation. It consists in tearing words from their mother context and setting them in rows – carrots and onions and beetroot and salsify next to one another – with roots shorn like those of celery to make them fit side by side, in an order determined not by nature but by some obscure Phoenician sailors who traded with Greeks in the long ago.[1] Half of the lexicographer's labor is spent repairing this damage to an infinitude of natural connections that every word in any language contracts with every other word, in a complex neural web knit densely at the center but ever more diffusely as it spreads outward. A bit of context, a synonym, a grammatical category, an etymology for remembrance's sake, and a cross-reference or two – these are the additives that accomplish the repair. But the fact that it is a repair always shows, and explains why no two dictionaries agree in their patchwork, unless they copy each other. Undamaged definition is impossible because we know our words not as individual bits but as parts of what Pawley and Syder (1983) call lexicalized sentence stems, hundreds of thousands of them, conveniently memorized to repeat – and adapt – as the occasion arises. And also as part of an associative network involving words of similar and opposite meaning, words of similar sound, similar spelling, similar register, and similar affect. A speaker who does not command this array, as Pawley and Syder point out, does not know the language, and there is little that a dictionary can do to promote fluency beyond offering a few hints.

Any word or formative will do as a case study, but I choose the suffix *-less* because of the rather assured way in which dictionaries treat it. And also because of its historic depth, with forgotten stems like *feck-*, *hap-*, and *list-* contributing their ancient association alongside the latest nonceword to prove eternal vitality, with stem and suffix coloring one another in ways no dictionary captures quite so well as we wish it might.

(Most of the references are to the *Oxford English Dictionary*, the *Century Dictionary*, and the *Merriam-Webster Third New International Dictionary*, abbreviated OED, C, and W3 respectively. The *Random House* and *American Heritage* dictionaries have little to say on the subject.)

A word first about the phonology. Though C states that *-less* is "applicable to any noun of which absence or destitution may be asserted", and OED says, more conservatively, "very freely attached to sbs [substantives – *Ed*.] to form adjs [adjectives – *Ed*.]", while W3 is

---

* Bolinger, D. (1985). 'Defining the indefinable', in Ilson, R. (ed.) *Dictionaries, Lexicography and Language Learning*. Oxford: Pergamon Press, 69–73. Reproduced with permission of Bruce Bolinger.
[1] Referring to the development of the alphabet by the Greeks after its invention by the Phoenicians. (*Ed*.)

simply silent on the matter, there are loose restrictions in colloquial English that conform rather closely to those of the comparative suffix *-er*, which OED explains in some detail. Venturesome speakers or writers sometimes extend *-er* beyond its normal limits (*unpleasanter, abtracter*), and *-less* is a shade freer still (and apparently was more so in the past, at least in writing – *resistless, remediless, husbandless, breakfastless*, all attested in OED), but for the most part *-less* is attached only to monosyllables or to disyllables with "light" second syllables, which contain reduced vowels without an overplus of consonants. *Skipperless*, not attested in OED, is better phonologically than *captainless*, which is attested. Forms like *card-caseless* (attested) and *drinking-glassless* (unattested) would be said only jokingly.

What concerns us more directly is meaning, and here we find, at the growing end, the literal sense of *-less* in a context of figure and ground, with "absence" applied to the figure. Thus one can have a *leafless twig* but not a **twigless leaf*, a *wickless lantern* but not a **lanternless wick*. The possibilities are broadly defined in the same way as the formula *X has (a) Y: A lantern has a wick, *A wick has a lantern. A hand has a finger* thus predicts *a fingerless hand*, whereas **An arm has a finger* predicts **a fingerless arm*. More narrowly, if a subpart is not apt to be conceived as figure – it may, for example, be too readily assimilated into the ground – it is not apt to take *-less*: we have *yolkless eggs* but not **whiteless eggs*, and *warless world* makes a better gestalt than *?peaceless world* (though OED attests *peaceless*). Thus *-less* is a shade more demanding of a sharp figure–ground relationship than is *have*. Given that relationship we are free to invent such unattested (by OED) forms as *moatless castle, mittenless hand, nounless clause, titless udder, zipperless jacket, doctorless clinic*, plus equally well-formed expressions that OED would probably regard as nonce, as in *This is the first hashless meal I've had in a week.*

That much is basic, and the association of adjective and noun is often so close that the noun is virtually presupposed by the adjective: *oarless* (*boat*), *motherless* (*child*), *rimless* (*glasses, tire*), *chinless* (*face, jaw*). This is coupled with a considerable amount of stereotyping. Though one might have a *horseless corral, horseless carriage* is the usual association, and similarly *strapless gown, beltless maxi, treeless plain, childless couple* (*marriage, family . . . –* but **childless society* is a bad gestalt), *landless peasant* (possessors are normally ground), *stainless steel, scoreless game, sleepless night.*

A clue to some of the grosser aspects of meaning is found in the attempts of dictionaries to define by synonym and antonym. C states that *-less* adjectives are "usually equivalent to the negative *un-* prefixed to an adjective in *-ful, -y, -ing,* or *-ed*, as *unhopeful, unwitty, unending, unmatched*". First, *-ful* adjectives are almost without exception gradable; the comparison readily applies: *very dreadful, youthful, playful, tearful, insightful, grateful* (the phrase *r-ful and r-less dialects*, with ungradable *r-ful*, was probably facetious to begin with). Adjectives in *-less*, though quite often gradable (*very fearless, tactless, useless*), are typically ungradable, either because what is missing must be totally missing if it is missing at all (**very collarless, supperless, sugarless, legless*), or because the adjective represents an ungradable extreme like *perfect* and *unique* (**very countless, *very ceaseless, *very deathless, ?very merciless*). Related to this is the fact that *-less* is attached to both concrete and abstract nouns, the former resulting in words that are often by definition ungradable, whereas *-ful* is almost uniformly attached to abstract nouns (an exception such as *manful* has *man* in an abstract sense). And even when *-ful* and *-less* are attached to the same noun, the result is seldom a good antonymic pair. *Useful* and *useless* might qualify, as would *harmful* and *harmless, cheerful* and *cheerless* (applied to "place" but not to "person"). But whereas *graceful* leans in the direction of movement, *graceless* leads towards manner and attitude. *Soulful* is almost restricted to "look" ("eyes", etc.), *soulless* applies to what is unfeeling generally. Even *sinful* and *sinless* do not quite match – a *sinless world* is a world in which there is no sin; a *sinful world* is a world that commits sin. And when those who work with the blind needed an antonym for *sightless* they did not resort to *sightful* but to *sighted*. What gives the several flavors to *-less* adjectives is the absolute vanishing of the figure from the ground. At the crudest level this produces the ungradable adjectives based mostly on concrete nouns. But it generates two main outgrowths found mostly with abstract nouns (though with a great deal of metaphorical extension from concrete nouns) which, depending on whether the noun designates an undesirable figure or a desirable one, can be labeled "freedom" and "deprivation". Add "absoluteness" to this and you tend to get adjectives that lean toward the extreme of the scale.

Deprivation seems to involve the principle of the "aching void". A large family of *-less* adjectives are typified by *hopeless* – they are negatively valued and cluster about such meanings as dejection, disorientation, and abandonment: *homeless, motherless, anchorless, rudderless, aimless, comfortless, loveless, joyless, meaningless, helpless, spiritless, feckless, hapless, remediless*. A related cluster is tied to "futility": *useless, fruitless, pointless, prof-itless, worthless*. Nearby are "weakness", "apathy", "awkwardness", "dulness", and other undesirable states, all expressed in a relatively extreme degree: *powerless, wordless, listless, graceless, tasteless, lifeless, senseless, luckless*. The sense of extremity can be seen by comparing *luckless* with its synonym *unlucky*. We say *He was unlucky in the game*; *luckless* is "permanently unlucky", and would not be used in that context. A number of *-less* words – mostly but not exclusively deverbal – refer to some extreme of measurement: *countless, numberless, measureless, fathomless, depthless, plumbless*. Even ungradable *-less* adjectives tend to be somewhat hyperbolic. We say *He was barefoot* or *unshod* but less likely *shoeless*, which would be a more extreme state of discalcement, perhaps that of not owning a pair. *To go to bed supperless* is a worse state of privation than *to go to bed without supper* – the latter would be more compatible with freedom to get up at 1 a.m. for a snack. *Baseless* and *groundless* are more potent than *unfounded*, *deathless* is so more than *undying*, *matchless* more so than *unmatched*. One who is *speechless* is thunderstruck, one who is *wordless* con-fronts the ineffable. To stand *motionless* is a more rigid pose than to stand *still* or *unmoving*. A *windowless house* is more than without windows: it is blind.

Other *-less* words are similarly stereotyped in a hyperbolic sense: *penniless* is matched only by *destitute* (*moneyless* is not fixed in this way), *faceless* is the extreme of anonymity. Of course, stereotyping can work in reverse, by overuse: *doubtless* is the weakest member of the series *doubtless, no doubt, undoubtedly, without doubt, without a doubt, without a shadow of a doubt*.

The potency of the aching void makes *-less* propitious for words used to denigrate: *witless, brainless, mindless, godless, mannerless, shiftless, spineless, merciless, heartless, shapeless, lawless, toothless, reckless, thoughtless, shameless*. (The curious near-synonymy with *shame-ful* results from "having no sense of shame" versus "crying shame upon").

The positively-valued adjectives are mostly the ones whose nouns (or occasionally verbs) designate something undesirable, whence the meaning "free from": *ageless, blameless, daunt-less, fearless, fadeless, faultless, guileless, peerless, spotless, scatheless, tireless*. Though there are weaker members of the set (*harmless, odorless, painless*) and of course many more that are ungradable (*warless, crimeless, stainless*), a high proportion of these adjectives are as strongly positive as those cited earlier are strongly negative. In this respect W3 and also the *Longman New Universal Dictionary* are misleading in the part corresponding to W3's definition 3: "unable or lacking power to be acted upon or to act (in a specified way) – in adjectives formed from verbs", with examples *resistless, dauntless, quenchless, tireless, fadeless, ceaseless*. "Lacking power" is precisely the opposite of what these adjectives imply, which is "too powerful to be resisted", "too powerful to be daunted", etc. One has or lacks power to act, not to be acted upon; by trying to cram too much in a single phrase the definition falsifies the majority of deverbal *-less* adjectives. (A secondary sense of *resistless* does fit: "unable to resist" rather than "too powerful to be resisted".) Again we find that some ungradable adjectives show the same tendency toward extremes as happened with the ungradables among the negatively-valued examples cited earlier. So a *smokeless industry*[2] is one that has no relationship with smoke (such as an electronics firm or a publishing house), whereas a *smoke-free industry* may be one that controls its emissions.

The strongly evaluative overtones of *-less* adjectives make them a natural choice for writing – and to a lesser extent speech – that lays some claim to lyricism, and authors seem to enjoy playing with the suffix. OED cites W.H. Hudson's *peaceful gnatless days*. There is an airy intensity about phrases like *shoreless sea, stormless sky, shadowless pond, brimless cup, faithless lover, endless desire, deathless affection, nameless dread, relentless hatred, seamless web, spaceless infinity, remorseless enemy, windless afternoon*. Metaphorical transfers are common: *breathless* for "eager", *faceless* for "anonymous", *brainless* for stupid. The poetic sweep of many *-less* words makes them unsuitable for humdrum settings. One may readily say *The expedition crossed a grassless plain* but not *Our neighbor has a grassless back yard*. This may also explain why some resist predicate position: *How far can you get in an oarless boat?* is normal, but *?The boat was oarless* is odd; we prefer *The boat had no oars*. What *-less* accomplishes is a transformation of *to have no* or *to be without* to a form that is syntactically and prosodically suitable for attributive position, which in turn lends the "characterizing" quality of that position, its solidity and permanence (see Bolinger, 1967). A *-less* adjective plus a noun is a picture frozen in place, and the freest use of *-less* is to form nonce words grouped in just such a collective still life: *If I were on a mountaintop, my wish would be to look down upon an autoless landscape, out to a rigless*[3] *sea, and up to a planeless sky.*

Much more could be said, but this account of sinuosities is enough to show how much we destroy them when we define. Some destruction is inevitable, for a dictionary must limit its aims. As Lakoff (1973) says, "The purpose of a dictionary ... is to fill in what the speaker cannot be expected to know already" – to which we must add, "and also to serve as a reminder of forgotten knowledge and an organizer of diffuse knowledge". To do the best within these limitations requires not only attention to logic and precision but sensitivity to affect. In that respect the most satisfactory definition of *-less* in the unabridged dictionaries[4] I have in front of me is from the shortest, the *Longman Dictionary of Contemporary English*. It employs five simple equivalents: (1) "lacking", which covers the negatively-valued "deprivation" sense; (2) "free from", which covers the positively-valued senses; (3) "without", which takes care of the most literal cases; and (4) "beyond" and (5) "that never ... s or that cannot be ... ed", which takes care of power and hyperbole. By contrast, the W3 definition not only imputes powerlessness where it should impute power, but chooses as example of the "free from" sense the word *doubtless*, which as we saw earlier is the least free from doubt of all the sentence adverbials that incorporate *doubt*. Many things can misrepresent a meaning, including an excess of erudition.

---

[2] The expression *smokestack industries* is now current in American English to refer to traditional heavy industries (with or without smokestack) such as the manufacture of steel or motor-cars. (*Ed.*)

[3] The reference here is to off-shore *oil-rigs*. (*Ed.*)

[4] That is, dictionaries (of any size) not shortened from longer ones. (*Ed.*)

14

More Than One Way to Skin a Cat: Why Full-Sentence Definitions Have Not Been Universally Adopted

MICHAEL RUNDELL*

I INTRODUCTION[1]

It is almost 20 years since the first COBUILD dictionary burst upon the scene and changed the face of lexicography. Its most important innovation – the systematic use of corpus data as the foundation of its description of English – has fundamentally altered the way dictionaries are compiled. Despite some initial resistance, corpus lexicography has become the norm, and few lexicographic enterprises in English would now be undertaken without a basis in primary linguistic data.[2] The effects of the corpus revolution are still being felt, as corpora grow larger and more diverse and the software for exploring them becomes increasingly powerful (see e.g. Kilgarriff *et al.* 2004; see also in this volume – *Ed.*). Most importantly, corpora are now available (or being developed) for dozens, if not hundreds, of languages, bringing the benefits of data-driven lexicography to an ever widening circle. There is no going back – but no-one who has worked with corpus data would ever want to go back.

Among COBUILD's other innovations, the most striking is its use of 'full-sentence definitions' (FSDs). As the name implies, FSDs present defining information in the form of a complete sentence in which the *definiendum* is embedded, for example:

confide If you **confide** in someone, you tell them a secret
confidential Information that is **confidential** is meant to be kept secret or private[3]

While this approach is not entirely original – FSDs can be found in early English dictionaries, from a time when lexicographic conventions had not yet hardened[4] – its use in the COBUILD range is both coherently motivated and systematically applied.

* Rundell, M. (2006). 'More than one way to skin a cat: why full-sentence definitions have not been universally adopted', in Corino, E., Marello, C., and Onesti, C. (eds), *Proceedings of the XIIth EURALEX International Congress*. Turin: Università di Torino, 323–338.

[1] Special thanks to my colleague Faye Carney for her insightful comments.
[2] In the U.S., however, resistance to corpus lexicography is still depressingly widespread.
[3] References to COBUILD are to the third (2001) edition unless otherwise specified.
[4] For example:

TRANSMUTATION *of Metals* [with *Alchymists*] or the *Grand Operation* (as they call it) is the Finding of the Philosopher's Stone
TRANSCENDENTAL *Curves* [in the *higher Geometry*] are such as cannot be defined by Algebraical Equations, or... (both from Bailey's *Dictionarium Britannicum*, 1730)

At the 2004 Euralex Congress, John Sinclair (2004) reiterated his faith in this approach, and wondered aloud why FSDs had not been taken up by other dictionaries. It is a good question. A notable feature of lexicography in general – and of English monolingual learners' dictionaries (MLDs) in particular – is the way that any innovation which looks likely to improve the product is sooner or later adopted by competitor dictionaries. Thus, in good Darwinian fashion, the standard model evolves and improves. The use of controlled defining vocabularies or of devices for indicating the frequency of headwords are cases in point, and the most obvious example of this process is the way that corpora were embraced, almost universally, soon after the publication of the first COBUILD dictionary. The fact that FSDs have *not* been universally copied is significant, and the inference must be that dictionary-makers are not entirely convinced of their value. In fact, FSDs *are* used to some degree by all the dictionaries that share the same market slot as COBUILD, and examples of these will be shown later. But it is true they are not used as the default style, so Sinclair's question deserves an answer.

The rest of this paper will:

- briefly outline the case for FSDs presented by Sinclair (1987a, 2004, 2005) and Hanks (1987)
- illustrate the benefits of this approach (comparing COBUILD's FSDs with conventional definitions used elsewhere)
- discuss the drawbacks of FSDs in order to explain why they have not been universally adopted
- conclude with some thoughts about the role and value of FSDs in a larger repertoire of defining strategies

2   THE CASE FOR FSDS

Ask any fluent speaker of English to tell you what **temerity** means, and nine times out of ten they will come back with a formulation that includes a phrase like 'if someone has the temerity to do something'. Corpus data confirms that the word has a strong preference for appearing in the pattern '**have the temerity**+TO-infinitive',[5] and in essence this provides the motivation for a defining approach based on complete sentences – an approach that 'places the word being explained in a typical structure' (Hanks 1987: 117). Traditional lexicographic practice, with its misconceived insistence on substitutability, simply defines the headword as (for example) 'foolish boldness; rashness' (LDOCE1), leaving the user to slot this explanation into an appropriate context. COBUILD rejects this approach because it fails to take account of an essential (one might say, a 'defining') fact about the word **temerity**.

The case for FSDs entails:

- a rejection of existing lexicographic conventions, since – as Hanks diplomatically argues – 'it may well be that their full significance is lost on many readers' (1987: 116);
- a move towards a less technical defining language, which 'is designed to read like ordinary English' (Sinclair *et al.* 1987: xvi), and which to some extent reflects the

---

[5] For example, in the diverse 250-million-word corpus I am currently using, this pattern occurs in almost 75% of all instances of **temerity** (only 31 of 118 instances are *not* like this).

folk-defining techniques that a teacher or parent might use to explain an unfamiliar lexical item (cf. Stock 1988);

- above all, a philosophical position regarding the language system (which Sinclair has been elaborating since the 1960s), in which a word's typical environment and behaviour are critical to any account of its semantics. Sinclair rejects the notion (implicit in the design of almost all dictionaries) of words as self-sufficient bearers of meaning, and insists that, for any lexical item, 'the characteristic cotext is part of the meaning, and so is relevant to the definition of the item' (2004: 5). Put simply, words almost never occur in isolation, so it makes no sense to define them in isolation.

Thus the adoption of FSDs in COBUILD is supported by clear theoretical and pedagogical arguments. It is worth saying at the outset that this paper does not seek to challenge the broad thrust of these arguments: they seem to me theoretically compelling, and every contact one has with language data shows (increasingly) their validity and relevance. My intention rather is to question whether this model of language *necessarily* implies the superiority of FSDs in all cases.

3   GOOD THINGS ABOUT FSDS

The various defining styles available in the FSD model, and the advantages these offer, are introduced and fully explained in Hanks (1987). There is no need to go over this, but it is worth mentioning a few cases where, it seems to me, FSDs clearly work better than any of the alternatives.

I have mentioned before the case of the phrasal verb **lay up** (Rundell 1998: 333; see also in this volume – *Ed.*), which nicely illustrates the advantages of the FSD over conventional styles. Compare:

lay sb up cause sb to stay in bed, not be able to work, etc. (OALD4)
lay up If someone is **laid up** with an illness, the illness makes it necessary for them to stay in bed (COBUILD3)

The COBUILD version is superior in every way: it reads like 'normal' prose (unlike the unnatural formula 'to cause someone to...'); it shows that (in this meaning) **lay up** is almost invariably passive; it specifies the reason *why* people are 'laid up' (illness); and it indicates that the verb is typically followed by a PP with **with** (*laid up* with *a bad cold* for example). The conventional definition fails on every one of these counts.

Another appealing feature of this style is that it allows for additional information to be added in a second sentence. Here, for example, the add-on enables the dictionary to account for the reciprocal use of the verb:

argue If one person **argues** with another, they speak angrily to each other about something that they disagree about. You can also say that two people **argue**.

COBUILD's definition for the verb **slim** indicates its preference for the progressive form:

slim If you are **slimming**, you are trying to make yourself thinner and lighter by eating less food

Though corpus data shows that **slim** is also common in the infinitive (*trying to slim, in order to slim, helped me to slim*, etc), it is certainly rare in any of the 'usual' tenses. Finally (though this is not intended to be an exhaustive list of the virtues of FSDs), it is worth mentioning definitions like the following, which conveys an idea of the illocutionary force of this expression:

When people refer to **the good old days**, they are referring to a time in the past when they think that life was better than it is now.

What is impressive about all these definitions is that they provide a much fuller picture of the target lexical items, yet without making unreasonable demands on users or requiring them to know any special conventions.

4   WHY DOESN'T EVERYONE USE FSDS?

While acknowledging the many positive aspects of FSDs, one needs also to be aware of potential disadvantages. These are, in summary:

- *length*: FSDs are usually longer than conventional definitions, and this has a number of consequences
- *overspecification*: it is a feature of FSDs that they specify typical contextual and colligational preferences, but this can sometimes make definitions unhelpfully restrictive
- *new conventions for old*: ironically, successful interpretation of some types of FSD requires familiarity with a new set of lexicographic conventions

4.1   Length

FSDs are almost always longer than conventional equivalents, often twice as long. Sinclair recognises this, and has a number of counter-arguments (2004: 5–6), but these are not altogether convincing. Definition length is a genuine problem because it tends to correlate with:

4.1.1   Reduced coverage

COBUILD dictionaries include significantly fewer headwords than other books of the same type. Whatever publishers may claim, the main advanced learners' dictionaries contain a roughly similar number of headwords – but COBUILD's coverage is far narrower. A like-for-like comparison of five randomly selected stretches of text, amounting to about 3% of the alphabet, shows COBUILD falling well behind its competitors. The aggregate figures are:

MED	OALD7	LDOCE4	COBUILD3
1415	1448	1364	1081

FIG. 1   Headword-list comparison of main MLDs

The mean of the other three dictionaries is 1409 headwords; COBUILD's headword count is 328 behind, so it has about 23% fewer headwords than its competitors. These are fairly small samples, and one could speculate that any of the three other dictionaries might end up with the largest headword list on a full count. But they are all the same ballpark, while COBUILD falls well short in each of the five samples. This is unlikely to be an aberration.[6]

These are not trivial differences. It is a perfectly reasonable publishing strategy to say: 'we have fewer headwords, but we tell you a lot more about the words that we *do* include',[7] but if the primary function of A–Z dictionaries is for decoding unfamiliar words, a marked reduction in coverage is bound to lead to fewer successful look-ups.

4.1.2   Increased complexity

'If the style of a dictionary is too difficult or too condensed for users, the work is useless' (Sinclair 1987a: xvi). Amen to that: the dense, formulaic language of many earlier dictionaries has few supporters in the MLD community. But being too condensed isn't the only way of being difficult. Problems can also arise when definitions are not condensed enough. Consider for example this definition of the noun **retreat**:

A **retreat** is a change in your position when you have decided that you do not want to do what you have agreed or promised to do, usually because it has become too difficult, too expensive, or too embarrassing (COBUILD1)

All of this is true, and there are no difficult words in the definition – but this is a challenging sentence for any learner to process. At 39 words, it is off the scale in terms of standard measures of readability like the Flesch test. Readability tests are no doubt a simplistic metric, but it is undeniable that longer definitions mean a heavier reading load (for users whose linguistic resources are limited), and generally entail increased complexity. Thus the abandonment of traditional conciseness can bring new problems for users, who may go from the frying pan of unpacking a dense, formulaic definition to the fire of processing something two or three times longer.

4.1.3   Problems with anaphora resolution

The FSD style (especially the 'if-definition') has a tendency to create sentences in which the word to which a pronoun refers is not altogether clear, for example:

necessitate If something **necessitates** an event, action, or situation, it makes it necessary
bind If one chemical or particle **is bound** to another, it becomes attached to it or reacts with it to form a single particle or substance

This can cause serious processing problems for learners, especially those whose first language (Japanese, for example) does not use pronouns in the same way as most European languages do.[8]

4.1.4   Prolixity and redundancy

A blanket commitment to FSDs – even where the application of a word is very broad and co-text cannot usefully be specified – sometimes leads to explanations that use a lot of words to say not very much. Take the following definition of **gaseous**:

---

[6] Counts were done on these stretches of text: *checkbook–chimneypot, heaped–hedgehog, pressure cooker–prime mover, turquoise–tzarism*, and the whole of the letter N. Adjustments were made for the fact that OALD and COBUILD have a single-entry structure (where LDOCE and MED divide headwords by POS), so that in the former dictionaries **nobody, preview, prey** count as two headwords, **heavy** and **prime** as three.

[7] This is a design feature of the *Longman Language Activator*, for example. As far as I know, though, COBUILD's publishers have never made such a claim.

[8] I am grateful to Akihiko Kawamura, who contributed to MED in its early stages, and drew our attention to this as a potential problem with FSDs.

You use **gaseous** to describe something that is in the form of a gas, rather than a solid or liquid

The equivalent definition in MED is almost identical, but it starts at the word 'in', so is half the length. This is not just an issue of bandying word counts. Language-learners who opt to use a monolingual dictionary commit themselves to processing text in another language: this is a challenging task at the best of times, so we owe it to our users not to force them to read more than they need to. To give another example: COBUILD's marketing literature draws attention to this entry for **fortunate** (presumably as a definition that the publishers wish to recommend):

If you say that someone or something is **fortunate**, you mean that they are lucky

What useful information is the learner being offered here? Arguably, a single word – and 'lucky' is not an adequate definition of **fortunate**, as we shall see later. Of course, the 'displacement' convention 'If you say...' (on which, more later) is intended to convey more about the way the word is typically used. But whether this is apparent to the average user is a very different matter (see 4.3 below).

A final example, the COBUILD definition for the phrasal verb **bump off**:

To **bump** someone **off** means to kill them

Here again, the definition contains a single content word. Though less long-winded than **fortunate**, it is a weak definition. The two things a learner needs to know about this word are, first, its register (noted by all the dictionaries) and second, that it denotes *murder* rather than just killing (noted in most of the dictionaries): you can't be bumped off by avian flu or in a car crash. To the basic 'murder' definition, LLA usefully sets the word in its most typical context (the murky criminal underworld) by adding:

especially because they [the victim] know about things you have done wrong or are dangerous to you.[9]

All of this casts doubt on the claim that the added length of FSDs is offset by their being more informative: 'Full sentence definitions are longer, to be sure, than their abbreviated counterparts. But they contain more information and present it in an immediately accessible form, rather than in a code which has to be learned anew for each dictionary' (Sinclair 2005: 428).[10] The definition of **fortunate** discussed above is much less informative than either of the following:

lucky compared with other people, so that life is always easier or more pleasant for you than for them (LLA)
lucky, especially because you have more advantages than other people (MED)

(Both these dictionaries, unlike COBUILD, divide the word into two senses: about people, and about events and situations.) Teasing out differences between close synonyms is never easy, but these definitions at least make a creditable attempt. Supported by examples reflecting recurrent patterns in text (such as 'not everyone is as fortunate as you', 'those less fortunate than ourselves', 'we were fortunate enough to...'), they are, overall, the better entries. Both definitions are conventional in style, but they can hardly be said to be framed in 'a code that has to be learned'.

---

[9] This definition was written about 15 years ago, drawing on a 30-million-word corpus. Having checked it against data an order of magnitude larger, I am gratified to see that it holds up well.

[10] Similarly: 'The structure of the full-sentence definition... provides even more detail than is found in other learner's dictionaries' (Barnbrook 2002: 47).

It goes without saying that counter-examples can always be found (there are plenty of excellent definitions in COBUILD), but the evidence for an automatic correlation between longer definitions and greater information value is not persuasive. These are independent variables, and it is not hard to find cases where an FSD is *both* longer *and* less informative than conventional equivalents.

4.2   Overspecification

A common problem with conventional definitions is that they are underspecified – that is, in trying to account for all possible instantiations of a word, they often resort to minimalist formulations that can be slotted into any conceivable context. Compare, for example, these two definitions of the word **absolute** when used as a noun:

Something that is absolute (*American Heritage Dictionary*, 3rd edition,1994)
a value or principle that is regarded as universally valid or which may be viewed without relation to other things (*Oxford Dictionary of English* 2005)

The best that can be said of the first definition is that it is easy to follow and infinitely substitutable. But it generalizes to the point of vacuity: it is, in other words, severely underspecified. The second definition is a 'typification' that reflects the majority of observable uses. As Hanks points out when explaining the COBUILD approach, definitions should be read as 'stating what is normally the case rather than what is necessarily the case' (1987: 118), a vitally important distinction. And of course 'stating what is normally the case' only becomes possible when we have access to corpus data.

Problems can arise, however, over the interpretation of 'normally'. This is an issue in definitions of all types, but it is especially acute when the primary objective is to place the *definiendum* in a typical context. The cases of **temerity** and **lay up** (above) are good examples of FSDs that accurately reflect the colligational and collocational preferences of these words. But if some conventional definitions are underspecified, FSDs risk the opposite danger: of *over*specifying typical contexts in ways that may cause confusion. Some examples follow:

innocence If someone proves their **innocence**, they prove that they are not guilty of a crime

This is COBUILD's sole explanation of the use of **innocence** in the sense of 'not being guilty'. Limiting the context to 'proving' one's innocence gives far too narrow an account of how the word is used. A Word Sketch for **innocence** shows that – when it is in the object position – words like **prove** and **establish** are fairly common, but words like **protest, proclaim, profess, maintain**, and **assert** are even more frequent. (Not to mention the many cases where **innocence** does not appear in this construction at all, e.g. *The issues were not the guilt or innocence of the accused.*)[11]

bundle 5 If someone is **bundled** somewhere, someone pushes them there in a rough and hurried way

We infer that the verb in this use is mainly used in the passive, but corpus data suggests otherwise. Of 877 instances of **bundle**-vb in a 250-million-word corpus there are 101 active uses of the verb in this pattern/meaning, and 109 passive uses. (The count excludes cases

---

[11] Similar problems arise at **forgiveness, approval** (1), **decision**, and **insight**. COBUILD defines **decision** with an explanation that begins: 'When you make a **decision**...' – a frequent pattern, to be sure, but representing only around 12%–13% of all uses of this noun. Similarly at **insight**, which starts 'If you gain **insight** or an **insight**...'. But cases where the subject is non-human, and the verbs are **provide, give, offer,** etc. are far more common.

where the particles **off** and **up** appear; these are treated separately as phrasal verbs in both COBUILD and MED.) So there is a marked preference for passivization (most transitive verbs passivize less frequently than this), and the entry in MED should in fact have attracted the code [often passive]. But I don't believe this justifies *defining* **bundle** passively and appearing to relegate other uses to the sidelines.

A final example:

> **cheat** If someone **cheats** you *out of* something, they get it from you by behaving dishonestly (emphasis mine – MR)

This is certainly a common pattern (found in at least 25% of cases where **cheat** takes an object) – but so is 'cheat someone *of* something' and (more to the point) so is the simple V+O pattern.[12] The principle that definitions should deal with 'the probable not the possible' is a sound one, and setting the boundary between a frequent pattern and an overwhelmingly marked preference isn't always easy. But the evidence presented here suggests that the requirement of specifying lexical and syntactic environments often leads to defining statements which appear to exclude a wide range of completely regular behaviours. This could be an inherent weakness in the model, and it certainly presents users with a problem of interpretation: for example, when 'prove' is used in the definition of **innocence**, or 'gain' in that of **insight**, should the user infer that this is the only (or the overwhelmingly most frequent) collocate, or simply one of many typical collocates?

4.3   New conventions for old

We have seen that many individual COBUILD definitions may be difficult for learners to process, while others may mislead by overspecifying typical co-texts. But most of the defining *styles* used by COBUILD are transparent (in the sense that you only need to be able to read English in order to understand what they are telling you).[13] There are a few cases, however, of definition styles where the full range of information the lexicographer sets out to convey is only retrievable if the user understands certain conventions unique to COBUILD. I will look briefly at three of these:

—*the If/When distinction*: most verb definitions begin with 'If', but a substantial minority begin with 'When'. For example:

> When a horse **gallops**, it runs ...
> If you **gallop**, you ride a horse that is galloping

The distinction is motivated rather than arbitrary: it is intended to say something to the user (Hanks 1987: 126). In most cases I can understand why one is used rather than another (though the entry for **break** has defeated me). I am more or less certain that the average learner (assuming s/he even notices this variation) will not pick up the difference the lexicographer intends.

—*the If you/If someone distinction*: Barnbrook (2002: 7–9) compares the entries for **prat** and **bastard**:

---

[12] The entry at **inform** has similar problems.

[13] Though the same can be said for definitions in other MLDs, which generally now avoid the kind of 'lexicographese' found, say, in 1980s editions of LDOCE and OALD.

If you call someone a **prat**, you mean that they are very stupid or foolish
If someone calls someone else a **bastard**, they are referring to them or addressing them in an insulting way

He notes: 'The difference between the "if you" at the beginning of the definition of "prat" and the "if someone" at the beginning of the definition of "bastard" is an implicit signal to the user that "bastard" is likely to be regarded as a stronger and more offensive word'. Again, the distinction is well-motivated, but anyone with experience of observing learners using MLDs will probably conclude that this 'implicit signal' is likely to remain implicit.

—*the 'displacement strategy'*: another influential feature of the first COBUILD dictionary was the attention paid to pragmatics and the various ways in which features such as speaker attitude, vagueness, and politeness are typically encoded. Many COBUILD definitions employ what Hanks (1987: 133) calls a 'displacement strategy' in order to account for this type of 'meaning'. Compare:

mug 1 A **mug** is a large deep cup with straight sides and a handle, used for hot drinks. . . .
3 If you say that someone is a **mug**, you mean that they are stupid and easily deceived by other people

The 'If you say . . .' introduction to the second definition exemplifies the displacement strategy, distinguishing this use from the simple denotative meaning signalled by the first definition.[14]
   A first observation is that it seems to have been difficult to establish guidelines as to when this style is used. The displacement strategy is employed, for example, at **inflammatory**, **controversial**, and **confrontational**, but not at **contentious**, **combative**, or **belligerent**; at **scrawny** and **plump**, but not at **svelte** or **chubby**; at **fabulous** but not at **stunning**; and so on. Secondly, this approach (inevitably) exacerbates the problems of length and complexity discussed above. Compare for example these entries for **confrontational**:

if you describe the way that someone behaves as **confrontational**, you are showing your
disapproval of the fact that they are aggressive and likely to cause an argument or dispute (COBUILD3)
tending to deal with people in an aggressive way that is likely to cause arguments, rather than discussing
things with them (OALD7)

It is not clear that the first definition contains more information; true, it alerts the user to the disapproving attitude, but a learner who encounters this word in context, then decodes it using the second definition, will infer that calling someone 'confrontational' is not a compliment.[15] It is to COBUILD's credit that they identified a problem which needs addressing – traditional lexicography's failure to account successfully for non-denotative meaning – and started the process of finding solutions. My own view is that these solutions do not deliver: they tend to expand already long definitions, and the information they aim to convey can only be fully understood by a user who has learned how these defining conventions work (since the conventions are not transparent).[16] Other dictionaries have tried different approaches (see for example the entries for **just good friends**, **idle rich**, and **nerd** in MED), and others will judge how successful they are. But this remains an area where more research is needed to find

---

[14] See also Sinclair 1987: xvi: 'The words "If you say that . . ." very often signal metaphoric, figurative, and other non-literal messages'.
[15] Meanwhile, the definition for **inflammatory**, which begins 'If you accuse someone of saying or doing **inflammatory** things . . .', risks overspecifying ('accuse' is a strong word to use here).
[16] The entry for **great** is an interesting case, with several different styles used for explaining the adjectival uses: 'You use **great** in order to', 'You say **great** in order to', 'You can describe someone who. . . as **great**', 'If you describe someone or something as **great**,' and so on.

solutions that really work. In approaching this – and any other aspect of defining – there is an important rule to keep in mind: what matters is not the lexicographer's intention but the user's interpretation.

5   MORE THAN ONE WAY TO SKIN A CAT

The FSD model arose in response to a set of objectives (see section 2) which are on the whole very good objectives. The question is whether they lead us, inescapably, to the wholesale abandonment of established lexicographic conventions in favour of the FSD. I would argue, rather, that FSDs represent a useful new strategy to add to other defining styles, but that the same objectives can often be achieved through other means – and in ways that make fewer demands on learners. Most of the main MLDs make quite frequent use of FSDs, but none except COBUILD uses them all the time. In the Macmillan dictionaries (the same may apply to other MLDs, but their Style Guides are not available to me), we recommend the use of FSDs in the following cases:

5.1   Defining verbs

- verbs (especially intransitive verbs) where it is critical to specify the typical range of *subjects*, for example:

  expire if an agreement, offer, or official document expires, the period of time during which it exists or can be used comes to an end (MED)

  The same style is used at: **pink** (of car engines), **abdicate**, **buzz** (if your head is buzzing with ideas...), and many others.
- some reflexive verbs: see for example both definitions of the verb **ally** ('if a country allies itself with another country, ...', 'if you ally yourself with someone...'); and some ergative verbs.
- transitive verbs that occur overwhelmingly in the passive: see for example the entries at **apprentice** ('if someone is apprenticed to another person, ...'), **beach** (of whales), **cheer** ('if you are cheered by something such as a piece of news...'). When passivization is merely frequent (rather than dominant), we tend to define in the active and add the note [often passive].

For most transitive verbs, subject-specification is not especially important, so a conventional style works perfectly well (and is more economical). For example:

assassinate to kill a famous or important person, especially for political reasons or for payment

5.2   Defining adjectives

FSDs tend to work well in the following cases:

- where the range of typical complements is narrow and worth specifying, for example:

  blistering blistering criticism is very severe

And similarly at **bounden** (duty), **isotonic** (drinks), **jobbing** (workers), **bouffant** (hair), and many others.

- where the word suggests a permanent characteristic, for example:

argumentative someone who is argumentative often argues or disagrees with people

- where a conventional definition cannot be achieved without unnatural and convoluted wording (adjectives are more problematic in this regard than most other word classes):

slippery a slippery surface, object etc is difficult to move on or hold because it is smooth, wet, or covered in something such as ice or oil

But the majority of adjectives can be handled successfully using conventional styles. Compare for example, these two definitions of **lonesome**:

unhappy because you are alone or because you have no friends (MED)
someone who is **lonesome** is unhappy because they do not have any friends or do not have anyone to talk to (COBUILD3)

A case of 'less is more', perhaps.

5.3   Other strategies

MED occasionally uses FSDs in other situations, when a traditional approach produces a more difficult expression.[17] Lexicographers are allowed to use their discretion but the Style Guide lists a series of conventional defining styles, and these are the recommended default. It is worth adding, finally, that information which COBUILD packs into its FSDs can often be conveyed (arguably more clearly) through a *combination* of a simple definition, a list of frequent collocates, and a set of examples. A case in point is the way the various uses of **badly** are explained in MED:

2 in a serious or severe way: *Her eye was cut quite badly.| One of the prisoners had been badly beaten by guards.|* **badly damaged/hurt/injured/wounded**: *Fortunately, none of the drivers was badly hurt.|* **badly hit/affected**: *London is one of the worst-affected areas.*[18]

To conclude on this point: MED – and this probably applies to other MLDs – uses FSDs systematically, for categories that gain most benefit from the approach. In many other cases, however, we prefer an accretive strategy: adding layers of information to a simpler definition, using devices such as add-on sentences, labelling, usage notes, transparent grammar codes, and glossed examples.

---

[17] They are almost never used for defining *nouns*, however: in very many cases, there is nothing useful to say about a noun's contextual preferences, and I am not convinced that the considerable extra length that the FSD approach adds is offset by much genuinely useful information.

[18] A similar approach is used in LDOCE4: see for example its entry for **shoulder** (verb), where collocates like **responsibility**, **blame**, and **burden** are listed ahead of a conventional definition.

6   CONCLUSIONS

The iconoclasm of the COBUILD project has been good for lexicography. COBUILD began by junking the whole repertoire of traditional defining practices, and out of this arose an imaginative set of new definition-types which have broadened lexicographers' options. Following the 'thesis-antithesis-synthesis' model, most learners' dictionaries have absorbed these lessons and use FSDs selectively – when they appear to be the most effective strategy. COBUILD also gave fresh impetus to a process already underway in the 1980s – starting perhaps with the *Collins English Dictionary* (1st edition 1979) – in which defining practices were re-evaluated with a view to humanising definitions and bringing them closer to 'normal prose'.[19] Sinclair talks about 'the cryptic messages that are still the most common form of definition' (2005: 428); this may be a fair description of earlier dictionaries, but it has little relevance to 21st century MLDs. This is a competitive and well-informed market, and if definitions in the other MLDs were all 'cryptic', learners would vote with their wallets and buy only COBUILD dictionaries.

The two papers in which Sinclair discusses FSDs raise important issues that deserve our attention. For example, how long can a definition be before the advantages of fuller information are offset by the difficulty of processing it? As linguistic data becomes more abundant and corpus-querying software more powerful, we can learn more and more about the meanings and typical uses of the words we have to define. This means we face difficult choices about what information to select (knowing what *not* to say is one of the hardest lexicographic skills), and the more help we can get with these decisions, the better. Consider for example this definition for **forge**:

If one person or institution **forges** an alliance or relationship with another, or if two people or institutions **forge** an alliance or relationship, they create it with a lot of hard work, hoping that it will be strong and lasting.

On the one hand, this is a more *informative* definition than anything found elsewhere: it tells us about typical subject-types and typical objects, about the verb's reciprocal use, and about some useful semantic features (hard work, the aim to make something lasting). On the other hand, it is 40 words long, and this is not a trivial objection – some users may baulk at reading it, most will find it difficult to follow. Suppose instead we said:

to create an alliance or relationship through a lot of hard work, hoping that it will be strong and lasting

This is half the length of the COBUILD definition and far easier to read. True, some information is lost, about typical subjects and reciprocity, but does this matter? The former point is, arguably, deducible through users' real-world knowledge ('alliances' are generally made by governments and corporations, not ordinary individuals); the latter could be conveyed using a grammar note; and both can be illustrated in well-chosen example sentences. I am reminded of Hanks' seminal paper on defining (1979), which discusses the notion of 'elegance' in definitions. Though Hanks only hints at what this means in this context, we can think of elegance (by analogy with mathematical proofs or computer programs, for example) as a quality that combines simplicity and economy with

---

[19] For example, the various non-transparent uses of parentheses in definitions of verbs and adjectives – criticised by Hanks (1987: 116) – have been abandoned in most MLDs.

effectiveness and adequacy.[20] Some FSDs are elegant in these terms, but too many are not.

Finally, we should consider Sinclair's own hypothesis about the non-adoption of FSDs: 'I have often wondered why full-sentence definitions (FSD) have not appealed more to lexicographers, until I realised recently that most of the additional information they provide comes from studying the corpus evidence' (2005: 427f.). In other words, most MLDs do not use FSDs because – unlike COBUILD – they do not really use corpus data (or at least, not properly). This assertion cannot go unchallenged. In Sinclair's view, COBUILD is 'still the only *corpus-driven* dictionary': the contrast is with a *corpus-based* dictionary, following the model proposed by Tognini-Bonelli (2001). As I understand it, a *corpus-based* approach sees the corpus mainly as a repository of examples with which to test and exemplify existing statements about language – rather than (as in a *corpus-driven* methodology) a source of data that can help us to radically reshape inherited descriptions. This sounds like a useful distinction when discussing methodologies for theoretical linguistics.[21] But as a description of what goes on in contemporary MLD lexicography, it is an outdated caricature. Sinclair describes COBUILD's aim as 'to write a dictionary that attempted to represent comprehensively the senses and uses of words and phrases *as they were found in a corpus*' (*ibid.*, author's own emphasis). Would any self-respecting lexicographer want to do anything else?

---

[20] Johnson, with characteristic foresight, comes close to defining this concept, when he talks about the need, in definitions, for 'brevity, fulness, and perspicuity' (*Plan* 1747 – see also in this volume, *Ed.*). That combination of brevity and 'fulness' is key.

[21] And it is actually a fair description of a transitional period (late 1980s–early 1990s) when established MLDs (OALD and LDOCE) grappled with the challenge of meshing the new insights from corpora with dictionaries that had been wholly written in the pre-corpus era.

PART VII
On Examples

15

Corpus-based versus Lexicographer Examples in Comprehension and Production of New Words

BATIA LAUFER*

I   INTRODUCTION

1.1   Word knowledge

In most linguistic analyses a word is described as a set of properties, or features (Lado 1972; Chomsky 1965; Gibson and Levin 1975; Richards 1976). Thus knowing a word would ideally imply familiarity with all its properties, as is often the case with an educated native speaker. When a person 'knows' a word, he/she knows the following: the word's pronunciation, its spelling, its morphological components, if any, the words that are morphologically related to it, the word's syntactic behaviour in a sentence, the full range of the word's meaning, the appropriate situations for using the word, its collocational restrictions, its distribution and the relation between the word and other words within a lexical set. (For a discussion of word knowledge see, for example, Nation 1990 and Laufer 1991).

Unlike an educated native speaker of a language, the foreign language learner knows a much smaller number of words. In some European countries and Israel lexical knowledge is about 2,000–3,000 word families, in some Asian countries 750–1,500 (Laufer 1991). In many cases, word knowledge is only partial, i.e. the learner may have mastered some of the word's properties but not the others. In fact, the plurality of word features to be learnt increases the probability of a word being only partially learnt.

One possible source of information about a totally new word or a partially learnt word is the learner's dictionary. The phonetic script shows the right pronunciation, the grammatical specifications provide information about the syntactic behaviour of the word, the derivatives in the entry show which words are morphologically related to the looked-up word. The definition explains the meaning, or meanings of the word, register specification adds information about the affective and pragmatic aspects of meaning. While each of the above-mentioned parts of the entry provides one piece of information about the word, the example illustrating the word combines in it most of the information the learner needs to have about the word. This is so because a correct and natural use of a word in a sentence, or several sentences, will necessarily bring out the grammatical, semantic, pragmatic and collocational characteristics of the word.

* Laufer, B. (1992). 'Corpus-based versus lexicographer examples in comprehension and production of new words', in Tommola, H., Varantola, K., Salmi-Tolonen, T., and Schopp, J. (eds.), *EURALEX 1992 Proceedings*. Tampere: University of Tampere, 71–76.

1.2   Corpus-based examples and lexicographer-written examples

Since the function of an example is to illustrate the most typical properties and contexts of the new word, it is often claimed that the lexicographer's best source on information about dictionary examples is a large corpus of language that comprises real language as used by native speakers. Such language corpora are indeed available in the major dictionary companies and are used by them in the compilation of lexical entries. An issue of contention is whether dictionary examples should be authentic, with minor modifications for low-frequency words, or whether they should be only corpus-oriented. In the latter case, the corpus would serve as a guideline for the lexicographer, but the lexicographer would be free to make up his/her own examples. Fox (1987) argues for the superiority of authentic examples over lexicographer-made examples. She points out that the latter are often isolated, self-contained sentences, because lexicographers tend to produce sentences with too much information in them. Communication, on the other hand, is context dependent and so are the authentic examples. Authentic examples are not only grammatically correct, but also situationally appropriate, as they were actually used in real life, unlike the made-up examples, which are sometimes odd and not very likely to occur in a communicative act. Artificial examples, Fox argues, may not reveal the most typical usage of a word. This usage is shown by concordances from which the authentic examples are taken.

However, one can question the argument that lexicographer-made examples are not natural enough. Lexicographers, who are educated native speakers of the language, are bound to have correct intuitions about their mother tongue, about the grammaticality of the word, its typical use and its typical environment. These intuitions are not necessarily less correct than the intuitions of those language users who are represented in the corpus and are therefore not less reliable. Second, even if we accept the argument that lexicographer-made examples are less natural than the authentic ones, we might still prefer to see them in learner's dictionaries if their pedagogic value proved to be greater than that of the authentic ones. Both teachers and learners expect the learner's dictionaries to clarify the meaning of new words in the best possible way and to help the learners use these words in speech and writing of their own. If 'artificial' examples are not different from authentic, or even better in attaining these objectives, one cannot sensibly argue against their inclusion in the learner's dictionary.

1.3   Previous research

The question of naturalness and pedagogic value as perceived by teachers of English was investigated by Maingay and Rundell (1990, 1991). A sample of 25 words was given to a group of EFL teachers. Each word was illustrated either by an authentic example or by a lexicographer-made example. The teachers were asked to state the source of each example and to evaluate its pedagogic value. The results showed that teachers were in general unable to distinguish between the two types of examples. There was also no correlation between the source of an example and its perceived pedagogic value. The first part of the experiment (distinguishing between authentic and made-up examples) was replicated with 'naive' native speakers, i.e. who were not language teachers. They too were in general unable to spot the source of the examples.

If native speakers consider 'artificial' examples to be just as natural as the 'natural' ones, then the naturalness argument put forward in favour of the authentic examples is not very convincing. The claim for the pedagogic superiority of the authentic examples is doubtful too, since they were not rated as superior to the made-up examples on the perceived value test. One should not forget, however, that the pedagogic value measured by Rundell and Maingay was the PERCEIVED value as judged by native speakers who were familiar with the words that were illustrated. In order to investigate the REAL pedagogic value of a teaching tool, we must test it by testing the performance of the learners who use it. If one teaching tool is better than another, then the use of the better tool should result in better performance by comparison with the use of a less successful tool. Therefore, if the authentic examples are superior to the lexicographer's examples, then illustration of new words by these examples should lead to better comprehension and use of these words than illustration of the same words by lexicographer's examples.

2   THE STUDY

2.1   Aims

The aim of the study was to examine the difference in the effectiveness of two types of examples in the dictionary entry: (a) examples taken from an authentic language corpus and (b) examples written by lexicographers for the particular entries. The dictionary we are interested in is the learner's dictionary and the user of the dictionary is an advanced foreign language learner whose proficiency is roughly equivalent to the Cambridge First Certificate of English.

2.2   The subjects

The subjects were two classes of altogether 57 adult EFL learners in the University of Haifa from different departments. At the time of the experiment they were taking a course in English for Academic Purposes which emphasized reading skills.

2.3   Test items

Twenty low-frequency words were chosen as the target words to be tested. The words were taken from the list of 25 words in the experiment by Maingay and Rundell (1990) and so were the two types of examples for each word. We used 20 words which were unfamiliar to the subjects. They were not a part of the high school syllabus and were not taught in the EFL university course prior to the experiment.

2.4   Procedure

The tests were taken during class time and each test was considered a regular language exercise similar to other exercises required in the course. The differences between the two types of examples were tested in two conditions: 1. the 'example only' condition and 2. the 'definition + example' condition. In condition 1 the subjects received a list of 20 target words and their illustrations. In condition 2 the subjects received the same 20 target words; only this time they were defined by a dictionary definition and also illustrated by an example. In condition 1, only comprehension of the new words was tested. In condition 2, we tested both comprehension and production of the new words. Comprehension was checked by students' translation of the target words; production by writing a sentence with each of the words. To compare the two types of examples, each test sheet included 10 items which were illustrated by authentic examples and 10 which were illustrated by lexicographer examples. To avoid a situation where all the students would have the same words illustrated by the same type of example, each half of the tests had a different ten words illustrated by the same type of example. This way, each word was tested by two types of examples and each student was exposed to two types of examples. The scoring procedure was as follows: for each correct translation or a correct use of word in a sentence the subject got 2 points, for an approximate translation or word use he got 1 point; for an incorrect – 0 points. Several days later one class (27 students were present) was also given the Vocabulary Levels Test (Nation 1983) which measures the size of the learner's passive vocabulary.

3   RESULTS

3.1   Condition 1 (examples only)

As stated earlier, only comprehension of the new words was tested. It was felt that the task of using a new word on the basis of an example only was too difficult. 26 subjects participated in experimental condition 1. The task of understanding the meaning of new words from the context of examples only was difficult, irrespective of whether the example was authentic or made up by a lexicographer. In the case of the authentic examples, out of the maximum score of 20 (10 words × 2 points), the mean score of the group was 2.15, range 0–8, sd 2.17; in the case of lexicographer examples, it was 4.15, range 0–11, sd. 3.27. The difference between the means of the two types of examples was significant ($z = 3.39$, $p = .007$, Wilcoxon Matched-pairs Signed-ranks test). This shows that the lexicographer's examples provided better clues to the understanding of the new words than the authentic ones. One should not forget, however, that no matter what examples were used, if the example was the only source of information, comprehension of the words was unsatisfactory.

3.2   Condition 2 (definition and example)

31 subjects took part in this experimental condition. The results for comprehension were as follows: understanding new words from definitions together with examples was much easier than understanding from examples only. In the case of words illustrated by authentic examples, the mean score was 9.32 (out of 20), sd 4.61, range 2–20. With words illustrated by lexicographer examples, the mean was 10.45, sd 4.28, range 0–18. The difference between the two means was significant ($z = 2.06$, $p = .038$). This shows that even if the new word is defined, the additional information which is provided by the lexicographer's example will contribute to the understanding of the word significantly more than the information provided in the authentic example.

   As mentioned before, in condition 2 (definition + example), subjects were required to write sentences with the target words. The 'production' results were as follows: with the authentic examples, the mean score was 7.36 (out of the maximum of 20), range 0–20, sd 5.03.

With the lexicographer examples, the mean was 8.36, sd 4.26, range 0–16. The difference between the two means was not significant ($z = -1.55$, $p = .12$). Thus, in production, unlike in comprehension, the subjects' performance was not significantly affected by the different type of the examples. A comparison was also made between comprehension scores in condition 1 (example only) and those in 2 (definition + example). With authentic examples, the comprehension scores were much higher in condition 2 ($z = -5.63$, $p = .0000$); the same was the case with lexicographer's examples ($z = 4.85$, $p = .0000$). This shows that an example alone cannot be expected to provide as much information as a definition with an example. (Another study which compared learners' comprehension of new words from definitions only with comprehension from examples only (Laufer 1992) suggests that examples alone provide less information than definitions alone).

3.3   Lexical level and the example-type

Since some learners took the vocabulary size test, we could calculate correlations between (a) lexical level and comprehension scores for each type of example and (b) lexical level and production scores for each type of example. A slightly higher correlation was found between lexical level and scores for words demonstrated by authentic examples than between lexical level and scores for words demonstrated by lexicographer's examples: between comprehension and authentic examples .45; between comprehension and lexicographer's examples .39; between production and authentic examples .55; between production and lexicographer's examples .49. This may suggest that the possible benefit from lexicographer's examples is less dependent on vocabulary level of the dictionary user than the benefit from authentic examples (even though the latter are modified for low-frequency words).

4   CONCLUSION

The basic concern of this study was the pedagogic value of two types of examples: authentic and lexicographer-made. It was assumed that if one type was superior to another, this superiority would be reflected in better learner performance on new words. Below is the summary of the findings. (1) Comprehension of new words is better when the words are both defined and illustrated than when they are only illustrated by an example. (2) Lexicographer's examples are more helpful in comprehension of new words than the authentic ones. In production of the new word, lexicographer's examples are also more helpful, but not significantly so. (3) The usefulness of made-up examples seems to be less dependent on the learner's general lexical knowledge than the usefulness of the authentic examples.

   The findings suggest that lexicographer-made examples are pedagogically more beneficial than the authentic ones (further studies would be useful to substantiate this claim). If this is so, can they be considered as unacceptable on the grounds of lack of naturalness? One would assume that a group of lexicographers working together and consulting a language corpus should be able to suggest examples which are typical, natural, thought-provoking and surrounded by a typical context. These are the main requirements stated in Fox (1987). As for the argument that one should only use examples that occurred in real life, we may ask ourselves how much of real-life communication is an exact duplicate of what has previously been said or written. Certainly, some of it is. But if our ultimate goal of language teaching is achieved, new words will be used by learners in new contexts, in sentences never heard before or never produced before. The use of words may be modelled on the patterns the learner studied, but it will not necessarily be identical to them. A lexicographer, one hopes, can provide learners with appropriate and effective models of vocabulary use.

ACKNOWLEDGEMENT

I would like to thank my student Hedva Brochstain for collecting the data and Hagai Kuppermintz for the statistical guidance in the analysis of the data.

PART VIII

On Grammar and Usage in Dictionaries

16

Recent Trends in English Pedagogical Lexicography[1]

MICHAEL RUNDELL*

PREFACE

I have to look in the dictionary to find out what a virgin is ... The dictionary says, Virgin, woman (usually a young woman) who is and remains in a state of inviolate chastity. Now I have to look up inviolate and chastity and all I can find here is that inviolate means not violated and chastity means chaste and that means pure from unlawful sexual intercourse. Now I have to look up intercourse and that leads to intromission ... I don't know what that means and I'm too weary going from one word to another in this heavy dictionary ... and all because the people who wrote the dictionary don't want the likes of me to know anything.

Frank McCourt, *Angela's Ashes* (1996), ch. XII, p. 333

I INTRODUCTION

The English monolingual learner's dictionary (MLD) currently occupies one of the most fiercely competitive marketplaces in the publishing world. The number of serious players at the advanced-learner level has now – with the recent appearance of US and Australian titles – reached double figures. This makes it all the more surprising that Hornby's *Idiomatic and Syntactic English Dictionary* (*ISED*: 1942) and its Oxford successors had the field virtually to themselves for over 30 years. Since Hornby's dictionary met its first real challenge, with the publication in 1978 of the first *Longman Dictionary of Contemporary English* (*LDOCE1*), the pace of change has been rapid – driven by a combination of theoretically-informed innovation, astonishing technological advances, and the creativity of dictionary-publishers in responding to the known and perceived needs of users.

If learner's dictionaries have undergone such profound changes, two questions arise. First, to what extent has the MLD moved on from the Hornby model? Or to put it another way, how much of what he and his fellow pioneers established is still recognizable in the dictionaries of today? Secondly, have all these changes actually improved the product, and are MLDs better than they were 50 years ago?

This paper is a response to these two questions. Hornby's legacy, and its profound influence on the development of the MLD as a distinct lexicographic category, will be briefly charted

* Rundell, M. (1998). 'Recent trends in English pedagogical lexicography', *International Journal of Lexicography*, 11(4): 315–342. Reproduced with permission of Oxford University Press.

[1] An earlier version of this paper was written as a discussion document for a workshop on 'Dictionaries for Foreign Language Learning' held in Gent, 13th–15th March 1998, under the auspices of the Dictionaries group within the EU's 'Thematic Network Project', chaired by Reinhard Hartmann.

in the next section. Following this, I will argue in the rest of the paper that there have indeed been significant improvements in MLDs, especially in the last decade or so. But, of course, if one makes the claim that improvements have occurred, then one is required to be explicit about the criteria on which this judgement is based: what constitutes 'quality' in this context, and how are we to measure it? Two possible answers are that improvement can be said to take place when:

- the *description* of a language that a dictionary provides corresponds more closely to reliable empirical evidence regarding the way in which that language is actually used
- the *presentation* of this description corresponds more closely to what we know about the reference needs and reference skills of the target user

What I will show in this paper is that there have been measurable advances in both these areas: the quality of information provided, and the strategies used for presenting it. Sections 3 and 4, therefore, will look first at the range and variety of linguistic data that is now available to dictionary-makers; and secondly at the opportunities for lexicographers and publishers to exploit this information and 'add value' to it in order to maximize its usefulness for learners and teachers. Section 5 will then detail some specific areas of recent improvement, and a final section will draw a few conclusions. What I hope to demonstrate here is that if the young Frank McCourt had had access to any of the current MLDs, most of his problems would have disappeared.

2   HORNBY'S LEGACY

2.1   The origins of the MLD

As Tony Cowie shows in more detail in Cowie (1998c) (see also Cowie 1999b), A.S. Hornby, Michael West, and H.E. Palmer augmented the established conventions of dictionary microstructure with a set of features that were specifically motivated by the needs of non-native learners of English. In the course of time, these features themselves acquired the status of convention, as the MLD developed into a distinct genre. The key elements in this emerging tradition included:

- Vocabulary control: Drawing on their own research into vocabulary control, begun in the 1920s and continued into the 1930s, Palmer, West, and Hornby came to see vocabulary limitation – in some sense – as central to the project of creating a learner-oriented dictionary. There are two separate strands here. In the first place, we have the notion that a learner's dictionary should aim to cover only a selected subset of the lexicon. This marks a major departure from the native-speaker dictionary (NSD) tradition, where a 'concise' edition of a dictionary is typically characterized not so much by a reduced headword list as by a more truncated description of the *same* vocabulary that would appear in an unabridged edition. In his preface to the first English MLD, the *New Method English Dictionary* (*NMED*, 1935), West explains how his book 'economises space by omitting the rare and highly technical words which the foreigner is unlikely to meet'. Palmer's *A Grammar of English Words* (1938), which was remarkable for being concerned almost entirely with the learner's *productive* needs, had a headword list limited to only 1,000 items. Hornby's dictionary, appearing in 1942, adopted much the same approach to the rare and technical as West's *NMED*. The converse of this, of course, is that this smaller list of items is given more detailed treatment, most obviously by Palmer (1938), though West, too, emphasizes 'the care devoted to the meaning and idioms of the commoner words'. The other important aspect of vocabulary control is the notion of a restricted 'defining vocabulary' (DV) – whether in the form of an explicit list, as pioneered by West in the *NMED* (whose definitions are all written using a DV of 1,490 common words), or in the form favoured by Hornby and his successors, where the use of simple vocabulary and grammatical structures is fundamental to the defining process. It would, as Cowie (1999b) observes, 'be no exaggeration to say that vocabulary limitation gave birth to the learner's dictionary'. What the young McCourt (see Preface) would have found, equipped with a good MLD, would be first, that words like **intromission** did not appear at all, and secondly that he did in any case not *need* such words because the definition for **virgin** would be sufficiently self-evident to obviate the need for further searching.

- Grammatical and syntactic information: The commitment to meeting the *encoding* needs of the users of an MLD entailed a more detailed description of grammatical categories and syntactic preferences than could be found in the average NSD (native speaker dictionary). Palmer's seminal encoding dictionary (1938) pointed the way forward by providing a systematic account of verb complementation. The importance of such a scheme for productive purposes was fully grasped by Hornby, whose verb pattern system was an elaboration and refinement of Palmer's.

- The role of examples: In the NSD tradition, citations and other illustrative examples have a clear and long-established set of functions. What Hornby and his colleagues saw was the special need – in an MLD – for examples that appeared extensively (rather than sporadically), and that had an overtly pedagogical character. All three early MLDs include in their example text minimal fragments such as article+adjective+complement (*a **serious** illness*), abstract infinitive phrases (*to **introduce** a new law*), and glosses to clarify anything not immediately transparent (*I have not an **idle** moment* = am always busy). In common with much of the material in language-teaching coursebooks, examples like this make no claim to replicate actual performance: rather, they function as templates that learners can use as a basis on which to model – with some degree of confidence – their own utterances. We will see later that corpus data has led to substantial changes in this area of lexicography, but the consciously pedagogical orientation of dictionary examples remains a distinctive feature of the MLD.

- Phraseology: Observers of the contemporary English language teaching scene can hardly have failed to notice the tremendous vogue that this aspect of language is currently enjoying. The buzzword in the ELT community (repeated almost to the point of tiresomeness) is 'chunking': that is, the tendency of writers and speakers to store, retrieve, and process language very largely in chunks (or pre-assembled multiword units of various kinds), rather than by stringing together individual words at the point of articulation. This revived concern with phraseology in all its forms dates back, in the UK, to the late 1970s (Alexander 1978; Cowie 1978; Mackin 1978). A much-quoted paper of the early 1980s is Pawley and Syder (1983), which sees the effective deployment of holistically stored units as one of the keys to 'native-like' fluency. And the work of Sinclair and other early corpus linguists (e.g. Sinclair 1991: 110ff.) has also been very influential here. But of course its roots go much deeper, and can be traced back not only to the Firthian academic tradition but also to the work done by Palmer and Hornby in the 1930s on collocations and other multiword expressions (Palmer 1933). Their research 'revealed the prevalence of ready-made sequences in everyday speech and writing, and helped pave the way for the strong upsurge of interest in phraseology of the 1980s and 1990s' (Cowie

1999b: 11). This work fed directly into the design and content of Hornby's first dictionary, and a concern for describing and explaining phraseology has been one of the key features of the MLD ever since (see also Cowie 1998a for a full survey of developments in this area).

To a remarkable degree, then, many of the defining characteristics of the MLD tradition – vocabulary control, pedagogically motivated examples, and a commitment to describing syntactic behaviour and phraseological units – are already prefigured in the dictionaries of West and Endicott (1935) and Palmer (1938), and are brought to fruition in Hornby's landmark work of 1942. Within a period of just seven years, the fundamentals of an MLD tradition were already in place.

2.2   *LDOCE1*: innovation within an established tradition

Hornby's *ISED* metamorphosed into the *ALD* (1948), which then remained unchallenged for 30 years as *the* English dictionary for advanced learners. Not surprisingly, therefore, both major new entrants to this field – *LDOCE1* in 1978 and *COBUILD1* in 1987 – consciously saw themselves as 'breaking the mould' established by Hornby. For Randolph Quirk, *LDOCE* marks a clear departure, and its editorial policy is 'untrammelled by a previous edition that might prescribe form or content and inhibit innovation' (Preface). It is worth considering briefly how far this aspiration is actually realized: how far, in reality, does *LDOCE* depart from the conventions established in the 1930s and 1940s, and conversely, how much of the existing tradition is absorbed into the new book?

   Vocabulary control remains a central concern, but *LDOCE* takes this a stage further. While Hornby has a general commitment to using the simplest possible language in his definitions, *LDOCE* – following the example of West – opts for an explicit controlled defining vocabulary (DV) of 2000 common words, which (with some minor adjustments over the years) is still used in all the main Longman MLDs. This approach has not been without its critics (see for example Jansen *et al.* 1987), and concern has been expressed that 'arbitrary' constraints on lexicographers' freedom to define can mean that they are 'forced to simplify and in some cases slightly distort meaning' (Fox 1989: 155). No doubt this is sometimes true, but the other side of this coin, as Quirk acutely observes (*ibid.*), is that 'the strict use of the defining vocabulary has in many cases resulted in fresh and revealing semantic analysis'. Certainly, any lexicographer who has worked within this tradition will confirm that the limitations of a DV frequently make it necessary to look beyond obvious synonyms in order to get at the deeper semantic core of a word or meaning. In reality, the problems that sometimes accompany this approach to defining arise not so much from the constraints of the DV itself as from its inexpert application. Inevitably, the high-frequency words that make up any DV list are often highly polysemous, and lexicographers have not always resisted the temptation to use such words in non-central or (worse) idiomatic meanings – as for example in *LDOCE1*'s definition of **disreputable**: 'having a *bad name*'.[2] But this is simply a bad definition, not an argument against using a DV. It is perfectly possible to produce a clear and precise explanation of the term even with a limited vocabulary, as the updated version in *LDOCE3* shows: 'a disreputable person or organization is not respected because they are thought to be involved in dishonest or illegal activities'.

---

[2] For a similar example, see **click**[2] **2** (v) in *LDOCE1*, defined as 'to fall into place', as in *Her joke suddenly clicked.*

LDOCE1 also introduced a new system of grammatical description, based on alphanumeric codes, which drew on Quirk *et al.*'s *Grammar of Contemporary English* (1972), and provided a powerful tool for describing complementation and other syntactic preferences and restrictions – not only for verbs but also for the other major word classes. The *LDOCE* coding system was, unquestionably, a considerable departure from Hornby and Palmer's 'verb patterns', as well as being (arguably) more transparent. But much of the information that the new codes aimed to provide was of course already catered for by the earlier systems.

Other innovations in *LDOCE1* include its improved coverage of function words and other high-frequency items. Prefiguring the developments at Birmingham a few years later, the *LDOCE1* team had access to the files of the Survey of English Usage – the 'ur-corpus' of English – and these were extensively mined for the preparation of entries for words such as **out**, **get**, and **there**. For the first time, too, there was a genuine effort to provide an even-handed account of *both* major varieties of English, and the extensive coverage of American English in *LDOCE* (in terms especially of lexis, but also of pronunciation, morphology, and even syntax) forms an influential new strand in the development of the MLD. This shift of the US variety from a marginal to a central position reflects a broader debt to the American lexicographic tradition, whose influence can be seen, for example, in the preference – typical of US collegiate dictionaries – for showing compound nouns and even phrasal verbs as full headwords rather than as 'nested' subentries. *LDOCE1* can fairly claim that it 'combines the best principles of British and American lexicography' (Introduction, viii), and in several important respects it takes the MLD into new territory. But underlying these changes, the core features of the Hornby model were not seriously altered with the arrival of *LDOCE1* in 1978, and even now one can argue that they remain substantially intact. The argument of this paper, however, is that if the broad parameters and overall goals of the MLD have changed relatively little over the last 50 years, there have nevertheless been enormous changes, and *improvements*, in both the quality of information provided and in its presentation. The sections that follow will examine the ideas and influences that have shaped these changes.

3   LEXICOGRAPHIC EVIDENCE

3.1   The 'Corpus Revolution': superior data for a description of the language

The quantum leap that took us from first-generation million-word English corpora (specifically, the Survey of English Usage and the Brown and LOB corpora) to huge databanks measured in hundreds of millions of words, is extensively documented and needs little amplification here (for an overview see Sinclair 1991; Rundell and Stock 1992; Rundell 1996). In corpus lexicography, size matters a lot. Experience has shown that 'the amount of corpus material needed in order to comprehensively account for the functional complexities of a developed natural language...is huge' (Clear 1996: 266). But the difference between the old and new dispensations is not one simply of quantity – important though that is – but one of quality as well. Individual judgement still plays a part in the design of corpus collections and (crucially) in the *analysis* of the material that the corpus throws up. But a key development from the lexicographer's point of view is that human selection is now replaced by dispassionate number-crunching at the vital stage where *appropriate units of language to be studied* are identified and extracted from a corpus – so eliminating at a (key)stroke the serious distortions that bedevilled older collections of hand-selected citations (on which see Murray 1977: 178). It is true that significant differences remain in the composition of the various corpora currently in use, and the debate on what constitutes a 'good' corpus shows no sign of slackening (see e.g. Biber 1993c [also in this volume – *Ed.*], McEnery and Wilson 1996: ch.3, for recent contributions). Nevertheless, it is fair to say that all the major UK dictionary-publishers now have access to large and diverse corpus resources which provide the raw materials for a far more reliable description of English than would have been possible for the pioneers of pedagogical lexicography.

3.2   Types of corpus: what is available?

While some resources are shared – the British National Corpus (BNC) being the most notable example – dictionary-publishers have on the whole developed their own heterogeneous data collections, whose compositions reflect, in varying degrees, opportunistic and principled approaches to data gathering. These now cover some or all of the following dimensions of language:

- general written text: for example, the Cambridge Language Survey (CLS) and the written-text components of the BNC and of Birmingham University's Bank of English (BoE);
- spoken text: for example, the spontaneous speech components of the BNC and BoE, the Longman Corpus of Spoken American English (following the BNC model), and most recently the CANCODE corpus being developed at the University of Nottingham (Carter and McCarthy 1995) and used by CUP lexicographers;
- varieties of English: for example, Australian newspapers in the BoE, the 'World English' components of the CLS and of the Longman–Lancaster Corpus (Summers 1993), and the 50-million-word Longman Written American Corpus (LWAC);
- learner text: for example, the Longman Learner Corpus, first developed in the late 1980s (Gillard and Gadsby 1998), and CUP's corpus of student exam texts (*CIDE*, p.viii);
- specialized text types: for example, print and broadcast journalism in BoE, ephemera and unpublished material in BNC and BoE.

3.3   What a corpus can do for the lexicographer

3.3.1   'Baseline' functions

Corpus-enquiry software, operating on large volumes of data, is very efficient at revealing the regular features of a language. Any linguistic feature that occurs more than a given number of times across a range of texts has a prima facie claim to be considered as part of the regular *system* of the language, as opposed to merely being a random event, and therefore becomes a candidate for being described in the dictionary. And while the analysis of meaning remains the core task of monolingual lexicography, attention is now increasingly being paid to the combinatorial behaviour of words: to phraseology, patterns of complementation, collocational and contextual preferences, and so on.

The KWIC concordance is still, in most situations, the central tool of corpus lexicography, but the software has become much more powerful. We now take for granted facilities like searching for multiword strings as well as for single words; searching according to word class (for example, to look at instances of the *adjective* **tense**, but not of the noun or verb); lemmatized searches (where specifying **tense**=*verb* as the search item generates concordances for **tensed**, **tensing**, and **tenses**); and searching user-defined subsets of a corpus (such as fiction written by women, or scientific text in a range of media). This much can be regarded as basic. And the more richly each constituent text in a corpus has been tagged – whether grammatically, or in terms of situational characteristics such as subject-field, medium, or the age and gender of the writer/speaker – then the more fine-grained the enquiries that can be made. Thus, for example, a part-of-speech tagged corpus with an SGML-aware enquiry tool enables us to distinguish **to**, the preposition, from **to**, the infinitive marker, so that we can look separately at sentences like:

I'm going to Boston

and

I'm going to buy a car.

Similarly, if we notice that the verb **taste** is frequently followed by an adjective (*it tastes great/disgusting/delicious* etc.), we can ask the software to search specifically for all instances of **taste** + (any) adjective, rather than trawling through a general concordance for the word.

3.3.2   Words in their environment

Lexicographers now find themselves increasingly well-equipped to identify patterns of co-occurrence that are of relevance to language learners. These include not only all forms of syntactic behaviour and collocational pairings, but also valuable information about typical context and selectional restrictions. A word like **adjudicate**, for example, is not especially problematic in strict semantic terms. But dictionary users need to know what sort of people **adjudicate**, and what it is that they **adjudicate** (or **adjudicate on**). And if the evidence suggests that expressions like 'called in to adjudicate' or 'brought in to adjudicate' are fairly common, what might this tell us about the circumstances in which adjudication typically takes place? Information of this kind adds considerable depth to our description, enabling us to locate words and meanings to quite precise places in the lexicon – with obvious benefits for dictionary users.

3.3.3   The need for automation

But as data collections grow exponentially, manual interaction with concordances (for anything but a sample of the full corpus) becomes correspondingly problematic. Hence the requirement for greater automation of the analysis process, so that if – for example – lexicographers are interested in collocation, they may now be 'happy to be presented with a list of collocations and some statistics [and] don't need to read 25,000 concordance lines to verify the information themselves' (Clear 1996: 268). Increasingly, then, concordances are complemented by a range of statistical tools that can, for example, identify regularly co-occurring items at a specified distance on either side of the node word and list them in order of significance. A good example is the mutual information (MI) technique (see for example Church and Mercer 1993: 18–21; or Church and Hanks 1990 in this volume – *Ed.*), which sometimes provides striking insights not only into collocational behaviour but, just as importantly, into meaning potentials. Stubbs (1996) notes the interesting case of the word **cause**. An MI search on this verb, using the BNC, lists the following as the ten most significant items appearing in its immediate environment: **grievous, consternation, furore, bodily, havoc, uproar, inconvenience, disruption, harm, distress.** All of which reveals – in a more graphic, more 'distilled' form than a concordance ever could – that **cause** has a 'strongly negative semantic prosody' (*ibid.* 173), thus compelling a re-evaluation of earlier descriptions. A simple enough point, perhaps, but one that appears to have eluded generations of lexicographers.

The development of more sophisticated tools is currently one of the growth areas in this field, and typical applications include the automatic identification of frequently-occurring multiword clusters or of vocabulary items that occur with significantly greater frequency in one particular text-type than in the corpus as a whole. The potential benefits for MLDs and their users are fairly obvious, while the reliability of frequency-based information is of course much greater now that the software can run on fully tagged and lemmatized corpora – rather than on raw data, as in the past. For lexicographers, all this helps to inform decisions regarding, *inter alia*, inclusion (for example, whether a particular headword, meaning, syntactic pattern, or phrasal unit is actually worth recording), register labelling, the order in which information is presented, and the depth of treatment that is appropriate for a given linguistic feature. And as we will see later, some MLDs now incorporate frequency information explicitly as well as implicitly. All of this has great potential value for learners of a language: broadly speaking, the more common a word is, the more important it is and the more worth learning, and the same point applies to more specific linguistic features too (though in practice the equation is not always quite so straightforward: see Kilgarriff 1997d).

3.4   An emerging methodology for corpus enquiry

The advent of large corpora has brought fundamental and irreversible changes to the process of dictionary making. This is not in question. It is worth making the point, however, that good corpus data is merely a prerequisite for better dictionaries: it does not in itself guarantee that good dictionaries will actually be produced – a point that will be developed in the next section. For lexicographers whose careers began in the pre-corpus era, the technological changes of the early 1980s were both exciting and empowering, as corpus data offered the possibility of producing a far more satisfying description of the language. Against this background, it is easy to see why the corpus was, initially, embraced so enthusiastically that – in some quarters at least – it was considered almost heretical to question anything that the concordances threw up. This 'fundamentalist' approach to the data is not without its problems, and a couple of examples of the tendency are worth mentioning here:

(1) **utter 1** When you **utter** sounds or words, you say them in order to communicate ideas and feelings. EG *Sam opened his mouth, then quickly shut it again without uttering a word... He seldom uttered, but when he did everyone listened.* (*COBUILD1*)

(2) **proxy... 3** If you do something **by proxy**, you arrange for someone else to do it for you. EG *You can create an international incident by proxy.* (*COBUILD1*)

My argument with case (1) focuses on the intransitive example, which is supported by a grammar code in the side column showing intransitivity as an option for this verb. A stray line in the corpus (which any fluent speaker would regard as atypical, if not aberrant) is thus made to justify a grammatical description of doubtful validity. In case (2), the example text presents a decontextualized scenario that is both difficult to retrieve and not remotely typical of the way this phrase is generally used. For the target users of this particular dictionary, the information provided here is seriously misleading. I make this point not in order to criticize colleagues at COBUILD, whose contribution to contemporary lexicography can scarcely be overstated. Rather, my intention is to show the dangers of an uncritical approach to corpus data. Both instances here reflect one 'order of reality' (to use Ronald Carter's phrase: Carter 1998: 47): this is undeniably 'real' English, in the sense that it derives from naturally-occurring data, but it is much less 'real' from a pedagogical perspective, in the sense that it is unlikely to meet the needs of the student user.

Significantly, too, both entries have been changed (greatly for the better) in *COBUILD2*, and now reflect norms of usage much more closely. It might be argued that this newer description is simply a product of the improved corpus resources now available, but this would be to miss the point: the original entries were simply inappropriate for the type of book they appear in. And while all of us are guilty of writing poor entries at one time or another, one is inclined to think that in cases like these the problems arise more from a flawed methodology than from a momentary lapse in concentration. The many improvements in *COBUILD*'s second edition seem to me to reflect a less dogmatic approach to corpus evidence, in which an appropriate balance is struck between the two 'orders of reality'. The novelty, in other words, has worn off, and a more coherent methodology for corpus lexicography is beginning to emerge.

3.5   A broadening of focus

One of the most striking developments of recent years is a shift towards (or perhaps a re-emergence of) a view of language-processing as a predominantly phrase-based rather than word-based operation – what Sinclair (1991: 110ff.) calls the 'idiom principle' (by contrast with the 'open-choice principle', which sees text as being generated by a process of combining individual vocabulary items in any way that satisfies the rules of grammar). There is a convergence here between data emerging from large corpora and ideas developed in areas such as phraseology and cognitive psychology, all pointing towards the notion that a great deal of language activity involves the manipulation of pre-assembled, more or less fixed, groups of words. For lexicographers who interrogate corpora on a regular basis, there has been a gradual shift in focus 'outwards' from the node. Corpus enquiry increasingly encompasses a broader span, looking not only at collocation and complementation, but also at the tendency of some concepts to be lexicalized through multiword units, and (following the notion of 'semantic prosody') at the way whole semantic classes can have discernible relationships with the node word at various points of valency. As we will see, this changing methodology is increasingly reflected in actual dictionary text.

4   PRESENTATION

With access to corpus data, what more do lexicographers need? Consider first the following definition from the respected *Merriam-Webster Collegiate Dictionary*:

(3) **catkin** a usu. long ament densely crowded with bracts

In terms of its *content*, this is unexceptionable: the definition is 'good' in so far as it accurately describes the definiendum. There is, however, an almost complete failure in the area of *presentation*. The definition would be incomprehensible to most non-specialist users (it is certainly incomprehensible to me), while a specialist user would be unlikely to need it at all. The important point to make here is that a definition cannot be said to be successful unless it scores well in both content *and* presentation. In this case, **catkin** has all the information it needs but its presentation is so obscure as to make the definition quite useless: it defines, but it does not explain.[3] It should be obvious from this – though the point is not always recognized – that the availability of better linguistic and factual data is merely a prerequisite for better dictionaries: it does not in itself guarantee that better dictionaries will be written.

---

[3] cf. Landau 1984: 131: 'If a definition fails in its basic purpose of giving the reader enough immediate information to enable him to surmise, at least approximately, its meaning in context, it is of no value whatsoever.'

To understand why this must be so, it is helpful to look at the schema proposed by Sue Atkins in her description of the lexicographer's task:

> In the first stage – the ANALYSIS process – the lexicographer analyzes the word, trying to discover as many relevant linguistic facts as possible. [This] should furnish the lexicographer with all the facts needed for the second stage of the process, which I will call SYNTHESIS. . . . During the synthesis stage, the compiler extracts from the collection of ordered facts those that are relevant to the particular dictionary being written. (Atkins 1992/3: 7ff – see also in this volume, *Ed.*)

For the analysis stage, corpus data and software tools are vitally important. In addition, theoretically-derived approaches to analysing the data, such as a frame-semantic classification (Fillmore and Atkins 1994), can often provide insights and help lexicographers to a better understanding of underlying regularities in the language. Nevertheless, the fact remains that some people are simply much better than others at analysing data. What lexicographers often refer to as *Sprachgefühl* is – though admittedly an ill-defined concept – an important factor in the success or failure of the analysis process.

Moving on to the synthesis stage, the demands on the lexicographer are even greater, and the process requires (*inter alia*):

- a clear idea of the needs, expectations, problems, and skills of the target user: for example, what sort of tasks will the dictionary be used for, what assumptions can we make about users' reference skills or their grasp of linguistic categories, what do we know about their preferred modes of learning or the types of language-transfer problems they typically experience, and so on;
- an understanding of the commercial/publishing constraints (time, space, cost, etc.) and how these impact on the editorial process;
- a sound grasp of the range of editorial strategies available for conveying certain categories of information, and the skill to use them successfully.

Collectively, these varied forms of knowledge contribute to a notion of 'lexicographic relevance': that is, the specific cluster of factors – unique to each individual dictionary project – that informs the decision-making process and enables the lexicographer to distinguish between information that is merely true and information that is relevant to a specific user group. (Thus in example (1) above, it is *true* that **utter** can be used intransitively, but it is not in this case *relevant*.)

And the more information that is available for us to process and in some way account for, the more important this notion of lexicographic relevance becomes. It acts as an essential filter between corpus and dictionary, and without it there is no guarantee that corpus-derived dictionary text will actually be pedagogically useful. All of which helps to explain why the arrival of corpus data has not in fact significantly diminished the role of human skill and human judgement in the dictionary-making process. And it is on this basis that I would argue that recent improvements in MLDs have at least as much to do with presentation (or, if you like, with the readiness of dictionary-makers to innovate and their commitment to meeting users' needs) as with the availability of more reliable language data.[4]

---

[4] Interestingly, now that the debate about the appropriate use of corpora has spread to the wider ELT community, Cook (1998: 58) makes a similar point with regard to the relationship between corpus data and teaching materials: 'Computer corpora – while impressive and interesting records of certain aspects of language use – can never be more than a contribution to our understanding of effective language teaching.'

5   SOME SIGNIFICANT RECENT DEVELOPMENTS

5.1   Navigation: finding the information you need

It is self-evident that dictionary users need to be able to quickly locate the information they are looking for – since consulting the dictionary may in itself disrupt their train of thought and 'loosen the link with the text [being read], especially when the search procedure takes some time' (Bogaards 1996: 284). Yet there is a good deal of evidence to show that the apparently straightforward operation of 'looking it up in the dictionary' often calls for considerable persistence and skill, and can itself be a source of error (Rundell 1999). Recent innovations reflect lexicographers' awareness of these problems and efforts to minimize them. These include:

5.1.1   *The use of frequency information as a guide to the ordering of meanings*
Most MLDs now organize multi-sense entries mainly on the basis of frequency, a strategy only made possible by the availability of large corpora. The logic of this is that the user, to locate the entry s/he is searching for, 'will on average have to scan the least amount of material if it is organized starting from the most frequently-occurring senses' (Scholfield 1999).

5.1.2   *Phraseology and canonical forms*
Corpus data has made a more phrasally-oriented approach both *possible* (in the sense that regular word combinations can be identified with some confidence) and *desirable* (in the sense that it is more helpful to users to present the whole string in which a given word most frequently occurs than to present fragments that have to be pieced together before they make sense). Thus, for example, most MLDs now describe the lexical unit **have a think** as a single item, rather than perpetuating the pretence that **think** is in any useful sense a noun (traditionally defined as 'an act of thinking'). Following the same logic, the fact that the BNC shows two instances of something being 'taken with *a fistful* of salt' is not allowed (as it is in many NSDs) to outweigh the fact that there are many dozens of examples of the prototypical **take something with a pinch of salt**: this is the citation form shown in most MLDs, and this approach is more calculated to accelerate the lookup process.[5] In this context, it is worth comparing here the entries for **lookout** in two editions of the same dictionary (see Appendix 1). Notice here that **keep a lookout** and **it's a bad lookout**, are now covered as complete phrases rather than treated as if their elements were infinitely combinable. Furthermore, the six different uses here are listed in frequency order: since **on the lookout** occurs much more often than any other use of this word, this is presumably the form in which users are most likely to encounter it, so this meaning is given first.

5.1.3   *Lexical relations*
Standard lexical relations, especially synonymy, hyponomy, and antonymy, appear to play an important part in the way concepts are stored and linked in the mental lexicon (e.g. Aitchison 1987: 72ff.). This helps to explain why they feature so prominently in most types of communication strategy used by language learners, most of whom will be familiar with the experience of defaulting to an opposite or superordinate term to encode an idea for which their lexical resources are limited – 'it wasn't interesting', for example, instead of 'it was boring'.

---

[5] For a similar example, compare the open-ended 'meaning' at **spot**[1] **6** in *LDOCE1:* 'an area of mind or feelings: *I have a soft spot for my old school'* with the treatment in *LDOCE3*, *COBUILD2*, and *ALD5*, all of which (correctly) focus on the typical instantiation of this meaning in the phrase **have a soft spot for**.

Information of this type has featured in MLDs for at least 20 years (rather sporadically, it must be said), but this is another area where more recent dictionaries have broken new ground. One thinks here of the symbols used in *COBUILD*'s 'side column' to show, for example, that the verb **intimate** is similar to **hint** and has **suggest** as its superordinate, and that the opposite of **off-the-peg** is **made-to-measure**;[6] of the Usage Notes (found in almost all MLDs) which disambiguate close synonyms; or of the 'Language Portraits' in *CIDE*, such as the one on 'Opposite and Negative Meanings' (p.991), which deals with the role of affixes in the formation of antonymous words.

5.1.4   Navigating longer entries

In most situations, the goal of the look-up exercise is to find information about a specific meaning or phrasal unit, rather than to learn everything about a particular headword. In the case of the more polysemous words, locating the right sense can be a major source of difficulty, and we know that many users 'solve' this problem simply by selecting the first sense they come to. In order to relieve users of the need to wade through large amounts of (irrelevant) text, both *CIDE* and *LDOCE3* have adapted a strategy already familiar in bilingual lexicography: for each separate sense, there is a short descriptor (variously called a 'Guideword' or 'Signpost') designed to give the user a general idea of the way the word is divided up; these can be scanned fairly quickly, and ideally the user is drawn to the appropriate sense without the need to perform a major reading task. Thus for example, the multi-sense item **tip** is signposted in *CIDE* with words such as END, INFORMATION, PAYMENT, and RUBBISH, and in *LDOCE3* with END, MONEY, ADVICE, UNTIDY, and HORSE RACE.

These approaches are not without their problems: the Guidewords or Signposts tend to rely on high-frequency superordinate terms, and these are sometimes too ambiguous or vague to facilitate effective searching. Certainly there is more work to be done here (see Herbst 1996: 350; and especially Bogaards 1998), but even if these systems do not always work perfectly, this is a well-motivated attempt to address a known problem, and we can look forward to further developments in this area.

5.1.5   *Onomasiological ('meaning to word') dictionaries*

Until recently, this tradition was represented in the pedagogical area only by Tom McArthur's pioneering *Longman Lexicon of Contemporary English* (1981, and still in print). But in the last five years, several new types of onomasiological dictionary have come onto the market:

- The so-called 'production dictionary', for which the prototype is the *Longman Language Activator* (1993). This is a conceptually organized reference resource designed specifically to meet the *encoding* needs of learners (in this case, fairly advanced learners). It is organized around what cognitive psychologists would call 'basic-level concepts' (about 1000 of them), and the look-up process essentially involves deciding on a broad meaning area, selecting the 'keywords' to which it is related, and then browsing and comparing sets of near synonyms (for details see Rundell and Ham 1994). An intermediate-level production dictionary, the *Longman Essential Activator*, was published in 1997.
- CUP's *Word Routes* series (starting 1994), a set of thematically-organized dictionaries which are bilingual but geared towards the learner of English. Rather as in *Roget's*

---

[6] Rather disappointingly, this feature has been somewhat downgraded in *COBUILD2*, despite some research evidence that 'the extra column, while largely unused as a source of grammatical information, is readily employed [by users] to suggest synonyms' (Harvey and Yuill 1997: 271).

Thesaurus, the overall structure according to which individual themes are organized is coherent but largely obscure, so that the usual way into the text is through one of the two indexes (one in English, one in the source language). The books cover many of the conceptual categories found in the *Activator* (with sets of words, for example, meaning **Easy**, **Forbid**, or **Persuade**), but (like the *Longman Lexicon*) they also deal with many concrete nouns, in sets such as **Farm Animals** and **Types of building**. (For a recent review, see Bruton 1997.)

- OUP's *Wordfinder Dictionary* (Trappes-Lomax 1997), a vocabulary-building tool that works somewhat like a reverse dictionary, and again covers both abstract concepts and concrete objects. The main entries are alphabetically arranged, and from the entry on **furniture**, for example, one can find words for specific pieces of furniture (thus: 'a piece of furniture with shelves which you keep books in: **bookcase**') but also words that describe the way furniture looks ('old and in bad condition because it has been used too much: **shabby**').

- Dictionaries on CD-ROM, such as the *Longman Interactive English Dictionary* (1993), the *COBUILD Dictionary on CD-ROM* (1996), the *Longman Interactive American Dictionary* (1997), and the *Oxford Advanced Learner's Dictionary on CD-ROM* (1997). Electronic products are still at a relatively early stage, though there have already been some impressive innovations in this medium. From a navigational point of view, the relevance of these dictionaries lies in the fact that – although they are still at present based on written-for-paper dictionaries – the electronic format largely frees users from the constraints imposed by alphabetical order. Thus, for example, locating an idiom such as **talk the hind legs off a donkey** (always a hit-and-miss procedure on paper) is simply a matter of keying parts of the phrase (e.g. **talk**, **hind**, and **donkey**) into a text search facility. Search routines can also enable the user to locate every definition that contains a particular genus word or expression: thus a full-text search on the string '*in & bad & condition*' in the electronic *ALD* yields a set of headwords that includes **ratty**, **fly-blown**, **derelict**, and **run-down**.

5.1.6 Navigation: some conclusions

We have seen here a number of initiatives designed to address the problems of 'findability', and the results generally look positive. Other macrostructural elements, too, have seen changes at the detailed level. With regard to homography, for example, the newer MLDs tend to use word class and orthographic form, rather than meaning and etymology, as the organizing principle. Only *ALD* still follows the older approach (which led, in *LDOCE1*, to no fewer than *nine* homographs for the word **tip**), but it is hard to see how this can be of much help to the average learner. In general, too, there is far less 'nesting' of derived forms, compounds, etc. than used to be common, so that *CIDE*'s policy of (for example) nesting **decisive** and **decision** under the headword **decide** now looks oddly retrogressive. Similarly, conflation of word classes into a single entry, a space-saving device used in many dictionaries, has largely been abandoned in the MLD, figuring now only in *CIDE* (e.g. in the entry for **cause**: *n*, *v* (to be) the reason why something, esp. something bad, happens). Other space-saving conventions, such as the use of the tilde (~) to replace the headword in examples, or the use of cut-back run-on forms (such as **-ogical** at the headword **ideology**) have also largely given way to more transparent approaches. These may look like minor tweakings of the macrostructure, but the cumulative effect is to make the dictionary easier to read and easier to get around. Finally, the old (*fig.*) label (described by Osselton 1995: 16 as 'hard to justify on linguistic grounds') is now in serious decline in all types of dictionary, and among MLDs is used only by *CIDE* (see for example the entries at **arid** and **swamp**). What characterizes most of these changes is a re-examination of macrostructural features inherited by MLDs from an earlier 'NSD tradition' (cf. Rundell 1988), and an abandonment of any that do not seem relevant.

5.2   Grammar and syntax

Since Palmer (1938) first introduced the notion of verb patterns, the provision of syntactic information has been fundamental to the MLD tradition (see 2.1 above). This sort of information can be conveyed both *explicitly* (typically through coding systems of one type or another) and *implicitly* (by being built in to the wording of definitions and examples). Two clear trends can be identified here: first, a move towards more transparent coding, and secondly a more systematic effort to ensure that information supplied in codes is mirrored in examples and (increasingly) in definitions too. Compare, for example, the following and note the changes over time:

> (4) **promise** 1 [T1,3,5a,b;V3;D1,5a;IØ] to make a promise to do or give (something) or that (something) will be done (*LDOCE1*: 1978)
> **promise** 1 [I, Tn,Tf, Dn·n, Dn·pr, Dn·f] ~**sth (to sb)** make a promise (to sb); assure (sb) that one will give or do or not do sth (*ALD4*: 1989)
> **promise** 1 [I;T] to tell someone that you will definitely do something or that something will happen: **promise (that)** *Hurry up! We promised that we wouldn't be late.* **promise sb (that)** *You promised me the car would be ready on Monday.* **promise to do sth** *The children promised to give us a hand with the packing* etc etc (*LDOCE3*: 1995)

Though considerable variation still exists among the different MLDs, what most current coding systems have in common is that they assume very little grammatical knowledge on the part of users, and they aim to satisfy users' needs in this department without requiring them to consult explanatory tables and charts. There is a trade-off here, in which a certain delicacy of description is sacrificed to the need for maximum clarity. So for example, the patterns represented by the sentences:

> *I warned him to leave*

and

> *I wanted him to leave*

which are actually distinct (for example in terms of passive transformation) and are coded differently in older dictionaries, are now treated purely in terms of their surface characteristics and therefore given the same code, for example:

> **want** (or **warn**) **sb to do sth** in *LDOCE3*, Vn.*to* inf in *ALD5*, and V n to-inf in *COBUILD2*

In general, the losses here seem to be outweighed by the gains. Furthermore, the use of examples and definitions to (subliminally) reinforce grammatical messages gives us another string to our bow, as for example in the following:

> (5) **argue 1** If you **argue** that something is true, you...*His lawyers are arguing that he is unfit to stand trial.* **2** If you **argue for** or **argue against** an idea or policy, you...*The report argues against tax increases*...**5** If one person **argues** with another, they speak angrily to each other about something that they disagree about. You can also say that two people **argue** : ...*They were still arguing*...(*COBUILD2*)

Developments here have been informed by a good deal of user research and user feedback, both about strategies of dictionary use and about the linguistic sophistication (or otherwise) of target users.[7] But they also reflect a view that – while we would all like more effort to be put into the development of users' reference skills (see e.g. Béjoint 1994: 166–7) – we would be unwise to produce dictionaries that relied on a more active engagement by users. On the whole, learners want to find information quickly and be able to grasp it immediately once they find it.

5.3   Meaning

In an influential paper written in 1981, Mahavir Jain identified meaning and context as areas where improvements were still needed in order for MLDs to meet learners' needs. In particular, he argued that, for students to operate successfully in the productive mode, the range and depth of grammatical information on offer needed to be matched by an equivalent level of lexico-semantic detail (Jain 1981: 275–6). With reference to the (then) leading MLDs – *ALD3* and *LDOCE1* – Jain demonstrated that simplified definitions were not enough: learners needed more information about selectional restrictions, typical context, appropriate register, and so on. In short, the scope of the MLD 'must be extended to include all such lexical-semantic information as has an important bearing on appropriate language use' (*ibid.* 284). At around the same time, the first steps in corpus lexicography were being taken by John Sinclair's COBUILD team in Birmingham, and the arrival of large corpora provided the raw materials for the kind of fine-grained descriptions that Jain was calling for.

5.3.1   Semantic analysis

The analysis of meaning – the core task of monolingual lexicography, and one of the most difficult – is from now on informed by large volumes of language data. This does not necessarily make the task any easier, but it does make possible a level of precision and detail that was previously unattainable in large areas of the lexicon (see e.g. Moon 1987b). Compare, for example, the following sets of definitions where, in each case, the first is from a pre-corpus dictionary, the second from a dictionary based on corpus evidence:

(6) **helpful** giving help; useful (*ALD4*)
   helpful If you describe someone as **helpful**, you mean that they help you in some way, such as doing part of your job for you or giving you advice or information (*COBUILD2*)
(7) **witness** be present at and see (*ALD3*)
   witness to see something happen, especially an accident, a crime, or an important event (*LEA*)
(8) **amicable** suitable between friends; friendly; peaceful (*LDOCE1*)
   amicable an **amicable** arrangement or solution is one where people who do not agree with each other are able to solve their problems in a friendly way (*LEA*)

The important trend here is not simply towards a finer level of detail. More significantly, MLDs are moving away from an NSD tradition in which there is a preference for underspecified, broadly substitutable definitions. Compare for example the definitions for the

---

[7] It is claimed in *LDOCE1* (Introduction: viii) that its codes represent 'a system which is easily remembered', but almost all the user feedback to Longman suggested that the opposite was true; the adoption by other publishers of simplified systems presumably reflects similar responses from users.

noun use of **absolute**, first in the (native-speaker) *Reader's Digest Great Illustrated Dictionary* (1984):

(9) Something that is absolute.

and secondly in *COBUILD2* (1995):

(10) An **absolute** is a rule or principle that is believed to be true, right, or relevant in all situations

The first definition is open-ended enough to cater for every possible instantiation of the word in text, but is somewhat unhelpful even in receptive mode (and practically useless as a basis for language production). The second, drawing on actual evidence of use, restricts itself to describing the word's most central usage, and thereby satisfies the needs of both the decoding and encoding user.

Disambiguation, both 'horizontal' (across sets of so-called synonyms) and 'vertical' (among the senses of polysemous words), has similarly felt the benefit of corpus data. As an example of the latter, compare the pre- and post-corpus entries for **false** (Appendix 2), the first rather vague and tentative, the second much more assured and precise. With regard to disambiguation among items in the same semantic area, pre-corpus dictionaries (even large scholarly ones) routinely relied on the use of synonym definitions, for example:

(11) **clever** quick to learn and understand
      intelligent clever and quick to understand
      bright clever
      brainy (*infml*) clever
      (all from *CULD* – but typical of most earlier dictionaries)

Current MLDs generally make a much better job of sets like this.

The various examples given here are simply random instances of an accretive process which is gradually transforming the quality of definitions and their usefulness to learners. Of course there is scope for further improvement (see e.g. Bogaards 1996: 291ff), but the trend towards more sharply-focused defining is clear and irreversible.

5.3.2 *Presentation: the structure and wording of definitions*

Access to more reliable linguistic data does not in itself lead automatically to better definitions. The following conversation throws light on another area where very important changes have been taking place. This is taken from a Caribbean novel, Sam Selvon's *A Brighter Sun* (London: Allan Wingate 1952), whose ambitious hero, Tiger, has been memorizing dictionary definitions in an effort to better himself. Here he is tormenting his long-suffering wife:

'I will catch you with a easy one now! . . . You know what a fish is?'
'But how? Is a thing that does live in the sea, and in river and pond too. It does swim, and people does eat it for food.'
'I know I would catch you! You really wrong this time! The dictionary ain't say anything like that! It says is a animal living in water, is a vertebrate cold-blooded animal having gills throughout life and limbs, if any, modified into fins. You see! . . . All the time I did think a fish was just like what you say, but now I find out for truth what it really is! . . . Look, hand me my small narcotic cylinders rolled in paper.'
'Cylinder? What is that? Is what you mean at all?'
Tiger chuckled, self-contented.
'Just extend the terminal part of your arm, the extent of space between where you is and which part it is not remote.'

'I beg you pardon, Tiger, but . . . this time you really tie me up.'
'All right, girl. Reach the cigarettes for me then.'

This neatly illustrates the point that dictionaries have traditionally operated in a self-contained universe of discourse, parallel to the world of 'normal' prose and even somewhat resembling it, but with its own distinct conventions and usages. *Merriam-Webster's Collegiate*, for example, gives for the first meaning of **pedantic** the definition 'of, relating to, or being a pedant'. Is this supposed to be English? As the extract above makes clear, the effect of such definitions can often be to hinder communication rather than to help it. A dictionary definition is a somewhat abstract construct at the best of times, so great efforts must be made to remove any obstacles to comprehension and accessibility. This is probably the biggest single challenge of pedagogical lexicography. Many earlier dictionaries do not seem concerned even to try, but recent MLDs have begun to move away from 'the technical character and syntactic clumsiness' of more traditional definitions (Herbst 1996: 326). In the first place, the use of a limited defining vocabulary has now become an almost standard feature of the MLD. But even more importantly, there has been a marked shift away from the conventions and metalanguage of traditional defining technique. The core meaning of 'pain', for example, is defined in *LDOCE1* – rather formally – as 'great discomfort of the body', but in *LDOCE3* this becomes 'the feeling you have when part of your body hurts'. One still occasionally comes across the more 'lexicographic' sort of definition even in the most recent MLDs, for example:

(12) **strict** greatly limiting someone's freedom to behave as they wish, and likely to cause them to be severely punished if disobeyed (*CIDE*)

But on the whole MLDs now aim for a defining language that approximates normal unmarked discourse.

Meanwhile the focus on typical contexts of use has been developed in various ways. *COBUILD*'s full-sentence definitions, drawing to some extent on well-known techniques of folk-defining, have been very influential here. In the dictionary's first edition (1987), the phrasal verb **lay up** is defined in these terms:

(13) If an illness **lays** someone **up**, it causes them to stay in bed

The definition immediately informs the reader about the typical subject of the verb, a point that users are left to deduce from the entry as a whole in the more conventional treatments found, for example, in the (more or less) contemporary *LDOCE2* and *ALD4*:

(14) **lay sbdy./sthg.** ↔ **up** . . . to keep indoors or in bed with an illness (*LDOCE2*)
     lay sb up cause sb to stay in bed, not be able to work, etc (*ALD4*)

But even within this new paradigm, further improvements have now been made: in its second edition, *COBUILD* not only dispenses with the rather unnatural 'cause someone to . . .' formula, but shifts the focus of the definition to the passive structure in which it most typically occurs – *and* shows the preposition that usually follows it:

(15) If someone **is laid up** with an illness, the illness makes it necessary for them to stay in bed

Definitions like this go a long way towards addressing the concerns raised by Jain. The explanation of **lay up** encapsulates the twin commitment to modelling definitions on 'normal English' and to supplying as much information as possible about a word's lexical, syntactic, and contextual environment.

A range of new definition styles is gradually being developed to meet these needs. Compare, for example, the way that (one meaning of) the verb **conduct** is covered in consecutive editions of *LDOCE*:

(16) to carry out or direct (*LDOCE2*)

(17) **conduct an experiment/survey/inquiry etc** to carry out a particular process, especially in order to get information or prove facts (*LDOCE3*)

Again, the emphasis is no longer on supplying a definition sufficiently broad (and therefore also sufficiently imprecise) to account for every possible occurrence. Rather, the aim is to describe what typically happens: in this case, corpus data shows that the usual objects of **conduct** (in this meaning) are actually quite limited and predictable, so these are highlighted at the beginning of the definition text. There is a delicate balance to be struck here because a definition that seeks to pin down typical contexts always runs the risk of being over-restrictive. The word **innocence**, for example, often means the fact of being not guilty of a crime. But a student who reads the definition:

(18) If someone proves their **innocence**, they prove that they are not guilty of a crime (*COBUILD2*)

may have difficulty matching this meaning to other perfectly plausible contexts, such as 'she was led away *protesting* her innocence'. It is legitimate, too, to point to the danger of wordiness in some types of 'natural-language' definition: for example *ALD5*'s more conventional definition of **scrumptious** ('esp of food: extremely enjoyable; DELICIOUS') uses only half as many words as *COBUILD2*'s ('If you describe food as **scrumptious**, you mean that it tastes extremely good') but it is equally clear and conveys all the information that is needed.[8] Clearly, we are still at the experimental stage with some of these new approaches to defining, and more user-research needs to be done to establish the pedagogic value of different styles. Nevertheless, the instinct to explain meaning in ways that are geared towards the user's needs and level of competence seems to me to be absolutely right.

5.4   Examples

Probably the most visible way in which dictionaries have changed under the impact of corpus data is the arrival of the corpus-derived dictionary example. There is a certain tension here between the desirability of showing authentic instances of language in use, and the need for examples that work as hard as possible for the user. As Cowie observes (1978: 131), Hornby long ago recognized that an invented example could include a range of information types, and 'pressure on space often requires that a given example sentence should fulfil several functions simultaneously'. On the other hand, critics of this approach can point with some justification to the many contrived, unnatural-sounding examples that littered pre-corpus MLDs and could not be seen as reliable models for students to emulate. Despite a certain amount of research into the issue (e.g. Laufer 1992; Humble 1998), the jury is still out on the relative merits of corpus-based and lexicographer-produced examples. But it is really no longer relevant to characterize the argument as a simple choice between the authentic and the invented. All reputable MLDs now base every aspect of their text on corpus data, so the differences now lie

---

[8] Similarly, compare these two definitions of **clothes horse**: 'If you describe someone, especially a woman, as a **clothes horse**, you mean that they are fashionable and think a lot about their clothes, but have little intelligence or no other abilities' (*COBUILD2*); 'a person who is more interested in clothes and fashion than anything else' (*CIDE*).

in the degree to which corpus material is 'processed' on its way into the examples. Compare the following examples for the core meaning of **kill**:

(19) *Careless driving kills. | He was killed with a knife. | Cancer kills thousands of people every year. | We need something to kill the weeds. (ALD5)*

More than 1,000 people have been killed by the armed forces. | Cattle should be killed cleanly and humanely. | The earthquake killed 62 people. | Heroin can kill. (*COBUILD2*)

Producing successful examples is a deceptively difficult skill, and both sets here do an excellent job. In a necessarily short space, they reveal (among other things):

- grammatical information (**kill** can be transitive or intransitive, and it is often used passively, in which case the agent is marked by **by**, the instrument by **with**)
- selectional restrictions: the subject of **kill** is often a human agent, but it can also be an illness, an event, a dangerous drug, or a type of behaviour; the object can be human, animal, or even vegetable
- a range of very typical contexts

There is not a great deal to choose between these accounts; the *COBUILD* examples have, characteristically, slightly more of the whiff of the corpus about them, but certainly not in a way that would cause problems for users. Most lexicographers would probably now agree that, where the corpus provides natural and typical examples that clearly illustrate the points that need to be made, there is no conceivable reason for not using them. The risk here, illustrated rather too often in *COBUILD1* but only very occasionally in *COBUILD2*, is that wholly authentic examples can sometimes show mystifyingly irretrievable contexts (for example in *COBUILD1*'s example at **gravitate**: *He gravitated, naturally, to Newmarket*); atypical uses (see **proxy** in (2) above); or too much irrelevant and – to the learner – distracting material (see Hausmann and Gorbahn's thoughtful analysis (1989) of *COBUILD1* for numerous instances). So there is still a place for the more 'pedagogical' example, typically now produced by modifying an actually occurring sentence, which allows the lexicographer to focus on specific linguistic points without baffling the user. But while clear philosophical differences remain in the publicly stated approaches of the different MLDs (compare for example the positions taken by Della Summers in the *Longman Language Activator* 1993: F10, and by John Sinclair in *COBUILD2* 1995: viii–ix), there is something not too far from a consensus in actual working practices.

5.5   Frequency information

In addition to frequency-based sense ordering (mentioned above), two current MLDs – *COBUILD2* and *LDOCE3* – provide quite detailed information about the frequency of the more common words in their respective headword lists. In the case of *LDOCE*, this is sometimes complemented by graphs that illustrate, among other things, the relative frequency of near synonyms across the written/spoken or British/American axes, or the relative frequency of the different complementation patterns of a verb. All of this is especially valuable for students operating in productive mode. If they are to make appropriate word choices, they need to know (for example) that certain types of cognates with words in their own languages (such as **commence**, **permit**, or **enter**) are actually rather uncommon in most types of English text, and would be almost aberrant in spoken discourse. Frequency symbols and frequency graphs provide helpful pointers here, and these new developments are merely the beginning of a trend which has a good deal further to run (see now Kilgarriff 1997d).

5.6   Illustrations

English dictionaries have featured illustrative material since as long ago as 1538 (Stein 1991: 101), and almost all MLDs – with the notable exception of the larger *COBUILD* dictionaries – make extensive use of illustrations. Earlier dictionaries used pictures mainly for representing concrete objects, either singly or in some sort of lexical set (such as vocabulary relating to cars or houses). Both these types of illustration are still widely used, but there have been several innovations in this area, many of them originating in the second edition of *LDOCE* (1987). These include: diagrams clarifying spatial or temporal concepts (such as **since** and **ago**); illustrations showing the related meanings of polysemous words; illustrations clarifying the differences between confusables like **borrow** and **lend** or **rob** and **steal**; illustrations that show the literal meanings of words which are often used metaphorically (such as **muzzle**, **boomerang**, or **pioneer**); illustrations showing cultural stereotypes (as for example of the stereotypical **burglar** in *LDELC*); and illustrations of what are sometimes called 'scripts', showing the various actions and events relating to a particular situation, with the associated lexis (see for example the 'script' for Driving a Car in *CIDE*). Illustrative material has thus become more closely integrated into the text of MLDs, and forms one of several strategies for helping users expand their vocabulary and successfully negotiate known areas of difficulty.

5.7   Other areas of improvement

5.7.1   Spoken English

The availability, in adequate quantity and quality, of data for ordinary conversational English has lagged almost 10 years behind developments in the area of written text. We are still, therefore, at a relatively early stage in terms of defining a methodology for exploiting these riches and translating the insights from spoken corpora into pedagogically-relevant dictionary text. Nevertheless, the impact of spoken corpora is beginning to be felt, for example in better coverage of spoken phraseology (see e.g. *LDOCE3*'s excellent entry for the verb **mean**) and in clearer guidance on appropriate situations of use, as in *COBUILD2*'s entry at **must**:

> (20)   **9** You use **must** in conversation in expressions such as '**I must say**' and '**I must admit**' in order to emphasize a point you are making.[9]

5.7.2   Pragmatics and speaker attitude

The illocutionary force of an utterance is not always retrievable from its surface meaning, so there is an opportunity here for the learner's dictionary to explain features like irony, euphemism, and understatement. Clearly there are limits to what dictionaries can do: for example, virtually any appreciative comment ('that's marvellous', 'you've been a great help, I must say', etc.) has the potential to be used ironically, so – in printed dictionaries at least – we have to confine ourselves to identifying those expressions that are *regularly* used in this way. Stylistic labels such as 'pejorative', 'ironic', or 'facetious' have long formed part of the lexicographer's repertoire, but current MLDs now often show speaker attitude in a more explicit fashion, for example:

---

[9]   See now Moon (1998b) for a recent discussion.

(21) If you describe something that someone has said as **pearls of wisdom**, you mean that it sounds very wise or helpful. People usually use this expression in a way that shows that, in fact, they mean the opposite of what they are saying (*COBUILD2*) **princely sum** an expression meaning a large amount of money, often used jokingly to mean a very small amount of money (*LDOCE3*)

5.7.3   *Register, regional variety, and genre*

There is nothing new about dictionaries marking words for extralinguistic features of this type, but here again we can see improvements in terms of both the quality of information and the way it is presented. With access to large and varied corpora, we can now give a reliable account of both major regional varieties of English, and as resources improve other Englishes will increasingly be covered too. With regard to stylistic values, Jain (1981: 283) questioned whether a simple label such as 'formal' actually conveyed much to learners. In reality, while some words and meanings are quite adequately characterized by a description of this type, there are in many cases other factors at play. Is it enough, for example, to say that **purchase** is merely a more 'formal' way of saying **buy**? Rather, corpus data suggests that this would be the usual item to select in certain well-defined contexts, as shown in this entry from *LLA*:

(22) **purchase** a word used especially in business meaning to buy something big or expensive such as a house, a piece of land, or shares in a company etc.

Improved corpus resources now make it possible to pin down appropriate contexts of use in fairly precise terms, such as '**aggregate** . . . a technical use in economics and sport' or 'Journalists sometimes use the word **slaying** to refer to a murder; used mainly in American English' (both from *COBUILD2*). Conventional style labels still have a useful role to play, but should not be used as an easy option in cases where more focused advice can be given.

6   RECENT DEVELOPMENTS: SOME CONCLUSIONS

The most obvious change of the past 20 years has been the application of corpus data to the dictionary-making process. And the emergence of 'corpus lexicography' as a distinct discipline has, to a very significant degree, taken place within the field of English (and specifically British) pedagogical lexicography. The impact of these developments on actual dictionary text has been profound, and it has by no means run its course. We can anticipate, for example, more systematic exploitation of learner corpus and spoken corpus resources, and we can confidently predict further improvements in corpus-enquiry software, perhaps especially in statistical tools. All of this is sure to yield more linguistic insights, so that the quality of information available to lexicographers will continue to improve. We are beginning, however, to see what the limits of automation might be, and which lexicographic tasks (perhaps most notably the analysis, discovery, and description of meaning) might ultimately turn out to be beyond the capabilities of computers.

Against this background, it is appropriate not to lose sight of the enormous contribution made by *human* ingenuity and innovation to the improvements that have undoubtedly taken place. The scope of the learner's dictionary has broadened considerably, now encompassing areas such as pragmatics, cultural allusion and encyclopedic information (see especially *LDELC* and the *ALD Encyclopedic Edition*), and guidance on every aspect of grammar and usage. This has taken the MLD into territory formerly occupied by mainstream English language teaching materials. There is, too, a greater readiness, in all areas of the text, to ignore the peripheral and focus on the typical, sometimes even to the extent of taking a prescriptive line when this can be pedagogically justified. All of this reflects a welcome move away from the inappropriate model of the native-speaker's 'dictionary of record' towards a more 'utilitarian' lexicography, in which the needs of the user take precedence over all other factors. One could argue that, for precisely this reason, the new generation of ESL dictionaries originating in the US are unlikely in the short term to challenge the dominance of the established British MLDs: for, not only are they not corpus-based – a severe handicap – but they also consciously see themselves as modelled on existing dictionaries for native-speakers.[10] As ever, we have much to learn from the far-sighted Dr. Johnson, who understood perfectly that 'it is not enough that a dictionary delights the critic, unless at the same time it instructs the learner; as it is to little purpose, that an engine amuses the philosopher by the subtlety of its mechanism, if it requires so much knowledge in its application, as to be of no advantage to the common workman' (Samuel Johnson, *The Plan of a Dictionary* 1747 – see also in this volume, *Ed.*). Whenever a pedagogical dictionary shows *systematic* failure (as opposed to the occasional lapses to which we are all subject), one can usually trace the cause back to a failure to consider the user, and almost all the examples of bad practice in this paper can be so interpreted. Conversely, those dictionaries whose design and content are informed primarily by an understanding of learners' needs and capabilities have progressively abandoned many of the features of the NSD: continuing the work begun by Palmer, West, and Hornby, they have created a distinctively different form of reference resource.

Six years ago, Reinhard Hartmann wrote: 'I feel we are only at the start of an exciting period of real problem-solving' (Hartmann 1992: 153). The paradox here (and this is what makes pedagogical lexicography such an absorbing field) is that really major advances have indeed been made in the intervening years, yet there are still grounds for believing that we are just at the start of more exciting developments still.

---

[10] For example, *The American Heritage English as a Second Language Dictionary* (Houghton Mifflin 1998) is 'adapted from the *American Heritage Student Dictionary*' (an NSD) and has 'authoritative definitions adapted from *The American Heritage Dictionary*'. Being 'authoritative' is no doubt important for an NSD, but one could argue that it is not the primary concern of definitions in an MLD.

APPENDIX I

lookout *n* **1** a future possibility: *It's not a good lookout for his family if he's going to work abroad* **2** the act of keeping watch **3** a place to watch from **4** a person who keeps watch **5 one's own lookout** a state of affairs one must take care of for oneself, without others' help: *If you want to go into that lion's cage, it's your own lookout* **6 on the lookout for** searching for
LDOCE1 (1978)

lookout *n* **1 be on the lookout for** to watch a place or situation continuously in order to find something you want or be ready for problems or opportunities: *Police were on the lookout for anyone behaving suspiciously.| We're always on the lookout for new business opportunities.* **2 keep a lookout** to keep watching carefully for something or someone, especially for danger: **keep a sharp/special lookout** *When you're driving keep a sharp lookout for cyclists.* **3** someonewhose duty is to watch carefully for something, especially danger: *A lookout reported an enemy plane approaching.* **4** a place for a lookout to watch from: *a coastguard lookout on the clifftop* **5 it's your/their own lookout** *BrE spoken* used to say that what someone has chosen to do is their own problem or risk, and no-one else's:*If he wants to ruin his health with all these drugs, that's his own lookout.* **6 be a poor/bad lookout for sb** *BrE spoken* used to say that something bad or unsatisfactory is likely to happen: *It'll be a poor lookout for James if she finds that letter.*
LDOCE3 (1995)

APPENDIX 2

false **1** not right, true or real: *a ~ alarm; ~ideas* ... **2** deceiving; lying: *give a ~ impression; bear/give ~ witness...* **3** not genuine; sham; artificial: *~ hair/teeth* ...
(*ALD3* 1974)

false 1 If something is **false**, it is incorrect, untrue, or mistaken: *It was quite clear that the President was being given false information...* **2** You use **false** to describe objects which are artificial but which are intended to look like the real thing or be used instead of the real thing... **3** If you describe a person or their behaviour as **false**, you are criticizing them for being insincere or for hiding their real feelings...
(*COBUILD2* 1995)

PART IX
On Bilingual Lexicography

17

Then and Now: Competence and Performance in 35 Years of Lexicography

B. T. SUE ATKINS*

ABSTRACT

This paper describes the process of writing a bilingual English–French dictionary in the late 1960s, and contrasts it with a similar task in the early 21st century, with all the benefits of a large text corpus and sophisticated query tools. The lexicography focuses on the entries for *cook* and *cooking*, designed for use both by an encoding English speaker and a decoding French speaker. Lexicographic evidence for the new entries comes from a 100-million-word corpus of British English, a small corpus of French for the words *cuire*, *cuisine*, *cuisiner*, *cuisinier*, and *cuisson*, and their inflected forms, and a small parallel corpus of English and French texts. The use of KWIC concordancing, the Word Sketch program and the FrameNet database is described in detail, together with the problems of equivalence encountered. An account is given of the way in which these problems are tackled and the dictionary entry is drafted.

I INTRODUCTION

Dictionaries exist...to provide a series of hints and associations connecting the unknown with the known.

So runs Bolinger's dictum, quoted by Patrick Hanks in his inspiring address to the 2000 Euralex Congress (Hanks 2000). However, about thirty-five years ago I began writing a dictionary whose *raison d'être* was – although I couldn't have said so then – to provide a series of hints *connecting the known with the unknown*. Eleven years and fifty-odd colleagues later, this had become the Collins–Robert English–French Dictionary (CREFD), now in its fifth edition and still going strong. It has latterly benefited from the linguistic resources of HarperCollins's Bank of English, and from an editorial eye more knowledgeable than my own, yet still I see in its entries the lingering ghosts of those I wrote in my first stumbling years as a lexicographer.

In this paper I shall consider how practical lexicography has changed over the past thirty-five or so years, and set these changes in the context of a handful of closely related English–French entries. I shall not concern myself with the great changes which the computer has brought to the consultation of the dictionaries, but solely with the writing of them. I shall look first at how the entries were written in 1967, and then at how they might be written in 2002. Any such comparison must include (as well as consideration of changes in the language itself):

* Atkins, B.T.S. (2002). 'Then and now: competence and performance in 35 years of lexicography', in Braasch, A., and Povlsen, C. (eds), *Proceedings of the Tenth EURALEX International Congress, EURALEX 2002*. Copenhagen: Center for Sprogteknologi, 1–28.

   (i) the technical skill and linguistic knowledge of the lexicographer;
  (ii) the instructions or guidelines given for the production of the dictionary;
 (iii) the sources of evidence on which lexicographic decisions are based;
 (iv) any reference works available for consultation;
  (v) aids to production of text; and
 (vi) the type of entry being compiled.

In this case, the first of these variables has changed radically, and the last remains the same: an English into French entry for an 'active' dictionary, i.e. one written for the encoding anglophone. Variables (ii) to (v) concern us here. I propose to focus on two specific entries, *cook* and *cooking*, to discover whether using present-day resources results in changes in the entries.

---

cook [...] **1** *n* cuisinier *m*, ière *f*.
she is a good ~ elle est bonne cuisinière, elle fait bien la cuisine; **to be head** *or* **chief** ~ **and bottle-washer** * (*in a household*) servir de bonne à tout faire; (*elsewhere*) être le factotum. **2** *cpd*: **cookbook** livre *m* de cuisine; (*Mil, Naut*) **cookhouse** cuisine *f*; (*US*) **cookout** repas *m* (cuit) en plein air. **3** *vt* **(a)** *food* (faire) cuire. (*fig*) **to** ~ **sb's goose** * faire son affaire à qn, régler son compte à qn; **(b)** (*Brit**: *falsify*) *accounts, books* truquer, maquiller.

4 *vi* [*food*] cuire; [*person*] faire la cuisine, cuisiner. **she** ~**s well** elle fait bien la cuisine, elle cuisine bien; **what's** ~**ing?**** qu'est-ce qui se mijote?*
✦**cook up*** *vt sep story, excuse* inventer, fabriquer.

cooking [...] **1** *n* cuisine *f* (*activité*). **plain / French** ~ cuisine bourgeoise / française. **2** *cpd* *utensils* de cuisine; *apples, chocolate* à cuire. **cooking foil** papier *m* d'aluminium; **cooking salt** gros sel, sel de cuisine.

FIG. 1   The entries in the CREFD first edition.

2   THEN

In 1967, in collaboration with my French colleague Marie-Noëlle Lamy, I wrote the entries shown in Figure 1 for the first edition of the CREFD, published in 1978. For this period, the parameters of comparison listed in (i) to (vi) above are simple to report. Neither she nor I had any experience of writing dictionaries, but we had both suffered at the hands of the bilingual dictionaries we had used as language students, and were determined to do better. We learned by trial and error, and it is to Collins's eternal credit that we were given scope to do so. When I began work in 1966, the French–English half of the dictionary had already been compiled (this early text was later scrapped), and the publishers were recruiting part-time home-workers to complete the other half. I was the eighth candidate interviewed that morning, and went home with a list of words beginning with H, and the brief to write bilingual entries for them all. No other instructions were given but I was encouraged to look at other dictionaries[1] which I had to supply myself, and make my own decisions. I started to collect citations in a small card-index box. Mistrusting the other bilingual dictionaries,

---

[1] The dictionaries I used as 'lexicographic evidence' were an early edition of the Concise Oxford English Dictionary, the Oxford Advanced Learner's Dictionary (1963), and the one-volume Harrap English and French Dictionary; later were added the Random House College Dictionary 2nd edition, and eventually the *Petit Robert*.

I enrolled a local francophone linguist as informant, and six months later returned the completed 'H' entries, only to discover that A–G (and of course I–Z) still awaited compiling, the first seven lexicographers having variously fallen by the wayside. I chose C as my next task, purely on the grounds that it contained a high proportion of words of Latin origin (with initial *con-*, *contra-* etc.) which I reckoned would make for speedy compiling. The principle of a bilingual editor pair working on the text was also established at that time, and eventually we were proud to claim, on publication, that all the English and all the French in the dictionary text had been written by native speakers. This principle was maintained by Collins on most of their subsequent major bilingual dictionaries. A year later, when C was finished, alarmed by the snail's pace at which the project was progressing, Collins agreed that I should write 'Compilers' Instructions' so that others could join the team, and the first version of the Style Guide came into being; over the years, enriched by many editors, it grew to 280 pages or so, and covered the lexicography of both directional halves of the dictionary.

2.1   Method of working

In writing the early English–French entries, our *modus operandi* was briefly as follows: I worked from a draft headword list supplied by the publishers. I read my reference dictionaries and tried to think up all the different constructions in which my headword might be found in each of its senses. I pencilled out a draft entry, over-rich in English examples, with suggestions for translations here and there, and notes explaining the reasoning behind the material and the way it was presented. Lamy supplied the missing French translations, often adapting the entry to include an equivalent I had not allowed for, or suggesting another example to clarify a point. We discussed the entry by telephone (living as we did in different parts of the country), she guarding the interests of the decoding francophone user and I those of the encoding anglophone reader. One of us copied out the finished entry legibly, underlining in red for primary bold type, green for secondary bold and black for italics. Our only aids to text production were pen and paper. The dictionary text was mailed weekly in manuscript sections to the publishers, where it was typed, and indeed set in stone, since before the days of photocopiers it was never possible to check back to see what we had written in an earlier section, far less to edit it, unless some serious error came to light. We did get a chance of authors' corrections at galley proof stage but almost every correction – or so memory tells me – had to be argued for individually.

2.2   The Entries

The 1967 entries are shown in Figure 1. There are a number of points of lexicographic technique which none of us would want to repeat – the treatment of compound nouns buried out of alphabetical order within a larger entry, the ubiquitous *fig* label, the ambiguous splitting of examples with *or*, and so on – but the then-and-now comparison will focus only on the content.

3   NOW

In 2002, much has changed. Lexicographic training has created a pool of skilled and adaptable editors, linguistically aware and able to compile entries speedily and efficiently; dictionary projects follow detailed Style Guides, which enshrine editorial decisions made at the design stage of the dictionary, and are nowadays often consulted online. With the advent of the computer in the 80s, many publishers installed sophisticated dictionary writing systems. These lead to a more rational approach to compiling (say, in lexical sets); they reduce the potential for errors and inconsistency by automating some routine tasks, removing a good deal of the drudgery along the way; they allow the lexicographers to look at already compiled text and to benefit from previous work by the team; they give the managing editors the opportunity of tailoring work packages to the skills and needs of the team members; they facilitate the editing process, reducing the steps in the text flow from initial editor to printed entry; and they monitor the timing and text length according to the project schedule.

And, more importantly, the computer opened the way to the lexicographers' corpus. The availability – from the early 1980s onwards – of large text corpora completely transformed our work. In this comparison I shall focus on the various sources of lexicographic evidence now available, and review the 1967 entries in the light of what is found there.

3.1   Aids to Bilingual Lexicography in 2002

The source-language editor drafting an English–French bilingual dictionary entry will normally begin with an analysis (see Atkins 1993 for a discussion of the analysis and synthesis stages of lexicography; see also in this volume – *Ed.*); this analysis should describe in as much detail as possible the behaviour of the English headword-lexeme[2] without any regard to a target language.[3] At this stage, therefore, the only corpus required is an English corpus; later in the process, when the target language appears, other corpora will be helpful: a corpus of current French is essential, and parallel English–French corpora could be useful.

3.2   Drafting the Framework

From the very rich analysis a 'framework' for the bilingual entry is extracted; much of the information in the framework is for internal use, and will not appear in the eventual entry. Potential dictionary senses are mapped out and standard information (e.g. parts of speech) inserted. Related multi-word expressions (idioms, compounds, phrasal verbs etc.) are included, together with other elements of the microstructure (e.g. labelling of register, style, domain etc.). The source-language editor will offer possible example sentences, and may make suggestions about translations. Notes may be added about the scope of specific source-language vocabulary items, possible faux amis or other translation problems, in an attempt to guide the target-language editor towards the best equivalents. This framework, rich in examples of usage, then goes to the target-language editor. Her responsibility is to propose equivalents, suggest amendments, and make sure that the entry does not mislead the French speaker, who has of course entirely different linguistic preconceptions from those of the English-speaking user.

---

[2] The lexeme *cook* unites the word-forms *cook, cooks, cooking* and *cooked*, and may be analysed into lexical units; we may think of a lexeme as corresponding to a dictionary headword, and a lexical unit to a dictionary sense.

[3] The *target language* is, for instance, French in an English-into-French bilingual dictionary entry, and the *source language* in such a dictionary is English.

I like	cooking	
these are meats and poultry (raw and	cooked	)
None of them except Mrs James, the	cook	, looked comfortable, Katherine mused.
She was totally independent, able to	cook	, wash, look after herself and her home
she would 've gone into the kitchen to	cook	a nice meal for Bina.
a	cook	able to produce basic dishes
I'm not much of a	cook	but it's fun, I like doing it
he's drawing two salaries and has me	cooking	for him.
piles of food which students attempt to	cook	for themselves to save money,
He peered into the sack and produced a	cooked	ham
Alice	cooked	herself eggs, drank tea, and…
she suddenly remembered the ox heart	cooking	in the oven for Ethel
Toma made fresh coffee and	cooked	me a man-sized breakfast of bacon…
She was sweeping the yard while Bella	cooked	the lunch and sang to the baby.

FIG. 2   Some KWIC concordances for *cook*.

3.3   Using KWIC Concordances

The first task of today's lexicographer, therefore, is to analyse the data: to discover and record significant facts about the headword, from the evidence of its behaviour available in a general corpus of current English. (The data we shall be using for *cook* is from the 100-million-word British National Corpus.[4]) The usual practice is to scan a few hundred randomly selected concordance lines, and try to see a pattern emerging of the senses of the word. Within these senses we then look further for structured information, including (a) the constructions in which the headword participates; (b) the words with which it co-occurs most significantly (its 'collocates'); (c) any multi-word expressions in which it is found; and (d) other aspects of linguistic behaviour such as register, stylistic, regional or pragmatic variation.

Our first view of the headword in the corpus is usually in the form of Key Word In Context (KWIC) lines, as shown in Figure 2. In this example, no distinction is made between noun and verb forms, although when wc know that the word belongs to more than one word class it is possible to select concordances for each one separately, by using the part-of-speech tags in the corpus; this can have the effect, however, of blurring correspondences between verbs and their nominalizations.

Figure 2 shows a simple KWIC screen, produced by the WordSmith Tools Concord program[5] with the lines sorted on the words to the right of the keyword: there are of course other programs which allow more sophisticated searches, such as XKWIC, which is part of the Corpus Workbench developed by the IMS at Universität Stuttgart, Germany, but these tend to be used in research projects rather than commercial publishing, where time is of the essence. From the few lines shown in Figure 2, we can already glean a lot of information about *cook*, but we have to spend a good deal of time thinking about it all, even though the 14 lines in our sample represent only 0.2% of the corpus examples. We note that the word has both noun and

---

[4]   See http://info.ox.ac.uk/bnc

[5]   WordSmith, by Mike Scott, is a useful, inexpensive corpus-querying utility; details of the program are available at http://www.liv.ac.uk/~ms2928/homepage.html. Dictionary publishers with large corpus resources tend to use more powerful concordancing software.

cook (v)   BNC freq= 2539

~ on		~ in		particle		and/or		object		subject	
~ on	30 0.2	~ in	152 1.0	particle up	75 4.8	and/or	120 1.3	object	1144 0.6	subject	1321 0.5
stove	3 7.4	wine	11 17.7			clean	14 16.0	meal	122 29.6	meal	11 12.5
fire	4 7.3	oven	10 14.5	particle through	16 6.1	eat	11 11.6	dinner	58 22.2	food	13 10.4
barbecue	2 5.7	pan	6 12.1			sew	5 9.7	supper	21 17.9	dish	6 9.0
~ for	123 1.6	sauce	2 11.3			wash	6 9.0	breakfast	26 17.9	potato	5 8.8
him	14 9.5	oil	6 9.8			prepare	6 8.1	lunch	26 16.8	kitchen	6 8.2
minute	12 9.1	kitchen	7 9.2			serve	5 7.0	food	62 16.8	microwave	3 7.5
us	7 8.0	skin	4 8.8			sleep	3 5.4	chicken	20 16.3	chef	4 7.3
them	8 7.1	butter	3 7.3			bake	2 4.9	pasta	12 15.5	onion	3 7.1
you	7 6.5	pot	4 6.1			shop	2 4.9	dish	20 15.4	fish	2 7.1
her	5 5.3	spice	2 5.8			mend	2 4.5	rice	14 13.8	mushroom	3 7.1
min	2 4.6	bedsit	2 5.7			modifier	404 0.6	steak	10 12.6	beef	3 6.7
.	20 4.5	fat	2 5.2			lightly	10 8.2	potato	16 12.5	rice	3 6.3
supper	2 4.1	saucepan	2 5.1			freshly	8 7.9	sausage	9 12.3	hour	2 6.1
me	4 4.1	microwave	3 4.8			evenly	5 7.1	vegetable	11 12.3	she	128 5.6
~ with	63 0.9	variety	3 4.6			tonight	9 6.5	onion	19 12.2	chicken	3 5.5
herb	4 9.0	juice	2 4.5			properly	7 5.2	turkey	7 11.3	lunch	3 5.5
								meat	12 11.1	dumpling	2 5.3

FIG. 3   Part of the Word Sketch for the verb *cook*.

verb uses, and in both of these word classes it seems to be polysemous. As a noun, it can refer to a profession (*Mrs James, the cook, looked comfortable*) and is also used when talking about someone's cooking skills (*I'm not much of a cook*). As a verb, it can be used transitively (*Bella cooked the lunch*) and intransitively (*the ox heart cooking in the oven*). There may be a case for two senses in the transitive verb (is *cooking ham* the same sense as *cooking breakfast*?), and it occurs with a benefactive indirect object (*cooked me a man-sized breakfast*) which can also be expressed with the preposition *for* (*cook a nice meal for Bina*).

Discovering a word's grammatical, semantic and combinatorial properties requires painstaking analysis of the data. However, there are 6,750 instances of the lexeme *cook* in the BNC, too many for a lexicographer to read carefully in the time available, and mostly we make do with random sampling. Moreover, reading through hundreds of corpus lines means that important points are bound to be missed. Indeed, some types of information can never be revealed by scanning KWIC lines. For instance, the points I picked up in the concordances contain nothing about collocates, yet these are of great interest, particularly if the dictionary is one for learners of the language, as is of course the case in bilingual lexicography for the encoding user.

Statistical programs are necessary to produce information on collocate patternings: Wordsmith has some collocate functionality (showing clusters of words – *e.g. know how to, to cook for, as well as* – in the context of *cook*; offering lists of word-forms with frequency statistics according to their position vis-à-vis the keyword; indicating the distribution of the keyword in the various texts in the corpus), but I want to look at the question of collocates through the lens of a different program devised specifically with lexicographers in mind, namely Adam Kilgarriff and David Tugwell's Word Sketches,[6] shown in Figure 3.

---

[6] See http://www.sketchengine.co.uk/ for demo version.

3.4   Using Word Sketches

The Word Sketch program (Kilgarriff and Tugwell 2001) combines information of two types: grammatical relations in the corpus, and statistically significant frequencies of cooccurrence. The screen shows ordered lists of significant grammatical relations, listing each in order of salience, with the count of corpus instances; clicking on the number of instances retrieves a selection of the actual corpus examples illustrating this pattern. This means that for the verb *cook*, seen in Figure 3, the construction with the particle **up** is highly salient (rating 4.8, where the norm is 1.0) and clicking on **75** produces corpus sentences of which the first few, together with the unique corpus address, are shown in Figure 4.

5845576	If the universe consisted of just the elements	cooked up	in the big bang, then…
6275223	how the chemical elements were	cooked up	in the turmoil ofcreation
8157260	thinking about eating, and	cooking	up plans for new diets up a…
28722307	Instead, it	cooked	deal with Du Pont that was to

FIG. 4   Some corpus examples of *cook* + particle *up*.

Using the Word Sketch enables us to get a fix on the verb *cook* much faster than with the simple KWIC concordances. The sense of processing something (*cooking ham*) and that of preparing something (*cooking breakfast*) show up clearly in the list of objects of the verb (in Figure 3, under the heading '**object 1144 0.6**'); the list of subjects to the right of it reminds me that food cooks (*meal, food, dish, potato*) and that people (*chef, she, I, you*) cook food; and the presence of nouns such as *meal, food* and *chicken* in both lists alerts me to the fact that this verb participates in the causative–inchoative alternation (see Atkins *et al.* (1988) for a discussion of this in relation to the verb *bake*). Also I notice – what I might have overlooked in a simple reading of KWIC lines – that appliances (*microwave*) and utensils can also be said to cook things. The list of prepositional objects following the high-salience **for** (*him, us, them, you* etc.) leaves me in no doubt of the existence of a benefactive, while – unlike the simple KWIC lines – the Word Sketch draws my attention to the possible importance to the act of cooking of the objects of the preposition *in*, and shows me at least three different lexical sets of nouns filling that slot: (1) *wine, sauce, oil* etc. (2) *oven, pan, pot* etc., and (3) *kitchen, bedsit* etc. How relevant are these to the bilingual entry? I make a note of this, to reflect on later. There is the intriguing list under the '**and/or**' heading, whose salience figure (1.3) shows me that *cook* is a verb which is found more often than the mean coordinated with another verb (*clean, eat, sew, wash* etc.). It is impossible to dig such information out of simple concordance lines, but it is something that I'll remember when drafting the bilingual entry (how do you translate *cook* in *She can cook and clean and sew?*). Finally, the presence of *goose* at the foot of the list of objects of the verb (not visible in Figure 3) reminds me of the phrase *to cook someone's goose*, a familiar but infrequent idiom of which there were no examples in my randomly selected set of 1,000 or so KWIC concordances.

The Word Sketch summary, combined with the ease of seeing the actual corpus examples it is based on, transforms the corpus-querying part of the analysis process: it radically reduces the time it takes to get an overview of the behaviour of the lexeme, to plan the senses that are likely to figure in the analysis entry, to look more closely at certain types of collocation in an effort to note everything of value, and to select sentences to exemplify points and possibly later to serve as examples in the dictionary entry. But even with such a tool, the lexicographer still has to disentangle the senses of polysemous words (many of them much more complex than *cook*), and cannot be sure of covering all the essential facts about the word. For assistance in these areas, we have to look to FrameNet.

3.5   Using FrameNet

The FrameNet project,[7] now in its second three-year phase, is currently building an online lexical resource, based on frame semantics and supported by corpus evidence, documenting the range of syntactic and semantic combinatory possibilities (the valence) of a word in each of its senses, through the manual annotation of example sentences. The database created during Phase 1 can be queried on the web.[8] The project is headed by Charles J. Fillmore, and follows the credo expressed in Fillmore (1995):

The proper way to describe a word is to identify the grammatical constructions in which it participates and to characterize all of the obligatory and optional types of companions (complements, modifiers, adjuncts, etc.) which the word can have in such constructions, in so far as the occurrence of such accompanying elements is dependent in some way on the meaning of the word being described.

This information is exactly what lexicographers need during the analysis stage of the process.

FrameNet is of course one resource among many: its authority rests on its sound theoretical foundation and the accuracy with which the database reflects the facts of language as evidenced in the corpus. The work in FrameNet (unlike standard dictionary compiling) is theory-informed, as well as data-driven. In the FrameNet entry there is, for each word sense, a table showing the various ways in which semantic roles, or 'frame elements', are syntactically expressed in the context of the target word. For each pattern there are supporting example sentences from the corpus, and the relevant definition from the Concise Oxford Dictionary is displayed (this last in order to locate the sense of the word for the human reader, for the entry is designed for use both by people and in a computer lexicon). Like a thesaurus, it groups words according to the semantic frames in which they participate, and work has begun on detailing the relations of semantic frames to each other. To quote the FrameNet website:

A frame is an intuitive construct that allows us to formalize the links between semantics and syntax in the results of lexical analysis. Semantic frames are schematic representations of situations involving various participants, props, and other conceptual roles, each of which is a frame element. The semantic arguments of a predicating word correspond to the frame elements of the frame, or frames associated with that word.

The objective of the FrameNet lexicographers is to record for each lexical unit (LU), or dictionary sense, every possible significant construction in which the target is found in the corpus, together with one or more corpus sentences in which the construction occurs. They aim at recording all the constructions necessary to a grammatical expression of the complex semantic range of the target word.

The FrameNet database contains three LUs for *cook* (so far – the entry is not yet complete), which may be roughly described as follows:

LU-1. heat and change the state of some foodstuff

---

[7] This research project, of considerable importance to professional lexicographers, is based in the International Computer Science Institute, Berkeley, California, and led by Charles J. Fillmore, whose work in frame semantics and construction grammar informs the lexicography. A full account of this project [was] given by the FrameNet team in an edition of the *International Journal of Lexicography* guest-edited by Thierry Fontenelle and published in December 2003.

[8] See http://www.icsi.berkeley.edu/~framenet/

(*cook the onions, the onions were cooking*)

LU-2. create a dish or a meal by doing that (also cook up)

(*she cooked him breakfast, she likes cooking*)

LU-3. invent (also cook up)

(*... spend hours cooking up exercise programmes*)

It will eventually also contain at least a fourth:

LU-4. alter (financial statements) with devious intent

(*accused him of cooking the sales returns*)

The first two senses (LU-1 and LU-2) will concern us in this paper.

3.5.1 The Apply_heat frame

The Apply_heat frame is defined in the FrameNet manual as follows (the names of frame elements are in small capitals):

The Cook applies heat to Food. Heat may be applied at a certain Temperature and for a certain Duration. A Cooking Instrument (generally indicated by a locative phrase) may also be specified. Some cooking methods involve the use of a Medium by which heat is transferred to the food. In some sentences more than one phrase may contain a food frame element. When one of these phrases is less grammatically prominent than the other, *i.e.* in a prepositional phrase, it is marked Food2 and the other is marked Food1.

The verbs *fry*, *bake* and *stew* all belong to this frame. Figure 5 shows how some of these frame elements may be instantiated in the context of these verbs:

Sally	fried	an egg	in butter.
Cook		Food	Medium
Joe	baked	the cookies	in the oven.
Cook		Food	Cookinstr
Ellen	stewed	the lamb shanks	with tomatoes and garlic.
Cook		Food1	Food2

FIG. 5 Elements in the Apply_heat frame.

3.5.2 FrameNet annotation

Within each lexical entry (the description of one lexical unit) every example sentence selected from the corpus is fully annotated with three types of information:

(1) the name of the frame element, or semantic role within the frame;
(2) the type of phrase to which the annotation tag is assigned; and
(3) the grammatical function of that phrase in relation to the target word.

Thus the sentence *Cook the meat in a saucepan over a high heat until browned* would be tagged as in Figure 6, where frame element names are shown above and grammatical information below their lexical realizations. This example is from the first LU in the lexical entry; it belongs to the Apply_heat frame (LU-1 above), as opposed to the Cook_creation frame (LU-2 above).[9]

---

[9] As the entry is not complete, the frame names are not yet finalized.

Target	Food	Container	Temperature	Duration
Cook	the meat	in a saucepan	over a high heat	until browned.
	NP Obj	PP Comp	PP Comp	Ssub Comp

FIG. 6   Sentence showing FrameNet annotation.

The annotation tags record information which is then stored in the database. For the example in Figure 6, this is:

cook is the target word (the fact that it is a verb is recorded elsewhere)
the meat, realizing the frame element FOOD, is a noun phrase functioning as the object of the target verb;
in a saucepan, the frame element CONTAINER, is a prepositional phrase functioning as a complement of the target verb
and so on for the other two frame elements, TEMPERATURE and DURATION.

The abstract information contained in this annotation is summarized in Figure 7; in FrameNet terms this constitutes a valence pattern.

Target	Food	Container	Temperature	Duration
	NP Obj	PP Comp	PP Comp	Ssub Comp

FIG. 7   A valence pattern for *cook* in the Apply_heat frame.

The complete description of this LU includes the full set of 18 valence patterns found in the corpus; these constitute the verb's valence. Figure 8 shows part of the list.

1	5 exx	Cook	FOOD	MEDIUM	
2	2 exx	Cook	FOOD	DURATION	
		--	NP Obj	PPComp	
3	1 exx	Cook	FOOD	MEDIUM	DURATION
		--	NP Obj	PP Comp	PPComp

FIG. 8   Part of the valence of *cook* in the Apply_heat frame.

Each valence pattern is exemplified in one or more corpus sentences which are called up by clicking on the 'exx' number, which indicates how many examples of the pattern have been annotated. The three valence patterns shown in Figure 8 are illustrated by the corpus sentences below:

1. She cooked the hash browns in oil.
2. Cook the duck for a further hour.
3. Cook pasta in boiling salted water for 10–12 minutes.

(In the last two sentences, the frame element COOK – the person cooking – is noted as being implicitly present, as subject of the imperative verb, but unrealized.)

Checking our first analyses and intuitions against the FrameNet entries for *cook* gives us some guidance on sense division. FrameNet offers us a structured set of facts about the lexeme-headword: these facts are already marshalled into LUs, although of course – depending on the requirements of the dictionary – we are at liberty to rework this sense division. FrameNet is however a great advance over most lexicographic resources, in that we can start from some idea of possible senses, and be fairly sure to find in the LU entry a summary of the essential elements of meaning, and the essential constructions, from which we may select what we want to include in our own dictionary entry. The FrameNet entry also offers us a direct route back into the corpus, for examples of usage: combined with the great number of corpus examples available via the Word Sketches, we will rarely need to scan KWIC lines at all. We have all we need to enable us to compile a thorough, even an exhaustive, account of the behaviour of our headword in our corpus. If the framework is correctly compiled, it should serve as a launching pad for any type of dictionary entry. A good framework should be dictionary-neutral. (This is in an ideal world, of course: in the rough and tumble of commercial publishing we never have time to create a full set of frameworks before launching on the dictionary proper.) The framework entry which results from this analysis is now ready to function as a launch-pad for our draft bilingual entry, as well as a source of information for the target-language editor, whose responsibility it is to supply the target-language items which go to make up half of the entry.

3.6   Drafting the source language entry for a bilingual dictionary

Our task as source-language editor is now to select from the wealth of facts at our disposal those most appropriate to the dictionary being compiled. We are writing a bilingual English-into-French dictionary entry, one which will not only help (passive) French speakers to understand an English text, but tell (active) English speakers enough to let them use the foreign language correctly. We must first work with the target-language editor, to tease out all the different little problems of equivalence which our headword presents in various contexts – until we do that we cannot know what information the English speaker will need. So we set about creating a very full draft: normally this is at least three times as long as the eventual entry. Already, on the basis of the framework, we must make 'keep or lose' decisions about grammatical constructions, collocates, example phrases and so on. At this stage we try to keep those items which are essential, those which are most likely to be useful if there is enough space, and those that have to be included in order not to mislead either the English or the French speaker. We then bundle it all up into a rough draft of an entry, already divided into senses – which may change before the entry becomes final – and complete with notes and suggestions for the target-language editor, who has to provide the equivalences throughout the entry.

3.7   Adding the target language material

Unlike English, there is no French national corpus available at low cost to researchers and lexicographers; nor is there (to the best of my knowledge) any structured corpus information like the Word Sketches or the FrameNet database to help us select the target language material for the *cook* and *cooking* entries. With the help of many colleagues, and by trawling the web, I assembled over 3,000 sentences containing *cuire, cuisine, cuisinier,* and *cuisson,* and their various inflected forms, and concordanced this little corpus using the WordSmith toolbox.

3.8   Using the French corpus

Even this cap-in-hand, unplanned, unbalanced, dubious corpus sheds many insights on problems which had clearly beset us in 1967, and we notice at once several surprising omissions of items which had a high profile in the French corpus. For instance, the '3 *vt*' section of the *cook* entry (see Figure 1) contains no reference to *laisser cuire,* yet there are a couple of screenfuls of such uses in the corpus (almost all in the imperative: *laissez cuire encore 10 minutes, laissez cuire plus longtemps si...*). Nor does this section mention *cuisiner,* whose transitive use is exemplified in the corpus (*le plat n'est cuisiné ni par nous ni pour nous*). However this transitive *cuisiner* is rare, except as a past participle adjective (*il s'agit aussi bien de plats cuisinés que de desserts*). Similar omissions are also to be found in the entry for *cooking,* where no mention is made of *cuisson,* yet according to corpus evidence it certainly has a strong claim to appear in the '1 *n*' section (*vérifiez la cuisson, continuez la cuisson, ne change pas de couleur à la cuisson, l'incomparable cuisson au micro-ondes, une cuisson à feu vif, pendant la durée de la cuisson* and so on) and in the '2 cpd' section (in phrases like *eau/jus/sauce/liquide de cuisson* and *mode/méthode/température de cuisson*).

3.9   Using parallel corpora

In principle, parallel corpora are interesting for the bilingual lexicographer, and certainly the pairs of sentences extracted for illustrative purposes from the French–English INTERSECT corpus[10] using the ParaConc program[11] shed a new light on the hunt for equivalences. However, few commercial dictionary-writing schedules allow time for the lexicographers to browse through data from parallel corpora, at least, not in the simple untreated pair format in which they are shown in Figure 9.

The principal use of parallel source- and target-language sentences for bilingual lexicographers must be to remind us of equivalents between items in the two languages. Their value of course is that these equivalent pairs occur in the course of text translation, and are not forced into marriage by dictionary compilers. Using parallel corpus data in this form is labour-intensive: each pair has to be read and evaluated. A number of the items in this list are redundant – **1** to **4** inclusive, for instance: no reminder is needed of the *cook–cuire* equivalence, either transitively or intransitively. (Information about semantic, syntactic and lexical context of the keywords may more readily be extracted from monolingual corpora.) The problem of redundant material could not be solved by the simple use of 'stop' words, since for instance excluding *cuire* would be too radical (it would certainly remove more than half the results of any search and make impossible any contrastive study of *cuire* and *faire cuire* and *laisser cuire*); and excluding a rarer word like *cuisiner* would lose us the interesting pair **8** as well as the straightforward **5**. We need a filter mechanism more open to niceties of grammatical and lexical context, if we are to justify this in terms of the dictionary budget.

From our tiny sample in the list above, this would be hard to do: **1** to **6** inclusive remind us rather unnecessarily of *cuire, cuisiner* and *préparer* as equivalents of *cook.* However, the editor of the *cook* entry might be pleased to notice *préparer vos repas* in **7**, as might

---

10   INTERSECT International Sample of English Contrastive Texts.
11   Available from Athelstan. Information at http://www.athel.com/

1	**a.** They take a long time to *cook.*	**b.** Ils mettent longtemps à *cuire.*
2	**a.** ...delighted by the sweet smell of the bread *cooking.*	**b.** ...toute ravie par la tendre odeur du pain en train de *cuire.*
3	**a.** When the cake *was cooked*...	**b.** Quand la galette *fut cuite*...
4	**a.** While the cake *cooked*...	**b.** Pendant que la galette *cuisait*...
5	**a.** in order to teach you how *to cook–*	**b.** pour vous apprendre à *cuisiner.*
6	**a.** She had *cooked* the ham and eggs	**b.** Elle avait *préparé* les œufs et le jambon
7	**a.** Do not *cook* or eat in your tent	**b.** Évitez de *préparer* et de prendre *vos repas* à l'intérieur de votre tente;
8	**a.** Some of the boys could very easily have *cooked their meals* in...	**b.** Certains garçons eussent fort bien *cuisiné* dans...
9	**a.** he was taking *his supper* home to Gargan *already cooked.*	**b.** *Tout prêt le dîner* qu'il emportait à Gargan.

FIG. 9   Extract from French–English parallel corpora.

the people compiling *préparer* and *repas*, while **8** is interesting in the context of the *cook* entry, as well as the entries for *meal* and *cuisiner*. The last pair in **9** illustrate the problems with the use of parallel corpora in commercial lexicography. The phrase *tout prêt le dîner* is too interesting to be summarily dismissed, but too far from any kind of context-free equivalence of *cook* to be of any use to the bilingual lexicographer (who however might spend quite a long expensive moment in reflection before coming to that conclusion). For the moment at least, parallel corpora might contribute more as a resource for the dictionary user rather than the dictionary writer: packaged on a CD-ROM with an electronic dictionary, they would form a fascinating source of alternative equivalences for the skilled translator.

A smarter program which would tailor the output of the concordancing program to our needs might persuade reference publishers to change their minds about the use of parallel corpora (after all, it took us years to persuade them to let us use corpora at all). However, as far as I know, nothing has been created specifically with dictionary-makers in mind, although there are of course programs which facilitate automatic extraction of candidate translations for machine translation lexicons. Lexicographers working on bilingual dictionaries need some bilingual form of the Word Sketch tool to help them use parallel corpus data within the time constraints of commercial dictionary production.

3.10   Looking back on the 1967 entries

Although the early entries seemed to give a reasonable account of *cook* and *cooking*, there are certain points in them that today I find difficult to understand. Why, for instance, had I included *to be head cook and bottle-washer*, already slightly dated, but omitted the more common *too many cooks (spoil the broth)*? Dr. Johnson, on being challenged to explain an error in his magnificent Dictionary, replied 'Ignorance, Madam, pure ignorance.' 'Incompetence' explains most of the bones I am picking with these entries today. The familiar phrase *to do the cooking* is nowhere to be seen. Why is there no sign of the past participle adjective *cooked* – especially since the compounds it forms present distinct translation problems: *cooked food* or *cooked meals* must be rendered as *plats* (= dishes) *cuisinés*, and *cooked breakfast*, not a regular part of the French day, requires a full gloss. As a dictionary user, I mistrust '3 vt' which implies that *faire cuire* and *cuire* are interchangeable, and I have the same problem with '4 vi' over *faire la cuisine* and *cuisiner*. I do not think that by using the *cook* entry anyone would be able to translate *to cook someone a meal* or *to cook breakfast for someone*, or *go and ask cook*, or *cook for 10 minutes in salted water*.

All in all, even before I looked at any lexicographic evidence I was not happy about the 1967 entries, and as I studied the corpus data, and looked at the FrameNet database, it became clear to me that the entries were poor because the source language editor (me) had no clear idea of how the words *cook* and *cooking* actually behaved in natural spoken and written language. I had plucked facts about them from my own native speaker's intuition and other people's dictionaries (one step away from their editors' intuitions); without the support of a massive reading programme there was no way for me, or my French colleague, to marshall all the necessary facts – semantic, syntactic, combinatorial, collocational – about *cook, cooking* etc. and their French equivalents. Without such an exhaustive analysis, we could not make a principled selection of the facts most appropriate for the Collins–Robert.

3.11   Understanding the English phenomena

What then are the essential points about the source-language headword which must be understood before a bilingual entry is to make sense? FrameNet analyses the verb *cook*, in its literal meanings (ignoring *cooking the books* and *cooking up an excuse*), as belonging to two different frames, provisionally named 'Apply_heat' and 'Cooking_creation'. This fundamental sense distinction escaped me in 1967, and is the key to most of the problems with the entries. It was to be made in relation to the verb *bake* in Atkins *et al.* (1988), after a study of corpus data, but that was far in the future. When I was drafting the English entry, it was not clear to me that when you talk about *cooking vegetables* or *cooking fish* this is a different sense from *cooking a meal* or *cooking dinner*. The knock-on effect of overlooking this fact led to the absence of *cuisiner* and *préparer* (used when talking about cooking dishes or meals), of the noun *cuisson* to contrast with *cuisine*, of the past participle *cuisiné* to contrast with *cuit*, and of *cooked meals* and *cooked dinners* and similar phrases.

In 2002, I start writing my entries with the benefit of an analysis of the similarities and differences between these two senses of the verb *cook*:

Sense 1   LU *cook* in FrameNet 'Apply_heat' frame, e.g.
              I cook the onions, the onions are cooking, cook until soft
Sense 2   LU *cook* in FrameNet 'Cooking_creation' frame, e.g.
              he cooked breakfast, he likes cooking

Sense 1 is a verb with both transitive and intransitive uses, designating the process of causing or undergoing a physical change involving heat, associated with the preparation of food. Sense

2, also a verb with both transitive and intransitive uses, designates the act of creating food, or (of the food itself) being created.

Having established this basic sense division, we must now try to assess in what formal ways the two senses differ. The two lexical units are thoroughly analysed and details recorded in great detail in the FrameNet database, using the type of annotation illustrated in Figure 6. We can therefore draw up a table of similarities and differences according to some of the relevant parameters, as shown in Figure 10.

The two lexical units in Figure 10 correspond to our sense 1 ('apply heat and change from raw state') and sense 2 ('create something else by doing that').

		LU 1 Apply_heat	LU 2 Creation
1	object of transitive	raw food	prepared food
2	subject of transitive	a) person b) oven *etc.*	person
3	subject of intransitive	food	person
4	'activity/achievement' interpretation	atelic	telic
5	causative/inchoative alternation	yes	no
6	benefactive indirect object	no	yes
7	benefactive PP-for	no	yes
8	omitted direct object interpreted as specific food already mentioned in discourse	yes	no
9	omitted direct object interpreted as indefinite 'food'	no	yes

FIG. 10   Similarities and differences in the two senses of verb *cook*.

Rows 1–3 in the table compare the semantic types of nouns which fill the subject and direct object slots of the LUs. As row 1 shows, food itself functions as the direct object in both senses; however, it would be more accurate to say that with sense 1 (*cook the peas in the usual way*) the food is something raw about to be processed, while with sense 2 (*I'm cooking a curry*) it is something which has been prepared by processing the raw foodstuffs. **Row 2** records that with sense 1 we can find the source of the heat (FrameNet's frame element 'Heating_Instrument') in subject position (*my new oven cooks meat really well*), as well as in a PP.comp (*I prefer to cook it in the microwave*), while this is not possible with sense 2 (**my new oven cooked me breakfast*).

Row 4: in considering senses 1 and 2, we notice that the object of *cook* in sense 1 is what is being processed, while the object of sense 2 is what is being produced by the process (and served and eaten). Our instinct is to distinguish these senses on the basis of the type of nouns filling the object slot – raw food (*meat, carrots, onions*) for sense 1, and prepared food (*pie, breakfast, meal*) for sense 2. For FrameNet, however, the distinction between sense 1 and sense 2 shown in row 4 does not inherently depend on the semantics of the noun filling the direct object slot: it depends on whether the event is construed as an activity (atelic) or an accomplishment (telic).[12] Thus, *cook the minced meat until browned* is clearly Apply_heat (sense 1), while *she cooked Sunday lunch in an hour* is clearly Cooking_creation (sense 2). Both of these examples may be rephrased with the same noun as direct object: *cook the potatoes until browned* (sense 1) and *she cooked the potatoes in an hour* (sense 2). The distinction depends on our knowledge that with the verb in sense 1, the potatoes are not the finished product, while with sense 2 they are what is produced by the process (and served up). For the sake of the poor dictionary users, however, the eventual bilingual entry must select quite distinct nouns to exemplify this difference: perhaps *meat, vegetables* for sense 1 and *meal, dish* for sense 2.

Row 5 highlights the fact that sense 1 (*while she was cooking the pasta/while the pasta was cooking*) participates in the causative–inchoative alternation (Levin 1993), discussed in relation to the verb *bake* in Atkins *et al.* (1988): the object of the transitive use in sense 1 becomes the subject of the intransitive, while in sense 2 it does not. In sentences like *breakfast was cooking*, we have to interpret *cooking* as 'being processed' (sense 1), not 'being produced' (sense 2).

In **rows 6 and 7**, we note that only sense 2 allows the person for whom the action is done (in FrameNet terminology, the frame element RECIPIENT) to be expressed both as the indirect object (*I cooked him a meal*) and as the prepositional object in the PP.comp (*I cooked a meal for him*).

Rows 8 and 9 focus on a problem which I found impossible to solve when I was writing the 1967 entries. I could think up sentences like *cook for 20 minutes or until browned,* and *she has been cooking all day,* and indeed could recognize that in some obscure way the direct object was unexpressed in both cases, but despite the obvious differences in the target language, I could not make a clear distinction in the meanings involved, and indeed omitted the *cook for 20 minutes* construction altogether, as the entry in Figure 1 shows. I probably could not decide where to put it – it would have looked uncomfortable grammatically in '3 vt' and ill at ease semantically in '4 vi'. It is for problems like this that every lexicographer needs a linguist on hand. Thanks to the sophisticated method which FrameNet has of distinguishing such constructions, this is no longer a problem. Sentences like *cook for 20 minutes* (an instance of the 'instructional imperative' discussed in Atkins *et al.* 1988) occur only in recipes. The omitted direct object is the specific foodstuff being cooked, which is known to the recipe reader. In FrameNet terms, this is treated as a case of Constructional Null Instantiation (CNI), where the grammatical construction licenses the omission of the (known) direct object. The situation is different in the case of *she has been cooking all day,* where the omitted direct object does not need to be specifically known to either the speaker or hearer for the sentence to be understood naturally. FrameNet terms this type of object omission Indefinite Null Instantiation (INI). As rows 8 and 9 show, both sense 1 and sense 2 allow null instantiation of the object, but in the first this is CNI and in the second INI. Our dictionary entry must make this clear, irrespective of whether these phenomena are mirrored in the target language.

3.12   The equivalences in the entries

Mention has already been made of some target-language omissions in the 1967 entries which became apparent as soon as a French corpus was available: *laisser cuire* and *cuisiner* from

---

[12] I owe this insight to Charles Fillmore.

the *cook* entry and *cuisson* from the *cooking* entry. There were however many other problems that had to be discussed with my francophone collaborator, Thierry Fontenelle,[13] before the bilingual entry could be fully drafted.

Starting from two senses of *cook* derived from the FrameNet analysis, we determined that sense 1 (change from raw state) would require a French equivalent using the verb *cuire*, while sense 2 (produce, create) would be translated by a more general verb like *préparer* (prepare) or even *faire* (make). Unlike the earlier version, the new entry would be quite explicit about these two senses, since I believe that an understanding of this would help the English-speaking user to appreciate why *cuire* (everyone's first choice as the French equivalent of *cook*) does not fit all contexts.

Having decided on the *cuire–préparer* distinction, we began our discussion of the real problems of equivalence. I had assembled FrameNet's account of the two senses of *cook*, together with the concordances from the French corpus for *cuire, cuisine, cuisiner,* and *cuisson* and their inflected forms. I had inserted sketchy English equivalents against some of the examples, added notes explaining the difficulties I envisaged for the anglophone user of these entries, and listed my principal queries for Fontenelle. I shall now summarize our discussions of each of these, using 'sense 1' to designate the Apply_heat sense, and 'sense 2' the Cooking_creation sense; this distinction was of course not made in the original entries. The revised draft of part of the entry for *cook* is shown in Figure 11.

---

cook
 I verb 1 (change from raw state)
 1a *vt* [*person*] *food* faire cuire, cuire; [*oven*] *food* cuire.
 1b *vi* [*food*] cuire. **the soup cooking on the fire** la soupe qui cuisait au feu.
 1c *vi* (*in recipes*) (faire) cuire, (+ *time expression*) laisser cuire. **cookin a hot oven** (faites)cuire à four très chaud; **cook for 10 minutes** laissez cuire pendant 10 minutes.
 2 (make meals, prepare)
 2a *vt meal, dish* (*prepare*) préparer, faire;

(*stressing actual cooking*) cuisiner. **to cook sb a meal, to cook a meal for sb** préparer un repas à qn.
 2b *vi* [*person*] (*generally*) faire la cuisine; (*stressing actual cooking*) cuisiner. **it's Paul who cooks** c'est Paul qui fait la cuisine; **to cook outside in the open** cuisiner en plein air; **she cooks well** elle fait bien la cuisine, elle cuisine bien; (*in lists*) **I can't sew or cook** je ne sais ni coudre ni cuisiner; **she used to cook for them** elle leur préparait des repas.

FIG. 11   Revised draft for the verb entry.

3.12.1   cook sense 1a vt : *cuire / faire cuire / laisser cuire / cuisiner*
This is a complex query, dealing as it does with four possible equivalences of *cook* in sentences like *I prefer to cook it in the microwave* and *cook the pasta in salted water for 10–12 minutes.*

---

[13] Thierry Fontenelle worked with me on the target-language problems discussed here. His contribution was all the more valuable because of his intimate knowledge of both the dictionary and FrameNet lexicography. His conversion of the Collins–Robert English–French Dictionary into a Mel'čukian-type electronic database is described in Fontenelle (1997), and his application of this database in a FrameNet perspective is discussed in Fontenelle (2000).

Setting aside for the moment the knotty problem of distinguishing between *cuire* and *faire cuire*, we turned first to *laisser cuire*, and noticed at once that in the many sentences where this expression was to be found, no direct object was ever expressed, although the verb phrase is transitive. We decided to pair this up with the instructional imperative (see below), since, like *cook* in this use, the omitted direct object was constructionally licensed. Here was another case of CNI.

We then looked at the concordances in which the verb *cuisiner* was used transitively: only seven out of more than 100 instances. When we checked the nouns[14] occurring in the direct object slot, we realised that *cuisiner* was in fact the equivalent of sense 2 (produce, create) and not of sense 1 (process from raw state).

We set about the task of discovering and transmitting to the dictionary user the difference (if any) between *cuire* in its transitive use, and *faire cuire*. We extracted a large number of facts from the corpus, spent a disproportionate amount of time discussing this problem, but made virtually no progress. This is frequently the case in lexicography: you spend hours puzzling something out, often discussing it with colleagues. Sometimes you come to understand a lot more about the behaviour of your headword, sometimes it remains opaque. When you do find yourself able to articulate a useful distinction, you then try to improve the entry, spend far too long inserting, deleting, and amending, and finally decide that it must be left as it is – not perfect, but the best that can be done given the space constraints.

In our study, we looked first at the semantic types of the nouns which occur in the direct object slot in corpus sentences, making lists[15] of most of the noun phrases found in that slot. We concluded tentatively that *cuire* seems to favour wheat-based products, but not exclusively, and *faire cuire* seems to favour vegetables, meat, fish, seafood, eggs, game . . . but again not exclusively. We considered the idea that substances such as bread or dough might be intuitively believed to cook in a different way from other substances such as fish, meat and eggs, so that *cuire* was more acceptable with the first group than with the second, which preferred *faire cuire*. We could find no solid evidence for this.

Turning next to grammatical context, we considered the types of noun phrases which occurred in the direct object slot with *cuire* and with *faire cuire* respectively, and in particular the types of determiner, but found no systematicity here either. We checked the use of these expressions in the past participle, but found nothing there either. Certain syntactic contexts seem to prefer *cuire* over *faire cuire* – manner adverbials, modal verbs, and infinitive constructions of purpose – but this might come about simply because *cuire* is less of a mouthful than *faire cuire*. Only in one aspect of their behaviour, the use in the imperative mood, was there any clear difference: we found no instance of *cuisez*, but many of *faites*

---

[14] These nouns included *d'autres denrées* (other foods), *des meringues* (meringues), *des spaghettis* (spaghetti), *les tartes à la crème* (custard tarts) and *les plats chinois* (Chinese dishes).

[15] With *cuire* the list included *son pain, le manioc, du pâté sablé, nos aliments, une pâte surgelée, des baguettes, du pain, des pâtons surgelés, le kouglof, le pain, un mets, les aliments, les saucisses, un poulet, deux repas quotidiens, le blé, confitures et gelées, les cocos, le pigeon, cabillaud, pain de campagne, le magret de canard, plat de côtes, le morceau de lotte, la crème* . . . In English: his bread, manioc, shortcrust pastry, our foodstuffs, frozen pastry, loaves, some bread, frozen dough sticks, kugelhopf, bread, a dish, foodstuffs, sausages, a chicken, two meals a day, wheat, jams and jellies, coconuts, pigeon, cod, some farmhouse bread, some breast of duck, dish of ribs, the piece of monkfish, cream.

With *faire cuire* we found *pommes de terre, l'agneau, toutes les espèces de poules, une viande, un poisson, les oeufs, leur petite soupe, ces deux légumes, des châtaignes, un oeuf, mon omelette, les fruits, mes champignons, du riz, des graines de blé, les artichauts, des pommes, le sucre, les filets de dorade, les canards, les pâtes, les tourteaux, la pâte, les petits oignons, les asperges, carottes et poireaux, les langoustines, les côtes d'agneau, leur frichti* . . . In English: potatoes, the lamb, all kinds of chicken, a piece of meat, a fish, eggs, their soup, these two vegetables, chestnuts, an egg, my omelette, fruit, my mushrooms, rice, wheat grains, artichokes, apples, sugar, bream fillets, ducks, pasta, crabs, pastry, little onions, asparagus, carrots and leeks, scampi, lamb chops, their grub . . .

cuire. However, we were forced to admit that we could not find any systematic differences, or even identify any consistent selectional preferences, in the use of these two expressions. In every concordance line we looked at, when the verb was transitive and used in the meaning of 'change state from raw to cooked', *cuire* was apparently substitutable for *faire cuire*, and vice versa.

> **3** *vt* **(a)** *food* (faire) cuire

Fig. 12   Part of original entry for *cook*.

We came to the conclusion that the 1967 entry, shown in Figure 12, though brief, had been correct. The bracketing of *faire*, according to the Style Guide, indicates that this is an optional element in the translation. Remembering, however, that on returning to the entry 35 years later I had been unable to trust it, I determined to expand this part a little, in order to reassure other dictionary users.

3.12.2   cook sense 1b vi *: cuire*

The concordances made it clear that *cuire* is the principal, and the safest, equivalent of *cook* in sentences like *a stew was put to cook in a saucepan*. There was no need for any further information in this section, but in order to distinguish it from the 'intransitive' use in the following section, we included a short example.

3.12.3   cook sense 1c vi *: instructional imperative*

The instructional imperative, superficially intransitive but essentially transitive with an unexpressed definite object, requires some thought: how to classify it, how much of the grammar to explain to anglophone or francophone users, and how to translate it. Following the Style Guide, we called it an intransitive verb. Like English, French has a similar pseudo-intransitive construction, so there was no need to explain the grammar to either the English or the French user. It was obvious from the evidence of the concordances that this was the place for *laisser cuire*. This translates as 'leave to cook', an unexceptionable phrase but one which does not occur much in the English corpus data we had.

   In our French corpus of some 2,000 sentences, *laisser cuire* was very prominent, and occurred exclusively in sentences like those in Figure 13.

Laissez	cuire	5 minutes, réservez.
Laissez	cuire	à petite ébullition pendant 2 heures.
Laissez	cuire	encore 10 minutes, passez au chinois.
Laissez	cuire	doucement 10 minutes…
Laissez	cuire	un petit peu jusqu'à ce que…

Fig. 13   Concordance lines for *laisser cuire*.

Every one of the *laisser cuire* lines occurred in the imperative (*laissez cuire*); every one came from a recipe;[16] none of them had an expressed direct object, and every one of them included a duration expression ('5 minutes', 'until…' etc.).

---

[16] The larger context available to us made us aware that in many cases an English recipe would not have used *cook* at all, but a more specific hyponym such as *simmer, fry, boil, bake* and so on – something to note about *laisser cuire* for the *cuire* entry, but not something to try to include in our *cook* entry.

However, we had many corpus examples, also from recipes, of *faites cuire* and of the bare infinitive *cuire* used as an imperative. As *(faire) cuire* is always a safe option, it was tempting to omit *laisser cuire*, which seemed to require a time expression, but the frequency of the latter phrase in the French corpus and its nigh-perfect match with the English recipe-ese usage earned it a place in the entry. However, unless we were sure (and we weren't) that the three phrases were interchangeable, we had to puzzle out what the differences were, and guide the user to the correct option.

A study of the corpus evidence leads to the conclusion that the difference between *(faire) cuire* on the one hand, and *laisser cuire* on the other is the following. *Faites cuire* and *cuire* occur in texts at the point in the instructions where the actual cooking process begins. *Laisser cuire* occurs where some previous instruction has initiated the cooking process, e.g.

> vérifiez la cuisson, laissez cuire plus longtemps si ...
> versez dans la sauce, laissez cuire encore 10 minutes[17]

It proved impossible to condense that information intelligibly, and we had to content ourselves with prefacing *laisser cuire* with '+ time expression', which was the truth, if not the whole truth.

3.12.4   cook sense 2a vt *: translation, including benefactives*

Our starting point in discussing the translations of *cook* was to make a systematic distinction between sense 1 (*cuire* etc.) and sense 2 (*préparer, faire*). Neither *préparer* nor *faire* appears in the 1967 entry, which indeed addresses only what we are calling sense 1 of the English verb. A study of the French corpus data and other material[18] left us in no doubt that *préparer* and *faire* must be offered as direct equivalents.

She would	cook	them all a good breakfast
Toma	cooked	me a man-sized breakfast
I came home to	cook	myself lunch
...to come home and	cook	three meals a week for her family
I'm	cooking	vegetable curry for them

FIG. 14   Concordance lines showing benefactives.

Figure 14 shows instances of the element RECIPIENT in the Cooking_creation frame (the person for whom the action is performed) expressed in two ways: as the indirect object of *cook* (*cook them all a good breakfast*) and within a prepositional phrase as the object of *for* (*cooking vegetable curry for them*). These constructions are part of the valence of our headword and it is therefore essential that anglophone dictionary users find in the entry enough information to allow them to produce the correct French equivalent; we added to '2 vt' an example phrase in the two formulations, see Figure 11.

3.12.5   cook sense 2b vi *: faire la cuisine / cuisiner*

There are a number of different points to be taken into consideration when producing the translations for this section of the entry. We know from the corpus that *cuisiner* (but not *faire*

---

[17] In English: check and cook longer if ..., pour into the sauce and cook for 10 minutes more.

[18] In researching this aspect of the translation, Fontenelle noted: "I was able to find more than 16,000 occurrences of *préparer + petit déjeuner* on Google. *Cuisiner + petit déjeuner* would not be found at all and *faire + petit déjeuner* would be found but much, much less frequently than *préparer*" – a comment which in itself more than justifies corpus use in lexicography.

la cuisine) functions like *cook* sense 2 in two significant respects. It has transitive uses (*le plat n'est cuisiné ni par nous ni pour nous*), even if these are much less salient than the transitive uses of *cook*. It also supports null instantiation of its indefinite object (INI): the corpus offers many superficially intransitive uses where the unexpressed object is indefinite (*la fille ne savait pas cuisiner*).

It is tempting to leave *cuisiner* as the only direct translation here, but *faire la cuisine* – literally 'do the cooking' – is simply too common to omit.[19] After comparing usages in the French corpus, Fontenelle came to the conclusion that on the whole these verb phrases are freely interchangeable, except that *cuisiner* focuses more on the actual cooking process, while *faire la cuisine* carries more the general idea of being responsible for preparing food. In particular, as the '**and/or**' list in the Word Sketch shown in Figure 3 indicates, *cook* often occurs in lists of activities, where *faire la cuisine* would be unlikely in French.[20] We added a couple of examples to try to indicate this distinction.

The FrameNet RECIPIENT can also be expressed with this intransitive use of *cook*, not however as an indirect object (which occurs only with transitives – see point 4) but in a prepositional phrase headed by *for* (*she was told to cook for the soldiers, I cook for you and I keep house for you*): we add an example to show this in the entry, thus demonstrating that it is impossible to improve a dictionary without adding to its length.

3.12.6   noun cook *as name and form of address*

Before we leave *cook*, we have to address an omission in '1 *n*' in the 1967 entry. The inclusion of the first example (*she is a good cook*) immediately after the direct translation (cuisinier *m*,ière *f*) implicitly distinguishes between the use of the noun as designating a member of a trade or profession (*he was a hotel cook, the cook and the gardener*), and the deverbal noun (*she's a good cook*), but it gives no help with the French equivalent of the 'bare' noun (*I must speak to cook*). This usage is pointed up in a column in the Word Sketch screen not visible in Figure 3. Nor does the 1967 entry include the use of *cook* as a form of address (*Good morning, Cook*). This turns out to pose a knotty problem of translation, and to do it justice in a dictionary would involve several more examples,[21] together with explanations for the English user. Manifestly, in 2002, to cover this point in enough detail would clearly demand a disproportionate amount of space in a general dictionary (as opposed to one for translators of historical novels). Figure 15 shows what the entry for the noun *cook* would have to look like if this point is to be covered, even inadequately.

3.12.7   cooked ptp adj *: cuit / cuisiné*

The past participle adjective *cooked* does not figure in the original entry, but since the only translation given for the transitive verb is (*faire*) *cuire*, the user must infer that the equivalent

---

[19] The French *cuisiner* and *faire la cuisine* almost exactly parallel in semantic nuance the English *cook* and *do the cooking*, the only difference being the relative salience of *faire la cuisine* in the French corpus and comparative infrequency of *do the cooking* in the English corpus. In a dictionary for encoding users, however, frequency matters (we are all looking for the most natural-sounding expression), and our entry must address this problem.

[20] For the same reason – related to analogy – that we would be reluctant to substitute *do the cooking* for *cook* in a list like *he can clean and cook and sew*.

[21] For *I must speak to cook* (or *Cook*), we would have to show options for the French translation depending on context. *Je dois parler à la cuisinière* (assuming a female cook) is what the employer – owner perhaps of a stately home or a private hotel – would say in general conversation, but if talking to another employee they are more likely to say *Je dois parler à Madame Duval,* or whatever the lady's name is. In the case of *Good morning, Cook* the French would have to be *Bonjour, Madame Duval. Madame* alone is too formal for an employer to use to someone working for her, and unlike *docteur etc.* the noun *cuisinier* cannot be used in vocatives.

cook noun

1 : to be a good *etc.* **cook** cuisiner bien, bien faire la cuisine; **she's a splendid cook** elle cuisine merveilleusement bien.

2 (*in home, hotel etc.*) cuisinier m, -ière f. (*used as a name*) **I must speak to Cook** je dois parler à la cuisinière; **good morning, Cook** ≈ bonjour, Madame Duval (*etc.*) (*using name in French*)

Fig. 15   Draft entry for noun *cook*.

of *cooked* is *cuit*. I probably thought so at the time that I wrote the entry. Figure 16 shows some corpus lines which seem to confirm that impression.

il est comestible	cuit,	mais vénéneux cru.
Il est consommé cru ou	cuit.	
La crème est	cuite	lorsqu'elle nappe la cuiller.
viande de cheval crue ou insuffisamment	cuite	
Ils empêchent les aliments	cuits	de rancir.

Fig. 16   Some corpus instances of *cuit*[22].

However, I also find in the French corpus the use of the past participle *cuisiné* as an adjective, particularly in the phrase *plats cuisinés* ('cooked food'). It seems that the past participles *cuit* and *cuisiné* reflect the sense distinctions already established between sense 1 of the verb (change from raw state) and sense 2 (prepare, produce), and this must be indicated in the entry for the past participle adjective, a draft of which is shown in Figure 17.

cooked   ptp adj

1 (*not raw*) *food* cuit. **cooked fruit / vegetables** légumes / fruits cuits; **cooked ham** jambon cuit.

2 (*prepared*) *meal, dish* cuisiné. **cooked meals, cooked food** plats cuisinés; **cooked breakfast** petit déjeuner complet à l'anglaise; **cooked dinners** (*as opp. to sandwiches*) repas chauds.

Fig. 17   Draft entry for *cooked*.

---

[22] In English: *it is edible cooked, but poisonous raw; it is eaten raw or cooked; the cream is cooked when it coats the spoon; horse meat raw or insufficiently cooked; they prevent cooked food from going bad.*

3.12.8 cooking n : *cuisine / cuisson*

In the framework for **cooking**, based on evidence in the English corpus, the noun has at least three senses:

1. the process of changing something from its raw state (*cooking method*);
2. the activity of producing food (*they share the cooking*);
3. the food produced (*his mother's cooking*).

Sense 1, the least frequent, is related to the Apply_heat sense of the verb; senses 2 and 3 are related to the Cooking_creation sense of the verb. According to the randomly selected sample of the BNC, sense 3 is by far the most salient. The candidates for inclusion as translations are the nouns *cuisine* and *cuisson*. We noted that the original entry contained no reference to *cuisson*, yet *cooking* is the only real English equivalent of this word, although in context it may be translated in many different ways, as the table in Figure 18 shows.

Vérifiez la cuisson, laissez cuire…	check to see if it is cooked…
Préparation : 30 mn. *Cuisson: 15 mn.*	Cooking time 15 minutes
…*ne change pas de couleur à la cuisson*	…does not change colour when cooked
l'incomparable *cuisson au micro-ondes*	…microwave cooking
…ail, persil, thym et laurier *avec* un concassé	…cooked together in white wine
de tomates *dans une cuisson au vin blanc*	
des fours à cuisson automatique	automatic ovens
après une heure de cuisson à feu très doux	…after simmering for an hour
La plancha permet une cuisson à feu vif	in the Plancha you can cook on
sans matières grasses	high heat without fat
le temps d'une mayonnaise ou *de la*	in the time it takes to… hard-boil
cuisson d'un oeuf dur	an egg
les consignes concernant *la cuisson d'un*	advice about ways of cooking a
plat spécifique	specific dish
Le micro-ondes est parfait *pour la cuisson*	…perfect for cooking carrots …
des carottes	

FIG. 18   Some English equivalents of *cuisson*.

The material in Figure 18 makes us wary of giving *cuisson* without explanation as a straight-forward equivalent of the noun *cooking*, and it will certainly pose serious problems for the lexicographer compiling the *cuisson* entry. We obviously cannot ignore it. Fontenelle points out that the default translation (always a priority for bilingual lexicographers) of the noun *cooking* is *cuisine*, which would translate the vast majority of the corpus instances of this word, such as those shown in Figure 19.

The difference in meaning and use between *cuisine* in its cooking sense (as opposed to 'kitchen') and *cuisson* were not initially apparent. The less familiar noun *cuisson* designates a process – it is of course the nominalisation of *cuire*, which corresponds to the change-from-raw-state sense of *cook*. *Cuisson,* but not *cuisine,* occurs with duration phrases (*la cuisson doit durer 5 minutes* 'it should cook for 5 minutes', *pendant la cuisson* 'during the cooking'), and is used to refer to specific cooking conditions, as in *cuisson rapide* ('fast cooking'). Historically, *cuisine* gave rise to *cuisiner* – explaining its sense of creating food, see points 4 and 7 above; it refers to the general activity relating to the preparation of meals (*la cuisine au gaz* 'gas

the loch provided water for	cooking	and drinking.
Natural gas is used for	cooking	
I hate the	cooking	and the cleaning
Molly's superb	cooking	
Microwave	cooking	is now back in vogue
he's an authority on Chinese	cooking	
the English use it in their	cooking	
her plain	cooking	is quite good
a taste for wine and continental	cooking	
the scents of north African	cooking	

FIG. 19   Some concordances of the noun *cooking*.

cooking', *la cuisine au micro-ondes* 'microwave cooking').[23] Our discussions end in the draft entry for *cooking* shown in Figure 20.

---

cooking
I noun
1 (*see vb 2: activity, food*) cuisine *f*. **to do the cooking** faire la cuisine; **French cooking** la cuisine française.
2 (*see vb 1: process*) cuisson *f*. **slow cooking** cuisson lente.
II modifier
1 de cuisine. **cooking smell / utensil** odeur *f* / ustensile *m* de cuisine.
2 de cuisson. **cooking liquid / method** liquide *m* / méthode *f* de cuisson.
3 *apples, chocolate etc*. à cuire.

FIG. 20   Draft entry for *cooking*.

When it comes to writing the dictionary entry, an accumulation of facts makes us change the sense division and ordering from the three senses in the framework, set out at the start of this section 8. First, the order of senses in the bilingual entry should if possible reflect frequency in the English corpus,[24] which means putting 'food produced' as the first sense in

---

[23] We find two disconcerting examples relating to the familiar phrase *microwave cooking*:

(a) La réfrigération et *la cuisine au micro-ondes* ont eu des répercussions importantes sur l'emballage... 'Refrigeration and microwave cooking have had serious repercussions on packaging...'
(b) Assaisonner le lièvre avec sel Vital: essayez aussi l'incomparable *cuisson au micro-ondes* (15 mn pour 500 g)... 'Season the hare with Vital salt: sample the incomparable microwave cooking...'

In (a) the topic is the change brought about in packaging by the development of refrigeration and microwave cooking – far removed from the heat and smells of the kitchen: here we have *la cuisine au micro-ondes*. The citation in (b) is from a recipe, instructions on cooking hare, and for this context *la cuisson au micro-ondes* is more appropriate.

[24] It is always better if possible to reflect source-language frequency in a bilingual dictionary: the commonest use probably generates the largest number of look-ups. However, the order of senses in the verb entry reflected the concept of 'basic' or 'core' sense (Apply_heat) from which a more complex sense (Cooking_creation) is derived.

the entry. Second, *cuisine* is far commoner than *cuisson* in the French corpus, which suggests that it is the 'safest' word for the English speaker to choose as a translation of *cooking*. Third, comparison of concordances for the English and French words makes it clear that the framework senses 2 and 3 of *cooking* should be translated by *cuisine*, and sense 1 by *cuisson*. Finally, since senses 2 and 3 have the same French equivalent, we can save space by collapsing them in the entry.[25]

4   CONCLUSION

In this paper I have tried to set out in detail the transfiguration wrought in practical lexicography by the advent of the computer. Writing dictionaries in 1967, even with the help of a citation bank on index cards, depended mainly on introspection and on discussion with one's colleagues and other informants – introspection again, at one remove. As Hanks (2000) points out, the entries that we wrote then reflected what he calls 'cognitive salience' – things that stand out in our minds when we think about language. Corpus lexicography has taught us that packing an entry with cognitively salient items does not produce a good description of naturally occurring language. We have no access through introspection to how the language really behaves out there in the linguistic community, or even to how we ourselves use language in speaking and writing. Idioms like *cook someone's goose* are cognitively salient, but extremely infrequent in corpus data. Expressions like *cook him breakfast* occur so frequently that they are not cognitively salient and are often overlooked in the dictionaries where they should occur, such as those for language learners.

But wealth of data alone does not make a good dictionary.[26] It simply swamps us with a dazzling array of facts and no systematic way of evaluating them. The craft of lexicography demands not only the ability to collect data, but also the ability to make sense of it. We have to be able to see the whole picture of how our headword behaves in natural language before we can decide what information is most needed by the people who will use the dictionary we are writing. Then we need to set out these facts in an intelligible and orderly way. Without a sound theoretical basis we cannot carry out these tasks successfully. The most significant difference, I believe, between the 1967 lexicography and that of today is that in the interval my approach to lexicography has benefited from the insights of linguistics.

In 2002, we have plenty of evidence about what Hanks calls 'socially salient' facts. A corpus like the BNC offers us literally thousands of citations for the core vocabulary of the language. Tools like the Word Sketch program, and resources like the FrameNet database, extract socially salient facts from this mass of data. Linguistic theory, particularly recent work in lexical semantics, can light the way to better lexicography. At last we are in a position to begin to reflect performance, and not our own competence, in our 21st century dictionary entries.

This logical approach makes it easier to guide the encoding user through the intricacies of the foreign language equivalents. The decision to follow logical order in the verb entry and frequency order in the noun entry rests on the need to communicate as efficiently as possible with the dictionary user. Lack of correspondence between entries for morphologically related verbs and nouns may disturb computers but rarely worries human users.

[25] This is a good example of why the 'senses' in a bilingual dictionary rarely reflect accurately the semantics of the source-language word.

[26] Michael Rundell pointed this out to me, having benefited himself from the contribution of linguistic theory to practical lexicography in the new Macmillan learners' dictionary (Rundell 2002).

ACKNOWLEDGEMENTS

I'm glad to have this opportunity of thanking my CREFD colleagues for many years of friendship and collaboration on this team-built dictionary: Richard Thomas, Collins's editorial director of the project; my French co-authors of the English–French entries, Marie-Noëlle Lamy, Hélène Lewis and Renée Birks, and our counterparts on the French–English side, Alain Duval, Rosemary Milne, Pierre-Henri Cousin and Lorna Sinclair Knight. Michel Poté's proto-type discussions on the letter H in 1967–8 were invaluable, as later were those with Geneviève McMillan. My warmest thanks go to Thierry Fontenelle, who acted as my francophone colleague for the 'Now' lexicography, for his knowledgeable and careful contribution to, and patience in, our electronic discussions on detailed points of equivalence. I am grateful to my colleagues on the FrameNet team at ICSI, Berkeley, under the leadership of Charles Fillmore, for their exhaustive analysis of *cook*. Many thanks, too, to everyone who helped me collect citations (in the absence of a French National Corpus) for *cuire* and related words : Kate Beeching, Pierrette Bouillon, Michael Clark, Marie-Hélène Corréard, Alain Duval, Thierry Fontenelle, Adam Kilgarriff, Raf Salkie, Penny Silva, Natalie Pomier, and Michael Rundell. Thierry Fontenelle, Valerie Grundy, Adam Kilgarriff, Miriam Petruck, Michael Rundell and Raf Salkie all made valuable comments on earlier versions of this paper. Finally, the 'Now' lexicography owes much to what I have learned over the past 15 years or so from many colleagues I've worked with, in particular two linguists, Charles Fillmore and Beth Levin, and two lexicographers, Patrick Hanks and Michael Rundell. Thank you all.

18

Equivalence in Bilingual Dictionaries

ALAIN DUVAL*

I   INTRODUCTION

All lexicographical reference books, such as monolingual dictionaries, bilingual dictionaries, multilingual glossaries or encyclopaedias, aim at creating bridges between what users know and what users do not know. Their goal is to show that there is equivalence between the entry word in the headword list from which the search starts and the body of the entry.

In monolingual dictionaries, the entry is always presented in the same pattern: a superordinate points to the broad semantic field and a specifier provides the meaning refinements which are typical of the headword and which enable users to distinguish it from all other hyponyms.

Thus, the compound word *easy chair*

a) applies to a piece of furniture
b) applies to a piece of furniture on which one can sit
c) applies to a piece of furniture with a back on which one can sit
d) applies to a piece of furniture with two arms and a back on which one can sit
e) applies to a piece of furniture with two arms and a back on which a single person can sit
f) applies to a comfortable, upholstered piece of furniture with two arms and a back on which a single person can sit

Therefore, equivalence is achieved with varying degrees of precision. Starting from the superordinate *furniture*, the specifier will bring a *sufficient number of elements* enabling users to distinguish between all possible hyponyms such as:

in b) stool/chair/sofa/armchair/easy chair
in c) chair/sofa/armchair/easy chair
in d) sofa/armchair/easy chair
in e) armchair/easy chair

In encyclopaedias, the article gives elements of information about the portion of the real world to which the headword applies. The sum total of these elements aims at bringing a certain level of culture.

Thus, in the article **Europe**, users will find indications on the geographical position of the continent, on the political entities which it is made of, on history, on economy, on

* Originally published as Duval, A. (1991). 'L'équivalence dans le dictionnaire bilingue', in Hausmann, F. J., Reichmann, O., Wiegand E., and Zgusta L. (eds.), *Wörterbücher/Dictionaries/Dictionnaires. Ein internationales Handbuch zur Lexikographie/An International Encyclopedia of Lexicography/Encyclopédie internationale de lexicographie,* 3. De Gruyter, Berlin-New York, 2817–2824. Reproduced with permission of Walter de Gruyter GMBH.

demography etc. Here too, equivalence is achieved with varying degrees of precision. However, since the aim is no longer to provide distinctions between several possible hyponyms (Africa/America/Asia/Europe), the notion of *sufficient number of elements* is replaced by the notion of *necessary number of elements*, depending on the size of the work and the cultural level one wishes to provide.

In bilingual dictionaries, the role of translations is to provide target-language equivalents of the source-language headword.

Users consider translations as synonyms of the headword in a foreign language. They believe that it is always possible to translate, and that it should not pose any problem. Indeed, the role of languages is to describe reality, which is intuitively thought to be the same for everyone. Therefore, equivalents should necessarily exist.

In fact, words being signs made up of a *signifié* which points to the real and a *signifiant* which points to its representation in language, equivalence problems will appear on two levels: does the real exist or not in the culture of the speakers of a particular language? Does the word which describes the real exist or not in the language of these speakers?

The examples used here to illustrate these points will be taken from a comparison between French and English, which may be the language pair having generated the largest production of bilingual reference books. Similar examples can obviously be found in varying degrees when comparing all other foreign languages.

2   EQUIVALENCE, REALITY AND LANGUAGE

The simplest case can be found when the *signifié* points to the same cultural reality and when the *signifiant* is a recognized item in the lexicon of both languages. For example:

F: *ordinateur*   E: *computer*

The lexical item here is monosemic and unambiguous in both languages. It is immediately understandable and usable by both categories of speakers.

Users tend to take it for granted that this is the most common case, even that it is the only one that can possibly exist. This way of seeing things has been generalized in small-size dictionaries. The two languages are considered to be two parallel codes with exact correspondence between the relevant items.

A different case is encountered when there is indeed an item present in the lexicon of both languages, while the reality it points to does not belong to the cultural universe of the target language speakers, or is not recognized as such by the majority of them. For example:

F: *le 14 juillet*   E: *Bastille Day*

The lexical item here too is monosemic and unambiguous in both languages, but most target-language speakers do not understand it readily. There is indeed equivalence on the level of language, but on the level of the real and of the network of associations of ideas linked to these words, equivalence will be perceived to a lesser or greater degree according to the degree of culture of the users.

More often than is generally thought, the real is only present in the cultural universe and the lexicon of source-language speakers. For example:

F: *ballotage*
E: *situation in a political election when no candidate has an absolute majority in the first ballot and people have to vote again*

The lexical item here too is monosemic and unambiguous, but it refers to reality only in the source language. Equivalence is achieved through a contextual gloss which amounts to a definition similar to the ones which are found in monolingual dictionaries.

It is worth noticing the uncomfortable status of this definition, which is a compromise between the pattern of a monolingual dictionary entry and that of an article in an encyclopaedia.

Typical of a monolingual dictionary are the superordinate and the specifier. However, the role of the latter is not to differentiate between several possible hyponyms, since the referent is in a foreign language.

Typical of an encyclopaedia are elements bringing a certain level of culture. However, there is an obvious logical impossibility in the very presence of the article since it is here to account for an absence of reality and the non-existence of the target language headword from which users usually start their search in the work.

The contextual gloss in the bilingual is therefore an equivalent with the structure of a monolingual dictionary entry and the content of an article in an encyclopaedia.

3   EQUIVALENCE, DENOTATION AND CONNOTATION

The translation of any given text (newspaper item, novel, poem) offers translators or demands of them varying degrees of equivalence, depending on the nature of the content: faithful translation, adaptation, transposition, recreation. These varying degrees can also be found in bilingual dictionaries, with the exception that the contextual environment must be hinted at as tersely as possible, given obvious constraints of space.

Perfect equivalence demands equal levels of denotation, i.e. reference to the same element of the real, and equal levels of connotation, i.e. reference to the same network of cultural associations linked to the words in both languages. Here again, users intuitively think that dictionary translations always provide perfect equivalence. In fact, depending on the nature of the problems, bilingual dictionaries cater for one or the other level in varying degrees.

The following examples have been taken from the Larousse Saturne bilingual. Only features which are relevant here are mentioned.

Example 1: The translation has the same denotative and connotative value as the headword.

F: *synovie*   E: *synovia*

The use of the word, its frequency and its technical character are felt to be the same by the users of both languages.

Example 2: The headword is given several translations, which are denotatively equivalent, but connotatively different.

F: *tibia*   E: *tibia, shinbone*

A large number of terms which have a scientific flavour are translated in English by a term with a Latin origin in the language of specialists, and by a word with a Saxon origin in everyday use. So, the latter translation will be used in standard conversation while a doctor or an anatomy professor will use the former. The two equivalents which are mentioned are therefore interchangeable as far as meaning is concerned, but not with respect to frequency and use.

Example 3: The translation is denotatively faithful to the headword but has no connotative relevance in the target language.

F: *étrille*   E: *swimming crab*

While the French word is fairly common and can be seen in fishmongers' shop windows or on restaurant menus, the English compound word can never be encountered in everyday use. It is not present in the wordlist of common monolingual dictionaries and can only be found in specialist zoology manuals. In this case, the bilingual dictionary provides an equivalent which is indeed accurate but restricted.

Example 4: The denotative value of the translation is only marginally acceptable while it is connotatively satisfactory.

F: *ministère de l'Intérieur*   E: *Home Office*

The French *signifié* bears no relation whatsoever to the English *signifié*. The former applies to a typically French entity while the latter applies to a typically British one. Connotatively however, what is described largely fulfils the same role in both countries and equivalence is therefore achieved on the levels of recognition of the phrase, frequency and association of ideas. This procedure has its limits though and is not without danger within the scope of a bilingual dictionary. It implies the use of a virtual superordinate, which is not present in the entry. The headword and the translation would each act as a hyponym in either language. If the procedure were pushed to the point of absurdity, one could end up with equivalents such as:

F: *président de la république*   E: *queen of England*

through the use of a virtual superordinate corresponding to:

head of state.

Example 5: The translation has no denotative value but tries to provide at least partial connotative equivalence.

F: *jeu de l'oie*   E: *snakes and ladders*

or:

F: *pain d'épices*   E: *gingerbread*

The French *signifié* has no exact counterpart in English and equivalence for translation purposes will be achieved through the semantic field, thanks to an item with the following features:

- The English *signifié* has no exact counterpart in French either,
- Its frequency in language use is approximately the same,
- It points to an element of the real which is felt to be very close, with maximum common characteristics.

In the former case, among the relevant features are the field of indoor games for children using a printed piece of cardboard, dice and counters.

The latter case refers to a similar type of soft, sweet, brown cake, with a distinctive, familiar flavour (aniseed for the former and ginger for the latter).

Equivalence here assumes the role of a kind of replacement value, of linguistic substitute.

The compiler is aware of the imperfect nature of the equivalents provided and often tries to narrow the gap between denotation and connotation by adding extra translation information. To keep to the culinary theme, here are three series with various characteristics:

F: *camembert*   E: *camembert*

In this example, there is only one translation. One considers that the equivalent, which is denotatively obvious, is just as obvious on the connotative level, as the word and the food are both supposed to be quite well known. The entry is evidently designed for the encoding needs of the source language speaker.

F: *munster*   E: *Munster, Munster cheese*

In this example, there are two translations. The former provides a denotative equivalent while the latter adds a connotative precision thanks to a superordinate indicating a semantic field, as the *signifié* might well be little known. This addition is mainly designed for the decoding needs of the target language speaker.

F: *girolle*   E: *mushroom, chanterelle*

In this example, there are again two translations. This time, connotative equivalence is devolved to the former which acts as a semantic field superordinate. Denotative equivalence is provided by the latter translation. The order in which the two translations appear is not haphazard. It has a discriminating value by implicitly warning the French source language speaker against the inconsiderate use of E: *chanterelle,* as the word as well as the plant are virtually unknown in English.

It should be stressed that the precision added in the last two examples is quite limited and that the superordinate is too far removed to provide sufficient semantic precision. However, it was felt to be a necessary addition by the compiler who did not want (or did not dare?) to offer the decoding English language speaker elliptical and baffling entries in the shape of:

F: *munster*   E: *Munster*
F: *girolle*   E: *chanterelle*

It is worth noting that any more elaborate gloss would have entailed sizeable encyclopaedic developments, which would have been totally disproportionate considering the relatively low frequency of the words in language.

4   EQUIVALENCE, EXTENSION AND COMPREHENSION

The words "extension" and "comprehension" are here taken with the meaning they have in logic. The extension of a concept refers to the set of logical objects to which the concept applies. The comprehension of a concept refers to the set of features which are peculiar to the concept. Thus, *furniture* will have far greater extension and far smaller comprehension than *easy chair* and conversely.

Let us examine the following English compound words and their French translations, taken from the Collins–Robert French dictionary:

   i) E: *traffic warden*
      F: *contractuel/-elle*

  ii) E: *lollipop man/lady*
      F: *contractuel/-elle*

 iii) E: *meter maid*
      F: *contractuelle*

Leaving aside problems of register, differences between British English and American English and metalinguistic material, which are not relevant here, one notices that the English compound words have one single equivalent in the target language, which would tend to show that they are synonymous. However, this is not the case at all.

Traffic warden and *contractuel/-elle* have roughly comparable extension and comprehension. They refer to people, mostly women or pensioners, assisting the police by dealing with traffic problems in towns.

Lollipop man/lady refers to one specific type of *contractuel/-elle*, looking after children crossing the street in front of their schools.

Meter maid refers to a female person specialized in monitoring the parking of cars.

In the last two cases, the source language has thus been artificially "extensionized" and the target language artificially "comprehensionized".

The information being presented in this raw state in a bilingual dictionary does not impair the quality of translation as such. Taking the English–French side of the dictionary, English speakers will be perfectly able to encode *lollipop man* into *contractuel* and French speakers will be perfectly able to decode *meter maid* into *contractuelle*. There will be no mistake in interpreting the meanings of the words, and no mistake in translating.

However, this can generate a potential mistake later on when English speakers, having memorized the information, automatically translate every occurrence of the word *contractuel* which they encounter in a French text by *lollipop man*, thus erroneously "comprehensionizing" the French, and when French speakers automatically use *meter maid* to encode *contractuelle*, thus erroneously "extensionizing" the English.

One may also notice that *traffic warden* takes the shape of a superordinate, the hyponyms of which being *lollipop man/lady* and *meter maid*. Consequently, the ambiguity will only appear in the English–French side, because in the French–English side, the headword *contractuel/-elle* is satisfactorily translated by *traffic warden*, with similar extension and comprehension.

Let us now examine the following words:

    E: *stoat*   F: *hermine*
    E: *ermine*   F: *hermine*

Here too the source language has erroneously been "extensionized" by the target language.

E: *stoat* refers to an animal with brown fur, roaming the southern part of a range, while E: *ermine* refers to the same species of animal in the northern part of that range, having white fur during the winter.

F: *hermine* refers to one or the other indiscriminately.

Unlike in the previous case, there is no immediate superordinate in English, whose direct hyponyms would be *stoat* and *ermine*.

Equivalence is therefore both accurate and misleading. It is misleading because the translation has more extension. However, it is accurate because all attempts at trying to "comprehensionize" the translation by adding a specifier such as:

E: *stoat*　　　　F: *hermine (in the south)*
E: *ermine*　　　 F: *hermine (with white winter fur)*

would have no relevance in the target language, which is blind to the shift of meaning.

In this case, English is far more analytical in describing the real and shows the inability of French to provide a sophisticated enough tool showing the differences.

Let us now examine the information from the point of view of the French source language:

F: *hermine*　　　　E: *ermine*; *stoat*

The opposite now appears in the equivalents provided. The target language erroneously "comprehensionizes" the source language. The two translations are not interchangeable. The full meaning of the source language headword can only be given by adding the meanings of each separate translation. In a way, the headword can be considered as a kind of foreign language superordinate.

In this case, French is far more synthetic in describing the real and shows the inability of English to provide a practical enough tool of classification.

Let us examine a final case with a word which has the same spelling in both languages:

F: *pneumothorax*　　　　E: *pneumothorax*

Reading monolingual French and English dictionaries shows that both *signifiants* refer to a same polysemic *signifié* which means either a disease or a surgical operation. The French headword and its English counterpart have therefore theoretically the same extension and the same comprehension.

In common use however, each language has "comprehensionized" the word by retaining one meaning only out of the two:

English has only retained the "disease" meaning;
French has only retained the "surgical operation" meaning.

The results are twofold:

Each word is practically a "faux ami" for the other because the translation does not
　　give a valid equivalent of the source language;
The disease being extremely rare, the English word is hardly ever used.

Consequently, in most bilinguals, *pneumothorax* appears in the French headword list but not in the English headword list.

In this case, perfect equivalence is indeed achieved diachronically in strict semantic terms, but synchronically, in everyday use, the cognate translation as such is totally inadequate.

5   EQUIVALENCE, LANGUAGE EVENTS AND SPEECH EVENTS

Translators of scientific journals have to remain as unobtrusive as possible and scrupulously stick to the appropriateness of the terms. They have to be transparent and impersonal and there is no room for any flight of fancy. Each term should be provided with an equivalent which is *a language event* generally duly recorded in technical glossaries.

Translators of fiction have to account both for the factual meaning of the text and for its spirit and flavour. They often have to show originality and literary talent, devise new coinages, which are unrecorded *speech events*, required for the genuine transposition of the text in the target language.

Dictionary editors are caught between the horns of a dilemma. As compilers of reference books, they have to stick to a norm and give an unbiased description of language which will enable users to take up this neutral information to fit their own purposes. In other words, their job is to record *language events*. However, in particular when dealing with set phrases and metaphors, equivalents do not always exist and they must then coin *speech events* of their own creation and impose them on users.

In order to illustrate this point, let us examine possible equivalents given to a well-defined set of figurative phrases: proverbs.

Examples will be taken from the inside cover of Harrap's New Shorter which regroups "50 famous English proverbs" and "50 famous French proverbs".

Some proverbs are duly recorded language events which belong to both the English proverb list and the French proverb list. For example:

E: *once bitten twice shy*
F: *chat échaudé craint l'eau froide*
F: *tout ce qui brille n'est pas or*
E: *all that glitters is not gold*

Every criterion of equivalence applies to these lexical items.

Other proverbs are duly recorded language events, but they appear in only one list. For example:

E: *all's well that ends well*
F: *tout est bien qui finit bien*
F: *tel père tel fils*
E: *like father like son*

The reason why they are not mentioned in the other list is arbitrary and only depended on the choices made for each list, which had been compiled separately. Here again every criterion of equivalence applies.

Other proverbs, which are listed in the source language, have no set equivalent in the target language. They are translated by neutral speech events. For example:

A: *people who live in glass houses shouldn't throw stones*
F: *il faut être sans défauts pour critiquer autrui*
F: *de deux maux il faut choisir le moindre*
E: *one must choose the lesser of two evils*

In these cases, the equivalents only give a denotative account of the meaning. They translate the letter and not the spirit of the proverb. Decoding users are allowed to understand the source language, but encoding users are deprived of the evocative flavour they wanted to give to their thinking. The dictionary editors did not have the necessary means of providing perfect equivalence and chose to play it safe by providing a risk-free gloss.

Some other proverbs have no set equivalent in the target language either and they are translated by calques. For example:

E: *too many cooks spoil the broth*
F: *trop de cuisiniers gâtent la sauce*
F: *l'habit ne fait pas le moine*
E: *it is not the cowl that makes the monk*

The calque's merit is to provide a more evocative translation, but the danger is that equivalence is achieved on the level of language, that of the linguistic sign, and not on the level of the concept. This poses two types of problems:

– Decoding users will learn very little from the translation, the metaphoric meaning of which they might more or less suspect, but without any absolute certainty since the concept does not exist in the target language.
– Encoding users will be wrongly led to believe that they are dealing with a genuine equivalent. They might intuitively have the uncomfortable feeling that this is all too good to be true and that the message they want to get across might be impaired by a translation which looks too ideally parallel in form.

Still other proverbs, which have no set equivalent in the target language, have been translated by purpose-built speech events. For example:

E: *you can't have your cake and eat it*
F: *on ne peut pas avoir le drap et l'argent*

Here, the translators were frustrated at being the passive witnesses of the shortcomings of the target language or they did not manage to think of a well-established equivalent, and so attempted to create their own coinage. They may also have thought that a valid equivalent existed but was now too uncommon because of its obsolete nature.

This concern is to be praised in literary translation but poses obvious problems in bilingual lexicography. Decoding users are left just as baffled by the translation as in the previous cases and encoding users are deprived of any means of intuitively sensing that there might be a potential danger, because the translators' coinage, i.e. the speech event, is deceptively presented as a language event and is, in a way, "a wolf in sheep's clothing".

Eventually, other proverbs take the shape of back translations: a speech event appears in the source language with all the characteristics of a language event, with the sole purpose of being translated in an ideal way by a proverb duly recorded in the target language. For example:

F: *c'est dans le malheur qu'on reconnait ses vrais amis*
E: *a friend in need is a friend indeed*

Encoding users will not be troubled by the phrase which they will never want to encode. They may be surprised at most to find it there.

Decoding users will not be surprised by the phrase as it is a perfectly logical speech event, and of course, they will not be misled by the translation which provides a kind of "excess equivalence".

However, the information might be misleading for decoding users once they have committed it to memory, because later on they may be tempted to reuse the pseudo equivalent when expressing themselves in the foreign language with the false conviction that they are producing a genuine set phrase.

6 CONCLUSION

Total equivalence between source language and target language, which is a legitimate requirement of dictionary users, is much more uncommon than one would think. It requires perfect balance between the real as it is perceived in the two cultures and the words in the language which describe it.

For want of total equivalence, dictionary editors can avail themselves of a series of means which enables them to provide relative equivalence by resorting to a subtle combination of denotation and connotation, by applying various degrees of extension and comprehension and by using set language events provided by both languages.

Meticulous metalinguistic labelling is therefore required in order to remove possible ambiguities in each translation and to warn users against the dangers of undue generalization. The degree of equivalence will thus be indicated and the usual mistakes associated with the indiscriminate use of bilingual dictionaries will partly be avoided.

PART X

On Tools for Lexicographers

19

Word Association Norms, Mutual Information, and Lexicography

KENNETH W. CHURCH AND PATRICK HANKS*

I MEANING AND ASSOCIATION

It is common practice in linguistics to classify words not only on the basis of their meanings but also on the basis of their co-occurrence with other words. Running through the whole Firthian tradition, for example, is the theme that "You shall know a word by the company it keeps" (Firth, 1957).

On the one hand, *bank* co-occurs with words and expression such as *money, notes, loan, account, investment, clerk, official, manager, robbery, vaults, working in a, its actions, First National, of England,* and so forth. On the other hand, we find *bank* co-occurring with *river, swim, boat, east* (and of course *West* and *South*, which have acquired special meanings of their own), *on top of the*, and *of the Rhine.*

(Hanks, 1987: 127)

The search for increasingly delicate word classes is not new. In lexicography, for example, it goes back at least to the "verb patterns" described in Hornby's *Advanced Learner's Dictionary* (first edition 1948). What is new is that facilities for the computational storage and analysis of large bodies of natural language have developed significantly in recent years, so that it is now becoming possible to test and apply informal assertions of this kind in a more rigorous way, and to see what company our words do keep.

2 PRACTICAL APPLICATIONS

The proposed statistical description has a large number of potentially important applications, including: (a) constraining the language model both for speech recognition and optical character recognition (OCR), (b) providing disambiguation cues for parsing highly ambiguous syntactic structures such as noun compounds, conjunctions, and prepositional phrases, (c) retrieving texts from large databases (e.g., newspapers, patents), (d) enhancing the productivity of computational linguists in compiling lexicons of lexico-syntactic facts, and (e) enhancing the productivity of lexicographers in identifying normal and conventional usage.

Consider the optical character recognizer (OCR) application. Suppose that we have an OCR device such as Kahan *et al.* (1987), and it has assigned about equal probability to having recognized "farm" and "form," where the context is either: (1) "federal __ credit" or (2) "some __ of." The proposed association measure can make use of the fact that "farm" is much

* Church, K.W., and Hanks, P. (1990). 'Word association norms, mutual information, and lexicography', *Computational Linguistics*, 16(1): 22–29. Reproduced with permission of the Association for Computational Linguistics.

more likely in the first context and "form" is much more likely in the second to resolve the ambiguity. Note that alternative disambiguation methods based on syntactic constraints such as part of speech are unlikely to help in this case since both "form" and "farm" are commonly used as nouns.

3   WORD ASSOCIATION AND PSYCHOLINGUISTICS

Word association norms are well known to be an important factor in psycholinguistic research, especially in the area of lexical retrieval. Generally speaking, subjects respond quicker than normal to the word "nurse" if it follows a highly associated word such as "doctor."

Some results and implications are summarized from reaction-time experiments in which subjects either (a) classified successive strings of letters as words and nonwords, or (b) pronounced the strings. Both types of response to words (e.g., BUTTER) were consistently faster when preceded by associated words (e.g., BREAD) rather than unassociated words (e.g., NURSE).

(Meyer *et al.* 1975: 8).

Much of this psycholinguistic research is based on empirical estimates of word association norms such as Palermo and Jenkins (1964), perhaps the most influential study of its kind, though extremely small and somewhat dated. This study measured 200 words by asking a few thousand subjects to write down a word after each of the 200 words to be measured. Results are reported in tabular form, indicating which words were written down, and by how many subjects, factored by grade level and sex. The word "doctor," for example, is reported on pp. 98–100 to be most often associated with "nurse," followed by "sick," "health," "medicine," "hospital," "man," "sickness," "lawyer," and about 70 more words.

4   AN INFORMATION THEORETIC MEASURE

We propose an alternative measure, *the association ratio*, for measuring word association norms, based on the information theoretic concept of *mutual information*. The proposed measure is more objective and less costly than the subjective method employed in Palermo and Jenkins (1964). The association ratio can be scaled up to provide robust estimates of word association norms for a large portion of the language. Using the association ratio measure, the five most associated words are (in order): "dentists," "nurses," "treating," "treat," and "hospitals."

What is "mutual information"? According to Fano (1961: 28), if two points (words), x and y, have probabilities $P(x)$ and $P(y)$, then their mutual information, $I(x,y)$, is defined to be

$$I(x,y) \equiv \log_2 \frac{P(x,y)}{P(x)P(y)}$$

Informally, mutual information compares the probability of observing x and y *together* (the joint probability) with the probabilities of observing x and y *independently* (chance). If there is a genuine association between x and y, then the joint probability $P(x,y)$ will be much larger than chance $P(x) P(y)$, and consequently $I(x,y) \gg 0$. If there is no interesting relationship between x and y, then $P(x,y) \approx P(x) P(y)$, and thus, $I(x,y) \approx 0$. If x and y are in complementary distribution, then $P(x,y)$ will be much less than $P(x) P(y)$, forcing $I(x,y) \ll 0$.

In our application, word probabilities, $P(x)$ and $P(y)$, are estimated by counting the number of observations of x and y in a corpus, $f(x)$ and $f(y)$, and normalizing by N, the size of the corpus. (Our examples use a number of different corpora with different sizes: 15 million words for the 1987 AP corpus, 36 million words for the 1988 AP corpus, and 8.6 million tokens for the tagged corpus.) Joint probabilities, $P(x,y)$, are estimated by counting the number of times that x is followed by y in a window of w words, $f_w(x,y)$, and normalizing by N.

The window size parameter allows us to look at different scales. Smaller window sizes will identify fixed expressions (idioms) and other relations that hold over short ranges; larger window sizes will highlight semantic concepts and other relationships that hold over larger scales. For the remainder of this paper, the window size, w, will be set to 5 words as a compromise; this setting is large enough to show some of the constraints between verbs and arguments, but not so large that it would wash out constraints that make use of strict adjacency.[1]

Since the association ratio becomes unstable when the counts are very small, we will not discuss word pairs with $f(x,y) \leq 5$. An improvement would make use of t-scores, and throw out pairs that were not significant. Unfortunately, this requires an estimate of the variance of $f(x,y)$, which goes beyond the scope of this paper. For the remainder of this paper, we will adopt the simple but arbitrary threshold, and ignore pairs with small counts.

Technically, the *association ratio* is different from *mutual information* in two respects. First, joint probabilities are supposed to be symmetric: $P(x,y) = P(y,x)$, and thus, mutual information is also symmetric: $I(x,y) = I(y,x)$. However, the association ratio is not symmetric, since $f(x,y)$ encodes linear precedence. (Recall that $f(x,y)$ denotes the number of times that word x appears *before* y in the window of w words, not the number of times the two words appear in either order.) Although we could fix this problem by redefining $f(x,y)$ to be symmetric (by averaging the matrix with its transpose), we have decided not to do so, since order information appears to be very interesting. Notice the asymmetry in the pairs below (computed from 36 million words of 1988 AP text), illustrating a wide variety of biases ranging from sexism to syntax.

Asymmetry in 1988 AP Corpus (N = 36 million)

x	y	$f(x,y)$	$f(y,x)$
doctors	nurses	81	10
man	woman	209	42
doctors	lawyers	25	16
bread	butter	14	0
save	life	106	8
save	money	155	8
save	from	144	16
supposed	to	982	21

Secondly, one might expect $f(x,y) \leq f(x)$ and $f(x,y) \leq f(y)$, but the way we have been counting, this needn't be the case if x and y happen to appear several times in the window. For example, given the sentence, "Library workers were prohibited from saving books from this heap of ruins," which appeared in an AP story on April 1, 1988, f (*prohibited*) $= 1$ and

---

[1] This definition $f_w(x,y)$ uses a rectangular window. It might be interesting to consider alternatives (e.g., a triangular window or a decaying exponential) that would weight words less and less as they are separated by more and more words.

$f(prohibited, from) = 2$. This problem can be fixed by dividing $f(x,y)$ by $w - 1$ (which has the consequence of subtracting $\log_2(w - 1) = 2$ from our association ratio scores). This adjustment has the additional benefit of assuring that $\sum f(x,y) = \sum f(x) = \sum f(y) = N$.

When $I(x,y)$ is large, the association ratio produces very credible results not unlike those reported in Palermo and Jenkins (1964), as illustrated in the table below. In contrast, when $I(x, y) \approx 0$, the pairs are less interesting. As a very rough rule of thumb, we have observed that pairs with $I(x,y) > 3$ tend to be interesting, and pairs with smaller $I(x,y)$ are generally not. One can make this statement precise by calibrating the measure with subjective measures. Alternatively, one could make estimates of the variance and then make statements about confidence levels, e.g., with 95% confidence, $P(x,y) > P(x)P(y)$.

Some Interesting Associations with "Doctor" in the 1987 AP Corpus ($N = 15$ million)

$I(x,y)$	$f(x,y)$	$f(x)$	x	$f(y)$	y
11.3	12	111	honorary	621	doctor
11.3	8	1,105	doctors	44	dentists
10.7	30	1,105	doctors	241	nurses
9.4	8	1,105	doctors	154	treating
9.0	6	275	examined	621	doctor
8.9	11	1,105	doctors	317	treat
8.7	25	621	doctor	1,407	bills
8.7	6	621	doctor	350	visits
8.6	19	1,105	doctors	676	hospitals
8.4	6	241	nurses	1,105	doctors

Some Uninteresting Associations with "Doctor"

$I(x,y)$	$f(x,y)$	$f(x)$	x	$f(y)$	y
0.96	6	621	doctor	73,785	with
0.95	41	284,690	a	1,105	doctors
0.93	12	84,716	is	1,105	doctors

If $I(x,y) \ll 0$, we would predict that x and y are in complementary distribution. However, we are rarely able to observe $I(x,y) \ll 0$ because our corpora are too small (and our measurement techniques are too crude). Suppose, for example, that both x and y appear about 10 times per million words of text. Then, $P(x) = P(y) = 10^{-5}$ and chance is $P(x)P(y) = 10^{-10}$. Thus, to say that $I(x,y)$ is much less than 0, we need to say that $P(x,y)$ is much less than 10^{-10}, a statement that is hard to make with much confidence given the size of presently available corpora. In fact, we cannot (easily) observe a probability less than $1/N \approx 10^{-7}$, and therefore, it is hard to know if $I(x,y)$ is much less than chance or not, unless chance is very large. (In fact, the pair *(a, doctors)* above appears significantly less often than chance. But to justify this statement, we need to compensate for the window size (which shifts the score downward by 2.0, e.g. from 0.96 down to -1.04) and we need to estimate the standard deviation, using a method such as Good (1953).)

5   LEXICO-SYNTACTIC REGULARITIES

Although the psycholinguistic literature documents the significance of noun/noun word associations such as doctor/nurse in considerable detail, relatively little is said about associations among verbs, function words, adjectives, and other non-nouns. In addition to identifying semantic relations of the doctor/nurse variety, we believe the association ratio can also be used to search for interesting lexico-syntactic relationships between verbs and typical arguments/adjuncts. The proposed association ratio can be viewed as a formalization of Sinclair's argument:

> How common are the phrasal verbs with *set*? *Set* is particularly rich in making combinations with words like *about*, *in*, *up*, *out*, *on*, *off*, and these words are themselves very common. How likely is *set off* to occur? Both are frequent words; *set* occurs approximately 250 times in a million words and *off* occurs approximately 556 times in a million words ... [T]he question we are asking can be roughly rephrased as follows: how likely is *off* to occur immediately after *set*? ... This is 0.00025 × 0.00055 $[P(x)P(y)]$, which gives us the tiny figure of 0.0000001375 ... The assumption behind this calculation is that the words are distributed at random in a text [at chance, in our terminology]. It is obvious to a linguist that this is not so, and a rough measure of how much *set* and *off* attract each other is to compare the probability with what actually happens ... *Set off* occurs nearly 70 times in the 7.3 million word corpus $[P(x,y) = 70/(7.3 \times 10^6) \gg P(x)P(y)]$. That is enough to show its main patterning and it suggests that in currently-held corpora there will be found sufficient evidence for the description of a substantial collection of phrases ...
>
> (Sinclair, 1987c: 151–152)

It happens that *set . . . off* was found 177 times in the 1987 AP Corpus of approximately 15 million words, about the same number of occurrences per million as Sinclair found in his (mainly British) corpus. Quantitatively, $I(set, off) = 5.9982$, indicating that the probability of *set . . . off* is almost 64 times greater than chance. This association is relatively strong; the other particles that Sinclair mentions have association ratios of: *about* (1.4), *in* (2.9), *up* (6.9), *out* (4.5), *on* (3.3) in the 1987 AP Corpus.

As Sinclair suggests, the approach is well suited for identifying phrasal verbs. However, phrasal verbs involving the preposition *to* raise an interesting problem because of the possible confusion with the infinitive marker *to*. We have found that if we first tag every word in the corpus with a part of speech using a method such as Church (1988), and then measure associations between tagged words, we can identify interesting contrasts between verbs associated with a following preposition *to/in* and verbs associated with a following infinitive marker *to/to*. (Part of speech notation is borrowed from Francis and Kučera (1982); in = preposition; to = infinitive marker; vb = bare verb; vbg = verb + ing; vbd = verb + ed; vbz = verb + s; vbn = verb + en.) The association ratio identifies quite a number of verbs associated in an interesting way with *to*; restricting our attention to pairs with a score of 3.0 or more, there are 768 verbs associated with the preposition *to/in* and 551 verbs with the infinitive marker *to/to*. The ten verbs found to be most associated before *to/in* are:

- *to/in:* alluding/vbg, adhere/vb, amounted/vbn, relating/vbg, amounting/vbg, revert/vb, reverted/vbn, resorting/vbg, relegated/vbn
- *to/to:* obligated/vbn, trying/vbg, compelled/vbn, enables/vbz, supposed/vbn, intends/vbz, vowing/vbg, tried/vbd, enabling/vbg, tends/vbz, tend/vb, intend/vb, tries/vbz

Thus, we see there is considerable leverage to be gained by preprocessing the corpus and manipulating the inventory of tokens. For measuring syntactic constraints, it may be useful to include some part of speech information and to exclude much of the internal structure of noun phrases. For other purposes, it may be helpful to tag items and/or phrases with semantic labels such as *person*, *place*, *time*, *body-part*, *bad*, etc. Hindle (personal communication) has found it helpful to preprocess the input with the Fidditch parser (Hindle 1983a,b) in order to identify associations between verbs and arguments, and postulate semantic classes for nouns on this basis.

6   APPLICATIONS IN LEXICOGRAPHY

Large machine-readable corpora are only just now becoming available to lexicographers. Up to now, lexicographers have been reliant either on citations collected by human readers, which introduced an element of selectivity and so inevitably distortion (rare words and uses were collected but common uses of common words were not), or on small corpora of only a million words or so, which are reliably informative for only the most common uses of the few most frequent words of English. (A million-word corpus such as the Brown Corpus is reliable, roughly, for only some uses of only some of the forms of around 4000 dictionary entries. But standard dictionaries typically contain twenty times this number of entries.)

The computational tools available for studying machine-readable corpora are at present still rather primitive. There are *concordancing* programs (see Figure 1), which are basically KWIC (key word in context) indexes (see Aho *et al.* 1988: 122) with additional features such as the ability to extend the context, sort leftwards as well as rightwards, and so on. There is very little interactive software. In a typical situation in the lexicography of the 1980s, a lexicographer is given the concordances for a word, marks up the printout with colored pens in order to identify the salient senses, and then writes syntactic descriptions and definitions.

Although this technology is a great improvement on using human readers to collect boxes of citation index cards (the method Murray used in constructing the Oxford English Dictionary a century ago), it works well if there are no more than a few dozen concordance lines for

rs Sunday, calling for greater economic reforms to	save China from poverty.
mmission asserted that "the Postal Service could	save enormous sums of money in contracting out individual c
Then, she said, the family hopes to	save enough for a down payment on a home.
e out-of-work steelworker, "because that doesn't	save jobs, that costs jobs."
"We suspend reality when we say we'll	save money by spending $10,000 in wages for a public works
scientists has won the first round in an effort to	save one of Egypt's great treasures, the decaying tomb of R
about three children in a mining town who plot to	save the "pit ponies" doomed to be slaughtered.
GM executives say the shutdowns will	save the automaker $500 million a year in operating costs a
rtment as receiver, instructed officials to try to	save the company rather than liquidate it and then declared
The package, which is to	save the country nearly $2 billion, also includes a program
newly enhanced image as the moderate who moved to	save the country.
million offer from chairman Victor Posner to help	save the financially troubled company, but said Posner stil
after telling a delivery-room doctor not to try to	save the infant by inserting a tube in its throat to help i
h birthday Tuesday, cheered by those who fought to	save the majestic Beaux Arts architectural masterpiece.
at he had formed an alliance with Moslem rebels to	save the nation from communism.
"Basically we could	save the operating costs of the Pershings and ground-launch
We worked for a year to	save the site at enormous expense to us," said Leveillee.
their expensive mirrors, just like in wartime, to	save them from drunken Yankee brawlers," Tass said.
ard of many who risked their own lives in order to	save those who were passengers."
We must increase the amount Americans	save."

FIG. 1   Short Sample of the Concordance to "Save" from the AP 1987 Corpus

a word, and only two or three main sense divisions. In analyzing a complex word such as "take," "save," or "from," the lexicographer is trying to pick out significant patterns and subtle distinctions that are buried in literally thousands of concordance lines: pages and pages of computer printout. The unaided human mind simply cannot discover all the significant patterns, let alone group them and rank in order of importance.

The AP 1987 concordance to "save" is many pages long; there are 666 lines for the base form alone, and many more for the inflected forms "saved," "saves," "saving," and "savings." In the discussion that follows, we shall, for the sake of simplicity, not analyze the inflected forms and we shall only look at the patterns to the right of "save."

Words Often Co-occurring to the Right of "save"

$I(x,y)$	$f(x,y)$	$f(x)$	x	$f(y)$	y
9.5	6	724	save	170	forests
9.4	6	724	save	180	$1.2
8.8	37	724	save	1,697	lives
8.7	6	724	save	301	enormous
8.3	7	724	save	447	annually
7.7	20	724	save	2,001	jobs
7.6	64	724	save	6,776	money
7.2	36	724	save	4,875	life
6.6	8	724	save	1,668	dollars
6.4	7	724	save	1,719	costs
6.4	6	724	save	1,481	thousands
6.2	9	724	save	2,590	face
5.7	6	724	save	2,311	son
5.7	6	724	save	2,387	estimated
5.5	7	724	save	3,141	your
5.5	24	724	save	10,880	billion
5.3	39	724	save	20,846	million
5.2	8	724	save	4,398	us
5.1	6	724	save	3,513	less
5.0	7	724	save	4,590	own
4.6	7	724	save	5,798	world
4.6	7	724	save	6,028	my
4.6	15	724	save	13,010	them
4.5	8	724	save	7,434	country
4.4	15	724	save	14,296	time
4.4	64	724	save	61,262	from
4.3	23	724	save	23,258	more
4.2	25	724	save	27,367	their
4.1	8	724	save	9,249	company
4.1	6	724	save	7,114	month

It is hard to know what is important in such a concordance and what is not. For example, although it is easy to see from the concordance selection in Figure 1 that the word "to" often comes before "save" and the word "the" often comes after "save," it is hard to say from examination of a concordance alone whether either or both of these co-occurrences have any significance.

Two examples will illustrate how the association ratio measure helps make the analysis both quicker and more accurate.

6.1   Example 1: "save ... from"

The association ratios (above) show that association norms apply to function words as well as content words. For example, one of the words significantly associated with "save" is "from." Many dictionaries, for example Merriam-Webster's Ninth, make no explicit mention of "from" in the entry for "save," although British learners' dictionaries do make specific mention of "from" in connection with "save." These learners' dictionaries pay more attention to language structure and collocation than do American collegiate dictionaries, and lexicographers trained in the British tradition are often fairly skilled at spotting these generalizations. However, teasing out such facts, and distinguishing true intuitions from false intuitions takes a lot of time and hard work, and there is a high probability of inconsistencies and omissions.

Which other verbs typically associate with "from," and where does "save" rank in such a list? The association ratio identified 1,530 words that are associated with "from"; 911 of them were tagged as verbs. The first 100 verbs are:

refrain/vb, gleaned/vbn, stems/vbz, stemmed/vbd, stemming/vbg, ranging/vbg, stemmed/vbn, ranged/vbn, derived/vbn, ranged/vbd, extort/vb, graduated/vbd, barred/vbn, benefiting/vbg, benefitted/vbn, benefited/vbn, excused/vbd, arising/vbg, range/vb, exempts/vbz, suffers/vbz, exempting/vbg, benefited/vbd, prevented/vbd (7.0), seeping/vbg, barred/vbd, prevents/vbz, suffering/vbg, excluded/vbn, marks/vbz, profiting/vbg, recovering/vbg, discharged/vbn, rebounding/vbg, vary/vb, exempted/vbn, separate/vb, banished/vbn, withdrawing/vbg, ferry/vb, prevented/vbn, profit/vb, bar/vb, excused/vbn, bars/vbz, benefit/vb, emerges/vbz, emerge/vb, varies/vbz, differ/vb, removed/vbn, exempt/vb, expelled/vbn, withdraw/vb, stem/vb, separated/vbn, judging/vbg, adapted/vbn, escaping/vbg, inherited/vbn, differed/vbd, emerged/vbd, withheld/vbd, leaked/vbn, strip/vb, resulting/vbg, discourage/vb, prevent/vb, withdrew/vbd, prohibits/vbz, borrowing/vbg, preventing/vbg, prohibit/vb, resulted/vbd (6.0), preclude/vb, divert/vb, distinguish/vb, pulled/vbn, fell/vbn, varied/vbn, emerging/vbg, suffer/vb, prohibiting/vbg, extract/vb, subtract/vb, recover/vb, paralyzed/vbn, stole/vbd, departing/vbg, escaped/vbn, prohibited/vbn, forbid/vb, evacuated/vbn, reap/vb, barring/vbg, removing/vbg, stolen/vbn, receives/vbz.

"Save ... from" is a good example for illustrating the advantages of the association ratio. *Save* is ranked 319th in this list, indicating that the association is modest, strong enough to be important (21 times more likely than chance), but not so strong that it would pop out at us in a concordance, or that it would be one of the first things to come to mind.

If the dictionary is going to list "save ... *from*," then, for consistency's sake, it ought to consider listing all of the more important associations as well. Of the 27 bare verbs (tagged "vb") in the list above, all but 7 are listed in the Cobuild dictionary as occurring with "from." However, this dictionary does not note that *vary, ferry, strip, divert, forbid,* and *reap* occur with "from." If the Cobuild lexicographers had had access to the proposed measure, they could possibly have obtained better coverage at less cost.

save X from Y (65 concordance lines)
1 save PERSON from Y (23 concordance lines)
1.1 save PERSON from BAD (19 concordance lines)

(Robert DeNiro) to	save Indian tribes[PERSON] from genocide[DESTRUCT[BAD]] at the hands of
"We wanted to	save him[PERSON] from undue trouble[BAD] and loss[BAD] of money,"
Murphy was sacrificed to	save more powerful Democrats[PERSON] from harm[BAD] .
"God sent this man to	save my five children[PERSON] from being burned to death[DESTRUCT[BAD]] and
Pope John Paul II to"	save us[PERSON] from sin[BAD]."

1.2 save PERSON from (BAD) LOC(ATION) (4 concordance lines)

rescuers who helped	save the toddler[PERSON] from an abandoned well[LOC] will be feted with a parade
while attempting to	save two drowning boys[PERSON] from a turbulent[BAD] creek[LOC] in Ohio[LOC]

2. save INST(ITUTION) from (ECON) BAD (27 concordance lines)

member states to help	save the EEC[INST] from possible bankruptcy[ECON][BAD] this year.
should be sought "to	save the company[CORP[INST]] from bankruptcy[ECON][BAD].
law was necessary to	save the country[NATION[INST]] from disaster[BAD].
operation "to	save the nation[NATION[INST]] from Communism[BAD][POLITICAL],
were not needed to	save the system from bankruptcy[ECON][BAD].
his efforts to	save the world[INST] from the likes of Lothar and the Spider Woman

3. save ANIMAL from DESTRUCT(ION) (5 concordance lines)

give them the money to	save the dogs[ANIMAL] from being destroyed[DESTRUCT],
program intended to	save the giant birds[ANIMAL] from extinction[DESTRUCT],

UNCLASSIFIED (10 concordance lines)

walnut and ash trees to	save them from the axes and saws of a logging company.
after the attack to	save the ship from a terrible[BAD] fire, Navy reports concluded Thursday.
certificates that would	save shoppers[PERSON] anywhere from $50[MONEY][NUMBER] to
	$500[MONEY][NUMBER]

FIG. 2   Some AP 1987 Concordance lines to "save ...from," roughly sorted into categories

6.2   Example 2: identifying semantic classes

Having established the relative importance of "save...from," and having noted that the two words are rarely adjacent, we would now like to speed up the labor-intensive task of categorizing the concordance lines. Ideally, we would like to develop a set of semi-automatic tools that would help a lexicographer produce something like Figure 2, which provides an annotated summary of the 65 concordance lines for "save...from."[2] The "save...from" pattern occurs in about 10% of the 666 concordance lines for "save."

Traditionally, semantic categories have been only vaguely recognized, and to date little effort has been devoted to a systematic classification of a large corpus. Lexicographers have tended to use concordances impressionistically; semantic theorists, AI-ers, and others have concentrated on a few interesting examples, e.g., "bachelor," and have not given much thought to how the results might be scaled up.

With this concern in mind, it seems reasonable to ask how well these 65 lines for "save...from" fit in with all other uses of "save"? A laborious concordance analysis was undertaken to answer this question. When it was nearing completion, we noticed that the tags that we were inventing to capture the generalizations could in most cases have been suggested

---

[2] The last unclassified line, "...save shoppers anywhere from $50..." raises interesting problems. Syntactic "chunking" shows that, in spite of its co-occurrence of "from" with "save," this line does not belong here. An intriguing exercise, given the lookup table we are trying to construct, is how to guard against false inferences such as that since "shoppers" is tagged [PERSON], "$50 to $500" must here count as either BAD or a LOCATION. Accidental coincidences of this kind do not have a significant effect on the measure, however, although they do serve as a reminder of the probabilistic nature of the findings.

by looking at the lexical items listed in the association ratio table for "save." For example, we had failed to notice the significance of time adverbials in our analysis of "save," and no dictionary records this. Yet it should be clear from the association ratio table above that "annually" and "month"[3] are commonly found with "save." More detailed inspection shows that the time adverbials correlate interestingly with just one group of "save" objects, namely those tagged [MONEY]. The AP wire is full of discussions of "saving $1.2 billion per month"; computational lexicography should measure and record such patterns if they are general, even when traditional dictionaries do not.

As another example illustrating how the association ratio tables would have helped us analyze the "save" concordance lines, we found ourselves contemplating the semantic tag ENV(IRONMENT) in order to analyze lines such as:

the trend to	save the forests[ENV]
it's our turn to	save the lake[ENV],
joined a fight to	save their forests[ENV],
can we get busy to	save the planet[ENV]?

If we had looked at the association ratio tables before labeling the 65 lines for "save...from," we might have noticed the very large value for "save...forests," suggesting that there may be an important pattern here. In fact, this pattern probably subsumes most of the occurrences of the "save [ANIMAL]" pattern noticed in Figure 2. Thus, tables do not provide semantic tags, but they provide a powerful set of suggestions to the lexicographer for what needs to be accounted for in choosing a set of semantic tags.

It may be that everything said here about "save" and other words is true only of 1987 American journalese. Intuitively, however, many of the patterns discovered seem to be good candidates for conventions of general English. A future step would be to examine other more balanced corpora and test how well the patterns hold up.

7   CONCLUSIONS

We began this paper with the psycholinguistic notion of word association norm, and extended that concept toward the information theoretic definition of mutual information. This provided a precise statistical calculation that could be applied to a very large corpus of texts in order to produce a table of associations for tens of thousands of words. We were then able to show that the table encoded a number of very interesting patterns ranging from *doctor...nurse* to *save...from*. We finally concluded by showing how the patterns in the association ratio table might help a lexicographer organize a concordance.

In point of fact, we actually developed these results in basically the reverse order. Concordance analysis is still extremely labor-intensive, and prone to errors of omission. The ways that concordances are sorted don't adequately support current lexicographic practice. Despite the fact that a concordance is indexed by a single word, often lexicographers actually use a second word such as "from" or an equally common semantic concept such as a time adverbial to decide how to categorize concordance lines. In other words, they use two words to *triangulate in* on a word sense. This triangulation approach clusters concordance lines together into word senses based primarily on usage (distributional evidence), as opposed to

---

[3] The word "time" itself also occurs significantly in the table, but on close examination it is clear that this use of "time" (e.g., "to save time") counts as something like a commodity or resource, not as part of a time adjunct. Such are the pitfalls of lexicography (obvious when they are pointed out).

intuitive notions of meaning. Thus, the question of what is a word sense can be addressed with syntactic methods (symbol pushing), and need not address semantics (interpretation), even though the inventory of tags may appear to have semantic values.

The triangulation approach requires "art." How does the lexicographer decide which potential cut points are "interesting" and which are merely due to chance? The proposed association ratio score provides a practical and objective measure which is often a fairly good approximation to the "art." Since the proposed measure is objective, it can be applied in a systematic way over a large body of material, steadily improving consistency and productivity.

But on the other hand, the objective score can be misleading. The score takes only distributional evidence into account. For example, the measure favors "set ... for" over "set ... down"; it doesn't know that the former is less interesting because its semantics are compositional. In addition, the measure is extremely superficial; it cannot cluster words into appropriate syntactic classes without an explicit preprocess such as Church's parts program or Hindle's parser. Neither of these preprocesses, though, can help highlight the "natural" similarity between nouns such as "picture" and "photograph." Although one might imagine a preprocess that would help in this particular case, there will probably always be a class of generalizations that are obvious to an intelligent lexicographer, but lie hopelessly beyond the objectivity of a computer.

Despite these problems, the association ratio could be an important tool to aid the lexicographer, rather like an index to the concordances. It can help us decide what to look for; it provides a quick summary of what company our words do keep.

20

The Sketch Engine

ADAM KILGARRIFF, PAVEL RYCHLY, PAVEL SMRŽ, AND DAVID TUGWELL*

I   INTRODUCTION

Word sketches are one-page automatic, corpus-based summaries of a word's grammatical and collocational behaviour. They were first used in the production of the Macmillan English Dictionary (Rundell 2002) and were presented at Euralex 2002 (Kilgarriff and Rundell 2002). Following that presentation, the most-asked question was "Can I have them for my language?" In response, we have now developed the Sketch Engine, a corpus tool which takes as input a corpus of any language (with appropriate linguistic markup), and which then generates, amongst other things, word sketches for the words of that language.

Those other things include a corpus-based thesaurus and "sketch differences", which specify, for two semantically related words, what behaviour they share and how they differ. We anticipate that sketch differences will be particularly useful for lexicographers interested in near-synonym differentiation.

In this paper we first provide, by way of background, an account of how corpora have been used in lexicography to date, culminating in a brief description of the word sketches as used in the preparation of the Macmillan dictionary. We then describe the Sketch Engine, including the preprocessing it requires, the approach taken to grammar, the thesaurus, and the sketch differences. We end with a note on our future plans.

I.I   A brief history of corpus lexicography

The first age of corpus lexicography was pre-computer. Dictionary compilers such as Samuel Johnson and James Murray worked from vast sets of index cards, their "corpus".

The second age commenced with the COBUILD project, in the late 1970s (Sinclair *et al.* 1987). Sinclair and Atkins, its devisers, saw the potential for the computer to do the storing, sorting and searching that was previously the role of readers, filing cabinets and clerks, and at the same time to make it far more objective: human readers would only make a citation for a word if it was rare, or where it was being used in an interesting way, so citations focused on the unusual but gave little evidence of the usual. The computer would be blindly objective, and show norms as well as the exceptions, as required for an objective account of the language. Since COBUILD, lexicographers have been using KWIC (keyword in context) concordances as their primary tool for finding out how a word behaves.

*Kilgarriff, A., Rychly, P., Smrž, P., and Tugwell, D. (2004). 'The Sketch Engine', in Williams, G., and Vessier, S. (eds.), *Euralex 2004 Proceedings*. Lorient: Université de Bretagne-Sud, 105–116.

For a lexicographer to look at the concordances for a word is a most satisfactory way to proceed, and any new and ambitious dictionary project will buy, borrow or steal a corpus, and use one of a number of corpus query systems (CQSs) to check the corpus evidence for a word prior to writing the entry. Available systems include WordSmith, MonoConc, the Stuttgart workbench and Manatee.

But corpora get bigger and bigger. As more and more documents are produced electronically, as the web makes so many documents easily available, so it becomes easy to produce ever larger corpora. Most of the first COBUILD dictionary was produced from a corpus of 8 million words. Several of the leading English dictionaries of the 1990s were produced using the British National Corpus (BNC), of 100m words. The Linguistic Data Consortium has recently announced its Gigaword (1,000m word corpus) – and the web is perhaps 10,000 times bigger than that, in terms of English language text (Kilgarriff and Grefenstette 2003 – see also in this volume, *Ed.*). This is good. The more data we have, the better placed we are to present a complete and accurate account of a word's behaviour. But it does present certain problems. Given fifty corpus occurrences of a word, the lexicographer can, simply, read them. If there are five hundred, it is still a possibility but might well take longer than an editorial schedule permits. Where there are five thousand, it is no longer at all viable. Having more data is good – but the data then needs summarizing.

The third age was marshalled in by Ken Church and Patrick Hanks's inauguration of the subfield of lexical statistics in 1989 (Church and Hanks 1990 – see also in this volume, *Ed.*). They proposed Mutual Information as a measure of the salience of the association between any two words. If, for the word we are interested in, we find all the other words occurring within (say) five words of it, and then calculate the salience of each of those words in relation to the node word, we can summarize the corpus data by presenting a list of its most salient collocates.

The line of enquiry generated a good deal of interest among lexicographers, and the corpus query tools all provide some functionality for identifying salient collocates, along these lines. But the usefulness of the tools was always compromised by:

- the bias of the lists towards overly rare items
- the lists being based on wordforms (*pigs*) rather than lemmas (*pig (noun)*).
- the arbitrariness of deciding how many words to left or right (or both) to consider
- assorted noise, of no linguistic interest, in the list
- the inclusion in the same list of words that might be the subject of a verb, the object of the verb, an adverb, another associated verb or a preposition.

The first issue is one of salience statistics. A number have been put forward, and modern CQSs choose the best, or offer a choice. The second is a matter of, first, lemmatizing the text, and then, applying the lists to lemmas rather than word forms. Here again, various CQSs provide options.

2   THE WORD SKETCH

The word sketch, in addition to using a well-founded salience statistic and lemmatization, addresses the remaining three questions. It does this by using grammar patterns. Rather than looking at an arbitrary window of text around the headword, we look, in turn, for each grammatical relation that the word participates in. In work to date, for English, we have used a repertoire of 27 grammatical relations, for Czech, 23 relations. The word sketch then provides one list of collocates for each grammatical relation the word participates in.

For a verb, the subject, the objects, the conjoined verbs (*stand and deliver, hope and pray*) modifying adverbs, prepositions and prepositional objects, are all presented in different lists. A (truncated) example is presented in Table 1. For each collocate, the lexicographer can click on the collocate to see the corpus contexts in which the node word and its collocate co-occur.

2.1   Corpus query systems

As noted above, corpus query systems play a large role in corpus lexicography. They are the technology through which the lexicographer accesses the corpus. State-of-the-art CQSs allow the lexicographer great flexibility, to search for phrases, collocates, grammatical patterns, to sort concordances according to a wide range of criteria, to identify "subcorpora" for searching in only spoken text, or only fiction. One reading of a word sketch is that it is simply an additional option for accessing the corpus, so should be integrated into a corpus query system to add to the existing armoury of corpus interrogation strategies. This was how we decided to proceed in developing the Sketch Engine. We took an existing CQS, Manatee, and added functionality to it.

3   THE SKETCH ENGINE

The Sketch Engine is a corpus query system which allows the user to view word sketches, thesaurally similar words, and "sketch differences", as well as the more familiar CQS functions. The word sketches are fully integrated with the concordancing: by clicking on a collocate of interest in the word sketch, the user is taken to a concordance of the corpus evidence giving rise to that collocate in that grammatical relation. If the user clicks on the word *toast* in the list of high-salience objects in the sketch for the verb *spread*, they will be taken to a concordance of contexts where *toast (n)* occurs as object of *spread (v)*.

3.1   Lemmatization

In order for the word sketch to classify lemmas, it must know, for each text word, what the corresponding lemma is. The Sketch Engine does not support this process; various tools are available for linguists to develop lemmatizers, and they are available for a number of languages (see e.g. Beesley and Karttunen 2003). If no lemmatizer is available, it is possible to apply the Sketch Engine to word forms, which, while not optimal, will still be a useful lexicographic tool.

3.2   POS-tagging

Similarly for part of speech (POS) tagging. This is the task of deciding the correct word class for each word in the corpus – of determining whether an occurrence of *toasts* is an occurrence of a plural noun or a 3rd person singular, present tense verb. A tagger presupposes a linguistic analysis of the language which has given rise to a set of the syntactic categories of the language, or tagset. Tagsets and taggers exist for a number of languages, and there are assorted well-tried methods for developing taggers. The Sketch Engine assumes tagged input.

TABLE I Word sketch for *pray* (v)

pray(v) BNC freq = 2455

~for	680	3.4	~to	142	1.1	and/or	179	1.7	modifier	338	0.5	object	183	-1.2	subject	1361	0.5
rain	12	19.8	god	32	24.0	hope	20	20.8	silently	15	13.3	god	13	10.5	we	306	12.3
soul	14	19.3	God	22	17.7	hop	13	15.5	together	35	9.3	God	11	9.6	petitioner	7	8.3
-	117	17.3	lord	16	11.4	fast	6	12.2	fervently	4	7.6	prayer	6	7.6	knee	5	6.9
God	11	16.5	saint	4	10.0	pray	16	11.2	aloud	6	7.5	day	9	3.8	congregation	4	6.8
peace	25	16.5	jesus	2	5.4	kneel	5	9.9	earnestly	5	7.3	heaven	2	3.3	i	263	6.2
miracle	8	13.9	emperor	2	5.2	read	9	9.5	inwardly	3	5.5	hook	2	3.3	she	130	5.8
him	26	13.7	Jesus	2	4.5	talk	6	7.4	hard	7	5.3	time	13	3.2	muslim	3	5.7
forgiveness	7	13.4	spirit	2	4.3	sing	4	6.4	daily	3	4.4	night	5	3.1	follower	3	5.0
you	23	13.2	image	2	4.0	watch	4	5.0	only	20	3.8	lord	2	2.7	Jesus	5	4.8
me	24	13.1	wind	2	3.9	live	3	3.9	continually	3	3.7	pardon	2	2.7	jew	3	4.5
deliverance	6	13.0	him	6	3.3	work	5	3.5	regularly	5	3.5	soul	2	2.4	church	7	4.5
them	23	12.2				wish	2	3.4	often	10	3.3	silence	3	2.4	fellowship	2	4.0
church	12	11.7				believe	2	2.9	ever	9	3.0				Singh	2	3.7
guidance	8	11.6				learn	2	2.8	secretly	2	2.7				Family	6	3.6
us	16	11.6				tell	2	2.3	quietly	3	2.4						
chance	5	10.3							still	11	2.3						

TABLE 2 Input format

`<s>`					
The	DET	the (det)	`<s>`		
cat	N-sing	cat (noun)	Kočka	N-sg-fem-nom	kočka
sat	V-past	sit (verb)	seděla	V-past-sg-fem-p3	sedět
on	PREP	on (prep)	na	PREP-loc	na
the	DET	the (det)	rohožce	N-sg-fem-loc	rohožka
mat	N-sing	mat (noun)	.	PUN	
.	PUN	.	`</s>`		
`</s>`					

3.3 Input format

The input format is as specified for the Stuttgart Corpus Tools: each word is on a new line, and for each word, there can be a number of fields specifying further information about the word, separated by lemmas. The fields of interest here are wordform, POS-tag and lemma. The fields are separated by tabs. Constituents such as sentences, paragraphs and documents may also be identified, between angle brackets, on a separate line, as in Table 2 above. (The bracketed word class following the word in the third column for English is one component of the lemma, the other being the string that forms the word. Thus, for current purposes, *brush (verb)* and *brush (noun)* are two different lemmas.)

Further information about these constituents can be appended as attributes associated with the constituents. The formalism is fully documented at

http://www.ims.uni-stuttgart.de/projekte/CorpusWorkbench/.

3.4 Grammatical relations

In order to identify the grammatical relations between words, the Sketch Engine needs to know how to find words connected by a grammatical relation in the language in question. The Sketch Engine countenances two possibilities.

In the first, the input corpus has been parsed and the information about which word-instances stand in which grammatical relations with which other word-instances is embedded in the corpus. Currently, dependency-based syntactically annotated corpora are fully supported. Phrase-structured trees need heads of phrases to be marked.

In the second, the input corpus is loaded into the Sketch Engine unparsed, and the Sketch Engine supports the process of identifying grammatical relation instances. In this approach, we distinguish two roles: a regular user such as a lexicographer, and an expert user, ideally a linguist with some experience and familiarity with computational formalisms. The expert user will then define each grammatical relation, using the Sketch Engine to test and develop it, and will load the grammatical relation set into the Sketch Engine. The Sketch Engine will then find all the grammatical relation instances and give all users access to word sketches.

The formalism for the grammatical relations is the formalism used for all searches that a user (expert or regular) might make on the corpus. It uses regular expression over POS-tags. An example: if we wish to define the English verb–object relation, we first note that, lexicographically, the noun we wish to capture is the head of the object noun phrase, and that this is generally the last noun of a sequence that may include determiners (DET), numbers

(NUM), adjectives (ADJ) and other nouns (N). We also note that the object noun phrase is, by default, directly after the verb in active sentences, and that the lexical verb (V) is generally the last verb of the verb group. Adverbs (ADV) may intervene between verb and object. Taken together, these give a first pass definition for a "verb–object" pair, as "a verb and the last noun in any intervening sequence of adverbs, determiners, numbers, adjectives and nouns". In the Sketch Engine formalism, using the tags given in brackets above, this is

```
1:"V" "(DET | NUM | ADJ | ADV | N)"* 2:"N"
```

The 1: and 2: mark the words to be extracted as the first and second arguments of the grammatical relation. |, (), and * are standard regular expression metacharacters. | is for disjunction and * indicates that the preceding term (here, the bracketed disjunction) occurs zero or more times.

The expert defines each grammatical relation in this way. Clearly, they need to be conversant with both the tagset and the grammar of the language. As the grammatical relations query language is the standard one for the CQS, they can use the CQS to test grammatical relation definitions and the process of grammatical relation development is well-supported. A definition can have multiple clauses: in our work on English, we have used separate clauses for objects realized as subjects of passives, and nouns which are objects of a verb in a relative clause. Czech sketches define several clauses to capture verbal modifiers in different grammatical cases.

While there are no limits to the sophistication with which one might define a grammatical relation, we have found that very simple definitions, such as the one above, while linguistically unsatisfactory, produce very useful results. While a simple definition will miss grammatically complex instances, it is generally the case that a small number of simple patterns cover a high proportion of instances, so the majority of high salience collocates are readily found, given a large enough corpus. Our use of word sketches to date suggests that POS-tagging errors are more frequently the source of anomalous output than weaknesses in the grammar. The use of sorting based on salience statistics means that occasional mis-analyses rarely result in wrong words appearing in collocate lists.

Verb–object, while frequently the most significant grammatical relation for describing the behaviour of nouns and verbs, is also a relatively complex one to identify. Others such as the relation between an adjective and the noun it modifies (which is usually the most significant one for adjectives) or between a word and others of the same word class that it occurs in conjunction with (*fish*/*chip*; *hope*/*pray*; *big*/*fat*), or between a content word and a following preposition, are generally simpler.

These kinds of methods have been widely used; a series of workshops on Finite State methods have been among the places at which Finite State (including regular-expression) approaches to grammatical analysis have been studied. Researchers such as Gahl (1998) have explored sophisticated syntactic querying within a CQS using the same formalism.

3.5   Grammatical relation definitions and free word order

The grammatical relations formalism is sequence-based, and is thereby more obviously suited to languages with a regular word order, such as English, and less clearly suited to a relatively free word order language such as Czech.

For Czech, the defined patterns were based on the grammar employed in SYNT – a robust deep parser for free Czech text (Smrž and Horák 2000). We started with complex patterns, following the complexity of rules in the grammar, aiming at high precision, and had few mismatches in the retrieved grammatical relations. However, the outcome was a large reduction in the number of identified occurrences of grammatical relations, which resulted in word sketches which were not very informative. So, in a stepwise process, we relaxed constraints, gaining recall at the expense of precision. In this way we found an improved tradeoff between the correctness of the patterns and the usability of the produced sketches.

The current definition of the subject relation for Czech is as below. The keyword DUAL specifies that there are two relations defined here: *is_subj_of* and its converse, *has_subj*, and a single instance of the relation contributes an *is_subj_of* relation to the noun and a *has_subj* relation to the verb. The strings following the equals sign are the names of the relations, separated by a slash. Each line introduces a new clause.

```
*DUAL
=is_subj_of/has_subj
        1:noun_nominative gap([NVZJP].*) 2:[verb_p3X & !aux_verb]
        1:noun_nominative gap([NVZJP].*) 2:[verb_passive & !aux_verb]
        2:[verb_p3X & !aux_verb] gap([NVZJP].*) 1:noun_nominative
        2:[verb_passive & !aux_verb] gap([NVZJP].*) 1:noun_nominative
```

The problem of free word order is addressed by the simple mechanism of gaps in these patterns. The object gap() matches up to 5 words differing in their categories from the given list.

Particular attention has been paid to the agreement constraints that are typical of Czech. Thus, the pattern for adjective modifiers must check that the noun and the corresponding adjective have the same case (c), number (n) and gender (g). The syntax below enforces the match.

```
*DUAL
=a_modifier/modifies
        2:adj adj_string 1:noun & 1.c = 2.c & 1.n = 2.n & 1.g = 2.g
        1:noun 2:adj & 1.c = 2.c & 1.n = 2.n & 1.g = 2.g
```

A 120-million-word Czech corpus, morphosyntactically tagged and automatically disambiguated, has been loaded into the Sketch Engine. Word-sketch patterns have been defined in an iterative process, starting from English-inspired patterns and adding more and more language-specific clauses. We have generated sketches for the 8875 most frequent Czech words; all those that occurred more than 1000 times in the corpus.

4   THESAURUS

A large set of grammatical relation instances is a rich representation of the lexicon of the language. We can go beyond looking at the behaviour of words one-headword-at-a-time, and use it to show patterns across groups of words.

In particular, when we find the pair of grammatical relation instances <*object, drink, beer*>, <*object, drink, wine*> we can use it as one piece of evidence for *beer* and *wine* being in the same thesaurus category. Here, we are building on a tradition of automatic thesaurus building that goes back to Karen Sparck Jones's thesis in the 1960s (republished as Sparck Jones 1986) and takes in Grefenstette (1994b) and Lin (1998). The Sketch Engine builds a thesaurus, in the form of a set of "nearest neighbours" for each word, using the mathematics for computing similarity as presented by Lin. The thesaurus developed in this way from the BNC is presented in Kilgarriff (2003b) and is available to view and to use at http://sketchengine.co.uk.

5   SKETCH DIFFERENCES

When viewing a thesaurus entry, one repeatedly wonders "what makes those words so similar?", or indeed, "how do those words differ?" We are in a position to answer this question well. The similarity was based on the "shared triples" (as *beer* and *wine* "share" the triple *<obj, drink, ?>*. What two words have in common are the shared triples that have high salience for both words. The difference between two near-synonyms can be identified as the triples which have high salience for one word, but no occurrences (or low salience) for the other. In the same way that we produced a one-page summary as a word sketch, here we can produce a one-page summary as a sketch difference.

A pair of near-synonyms we explored using the first prototype sketch difference engine were English adjectives *clever* and *intelligent* (see Table 3). The contrast between the words was immediately apparent. Whereas to call someone intelligent is straightforwardly complimentary, if we call them clever, we may well be implying they are a "clever dick" or "too clever for their own good". *Clever*, but not *intelligent*, is often found conjoined with *cunning* or preceded by *bloody*, or modifying *swine* or *bastard*.

We also observe a phenomenon which has been striking in all our thesaurus work: long words tend to go with long words, and short ones with short. *Intelligent* appears to be at home in text types with many long words, whereas *clever* is to be found in less formal genres, amongst shorter words.

We believe the sketch differences provide useful summaries for researchers interested in how pairs of near-synonyms differ.

6   EVALUATION OF CZECH WORD SKETCHES

The goal for the Czech word sketches was to explore whether it might be possible to substitute standard lexicographic corpus searching by examining only the sketches. We randomly chose 50 words and compared automatically generated sketches with the information given by the biggest two Czech dictionaries (*Slovník spisovné ceštiny* and *Spisovném slovníku jazyka ceského*).

Only eight entries contained data that could not be worked directly from the generated sketches. (Idioms in the dictionary were excluded from our comparison here). Moreover, all these cases were generalizations of basic senses that could not be found easily in the corpus and that would probably be missed even with detailed corpus searching. We believe that such results justify future Czech lexicographic projects based on word sketches for the description of the core of the language.

7   AVAILABILITY, WEB SERVICES

The Sketch Engine is available as a commercial product. It is implemented in C++ and Python. It is designed for use over the web, with a server holding the data and queries issued to the server from a web browser, and with the browser presenting query results. At the time of writing, corpora of Czech, Irish and English have been loaded into the Sketch Engine. The

TABLE 3 Sketch difference for *clever* (*adj*) and *intelligent* (*adj*)

Correspondence of clever (a) with intelligent (a)

Shared Patterns

andor			
witty	13.7	6	12
resourceful	12.0	4	3
ambitious	10.6	7	6
quick	10.2	8	7
amusing	9.9	6	2
well-read	9.9	2	2
articulate	9.8	2	15
modifies			
girl	16.3	74	11
boy	15.7	71	7
man	14.3	56	68
use	10.5	18	15
chap	10.2	10	1
people	9.5	28	62
woman	8.7	22	36
subject			
he	9.5	98	49
modifier			
incredibly	5.3	5	3

"Clever (a)" patterns

adj_comp			modifies		
box	3.3	4	dick	4.7	15
get	2.7	15	trick	4.4	21
andor			clog	4.1	9
little	3.8	22	idea	4.1	30
cunning	3.2	5	folly	3.9	10
bloody	2.6	7	chap	3.7	10
subtle	2.5	4	ploy	3.6	7
modifier			boy	3.4	71
very	5.6	278	lawyer	3.2	8
too	4.4	83	bastard	3.0	7
fiendishly	3.2	5	pass	3.0	7
extraordinarily	2.5	6	girl	3.0	74
subject			pun	3.0	4
you	4.4	85	swine	3.0	4
boxing	3.7	7	piece	2.9	9
			fellow	2.9	6
			thing	2.8	17
			lass	2.8	4
			move	2.8	8
			Hans	2.7	3

"Intelligent (a)" patterns

andor			modifies		
sensitive	4.7	27	being	4.6	34
adaptive	3.0	5	hub	4.4	14
attractive	2.9	9	life	4.0	28
alert	2.7	5	network	4.0	18
honest	2.6	7	conversation	3.7	13
articulate	2.5	15	person	3.6	18
educated	2.5	4	system	3.6	35
cultured	2.5	3	robotic	3.3	4
thinking	2.5	6	electronics	3.0	5
energetic	2.5	4	behaviour	3.0	10
delightful	2.5	4	robot	2.8	4
human	2.5	12	modem	2.7	3
dedicated	2.5	4	subsystem	2.7	3
tutoring	2.5	2	lifeform	2.6	2
modifier			animal	2.6	7
highly	4.9	66	plug	2.5	3
obviously	2.8	8	**subject**		
			she	3.4	30
			humm	2.8	4

authors are willing to host clients' corpora on their specialist server, and to work with clients on the data preparation.

8   FUTURE PLANS

1. The software does not yet properly support lexicographic research into multi-word items. When investigating, for example, English phrasal verbs, one would like to explore the grammatical relations and collocations that the phrasal unit entered into. Currently, this is supported only indirectly and minimally. We plan to allow a user to explore a multi-word item (provided it is captured as a grammatical relation triple) as follows. Let us take the English phrasal verb *make up* and assume it is captured as the triple *<following prep, make, up>*.

The lexicographer first calls up the word sketch for *make* and finds *up* amongst the collocates in the *following prep* list. They select that preposition and request a word sketch for the triple. The sketch engine then identifies all instances of *make* and *up* occurring in *<following prep, make, up>*, finds what other grammatical relations those instances participate in, and summarizes them in a new "multiword sketch".

2. The sketch difference currently contrasts two related words. A comparable task is to look at the same word, in different sets of texts, for example contrasting the use of a word in texts from one era and another, or in written and spoken texts, or in "original" texts and in translations. We plan to extend sketch difference functionality to make comparisons based on different subcorpora possible.

21

The Future of Linguistics and Lexicographers: Will there be Lexicographers in the Year 3000?

GREGORY GREFENSTETTE*

I   INTRODUCTION

Lexicology has been posed as a science ever since the 18th century. In the article *Grammaire* from Diderot and D'Alembert's Encyclopedia, lexicology is described as the explanation of three aspects of knowledge about each of the words from a language: its Material, its Value, and its Etymology. The Material is described as how a given word is put together: the syllables that compose it, how it is pronounced. The Value of a word is divided into three parts: the fundamental sense (proper or figurative), the specific sense (now called the part-of-speech), and the accidental sense (morphological variants of the word). The Etymology concerns the rules by which new words are formed, as well as the historical sources of a word interesting as an aid to understanding the word's current meaning. Lexicology dealt with words taken in isolation, while syntax concerned words in the context of other words. The section ends: *"Tels sont les points de vue fondamentaux auxquels on peut rapporter les principes de la Lexicologie. C'est aux dictionnaires de chaque langue à marquer sur chacun des mots qu'ils renferment, les décisions propres de l'usage, relatives à ces points de vue."*

Looking at modern dictionaries, we find that lexicographers in every language have taken these words to heart. The same principles are found in today's dictionary entries. The Material is presented in a word's spelling, pronunciation, and syllabification. The Etymology is often covered by a succinct presentation of the word's origins. Two of the three parts of the word's Value, the part-of-speech and special morphological variants, are almost invariably included in the entry. The remaining point of view on a word, a description of the fundamental sense, composes the meat of the dictionary entry, and, to mix the culinary metaphor, is the bread-and-butter of the lexicographer.

In this paper I discuss what help the field of Computational Linguistics will bring to this task of describing the fundamental meaning of a word, and how the tools that will foreseeably be developed in this field may radically alter this two-hundred-year-old image of lexicographical description.

* Grefenstette, G. (1998). 'The future of linguistics and lexicographers: will there be lexicographers in the year 3000?', in Fontenelle, T., Hiligsmann, P., Michiels, A., Moulin, A., and Theissen, S. (eds.), *Proceedings of the Eighth EURALEX Congress*. Liège: University of Liège, 25–41.

2   LINGUISTICS, COMPUTATIONAL LINGUISTICS,
AND APPROXIMATE LINGUISTICS

It is clear that one of the things that a computer can do well is treat a large amount of data, and that, with more and more text becoming available online, there is a lot of data with which a computer could work.[1] What is not clear is why Linguistics and, more recently and more blamably, Computational Linguistics have been so slow in providing adequate computer tools for aiding lexicographers in their task of describing word meaning.

Linguists used to be polyglots who were able to cite and qualitatively compare lexical and grammatical similarities and differences between languages. The systems that were devised in this old school of Linguistics mixed semantics, history, phonetics, into rules that were comprehensible to humans but not formally specifiable.

The idea of mathematical or computational linguistics appeared after the advent of the computer and following the mathematical classification of formal languages that Chomsky (1956) produced. There was a certain heady glory in the idea that man's languages could be reducible to mathematical principles, now implementable in such calculating machines as were only a dream in Pascal's time. This computational idea was new, exciting, and à propos as Universities grew and were restructured during the academic buildup of the 1960s. Purveyed by these new, young linguists, the idea that all languages were merely variations on a set of formal principles, and that discovery of the parametric settings for each principle might be determined, became the dominant theory in Linguistics and in Linguistics departments. Poor working lexicographers, with their down-to-earth questions about one particular language's vocabulary, were left in the dust as the linguists of the new generation pursued the more glorious goal of uniting the world's languages.

By the end of the 1980s two conflicting schools of computational linguistics were sharing the stage: the universal grammar school of Chomskian linguistics, and the no-grammar school of corpus linguistics. Here, if the reader permits, I will digress into a metaphorical comparison of these schools, inspired by Umberto Eco's comparison of the pre-Windows worlds of the DOS and of the Macintosh to Protestantism and Catholicism.[2] In my metaphor, one can map the Chomsky-inspired school to the communist ideology; and the corpus-based school, of which the late IBM research (Brown *et al.* 1992) was the most flamingly brilliant example, to pure capitalism.

The communist ideology is firmly anchored in the belief that there is a unifying logic underlying human life, a logic that can be understood, a logic of which one can tease the thesis and anti-thesis from objective historical events by the power of reason. Understanding this logic leads to perceiving the communist ideal, the final classless unity to which humankind is tending in its spiraling crises of production and revolution. In the same Utopian vein, we find

---

[1] For example, the AltaVista web browser has encountered the word *the* 1.4 billion times in its latest monthly trawl of the Internet. With its frequency of about 1 per 7 English words, we can roughly estimate that there are 10 billion English words to be computationally digested on the Web pages accessible through AltaVista. The words are certainly there, accessible for lexicographical study, in this large distributed corpus.

[2] See http://www.pcuf.fi/~pjt/pink/catholic-mac.html. Here is an excerpt: "The fact is that the world is divided between users of the Macintosh computer and users of MS-DOS compatible computers. I am firmly of the opinion that the Macintosh is Catholic and that DOS is Protestant. Indeed, the Macintosh is counter-reformist and has been influenced by the 'ratio studiorum' of the Jesuits. It is cheerful, friendly, conciliatory, it tells the faithful how they must proceed step by step to reach – if not the Kingdom of Heaven – the moment in which their document is printed. It is catechistic: the essence of revelation is dealt with via simple formulae and sumptuous icons. Everyone has a right to salvation. DOS is Protestant, or even Calvinistic. It allows free interpretation of scripture, demands difficult personal decisions, imposes a subtle hermeneutics upon the user, and takes for granted the idea that not all can reach salvation. To make the system work you need to interpret the program yourself: a long way from the baroque community of revelers, the user is closed within the loneliness of his own inner torment."

the linguistic endeavor to understand the underlying parameters whose discovery will render the masses of languages simply variations of one universal language. The Chomskian linguist is out there, searching for truth among the conflict. Not concerned by the trivial, quotidian of languages, the Chomskian is looking for hidden currents, running through history and cultures, because their discovery will solve the divisions, and bring about the golden age. On the darker side, we find the same fanaticism concerning the unadulterated truth of the believer's path. Just as factions among the far left (and the far right) are violently opposed to deviance from their party line, we find a plethora of acronyms (GB, HPSG, CG, LFG...), covering groups who ostracize and disparage their philosophical neighbors.[3]

The competing school of corpus linguists can be compared to pure capitalism in that they feel that the market (corpus) has its own self-defining logic (Adam Smith's *the Invisible Hand of God*) that should not be impeded by outside theories. Contrary to the Chomskian school, motivated by the goal of making all languages one, the corpus linguistic approach is undirected, taking an empirical approach of "seeing what is in the corpus." It is concerned with maximizing what can profitably be extracted from the corpus, and in this sense, in order to increase its gains, its market must continually expand, encompassing ever larger corpora.

What is needed is a middle way between these two extremes of laissez-faire and linguistic *dirigisme*, that is, a recognition that there is some structure in text that can be recognized by machines, and that this recognition can be done in a useful way before the final goal of ultimate language unity is achieved. This middle linguistic ground is somewhat like the social-democratic approach of Western Europe: not theoretically pure, but containing a smattering of principles; recognizing market forces, but ready to stick a political hand into the market. In lexicography, this approach has been attempted by a few computer scientists, such as Kenneth Church,[4] who has taken the time to sit and watch eminent lexicographers at work, seeing

---

[3] Ivan Sag raged against the hubris of the Chomskians in a 1993 interview (http://www.let.uu.nl/~Anne-Marie.Mineur/personal/Ta/Sag.html) in which he bemoaned that GB (Government & Binding) practitioners "can simply condemn a whole tradition to irrelevance, like Relational Grammar, whose systematizations of complex grammatical systems constitute to my mind a long-lasting and significant contribution to the field of syntax. It is an anti-intellectual attitude, and in fact I think it is dangerous for the entire field of linguistics." He complained that GB "also has heresy – essentially what everyone else in linguistics does, not to mention the work on language done in other fields, e.g. psychology or computer science." Bob Carpenter, in a 1995 interview (http://www.let.uu.nl/~Anne-Marie.Mineur/personal/Ta/Carpenter.html), describes the theoretical correctness that this school of Linguistics searches for: "I really hated HPSG (Pollard and Sag 1987) at that time, because to me it looked like a complete Frankenstein theory. Not because it is built up from all these other grammar formalisms, like LFG and GPSG and CG and all that, but I had a real bias against the fact that it was using different sorts of mechanisms to do everything. You can look at Categorial Grammar, and you can say there is a pure logical reasoning mechanism on which everything is based. But in HPSG that uniformity comes only at the level of the feature structure logic. It is important not to confuse the kind of underlying attribute-value logic formalism with the linguistic theory. In HPSG there is this whole linguistic theory that contains things like the Head Feature Principle and the Quantifier Binding Condition and Principle A of the Binding Theory. That is the linguistic theory. HPSG should not be criticized on the fact that it is based on a Turing-powerful constraint resolution system. You just cannot do in the linguistic theory, everything you can do in the underlying theory. Shieber originally pointed this out in the context of PATR." He continues with a description of how none of the theories propounded in this linguistic school are aimed at producing anything practical for NLP: "Now of course no linguistic theory, GB, HPSG, any of these, have really laid out a meta-theory of what really counts as a grammar. You will never find anybody saying: 'A GB grammar is the following thing: one of these versions of this, one of these versions of that.' They talk about it that way, they say it is somehow parameterized, but you never actually see a list of parameters. No one can make a proposal so that someone will stand up in the audience and say: 'Ah, but that is not a GB grammar!' Similarly, I could add a bunch of features and devices to HPSG and no one could say: 'That is not HPSG.' You can say that it is not in the spirit of HPSG, or not in the spirit of GB, but it is really all just a matter of esthetics. So I think insofar as people really want to make theories of a universal grammar, then they should be honest and lay out the possible grammars. Again, GPSG perhaps came the closest to this goal in spirit, but it didn't really excite many linguists. Once you lay something out concretely, it's just a little too easy to see where it falls down."

[4] See the description of his invited talk to the European Association of Computational Linguistics in 1993 at http://www.let.uu.nl/~Anne-Marie.Mineur/personal/Ta/Church.html.

what parts of their task might be readily computerizable, using a "combination of data and theory." Lexicographers such as Jeremy Clear (1994) have also explored this middle ground, attacking their real problems of lexicography, particularly the search for a description of words' fundamental meanings, with the computer.

This middle approach can be named *approximate linguistics*. Not perfect, but not bad. Until now, the use of computer parsers in lexicography has been considered limited by the unavailability of swift, robust parsers with which to process large corpora of naturally occurring texts. This dearth of practical parsers can be explained by the aptitude of linguists to consider the inability to properly treat the least counter-example as a fundamental flaw in a parser, so, they consider, no parser can yet be proposed; it has also been sustained by the highly publicized belief in the all-computational camp that no parser is needed, since statistics can find any structure in a large enough corpus. Bridging these two extremes, approximate linguistics is based on the idea that higher linguistic analyses such as those to be produced by perfect full-sentence parsing, can be represented more or less faithfully by imperfect systems, that the accuracy of the approximations produced by these systems can be measured, and that the approximations can be successively refined by incremental improvements to the system to reduce error to desired proportions. In the next sections I illustrate an approximate linguistics approach to a lexicographical problem, showing both how the desired answers become clearer and clearer as more linguistic knowledge is injected into the system, and how one higher level linguistic analysis can be approximated by lower level functions.

3   APPROXIMATE LINGUISTICS AND LEXICOGRAPHY

One of the principal tasks of lexicography, as stated above, is to describe the fundamental sense of a given word. Currently, a lexicographer does this by seeing how the word is ordinarily used in the language, calling upon intuition or upon corpus citations (Kilgarriff 1992: 51). When a corpus is being used, the idea of ordinary use shifts somewhat, becoming quantifiable. How a word is ordinarily used in a corpus brings in the idea of frequency, how often a word is used in a certain way, and the idea of relative frequency, how often it is being used one way as opposed to another. Now, having shifted the problem of fundamental meaning to ordinary meaning to a process involving counting, let us see how the computer enters the picture.

We can observe that the computer is very good at counting, but unfortunately not very good at knowing *what* to count. Contrary to what a small child can do, a computer can only count things which are made to look exactly alike. One programming task, then, involved in making language-related things countable by computer, is transforming them, abstracting away surface differences between two variant manifestations of the same phenomenon until the computer can see them as the same string of characters, of zeroes and ones in the same pattern. This is actually one of the aims of a complete parser: to produce a unique internal structure so that different sentences, even in different languages (Butt *et al.* 1999), can be matched, compared, and counted by a computer. Until such parsers become widely available, the abstraction process provided by them can be approximated using existing technology involving lesser text-processing means, by approximate linguistics. The successfulness of these approximations depends, as we will see, on the amount of linguistic information included in the technology.

3.1   Abstraction levels and approximate linguistic tools

If one thinks of the process of abstracting away surface differences in text as a linguistic process, then one can consider that there is a continuum of abstraction levels between the original text and the completely parsed version (whatever that might be) of a text. In the first steps of computer treatment of text, converting physically printed text into an electronic form, some meaning-carrying aspects of the text are regularly abstracted away. The meaning carried by differences in fonts, in type size, and in page layout often disappears in the electronic ASCII version of a text. For corpus analysis, this loss of information carries the advantage that the computer can now compare two strings of characters in an electronic corpus, rather than comparing pixel equalities, in order to determine whether the two words are the same. This first level of text abstraction requires linguistic information, either on the part of the person who retyped in the text and who was able to correctly recognize each letter, or by the optical character reading program, programs which commonly contain character-level language models.

Here are some other more evident linguistically-informed levels of abstraction which erase surface differences in words:

- tokenization – deciding where to find the boundaries of the objects to be compared,
- lemmatization – conflating inflected forms of words to normalized lemmas,
- part-of-speech tagging – abstracting away from individual words to grammatical classes of words,
- shallow parsing – abstracting away from positional information to syntactic function,
- semantic tagging – abstracting away from individual words to semantic classes.

Each of these tasks can be attacked more or less successfully with different computer tools. The tools used for one level can be stretched to perform tasks on a higher level. Just as when one only has one tool, like a screwdriver, one uses it as a hammer, a knife, or whatever is needed, so one can make do with unadapted computer tools to perform linguistic tasks. To illustrate what different levels of abstraction can provide to the lexicographer using current technology, let us consider a typical lexicographic problem. Suppose that the lexicographer has a large corpus of English text, and is working on the fundamental meaning of the word *check*. More precisely, suppose that she is currently looking for the typical arguments of the verb *check*, an interesting example since the verbal and nominal forms of the word are written the same: to *write a check*, to *check*. Further suppose that, in order to grasp the ordinary senses for *check*, she is looking for the common direct objects (what can be *checked*) and the common objects of prepositional adjuncts (e.g., what can be *checked for*) of the verb *check*. If a full parser existed that could treat the entire corpus, one might then parse the corpus and the results of the parser would indicate these common arguments with precision. In the next few sections, I show what different levels of abstraction, made possible by incrementally more complicated linguistic tools, provide as an answer to this task. We shall see that simple tools provide an answer, but the answers become clearer as more linguistic knowledge is added, and as the approximations more accurately approach the goal of complete parsing.

3.2   Tokenization as an approximation to parsing

In this task of finding common arguments of a word, tokenization is the simplest tool that can be used to approximate parsing. Tokenization defines the boundaries of the units that will be counted by the computer, and allows us to recognize contiguous but separate units. In printed languages which use spaces, the techniques of tokenization usually involve using regular expressions to describe contexts where the input string needs to be separated into units (Karttunen *et al.* 1996). Since tokenization is a well-known problem in computer science, being an inherent part of computer language compiler construction, many computer-based tools have been developed that can be used for tokenizing, e.g. *lex*, *awk*, and *perl*.[5] A tokenizer for a natural human language contains simple linguistic information about how words are formed in that language: what characters are letters, what characters are numbers, what characters are punctuation, what elements of punctuation can appear within a word (like the apostrophe or the hyphen in English.) The more linguistic information the tokenizer has access to, the better the results (Grefenstette and Tapanainen 1994).

As a first approach to our lexicographical problem, we can process our corpus in the following way: whenever the token *check* appears we store the next three tokens that occur in the input. This simple heuristic is based on the rudimentary linguistic knowledge that English verbal arguments and adjuncts generally occur shortly after the verb, so this three-token window is where we are likely to find the arguments we want. Once we have gone through the whole corpus, we count each occurrence of each token found in this small window, and then sort the tokens according to frequency. The computer is good at this counting and sorting. This same heuristic is similar to that used by practicing lexicographers visually scanning right-sorted KWIC (Key Word In Context) files for regularities. Table 1 shows the most common tokens extracted using this windowing technique for the token *check* over the British National Corpus.[6] (Here, even for this simple task, we can use different levels of approximation. The simplest tokenizer just splits words on spaces. The first three columns in Table 1 use this space-only approach. The last column uses a slightly more informed tokenizer integrating English word-structure knowledge to divide the input text into separate tokens.) The first column gives the most frequent tokens found in this three-word window, with their frequency. This list is not very interesting for finding the direct objects and objects of prepositional adjuncts of *check*. We find *check it* and *check this* but this does not tell us very much about what the typical arguments of the verb *check* are. There is interesting information about *check* nonetheless: we find that the most likely prepositions associated with *check* are *on*, *of*, *out*, *with*, and that *check* seems to subcategorize for subclauses introduced by *that* and *whether*. This is interesting, but not what we were looking for. One improvement to this simple approach is found in subsequent columns from which are removed a list of common function words, called stopwords in the Information Retrieval community. Stopword lists[7] are comprised of personal pronouns, articles, prepositions, conjunctions, etc., the closed-class function words of the language. For English such a list runs to about one hundred words. Of course, such a list can be counted as a slight injection of linguistic knowledge into the system. Filtering out such words provides a much cleaner list using this simple three-word window technique. Column two in Table 1 shows a more plausible list of common objects of *check*: *lists, things, progress, details, accuracy…*

Column three introduces a minor linguistic fact, i.e. that upper and lower case distinctions do not affect meaning inordinately in English, since such typographical variations can appear

---

[5] See the following websites for free versions of these tools: http://www.cs.columbia.edu/~royr/tools.html, http://w4.lns.cornell.edu/public/compdoc/info/gawk/gawk_1, http://www-cgi.cs.cmu.edu/cgi-bin/perl-man.

[6] The British National Corpus (BNC) is a 100 million word collection of samples of written and spoken language from a wide range of sources, designed to represent a wide cross-section of current British English, both spoken and written. See http://info.ox.ac.uk:80/bnc/. A version of this corpus, retagged using Xerox taggers (http://www.xrce.xerox.com/research/mltt/Tools/pos.html) was used for this paper.

[7] Available via FTP in the directory /pub/med/smart/ at ftp.cs.cornell.edu.

TABLE I Finding and counting the three words appearing after the token *check* in order to find the arguments of the verb *check*

Space-only		No Stopwords		No Case Distinction		Tokenizer	
1753	the	55	list	65	list	92	list
722	that	24	make	30	carefully	40	carefully
620	on	23	things	29	local	34	progress
398	and	22	carefully	26	make	28	things
336	of	21	progress	24	things	28	local
317	out	21	local	24	details	28	details
281	with	20	details	21	progress	25	price
272	for	19	own	21	price	25	make
257	your	19	accuracy	21	erm	25	lists
242	it	18	blood	20	own	24	accuracy
217	to	16	new	20	new	21	facts
195	in	16	made	20	back	21	erm
185	is	16	back	19	lists	21	balance
180	a	15	time	19	accuracy	21	back
172	you	15	spelling	18	time	20	water
152	whether	15	facts	18	blood	20	spelling
131	if	14	sure	17	spelling	20	own
122	all	14	lists	17	made	20	number
120	their	14	information	17	level	20	new
116	.	14	erm	17	facts	20	made
112	up	14	ensure	17	ensure	19	information
112	his	13	water	16	water	18	action
104	this	11	validity	16	number	17	shirt
99	before	11	suit	15	sure	17	level
90	they	11	quality	15	information	17	increase
89	are	11	points	15	balance	17	ensure
84	at	11	list,	14	increase	17	doctor
81	what	11	doctor	14	doctor	17	blood
80	by	11	data	14	correct	16	work
79	I	11	actual	13	work	16	time

Columns 1 to 3 use just spaces to find tokens. Column 4 uses a linguistically motivated tokenizer for English. Stopwords (closed-class words) are removed from columns 2 to 4. Columns 3 and 4 ignore case distinctions. As more linguistic information is added, the lists present the possible arguments more cleanly and more completely. Note: *erm* comes from the recorded speech in the BNC.

in headers, or in quoted speech. The input corpus for columns three and four has been transliterated into lower case, so we find more instances of both *check* as well as its possible arguments.

The final refinement shown in Table 1 is the result of using a proper English tokenizer and not just spaces to separate words. We see that the count for *checking a list* rises to 92 from column two's 55 count, since now we find cases where periods, commas, and parenthesis were stuck to *list*, effectively hiding it from our computer which could not recognize in column two that the two strings *list* and *list)* [with a postpended parenthesis] were the same word. What we see in the four columns of Table 1 are that little injections of linguistic knowledge make the lexicographer's task easier, by making surface differences disappear. These little improvements become especially evident as we go further down the list. For example, we see that *check . . . shirt* appears whereas in the simpler approaches we would have had to scan further down the list to find it.

The results seem rather noisy, and require a certain patience and habit in order to extract any information. One can derive even from this noisy data that *details* and *prices* seem to be common arguments of *check*. But the confusion between nominal forms and verbal forms renders speculative any conjectures about whether *number* is a common argument of the verb *check* or whether it appears in a common noun phrase such as *check number*. In addition to confusing verbal and nominal forms of *check*, Table 1 ignores variant verbal forms of *check*. The next level of linguistic refinement, lemmatization, addresses this problem.

3.3   Adding morphological analysis and lemmatization to the approximation

A next level of linguistic sophistication, beyond tokenizers and lists of function words, is the ability to morphologically analyze and to lemmatize surface forms of words into some canonical form, for example, masculine singular for nouns, or an infinitive form for verbs. This requires the linguistic resources of a lexicon and an analyzer, but thanks to the efforts of computational linguists and lexicographers (Karttunen 1983; Chanod 1994) over recent years, these basic resources are becoming available in more and more languages.[8]

The last column of Table 2 shows the lemmas found after the lemmatized forms of the word *check*. We can approximate a lemmatizer, tediously, by explicitly detailing the forms we are looking at, such as are given in the first four columns of Table 2. The fifth column accumulates all four forms into one total column. The lemma-derived list in the sixth column is not all that very different at first glance from the fifth column, yet we have included a relatively expensive resource, a morphological analyzer and lemmatizer, in the process. In fact, the greatest difference comes in the numbers. Thus, in the same corpus, after lemmatization, the number of recognized instances of *check . . . spelling* grows from 27 to 39. This growth comes from the fact that the lemmatizer allows the computer to match variants such as *check my spellings* and *checked my spelling* to a single form *check . . . spelling*, abstracting away morphological variation and intervening words within the window. The number of recognized instances of the desired phenomena grows as more linguistic information is added. Since the number of recognized instances grows, we can consider rarer phenomena. The morphological analysis and lemmatization, by abstracting away differences, improves the counts of the data.

Another advantage provided by a lemmatizer that returns the possible parts of speech as well as the lemmas, is that one can start to reason in terms of part-of-speech as well as in terms of strings. For example, one finds the most common prepositions in this window of three words after any form of the word *check* to be those given in Table 3. We will see the usefulness of this abstraction to part-of-speech as well as the improvement in recognition due to the abstraction derived from lemmatization in the next section.

3.4   Adding part-of-speech tagging to the approximation

Table 2 shows a confusion between verbal and nominal uses of *check*. In order to distinguish these uses when the surface form is *check* used as a noun or *check* used as a verb, we can supplement the tokenizer, morphological analyzer and lemmatizer, with one additional

---

[8] See http://www.xrce.xerox.com/research/mltt/Tools/morph.html for online morphological analyzers for most Western European languages.

TABLE 2   Approximating a lemmatizer by explicitly listing forms

checking	*checked*	*checks*	*check*	*check, -ed, -s,-ing*	*lemmas*
17 watch	71 watch	58 balances	92 list	107 list	137 list
11 time	18 ensure	45 made	40 carefully	95 watch	118 make
10 records	17 hotel	21 carried	34 progress	67 made	98 watch
8 checking	16 carefully	7 performed	28 things	62 carefully	83 balance
7 stock	15 regularly	7 ensure	28 local	61 balances	62 carefully
7 progress	14 time	7 controls	28 details	49 make	57 number
7 erm	14 shirt	6 three	25 price	47 progress	51 ensure
7 back	14 checked	6 new	25 make	45 ensure	47 progress
6 times	13 number	6 make	25 lists	41 time	46 detail
6 quality	12 using	6 checks	24 accuracy	41 number	45 record
6 procedure	12 sure	6 built	21 facts	40 local	45 level
6 number	12 make	5 people	21 erm	37 things	44 shirt
6 make	11 list	5 gas	21 balance	37 back	44 price
6 local	9 three	5 files	21 back	36 erm	43 use
6 information	9 state	5 credit	20 water	36 carried	42 thing
6 facts	9 records	5 car	20 spelling	35 records	41 time
6 accounts	8 room	4 work	20 own	34 information	40 local
5 understanding	7 yesterday	4 traders	20 number	34 details	40 carry
5 system	7 times	4 take	20 new	34 accuracy	39 spelling
5 supplies	7 shirts	4 successful	20 made	33 new	38 car
5 purposes	7 rechecked	4 required	19 information	31 shirt	37 back
5 possible	7 pulse	4 regularly	18 action	31 facts	36 work
5 people	7 information	4 patients	17 shirt	29 regularly	36 erm
5 old	7 file	4 levels	17 level	28 water	34 information
5 notes	7 car	4 going	17 increase	28 sure	34 file
5 names	7 approved	4 data	17 ensure	28 price	34 accuracy
5 movements	6 tables	4 cracks	17 doctor	28 lists	33 new
5 items	6 street	4 black	17 blood	28 car	33 fact
5 claims	6 statistical	4 appliances	16 work	27 times	32 name

Columns 1 to 4 show the tokens appearing within 3 words after various forms of *check*. Column 5 unions these lists. The last column gives the lemmas after any form of the lemma *check*. This last treatment finds more corpus samples.

linguistic tool: a part-of-speech disambiguator.[9] Part-of-speech taggers have been around for thirty years, based on hand-written rules and statistics, attaining correct tag rates of 95% to 99% according to the languages (Karlsson *et al.* 1995; Schiller 1996). Using such a tool is important for our problem since the identical nominal and verbal forms are both frequent. On top of the linguistic information contained in morphological analyzers and lemmatizers about word forms, part-of-speech taggers contain models of word sequences to be found in the language. These models are either derived from introspection by linguists, or from a training set of manually tagged text (Church 1988). Using this linguistic tool allows us to further

[9] The Common Lisp source for version 1.2 of the Xerox part-of-speech tagger is available for anonymous FTP from parcftp.xerox.com in the file pub/tagger/tagger-1-2.tar.Z. Another freely available English tagger, developed by Eric Brill (http://www.cs.jhu.edu/~brill), uses rules based on surface strings and tags.

TABLE 3   Prepositions in a three-word window after the lemma *check* in the British National Corpus

instances	preposition
1050	on
652	for
619	of
582	with
507	to

approximate perfect parsing, since now we can distinguish between verbal and nominal uses of *check* and look for arguments of the verb.

The first column of Table 4 shows the results of applying the three-word, window-based, parsing approximation technique to verbal uses of *check*, and enables us to consider, if we wish, only nominal arguments to the verb. Here the solution to our original problem becomes even clearer. We see that one checks watches, the time, progress; details, lists, records, files; names, information, the car, levels, spelling, etc. From this list of potential arguments we see that some of the words appearing in the last column of Table 3, which came from a lemmatizer

TABLE 4   Once we can use a part-of-speech tagger with the morphological analyzer and lemmatizer, rarer phenomena can be more accurately counted. We can specify what nouns appear after the verbal use of *check* in column 1. In Columns 2 and 3, we can find nouns appearing after certain prepositions after verbal uses of *check*. This additional tool provides a closer approximation to full parsing

Nouns after check ...		nouns found after check ... on ...		nouns found after check ... for ...	
97	watch	28	progress	21	sign
51	time	12	movement	14	error
44	number	11	thing	12	accuracy
43	progress	11	number	11	leak
37	record	9	file	11	damage
35	detail	8	use	10	check
33	thing	8	time	8	consistency
33	list	8	quality	7	time
32	accuracy	8	people	7	possible
31	fact	8	level	7	level
30	check	8	activity	7	correct
29	level	7	make	5	square
29	information	7	car	5	pulse
27	name	6	record	5	free
27	date	6	performance	5	flight
27	car	6	material	5	fingerprint
25	hotel	6	health	5	detail
23	work	6	gas	5	crack
23	spelling	6	child	4	wear
22	file	6	calculator	4	virus

without a part-of-speech tagger, disappear. For example, *balance* is no longer present. This is because *balance* is almost exclusively found in the nominal expression *checks and balances*. The additional linguistic processing refines the search.

This additional tool allows us to more accurately consider more specific and rarer phenomena. The second and third columns of Table 4 show the nouns appearing in a window of three words after the most common prepositions found in Table 3, *on* and *for*, themselves appearing within three words of a verbal use of *check*. From this, the lexicographer can be led to discover common uses involving prepositions: *check on progress/performance*, *check on car/gas/health/child*, or *check for damage/wear/crack*, etc. These samples are relatively rare in the corpus, and would have been farther down the list in Tables 1 and 2 where they would have been swamped in noise, but here as the approximations to full linguistic analysis improve, they become evident.

3.5   Shallow parsing as an approximation to full parsing

As the previous sections have shown, some aspects of syntax can be approximated by simple position information, i.e. the window appearing after the word being examined. We have been supposing that words appearing in this window probably play some role as an argument. Other words appearing in the window are abstracted away so that different surface configurations can be made to look equal for the computer.

A further linguistic refinement that can be applied is to use regular patterns of the tags provided by the part-of-speech disambiguator to partially recreate the syntactic structure of the sentence. Recognizing nominal chains and verbal chains as sequences of part-of-speech tags allows us to recognize certain syntactic relations, such as government of a noun by a preposition, or the voice of a verbal chain. This classification allows us to further pinpoint possible objects and prepositional arguments while eliminating others. This area of computational linguistics (Debili 1982; Abney 1991; Grefenstette 1994b; Ait-Mokhtar and Chanod 1997) is gaining more attention and more respect as work progresses on creating such low-level parsers in a number of languages. Using such a low-level syntactic pattern extractor (Grefenstette 1998) built using finite-state regular expressions and transducers, we can analyze the corpus at a higher level of abstraction.

Table 5 shows the improvement in the data that the shallow parser tool gives over the lower-level 3-word window approximation for the pattern *check...with....* As before, the lists become cleaner as noise becomes more properly eliminated. One can see, in the first column, that in the corpus people *check with* their bosses, editors, and banks. This shallow parsing information can be used to extract the corresponding KWIC lines automatically for the lexicographer, as shown in Table 6.

Table 7 shows the lemmas identified as direct objects that are extracted using a low-level parser over the same BNC corpus used throughout this presentation. Though noise persists, as is the case with all the previous approximations to full linguistic parsing, the lists produced are more precise. In both columns of Table 7, there is much overlap with the most frequent cases, but the focusing power of adding more linguistic knowledge appears more clearly at the end of the list where one discovers only with the low-level parser that one can *check symptoms, signs, shoes, security*. These lemmas would also appear further down the list of the second column but they would be swamped in the noise there and be harder to discern.

TABLE 5 Comparing results returned with a shallow parser to those returned by a window-based approximation to parsing

parsed check ... with ...		3 words after check ... with ...	
20	office	19	local
8	doctor	19	doctor
7	authority	13	office
5	agent	12	level
4	number	9	spirit
4	manager	7	bank
4	detector	6	manager
4	company	6	erm
4	bank	6	company
3	staff	6	check
3	police	6	authority
3	hotel	5	travel
3	editor	5	police
3	consulate	5	agent
3	centre	4	time
3	boss	4	radio
3	association	4	parent
2	time	4	own
2	thermometer	4	manufacturer
2	test	4	language

The initial problem of finding arguments for the verb *check* has been treated with a sequence of increasingly sophisticated linguistic tools: from tokenizers, to eliminating a list of stopwords, to morphological analyzers and lemmatizers, to part-of-speech disambiguators, and finally to low-level parsers. The results obtained in Tables 1 to 7 show a gradual focusing in which more noise is eliminated and in which more infrequent phenomena are brought to light as more linguistic information is incorporated into the process.

3.6   Semantic tags

One further linguistic refinement, this time using the WordNet thesaurus as a linguistic resource (Miller *et al.* 1990 – see also in this volume, *Ed.*), is shown in Table 8. This table shows the semantic tags associated with each of the most frequent direct objects recognized for *check*. Semantic tags are not as well defined as grammatical tags where the classes are more constrained and better understood (Bolinger 1965). Ideally, a semantic part-of-speech tagger would use context, as a grammatical part-of-speech tagger does, in order to choose the most likely tag. This research area has had limited success (Segond *et al.* 1997), impeded by a lack of semantic dictionaries and due to the fact that the problem is no longer one of simple structure but also of meaning.

The only conclusion to be drawn from Table 8 is that the direct object of *check* is likely to be something classified as a *communication* or an *artifact*, but the meanings of these semantic tags are not very clear in themselves.

TABLE 6 KWIC lines associated with *check...with* (*bank* or *editor* or *boss*) returned by the shallow parser

shops and other establishments abroad	check with your bank for details .
So it is essential to	check with your travel agent or bank on
No, cheque - but it 's good - Josh	checked with the bank, called Hnatiuk
this was a good idea but would have to	check with his immediate boss
Universe editor Anne Noels	checked with bosses about the ban in
It is sensible, however, to	check with editors of really specialist
On being told by the manager to	check with the bank, he pretended to
Then, posing as a relative, she	checked with the editor .
She	checked with all the contributing editors
with drivers stranded in France	checking in with their boss.

TABLE 7   Parsing vs. Window

80	watch		92	list
44	number		84	check
33	record		40	carefully
33	detail		34	progress
30	time		28	things
30	item		28	local
30	fact		28	details
29	level		25	price
29	date		25	make
27	accuracy		25	lists
24	list		24	accuracy
22	work		21	facts
...	...		...	...
17	condition		17	ensure
17	answer		17	doctor
16	story		17	blood
16	room		16	work
...	...		...	...
4	symptom		5	vehicle
4	structure		5	various
4	string		5	use
4	status		5	ups
4	slide		5	trading
4	sign		5	traders
4	shoe		5	table
4	setting		5	supplier
4	security		5	suitability
4	seal		5	still

Looking for direct object collocates of *check*. The first column shows nouns extracted as direct objects by a low-level parser, the second column shows words within a window of three words after *check*. In the first column, we see that noise coming from prepositional objects (*check with doctor*), and noise coming from non-recognition of structure (*check your blood pressure*) which clutter the list supplied with the simpler approximation, disappears from the first column. Even much further down the list, one can capture rarer but true arguments more often with the shallow parser.

4   EXTRAPOLATION TO THE FUTURE

So far, I have presented the historical argument that the main task of the lexicographer is to describe the usual meanings of the words in a language. I have also argued that classical linguistics (1956–present) has not been supplying the tools necessary for this task because it has been concentrating on the universal (universal grammar formalisms or universal statistical techniques) and not on the everyday routine. Springing up, and gaining weight in computational linguistics, are techniques that can be called approximate linguistics, i.e.

TABLE 8 The WordNet semantic tags associated with the most common direct objects of a verbal form of *check*

direct object of *check*		WordNet semantic tags associated with word
80	watch	act, artifact, time
44	number	attribute, artifact, communication, group, quantity
33	record	act, communication, possession, quantity
33	detail	cognition, communication, group, relation
30	time	Tops, event, time
30	item	artifact, communication
30	fact	cognition, state, communication
29	level	attribute, artifact
29	date	person, group, food, time
27	accuracy	attribute
24	list	communication
22	work	act, artifact, phenomenon
22	thing	attribute, act, artifact, cognition, communication, event, feeling, state
22	spelling	communication
22	position	act, attribute, cognition, location
22	name	communication, person, group, state
22	file	artifact, communication, group
20	shirt	artifact
20	result	event
19	pressure	attribute, cognition, phenomenon
18	progress	act, event
18	figure	act, attribute, artifact, cognition, shape, possession, communication
18	car	artifact
17	price	attribute, communication, possession
17	information	cognition, communication
17	equipment	artifact
17	condition	communication, state
17	answer	act, communication
16	story	communication
16	room	artifact, group, quantity, state

The semantic tags *communication* (16 of 31 words) and *artifact* (12 of 31) appear most frequently. Choosing between the semantic tags using context is a problem akin to part-of-speech disambiguation, but on a much larger scale, as the ambiguity of words is greater than with grammatical tags, and because there are many more potential semantic tags than grammatical ones.

approximations to linguistic theory that are both incrementally perfectible as well as being robust and immediately useful.

The previous section gives a hint of what approximate linguistics can offer working lexicographers today in their task of describing some fundamental sense of a word. Though the tools used there have not all been packaged as a shrink-wrapped product with lively colors and series of ergonomic pull-down menus, all the tools exist today from a variety of resource providers and in a variety of languages: corpora, tokenizers, morphological analyzers and lemmatizers, part-of-speech taggers, shallow parsers, and assorted bookkeeping tools which count, sort, calculate co-occurrence statistics (mutual information, t-scores, etc.), and so on. These tools allow the lexicographer to see what words co-occur with a given word, to examine what syntactic structures the word occurs in, what other words enter into what syntactic relations with the word and how often, and to retrieve all the corpus lines corresponding to any of these configurations.

Let us return to the question of corpus size, which is one of the major aspects of the theory-less corpus linguistics approach. All the tables and charts in this paper were derived from the 100-million-word British National Corpus. In this large corpus, the lemma *check* appears about 13,000 times. This great number of occurrences allows us to aid our imaginary lexicographer by showing the common arguments of the word *check* as a verb. With little linguistic information, e.g. stopwords, we already get some answers; as more linguistic information is added to the system, the results become clearer, and rarer phenomena can be considered, as can be seen at the bottom of the first column of Table 7. As an example of how more complex structures become rarer, in our Xerox-parsed version of the BNC, there are 4854 instances of *check* with a direct object; when we consider prepositional adjuncts, a structure that involves three words: the verb *check*, a preposition, and the object of the preposition, there are 2893 cases; when we consider the more specific structure of prepositional adjuncts to *check* beginning with the preposition *with*, there are only 417 cases (see Table 5). In true Zipfian fashion, the more complicated the structure, the rarer it is. The rarer something is, the more text you need to find it reliably. Now, on the AltaVista Web browser in Spring of 1998, there were 13 million indexed occurrences of a form of *check,* one thousand times more data than was used for the data appearing in this presentation. The data is there for extracting all the information one might want about a word in more and more complicated patterns.

Will we need lexicographers in the future? What are lexicographers needed for now? According to Adam Kilgarriff (1992), the ideal lexicographer must (i) gather a corpus of citations for a given word, (ii) divide the citations into clusters, (iii) decide why the cluster members belong together, and (iv) code their conclusions into a dictionary definition. As for the first two steps, we can easily predict that approximations to proper parsing that computational linguistics can provide will become more and more accurate, that the structures that will be recognized will be more and more complex, that the corpus to which the techniques will have access will be bigger and bigger, and that more and more usage patterns of words can be extracted from this text corpus. The computer will have better numbers to count with, to cluster with, to separate with. This leaves the rational steps of three and four, synthesizing and explaining. Synthesizing means finding a higher level description of the things found in certain positions. Table 8, the WordNet semantic abstractions, shows that this goal is far from being satisfied. It is something that humans are eminently good at, but machines still poor. Explaining what makes a cluster coherent in a way understandable for a human is beyond the scope of a computer. It means drawing distinctions and contrasts between shared experiences and expectations, explaining what makes this group different from other groups that the human user knows. In this sense, that of providing shortcuts to understanding to other users, a lexicographer will always be needed.

Yet it might also happen that lexicographers may be needed less and less for some of the tasks that they spend much time on now. What if end-users had access to clustered and filtered KWIC lines when they wondered how a word was used? What if the computer was able to analyze any word in context, extract all the patterns that the word was found in, cluster them in a coherent way,[10] and display these further examples succinctly for the user? For translation dictionaries, for knowing the patterns that words appear in, with what preposition, what if patterns were able to be pre-digested and scanned by the user, could they induce meaning from these examples? Would the user need a human-supplied explanation? I believe that in the coming years we shall see a new way of looking at the lexicon that is no longer

---

[10] See the lexicons derived by the DECIDE project and cited in Grefenstette *et al.* (1996).

two-dimensional: a list of words, and their explanations, but rather three and four and five dimensional in which information is stored about how each word is used with each other word, and how that pair of words is used with a third word, and that triple with a fourth word. This vision requires massive data structures and robust linguistic-approximation tools to fill them, and a new way of sifting and handling this data. It also requires a lot of disk space, but this, contrary to the space requirements that governed paper dictionaries, is now the least of our concerns when we remain in the electronic world.

But paper still has a long life in front of itself, and as long as things are printed we will need the reasoned condensations that only lexicographers provide.

PART XI

On Semantic Networks and Wordnets

22

Introduction to WordNet: An On-line Lexical Database[1]

GEORGE A. MILLER, RICHARD BECKWITH,
CHRISTIANE FELLBAUM, DEREK GROSS,
AND KATHERINE J. MILLER*

I INTRODUCTION

Standard alphabetical procedures for organizing lexical information put together words that are spelled alike and scatter words with similar or related meanings haphazardly through the list. Unfortunately, there is no obvious alternative, no other simple way for lexicographers to keep track of what has been done or for readers to find the word they are looking for. But a frequent objection to this solution is that finding things on an alphabetical list can be tedious and time-consuming. Many people who would like to refer to a dictionary decide not to bother with it because finding the information would interrupt their work and break their train of thought.

In this age of computers, however, there is an answer to that complaint. One obvious reason to resort to on-line dictionaries – lexical databases that can be read by computers – is that computers can search such alphabetical lists much faster than people can. A dictionary entry can be available as soon as the target word is selected or typed into the keyboard. Moreover, since dictionaries are printed from tapes that are read by computers, it is a relatively simple matter to convert those tapes into the appropriate kind of lexical database. Putting conventional dictionaries on line seems a simple and natural marriage of the old and the new.

Once computers are enlisted in the service of dictionary users, however, it quickly becomes apparent that it is grossly inefficient to use these powerful machines as little more than rapid page-turners. The challenge is to think what further use to make of them. WordNet is a proposal for a more effective combination of traditional lexicographic information and modern high-speed computation.

* Miller, G, Beckwith, R., Fellbaum, C., Gross, D., and Miller, K. (1990). 'Introduction to WordNet: an on-line lexical database', *International Journal of Lexicography*, 3(4): 235–244. Reproduced with permission of Oxford University Press.

[1] Preparation of these five papers was supported in part by contract N00014-86-K-0492 with the Office of Naval Research and in part by a grant from the James S. McDonnell Foundation. The work on WordNet was done in collaboration with Amalia Bachman, Marie Bienkowski, Patrick Byrnes, Roger Chaffin, George Collier, Michael Colon, Melanie Cook, Fiona Cowie, Brian Gustafson, P. N. Johnson-Laird, Yana Kane, Judy Kegl, Benjamin Martin, Elana Messer, Antonio Romero, Daniel Teibel, Anton Vishio, Pamela Wakefield, and Benjamin Wilkes. The views and conclusions contained herein are those of the authors and should not be represented as official policies of ONR, the McDonnell Foundation, or Princeton University.

Correspondence concerning these papers should be addressed to George A. Miller, Department of Psychology, Princeton University, Princeton, NJ 08544-1010.

This, and the accompanying four papers,* is a detailed report of the state of WordNet as of 1990. In order to reduce the unnecessary repetition, the papers are written to be read consecutively.

2 PSYCHOLEXICOLOGY

Murray's *Oxford English Dictionary* (1928) was compiled "on historical principles" and no one doubts the value of the *OED* in settling issues of word use or sense priority. By focussing on historical (diachronic) evidence, however, the *OED*, like other standard dictionaries, neglected questions concerning the synchronic organization of lexical knowledge.

It is now possible to envision ways in which the omission might be repaired. The 20th Century has seen the emergence of psycholinguistics, an interdisciplinary field of research concerned with the cognitive bases of linguistic competence. Both linguists and psycholinguists have explored in considerable depth the factors determining the contemporary (synchronic) structure of linguistic knowledge in general, and lexical knowledge in particular – Miller and Johnson-Laird (1976) have proposed that research concerned with the lexical component of language should be called psycholexicology. As linguistic theories evolved in recent decades, linguists became increasingly explicit about the information a lexicon must contain in order for the phonological, syntactic, and lexical components to work together in the everyday production and comprehension of linguistic messages, and those proposals have been incorporated into the work of psycholinguists. Beginning with word association studies at the turn of the century and continuing down to the sophisticated experimental tasks of the past twenty years, psycholinguists have discovered many synchronic properties of the mental lexicon that can be exploited in lexicography.

In 1985 a group of psychologists and linguists at Princeton University undertook to develop a lexical database along lines suggested by these investigations (Miller, 1985). The initial idea was to provide an aid to use in searching dictionaries conceptually, rather than merely alphabetically – it was to be used in close conjunction with an on-line dictionary of the conventional type. As the work proceeded, however, it demanded a more ambitious formulation of its own principles and goals. WordNet is the result. Inasmuch as it instantiates hypotheses based on results of psycholinguistic research, WordNet can be said to be a dictionary based on psycholinguistic principles.

How the leading psycholinguistic theories should be exploited for this project was not always obvious. Unfortunately, most research of interest for psycholexicology has dealt with relatively small samples of the English lexicon, often concentrating on nouns at the expense of other parts of speech. All too often, an interesting hypothesis is put forward, fifty or a hundred words illustrating it are considered, and extension to the rest of the lexicon is left as an exercise for the reader. One motive for developing WordNet was to expose such hypotheses to the full range of the common vocabulary. WordNet presently contains approximately 54,000 different lexical entries organized into some 48,000 sets of synonyms (Beckwith, Fellbaum, Gross, and Miller, 1990), and only the most robust hypotheses have survived.

The most obvious difference between WordNet and a standard dictionary is that WordNet divides the lexicon into four categories: nouns, verbs, modifiers, and function words. Actually, WordNet contains only nouns, verbs, and adjectives. Adverbs are omitted on the assumption that most of them merely duplicate adjectives; the relatively small set of English function

---

*Miller (1990b), Gross and Miller (1990), Fellbaum (1990) and Beckwith and Miller (1990) are not included in this volume. They are available in the Special Issue of the *International Journal of Lexicography* devoted to WordNet (Winter 1990) – *Ed.*

words is omitted on the assumption (supported by observations of the speech of aphasic patients: Garrett, 1982) that they are probably stored separately as part of the syntactic component of language. The realization that syntactic categories differ in subjective organization emerged first from studies of word associations. Fillenbaum and Jones (1965), for example, asked English-speaking subjects to give the first word they thought of in response to highly familiar words drawn from different syntactic categories. The modal response category was the same as the category of the probe word: noun probes elicited noun responses 79% of the time, adjectives elicited adjectives 65% of the time, and verbs elicited verbs 43% of the time. Since grammatical speech requires a speaker to know (at least implicitly) the syntactic privileges of different words, it is not surprising that such information would be readily available. How it is learned, however, is more of a puzzle: it is rare in connected discourse for adjacent words to be from the same syntactic category, so Fillenbaum and Jones's data cannot be explained as association by contiguity.

The price of imposing this syntactic categorization on WordNet is a certain amount of redundancy that conventional dictionaries avoid – words like *back,* for example, turn up in more than one category. But the advantage is that fundamental differences in the semantic organization of these syntactic categories can be clearly seen and systematically exploited. As will become clear from the papers following this one, nouns are organized in lexical memory as topical hierarchies, adjectives are organized as N-dimensional hyperspaces, and verbs are organized by a variety of entailment relations. Each of these lexical structures reflects a different way of categorizing experience; attempts to impose a single organizing principle on all three would badly misrepresent the psychological complexity of lexical knowledge.

The most ambitious feature of WordNet, however, is its attempt to organize lexical information in terms of word meanings, rather than word forms. In that respect, WordNet resembles a thesaurus more than a dictionary, and, in fact, Laurence Urdang's revision of Rodale's *The Synonym Finder* (1978) and Robert L. Chapman's revision of *Roget's International Thesaurus* (1977) have been helpful tools in putting WordNet together. But neither of those excellent works is well suited to the printed form. The problem with an alphabetical thesaurus is redundant entries: if word W_x and word W_y are synonyms, the pair should be entered twice, once alphabetized under W_x and again alphabetized under W_y. The problem with a topical thesaurus is that two look-ups are required, first on an alphabetical list and again in the thesaurus proper, thus doubling a user's search time. These are, of course, precisely the kind of mechanical chores that a computer can perform rapidly and efficiently.

WordNet is not merely an on-line thesaurus, however. In order to appreciate what more has been attempted in WordNet, it is necessary to understand its basic design (Miller and Fellbaum, 1991).

3   THE LEXICAL MATRIX

Lexical semantics begins with a recognition that a word is a conventional association between a lexicalized concept and an utterance that plays a syntactic role. This definition of "word" raises at least three classes of problems for research. First, what kinds of utterances enter into these lexical associations? Second, what is the nature and organization of the lexicalized concepts that words can express? Third, what syntactic roles do different words play? Although it is impossible to ignore any of these questions while considering only one, the emphasis here will be on the second class of problems, those dealing with the semantic structure of the English lexicon.

TABLE I   Illustrating the concept of a lexical matrix: F_1 and F_2 are synonyms; F_2 is polysemous.

Word Meanings	Word Forms						
	F_1	F_2	F_3	.	.	.	F_n
M_1	$E_{1,1}$	$E_{1,2}$					
M_2		$E_{2,2}$					
M_3			$E_{3,3}$				
.				.			
.					.		
.						.	
M_m							$E_{m,n}$

Since the word "word" is commonly used to refer both to the utterance and to its associated concept, discussions of this lexical association are vulnerable to terminological confusion. In order to reduce ambiguity, therefore, "word form" will be used here to refer to the physical utterance or inscription and "word meaning" to refer to the lexicalized concept that a form can be used to express. Then the starting point for lexical semantics can be said to be the mapping between forms and meanings (Miller, 1986). A conservative initial assumption is that different syntactic categories of words may have different kinds of mappings.

Table I is offered simply to make the notion of a lexical matrix concrete. Word forms are imagined to be listed as headings for the columns; word meanings as headings for the rows. An entry in a cell of the matrix implies that the form in that column can be used (in an appropriate context) to express the meaning in that row. Thus, entry $E_{1,1}$ implies that word form F_1 can be used to express word meaning M_1. If there are two entries in the same column, the word form is polysemous; if there are two entries in the same row, the two word forms are synonyms (relative to a context).

Mappings between forms and meanings are many:many – some forms have several different meanings, and some meanings can be expressed by several different forms. Two difficult problems of lexicography, polysemy and synonymy, can be viewed as complementary aspects of this mapping. That is to say, polysemy and synonymy are problems that arise in the course of gaining access to information in the mental lexicon: a listener or reader who recognizes a form must cope with its polysemy; a speaker or writer who hopes to express a meaning must decide between synonyms.

As a parenthetical comment, it should be noted that psycholinguists frequently represent their hypotheses about language processing by box-and-arrow diagrams. In that notation, a lexical matrix could be represented by two boxes with arrows going between them in both directions. One box would be labeled "Word Meaning" and the other "Word Form"; arrows would indicate that a language user could start with a meaning and look for appropriate forms to express it, or could start with a form and retrieve appropriate meanings. This box-and-arrow representation makes clear the difference between meaning:meaning relations (in the Word Meaning box) and word:word relations (in the Word Form box). In its initial conception, WordNet was concerned solely with the pattern of semantic relations between lexicalized concepts; that is to say, it was to be a theory of the Word Meaning box. As work proceeded, however, it became increasingly clear that lexical relations in the Word Form box could not be ignored. At present, WordNet distinguishes sharply between semantic relations and lexical relations; the emphasis is still on semantic relations between meanings, but lexical relations between words are also included.

Although the box-and-arrow representation respects the difference between these two kinds of relations, it has the disadvantage that the intricate details of the many:many mappings between meanings and forms are slighted, which not only conceals the reciprocity of polysemy and synonymy, but also obscures the major device used in WordNet to represent meanings. For that reason, this description of WordNet has been introduced in terms of a lexical matrix, rather than as a box-and-arrow diagram.

How are word meanings represented in WordNet? In order to simulate a lexical matrix it is necessary to have some way to represent both forms and meanings in a computer. Inscriptions can provide a reasonably satisfactory solution for the forms, but how meanings should be represented poses a critical question for any theory of lexical semantics. Lacking an adequate psychological theory, methods developed by lexicographers can provide an interim solution: definitions can play the same role in a simulation that meanings play in the mind of a language user.

How lexicalized concepts are to be represented by definitions in a theory of lexical semantics depends on whether the theory is intended to be constructive or merely differential. In a constructive theory, the representation should contain sufficient information to support an accurate construction of the concept (by either a person or a machine). The requirements of a constructive theory are not easily met, and there is some reason to believe that the definitions found in most standard dictionaries do not meet them (Gross, Kegl, Gildea, and Miller, 1989; Miller and Gildea, 1987). In a differential theory, on the other hand, meanings can be represented by any symbols that enable a theorist to distinguish among them. The requirements for a differential theory are more modest, yet suffice for the construction of the desired mappings. If the person who reads the definition has already acquired the concept and needs merely to identify it, then a synonym (or near synonym) is often sufficient. In other words, the word meaning M_1 in Table 1 can be represented by simply listing the word forms that can be used to express it: $\{F_1, F_2, \ldots\}$. (Here and later, the curly brackets, "{" and "}", surround the sets of synonyms that serve as identifying definitions of lexicalized concepts.) For example, someone who knows that *board* can signify either a piece of lumber or a group of people assembled for some purpose will be able to pick out the intended sense with no more help than *plank* or *committee*. The synonym sets, {*board, plank*} and {*board, committee*} can serve as unambiguous designators of these two meanings of *board*. These synonym sets (synsets) do not explain what the concepts are; they merely signify that the concepts exist. People who know English are assumed to have already acquired the concepts, and are expected to recognize them from the words listed in the synset.

A lexical matrix, therefore, can be represented for theoretical purposes by a mapping between written words and synsets. Since English is rich in synonyms, synsets are often sufficient for differential purposes. Sometimes, however, an appropriate synonym is not available, in which case the polysemy can be resolved by a short gloss, e.g., {*board*, (a person's meals, provided regularly for money)} can serve to differentiate this sense of *board* from the others; it can be regarded as a synset with a single member. The gloss is not intended for use in constructing a new lexical concept by someone not already familiar with it, and it differs from a synonym in that it is not used to gain access to information stored in the mental lexicon. It fulfills its purpose if it enables the user of WordNet, who is assumed to know English, to differentiate this sense from others with which it could be confused.

Synonymy is, of course, a lexical relation between word forms, but because it is assigned this central role in WordNet, a notational distinction is made between words related by synonymy, which are enclosed in curly brackets, "{" and "}", and other lexical relations, which will be enclosed in square brackets, "[" and "]". Semantic relations are indicated by pointers.

WordNet is organized by semantic relations. Since a semantic relation is a relation between meanings, and since meanings can be represented by synsets, it is natural to think of semantic relations as pointers between synsets. It is characteristic of semantic relations that they are reciprocated: if there is a semantic relation R between meaning $\{x, x', \ldots\}$ and meaning $\{y, y', \ldots\}$, then there is also a relation R' between $\{y, y', \ldots\}$ and $\{x, x', \ldots\}$. For the purposes of the present discussion, the names of the semantic relations will serve a dual role: if the relation between the meanings $\{x, x', \ldots\}$ and $\{y, y', \ldots\}$ is called R, then R will also be used to designate the relation between individual word forms belonging to those synsets. It might be logically tidier to introduce separate terms for the relation between meanings and for the relation between forms, but even greater confusion might result from the introduction of so many new technical terms.

The following examples illustrate (but do not exhaust) the kinds of relations used to create WordNet.

4   SYNONYMY

From what has already been said, it should be obvious that the most important relation for WordNet is similarity of meaning, since the ability to judge that relation between word forms is a prerequisite for the representation of meanings in a lexical matrix. According to one definition (usually attributed to Leibniz) two expressions are synonymous if the substitution of one for the other never changes the truth value of a sentence in which the substitution is made. By that definition, true synonyms are rare, if they exist at all. A weakened version of this definition would make synonymy relative to a context: two expressions are synonymous in a linguistic context C if the substitution of one for the other in C does not alter the truth value. For example, the substitution of *plank* for *board* will seldom alter truth values in carpentry contexts, although there are other contexts of *board* where that substitution would be totally inappropriate.

Note that the definition of synonymy in terms of substitutability makes it necessary to partition WordNet into nouns, adjectives, and verbs. That is to say, if concepts are represented by synsets, and if synonyms must be interchangeable, then words in different syntactic categories cannot be synonyms (cannot form synsets) because they are not interchangeable. Nouns form nominal concepts, adjectives form adjectival concepts, verbs form verbal concepts. In other words, the use of synsets to represent word meanings is consistent with psycholinguistic evidence that nouns, verbs, and modifiers are organized independently in semantic memory. An argument might be made in favor of still further partitions: some words in the same syntactic category (particularly verbs) express very similar concepts, yet cannot be interchanged without making the sentence ungrammatical.

The definition of synonymy in terms of truth values seems to make synonymy a discrete matter: two words either are synonyms or they are not. But as some philosophers have argued, and most psychologists accept without considering the alternative, synonymy is best thought of as one end of a continuum along which similarity of meaning can be graded. It is probably the case that semantically similar words can be interchanged in more contexts than can semantically dissimilar words. But the important point here is that theories of lexical semantics do not depend on truth-functional conceptions of meaning; semantic similarity is sufficient. It is convenient to assume that the relation is symmetric: if x is similar to y, then y is equally similar to x.

The gradability of semantic similarity is ubiquitous, but it is most important for understanding the organization of adjectival meanings.

5   ANTONYMY

Another familiar relation is antonymy, which turns out to be surprisingly difficult to define. The antonym of a word x is sometimes *not-x*, but not always. For example, *rich* and *poor* are antonyms, but to say that someone is not rich does not imply that they must be poor; many people consider themselves neither rich nor poor. Antonymy, which seems to be a simple symmetric relation, is actually quite complex, yet speakers of English have little difficulty recognizing antonyms when they see them.

Antonymy is a lexical relation between word forms, not a semantic relation between word meanings. For example, the meanings {*rise, ascend*} and {*fall, descend*} may be conceptual opposites, but they are not antonyms; [*rise/fall*] are antonyms and so are [*ascend/descend*], but most people hesitate and look thoughtful when asked if *rise* and *descend*, or *ascend* and *fall*, are antonyms. Such facts make apparent the need to distinguish clearly between lexical relations between word forms and semantic relations between word meanings. Antonymy provides the central organizing principle for the adjectives in WordNet, and the complications that arise from the fact that antonymy is a lexical relation with important semantic consequences are better discussed in that context (Gross and Miller, 1990).

6   HYPONYMY

Unlike synonymy and antonymy, which are lexical relations between word forms, hyponymy/hypernymy is a semantic relation between word meanings: e.g., {*maple*} is a hyponym of {*tree*}, and {*tree*} is a hyponym of {*plant*}. Much attention has been devoted to hyponymy/hypernymy (variously called subordination/superordination, subset/superset, or the ISA relation). A concept represented by the synset $\{x, x', \dots\}$ is said to be a hyponym of the concept represented by the synset $\{y, y', \dots\}$ if native speakers of English accept sentences constructed from such frames as *An x is a (kind of) y*. The relation can be represented by including in $\{x, x', \dots\}$ a pointer to its superordinate, and including in $\{y, y', \dots\}$ pointers to its hyponyms.

Hyponymy is transitive and asymmetrical (Lyons, 1977, vol. 1), and, since there is normally a single superordinate, it generates a hierarchical semantic structure, in which a hyponym is said to be below its superordinate. Such hierarchical representations are widely used in the construction of information retrieval systems, where they are called inheritance systems (Touretzky, 1986): a hyponym inherits all the features of the more generic concept and adds at least one feature that distinguishes it from its superordinate and from any other hyponyms of that superordinate. For example, *maple* inherits the features of its superordinate, *tree*, but is distinguished from other trees by the hardness of its wood, the shape of its leaves, the use of its sap for syrup, etc. This convention provides the central organizing principle for the nouns in WordNet.

7   MERONYMY

Synonymy, antonymy, and hyponymy are familiar relations. They apply widely throughout the lexicon and people do not need special training in linguistics in order to appreciate them.

Another relation sharing these advantages – a semantic relation – is the part–whole (or HASA) relation, known to lexical semanticists as meronymy/holonymy. A concept represented by the synset $\{x, x', \dots\}$ is a meronym of a concept represented by the synset $\{y, y', \dots\}$ if native speakers of English accept sentences constructed from such frames as *A y has an x (as a part)* or *An x is a part of y.* The meronymic relation is transitive (with qualifications) and asymmetrical (Cruse, 1986), and can be used to construct a part hierarchy (with some reservations, since a meronym can have many holonyms). It will be assumed that the concept of a part of a whole can be a part of a concept of the whole, although it is recognized that the implications of this assumption deserve more discussion than they will receive here.

These and other similar relations serve to organize the mental lexicon. They can be represented in WordNet by parenthetical groupings or by pointers (labeled arcs) from one synset to another. These relations represent associations that form a complex network; knowing where a word is situated in that network is an important part of knowing the word's meaning. It is not profitable to discuss these relations in the abstract, however, because they play different roles in organizing the lexical knowledge associated with different syntactic categories.

8   MORPHOLOGICAL RELATIONS

An important class of lexical relations are the morphological relations between word forms. Initially, interest was limited to semantic relations; no plans were made to include morphological relations in WordNet. As work progressed, however, two facts became increasingly obvious: (1) synonymy and antonymy are lexical relations between word forms, not semantic relations between word meanings, and (2) if WordNet was to be of any practical use to anyone, it would have to deal with inflectional morphology. For example, if someone put the computer's cursor on the word *trees* and clicked a request for information, WordNet would reply that the word was not in the database. A program was needed to strip off the plural suffix and then to look up *tree*, which certainly is in the database.

Although the inflectional morphology of English is relatively simple, writing a computer program to deal with it proved to be a more complex task than had been expected. Verbs are the major problem, of course, since there are four forms and many irregular verbs. But the software has been written and is presently available as part of the interface between the lexical database and the user. In the course of this development it became obvious that programs dealing with derivational morphology would greatly enhance the value of WordNet, but that more ambitious project has not yet been undertaken.

The three papers following this introduction have little to say about lexical relations resulting from inflectional morphology, since those relations are incorporated in the interface to WordNet, not in the central database.

PART XII
On Dictionary Use

23

Monitoring Dictionary Use

B. T. S. ATKINS AND KRISTA VARANTOLA *

I   SETTING THE STUDY IN CONTEXT

There are two direct routes to more effective dictionary use: the first is to radically improve the dictionary; the second is to radically improve the users. If we are to do either of these things – and obviously we should try to do both – the *sine qua non* of any action is a very detailed knowledge of how people use dictionaries at present. What do people actually do when they use a dictionary in the privacy of their own home? At the moment, we have no way of discovering this: dictionary use is a highly individual activity. We know from our own experience that the main steps include deciding which entry to look up, searching the entry for the information needed (usually not consciously articulated at this point), and either selecting what one hopes is the correct information, or moving on to another entry, perhaps in another dictionary. Yet there are many aspects of our use of dictionaries that we cannot describe in any detail. What kind of information do we usually look for? How do we decide where to look for it? What strategies do we adopt when the dictionary does not tell us exactly what we want to know?

A number of projects have had as their goal to add to the facts known about how people use dictionaries. Béjoint (1981, 1988, and 1989) discusses from the language teacher's perspective the way in which language students use dictionaries, and the skills they require if they are to do this effectively. Hatherall (1984) also studies the way in which students use dictionaries, and applies the knowledge gained to make some proposals about the contents and format of dictionary entries and about skills required by dictionary users. Hartmann (1989) discusses *inter alia* a taxonomy of dictionary reference acts and offers a flowchart for lexical look-up strategies.

Meara and English (1988) report on their use of a corpus of lexical errors in an attempt – supported by the Longman Group – at an analysis of the effectiveness of a learners' dictionary, the Longman Dictionary of Contemporary English. Bogaards's studies (Bogaards 1990 and 1992) describe various strategies employed by dictionary users in their search for multi-word expressions in bilingual dictionaries. Mitchell (1983a) analyses potential difficulties in using a dictionary, and offers a series of "assessment units" designed to help identify the aspects of dictionary use that school students find difficult; subsequently (Mitchell 1983b) she reports the findings from school trials of five of the assessment units. Laufer and Melamed (1994) examine monolingual, bilingual, and "bilingualized" dictionaries from the point of view of how effective these are, for what purposes and for what type of users.

The EURALEX and AILA Research Project into Dictionary Use described in Atkins *et al.* (1987), Atkins and Knowles (1990), and Atkins and Varantola (1998), consisted of a study of

* Atkins, B.T.S., and Varantola, K. (1997). 'Monitoring dictionary use', *International Journal of Lexicography*, 10(1): 1–45. Reproduced with permission of Oxford University Press.

dictionary use by many different types of user in four linguistic communities. It concentrated on the effectiveness of dictionary use and the factors which contribute to this, and made it clear that while it was possible to tell when someone had taken the correct information from a dictionary, and when they had not, it was not possible to know how this came about. Further research was needed into what people actually do when they consult a dictionary.

1.1   The EURALEX Workshop on Dictionary Use (Oxford 1991)

This paper reports primarily on a methodology devised to record just that: what people do when they consult a dictionary. We give a detailed account of the process of monitoring dictionary use, and include the documents devised for this purpose, and describe the data gathered by this means. Looking at some questions to which answers are needed if the true process of dictionary consultation is to be described, we draw on the results of two applications of the methodology, one at the EURALEX Workshop on Dictionary Use held in Oxford in September 1991[1] and the other carried out by Varantola among students of translation at the Department of Translation Studies, University of Tampere, in the spring of 1993. Atkins and Varantola (1992) and Varantola and Atkins (1993) gave preliminary reports on this work. The methodology was subsequently applied in a third study carried out by Kristen Mackintosh under the supervision of Ingrid Meyer at the University of Ottawa, and described in Mackintosh's MA thesis.

Our aim was to monitor the dictionary look-up process in as natural a situation as possible. In other words, we wanted to find out what people really do when they use a dictionary to solve a linguistic problem, in this case when trying to translate a text either out of or into their native language. Our study, then, is a first attempt to look at this very complex process in some detail. It is the paper equivalent of the "think-aloud" protocol discussed in, for instance, Krings (1986). The "paper approach" adopted in the present study not only facilitated the collection of similar information from a much larger group of people, but also structured the information in such a way as to allow it to be collated in an electronic database.

We tried to record step by step what went on when people turned to a dictionary for help with a problem of translation. We did not attempt to discover in these experiments how "successful" the look-ups were, by rating the choices made as correct or incorrect, as in normal circumstances dictionary users translating into a foreign language rarely know immediately whether they have got the correct solution. However, they often know if they feel satisfied with the information they got. For our purposes, then, it was appropriate to record the level of user satisfaction after each search.

Since our focus was on the strategies of dictionary use and not on the dictionary users' skills in translation, we did not ask the participants to produce a written translation, simply to look up any expressions they felt were necessary to allow them to translate the passage. We set no targets for completion, and few participants went through the whole text: most concentrated on a thorough preparation of a relatively short passage. The participants worked in pairs, one

[1] We want to thank all those who contributed to the EURALEX Oxford workshop: those who helped to organize it, particularly Oxford University Press who provided secretarial facilities and on whose premises it was held; the participants; the publishers who generously donated the dictionaries which were used there; and Henri Béjoint and his students at Université Lyon-Lumière for help with devising the forms and testing the prototypes. Our thanks go too to the Tampere students who carried out the second experiment, to Patricia Thomas for providing additional data, and to John Atkins for comments on an earlier version of this paper and valued help with its production. Finally, we are grateful for the meticulous constructive comments which we received from Robert Ilson and from our two, formerly anonymous, reviewers, Hilary Nesi and Ingrid Meyer, and one still anonymous statistician-reviewer. Any errors, misinterpretations, and infelicities which remain are entirely our own.

partner using dictionaries, and the other recording every step of this activity on forms designed for this purpose. The data so gathered was keyed into a database held in dBaseIII Plus; it was subsequently transferred into a Reflex database for ease of cross-tabulation. The unrepresentative nature of the participants group (there were no naive dictionary users amongst them) means that the data tells us, not about how the average dictionary user behaves, but how the skilled dictionary user solves problems. However, the database, which records details of 1,000 dictionary look-ups made by 103 people, throws up a number of extremely interesting questions both for teachers of dictionary skills and for lexicographers, by revealing individual strategies for handling frustrating situations. We show how the methodology described in this paper may be used to provide answers to some basic questions about dictionary use, including:

- how did people consult dictionaries?
- what kind of information were the users looking for?
- what was the most helpful component in the dictionary entry?
- did the users find what they were looking for?
- were people satisfied with what they got?
- what did people do when frustrated?
- when did people choose to use an L2 monolingual dictionary?

2   METHODOLOGY

The database which will be queried later in this paper records the results of studying the two groups mentioned above, which we shall call the Oxford group and the Tampere group. Before describing the methodology applied, it is appropriate to set these two studies in context.

The 71 Oxford Workshop participants were all experienced dictionary users, many of them lexicographers: 38 people had English as their mother tongue (L1), six German, five Danish, five French, three Norwegian, three Spanish, two Dutch, two Swedish, and one each Czech, Hungarian, Italian, Korean, Polish, Russian, and Turkish. 34 participants assessed their command of their selected L2 as "advanced", 23 as "intermediate", 11 as "beginner", and three did not specify. They were given the choice of translating from L1 into L2 (mother tongue into foreign language) or vice versa. There were over a hundred dictionaries available for them to choose from, and they were encouraged to use as many as they wanted. They could also choose the translation text from among three texts of varying levels of difficulty (previously assessed as "easy", "intermediate", or "difficult" by experienced language teachers)[2] in any of the languages represented at the workshop. The participants were encouraged to choose an L1–L2 translation task, and one that looked difficult to them. 54 did choose an L1–L2 translation, the other 17 working from L2 into their own language. Every translation task involved English as one of the languages.

In the Tampere experiment the methodology was basically the same. The main differences were that the 32 Tampere participants were all Finnish speakers, and all using the same Finnish text and translating it into English (L1–L2). These were students following an intermediate course in L1–L2 translation. A separate group of students (following a lexicography course) acted as recorders. Six dictionaries, one two-volume bilingual and four English monolingual, were available.

---

[2] The choice was included in order to make the translation task more natural, since the participants' knowledge of the various target languages was unpredictable: had everyone used the same text the results of the study would have been just as informative, but the process would have been less enjoyable for those who took part.

The methodology described in this section is suitable for any group of participants, whatever their languages or linguistic knowledge, provided that the dictionaries are being used for the purpose of translation into or out of a foreign language. The first task of the project was to gather the minimum information about each participant that would allow a sensible assessment of the results, and a form ("Cover Sheet", in Appendix 1) was devised to record this. The participants were then divided into pairs consisting of a "dictionary user" and a "recorder"; the dictionary user selected a passage for translation, chose the dictionaries to be used, and started on the translation; the recorder recorded each step of the operation on a "Recording Sheet" (shown in Appendix 2). In preparing the recording sheets we relied heavily on our experience in teaching translation studies (Varantola) and in practical lexicography (Atkins).

2.1   The user profile: the Cover Sheet

For each dictionary user in the experiments there was a Cover Sheet, which headed the data produced by that person. This form (see Appendix 1) is almost self-explanatory.

The square in the top right hand corner, entitled "Dictionary User's Badge Number", asks for the unique identifying number which was assigned to every participant, in the form of a number on the name badge they received. The forms otherwise remained anonymous: no participant was asked for his or her name.

Question 1 asks for information about the dictionary users' mother tongue.

Question 2 asks for the users' own assessment of their level of competence (beginner, intermediate, advanced) in the L2 of their choice, regardless of whether they are performing an L1–L2 or L2–L1 translation task.

Question 3 relates to the actual translation task being performed.

Question 4 asks for information about the language of the translation passage selected; the column headed "Difficulty" refers to the three levels of assessed difficulty of the passages available.

Question 5 asks for information about all the dictionaries that were used in the course of the translation work being recorded. This was principally to allow the database to distinguish between monolingual and bilingual dictionaries. It also made it possible for the results of any particular search to be checked out against the dictionary being used; this may be followed up at a later stage, if it proves a promising avenue of research.

This form is of necessity brief: time was short, and as much as possible had to be devoted to the business of recording the steps in the look-up process. For that reason, the participants had to assess their own linguistic competence in their chosen L2, and this is rather unsatisfactory. A more objective method of assessing L2 competence would have been preferable. The research project described in Atkins and Knowles (1990) contained a one-hour "Placement Test" which all participants completed, and which allowed for an objective assessment of their competence in L2 (which for all of them was English). Lack of a common L2 made such an assessment impossible in Oxford, even had there been time. In Tampere, no such assessment was required, as the group was homogeneous: they were all students of translation studies with similar advanced linguistic skills.

Our determination to keep the Cover Sheet short[3] prevented us from eliciting other facts about the participants that might have been interesting: whether they had ever received any training in the use of dictionaries; whether they had actually used a dictionary in the past

---

[3] The research described in Atkins and Knowles (1990) elicited a much more detailed user profile.

month; whether they were professional linguists (translators, interpreters, language teachers, lexicographers etc.) or not. However, the minimalist Cover Sheet served its purpose well. The question which gave the most trouble was Question 5: many people did not manage to identify the dictionaries accurately enough for it to be clear which version (standard, concise etc.) or edition of the named dictionary was being used.

2.2 The dictionary searches: the Recording Sheets

The two Recording Sheets are shown in Appendix 2: one is for L1–L2 and the other for L2–L1. The slight difference is to be found in the options to choose from in Question 4, which relates to the reason for the look-up. These forms seek detailed information about what was going on during the use of dictionaries as a translation aid. The instructions on how to record this (the "Recorder's Notes") are included in Appendix 2.

It is important to distinguish between what was called a "look-up" and a "search". A look-up, as the word implies, designates the looking up of one entry, once, in one dictionary. Every time another headword was turned to, whether in the same dictionary or in another one, a new look-up started. The term "search" designates the group of look-ups (or single look-up) relating to one specific problem in the translation passage; a search could lead from one dictionary to another and back to the first, and all of these look-ups would be recorded as part of the same search. When a new problem was broached, a new search started.

The Recording Sheet was used to record details of a single look-up, and every look-up had its own Recording Sheet. A brief account follows of the contents of this form (see Appendix 2).

The box in the top right corner once again contains the participant's unique identification number. This is used to link in the database the two sets of data, User Profile (from the Cover Sheet) and Dictionary Use (from the Recording Sheets). The box below it holds (in the left section) the Search Number and (right section) the Look-up Letter. These are assigned in chronological order by the person recording the look-up. Thus the first search is number 1, and the first look-up of each search is A. "3B" in this box therefore indicates that the look-up being recorded on the form is the second look-up ("B") of the third search ("3") carried out by one particular participant.

Question 1 asks for a statement of the expression which made the participant go to the dictionary in the first place. Apparently no one had any problems with this question, and the information given turned out to be correct when it was checked.

In **Question 2**, the users were asked to identify the actual dictionary being used in that particular search, by the identification letter assigned to it on the Cover Sheet (A–D). When the database was keyed, the information given here was converted into a unique number identifying each individual dictionary; this also indicated whether the dictionary in question was bilingual, monolingual for learners, or monolingual for native speakers, and what the language(s) involved were.

Question 3 asks for information about the headword of the entry to which the users turned in this particular look-up.

Question 4 proved one which gave some participants problems, although the great majority answered it competently. It offers options on the reason for which they had turned to the dictionary. Was it, for example, because they simply had no idea how the expression was rendered in the other language? Or was it that they had some idea, but wanted reassurance? Another possible reason for the dictionary look-up, which applies only to a translation into a foreign language (L1–L2), was a need for information about a foreign word; this information could relate to the word's grammar, spelling, collocational options, register, style, regional variety, or other aspects of its use.

Question 4 was problematic for the recorders and participants because it gave too many alternatives to choose from; dictionary consultation is complex, and many participants (despite being asked for a single answer) gave several alternatives in their response. It would have been simpler, and the answers more informative, if this question had asked for the *principal* reason for which the dictionary was consulted.

In **Question 5**, participants were asked whether they thought they had unequivocally found what they were looking for ("Yes"); if they had some reservations about it they responded "Yes, but"; if they had not found it, they answered "No". It should be noted that no attempt was made to discover whether the participants were correct in their estimate of the situation.

Question 6 was used in an attempt to discover which (if any) component of the dictionary entry had produced the useful information, and some components were suggested as an indicator of the kind of response expected. Here again, the question obviously proved difficult to answer, and might have produced clearer responses if participants had simply been asked to name the single part of the entry that had been most helpful.

Question 7 sought to discover what the dictionary user did next, which of course depended on the outcome of the current look-up: the options were to choose a translation and end the search, or to continue it either by looking up another entry in the same dictionary or by moving to another dictionary. One omission in Question 7 showed up as soon as queries started to be made to the database: Question 7 should have included the option "moving to an entry in a different type of dictionary". Given the current structure of the database, it is not possible to infer this fact by cross-tabulation of other responses.

If they moved to another dictionary, they were asked in **Question 8** to explain this move; this could be the result of many different factors: lack of any information or adequate information in the first dictionary, unintelligibility of the first dictionary, or sheer lack of confidence in the information offered. In the event, this question provided the least variation in response of all the questions: the great majority of participants gave as their reason for moving on the fact that they needed more information about the point that had puzzled them in the first place ("B").

Question 9 invites an account of the satisfaction level of those who were ending the search. Were they convinced that they had got the right information, or doubtful about this, or were they sure they had not been successful?

Question 10 offers space for further comments: most of those proved to relate to the user's needs for a different type of dictionary, or simply for a better dictionary of the same type as the one being used.

To summarize: although the questionnaire proved to have some minor shortcomings in practice, the Cover Sheet and Recording Sheets proved adequate for their purpose: there were few spoilt answers. Some of the questions could be fine-tuned for a homogeneous group, but there is a nice balance to be maintained between tedious hair-splitting and gathering a sufficient amount of useful information to form the basis of constructive thinking about dictionary use.

3   DATABASE QUERY: HOW DO PEOPLE CONSULT DICTIONARIES?

The information collected by this method lends itself to a detailed study of the way in which individuals use their dictionaries. Using a statistical program to query the database, we asked questions about the translation problems that sent people to their dictionary, the kind of information they were looking for, whether or not they found it and if so in what section of the dictionary entry, the strategies they used when frustrated, and what they felt about the experience: in Sections 3–9 we discuss in some detail the information which the database can provide in answer to these questions. The full database holds the results of both the Oxford and Tampere experiments, but when the different nature of the two groups appeared to affect the interpretation, the results from the two sources are discussed separately.

In this section, we examine three fairly typical instances of dictionary use, and comment briefly on the strategies being employed.

The fact that the database tells us exactly what dictionary was being consulted at any given moment, and exactly what the object of the search was, allows us to reconstruct the situation in considerable detail, resulting in information which should be of particular interest to teachers wishing to learn how their students actually use their dictionaries, as a preliminary to teaching dictionary skills.

The 574 searches recorded in the database involved 1,000 look-ups, and each was subtly different from every other. The method of enquiry allows each of these to be studied in great detail, as may be seen from the following case studies, which are included to give some idea of the potential of this type of database query.

3.1   Case study: single-word target not in the dictionary

We start with the classic case of a dictionary user hunting in vain for an item in a dictionary, searching for information in two L2 monolingual dictionaries as well as in both directions of a bilingual dictionary.

A Danish participant wanted to know what *to'er* was in English. (This designates an apartment with two rooms; the English equivalent would be something like "two-roomer", which is not at all as established as the Danish term, and which one would not expect to find figuring explicitly in any dictionary.) An additional problem was that *to'er* is a colloquial expression; an attempt at paraphrase in English would probably have resulted in *"two-er", and the user was rightly wary of this. The search consisted of five look-ups.

Look-up 1
Looked up: *to'er* in Danish–English bilingual dictionary
Found: *to'er* was not in the dictionary

Look-up 2
Looked up: *toværelses* (= "two-room flat", unmarked for register) in the same bilingual dictionary
Found: the entry exists (see Figure 1), but contains no information about informal variants in English; the asterisk before the last phrase is a device used in this particular dictionary to indicate an untranslated example.

> **toværelse(r)s** adj.: ~ **lejlighed** two-room flat; (amr.) three-room apartment *(idet køkkenet regnes med som værelse i USA);* * a two-roomed house.

FIG. 1   Entry for *toværelses* in Danish–English dictionary

Look-up 3
Looked up: "two-room flat" (gleaned from Look-up 2) in English monolingual dictionary A (a desk-size native-speaker dictionary)
Found: "two-room flat" was not in the dictionary

Comment: presumably the Danish user was hoping to find an informal English synonym for "two-room flat"

Look-up 4
Looked up: "two-room flat" in English monolingual dictionary B (also a desk-size native-speaker dictionary)
Found: "two-room flat" was not in the dictionary

Look-up 5
Looked up: "flat" in English–Danish bilingual dictionary
Found: the entry exists (see Figure 2), but contains no information about colloquial variants of the English term
Comment: The search ended there, leaving the user frustrated.

> **flat** *sb* **1.** (*Brit.*) lejlighed; bolig; **residence** ~ beboelseslejlighed. **2.** (*U.S.*) (lejlighed i) lejekaserne; del af etage indrettet til beboelse.

FIG. 2   Entry for noun *flat* in English–Danish dictionary

3.2   Case study: Multi-word target partially in the dictionary

An English participant wanted to find the French equivalent of "low wage earner". The search (using two bilingual English–French dictionaries) consisted of five look-ups:

Look-up 1
Looked up: "low" in English–French bilingual dictionary **A**
Found: the entry exists (see Figure 3), but "low wage earner" is not explicitly given

> **low**...
>
> (c) *wage, rate* bas (*f* basse), faible; *price* bas, modéré, modique...
> **people of** ~ **income** les gens aux faibles revenus;...

FIG. 3   Extract from *low* entry in English–French dictionary A

Look-up 2
Looked up: "wage" in the same bilingual dictionary (**A**)
Found: no satisfactory answer; although the dictionary entry (see Figure 4) includes the compound item "wage earner" with two additional examples of its use, it does not include the phrase "low wage earner".
Comment: "low wage earner" was not in this dictionary as a translated item, although there is a section (shown in Figure 3) in the entry for "low" where the relevant sense of this adjective is extensively translated, and which includes as its very first collocating noun the word "wage". The anglophone user had described himself or herself as having "advanced" competence in French, and therefore must have realized that it is impossible in that language to put together "salarié" and "bas" to form the equivalent of "low wage earner", because of course the constituents of the English phrase are "((low wage) earner)". A low wage earner is a "salarié" whose "salaire" is "bas". Spotting "il est bien payé" given as a translation

> **wage** ... **1** *n* salaire *m*, paye *f or* paie *f;[domestic servant]*
> gages *mpl*. **hourly/weekly** ~ salaire horaire/hebdomadaire; ...
> **he gets a good** ~ il est bien payé, il a un bon salaire;... **2** *cpd*: ...**wage**
> **earner** salarié(e) *m(f)*; **she is the family wage earner** c'est elle qui fait
> vivre sa famille *or* qui est le soutien sa famille; **we are both wage**
> **earners** nous gagnons tous les deux notre vie;...

FIG. 4   Extract from *wage* entry in English-French dictionary A

of "he gets a good wage", the user might have given up at this point and composed some kind of paraphrase of "low wage earners" such as "ceux qui ne sont pas bien payés", but instead chose to continue the search. It is conceivable that the user's behaviour in this instance was influenced by the abnormal circumstances of the dictionary use: despite our attempts to reproduce as far as possible a natural use of dictionaries, an experiment like this one cannot of course be completely faithful to the real-world event in all aspects of the process.

Look-up 3
Looked up: "earner" in the same bilingual dictionary
Found: the word was not in the dictionary

Look-up 4
Looked up: "wage" in another English–French bilingual dictionary (B)
Found: here again (see Figure 5) "wage earner" was in the dictionary, but no indication of a way of translating "low wage earner".

> **wage** ... **1** *n* salaire *m*, paye *f or* paie *f;[servant]* gages *mpl*.
> **hourly/weekly** ~ salaire horaire/hebdomadaire; ...   **2** *cpd*:...**wage**
> **earner** salarié(e) *m(f)*; **the family wage earner** le soutien de la
> famille; ...

FIG. 5   Extract from *wage* entry in English-French dictionary B

Comment: This dictionary was an abridged version of the previous bilingual dictionary consulted during this search: an indication of either extreme naivety or extreme desperation on the part of the user. There were many different bilingual and monolingual French and English dictionaries available in the room, and it is hard to see a logic in searching an abridged dictionary for an item which did not exist in its unabridged version.

Look-up 5
Looked up: "earner" in the second bilingual dictionary (B)
Found: the word was not in the dictionary
Comment: At the end of this search the user noted that he or she would have to resort to a paraphrase. This decision was clearly the correct one, and the delay in making it is difficult to understand.

3.3   Case study: idiom target, partially in the dictionary

An English user wanted to find out how to adapt the German equivalent of the English idiom "to put all one's eggs in one basket", in order to put into German the concept expressed in the sentence (on the topic of nuclear versus fossil fuels) "Even the most ardent nuclear fan would not wish to put all our eggs in the nuclear basket". The search consisted of three look-ups, all in the same bilingual dictionary.

Look-up 1
Looked up: "put" in an English–German bilingual dictionary
Found: "to put all one's eggs in one basket" is perhaps understandably not to be found in the entry for "put", which is too long to cite here, and which contains virtually no idioms

Look-up 2
Looked up: "basket" in the same bilingual dictionary
Found: this entry contained no idiomatic material either

Look-up 3
Looked up: "put" again, in the same bilingual dictionary
Found: still no success. Search abandoned.
Comment: Here, instead of looking under "egg", which seems the obvious next step (and the idiom is actually there, in this dictionary), the user returned to "put" and presumably read the very long entry more carefully.

3.4   What a search involves

A careful study of individual searches, such as those described above, gives some idea of what is involved in consulting a dictionary: for instance, these case studies throw some light on dictionary users' strategies for handling the frustrating situation of not finding what you want in a dictionary entry. Sometimes the tactics employed (such as those in 3.1) are sophisticated and sensible; sometimes (as in 3.2) with the benefit of hindsight the user might have wished to give up earlier; sometimes (as in 3.3) a more intelligent search strategy would have found the item in the dictionary. (At the very least, 3.3 makes a good case for the teaching of dictionary skills.)

The methodology devised for this experiment is thus powerful enough to allow language teachers to investigate in some depth the way their students use dictionaries. We shall now take a brief look at the broader picture.

TABLE I   Length of searches in terms of number of look-ups

Number of look-ups in the search	Number of such searches	Percentage of total
1 look-up	309	57%
2 look-ups	133	25%
3 look-ups	46	9%
4 look-ups	25	5%
5 look-ups	14	2.6%
6 look-ups	6	1.1%
7 look-ups	3	0.6%
8 look-ups	1	0.2%
Total	**537**	**~ 100%**

The 103 dictionary users (Oxford and Tampere combined) managed to complete exactly 1,000 dictionary look-ups during the time they had at their disposal. All the look-ups by one individual with the object of finding a translation for one particular expression in the text formed one "search" in our experiment.

Altogether, 574 searches were recorded. In other words, the users deployed 1,000 look-ups in trying to solve 574 problems. Of the 574 searches, 37 ended prematurely when time was called at the end of a session. The actual length (in number of look-ups per search) of the remaining 537 searches recorded in the database was as shown in Table 1.

Table 1 shows that more than half the searches recorded (57%) consisted of a single look-up, but one out of the 537 comprised eight separate dictionary operations.

Unfortunately, the way in which we keyed the information into the original dBaseIII Plus database does not allow us to extract figures relating to the sequence of various types of look-ups within a search: it is for example impossible for us to say from the database in its current format what the predominant patterns were in the searches recorded there. Without much detailed effort and manual re-ordering of our database, we cannot check our hypothesis that many searches which began with a quest for a direct L2 translation changed into a secondary hunt for confirmation of this, or for grammatical or collocation information about that translation. Nor will the database tell us whether the searches accounted successful by the searchers actually delivered the appropriate information, as pointed out above. We cannot therefore identify truly successful searches, simply those that the users thought were successful.

One of the things the database can, however, tell us is something about how the total number of look-ups breaks down among the various types of users.

The Oxford group contained 34 advanced L2 speakers, 23 intermediate, 11 beginners and three unspecified; the Tampere group consisted of 32 advanced L2 speakers. Contrasting the Oxford users only, according to their L2 skills, Table 2 shows the mean number of look-ups per user of each type.

TABLE 2   Number of look-ups according to users' L2 skills

Groups of users according to L2 skills		Total number of look-ups per group	Mean number of look-ups per group
Advanced	34 users	239	7.03
Intermediate	23 users	192	8.3
Beginners	11 users	62	5.6
Unspecified	3 users	17	—
Total	**71**	**510**	**7.2**

It might be concluded that the Advanced users with a mean of 7.03 look-ups per user worked more slowly than the Intermediate group, where the mean number of look-ups per user was 8.3. However, this conclusion would be valid only if all participants spent the same amount of time as users (as opposed to acting as recorders). This was not the case, as the chart in Figure 6 shows.

From Figure 6 it may be seen that two participants performed only one look-up each, and at the other end of the scale seven participants performed 12 or more look-ups each during the session. It is clear from this disparity that all the participants did not spend the same amount of time as dictionary user (as opposed to recorder). Some clearly must have performed as the dictionary user for the bulk of the time available. This means that the figures in the right-hand column of Table 2 ("Mean number of look-ups per group") is not informative. However, the

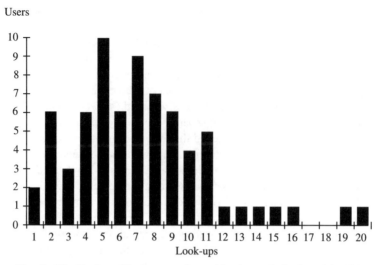

FIG. 6   Distribution of look-ups performed by the 71 Oxford participants

median number of look-ups (seven), if performed over half an hour, does seem intuitively probable. We include this discussion in order to alert other researchers who might adopt our methodology to the need for control over the amount of time which each participant spends on the two roles (dictionary user *v* recorder).

In the Tampere group, this problem did not arise. The students spent approximately 45 minutes on the exercise, acting all the time as dictionary users, and another group acted as recorders.

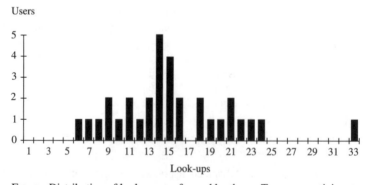

FIG. 7   Distribution of look-ups performed by the 32 Tampere participants

The chart in Figure 7 shows a much more even distribution of look-ups per user in the 32 members of the Tampere group, where the median of 14.5 look-ups in 45 minutes is the equivalent of 9.7 look-ups in half an hour. This compares favourably with the Oxford median of seven per half-hour, but it must be remembered that some time was lost in Oxford because of the change of roles, and that the dictionary users did not have as long as the homogeneous group of Tampere users to get used to the task. Of course, this says nothing about whether they were doing so efficiently, and evaluating the results accurately.

TABLE 3   Variation in types of information sought according to type of translation task

Type of information sought	Number of look-ups for L1–L2 translation		Number of look-ups for L2–L1 translation	
Q.4 = 'A' Seeking an L2 translation	396	43%	53	59%
Q.4 = 'B' Checking word as L2 translation	309	34%	29	32%
Q.4 = 'C' Seeking grammar of L2 word	34	4%	4	4%
Q.4 = 'D' Seeking collocations of L2 word	102	11%	4	4%
Q.4 = 'E' Other types of information	44	5%	—	—
Unspecified	25	3%	—	—
Total	**910**	**~ 100%**	**90**	**~ 100%**

4 DATABASE QUERY: WHAT KIND OF INFORMATION ARE USERS LOOKING FOR?

Lexicographers (if they are to write more helpful entries) and language teachers (if they are to improve their students' dictionary skills) need not only to know the kind of information that dictionary users are looking for, but to have some idea of what users most frequently need to find out from their dictionaries. Question 4 on the Recording Sheet (L1–L2) attempted to gather such information, giving users a choice between five different types of information:

A: L2 translation of L1 term (or vice versa)
B: confirmation of a known L2 term as the good translation
C: grammatical information about the L2 term
D: information about collocational behaviour of the L2 term
E: other information

4.1   Translation task: L1–L2 versus L2–L1

People attempting to translate into their own language rarely if ever consult a dictionary about the grammatical and collocational behaviour of an L2 word. Any meaningful query to the database about types of information must take into account the differences between L1–L2 and L2–L1 translation. When the type of translation task is taken into account, the statistics are as shown in Table 3.

Predictably, the commonest L1–L2 look-up was to find a foreign language translation unknown to the user; the next commonest had as its aim to check that an L2 word thought to be a good translation was actually acceptable. We were, however, surprised to note that, roughly, only one in ten look-ups was in search of collocational information (e.g. was the L2 adjective they had in mind really used to modify the L2 noun that their L1 context required, and so on), and fewer than one in 20 look-ups had grammatical information as its goal. See Section 7 for information about how satisfied these people were with what they found.

As was to be expected, people translating into their own language (L2–L1 Recording Sheet) had limited needs from their dictionary: either they did not know the L2 word and had to find the L1 equivalent (Q.4: A), or they thought they knew it and had to check (Q.4: B).

It is comparatively easy, if there are no insuperable space constraints, for a lexicographer to make sure that the grammatical information in a dictionary entry is fairly comprehensive. It is much less easy, and requires much more space, to make the collocation information even remotely adequate. The fact that many more users are seeking the latter type of information than the former is a challenge to lexicographers and language teachers alike. The need for collocational information in dictionaries for L2 speakers is mentioned again in Section 8.3.

4.2   Level of users' L2 skills

It would be reasonable to think that the type of information looked up in the dictionary might vary to some extent according to the users' knowledge of the foreign language in question. Focusing more specifically on the L2 language skills of the seekers gives the results shown in Table 4, where the total number of look-ups is 983 and not 1,000, because 17 look-ups were performed by users who did not specify their L2 skills.

TABLE 4   Variation in types of information sought according to users' L2 skills

Type of information sought	Look-ups by those with advanced L2 skills		Look-ups by those with intermediate L2 skills		Look-ups by those with beginner L2 skills	
Q.4 = 'A' Seeking an L2 translation	299	41%	87	45%	49	79%
Q.4 = 'B' Checking word as L2 translation	273	37%	56	29%	8	13%
Q.4 = 'C' Seeking grammar of L2 word	23	3%	11	6%	4	6%
Q.4 = 'D' Seeking collocations of L2 word	76	10%	29	15%	1	1%
Q.4 = 'E' Other types of information	36	5%	8	4%	—	—
Unspecified	22	3%	1	—	—	—
Total	**729**	**~ 100%**	**192**	**~ 100%**	**62**	**~ 100%**

The figures in the first row of Table 4 (Advanced 41% versus Intermediate 45% versus Beginners 79%) seem to support the intuition that those with least L2 knowledge will make most use of the direct-translation facility which the dictionary offers. It should however be pointed out in this regard that most of the Beginners chose to do a translation into their own language rather than into a foreign language, and that fact must also be reflected in these figures.

4.3   Position of look-up in search process

Finally, one might speculate that the first look-up in a search might be a quest for an L2 translation (we shall call this **primary information**), and that once the L2 word had been found this would change to a quest for confirmation of the chosen translation, grammatical or collocational facts about it, etc. (we shall call this **secondary information**). As explained in Section 3.4, it is not possible to determine from the current database whether this did in fact happen.

However, a comparison of the number of first, second, and subsequent look-ups against this broad division of information types sought (primary versus secondary information) gives the statistics in Table 5, where only these two broad types of information have been considered: those answering "A" to Question 4 were seeking for primary information, and those answering "B", "C", "D", or "E" were seeking for secondary information.

TABLE 5   Comparison of broad types of information sought according to the position of look-up in search process

Type of information sought	Look-up 1		Look-up 2		Look-up 3		Look-up 4		Look-ups 5–8	
Primary	295	51%	97	40%	28	29%	19	39%	10	26%
Secondary	271	47%	137	57%	63	64%	30	61%	25	64%
Unspecified	8	2%	6	2%	7	7%	—	—	4	10%
Total	**574**	**100%**	**240**	**~100%**	**98**	**100%**	**49**	**100%**	**39**	**100%**

As might be expected, the secondary information takes on increasing prominence as the search continues (47% of first look-ups, 57% of second look-ups, and 64% of third look-ups).

5   DATABASE QUERY: WHERE DO USERS FIND THE INFORMATION THEY NEED?

Lexicographers in particular are keen to know in which part of the entry the user is most likely to find the information sought. To a certain extent, naturally, this depends on the kind of information needed, but often a lexicographer has a choice of how to include a specific piece of information: for instance, a fact destined to help the user identify the sense of the headword being treated in a particular section of the entry could be encoded as a metalinguistic note, or an example of usage, or a semantic domain label, and so on.

TABLE 6   Location of answers to successful look-ups for different translation tasks

Location of answers	Successful look-ups for L1–L2 translation		Successful look-ups for L2–L1 translation	
headword translation	232	44%	27	42%
example (+ translation)	65	12%	5	8%
definition	46	9%	12	19%
idiom (+ translation)	29	5%	8	12%
compound (+ translation)	17	3%	1	2%
other	5	1%	1	2%
unspecified	134	25%	10	16%
Total	**528**	**~100%**	**64**	**~100%**

Information about the helpfulness of the various dictionary entry components was requested in Question 6 of the Recording Sheets, which asked users who had found what they needed (i.e. those who had replied either "Yes" or "Yes, but ..." to Question 5) to identify the section of the entry which had provided the facts. Many people who answered "Yes, but ..." to Question 5 had not given any information for Question 6; for 144 such look-ups (24% of the total of 592 (528 + 64) successful look-ups: see Table 6 below), Question 6 was left blank.

In designing the questionnaire, "headword translation" was intended to refer only to that section in bilingual dictionaries, and "definition" only to the definitions in monolingual dictionaries. However, some users clearly interpreted "definition" as referring to the headword translation (since as Table 7 shows, it is recorded as having been of use to bilingual dictionary users), and indeed in some languages these are alternative terms to denote the translation material. This ambiguity was unfortunately not foreseen in the wording of the questions, but should be borne in mind by others using our methodology. The brackets round "+ translation" in this section reflect the fact that in monolingual dictionaries no translations are included.

The type of query discussed here in Section 5 is, we believe, a good illustration of the power of this database. Sections 5.1 to 5.3 illustrate how it is possible to place different conditions on the query, as various parameters are reviewed.

5.1   Dictionary component and type of translation task

We look first at the overall figures, distinguishing dictionary components and translation tasks.

As Table 6 shows, in 44% of all successful L1–L2 look-ups and in 42% of successful L2–L1 look-ups the user found the information in the translation of the headword. If "definition" is construed as "translation", this proportion increases. The figures given are, however, rather crude, and ignore a number of variables, such as the type of dictionary used, or of information sought: all important aspects of dictionary consultation which have to be taken into account.

TABLE 7   Location of answers to successful look-ups using bilingual dictionaries for different translation tasks

Location of answers in bilingual dictionaries	In successful look-ups for L1–L2 translation		In successful look-ups for L2–L1 translation	
headword translation	220	53%	27	64%
example (+ translation)	48	11%	1	2%
definition	10	2%	1	2%
idiom (+ translation)	26	8%	6	14%
compound (+ translation)	16	4%	—	—
other	4	1%	—	—
unspecified	92	22%	7	17%
Total	**416**	~ **100%**	**42**	~ **100%**

The great majority of the participants used bilingual rather than monolingual dictionaries (this is shown in Table 21 below). Therefore we decided to look specifically at successful look-ups with a bilingual dictionary, distinguishing between the two types of translation task; as Table 7 shows, here the role of the headword translation predictably increases and that of definition is reduced. Other changes appear insignificant.

TABLE 8   Distribution of look-ups according to narrowing conditions

Translation tasks	Total number of look-ups	Successful look-ups in all dictionaries	Successful look-ups in bilinguals only
L1–L2	910	528	416
L2–L1	90	64	42
Total	**1,000**	**592**	**458**

5.2   Type of dictionary used

Table 8 shows the varying number of look-ups according to narrowing conditions, namely first the overall figures, then figures of successful look-ups (*i.e.* where users responded "yes" or "yes, but..." to Question 5: see Section 6), and in the last column the figures of successful look-ups in bilingual dictionaries.

Our figures show (see Table 9) that overall the bilingual dictionary (with a 64% success rate) proved more useful than the monolingual (successful in only 48% of look-ups).

It may be relevant to remember, in connection with Table 9, that an L2 monolingual look-up would often follow a series of unsuccessful bilingual look-ups.

TABLE 9   Success rate of bilingual versus L2 monolingual dictionaries

Type of dictionary consulted	Look-ups in bilingual dictionaries		Look-ups in monolingual dictionaries		Look-ups where dictionary unspecified	
Successful	458	64%	134	48%	—	—
Unsuccessful	253	35%	147	52%	—	—
Unspecified	3	—	—	—	5	100%
Total	**714**	**~ 100%**	**281**	**100%**	**5**	**100%**

5.3   Type of information sought

Another factor which could affect the place where information might be found in the dictionary entry is the type of information (primary or secondary) being sought. Table 10 shows the results of this query.

It will have been noted from the figures in Table 8 that the total number of successful look-ups was 592; in Table 10 the total is however 583 (256 + 327), because 9 of the look-ups were performed by users who did not specify the type of information they were looking for. Table 10 seems to indicate that a user looking for secondary information about a specific word needs to spread the net wider in the dictionary entry than a user seeking a simple translation.

6   DATABASE QUERY: DO USERS FIND WHAT THEY LOOK UP?

One of the main things which both lexicographers and teachers need to know (and which lexicographers at least rarely get the chance of finding out) is what kind of success rate users have in their dictionary searches. Question 5 on the Recording Sheet asked users to say whether their look-up had been successful; they were given the choice of saying that they

TABLE 10   Location of answers to successful look-ups according to types of information sought

Answer to query was found in ...	In successful look-ups for primary information		In successful look-ups for secondary information	
headword translation	123	48%	133	41%
example (+ translation)	22	9%	46	14%
definition	16	6%	40	12%
idiom (+ translation)	24	9%	13	4%
compound (+ translation)	11	4%	7	2%
other	—	—	6	2%
unspecified	60	23%	82	25%
Total	**256**	**~ 100%**	**327**	**~ 100%**

had found what they were looking for (shown as answer "Yes" in Table 11), that they had found something useful but not exactly what they need (answer "Yes, but..."), or that the look-up had failed (answer "No").

It should be remembered that the figures here do not tell us whether user expectations of dictionary contents were reasonable, whether their search techniques were adequate, or whether what they found was a correct solution to their translation problem. Only close study of the individual search patterns will give that information, and such a detailed investigation is not part of our present brief. The material discussed in Sections 6.1–6.3, and illustrated in Tables 11–13 inclusive, all relates essentially to the 1,000 look-ups being analysed, although the totals in these tables, for reasons given in the text, do not always add up to 1,000.

6.1   Overall

The responses to Question 5 over the 1,000 look-ups performed by the 103 participants are summarized in Table 11, showing that only slightly over one third were wholly satisfactory.

TABLE 11   Success ratings of dictionary look-ups

Answer to Q.5 Did they find it?	Out of 1,000 look-ups	
Yes	373	37%
Yes, but...	219	22%
No	400	40%
No response	8	1%
Total	**1,000**	**100%**

Why, in 40% of the cases, did the user believe that the look-up had failed? In order to answer that question one would need to be able to generalize from the searches recorded, in an attempt to discern recurring patterns. As explained in Section 3.4, this is unfortunately not possible.

6.2   Translation task: L1–L2 versus L2–L1

It is arguable that the direction of the translation, into or out of one's native language, would have an effect on the success of the look-up. Out of the 1,000 individual look-ups in the database, 910 (91%) related to a translation task into a foreign language, and only 90 (9%) to a translation from the foreign language into one's mother tongue. The imbalance means that comparison of the two sets cannot do more than indicate a possible trend, which may be worth following up later; the comparative figures are given in Table 12.

TABLE 12   Success ratings of dictionary look-ups according to type of translation task

Answer to Q.5: Did they find it?	In look-ups for L1–L2 translation		In look-ups for L2–L1 translation	
Yes	323	35%	50	55%
Yes, but...	205	22%	14	15%
No	374	41%	26	29%
No response	8	1%	—	—
Total	**910**	~ **100%**	**90**	~ **100%**

Predictably, it proved easier to translate into one's own language rather than the other way around. 55% of the look-ups for L2–L1 translation were accounted wholly successful, compared with 35% of L1–L2 look-ups. Presumably, people performing the latter task needed, and were hoping for, more information than their dictionary provided. Similarly, only 29% of the L2–L1 translators believed that their dictionary had totally failed them, as opposed to 41% of the L1–L2 translators. As noted above, however, the numbers of L2–L1 tasks are comparatively small, and further research is needed in order to discover whether the figures in Table 12 provide a true picture of what happens during the dictionary consultation process.

6.3   Level of Users' L2 skills

It could be that the level of the user's L2 skills would have an effect on the success of the look-up. 729 out of the 1,000 look-ups were carried out by the 66 advanced speakers of L2, 192 by the 23 intermediate speakers, and 62 by the 11 beginners. Three people (accounting for 17 look-ups) did not specify their L2 skills. The figures in Table 13 therefore relate to the

TABLE 13   Success ratings of dictionary look-ups according to level of users' L2 skills

Answer to Q.5: Did they find it?	In look-ups by those with advanced L2 skills		In look-ups by those with intermediate L2 skills		In look-ups by those with beginner L2 skills	
Yes	237	32%	94	49%	29	47%
Yes, but...	180	25%	28	15%	11	18%
No	306	42%	68	35%	22	35%
No response	6	1%	2	1%	—	—
Total	**729**	**100%**	**192**	**100%**	**62**	**100%**

983 look-ups (729 + 192 + 62) for which the users' L2 skills are known, rather than the full total of 1,000 look-ups.

The differences between those answering "Yes" and those answering "Yes, but…" are interesting here. Those with advanced L2 skills are clearly more reluctant to say that they have definitely found what they are looking for (32% as against 49% of the intermediate group). This could be because the information the advanced users wanted was more complex and elusive, or because experience has taught them to mistrust their dictionaries, or because they are more aware than the others of the niceties of collocational fit, or of the other pitfalls lying in wait for those writing in a foreign language.

6.4   Type of information sought for L1–L2 translation only

The type of information being sought might reasonably be expected to have a bearing on the success rate of the search. In looking at this aspect of dictionary use, we decided to isolate the L1–L2 translation task, for which more sophisticated dictionary skills are needed than those required for L2–L1 translation. The figures in Sections 6.4.1–2 therefore relate to the 910 look-ups (see Table 12) carried out during the process of translating out of one's mother tongue into a foreign language.

6.4.1   *Two types of information: primary versus secondary*
396 of the total of 910 L1–L2 look-ups involved primary information and 489 involved secondary (see Section 4.3 above for what these terms mean): in 25 cases not enough detail was given to identify the type of information sought. Looking first at the success rate of look-ups in the broad context of either primary or secondary information, we obtain the figures in Table 14, where the total number of look-ups is 885 (396 + 489), which together with the 25 mentioned above represents the 910 L1–L2 look-ups.

TABLE 14   Success ratings of dictionary look-ups according to broad types of information sought

Answer to Q.5: Did they find it?	In look-ups for primary information		In look-ups for secondary information	
Yes	124	31%	191	39%
Yes, but…	92	23%	112	23%
No	179	45%	181	37%
Unspecified	1	—	5	1%
Total	**396**	**~ 100%**	**489**	**100%**

The figures in Table 14 suggest that the broad type of information sought does in fact make some difference to the success of the look-up. People who go to the dictionary looking for information about a word they already have in mind are more likely to succeed than those with no clear idea of the translation they need. Only 37% of the former, the secondary information look-ups, failed; of primary information look-ups, the failure rate was 45%.

6.4.2   *Four different types of information*
The database allows a more detailed query relating to the types of information being sought during L1–L2 translation and recorded in Question 4 on the Recording Sheets. When such

TABLE 15 Success ratings of dictionary look-ups according to specific types of information sought

Answer to Q5: Did they find it?	(Q.4 = "A") Seeking an L2 translation		(Q.4 = "B") Checking word as L2 translation		(Q.4 = "C") Seeking grammar of L2 word		(Q.4 = "D") Seeking collocations of L2 word		(Q.4 = "E") Seeking other information	
Yes	124	31%	127	41%	16	47%	39	38%	9	20%
Yes, but …	92	23%	78	25%	6	18%	22	22%	6	14%
No	179	45%	102	33%	12	35%	39	38%	28	64%
Unspecified	1	—	2	1%	—	—	2	2%	1	2%
Total	**396**	**~ 100%**	**309**	**100%**	**34**	**100%**	**102**	**100%**	**44**	**100%**

a query is made, the results are as shown in Table 15, which again omits the 25 unspecified look-ups, giving a total of 885 (396 + 309 + 34 + 102 + 44) instead of the expected 910.

At first glance the figures in Table 15 do not look very interesting: it obviously proved somewhat more difficult (as is also seen in Table 14) to find the L2 translation of an L1 word (primary information) than to confirm a hunch about an L2 term, or to find information about its grammar or its collocability (secondary information). However, as there was a considerable difference in the number of look-ups targeting the various types of information, the 38% failure in attempts to find collocational information represents much more user frustration than the 35% failure to find grammatical information. The former percentage reflects 39 look-ups, while the latter reflects only 12.

We also looked to see whether there is a difference in the *failure* rating between people who were looking for primary information and those who were looking for secondary information, taking into account their different L2 skills, but no clear pattern emerged.

7   DATABASE QUERY: ARE PEOPLE SATISFIED WITH WHAT THEY GET?

Information about the satisfaction rate of the user is based on answers to Question 9 in the Recording Sheets, which asked users to say whether they were satisfied or not with the results they had obtained in that particular search. Question 9 was completed at the end of each search (not each look-up) and so relates to a single problem which a user was trying to solve. There were 574 searches in all, out of which 537 were completed. The material in this section (Tables 16–20 inclusive) relates to these 537 searches, showing different aspects of the same data.

7.1   Overall figures

Looking at the satisfaction rating across all participants in this experiment gives the results shown in Table 16.

TABLE 16   Overall satisfaction rate at end of search

Dictionary users' evaluation of results	Out of 537 searches	
Satisfied	319	59%
Doubtful	131	24%
Not satisfied	71	13%
No response	16	3%
Total	**537**	**~ 100%**

The fact that in 59% of the cases the dictionary users pronounced themselves satisfied with the results of their search is encouraging.

7.2   Translation task

Did the direction of the translation task make a difference to the satisfaction rate?

Of the 537 completed searches, 473 related to L1–L2 translation tasks and 64 to L2–L1 tasks. The database offers the figures shown in Table 17, resulting from a correlation of

TABLE 17   Satisfaction rate for different translation tasks

Dictionary users' evaluation of results	In searches for L1–L2 translation		In searches for L2–L1 translation	
Satisfied	273	58%	46	72%
Doubtful	117	25%	14	22%
Not satisfied	67	14%	4	6%
No response	16	3%	—	—
Total	**473**	**100%**	**64**	**100%**

Question 9 on the Recording Sheet (user satisfaction rating) and Question 3 on the Cover Sheet (type of translation task being performed).

It is clear from the figures in Table 17 that people translating into their own language were more satisfied with the performance of their dictionaries than people translating into a foreign language. This is understandable. Much more information is needed, of course, for the latter task.

7.3   Level of users' L2 skills

The question also arises whether the users' level of L2 skills makes a difference to the way in which they view the performance of their dictionary. One might hypothesize that the more the users know about the foreign language, the less easy they are to please. We saw in Section 6.3 that on the basis of look-ups (as opposed to searches, on which satisfaction ratings were requested), the advanced L2 speakers were more reluctant than others to say that they had definitely found what they were looking for.

In response to Question 2 on the Cover Sheet, 66 of the participants rated themselves as having advanced L2 knowledge, 23 as having intermediate skills, and 11 described themselves as beginners. Three users did not specify their L2 level.

An analysis of the satisfaction rating (Question 9 on Recording Sheet) taking into account the users' L2 skills gives the results shown in Table 18.

The "Not satisfied" figures show little variation ascribable to the users' different levels of L2 skills. Where these do seem to make a difference is in the users' assessment of whether they got all of what they had hoped for, and whether they believed it to be correct. 29% of the advanced L2 speakers expressed reservations about that, as compared with 14% of the intermediate speakers and 22.5% of the beginners. The "Satisfied" figures also show some difference. Although the "Beginners" numbers are small, this exercise illustrates the potential of a database of this type.

7.4   Type of information sought

In Section 4.3 we made a broad distinction between primary information and secondary information: participants answering "A" to Question 4 in the Recording Sheet were considered to be seeking primary information, while those answering "B", "C", "D", or "E" were seeking secondary information. These distinctions form the basis for the figures in Table 19, which shows the comparative satisfaction rates for the last look-ups of each type of search.

TABLE 18 Satisfaction rate against level of L2 skills

Dictionary users' evaluation of results	In searches by those with advanced L2 skills		In searches by those with intermediate L2 skills		In searches by those with beginner L2 skills		In searches by those with unspecified L2 skills	
Satisfied	201	56%	80	65%	26	65%	12	92%
Doubtful	104	29%	17	14%	9	22.5%	1	8%
Not satisfied	51	14%	16	13%	4	10%	—	—
No response	5	1%	10	8%	1	2.5%	—	—
Total	**361**	**100%**	**123**	**100%**	**40**	**100%**	**13**	**100%**

TABLE 19   Satisfaction rates according to broad types of information sought

Dictionary users' evaluation of results	Primary information		Secondary information		Unspecified information	
Satisfied	131	61%	182	59%	6	50%
Doubtful	46	21%	81	26%	4	33%
Not satisfied	33	15%	36	11%	2	16%
No response	5	2%	11	3%	—	—
Total	**215**	**~ 100%**	**310**	**~ 100%**	**12**	**~ 100%**

These figures which distinguish among the various types of information show little difference in the satisfaction rate of the respective groups.

7.5   Translators versus others

Finally, the satisfaction levels of trainee translators (as represented by the 32 members of the homogeneous group from Tampere) was compared with that of the 54 in the Oxford group who were performing the same L1–L2 translation task, and the results are shown in Table 20. Some of these may very well have been qualified translators, of course, but there was a high proportion of professional lexicographers and practising academics in the group. Tampere had 230 completed searches, as against Oxford's 243: roughly comparable figures.

More trained translators expressed doubt over the success of their search. Their training undoubtedly leads them to be wary of possible translation traps: they were fully satisfied only if they got multiple confirmation from various sources that their choice was a correct or adequate one for the particular context.

TABLE 20   Rates of satisfaction with the result of L1–L2 translation task queries

Dictionary users' evaluation of results	Oxford group		Tampere group	
Satisfied	157	65%	116	50%
Doubtful	39	16%	78	34%
Not satisfied	33	14%	34	15%
No response	14	6%	2	1%
Total	**243**	**~ 100%**	**230**	**100%**

8   DATABASE QUERY: WHAT DO PEOPLE DO WHEN FRUSTRATED?

Out of the total 1,000 look-ups, 400 were unsuccessful, that is to say, in these the users did not find what they were looking for (see Section 6.1). Of course, the failure rate of 40% cannot be due only to some inadequacy on the part of the dictionaries involved: inadequate strategies and unrealistic expectations on the part of the user must also contribute to this figure.

In order to determine what dictionary users do when they do not find an answer to their problem, we decided to make some individual case studies. As explained in Section 3.4 above, it was not possible for us to detect trends automatically by querying the database on this point.

The Tampere group was much more homogeneous than the Oxford group: in the former, all members had relatively similar L2 skills, spoke the same mother tongue (Finnish), were using the same set of dictionaries, and were translating the same text.

This was obviously a good basis for a pair of contrastive case studies.

In this section we look at the way the Finnish translators handled their frustrations with problems of L1–L2 translation.

In recording the work of the Tampere group, a separate field was included in which was noted a unique reference number, identifying each of the 39 expressions in the text which had given rise to a search. The existence of this field tells us how many times each of these expressions caused a problem, and of course helps to identify the most problematic of these items. The case studies below discuss two of the most frequent causes of problems.

8.1   Case study: Selecting an appropriate translation from among L2 alternatives

The Finnish expression *apuväline* posed a problem of translation into English. Its meaning is rendered in the dictionary that the students used as: *instrument, medium, vehicle, facilities*. In a passage discussing the design of a work station environment, the word occurred in this context: "Oman tietokoneen ääressä tehdään paljon töitä, mutta vasta työntekijöiden niska- ja hartiaseudun vaivat vat herättäneet *apuvälineiden* keksijät" ("A lot of people work at their own PCs, but it was only when computer operators in the workplace complained of neck and shoulder pains that the interest of the accessory designers was aroused"). Here, *apuväline* would cover such items as adjustable chairs, back supports, wrist rests, foot rests, document holders, and so on, which, in an office supplies catalogue, come under the heading of *accessories*. This excellent equivalent of the Finnish term is not under *apuväline* in the Finnish–English dictionary used by all the students. It is therefore all the more interesting to attempt to discover what strategies the students employed in an effort to find a satisfactory translation.

Here is a summary of the searches performed by three different users in an attempt to find an appropriate translation of *apuväline*. As noted above, they all had the same two-volume bilingual dictionary, and there were four monolingual English dictionaries available.

(1) USER A
Look-up 1
Looked up: *apuväline* in the bilingual dictionary
Found: *instrument, medium, vehicle, facilities*

Look-up 2
Looked up: *facility* in monolingual English dictionary A

Look-up 3
Looked up: *instrument* in monolingual English dictionary A

Look-up 4
Looked up: *aid* in monolingual English dictionary A
Look-up 5
Looked up: *help* in monolingual English dictionary A

Look-up 6
Looked up: *medium* in monolingual English dictionary A
Look-up 7
Looked up: *aid* in monolingual English dictionary B

Outcome: The user noted the outcome as a failure to find the correct English translation for *apuväline*.

Comment: Initially, the user followed a fairly orthodox path: faced with four alternatives, he checked out what seemed to be the two most likely candidates in a monolingual dictionary, but decided from the definitions and examples there that neither was a suitable translation for *apuväline*.

He then thought up two English words which might have been appropriate, *aid* and *help*, and looked them up in the same monolingual dictionary, without making much progress in his task.

Reverting to the original four alternatives, he selected a third, *medium*, and consulted the same monolingual dictionary, but this led him to believe that the word was not a good choice. As a last resort in what had clearly become a despairing impasse, he returned to one of the words he had thought up for himself, *aid*, and looked it up in a different monolingual dictionary.

He then gave up.

(2) USER B
Look-up 1
Looked up: *apuväline* in the bilingual dictionary
Found: *instrument, medium, vehicle, facilities*

Look-up 2
Looked up: *instrument* in monolingual English dictionary B

Look-up 3
Looked up: *medium* in monolingual English dictionary B

Look-up 4
Looked up: *apuväline* in the bilingual dictionary

Outcome: The user noted that a useful example had been found, and believed that the correct translation had probably been chosen. However, as this was the word *medium*, this was an incorrect assumption.

Comment: Like User A, User B began in an orthodox manner, gleaning four alternatives from the bilingual dictionary and checking two of these, *facility* and *medium*, in a monolingual dictionary. Dissatisfied with the result, and presumably believing she might have missed something in the first look-up, she then returned to the bilingual dictionary and reread the entry for *apuväline*. Her cumulative impression of the search led her to select (wrongly) the English word *medium* as a translation.

(3) USER C
Look-up 1
Looked up: *apuväline* in the bilingual dictionary
Found: *instrument, medium, vehicle, facilities*

Look-up 2
Looked up: *instrument* in monolingual English dictionary B

Look-up 3
Looked up: *medium* in monolingual English dictionary B

Look-up 4
Looked up: *vehicle* in monolingual English dictionary B

Look-up 5
Looked up: *facility* in monolingual English dictionary B

Outcome: The user noted that a useful example had been found, and believed that the correct translation had probably been chosen. However, as this was the word *facility*, this was an incorrect assumption.

Comment: Like the others, User C started with the bilingual dictionary. Unlike her colleagues, however, she carefully checked all the four alternatives in a monolingual dictionary, coming to the (mistaken) conclusion that the English word *facility* was probably the correct choice. Her hesitation however is shown in her assessment of the outcome: to Question 5 in the Recording Sheets ("Did you find what you are looking for?") she answered "Yes, but...".

Conclusion: We would suggest that the ways in which these three students dealt with the same problem highlight the responsibility of bilingual dictionaries. Had the bilingual dictionary which offered *instrument, medium, vehicle, facilities* as translations for *apuväline* differentiated the English equivalents, some at least of the subsequent dictionary consultation might have proved unnecessary.

The four English words are by no means even partially synonymous, *medium* and *vehicle* being semantically the closest neighbours, but still having very distinct meanings. They are certainly different enough to support some semantic differentiation, which would have helped the Finnish speaker choose among them in the light of the context in which the translation would be used.

Probably the most useful way of giving that type of information is in example sentences. The bilingual dictionary entry held no examples at all. More information differentiating the L2 terms would have helped all three users.

8.2   Case study: Translating a multi-word expression

In this case study, the problem consists of translating into English a multi-word expression in Finnish. This is *niska- ja hartiaseudun vaivat*, and it was found in the context cited and translated in section 8.1: "Oman tietokoneen ääressä tehdään paljon töitä, mutta vasta työntekijöiden *niska- ja hartiaseudun vaivat* vat herättäneet apuvälineiden keksijät".

The Finnish word *niska* means "neck"; *ja* means "and"; *hartia* means "shoulder"; *seutu* means "region" and is in the genitive case in this compound; and *vaivat* is a plural form of a word variously rendered in English by *aches, pains,* or *troubles*.

The problem for the Finnish students, who undoubtedly could translate all of the individual component words into English, was to determine the combinatory potential of the English terms; in particular they needed to know:

- whether *niska- ja hartiaseudun* should be translated as *neck and shoulder* or *neck and shoulder region* within the English multi-word expression; and
- what in the context of *neck and shoulder* would be the most appropriate English translation of *vaivat*.

Two different approaches to finding the information are described below.

(1) USER A
Look-up 1
Looked up: *niska* in the bilingual dictionary
Found: *neck*

Look-up 2
Looked up: *hartia* in the bilingual dictionary
Found: *shoulder*

Look-up 3
Looked up: *vaiva* in the bilingual dictionary
Found: *trouble, complaint, ailment, affliction* and, in phrasal examples, expressions such as *stomach pains* and *back pains*

Outcome: The user abandoned the search, apparently no further advanced in the search for the translation of *niska- ja hartiaseudun vaivat*.

Comment: As regards the first two look-ups, the user undoubtedly knew the English for *niska* and *hartia*. One is forced to the conclusion that she was looking for a translation of the whole phrase, or at least for *niskaseudun vaivat (neck pains)* or *hartiaseudun vaivat (shoulder pains)*. When neither of these was forthcoming, she turned to the entry for *vaiva*, presumably in search of the same information.

(2) USER B
Look-up 1
Looked up: *neck* in the bilingual dictionary
Found: *kaula, niska (kaula* refers to the whole, or the front, of the neck, whereas *niska* designates the nape of the neck)

Look-up 2
Looked up: *neck* in monolingual dictionary C

Look-up 3
Looked up: *niska* in the bilingual dictionary
Found: *neck*

Look-up 4
Looked up: *hartia* in the bilingual dictionary
Found: *shoulder*

Look-up 5
Looked up: *seutu* in the bilingual dictionary
Found: *region*, and, in phrasal examples, expressions such as *abdominal region* and *heart region*

Look-up 6
Looked up: *region* in monolingual dictionary B

Outcome: User B described himself as satisfied that he had found the correct way to translate the Finnish expression *niska- ja hartiaseudun vaivat*. (Whether he had in fact done so is not known.)

Comment: This user looked up the components of the Finnish expression in linear order. The search is typical of many such searches, both with regard to this expression and to many others in the text.

8.3   Discussion

It is interesting to note that the kind of expressions which caused most of the problems were not "hard words" (difficult or rare terms which the students might be forgiven for never having encountered before), but (i) (see 8.1) very general words whose translation is highly context-dependent, or (ii) (see 8.2) combinations of extremely basic terms which all the students knew. In their comments on their experiences, the Tampere students frequently expressed their desire for more comprehensive coverage in the examples section of the entries, and in particular for more information about collocation in English.

We have suggested in our comments on the cases in 8.1 that the bilingual dictionary could do more to help students with this type of problem. However, there is a physical limit to the amount of information which a bilingual dictionary can contain. The possible contexts of *apuväline* are so varied that it would be virtually impossible to include them all in a dictionary. Similarly, the possible combinations of *vaiva* with names of parts of the body are too numerous to include them all.

Atkins (1991a: 53 ff) discussed the insuperable problems for a bilingual lexicographer raised by words like *apuväline*; words having a very general meaning which it is easy, depending on the context in which it occurs, for a reader to interpret in a number of different specific ways: the example chosen by Atkins was *facility*. This semantic generality coupled with possible contextual specificity means that these words normally have many different equivalents in another language.

Varantola (1994) suggested that a monolingual corpus, rather than a bilingual or monolingual dictionary, was the right place to start in the search for appropriate translations for highly context-dependent equivalents, or for information about the combinatory properties of basic terms. A dictionary is not enough, for an advanced student of a foreign language. But a dictionary is essential as a starting point in many of such a student's searches. The combination of a comprehensive bilingual dictionary (together with other reference works, including specialist dictionaries as appropriate) and a selected monolingual L2 corpus in which the examples are broadly differentiated according to word senses would offer advanced language practitioners a powerful translating tool. Many would also appreciate a similarly selected and differentiated L1 monolingual corpus, for often a translator needs a certain amount of reassurance about his or her own language.

9   DATABASE QUERY: WHEN DO PEOPLE USE AN L2 MONOLINGUAL DICTIONARY?

TABLE 21   Choice of bilingual or L2 monolingual dictionary

Dictionary type consulted	Out of 1000 look-ups	
Bilingual	714	71%
L2 monolingual	281	28%
Unspecified	5	—
Total	**1,000**	**~ 100%**

One of the interesting aspects of the use of dictionaries for translation purposes is the amount of weight which the user gives to a bilingual dictionary compared with a monolingual dictionary. The large multilingual research project into the use of dictionaries for L2 purposes described in Atkins and Knowles (1990) found a distinct preference for bilingual over L2 monolingual dictionaries: 57.9% of the 740 participants claimed to use a bilingual dictionary nearly every week, while only 30.8% made the same claim for an L2 monolingual dictionary; only 0.4% said that they never used a bilingual dictionary, as compared with 27% who never used an L2 monolingual dictionary. It was clear that, overall, the bilingual dictionary was the preferred reference work for most tasks with most people. Our database also shows this trend: see Table 21.

9.1   For different translation tasks?

In this context, however, it is interesting to ask how the different tasks (translating from L1 to L2, and from L2 to L1) affect the figures. There were 1,000 look-ups in all, and Table 22 shows how these were distributed between bilingual and L2 monolingual dictionaries.

As Table 22 shows, 27% of the total L1–L2 translation tasks were performed with the aid of an L2 monolingual dictionary, whereas in the case of L2–L1 translations, an L2 monolingual dictionary was chosen for 37% of the total. This confirms one's intuitions that an L2 monolingual dictionary would offer more help to people trying to understand the foreign language than to those trying to express a concept in it.

TABLE 22   Dictionary choices for different translation tasks

Dictionary type consulted	In look-ups for L1–L2 translation		In look-ups for L2–L1 translation	
Bilingual	657	72%	57	63%
L2 monolingual	248	27%	33	37%
Unspecified	5	—	—	—
Total	**910**	~ **100%**	**90**	**100%**

9.2   For different types of searches?

The type of information needed might also affect a user's choice between a bilingual and an L2 monolingual dictionary. It was possible to focus on a uniform group of people (all with advanced level of L2) performing the same task (L1–L2 translation). By comparing their replies to Question 4 on the Recording Sheet ("Why do you need the dictionary?") it is possible to see whether the type of search reflects a difference in the kind of dictionary chosen.

693 of the total of 910 look-ups for an L1–L2 translation were performed by Advanced users, and in 22 of these cases the users did not specify the type of information being sought, leaving 671 look-ups to be included in this calculation. The base figures (290 + 253 + 20 + 72 + 36) in Table 23 total 671. This table highlights rather nicely the fact that when looking for primary information (an unknown translation) people tend to go to the bilingual dictionary, whereas the monolingual dictionary comes into play as their need for secondary information grows.

The figure of 19% for people who looked in L2 monolingual dictionaries for an L2 translation without having a specific L2 expression in mind requires perhaps some elucidation: such look-ups tended to occur after a bilingual dictionary had produced several candidate L2 translations, and the user was turning to an L2 monolingual dictionary in order to choose from amongst them.

9.3   Because of different linguistic skills?

Atkins and Knowles (1990) pointed out that the individual's competence in L2 must influence the choice: the more advanced the user's knowledge, the more likely the choice of an L2 monolingual dictionary. Our database provided the statistics shown in Table 24 for 983 look-ups: cf. 6.3.

TABLE 23 Dictionary choices for L1–L2 translation task by users with advanced L2 skills

Dictionary type consulted	(Q.4 = "A") Seeking an L2 translation		(Q.4 = "B") Checking word as L2 translation		(Q.4 = "C") Seeking grammar of L2 word		(Q.4 = "D") Seeking collocations of L2 word		(Q.4 = "E") Seeking other information	
Bilingual	235	81%	167	66%	8	40%	23	32%	19	53%
L2 monolingual	54	19%	85	34%	12	60%	48	67%	17	47%
Unspecified	1	—	1	—	—	—	1	1%	—	—
Total	**290**	**100%**	**253**	**100%**	**20**	**100%**	**72**	**100%**	**36**	**100%**

TABLE 24   Distribution of bilingual vs. L2 monolingual use taking account of users' L2 skills

Dictionary type consulted	In look-ups by those with advanced L2 skills		In look-ups by those with intermediate L2 skills		In look-ups by those with beginner L2 skills	
Bilingual	474	65%	169	88%	54	87%
L2 monolingual	250	34%	23	12%	8	13%
Unspecified	5	1%	—	—	—	—
Total	**729**	**100%**	**192**	**100%**	**62**	**100%**

The figures in Table 24 do seem to support the claim that monolingual dictionaries were used more often by users with advanced L2 skills.

It seemed sensible to combine the parameters studied in Sections 9.2 and 9.3 and look at figures for the use of (say) L2 monolingual dictionaries, taking into account both the kind of information sought and the level of users' L2 knowledge. However, the figures for L2 monolingual dictionary use by Intermediate users and Beginners (12% of 192, or 23 for Intermediate, 13% of 62, or 8 for Beginners, see Table 24) are so small that this would not be a worthwhile operation with the current database.

9.4   Because of what has gone before in the search?

More interesting perhaps are the contrastive figures for the various percentages of look-ups in a bilingual dictionary, depending on where the look-up came in the search process; these are given in Tables 25 and 26 (cf. Table 9).

TABLE 25   Selection of bilingual or monolingual dictionary during a single look-up by the Oxford group

Position in search	Oxford group Bilingual		Oxford group Monolingual		Total	
Look-up 1	291	88%	38	11%	329	~ 100%
Look-up 2	80	71%	32	29%	112	100%
Look-up 3	26	65%	14	35%	40	100%
Look-up 4	10	59%	7	41%	17	100%
Look-ups 5–8	6	54%	5	45%	11	~ 100%
Total	**413**		**96**		**509**	

In Tables 25 and 26, we see a common trend in the two groups, but also a distinct divergence between them. The common trend is that as the search progresses, less use is made of the bilingual and more of the monolingual dictionary. In Oxford (Table 25), the bilingual figures drop from 88% through 71%, 65%, and 59% to 54%; in Tampere (Table 26) they drop from 86% through 47% and 24%, with a hiccup at 41%, to 21%. The two columns of monolingual figures rise correspondingly. The divergence lies in the fact that, while the mixed-level Oxford group remains faithful to the bilingual dictionary (88% of first look-ups and 71% of second look-ups), the advanced Tampere users quickly move on to monolinguals (86% bilingual in first look-up, only 47% in second look-up). One has the intuition that the surprising reversion to the bilingual dictionary in 41% of the 4th look-ups in Tampere was caused by users believing they must have missed something in an earlier bilingual consultation, and going back to recheck.

TABLE 26   Selection of bilingual or monolingual dictionary during a single look-up by the Tampere group

Position in search	Tampere group Bilingual		Tampere group Monolingual		Total	
Look-up 1	208	86%	33	14%	241	100%
Look-up 2	60	47%	67	53%	127	100%
Look-up 3	14	24%	44	76%	58	100%
Look-up 4	13	41%	19	59%	32	100%
Look-ups 5–8	6	21%	22	79%	28	100%
Total	**301**		**185**		**486**	

Tantalizing questions of detail arise. Why does a user move from bilingual to monolingual dictionary in the middle of a search? Why does the same user start one search with a bilingual dictionary and the next search with a monolingual? The database contains enough detailed information to allow these questions to be answered, but to do so would require much time-consuming cross-checking against the actual dictionaries used for each look-up.

IO   CONCLUSION

In this paper we have given an account of an experiment into the recording of dictionary use for translation purposes, explaining how it was carried out, and pointing out the strengths and weaknesses of the resultant database as a source of information about the process.

The weaknesses have been touched on at the appropriate point in the discussion of the queries, notably in Sections 2.1 (on the optimal amount of information requested in the Cover Sheet), 2.2 (on the content of Questions 4, 6, 7 in the Recording Sheet), 3.2 (on how such an experiment could really reflect 'natural' dictionary usage), 3.4 and 6.1 (the last two on infelicities in the database design). The queries which could not be made to the database in its present state include the following:

- did searches tend to start with a quest for a translation and go on to a quest for peripheral information?
- was the use of an L2 monolingual dictionary a last resort, or were monolinguals a regular step in search strategies?

When applied to linguistically-motivated searches of this nature, statistics have rarely any value other than that of indicating possible trends in the behaviour of the groups involved. We believe, however, that the strengths of this study are demonstrated by the extent and detail of the answers which may be derived from the database, as exemplified in Sections 3–9 above. The database is powerful and flexible: other researchers may wish to use it as a launchpad for their own studies, since it is easy to add or remove fields without invalidating the data, if this is done carefully.

A comprehensive and representative survey would undoubtedly provide a highly informative resource for lexicographers, both those working on bilingual dictionaries and those whose work is in their own language alone. Moreover, such a database would be of equal service to language teachers and teachers of translation. We have found that it has told us a great deal about how dictionaries are used for assistance with translation problems. One fact that has impressed us is the amount of reassurance sought from their dictionaries, particularly about L2 collocation, by even the most skilled of non-native L2 speakers, however experienced in translation they may be.

We believe that dictionary skills must be taught, carefully and thoroughly, if dictionary users are to extract from their dictionaries the information which lexicographers have put into them. Teachers will be better able to carry out such teaching if they are fully aware of exactly what their students are doing with their dictionaries, what they expect from them, and how easily they are satisfied during the process of consultation.

This is the type of knowledge that we have tried to elicit in the course of the Oxford and Tampere experiments.

The objective of these was to provide a basis from which to continue the study of students' dictionary use habits, in order both to help them to develop better skills in this regard, and to inform dictionary-makers of users' more specific needs. Some of the latter pose almost insoluble problems for compilers of desk-sized print dictionaries, but the situation will change when new dictionaries are compiled for electronic access only. The EURALEX Oxford and Tampere experiments were intended to be a first step towards transforming the print dictionary into an electronic one, by highlighting various types of lexicographical information which might be improved, or added, at that time. One of these is clearly lexical collocation, and another the syntactic environment in which a word is used. It is also clear that a dictionary without space problems could usefully provide more, fuller, and more intelligible guidance to help the users in their decision-making process. This study also provides some leads on what such a dictionary might do to combat user frustration.

APPENDIX I

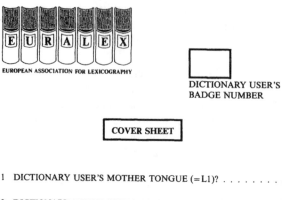

EUROPEAN ASSOCIATION FOR LEXICOGRAPHY

[ ] DICTIONARY USER'S
BADGE NUMBER

COVER SHEET

1 DICTIONARY USER'S MOTHER TONGUE (=L1)? . . . .

2 DICTIONARY USER'S OWN ASSESSMENT OF L2 LEVEL
   (tick one box)

   | beginner | | intermediate | | advanced |

3 TASK BEING PERFORMED *(tick one box)*

   | L1 → L2 translation | | L2 → L1 translation |

4 TEXT BEING TRANSLATED

   Answers here should identify   Language   Difficulty
   the translation passage as e.g.
   'Italian 1', or 'English 3' etc.   . . . .

5 DICTIONARY OR DICTIONARIES BEING USED

   When the Dictionary User selects a dictionary, write on one of the lines below
   a brief form of its title (enough to identify it) and the name of the publisher
   and use the letter thus assigned to it to indicate that dictionary in the
   'Dictionary Used' box on the Recording Form.

   NB: You may need to complete only one or two of the lines below.

	TITLE	PUBLISHER
A	. . . .	. . . .
B	. . . .	. . . .
C	. . . .	. . . .
D	. . . .	. . . .

APPENDIX 2

L1 → **L2**	DICTIONARY USER BADGE NUMBER ☐
own language other language	SEARCH NUMBER &
RECORDING SHEET	LOOK-UP LETTER ☐
	(see Recorder's Notes)

1 WHAT MADE THE DICTIONARY USER GO TO THE DICTIONARY?
(answer this only for the first look-up of any search: copy the word(s) from the translation text that sent Dictionary User to dictionary; you might want to include a short context and circle the actual problem)
. . . .

2 WHAT DICTIONARY ARE THEY USING?
(give identification letter)

3 WHAT ENTRY ARE THEY LOOKING UP?
(write in capital letters the headword heading the entry being looked at)
. . . .

4 WHY DO THEY NEED IT? *(circle a letter)*
  A   they don't know what the L2 equivalent of the problem expression is
  B   they think they know what it is, but want to check
  C   they know it but want grammatical information about it
      (e.g. gender, complementation structures, correct preposition to use, etc; specify if necessary)
      . . . .
  D   they know it but want to find other help with using it
      (e.g. typical examples of use; collocates; spelling; register, style or usage constraints etc; specify)
      . . . .
  E   other *(specify)*
      . . . .

5 HAVE THEY FOUND WHAT THEY WERE LOOKING FOR?
(circle one: 'yes', 'yes, but...' or 'no')   yes   yes-but   no

6 IF YES, WHERE DID THEY FIND IT?
(in definition, headword translation, example, idiom, compound, phrasal verb or the translation of any of these, style indicator, usage note etc; say which)
. . . .

7 WHAT ARE THEY DOING NEXT? *(circle a letter)*
  A   moving on to another dictionary
  B   choosing a translation and ending this search *(go to 9)*
  C   moving to another entry in the same dictionary

8 IF THEY ARE MOVING TO ANOTHER DICTIONARY, WHY?
(circle a letter)
  A   the headword they're looking for is not in this dictionary
  B   they need more information about the point noted in Section 4 above
  C   they need more information about something else *(say what)*
      . . . .
  D   they can't understand this dictionary *(say why)*
      . . . .
  E   they don't trust this dictionary *(say why)*
      . . . .
  F   other . . . .
      . . . .

9 IF THEY ARE ENDING THIS SEARCH, HOW DO THEY FEEL?
  A   satisfied they got the right information
  B   doubtful about whether they got the right information
  C   sure they didn't get the right information

10 ANY OTHER COMMENTS
(from either Recorder or Dictionary User, e.g. how the dictionary could be made more useful; specific dictionary skills that could be taught; ways in which this Recording Sheet could be improved, etc.)
. . . .
. . . .
. . . .

L2 → L1	DICTIONARY USER BADGE NUMBER	☐
other language own language RECORDING SHEET	SEARCH NUMBER & LOOK-UP LETTER *(see Recorder's Notes)*	⊡

1 WHAT MADE THE DICTIONARY USER GO TO THE DICTIONARY?
(answer this only for the first look-up of any search: copy the word(s) from the translation text that sent Dictionary User to dictionary; you might want to include a short context and circle the actual problem)
. . . .

2 WHAT DICTIONARY ARE THEY USING?
(give identification letter)

3 WHAT ENTRY ARE THEY LOOKING UP?
(write in capital letters the headword heading the entry being looked at)
. . . .

4 WHY DO THEY NEED IT? *(circle a letter)*
  A   to find the meaning of the L2 expression
  B   to check that the L2 expression means what they think it means
  C   other *(specify)*

. . . .
. . . .

5 HAVE THEY FOUND WHAT THEY WERE LOOKING FOR?
(circle one: 'yes', 'yes, but...' or 'no')   yes   yes-but   no

6 IF YES, WHERE DID THEY FIND IT?
(in definition, headword translation, example, idiom, compound, phrasal verb or the translation of any of these, style indicator, usage note etc; say which)
. . . .

7 WHAT ARE THEY DOING NEXT? *(circle a letter)*
  A   moving on to another dictionary
  B   choosing a translation and ending this search *(go to 9)*
  C   moving to another entry in the same dictionary

8 IF THEY ARE MOVING TO ANOTHER DICTIONARY, WHY?
(circle a letter)
  A   the headword they're looking for is not in this dictionary
  B   they need more information about the point noted in Section 4 above
  C   they need more information about something else *(say what)*
. . . .
  D   they can't understand this dictionary *(say why)*
. . . .
  E   they don't trust this dictionary *(say why)*
. . . .
. . . .
  F   other . . . .
. . . .

9 IF THEY ARE ENDING THIS SEARCH, HOW DO THEY FEEL?
  A   satisfied they got the right information
  B   doubtful about whether they got the right information
  C   sure they didn't get the right information

10 ANY OTHER COMMENTS
(from either Recorder or Dictionary User, e.g. how the dictionary could be made more useful; specific dictionary skills that could be taught; ways in which this Recording Sheet could be improved, etc.)
. . . .
. . . .
. . . .

RECORDER'S NOTES

Start a new *COVER SHEET* for each dictionary user.
Use same cover sheet for all searches done by one person.

A *SEARCH* means all the dictionary use related to one specific problem in the translation passage; the search may lead from one dictionary to another and back to the first – it should all be recorded as part of the same search.

A *LOOK-UP* refers to looking up one single entry in a dictionary. Record the look-ups on *RECORDING SHEETS*. There are two types of Recording Sheet – one for L1→L2 translation and another for L2→L1 translation. Please be sure to use the correct one.

SEARCH NUMBER and *LOOK-UP LETTER* box on Recording Sheet
Every individual search gets a new number, e.g. 1, 2, 3 ...
Within a search, each look-up gets a letter, e.g. A, B, C ...
So the first recording sheet for the first search is marked 1A, the next sheet for the same search is 1B, and so on. Start a new look-up letter when the Dictionary User turns to another headword, whether it is in the same dictionary or a different one. When they move to a new problem, this becomes search number 2, and the look-ups within it will be 2A, 2B, etc.

When one person stops being the Dictionary User, clip together all their Recording Sheets with their COVER SHEET on top.

Don't spend a lot of time puzzling about the Recording Sheet. If it's not clear what to answer, or where to put something, use the space marked 'OTHER'.

Remember the *DICTIONARY USER'S BADGE NUMBER* box in top right corner of each page. This number is crucial and must be inserted on the Cover Sheet and on every Recording Sheet. Without it there is no link between the record and what it is recording.

References

A. Dictionaries

American Heritage Dictionary of the English language, 3rd edn. (1994). Boston: Houghton Mifflin.

Atkins, B.T.S., and Duval, A. (eds.) (1978). *Collins–Robert French–English, English-French Dictionary*. Paris: Le Robert/Glasgow: Collins. [2nd edition – 1987].

Benson, M., Benson, E., and Ilson, R. (1986). *The BBI Combinatory Dictionary of English: A Guide to Word Combinations*. Amsterdam and Philadelphia: John Benjamins.

Collin, P., Knox, H., Ledésert, M., and Ledésert, R. (eds.) (1982). *Harrap's New Shorter French and English Dictionary*. London/Paris: Harrap.

Corréard, M-H., and Grundy, V. (eds.) (1994). *The Oxford–Hachette French Dictionary (French–English, English–French)*. Paris: Hachette; Oxford: Oxford University Press.

Cowie, A.P., Mackin, R., and McCaig, I. (1983). *Oxford Dictionary of Current Idiomatic English*, vol. 2. Oxford: Oxford University Press.

Dubois, M.-M., Cestre, C., Shuey, B., Keen, D., and James, I. (eds.) (1981). *Larousse Saturne 1981 – Dictionnaire français–anglais Saturne*. Nouv. éd. augm. de 10,000 termes par Michèle Beaucourt/ Jacqueline Blériot/David Jones. Paris: Larousse.

Hanks, P. (ed.) (1986). *Collins Dictionary of the English Language*, 2nd edn. London: Collins.

Hornby, A.S. (1942). *Idiomatic and Syntactic English Dictionary*. Tokyo: Kaitakuska. (ISED)

—— (1948). *The Advanced Learner's Dictionary*. Oxford: Oxford University Press.

Johnson, S. (1755). *A Dictionary of the English Language* (First folio edition). London.

Kirkpatrick, E.M. (ed.) (1980). *Chambers Universal Learners' Dictionary*. Edinburgh: W&R Chambers. (CULD)

LLA. *Longman Language Activator* (1993). Harlow: Longman.

OALD 3, 4, 5, 7. *Oxford Advanced Learner's Dictionary*, Editions 3 (1974), 4 (1989), 5 (1995), 7 (2005). Oxford: Oxford University Press.

OED. *Oxford English Dictionary: A New English Dictionary on Historical Principles* (1928). Oxford: Oxford University Press.

Procter, P. (ed.) (1978). *Longman Dictionary of Contemporary English*. Harlow: Longman. (LDOCE) [2nd edn. – LDOCE 2 – ed. D. Summers (1987); LDOCE3, ed. D. Summers (1995); LDOCE 4, ed. D. Summers (2003).

—— (ed.) (1995). *Cambridge International Dictionary of English*. Cambridge: Cambridge University Press. (CIDE)

Roget's International Thesaurus 4th edn. (1977). New York: Harper and Row.

Rundell, M. (ed.) (2002). *Macmillan English Dictionary for Advanced Learners*. Oxford: Macmillan. (MED)

Sinclair, J., Hanks, P., Fox, G., Moon, R., and Stock, P. (eds.) (1987). *Collins Cobuild English Language Dictionary*. London and Glasgow: Collins. (COBUILD) [COBUILD 2 (1995); COBUILD 3 (2001)].

Soanes, C., and Stevenson, A. (eds.) (2005). *Oxford Dictionary of English*, 2nd edn., revised. Oxford: Oxford University Press.

Summers, D. (ed.) (1992). *Longman Dictionary of English Language and Culture*. London: Longman. (LDELC)

—— (ed.) (1993). *Longman Language Activator*. London: Longman. (LLA)

—— and Rundell, M. (eds.) (1997). *Longman Essential Activator*. London: Longman. (LEA).

The Synonym Finder. 1978. Emmaus, PA: Rodale Press.

Trappes-Lomax, H. (1997). *Oxford Learner's Wordfinder Dictionary*. Oxford: Oxford University Press.

Webster's New International Dictionary of the English language, 2nd edn. (1934). Unabridged. (W2)

Wehmeier, S. (1993). *Oxford Wordpower Dictionary*. Oxford: Oxford University Press.

West, M., and Endicott, J.-G. (1935). *New Method English Dictionary*. London: Longmans, Green. (NMED)

B. Other literature

Works by three or more authors are listed in date order after all works by the first-named author alone or with one other author.

Abney, S. (1991). 'Parsing by Chunks', in Berwick, R., Abney, S., and Tenny, C. (eds.) *Principle-Based Parsing*. Dordrecht: Kluwer, 257–278.

Agirre, E., Ansa, O., Hovy, E., and Martinez, D. (2000). 'Enriching very large ontologies using the WWW', in *Proceedings of the Ontology Learning Workshop of the European Conference on Artificial Intelligence (ECAI)*, Berlin, Germany.

Ahlswede, T., and Evens, M. (1988). 'Generating a relational lexicon from a machine-readable dictionary', *International Journal of Lexicography*, 1(3): 214–237.

Aho, A., Kernighan, B., and Weinberger, P. (1988). *The AWK Programming Language*. Boston, MA: Addison-Wesley.

Aisenstadt, E. (1979). 'Collocability restrictions in dictionaries', *ITL*, 45–46: 71–74.

Aitchison, J. (1987). *Words in the Mind*. Oxford: Blackwell.

Ait-Mokhtar, S., and Chanod, J.P. (1997). 'Incremental finite-state parsing', *ANLP'97*. Washington: Association for Computational Linguistics, 72–79.

Alexander, R.J. (1978). 'Fixed expressions in English: a linguistic, psycholinguistic, sociolinguistic and didactic study. Part 1', *Anglistik und Englischunterricht*, 6: 171–188.

——(1987). 'Problems in understanding and teaching idiomaticity in English', *Anglistik und Englischunterricht*, 32: 105–122.

Alonso Ramos, M., and Tutin, A. (1992). 'A classification and description of the lexical functions of the Explanatory Combinatorial Dictionary for the treatment of LF combinations', in Haenelt, K., and Wanner, L. (eds.), *Proceedings of the International Workshop on the Meaning-Text Theory*. Darmstadt, Arbeitspapiere der GMD, 671, 187–196.

Amsler, R.A. (1980). *The Structure of the Merriam-Webster Pocket Dictionary*. PhD thesis, University of Texas at Austin.

Apresjan, J.D. (1973). 'Regular polysemy', *Linguistics*, 142: 5–32.

——(1974). *Lexical semantics: Means of Synonymy in Language*. Moscow: Nauka.

——(1992a). 'Systematic lexicography', in Tommola, H. *et al.* (eds.), *EURALEX '92 Proceedings 1–2*: Studia Translatologica: Publications of the Department of Translation Studies, University of Tampere, Finland, 3–16.

——(1992b). 'Lexicographic portraits and lexicographic types', in Guiraud-Weber M., and Zaremba, C. (eds.), *Linguistique et Slavistique. Mélanges offerts à Paul Garde*. Paris: Université de Provence, 360–76.

——(1995a). 'Theoretical linguistics, formal models of language and systemic lexicography', in Ik-Hwan Lee (ed.), *Linguistics in the Morning Calm*. Seoul: Hanshin Publishing Company, 3–30.

——(1995b). *Integral'noe opisanie iazyka i sistemnaia leksikographiia [An Integrated Description of Language and Systematic Lexicography]*. Moscow: Iazyki russkoi kul'tury.

——(2000). *Systematic Lexicography*. Oxford: Oxford University Press.

Arnold, I.V. (1986). *The English Word*, 2nd edn. Moscow: Vysšaja Škola. (1st edn. 1973)

Atkins, B.T.S. (1991a). 'Corpus lexicography: the bilingual dimension', in Zampolli, A., Cignoni, L. and Peters, C. (eds.), *Computational Lexicology and Lexicography*. Pisa: Giardini, Vol. 1: 43–64.

——(1991b). 'Building a lexicon: the contribution of lexicography', *International Journal of Lexicography*, 4(3): 167–204.

——(1992). 'Putting lexicography on the professional map', in Alvar Ezquerra, M. (ed.), *Proceedings of EURALEX '90*. Barcelona: Biblograf SA, 519–526.

——(1992/3). 'Theoretical lexicography and its relation to dictionary-making', in Frawley, W. (ed.) *Dictionaries: the Journal of the Dictionary Society of North America*, 14: 4–43.

——(1993). 'Tools for computer-aided corpus lexicography: the Hector project', *Acta Linguistica Hungarica*, 41: 5–72.

——(1996). *Assessment Report on the Efficiency of the DECIDE Toolbox – The DECIDE lexicon and toolbox in the lexicographer's workstation*, Deliverable D-9 of the DECIDE project, 21 pp. Liège/Stuttgart/Luxembourg.

——(ed.) (1998). *Using Dictionaries: Studies of Dictionary Use by Language Learners and Translators*. Tübingen: Niemeyer.

——and Christ, O. (1995). '*Case study*: developing a dictionary entry for the perception reading of the verb "survey" with Support of the IMS Corpus Query Tools, DELIS Cookbook'. DELIS Internal document, Oxford University Press and University of Stuttgart, M. 81 pp.

——and Hulstijn, J.H. (1998). 'Empirical research on dictionary use in foreign-language learning: an overview', in Atkins (1998) *Using Dictionaries: Studies of Dictionary Use by Language Learners and Translators*. Tübingen: Niemeyer, 7–20.

——and Knowles, F.E. (1990). 'Interim report on the EURALEX/AILA research project into dictionary use', in Magay, T., and Zigany, J. (eds.), *Proceedings of BudaLex '88*. Budapest: Akademiai Kiado, 381–392.

——and Levin, B. (1991). 'Admitting impediments', in Zernik, U. (ed.), *Lexical Acquisition: Using On-Line Resources to Build a Lexicon*. Hillsdale, NJ: Lawrence Erlbaum Associates, 233–262.

——and Rundell, M. (forthcoming, 2008). *Oxford Guide to Practical Lexicography*. Oxford: Oxford University Press.

——and Varantola, K. (1992). 'First report on the EURALEX 1991 Oxford Workshop into the Use of Dictionaries for Translation.' Paper presented at the *Fifth EURALEX International Congress*, University of Tampere, Finland.

————(1998). 'Language learners using dictionaries: the final report on the EURALEX/AILA research project on dictionary use', in Atkins, B.T.S. (ed.), *Using Dictionaries: Studies of Dictionary use by Language Learners and Translators*. Tübingen: Niemeyer, 21–82.

——Lewis, H., Summers, D., and Whitcut, J. (1987). 'A research project into the use of learners' dictionaries', in Cowie, A.P. (ed.), *The Dictionary and the Language Learner*. Tübingen: Niemeyer, 29–43.

——Kegl, J., and Levin, B. (1988). 'Anatomy of a verb entry: from linguistic theory to lexicographic practice', *International Journal of Lexicography*, 1(2): 84–126.

——Clear, J.H., and Ostler, N. (1992). 'Corpus design criteria', *Journal of Literary and Linguistic Computing*, 5(1): 1–16.

——Levin, B., and Song, G. (1996). 'Making sense of corpus data: a case study', in Gellerstam, M., Järborg, J., Malmgren, S.-G., Norén, K., Rogström, L., and Papmehl, P. (eds.), *Euralex'96 Proceedings*. Gothenburg: Gothenburg University, Department of Swedish, 345–354.

——Fillmore, C., and Johnson, C. (2003a). 'Lexicographic relevance: selecting information from corpus evidence', *International Journal of Lexicography*, Special Issue on FrameNet, 16(3): 251–280.

——Rundell, M., and Sato, H. (2003b). 'The contribution of FrameNet to practical lexicography', *International Journal of Lexicography*, Special Issue on FrameNet, 16(3): 333–357.

Ayto, J.R. (1983). 'On specifying meaning: semantic analysis and dictionary definitions', in Hartmann R.R.K. (ed.), *Lexicography: Principles and Practice*. London: Academic Press, 89–98.

——(1984). 'The vocabulary of definition', in Goetz, D., and Herbst, Th. (eds.), *Theoretische und praktische Probleme der Lexikographie*. Munich: Max Hueber, 50–62.

——(1988). 'Fig. leaves: metaphor in dictionaries,' in Snell-Hornby, M. (ed.), *ZuriLEX '86 Proceedings*. Tübingen: Francke, 49–54.

Baayen, H. (2001). *Word Frequency Distributions*. Dordrecht: Kluwer.

Baker, C., Fillmore, C.J., and Lowe, J.B. (1998). 'The Berkeley FrameNet project', *COLING-ACL*, Montreal, 86–90.

Banko, M., and Brill, E. (2001). 'Scaling to very very large corpora for natural language disambiguation', *Proceedings of the 39th Annual Meeting of the Association for Computational Linguistics and the 10th Conference of the European Chapter of the Association for Computational Linguistics*, Toulouse, 26–33.

Barnbrook, G. (2002). *Defining Language: A Local Grammar of Definition Sentences*. Amsterdam: John Benjamins.

Bauer, D., Segond, F., and Zaenen, A. (1994). 'Enriching an SGML-tagged bilingual dictionary for machine-aided comprehension.' Rank Xerox Research Centre Technical Report, MLTT, 11, Meylan.

Baugh, S., Harley, A., and Jellis, S. (1996). 'The role of corpora in compiling the Cambridge International Dictionary of English', *International Journal of Corpus Linguistics*, 1(1): 39–59.

Beaudouin, V., Fleury, S., Habert, B., Illouz, G., Licoppe, C., and Pasquier, M. (2001). 'TyPWeb: décrire la toile pour mieux comprendre les parcours', *CIUST'01, Colloque International sur les Usages et les Services des Télécommunications*, Paris, June. http://www.cavi.univ-paris3.fr/ilpga/ilpga/seury/typweb.htm.

Beckwith, R., and Miller, G. (1990). 'Implementing a Lexical Network', *International Journal of Lexicography (special issue)*, 3(4): 302–312.

——Fellbaum, C., Gross, D., and Miller, G.A. (1990). 'WordNet: a lexical database organized on psycholinguistic principles', in Zernik, U. (ed.), *Lexical Acquisition: Using On-line Resources to Build a Lexicon*. Hillsdale, NJ: Erlbaum.

Beesley, K.R. (1988). 'Language identifier: a computer program for automatic natural-language identification of on-line text', *Language at Crossroads: Proceedings of the 29th Annual Conference of the American Translators Association*, Oct 12–16: 47–54.

—— and Karttunen, L. (2003). *Finite-State Morphology*. Stanford: Center for the Study of Language and Information (CSLI).

Béjoint, H. (1981). 'The foreign student's use of monolingual English dictionaries: a study of language needs and reference skills', *Applied Linguistics*, 2(3): 207–222.

——(1988). 'Psycholinguistic evidence and the use of dictionaries by L2 learners', in Snell-Hornby, M. (ed.), *ZuriLEX '86 Proceedings*. Tübingen: Francke Verlag.

——(1989). 'The teaching of dictionary use', in Hausmann, F.-J., Reichmann, O., Wiegand, H.E., and Zgusta, L. (eds.), *Wörterbücher/Dictionaries/Dictionnaires: An International Encyclopedia of Lexicography*, Vol. 1. Berlin: de Gruyter, 208–215.

——(1994). *Tradition and Innovation in Modern English Dictionaries*. Oxford: Clarendon Press.

—— and Thoiron, P. (ed.) (1996). *Les Dictionnaires Bilingues*. Louvain-la-Neuve: Duculot.

Benson, M. (1985). 'Collocations and idioms', in Ilson, R. (ed.), *Dictionaries, Lexicography and Language Learning*. ELT Documents, 120. Oxford: Pergamon Press, 61–68.

——(1989). 'The structure of the collocational dictionary', *International Journal of Lexicography* 2(1): 1–14.

Biber, D. (1986). 'Spoken and written textual dimensions in English: resolving the contradictory findings', *Language*, 62: 384–414.

——(1988). *Variation across Speech and Writing*. Cambridge: Cambridge University Press.

——(1989). 'A Typology of English texts', *Linguistics*, 27: 3–43.

——(1990). 'Methodological issues regarding corpus-based analyses of linguistic variation', *Literary and Linguistic Computing*, 5: 257–269.

——(1992). 'On the complexity of discourse complexity: a multidimensional analysis', *Discourse Processes*, 15: 133–163.

——(1993a). 'An analytical framework for register studies', in Biber, D., and Finegan, E. (eds.), *Sociolinguistic Perspectives on Register*. New York: Oxford University Press.

——(1993b). 'Using register-diversified corpora for general language studies', *Computational Linguistics*, 19(2): 219–242.

——(1993c). 'Representativeness in corpus design', *Linguistic and Literary Computing*, 8(4): 243–257. [Also in this volume]

—— and Finegan, E. (1986). 'An initial typology of English text types', in Aarts, J., and Meijs, W. (eds.), *Corpus Linguistics 2*. Amsterdam: Rodopi, 19–46.

—— and Hared, M. (1992). 'Dimensions of register variation in Somali', *Language Variation and Change*, 4: 41–75.

Bogaards, P. (1990). 'Où cherche-t-on dans le dictionnaire?', *International Journal of Lexicography*, 3(2): 79–102.

——(1992). 'A la recherche de collocations dans le dictionnaire de langue étrangère', *Actas do XIX Congreso Internacional de Linguistica e Filoloxia Romanicas*. A Coruña: Corufla, Fundacion Pedro Barrié de la Maza, Conde de Fenosa, 175–185.

——(1996). 'Dictionaries for learners of English', *International Journal of Lexicography*, 9(4): 277–320.

——(1998). 'Scanning long entries in learners' dictionaries', in Fontenelle, T., *et al.* (eds.) *EURALEX'98 Proceedings*. Liège: University of Liège, 555–562.

Boguraev, B. (1991). 'Building a lexicon: the contribution of computers', *International Journal of Lexicography*, 4(3): 227–260.

——(1994). 'Machine-readable dictionaries and computational linguistics research', in Zampolli, A., Calzolari, N., and Palmer, M. (eds.), *Current Issues in Computational Linguistics: in Honour of Don Walker*. Series *Linguistica Computazionale*, IX–X. Dordrecht: Kluwer, 119–154.

——and Briscoe, T. (1989). *Computational Lexicography for Natural Language Processing*. London and New York: Longman.

————Carroll, J., and Copestake, A. (1992). 'Database models for computational lexicography', in *EURALEX'90 Proceedings*. Barcelona: Biblograf, 59–78.

Bolinger. D. (1965). 'The Atomization of meaning', *Language*, 41(4): 455–473.

——(1967). 'Adjectives in English: attribution and predication', *Lingua*, 18: 1–34.

——(1976). 'Meaning and memory', *Forum Linguisticum*, 1(1): 1–14.

——(1985). 'Defining the indefinable', in Ilson, R. (ed.), *Dictionaries, Lexicography and Language Learning*. ELT Documents, 120. Oxford: Permagon Press, 69–73. [Also in this volume]

Briscoe, E.J., and Carroll, J. (1997). 'Automatic extraction of subcategorization from corpora', *Proc. Fifth Conference on Applied Natural Language Processing*, Washington, DC: 356–363.

——Copestake, A., and Boguraev, B. (1990). 'Enjoy the paper: lexical semantics via lexicology', *COLING 90 Proceedings*, volume 2, Helsinki: 42–47.

——De Paiva, V., and Copestake, A. (eds.) (1993). *Inheritance, Defaults and the Lexicon*. Cambridge: Cambridge University Press.

Brown, P., and Fraser, C. (1979). 'Speech as a marker of situation', in Scherer, K. R. and Giles, H. (eds.), *Social Markers in Speech*. Cambridge: Cambridge University Press, 33–62.

——Della Pietra, S., Della Pietra, V., and Mercer, R. (1991). 'Word-sense disambiguation using statistical methods', *Proceedings of the 29th Conference of the Association of Computational Linguistics*, Berkeley, California, 264–270.

——Della Pietra, V. J., deSouza, P.V., Lai, J.C., and Mercer, R.L. (1992). 'Class-based *n*-gram models of Natural Language,' *Computational Linguistics*, 18(4): 467–479.

Bruton, A. (1997). 'Review of *Cambridge Word Selector*', *International Journal of Lexicography*, 10(4): 339–342.

Buitelaar, P., and Sacaleanu, B. (2001). 'Ranking and selecting synsets by domain relevance', *Proc. Workshop on WordNet and Other Lexical Resources: Applications, Extensions and Customizations*. Pittsburgh: NAACL.

Burnard, L. (1995). *The BNC Reference Manual*. Oxford University Computing Service.

Butt, M., King, T., Niño, M., and Segond, F. (1999). *A Grammar Writer's Cookbook*. Stanford, CA: CSLI Publications.

Cartes, R. (1989). 'Discovering relationships among word senses', *Dictionaries in the Electronic Age: Proceedings of the Fifth Annual Conference of the UW Centre for the New Oxford English Dictionary*, Oxford, 67–79.

——Calzolari, N., Chodorow, M., Klavans, J., Neff, M., and Rizk, O. (1987). 'Tools and methods for computational lexicology', *Computational Linguistics*, 13(3–4): 219–240.

Calzolari, N. (1984). 'Detecting patterns in a lexical database', *Proceedings of the 10th International Conference on Computational Linguistics*, COLING'84, Stanford, CA, 170–173.

——(1988). 'The dictionary and the thesaurus can be combined', in Evens, M. (ed.) *Relational Models of the Lexicon*. Cambridge: Cambridge University Press, 75–96.

Carter, R. (1987). *Vocabulary: Applied Linguistic Perspectives*. London: Allen and Unwin.

Carter, R. (1998). 'Orders of Reality: CANCODE, communication and culture', *ELT Journal*, 52(1): 43–56.

—— and McCarthy, M. (eds.) (1988). *Vocabulary and Language Teaching*. London: Longman.

————(1995). 'Grammar and the spoken language', *Applied Linguistics*, 16(2): 141–158.

Cavaglia, G. (2002). 'Measuring corpus homogeneity using a range of measures for inter-document distance', *Third International Conference on Language Resources and Evaluation (LREC)*, Las Palmas de Gran Canaria, Spain, May, 426–431.

Čermak, F. (2001). 'Substance of idioms: perennial problems, lack of data or theory?', *International Journal of Lexicography*, 14(1): 1–20.

Chanod, J.P. (1994). 'Finite-state composition of French verb morphology.' Technical Report MLTT-005. Xerox Research Centre Europe, Meylan, France, http://www.xrce.xerox.com/publis/mltt/mltt-005.ps

Chodorow, M., Byrd, R., and Heidorn, G. (1985). 'Extracting semantic hierarchies from a large on–line dictionary', *Proceedings of the Association for Computational Linguistics*, Chicago, 299–304.

Chomsky, N. (1956). 'Three models for the description of language', *IRE Transactions on Information Theory* IT, 2:3, 113–124.

——(1965). *Aspects of the Theory of Syntax*. Cambridge, MA: The MIT Press.

Choueka, Y. (1988). 'Looking for needles in a haystack, or locating interesting collocations in large textual databases', in *Proceedings of the RIAO International Conference on User-Oriented Content-Based Text and Image Handling*. Cambridge, MA, 609–623.

Christ, O. (1994). 'A modular and flexible architecture for an integrated corpus query system', in Kiefer, F. Kiss, G. and Pajzs J. (eds.), *COMPLEX'94 – Papers in Computational Lexicography*. Budapest: Research Institute for Linguistics, Hungarian Academy of Sciences, 23–32.

Church, K.W. (1988). 'A Stochastic parts program and noun phrase parser for unrestricted texts', in *Proceedings of the Second Conference on Applied Natural Language Processing*, Austin, Texas: Association for Computational Linguistics, 136–43.

—— and Hanks, P. (1990). 'Word association norms, mutual information, and lexicography', *Computational Linguistics*, 16(1): 22–29. [Also in this volume]

—— and Mercer, R. (1993). 'Introduction to the special issue on computational linguistics using large corpora', *Computational Linguistics*, 19(1): 1–24.

—— Gale, W., Hanks, P., and Hindle, D. (1990). 'Using statistics in lexical analysis', in Zernik, U. (ed.), *Lexical Acquisition: Using On-Line Resources to Build a Lexicon*. Hillsdale, NJ: Lawrence Erlbaum Associates, 115–164.

——————and Moon, R. (1994). 'Lexical substitutability', in Atkins, B.T.S., and Zampolli,A. (eds.), *Computational Approaches to the Lexicon*. Oxford: Oxford University Press, 153–177.

Clark, E.V., and Clark, H. (1979). 'When nouns surface as verbs', *Language*, 55(4): 767–811.

Clear, J.H. (1988). 'Trawling the language: monitor corpora', in Snell-Hornby, M. (ed.), *ZuriLEX '86 Proceedings*. Tübingen: Francke.

——(1992). 'Corpus Sampling', in G. Leitner (ed.), *New Dimensions in Corpus Linguistics: Proceedings of the 11th ICAME Conference*. Berlin: Walter de Gruyter, 21–31.

——(1994). 'I can't see the sense in a large corpus', in Kiefer, F., Kiss, G., and Pajzs, J. (eds.), *Papers in Computational Lexicography: COMPLEX '94*. Budapest: Research Institute for Linguistics, Hungarian Academy of Sciences, 33–48.

——(1996). 'Technical implications of multilingual corpus lexicography', *International Journal of Lexicography*, 9(3): 265–273.

Cook, G. (1998). 'The uses of reality: a reply to Ronald Carter', *ELT Journal*, 52(1): 57–63.

Cop, M. (1988). 'The function of collocations in dictionaries', in Magay, T., and Zigany, J. (eds.), *BudaLEX'88 Proceedings: Papers from the EURALEX Third International Congress*. Budapest: Akademiai Kiado, 35–46.

Copestake, A., and Briscoe, E. (1995). 'Semi-productive polysemy and sense extension', *Journal of Semantics*, 12(1): 15–67.

CorpusBench. (1993). *CorpusBench Manual*. Copenhagen: Textware A/S.

Cottrell, G.W. (1989). *A Connectionist Approach to Word Sense Disambiguation*. London: Pitman.

Coulmas, F. (ed.) (1981). *Conversational Routine*. The Hague: Mouton.

Cowie, A.P. (1978). 'The place of illustrative material and collocations in the design of a learner's dictionary', in Strevens, P. (ed.), *In Honour of A.S. Hornby*. Oxford: Oxford University Press, 127–139.

——(1981). 'The treatment of collocations and idioms in learners' dictionaries', *Applied Linguistics*, 2(3): 223–35.

——(1986). 'Collocational dictionaries – a comparative view', in Murphy, M. J. (ed.), *Proceedings of the Fourth Anglo-Soviet English Studies Seminar*. London: The British Council.

——(1988). 'Stable and creative aspects of vocabulary use', in Carter, R., and McCarthy, M. (eds.), *Vocabulary and Language Teaching*. London: Longman, 126–137.

——(ed.) (1998a). *Phraseology: Theory, Analysis, and Applications*. Oxford: Clarendon Press.

——(1998b). 'Phraseological dictionaries: some east–west comparisons', in Cowie, A.P. (ed.), *Phraseology: Theory, Analysis, and Applications*. Oxford University Press, Oxford, 209–228.

——(1998c). 'A.S. Hornby: a centenary tribute', *International Journal of Lexicography*, 11(4): 251–268.

——(1999a). *English Dictionaries for Foreign Learners: A History*. Oxford: Clarendon Press.

——(1999b). 'Learners' dictionaries in a historical and a theoretical perspective', in Herbst, T., and Popp, K. (eds.), *The Perfect Learners' Dictionary (?)*, Lexicographica Series Maior 95. Tübingen: Niemeyer, 3–13.

——(ed.) (forthcoming). *Oxford History of English Lexicography*. Oxford: Oxford University Press.

——Mackin R., and McCaig, I.R. (1983). 'General Introduction', *Oxford Dictionary of Current Idiomatic English, Vol 2: Phrase, Clause and Sentence Idioms*. Oxford: Oxford University Press.

Cruse, D.A. (1986). *Lexical Semantics*. Cambridge: Cambridge University Press.

——(1995). 'Polysemy and related phenomena from a cognitive linguistic viewpoint', in St. Dizier, P. and Viegas, E. (eds.), *Computational Lexical Semantics*. Cambridge: Cambridge University Press. 33–49.

Daille, B., and Williams, G. (eds.) (2001). *Proceedings of the Workshop on Collocation: Computational extraction, analysis and exploitation*, 39th Annual Meeting and 10th Conference of the European Chapter of the Association for Computational Linguistics (ACL2001), Toulouse.

Debili, F. (1982). *Analyse Syntaxico-Sémantique Fondée sur une Acquisition Automatique de Relations Lexicales-Sémantiques*. PhD thesis, University of Paris XI.

Dolan, W.B. (1994). 'Word sense ambiguation: clustering related senses', *COLING 94*, Kyoto: Association for Computational Linguistics, 712–716.

Dolezal, F. (1984). 'The construction of entries in the Alphabetical Dictionary (1688) of John Wilkins and William Lloyd', in Hartmann, R.R.K. (ed.), *LEXeter '83 Proceedings*. Tübingen: Niemeyer, 67–72.

——and McCreary, D.R. (1999). *Pedagogical Lexicography Today: A Critical Bibliography on Learners' Dictionaries with Special Emphasis on Language Learners and Dictionary Users*. Lexicographica Series Maior 96. Tübingen: Max Niemeyer.

Dufour, N. (1997). 'Merging two DEFI dictionaries', DEFI Technical Report, Liège.

Dumais, S., Banko, M., Brill, E., Lin, J., and Ng, A. (2002). 'Web question answering: is more always better?', *Proceedings of the 25th ACM SIGIR*. Tampere, Finland, 291–298.

Duranti, A. (1985). 'Sociocultural dimensions of discourse', in van Dijk, T. (ed.), *Handbook of Discourse Analysis*,Vol. 1. New York: Academic Press, 193–230.

Duval, A. (1986). 'La métalangue dans les dictionnaires bilingues', *Lexicographica*, 2: 93–100.

——(1990). 'Nature et valeur de la traduction dans les dictionnaires bilingues', *Cahiers de Lexicologie*, 56–57: 27–33.

Engwall, G. (1994). 'Chance or Choice: Criteria for Corpus Selection', in Atkins, B.T.S., and Zampolli, A. (eds.), *Computational Approaches to the Lexicon*, Oxford: Oxford University Press, 49–82.

Evert, S., and Krenn, B. (2001). 'Methods for the qualitative evaluation of lexical association measures', *Proceedings of the 39th Annual Meeting of the Association for Computational Linguistics*. Toulouse, 188–195.

Fano, R. (1961). *Transmission of Information*. Cambridge, MA: MIT Press.

Farwell, D., Guthrie, L., and Wilks, Y.A. (1993). 'Using machine-readable dictionaries for the creation of lexicons', *Proceedings of the AAAI Spring Symposium on Building Lexicons for Machine Translation*. Stanford University, CA, 100.

Fellbaum, C. (1990). 'English verbs as a semantic net', *International Journal of Lexicography* (Special Issue), 3(4): 278–301.

——(ed.) (1998). *WordNet: An Electronic Lexical Database*. Cambridge, MA: MIT Press.

Ferguson, C.A. (1976). 'The structure and use of politeness formulas', *Language in Society*, 5: 137–151.

Fernando, C. (1996). *Idioms and Idiomaticity*. Oxford: Oxford University Press.

——and Flavell, R. (1981). *On Idiom: Critical Views and Perspectives*. (Exeter Linguistic Studies, 5). Exeter: University of Exeter.

Fillenbaum, S., and Jones, L.V. (1965). 'Grammatical contingencies in word association', *Journal of Verbal Learning and Verbal Behavior*, 4: 248–55.

Fillmore, C.J. (1972). 'A grammarian looks at sociolinguistics', *Georgetown University Monographs on Language and Linguistics*, 25. Washington, DC: Georgetown University Press, 275–287.

——(1975a). 'Santa Cruz lectures on deixis 1971 ', reproduced by the Indiana University Linguistics Club; the lecture 'Coming and going', under the title 'How to know whether you're coming or going', was revised and reprinted in Karl Hyldgaard-Jensen (ed.), *Linguistik 1971*. Königstein: Athenaeum-Verlag, 369–379.

——(1975b). 'An alternative to checklist theories of meaning', in Cogen, C., *et al.* (eds.), *Proceedings of the First Annual Meeting of the Berkeley Linguistics Society*. Berkeley, CA: UC Press, 123–131.

——(1977a). 'Topics in Lexical Semantics', in Cole, R. (ed.), *Current Issues in Linguistic Theory*. Bloomington, IN: Indiana UP, 76–138.

——(1977b). 'Scenes-and-frames semantics', in Zampolli, A. (ed.), *Linguistic Structures Processing*. Fundamental Studies in Computer Science, No. 59. Amsterdam: North Holland, 55–79.

——(1977c). 'The need for a frame semantics in linguistics', in Karlgren, H. (ed.), *Statistical Methods in Linguistics*. Stockholm: Språkförlaget Skriptor, 5–29.

——(1978). 'On the organization of semantic information in the lexicon', in D. Farkas *et al.* (eds.), *Papers from the Parasession on the Lexicon*. Chicago Linguistic Society, 148–173.

——(1982a). 'Towards a descriptive framework for spatial deixis', in Jarvella, R.J., and Klein, W. (eds.), *Speech, Place, and Action*. New York: John Wiley and Sons.

——(1982b). 'Frame semantics', in The Linguistic Society of Korea (ed.), *Linguistics in the Morning Calm*. Seoul: Hanshin Publishing Co., 111–137.

——(1985). 'Frames and the semantics of understanding', *Quaderni di Semantica*, 6: 222–254.

——(1988). Keynote lecture, British Association for Applied Linguistics conference, Exeter, September.

——(1995). 'The hard road from verbs to nouns', in Chen, M., and Tzeng, O. (eds.), *In Honour of William S-Y Wang: Interdisciplinary Studies on Language and Language Change*. Taipei: Pyramid Press, 105–129.

——and Atkins, B.T.S. (1992). 'Towards a Frame-based lexicon: the semantics of RISK and its neighbors', in Lehrer, A., and Kittay, E. (eds.), *Frames, Fields, and Contrasts*. Hillsdale, NJ: Erlbaum, 75–102.

————(1994). 'Starting where the dictionaries stop: the challenge of corpus lexicography', in Atkins, B.T.S., and Zampolli, A. (eds.), *Computational Approaches to the Lexicon*. Oxford: Oxford University Press, 350–393.

——Kay, P., and O'Connor, M.C. (1988). 'Regularity and idiomaticity in grammatical constructions: the case of *let alone*', *Language*, 64(3): 501–538.

——Johnson, C., and Petruck, M. (2003a). 'Background to FrameNet', *International Journal of Lexicography*, Special Issue on FrameNet, 16(3): 235–250.

——Petruck, M., Ruppenhofer, J., and Wright, A. (2003b). 'FrameNet in action: the case of attaching', *International Journal of Lexicography*, Special Issue on FrameNet, 16(3): 297–332.

Firth, J. (1957). 'A synopsis of linguistic theory 1930–1955', *Studies in Linguistic Analysis*, Philological Society, Oxford; reprinted in Palmer, F. (1968, ed.), *Selected Papers of J.R. Firth*, Harlow: Longman, 168–205.

Fletcher, W. (2004). 'Facilitating the compilation and dissemination of ad-hoc web corpora', in Aston, G., Bernardini, S., and Stewart, D. (eds.), *Corpora and Language Learners*. Amsterdam: Benjamins, 273–300.

Folch, H., Heiden, S., Habert, B., Fleury, S., Illouz, G., Lafon, P., Nioche, J., and Prévost, S. (2000). 'TyPTex inductive typological text classification by multivariate statistical analysis for NLP systems tuning/evaluation', *Second Language Resources and Evaluation Conference*, Athens, Greece: ELRA, 141–148.

Fontenelle, T. (1992). 'Collocation acquisition from a corpus or from a dictionary: a comparison', in Tommola, H., Varantola, K., Salmi-Tolonen, T., and Schopp J. (eds.), *EURALEX'92 Proceedings I-II, Fifth EURALEX International Congress*. Studia Translatologica, Ser. A, Vol. 1. Tampere: University of Tampere, 220–228.

——(1997). *Turning a Bilingual Dictionary into a Lexical-Semantic Database*. Lexicographica Series Maior 79. Tübingen: Max Niemeyer Verlag.

——(1998). 'Discovering significant lexical functions in dictionary entries', in Cowie, A.P. (ed.), *Phraseology: Theory, Analysis, and Applications*. Oxford: Oxford University Press, 189–207.

——(2000). 'A bilingual lexical database for frame semantics', *International Journal of Lexicography*, 13(4): 232–248.

——(ed.) (2003). Special issue on FrameNet and frame semantics, *International Journal of Lexicography*, 16:3.

——(forthcoming). 'Linguistic research and learners' dictionaries: The *Longman Dictionary of Contemporary English*', in Cowie, A.P. (ed.), *Oxford History of English Lexicography*. Oxford: Oxford University Press.

Fox, G. (1987). 'The case for examples', in Sinclair, J. (ed.), *Looking Up: An Account of the COBUILD Project in Lexical Computing*. London: Collins, 137–149.

——(1989). 'A vocabulary for writing dictionaries', in Tickoo, M. (ed.), *Learners' Dictionaries: State of the Art*. Singapore: SEAMEO Regional Language Centre, 153–171.

Francis, W.N. (1980). 'A tagged corpus – problems and prospects', in Greenbaum, S., Leech, G., and Svartvik, J. (eds.), *Studies in English Linguistics, for Randolph Quirk*. London: Longman, 192–209.

——and Kučera, H. (1964/1979). *Manual of Information to Accompany a Standard Corpus of Present-Day Edited American English, for use with Digital Computers*. Department of Linguistics, Brown University.

————(1982). *Frequency Analysis of English Usage*. Boston: Houghton Mifflin Company.

Fraser, B. (1970). 'Idioms within a transformational grammar', *Foundations of Language*, 6: 22–42.

Frawley, W. (1988). 'New forms of specialized dictionaries', *International Journal of Lexicography*, 1(3): 189–213.

——(1989). 'The dictionary as text', *International Journal of Lexicography*, 2(3): 231–248.

Fujii, A., and Ishikawa, T. (2000). 'Utilizing the world wide web as an encyclopedia: extracting term descriptions from semi-structured texts', in *Proceedings of the 38th Meeting of the ACL*, Hong Kong, October, 488–495.

Gahl, S. (1998). 'Automatic extraction of subcategorization frames for corpus-based dictionary-building', in Fontenelle, T. *et al.* (eds.), *EURALEX'98 Proceedings*. Liège, 445–452.

Gale, W., Church, K.W., and Yarowsky, D. (1992). 'Estimating upper and lower bounds on the performance of word-sense disambiguation programs', *Proceedings of the 30th ACL*, 249–156.

Garrett, M.F. (1982). 'Production of speech: observations from normal and pathological language use', in Ellis, A. (ed.), *Normality and Pathology in Cognitive Functions*. London: Academic Press, 19–76.

Garside, R., Leech, G., and Sampson, G. (1987). *The Computational Analysis of English*. London: Longman.

Geeraerts, D. (1990). 'The lexicographical treatment of prototypical polysemy', in Tsohatzidis, S. (ed.), *Meanings and Prototypes: Studies in Linguistic Classification*. London: Routledge, 195–210.

——(1993). 'Vagueness's puzzles, polysemy's vagueness', *Cognitive Linguistics*, 4(3): 223–272.

Gibson, E.J. and Levin, H. (1975). 'On the perception of words: an application of some basic concepts', in Gibson, E.J., and Levin, H. (eds.), *The Psychology of Reading*. Cambridge, MA: The MIT Press.

Gildea, D. (2001). 'Corpus variation and parser performance', Lee, L., and Harman, D. (eds.), *Proceedings of the 2001 Conference on Emprical Methods in NLP*. Pittsburgh, PA, 167–202.

Gillard, P., and Gadsby, A. (1998). 'Using a learner corpus in compiling ELT dictionaries', in Granger, S. (ed.), *Learner English on Computer*. Harlow: Addison Wesley Longman, 159–171.

Gläser, R. (1986). *Phraseologie der englischen Sprache*. Leipzig: Verlag Enzyklopädie.

——(1988). 'The grading of idiomaticity as a presupposition for a taxonomy of idioms', in Hüllen, W., and Schulze, R. (eds.), *Understanding the Lexicon: Meaning, Sense and World Knowledge in Lexical Semantics*. Tübingen: Niemeyer.

Good, I.J. (1953). 'The population frequencies of species and the estimation of population parameters', *Biometrika*, 40: 237–264.

Greenbaum, S. (1974). 'Some verb-intensifier collocations in American and British English', *American Speech*, 49(1–2): 79–89.

Greenwood, M., Roberts, I., and Gaizauskas, R. (2002). 'University of Sheffield TREC 2002 Q&A system', in Voorhees, E., and Buckland, L.P. (eds.), *The Eleventh Text REtrieval Conference (TREC-11)*, Washington. U.S. Government Printing Office. NIST Special Publication 500: 251.

Grefenstette, G. (1994a). 'Corpus-derived first, second and third-order word affinities', *EURALEX'94 Proceedings*. Amsterdam: Vrije Universiteit, 279–290.

——(1994b). *Explorations in Automatic Thesaurus Discovery*. Boston: Kluwer Academic Press.

——(1995). 'Comparing two language identification schemes', *Proceedings of the 3rd International Conference on the Statistical Analysis of Textual Data* (JADT'95), Rome, 263–268.

——(1998). 'Light parsing as finite state filtering', in Kornai, A. (ed.), *Extended Finite State Models of Language*. Cambridge: Cambridge University Press, 89–94.

——(1999). 'The WWW as a resource for example-based MT tasks.' Invited Talk, ASLIB: *Translating and the Computer* conference, London, October.

——(2001). 'Very large lexicons', in Daelemans *et al.* (eds.), *Computational Linguistics in the Netherlands 2000: Selected Papers from the Eleventh CLIN Meeting*. Language and Computers 37. Amsterdam: Rodopi.

——and Nioche, J. (2000). 'Estimation of English and non-English language use on the WWW', *Proc. RIAO (Recherche d'Informations Assistée par Ordinateur)*. Paris: Collège de France, 237–246.

——and Tapanainen, P. (1994). 'What is a word, what is a sentence? Problems of tokenization', in Kiefer, F., Kiss, G., and Pajzs, J. (eds.), COMPLEX'94: *Papers in Computational Lexicography*. Budapest: Research Institute for Linguistics, Hungarian Academy of Sciences, 79–87.

——Heid, U., Schulze, B.M., Fontenelle, T., and Gérardy, C. (1996). 'The DECIDE project: multilingual collocation extraction', in Gellerstam, M. *et al.* (eds.), Euralex '96 Proceedings. University of Göteborg, 93–107.

Gross, D., and Miller, K. (1990). 'Adjectives in WordNet', *International Journal of Lexicography* (Special Issue), 3(4): 265–277.

——Kegl, J., Gildea, P., and Miller, G. A. (1989). *A Coded Corpus and Commentary on Children's Dictionary Strategies*. Princeton, NJ: Cognitive Science Laboratory Report 39.

Guthrie, J.A., Guthrie, L., Wilks, Y., and Aidinejad, H. (1991). 'Subject-dependent co-occurrence and word sense disambiguation', in *Proceedings of the 29th Annual Meeting of the Association for Computational Linguistics*, Berkeley, CA, 146–152.

Guthrie, L., Slator, B.M., Wilks, Y., and Bruce, R. (1990). 'Is there content in empty heads?', *Proceedings of the 13th International Conference on Computational Linguistics* (*COLING 90*), volume 3. Helsinki, 138–143.

Halliday, M.A.K., and Hasan, R. (1989). *Language, Context, and Text: Aspects of Language in a Social-semiotic Perspective*. Oxford: Oxford University Press.

Hanks, P. (1979). 'To what extent does a dictionary definition define?', in Hartmann, R.R.K. (ed.), *Dictionaries and Their Users*. Exeter: University of Exeter, 32–38.

——(1987). 'Definitions and explanations', in Sinclair, J.M. (ed.), *Looking Up*. London: Collins, 116–136.

——(1988). 'Typicality and meaning potentials', in Snell-Hornby, M. (ed.), *ZuriLEX '86 Proceedings*. Tübingen: Francke, 37–47.

—— (1990). 'Evidence and intuition in lexicography', in Tomaszczyk, J., and Lewandowska-Tomasczcyk, B. (eds.), *Meaning and Lexicography*. Amsterdam and Philadelphia: John Benjamins, 31–41.

—— (1994). 'Linguistic norms and pragmatic exploitations, or why lexicographers need Prototype Theory, and vice versa', in Kiefer, F., Kiss, G., and Pajzs, J. (eds.), *Papers in Computational Lexicography: COMPLEX '94*. Budapest: Research Institute for Linguistics, 89–113.

—— (2000). 'Contributions of lexicography and corpus linguistics to a theory of language performance', in Heid, U. *et al.* (eds.), *Proceedings of the Ninth Euralex International Congress*. Stuttgart, Germany: IMS, Stuttgart University, I: 3–13.

—— (2005). 'Johnson and modern lexicography', *International Journal of Lexicography*, 18(2): 243–266.

—— and Pustejovsky, J. (2005). 'A pattern dictionary for natural language processing', in Fontenelle, T. (ed.), *Revue Française de Linguistique Appliquée* – Numéro spécial: *Dictionnaires: nouvelles approches, nouveaux modèles*, December 2005, Vol. X-2: 63–82.

Harris, R. (1982). 'The history men', *The Times Literary Supplement*. No. 4, 144: 935–936.

Hartmann, R.R.K. (1989). 'Sociology of the dictionary user', in Hausmann, F.-J., Reichmann, O., Wiegand, H.E., and Zgusta, L. (eds.), *Wörterbücher/Dictionaries/Dictionnaires: An International Encyclopedia of Lexicography*, Vol. 1. Berlin: de Gruyter, 102–112.

—— (1992). 'Lexicography, with particular reference to English learners' dictionaries', *Language Teaching*, 25(3): 151–159.

—— and James, G. (1998). *Dictionary of Lexicography*. London/New York: Routledge.

Harvey, K., and Yuill, D. (1997). 'A study of the use of a monolingual pedagogical dictionary by learners of English engaged in writing', *Applied Linguistics*, 18(3): 253–278.

Hatherall, G. (1984). 'Studying dictionary use: some findings and proposals', in Hartmann, R.R.K. (ed.), *LEXeter '83 Proceedings*, Lexicographica Series Maior No.1. Tübingen: Niemeyer, 183–189.

Hausmann, F.J. (1979). 'Un dictionnaire des collocations est-il possible?', *Travaux de Linguistique et de Littérature*, 17(1): 187–195.

—— (1989). 'Le dictionnaire de collocations', in Hausmann, F.J., Reichmann, O., Wiegand, H.E., Zgusta, L. (eds.), *Wörterbücher/Dictionaries/Dictionnaires*, vol. 1. Berlin: de Gruyter, 1010–1019.

—— and Gorbahn, A. (1989). 'COBUILD and LDOCE 2: A comparative review,' *International Journal of Lexicography*, 2(1): 44–56.

Hawking, D., Voorhees, E., Craswell, N., and Bailey, P. (1999). 'Overview of the TREC8 Web Track', in *Eighth Text REtrieval Conference (TREC-8)*. Gaithersburg, MA, 131–150.

Hearst, M.A. (1991). 'Noun homograph disambiguation using local context in large text corpora', *Using Corpora: Proceedings of the Seventh Annual Conference of the UW Centre for the New OED*. Waterloo, Canada, 1–22.

Heid, U. (1994). 'On ways words work together – topics in lexical combinatorics', in Martin, W., Meijs, W., Moerland, M., ten Pas, E., van Sterkenburg, P., and Vossen, P. (eds.), *EURALEX'94 Proceedings*. Amsterdam: Vrije Universiteit, 226–257.

—— (1996). 'Using lexical functions for the extraction of collocations from dictionaries and corpora', in Wanner, L. (ed.), *Lexical Functions in Lexicography and Natural Language Processing*. Amsterdam and Philadelphia: John Benjamins, 115–146.

Henry, G.T. (1990). *Practical Sampling*. Newbury Park, CA: Sage.

Herbst, T. (1996). 'On the way to the perfect learners' dictionary: a first comparison of *OALD5*, *LDOCE3*, *COBUILD2* and *CIDE*', *International Journal of Lexicography*, 9(4), 321–357.

—— and Popp, K. (ed.) (1999). *The Perfect Learners' Dictionary (?)*, Lexicographica Series Maior 95. Tübingen: Niemeyer.

Heylen, D. (1995). 'Lexical functions, generative lexicons and the world', in Saint-Dizier, P., and Viegas, E. (eds.), *Computational Lexical Semantics*. Cambridge: Cambridge University Press, 125–140.

Hindle, D. (1983a). 'Deterministic parsing of syntactic non-fluencies', in *Proceedings of the 21st Annual Meeting of the Association for Computational Linguistics*, 123–128.

Hindle, D. (1983b). 'User manual for Fidditch, a deterministic parser.' Naval Research Laboratory Technical Memorandum #7590–142.

Hindle, D. (1994). 'A parser for text corpora', in Atkins, B.T.S., and Zampolli, A. (eds.), *Computational Approaches to the Lexicon*. Oxford: Oxford University Press, 103–153.

Hofland, K., and Johansson, S. (1982). *Word Frequencies in British and American English*. Bergen, Norway: Norwegian Computing Center for the Humanities.

Householder, F.W. *et al.* (1964). *Some Classes of Verbs in English*. Bloomington, IN: Indiana University Linguistics Club.

——(1965). *More Classes of Verbs in English*. Bloomington, IN: Indiana University Linguistics Club.

Humble, P. (1998). 'The use of authentic, made-up, and "controlled" examples in foreign language dictionaries', in Fontenelle, T. *et al.* (eds.), *EURALEX'98 Proceedings*. Liège: University of Liège, 593–599.

Hymes, D.H. (1974). *Foundations in Sociolinguistics*. Philadelphia: University of Pennsylvania Press.

Iannucci, J.E. (1975). 'Meaning discrimination in bilingual dictionaries', in Householder, F.W., and Saporta, S. (eds.), *Problems in Lexicography*. Bloomington, IN: Indiana University Press.

Ide, N., Véronis, J., and Le Maître, J. (1991). 'Outline of a database model for electronic dictionaries', *RIAO'91 Conference Proceedings: Intelligent Text and Image Handling*. Barcelona, 375–393.

——Le Maître, J., and Véronis, J. (1994). 'Outline of a Model for Lexical Databases', in Zampolli, A., Calzolari, N., and Palmer, M. (eds.), *Current Issues in Computational Linguistics: in Honour of Don Walker*. Series *Linguistica Computazionale*. IX–X: 283–320.

Ilson, R.F. (n.d.) *Lexicography: the description of a discipline*. London: Longman Group.

Ilson, R.F. (1984). 'The communicative significance of some lexicographic conventions', in Hartmann, R.R.K. (ed.), *LEXeter '83 Proceedings*. Tübingen: Niemeyer, 80–86.

Ipeirotis, P.G., Gravano, L., and Sahami, M. (2001). 'Probe, count, and classify: categorizing hidden web databases', in *Proceedings of the SIGMOD Conference*, Vol. 30, No. 2. New York: ACM Press, 67–78.

Jackendoff, R.S. (1990). *Semantic Structures*. Cambridge, MA: MIT Press.

Jain, M.P. (1981). 'On meaning in the foreign learner's dictionary', *Applied Linguistics*, 2(3): 274–286.

Jansen, J., Mergeai, J.P., and Vanandroye, J. (1987). 'Controlling LDOCE's controlled vocabulary', in Cowie, A.P. (ed.), *The Dictionary and the Language Learner*. Tübingen: Max Niemeyer Verlag, 78–94.

Jelinek, F. (1985). *Self-organized Language Modeling for Speech Recognition*. Yorktown Heights, VA: Technical Report, IBM.

Jensen, K., and Binot, J.-L. (1987). 'Disambiguating prepositional phrase attachment by using on-line dictionary definitions', *Computational Linguistics*, 13: 251–260.

Johansson, S. (1980). 'The LOB corpus of British English texts: presentation and comments', *Journal of the Association of, Literary and Linguistic Computing*, 1: 25–36.

——(ed.) (1982). *Computer Corpora in English Language Research*. Bergen, Norway: Norwegian Computing Center for the Humanities.

——Leech, G. N., and Goodluck, H. (1978). *Manual of information to accompany the Lancaster–Oslo/Bergen Corpus of British English, for use with digital computers*. Department of English, University of Oslo.

Johnson, S. (1747). *The Plan of a Dictionary of the English Language*. London: Knapton. [Also in this volume]

Jones, R., and Ghani, R. (2000). 'Automatically building a corpus for a minority language from the web', *Proceedings of the Student Workshop of the 38th Annual Meeting of the Association for Computational Linguistics*, 29–36.

Jones, S., and Sinclair, J. (1974). 'English lexical collocations. A study in computational linguistics', *Cahiers de Lexicologie*, 24: 15–61.

Jorgensen, J.C. (1990). 'The psychological reality of word senses', *Journal of Psycholinguistic Research*, 19(3): 167–190.

Kahan, S., Pavlidis, T., and Baird, H. (1987). 'On the recognition of printed characters of any font and size', *IEEE Transactions PAMI*, 274–287.

Kalton, G. (1983). *Introduction to Survey Sampling*. Newbury Park, CA: Sage.

Karlgren, J., and Cutting, D. (1994). 'Recognizing text genres with simple metrics using discriminant analysis', *Proc. COLING-94*, Kyoto, Japan, 1071–1075.

Karlsson, F., Voutilainen, A., Heikkilä, J., and Anttila, A. (eds.). (1995). *Constraint Grammar: A Language-independent System for Parsing Unrestricted Text*, volume 4 of *Natural Language Processing*. Berlin and New York: Mouton de Gruyter.

Karttunen, L. (1983). 'KIMMO: a general morphological processor,' *Texas Linguistics Forum*, 22: 163–186.

——Chanod, J.P., Grefenstette, G., and Schiller, A. (1996). 'Regular expressions for language engineering', *Natural Language Engineering*, 2(4): 305–328.

Kay, P. (1984). 'The kinda/sorta construction', in Brugman, C. *et al.* (eds.), *Proceedings of the Tenth Annual Meeting of the Berkeley Linguistics Society*. Berkeley, CA: UC Press, 157–171.

——(1989). 'Contextual operators: *respective, respectively,* and *vice versa'*, in Hall, K., Meacham, M., and Shapiro, R. (eds.), *Proceedings of the Fifteenth Annual Meeting of the Berkeley Linguistics Society*. Berkeley, CA: UC Press, 181–192.

——(1990). 'Even', *Linguistics and Philosophy*, 13: 59–111.

Keller, E. (1979). 'Gambits: conversational strategy signals', *Journal of Pragmatics*, 3: 219–237.

Keller, F., and Lapata, M. (2003). 'Using the web to obtain frequencies for unseen bigrams', *Computational Linguistics, Special Issue on the Web as Corpus*, 29(3): 459–484.

Kessler, B., Nunberg, G., and Schütze, H. (1997). 'Automatic detection of text genre', in Cohen, P., and Wahlster, W. (eds.), *Proceedings of the 35th Annual Meeting of the ACL and 8th Conference of the EACL*. Madrid, 32–38.

Kilgarriff, A. (1992). *Polysemy*. PhD thesis, University of Sussex, CSRP 261, School of Cognitive and Computing Sciences, Brighton.

——(1993). 'Dictionary word sense distinctions: an enquiry into their nature', *Computers and the Humanities*, 26(1.2): 365–387.

——(1997a). 'Evaluating word sense disambiguation programs: progress report', in Gaizauskas, R. (ed.), *Proc. SALT Workshop on Evaluation in Speech and Language Technology*, Sheffield, June: 114–120.

——(1997b). 'Foreground and background lexicons and word sense disambiguation for information extraction', in *Proc. Workshop on Lexicon-Driven Information Extraction*, Frascati, Italy, July: 51–62.

——(1997c). 'What is word sense disambiguation good for?', in *Proc. Natural Language Processing in the Pacific Rim (NLPRS '97)*, Phuket, Thailand, December: 209–214.

——(1997d). 'Putting frequencies in the dictionary', *International Journal of Lexicography*, 10(2): 135–155.

——(1997e). 'I don't believe in word senses', *Computers and the Humanities*, 31(2): 91–113, [Also this volume].

——(2001). 'Comparing corpora', *International Journal of Corpus Linguistics*, 6(1): 1–37.

——(2003a). 'Linguistic search engine', in Simov, K. (ed.), *Shallow Processing of Large Corpora: Workshop Held in Association with Corpus Linguistics 2003*, Lancaster, March, 53–58.

——(2003b). 'Thesauruses for Natural Language Processing', *Proceedings of Natural Language Processing and Knowledge Engineering (NLPKE)*. Beijing, China, Oct 2003.

——(2006). 'Collocationality (and how to measure it)', in Corino, E., Marello, C., and Onesti, C. (eds.), *Proceedings of the XIIth EURALEX International Congress*. Tonino: Università di Torino, 997–1004.

——and Gazdar, G. (1995). 'Polysemous relations', in Palmer, F. (ed.), *Grammar and Meaning: Essays in Honour of Sir John Lyons*. Cambridge: Cambridge University Press, 1–25.

——and Grefenstette, G. (2003). 'Web as corpus: introduction to the special issue', *Computational Linguistics*, 29(3), 333–348. [Also in this volume]

——and Rundell, M. (2002). 'Lexical profiling software and its lexicographic applications – a case study', in Braasch, A., and Povlsen, C. (eds.), *EURALEX 2002 Proceedings*. Copenhagen: Center for Sprog Teknologi, 807–818.

——and Tugwell, D. (2001). 'Word Sketch: extraction and display of significant collocations for lexicography', *ACL Workshop on Collocation*, Toulouse, July 7 2001: available online from http://wasps.itri.bton.ac.uk/, or as ITRI technical report ITRI-01-12 from http://www.itri.bton.ac.uk/techindex.html.

Kilgarriff, A. Rychly, P., Smrž, P., and Tugwell, D. (2004). 'The Sketch Engine', in Williams, G., and Vessier, S. (eds.), *Proceedings of the Eleventh EURALEX Congress*. Lorient, France: Université de Bretagne-Sud, 105–116. [Also in this volume]

Kiparsky, P., and Kiparsky, C. (1971). 'Fact', in Steinberg, D., and Jakobovits, L. A. (eds.), *Semantics: An Interdisciplinary Reader in Philosophy, Linguistics and Psychology*. Cambridge: Cambridge University Press, 345–369.

Kipfer, B. (1984). 'Methods of ordering senses within entries', in Hartmann, R.R.K. (ed.), *LEXeter '83 Proceedings*. Tübingen: Niemeyer, 101–109.

Kittredge, R., and Lehrberger, J. (1982). *Sublanguage: Studies of Language in Restricted Semantic Domains*. Berlin: De Gruyter.

Kjellmer, G. (1993). 'Multiple meaning and interpretation: the case of *sanction*', *Zeitschrift für Anglistik und Amerikanistik*, 41(2): 115–123.

Klappenbach, R. (1968). 'Probleme der Phraseologie', *Wissenschaftliche Zeitschrift der Karl-Marx-Universität*, 17(5): 221–227.

Klavans, J., and Tzoukermann, E. (1995). 'Dictionaries and corpora: combining corpus and MRD data for building bilingual lexicons', *Machine Translation*, 10:3: 185–218.

——Chodorow, M., and Wacholder, N. (1993). 'Building a knowledge base from parsed definitions', in Jensen, K., Heidorn, G., and Richardson S. (eds.), *Natural Language Processing: The PLNLP Approach*. Boston: Kluwer, 119–133.

Korhonen, A. (2000). 'Using semantically motivated estimates to help subcategorization acquisition', *Proc. Joint Conf. on Empirical Methods in NLP and Very Large Corpora*. Hong Kong: ACL SIGDAT, 216–223.

Kraaij, W., Nie, J.-Y., and Simard, M. (2003). 'Embedding web-based statistical translation models in cross-language information retrieval', *Computational Linguistics, Special Issue on the Web as Corpus*, 29(3): 381–420.

Krenn, B., and Evert, S. (2001). 'Can we do better than frequency? A case study on extracting PP-verb collocations', in Daille, B., and Williams, G. (eds.), *Proceedings of the Workshop on Collocation: Computational Extraction, Analysis and Exploitation*. 39th Annual Meeting and 10th Conference of the European Chapter of the Association for Computational Linguistics (ACL2001), Toulouse, 39–46.

Krings, H.B. (1986). *Was in den Köpfen von Übersetzern vorgeht. Eine empirische Untersuchung zur Struktur des Übersetzungsprozesses an fortgeschrittenen Französischlernern*. Tübinger Beiträge zur Linguistik 291. Tübingen: Narr.

Kromann, H., Riiber, T., and Rosbach, P. (1984). 'Active and passive bilingual dictionaries', in Hartmann, R.R.K. (ed.), *LEXeter '83 Proceedings*. Tübingen: Niemeyer, 207–215.

Krovetz, R. (1996). 'Surprises under the hood: an investigation of word meanings and information retrieval', *Computational Linguistics*, Special Issue on Word Sense Disambiguation.

Labov, W. (1973). 'The boundaries of words and their meanings', in Bailey, C.J., and Shuy, R. (eds.), *New Ways of Analyzing Variation in English*. Washington, DC: Georgetown University Press, 340–373.

Lado, R. (1972). 'Patterns of difficulty in vocabulary', in Allen, H.B., and Campbell, R.N. (eds.), *Teaching English as a Second Language*. New York: McGraw Hill, 346–354.

Lakoff, G. (1987). *Women, Fire, and Dangerous Things*. Chicago: University of Chicago Press.

——and Johnson, M. (1980). *Metaphors We Live By*. Chicago: University of Chicago Press.

Lakoff, R. (1973). 'Lexicography and generative grammar II: context and connotation in the dictionary', *Annals of the New York Academy of Sciences*, Vol. 211 (8 June 1973), 144–153.

Landau, S (1984). *Dictionaries: the Art and Craft of Lexicography*. New York: Charles Scribner's Sons. (2nd edition, Cambridge University Press, 2001).

Landes, S., Leacock, C., and Tengi, R. (1998). 'Building semantic concordances', in Fellbaum, C. (ed.), *WordNet: An Electronic Lexical Database*. Cambridge, MA: MIT Press.

Laufer, B. (1991). 'Knowing a word: what is so difficult about it?', *English Teachers' Journal*, 42: 82–88.

——(1992). 'The effect of dictionary definitions and examples on the use and comprehension of new L2 words', *Cahiers de Lexicologie*, 63: 131–142.

——and Melamed, L. (1994). 'Monolingual, bilingual and "bilingualized" dictionaries: which are more effective, for what, and for whom?', in Martin, W., Meijs, W., Moerland, M., ten Pas, E., van

Sterkenburg, P., and Vossen, P. (eds.), *EURALEX 1994 Proceedings*, Amsterdam: Vrije Universiteit, 565–576.

Lawrence, S., and Lee Giles, C. (1999). 'Accessibility of information on the web', *Nature*, 400: 107–109.

Leech, G. (1974). *Semantics*. Harmondsworth: Penguin.

Leitner, G. (1990). 'Corpus design – problems and suggested solutions', *Working Paper in ICE Newsletter 1* (May 1990). International Corpus of English, University College London.

Lesk, M. (1986). 'Automatic sense disambiguation using machine readable dictionaries: how to tell a pine cone from an ice cream cone', *Proceeding of the 1986 SIGDOC Conference*. Toronto, Canada: ACM Press, 24–26.

Levi, J. (1982). 'Complex nominals: new discoveries, new questions', in Hattori, S., and Inoue, K. (eds.), *Proceedings of the XIIIth International Congress of Linguists*, Tokyo, 183–197.

Levin, B. (1993). *English Verb Classes and Alternations: A Preliminary Investigation*. Chicago: University of Chicago Press.

——and Rappoport Hovav, M. (1991). 'Wiping the slate clean: a lexical semantic exploration', *Cognition*, 41: 123–151.

——Song, G., and Atkins, B.T.S. (1997). 'Making sense of corpus data: a case study of verbs of sound', *International Journal of Corpus Linguistics*, 2(1): 23–64.

Lin, D. (1998). 'Automatic retrieval and clustering of similar words', *Proceedings of the Joint 17th International Conference on Computational Linguistics and 36th Annual Meeting of the ACL*, Montreal, 768–774.

Lipka, L. (1974). 'Probleme der Analyse englischer Idioms aus struktureller und generativer Sicht', *Linguistik und Didaktik*, 20: 274–285.

——(1990). *An Outline of English Lexicology*. (Forschung und Studium Anglistik, 3.) Tübingen: Max Niemeyer.

Lyons, J. (1969). *Introduction to Theoretical Linguistics*. Cambridge: Cambridge University Press.

——(1977). *Semantics*. Vols. 1 and 2. Cambridge: Cambridge University Press.

Mackin, R. (1978). 'On collocations: "Words shall be known by the company they keep"', in Strevens, P. (ed.), *In Honour of A.S. Hornby*. Oxford: Oxford University Press, 149–165.

Magerman, D., and Marcus, M.P. (1990). 'Parsing a natural language using mutual information statistics', *Proceedings of AAAI 90*. American Association for Artificial Intelligence, 984–989.

Maingay, S., and Rundell, M. (1990). 'What makes a good dictionary example?' Paper presented at the 24th IATEFL Conference, Dublin.

————(1991). 'What we have learnt about writing dictionaries from students and teachers.' Paper presented at the 25th IATEFL Conference, Exeter.

Manning, C., and Schütze, H. (1999). *Foundations of Statistical Natural Language Processing*. Cambridge, MA: MIT Press.

Marcus, M.P. (1980). *A Theory of Syntactic Recognition for Natural Language*. Cambridge, MA: MIT Press.

McArthur, T. (1987). *Worlds of Reference*. Cambridge: Cambridge University Press.

McCawley, J.D. (1986). 'What linguists might contribute to dictionary-making if they could get their act together', in Bjarkman, P.C., and Raskin, V. (eds.), *The Real-World Linguist: Linguistic Applications in the 1980s*. Norwood, NJ: Ablex, 3–18.

McDermott, A., and Moon, R. (2005). 'Introduction: Johnson in context', *International Journal of Lexicography*, 18(2): 153–155.

McEnery, T., and Wilson, A. (1996). *Corpus Linguistics*. Edinburgh: Edinburgh University Press.

McRoy, S.W. (1992). 'Using multiple knowledge sources for word sense discrimination', *Computational Linguistics*, 18(1), 1–30.

Meara, P., and English, F. (1988). 'Lexical errors and learners' dictionaries.' Paper presented at the 1988 IATEFL Conference. Microfiche, Educational Resources Information Centre: ERIC ED 654 321.

Mel'čuk, I. (1988). 'Semantic description of lexical units in an explanatory combinatorial dictionary: basic principles and heuristic criteria', *International Journal of Lexicography*, 1(3): 165–88.

——(1998). 'Collocations and lexical functions', in Cowie, A.P. (ed.), *Phraseology: Theory, Analysis, and Applications*. Oxford: Oxford University Press, 23–53.

Mel'čuk, I. and Zholkovsky, A. (1988). 'The explanatory combinatorial dictionary', in Evens, M. (ed.), *Relational Models of the Lexicon: Representing Knowledge in Semantic Networks*. Studies in Natural Language Processing. Cambridge: Cambridge University Press, 42–74.

——Arbatchewsky-Jumarie, N., Dagenais, L., Elnitsky, L., Iordanskaja, L., Lefebvre, M.N., Mantha, S., Lessard, A. (1984/1988/1992). *Dictionnaire Explicatif et Combinatoire du Français Contemporain: Recherches Lexico-Sémantiques I, II, III*. Montreal: Les Presses de l'Université de Montréal.

——Clas, A., and Polguère, A. (1995). *Introduction à la lexicologie explicative et combinatoire*. Collection 'Universités Francophones', AUPELF-UREF, Duculot.

Meyer, D., Schvaneveldt, R., and Ruddy, M. (1975). 'Loci of contextual effects on visual word-recognition', in Rabbitt, P., and Dornic, S. (eds.), *Attention and Performance V*. London, New York, San Francisco: Academic Press. 98–118.

Meyer, I. (1990). 'Interlingual meaning-text lexicography: towards a new type of dictionary for translation', in Steele, J. (ed.), *Meaning-Text Theory: Linguistics, Lexicography and Implications*. Ottawa: University of Ottawa Press, 175–270.

Michiels, A. (1982). *Exploiting a Large Dictionary Database*. PhD thesis, University of Liège, mimeographed.

——(1995a). 'Introducing HORATIO', in Alberto, P., and Bennett, P. (eds.), *Lexical Issues in Machine Translation*. Studies in Machine Translation and Natural Language Processing, Vol. 8, European Commission, Luxembourg, 77–91.

——(1995b). 'Feeding LDOCE entries into HORATIO', in Alberto, P., and Bennett, P. (eds.), *Lexical Issues in Machine Translation*. Studies in Machine Translation and Natural Language Processing, Vol. 8, European Commission, Luxembourg, 93–115.

——(1995c). *HORATIO: A Middle-sized NLP Application in Prolog*. L3, Liège: Liège Language and Literature.

——(1996). 'An experiment in translation selection and word sense discrimination using the meta-linguistic apparatus of two computerized dictionaries.' DEFI Technical Report, University of Liège.

——and Dufour, N. (1996). 'From SGML tapes to DIC clauses: identifying multi-word units for context-sensitive lookup.' DEFI Technical Report, Liège.

——and Noël, J. (1984). 'The pro's and con's of a controlled defining vocabulary in a learner's dictionary', in *LEXeter'83 Proceedings*. Tübingen: Max Niemeyer Verlag, 386–394.

Mihalcea, R., and Moldovan, D. (1999). 'A method for word sense disambiguation of unrestricted text', *Proceedings of the 37th Meeting of ACL*. Maryland, June: 152–158.

Miller, G.A. (1985). 'WordNet: a dictionary browser', *Information in Data: Proceedings of the First Conference of the UW Centre for the New Oxford Dictionary*. Waterloo, Canada: University of Waterloo.

——(1986). 'Dictionaries in the mind', *Language and Cognitive Processes*, 1: 171–85.

——(1990a). 'WordNet: an on-line lexical database', *International Journal of Lexicography (Special Issue)*, 3(4): 235–312.

——(1990b). 'Nouns in WordNet: a lexical inheritance system', *International Journal of Lexicography (Special Issue)*, 3(4): 245–264.

——and Fellbaum, C. (1991). 'Semantic networks of English', *Cognition*, 41: 1–3, 197–229.

——and Gildea, P. (1987). 'How children learn words', *Scientific American*, 257(3): 94–99.

——and Johnson-Laird, P.N. (1976). *Language and Perception*. Cambridge, MA: Harvard University Press.

——Beckwith, R., Fellbaum, C., Gross, D., and Miller, K. (1990). 'Introduction to WordNet: an on–line lexical database', *International Journal of Lexicography*, 3(4): 235–244. [Also in this volume]

Mitchell, E. (1983a). 'Search-do reading: (2) using a dictionary. A preliminary analysis', Working Paper 20: *Formative Assessment of Reading Strategies in Secondary Schools*. Aberdeen: Aberdeen College of Education.

——(1983b). 'Search-do reading: (3) Difficulties in using a dictionary', *Working Paper 21: Formative Assessment of Reading Strategies in Secondary Schools*. Aberdeen: Aberdeen College of Education.

Mitchell, T.F. (1971). 'Linguistic "goings-on": collocations and other lexical matters arising on the syntagmatic record', *Archivum Linguisticum*, 2: 35–69.

Moon, R. (1987a). 'Monosemous words and the dictionary', in Cowie, A.P. (ed.), *The Dictionary and the Language Learner*. (Lexicographica Series Maior 17.) Tübingen: Max Niemeyer, 173–182.

——(1987b). 'The analysis of meaning', in Sinclair, J.M. (ed.), *Looking Up: An Account of the COBUILD Project*. London: Collins, 86–103.

——(1988). 'Time and idioms', in Snell-Hornby, M. (ed.), *ZuriLEX '86 Proceedings*. Tübingen: Francke, 107–123.

——(1989). 'Objective or objectionable? Ideological aspects of dictionaries', *English Language Research*, 3: Language and Ideology: 59–94.

——(1998b). 'On using spoken data in corpus lexicography', in Fontenelle, T. *et al.* (eds.), *Euralex'98 Proceedings*. Liège: University of Liège, 347–355.

Murray, K.M.E. (1977). *Caught in the Web of Words: James Murray and the Oxford English Dictionary*. New Haven, CT: Yale University Press.

Nagao, M. (1984). 'A framework of a mechanical translation between Japanese and English by analogy principle', in Elithorn, A., and Banerji, R. (eds.), *Artificial and Human Intelligence*. Amsterdam: North-Holland, 173–180.

Nation, I.S.P. (1983). 'Testing and teaching vocabulary', *RELC Journal* (Guidelines), 12–24.

——(1990). *Teaching and Learning Vocabulary*. New York: Newbury House.

Neff, M., and McCord, M. (1990). 'Acquiring lexical data from machine-readable dictionary resources for machine translation', *Proceedings of the 3rd International Conference on Theoretical and Methodological Issues in Machine Translation of Natural Language*, University of Texas at Austin, 85–90.

Newmeyer, F.J. (1972). 'The insertion of idioms', *Papers from the 8th Regional Meeting*. Chicago Linguistic Society, Chicago, IL.

Nida, E.A. (1997). 'The molecular level of lexical semantics', *International Journal of Lexicography*, 10(4): 265–274.

Nirenburg, S. (1989). 'Lexicons for computer programs and lexicons for people', *Dictionaries in the Electronic Age, Proceedings of the Fifth Annual Conference of the UW Centre for the New Oxford English Dictionary*. Oxford, 43–65.

Nunberg, G. (1978). *The Pragmatics of Reference*. Bloomington, IN: University of Indiana Linguistics Club.

——(1994). 'The once and future dictionary'. Presentation at *The Future of the Dictionary Xerox Workshop*, Uriage-les-Bains, France, October.

——and Zaenen, A. (1992). 'Systematic polysemy in lexicology and lexicography', in Tommola, H., Varantola, K., Salmi-Tolonen, T., and Schopp J. (eds.), *EURALEX'92 Proceedings I-II, Fifth Euralex International Congress*. Studia Translatologica, Ser. A, Vol.1, University of Tampere, 387–396.

Osselton, N.E. (1995). *Chosen Words: Past and Present Problems for Dictionary Makers*. Exeter: University of Exeter Press.

Ostler, N., and Atkins, B.T.S. (1992). 'Predictable meaning shift: some linguistic properties of lexical implication rules', in Pustejovsky, J., and Bergler, S. (eds.), *Lexical Semantics and Commonsense Reasoning*. New York: Springer-Verlag, 87–98.

Palermo, D., and Jenkins, J. (1964). *Word Association Norms*. Minneapolis: University of Minnesota Press.

Palmer, F.R. (ed.) (1968). *Selected Papers of J.R. Firth, 1952–59*. London: Longman.

Palmer, H.E. (1933). *Second Interim Report on English Collocations*. Tokyo: Kaitakusha.

——(1938). *A Grammar of English Words*. London: Longmans, Green.

Pawley, A. (1985). 'Lexicalization', in Tannen, D., and Alatis, J.E. (eds.), *Language and Linguistics: The Interdependence of Theory, Data and Application*. (Georgetown Round Table on Language and Linguistics.) Washington, DC: University of Georgetown, 98–120.

——and Syder, F.H. (1983). 'Two puzzles for linguistic theory: nativelike selection and nativelike fluency', in Richards, J.C., and Schmidt, R.W. (eds.), *Language and Communication*. London: Longman, 191–226.

Peters, A. (1983). *The Units of Language Acquisition*. Cambridge: Cambridge University Press.

Peters, C. (ed.) (2001). *Cross-Language Information Retrieval and Evaluation.* CLEF 2000 Workshop, Lisbon, Portugal, September 21–22, 2000, Revised Papers, Lecture Notes in Computer Science: Springer.

Petitpierre, D., Robert, D., and Warwick-Armstrong, S. (1994). 'DICO: a network-based dictionary consultation tool.' Poster presented at the EURALEX'94 International Congress, Vrije Universiteit Amsterdam.

Picchi, E., Peters, C., and Marinai, E. (1992). 'the Pisa lexicographic workstation: The bilingual components', in Tommola, H., Varantola, K., Salmi-Tolonen, T., and Schopp, J. (eds.), *EURALEX'92 Proceedings I-II, Fifth Euralex International Congress.* Studia Translatologica, Ser.A, Vol.1, University of Tampere, 277–285.

Polanyi, M. (1958). *Personal Knowledge: Towards a Post-Critical Philosophy.* Chicago, IL: University of Chicago Press.

Pollard, C.J., and Sag, I.A. (1987). *Information-Based Syntax and Semantics: Volume I, Fundamentals.* Volume 13 of *CSLI Lecture Notes.* Stanford, CA: CSLI.

Pustejovsky, J. (1991). 'The generative lexicon', *Computational Linguistics,* 17(4): 409–441.

——(1995). *The generative lexicon.* Cambridge, MA: MIT Press.

Quine, W. (1969). 'Speaking of objects', in Quine, W. (ed.), *Ontological Relativity.* New York: Columbia University Press, 1–25.

Quirk, R., Greenbaum, S., Leech, G., and Svartvik, J. (1972). *A Grammar of Contemporary English.* London: Longman.

————————(1985). *A Comprehensive Grammar of the English Language.* London: Longman.

Raiffa, H. (1970). *Decision Analysis: Introductory Lectures on Choices under Uncertainty.* Reading, MA: Addison Wesley.

Resnik, P. (1999). 'Mining the web for bilingual text', *Proceeding of the 37th Meeting of ACL.* Maryland, June: 527–534.

——and Smith, N. (2003). 'The web as a parallel corpus', *Computational Linguistics, Special Issue on the Web as Corpus,* 29(3): 349–380.

——and Yarowsky, D. (1997). 'A perspective on word sense disambiguation methods and their evaluation', in Light, M. (ed.), *Tagging Text with Lexical Semantics: Why, What and How?* Washington, DC: SIGLEX (Lexicon Special Interest Group) of the ACL, 79–86.

Rey, A. (1977). *Le lexique, images et modèles.* Paris: Armand Colin.

Richards, J.C. (1976). 'The role of vocabulary teaching', *TESOL Quarterly,* 10: 77–89.

Rigau, G., Magnini, B., Agirre, E., Vossen, P., and Carroll, J. (2002). 'Meaning: a roadmap to knowledge technologies', *Proceedings of COLING Workshop on A Roadmap for Computational Linguistics.* Taipei, Taiwan, 1–7.

Roland, D., Jurafsky, D., Menn, L., Gahl, S., Elder, E., and Riddoch, C. (2000). 'Verb subcategorization frequency differences between business-news and balanced corpora: the role of verb sense', *Proc. Workshop on Comparing Corpora,* 38th ACL, Hong Kong, October, 28–34.

Rundell, M. (1988). 'Changing the rules: why the monolingual learner's dictionary should move away from the native-speaker tradition', in Snell-Hornby, M. (ed.), *ZüriLEX '86 Proceedings.* Tübingen: Franke Verlag, 127–137.

——(1996). 'Computer Corpora and their impact on lexicography and language teaching', in Mullings, C. *et al.* (eds.), *New Technologies for the Humanities.* London: Bowker-Saur, 198–216.

——(1998). 'Recent trends in English pedagogical lexicography', *International Journal of Lexicography,* 11(4): 315–342. [Also in this volume]

——(1999). 'Dictionary use in production', *International Journal of Lexicography,* 12(1): 35–53.

——(2002). 'Good old-fashioned lexicography: human judgement and the limits of automation', in Corréard, M.-H. (ed.), *Lexicography and Natural Language Processing – in Honour of B.T.S. Atkins.* Euralex, 142–146.

——and Ham, N. (1994). 'A new conceptual map of English', in Martin, W. *et al.* (eds.), *EURALEX '94 Proceedings.* Amsterdam, 172–180.

——and Stock, P. (1992). 'The corpus revolution', *English Today,* 8(2): 9–14; 8(3): 21–32; 8(4): 45–51.

Santamaría, C., Gonzalo, J., and Verdejo, F. (2003). 'Automatic association of web directories with word senses', *Computational Linguistics, Special Issue on the Web as Corpus*, 29(3): 485–502.

Schiller, A. (1996). 'Multilingual part-of-speech tagging and noun phrase mark-up', *15th European Conference on Grammar and Lexicon of Romance Languages*, Munich, Sept 19–21.

Scholfield, P. (1999). 'Dictionary use in reception', *International Journal of Lexicography*, 12(1): 13–34.

Schulze, B. (1996). *Macroprocessor User Guide*. IMS Universität Stuttgart, internal document.

——and Christ, O. (1994). *The IMS Corpus Workbench*. Stuttgart: Institut für maschinelle Sprachverarbeitung, Universität Stuttgart.

Schütze, H., and Pederson, J.O. (1995). 'Information retrieval based on word senses', *Proceedings, ACM Special Interest Group on Information Retrieval*.

Segond, F., and Breidt, E. (1996). 'IDAREX: description formelle des expressions à mots multiples en français et en allemand dans le cadre de la technologie des états finis', in Clas, A., Thoiron, P., and Béjoint H. (eds.), *Lexicomatique et Dictionnairiques* (Actes du Colloque de Lyon 1995), AUPELF-UREF, and FMA, Beyrouth, 93–104.

——and Zaenen, A. (1994). 'Multi-word expressions in bilingual dictionaries and in Compass.' Paper read at the workshop on 'The Future of the Dictionary' co-sponsored by Rank Xerox Research Centre and Acquilex-II, Grenoble.

——Schiller, A., Grefenstette, G., and Chanod, J.P. (1997). 'An experiment in semantic tagging using Hidden Markov Model tagging', in Vossen, P., Adriaens, G., Calzolari, N., Sanfilippo, A., and Wilks, Y. (eds.), *ACL'97 Workshop on Information Extraction and the Building of Lexical Semantic Resources for NLP Applications* (Madrid, July 7–12), 78–81.

Sekine, S. (1997). 'The domain dependence of parsing', *Proc. Fifth Conference on Applied Natural Language Processing*. Washington, DC: ACL, 96–102.

Sinclair, J.M. (1987a). 'Editor's introduction' in *Collins Cobuild English Language Dictionary*. London and Glasgow: Collins.

——(ed.) (1987b). *Looking Up: An Account of the COBUILD Project in Lexical Computing*. London: Collins.

——(1987c). 'The nature of the evidence', in Sinclair, J.M. (ed.), *Looking Up: An Account of the COBUILD Project in Lexical Computing*. London and Glasgow: Collins 150–159.

——(1991). *Corpus, Concordance, Collocation*. Oxford: Oxford University Press.

——(2004). 'In praise of the dictionary', in Williams, G., and Vessier, S. (eds.), *Proceedings of the Eleventh EURALEX Congress*. Lorient, France: Université de Bretagne-Sud, 1–12.

——(2005). 'To complement the dictionary', in Blatná, R., and Petkevič, V. (eds.), *Jazyky a jazykovĕda: Sborník k 65. narozeniná prof. Františka Čermá*. Prague: Charles University, 417–444.

Slator, B.M. (1988). 'Lexical semantics and a preference semantics parser'. Technical Report MCCS-88–16, Computing Research Laboratory, New Mexico State University, New Mexico.

Smadja, F. (1991). 'Macrocoding the lexicon with co-occurrence knowledge', in Zernik, U. (ed.), *Lexical Acquisition: Using On-Line Resources to Build a Lexicon*. Hillsdale, NJ: Lawrence Erlbaum Associates, 165–189.

——(1993). 'Retrieving collocations from text: Xtract', *Computational Linguistics*. 19(1): 143–177.

Smrž, P., and Horák, A. (2000). 'Large scale parsing of Czech', *Proceedings of Efficiency in Large-Scale Parsing Systems Workshop, COLING'2000* (1st edn.) Saarbrücken: Universität des Saarlandes, 43–50.

Snell-Hornby, M. (1984). 'The bilingual dictionary – help or hindrance?', in Hartmann, R.R.K. (ed.), *LEXeter '83 Proceedings*. Tübingen: Max Niemeyer Verlag, 274–281.

——(1986). 'The bilingual dictionary – victim of its own tradition', in Hartmann, R.R.K. (ed.), *The History of Lexicography*. Amsterdam and Philadelphia: John Benjamins, 207–218.

——(1990). 'Dynamics in meaning as a problem for bilingual lexicography', in Tomaszczyk, J.B., and Lewandowska-Tomaszczyk, B. (eds.), *Meaning and Lexicography*. Amsterdam and Philadelphia: John Benjamins, 200–226.

Sparck Jones, K. (1986). *Synonymy and Semantic Classification*. Edinburgh: Edinburgh University Press.

Stein, G. (1991). 'Illustrations in dictionaries', *International Journal of Lexicography*, 4(2): 99–127.

Steiner, R.J. (1971). 'A cardinal principle in lexicography: equivalence', *Tijdschrift van het Instituut voor Toegepaste Linguïstiek* 14: 23–28.

Steiner, R.J. (1984). 'Guidelines for reviewers of bilingual dictionaries', *Dictionaries: Journal of the Dictionary Society of North America*, 6: 166–181.

Stock, P. (1984). 'Polysemy', in Hartmann, R.R.K. (ed.), *LEXeter '83 Proceedings*. Tübingen: Niemeyer, 131–140. [Also in this volume]

——(1988). 'The structure and function of definitions', in Snell-Hornby, M. (ed.), *ZuriLEX '86 Proceedings*. Tübingen: Francke Verlag, 81–90.

Stubbs, M. (1996). *Text and Corpus Analysis*. Oxford: Blackwell.

Sudman, S. (1976). *Applied Sampling*. New York: Academic Press.

Summers, D. (1988). 'The role of dictionaries in language learning', in Carter, R.A., and McCarthy, M. (eds.), *Vocabulary and Language Teaching*. London: Longman, 111–125.

——(1993). 'Longman/Lancaster English Language Corpus – criteria and design', *International Journal of Lexicography*, 6(3): 181–208.

Sweetser, E. (1990). *From Etymology to Pragmatics: Metaphorical and Cultural Aspects of Semantic Structure*. Cambridge: Cambridge University Press.

Taylor, J. (1989). *Linguistic Categorization: Prototypes in Linguistic Theory*. Oxford: Oxford University Press.

ten Hacken, P. (1990). 'Reading distinction in machine translation', in Karlgren, H. (ed.), *COLING '90*, Helsinki, 162–166.

Thumb, J. (2004). *Dictionary Look-up Strategies and the Bilingualised Learner's Dictionary*. Lexicographica Series Maior 117. Tübingen: Niemeyer.

Tognini-Bonelli, E. (2001). *Corpus Linguistics at Work*. Amsterdam/Philadelphia: John Benjamins.

Tono, Y. (2001). *Research on Dictionary Use in the Context of Foreign Language Learning – Focus on Reading Comprehension*. Lexicographica Series Maior 106. Tübingen: Niemeyer.

Touretzky, D.S. (1986). *The Mathematics of Inheritance Systems*. Los Altos, CA: Morgan Kaufmann.

Van Sterkenburg, P. (ed.) (2003). *A Practical Guide to Lexicography*. Amsterdam/Philadelphia: John Benjamins.

Varantola, K. (1994). 'The dictionary user as decision-maker', in Martin, W., Meijs, W., Moerland, M., ten Pas, E., van Sterkenburg, P., and Vossen, P. (eds.), *EURALEX 1994 Proceedings*. Amsterdam: Vrije Universiteit, 606–611.

——(2000). 'Translators and disposable corpora', *Proc. CULT (Corpus Use and Learning to Translate)*, Bertinoro, Italy, November.

——and Atkins, B.T.S. (1993). 'Report on EURALEX dictionary use database (Oxford 1991 and Tampere 1993 results).' Paper presented at AILA 1993 World Conference, Amsterdam, The Netherlands.

Vendler, Z. (1967). 'Verbs and Times', in Vendler, Z. (ed.), *Linguistics in Philosophy*. Ithaca: Cornell University Press, 97–121.

——(1972). *Res Cogitans*. Ithaca: Cornell University Press.

Véronis, J., and Ide, N. (1990). 'Word sense disambiguation with very large neural networks extracted from machine readable dictionaries', *COLING '90*, volume 2, Helsinki, 389–394.

————(1994). 'From dictionaries to knowledge bases...and back.' Paper read at the workshop on 'The Future of the Dictionary' co-sponsored by Rank Xerox Research Centre and Acquilex-II, Grenoble (abstract published under the title 'Machine-readable dictionaries: have we wasted our time?', in *Cambridge Language Reference News*, 1994, Cambridge University Press, Number 4, 1).

Villasenor-Pineda, L., Montes y Gómez, M., Pérez-Coutino, M., and Vaufreydaz, D. (2003). 'A corpus balancing method for language model construction', *Fourth International Conference on Intelligent Text Processing and Computational Linguistics (CICLing-2003)*, Mexico City, 393–401.

Volk, M. (2001). 'Exploiting the WWW as a corpus to resolve PP attachment ambiguities', *Proc. Corpus Linguistics 2001*, Lancaster, UK, 601–606.

Vossen, P. (1992). 'The automatic construction of a knowledge base from dictionaries: a combination of techniques', in Tommola, H., Varantola, K., Salmi-Tolonen, T., and Schopp J. (eds.), *EURALEX'92 Proceedings I–II, Fifth Euralex International Congress*. Studia Translatologica, Ser.A, Vol.1, University of Tampere, 311–326.

——(1996). 'Right or wrong: combining lexical resources in the EuroWordNet Project', in Gellerstam, M. *et al.*, *EURALEX'96 Proceedings*. Gothenburg: Göteborg University, 715–730.

——(ed.) (1998). *EuroWordNet: A Multilingual Database with Lexical Semantic Networks for European Languages*. Dordrecht: Kluwer.

——(2001). 'Extending, trimming and fusing WordNet for technical documents', *Proceedings of the NAACL 2001 Workshop on WordNet and Other Lexical Resources*, Pittsburgh, June. http://www.seas. smu.edu/rada/mwnw/papers/WNW-NAACL-105.pdf.

——Meijs, W., and Den Broeder, M. (1989). 'Meaning and structure in dictionary definitions', in Boguraev, B., and Briscoe, E. (eds.), *Computational Lexicography for Natural Language Processing*. London and New York: Longman, 171–192.

Wanner, L. (1996). *Lexical Functions in Lexicography and Natural Language Processing*. Amsterdam/ Philadelphia: John Benjamins Publishing.

Way, A., and Gough, N. (2003). '*wEBMT*: developing and validating an example-based machine translation system using the World Wide Web', *Computational Linguistics, Special Issue on the Web as Corpus*, 29(3): 421–457.

Weinreich, U. (1969). 'Problems in the analysis of idioms', in Puhvel, J. (ed.), *Substance and Structure of Language*. Berkeley, CA: University of California Press.

Wierzbicka, A. (1985). *Lexicography and Conceptual Analysis*. Ann Arbor, MI: Karoma.

——(1987). *English Speech Act Verbs: A Semantic Dictionary*. Sydney: Academic Press.

——(1988). 'The semantics and lexicography of "Natural Kinds"', in Hyldgaard-Hensen, K., and Zettersten, A. (eds.), *Symposium on Lexicography III*. Tübingen: Niemeyer, 155–182.

——(1992). 'What are the uses of theoretical lexicography?', in Frawley, W. (ed.), *Dictionaries: Journal of the Dictionary Society of North America* (DSNA) 14, 44–78.

Wilks, Y. (2004). 'On the ownership of text', *Computers and the Humanities*, 38(2): 115–127.

——Fass, D., Guo, C.-M., McDonald, J., Plate, T., and Slator, B. (1989). 'A tractable machine dictionary as a resource for computational semantics', in Boguraev, B., and Briscoe, E. (eds.), *Computational Lexicography for Natural Language Processing*. London and New York: Longman, 193–228.

——Slator, B., and Guthrie, L. (1996). *Electric Words: Dictionaries, Computers, and Meanings*. Cambridge, MA and London: MIT Press.

Williams, B. (1978). *A Sampler on Sampling*. New York: John Wiley and Sons.

Williams, J.N. (1992). 'Processing polysemous words in context: evidence for interrelated meanings', *Journal of Psycholinguistic Research*, 21: 193–218.

Wittgenstein, L. (1953). *Philosophical Investigations*. Oxford: Basil Blackwell.

Xu, J.L. (2000). 'Multilingual search on the World Wide Web', *Proc. Hawaii International Conference on System Science HICSS-33*, Maui, Hawaii, January.

Yarowsky, D. (1992). 'Word-sense disambiguation using statistical models of Roget's categories trained on large corpora', in *Proceedings of the 14th International Conference on Computational Linguistics (COLING '92)*, 454–460.

——(1995). 'Unsupervised word sense disambiguation rivaling supervised methods', in *Proceedings of the 33rd Meeting of the ACL*. MIT, 189–196.

Zgusta, L. (1971). *Manual of Lexicography*. (Janua Linguarum. Series Maior, 39.) The Hague: Mouton.

——(1979). 'Equivalents and explanations in bilingual dictionaries', in Jazayery, M.A., Polomé, E.C., and Winter, W. (eds.), *Linguistic and Literary Studies in Honor of Archibald A. Hill*. Vol. 2. Lisse, Netherlands: Peter de Ridder.

——(1984). 'Translation equivalence in the bilingual dictionary', in Hartmann, R.R.K. (ed.), *LEXeter '83 Proceedings*. Tübingen: Max Niemeyer Verlag, 147–154.

Zheng, Z. (2002). 'AnswerBus question answering system', in Voorhees, E.M., and Buckland, L.P. (eds.), *Proceedings of HLT Human Language Technology Conference (HLT 2002)*, San Diego, CA, March 24–27.

Zwicky, A.M., and Sadock, J.M. (1975). 'Ambiguity tests and how to fail them', *Syntax and Semantics*, 4(1): 1–36.

Index

Abney, S. 317
active dictionary 248
addressees 69
Agirre, E. 92
Ahlswede, T. 178, 188
Aisenstadt, E. 164–65, 173
Aitchison, J. 231
Ait-Mokhtar, S. 317
Alexander, R. 163, 166, 175, 223
Alonso Ramos, M. 189
AltaVista 93–96, 322
ambiguity tests 139, 145
Amsler, R. 169, 188
analysis process 230; *see also* synthesis
analysis of meaning 235
analysis vs. synthesis 33
anaphor 115
anaphoric element 120
ANLT 97
annotated corpora 301
antonymy 14, 333
Apply_heat frame 255, 260
approximate linguistics 310, 320
Apresjan, J. 3, 40–42, 44, 48, 51–60, 111, 138
armchair linguistics 105–22
Arnold, I. 163
association measure 285; *see also* mutual information
association ratio 286–87, 292, 295
atelic vs. telic 261–62
Atkins, B.T.S. 3–5, 10–11, 14–15, 31–50, 51, 90, 93, 99, 108, 125, 135, 138, 144–45, 169, 185, 230, 247–72, 297, 337–75
authenticity of data 107
autohyponymy 149
Ayto, J. 8, 45, 143–44, 153–54

Baayen, H. 99
Baker, C. 92
bank (senses) 125–29, 154–56
Bank of English 226
Banko, M. 92
base (of collocation) 173–75; *see also* collocator
Bauer, D. 171, 188
Baugh, S. 12
BBI dictionary 174
Beaudouin, V. 99
Beckwith, R. 14, 327–34
Beesley, K. 93, 299
Béjoint, H. 11, 143, 235, 337
benefactive 266
Benson, M. 7, 163, 165, 167, 174
Biber, D. 4, 38–39, 63–87, 98–99, 226
bilingual corpora 100
bilingual dictionaries 169–70, 247–72, 273–82, 345, 353
bilingual lexicography 10, 44
bilingualized dictionaries 337
Binot, J.-L. 136

BNC, *see* British National Corpus
Boas, H. 52
Bogaards, P. 15, 231–32, 236, 337
Boguraev, B. 13, 138, 169–70, 175, 188
Bolinger, D. 8, 163, 193–96, 247, 318
Breidt, E. 188
Brill, E. 92
Briscoe, E. 13, 92, 138, 170
British National Corpus (BNC) 42, 90, 93, 97, 100, 126, 146, 226, 298, 312, 322
Brown corpus 64, 66, 86, 90, 100, 136, 186
Buitelaar, P. 99
Burnard, L. 90
Butt, M. 310
Byrd, R. 170

Calzolari, N. 170, 188
Cambridge International Dictionary of English, *see* CIDE
Cambridge Language Survey 226
CANCODE corpus 226
Carroll, J. 92
Carter, R. 163, 226, 228
causative-inchoative alternation 8, 11, 262
Cavaglia, G. 99
Čermak, F. 7
Chanod, J.-P. 314, 317
check (Hanks' analysis) 131–33; (Grefenstette's analysis) 311–23
checklist theory 125
Chklovski, T. 91
Chodorow, M. 170
Chomsky, N. 213, 308
Choueka, Y. 173
Christ, O. 145, 185
chunking 223
Church, K. 12, 39, 91, 126, 136, 173, 227, 285–95, 298, 309, 315
CIDE 12, 232
Clark, E. 41
Clear, J. 38, 99, 136–37, 225, 227, 310
COBUILD 8, 9, 12, 90, 144, 170, 197, 200–05, 208–09, 224, 239, 297; definitions 204; on CD-ROM 233; *see also* full-sentence definition
cognate translation 279
cognitive linguistics 137–38
cognitive salience 271
colligation 157
colligational patterning 160
Collins-Robert English-French Dictionary 7, 11, 169, 247–72
collocate 132, 251, 299; patterning 252
collocation 6, 7, 12, 47, 148, 164, 173, 186, 223, 227, 349, 371; base vs. collocation 173; and translation 183; collocation extraction 182
collocational constraints 172
collocational database 182
collocational dictionary 174